Phase Blue
A Systems Approach to College English

James Burl Hogins

Robert E. Yarber

San Diego Mesa College

D1304708

College Learning Systems

Science Research Associates, Inc., 259 East Erie Street, Chicago, Illinois 60611

A Subsidiary of IBM

Developed at the Palo Alto Center

Acknowledgments

Preface

Phase Blue is the first step in making an educational dream come true. It offers, for the first time, a systems approach to freshman English—one that provides several points of access to the study of reading, writing, and rhetoric. This approach is flexible enough to be easily adapted to each instructor's teaching style; in addition, it provides behavioral objectives for the course, a method of evaluating whether these goals have been achieved, and a procedure for recycling the student through appropriate parts of the system if a review is shown to be necessary.

In addition to this anthology of readings and the annotated version, there are six components that are designed to complement each other in the teaching-learning process: stimulus tapes, critique tapes, overhead projector transparencies, student book, instructor's guide, and a classroom assessment program.

The anthology can be used independently; however, the other components provide in their totality an enriched and innovative program that will help the student master freshman English.

There are sixty-four selections grouped into ten units ranging from "The 70s: In Pursuit of Dreams" and "The Student and His Language" to "The Black Rage." In order to make learning as meaningful as possible for the student, we have provided supporting apparatus with these selections: headnotes, discussion questions, writing assignments, suggested library research, questions on rhetoric (with answers in the *Instructor's Guide*), and definitions of difficult words. A feature that many teachers will find helpful is the Guide to Rhetoric, which lists eighteen principles of composition with paragraph and page numbers of places in the essays that illustrate these principles.

It is customary for authors to express their gratitude to their wives, children, and colleagues; and to all of these we wish to record our appreciation. But two individuals especially deserve our gratitude and thanks: Carroll Edwards and Helen Friend.

James Burl Hogins
Robert E. Yarber

San Diego Mesa College

Contents

1 The 70s: In Pursuit of Dreams

If our fears are realized, the coming decade will be a time of continuing violence, class and racial hatred and mistrust, and depletion of our natural and human resources. If our dreams are fulfilled, however, the 1970s will bring many great advances.

The poor dream of being freed from poverty. The diseased dream of being made well. The disenfranchised dream of being allowed to participate. We all dream of peace, freedom, and prosperity.

These concerns, which are common to all people, are reflected in the articles that follow.

2 Visions of the Future

At the beginning of this century only a few dreamers believed that man could fly; now some airlines are buying jets that can carry more than four hundred passengers and fly from Los Angeles to London in less than six hours. Seventy-five years ago motion pictures were a novelty, a popular attraction in penny arcades; now men have transmitted back to earth pictures of their first steps on the moon. The scientific speculation that just a few decades ago centered on the origin of life on earth has now shifted to the possibility of encountering life in outer space.

The technological achievements of the first two-thirds of this century have been astounding. But what of the next thirty years? Will the new technology enslave us or set us free? Will the nations of the world find a greater measure of political freedom and economic security? Will the oppressed minorities of the world find the freedom and dignity that should be the birthright of all men?

3 Dialog between the Generations

In a rapidly changing world, one factor remains constant: children are still critical of their parents; parents continue to be confused and bewildered by the actions of their offspring. But perhaps, as some critics have suggested, the current generation gap is wider, more difficult to breach, than any that has preceded it.

In the following section you will hear voices from both sides of the gap. Listen carefully; you may be surprised at what you hear.

4 The Student and His Language

It is easy to understand why the student worries about his language: his composition papers are returned splattered with red ink; his speech is corrected at every turn. He is told to write one kind of English in the classroom, but he reads another kind in the works of successful authors; he's urged to be succinct and direct, but he finds his textbooks often wordy and poorly organized. His confusion is compounded because all too often he gets the impression that mastery of English is merely a matter of memorizing a long list of dos ("do write clearly") and don'ts ("don't mix metaphors").

What is "good" English and what is not? The student may learn some answers to this question from the following selections as well as something about the history of his language and about different views on how words should be used.

5 Violence in America

Violence and crime are increasing in America: national leaders are murdered on our streets, college students refuse to obey the law, ghetto residents and police engage in open warfare. One can only hope that the current unrest will have some beneficial side effects, that it will cause us to reassess our thinking and establish new private and national priorities.

The selections in this unit offer no solutions to the problem of law and order in America; they merely reflect the attempts of concerned citizens to explain—or justify—some aspects of our present state of civil disorder.

6 Religion and Philosphy: Evaluations

What is the nature of reality? What is the purpose of life? Is there a Supreme Being? Men throughout the ages have pondered these questions. But they are not solely the province of the philosopher. The college student also faces them. He answers them even in refusing to answer them. These are not abstract matters; they are not just word games. The answers to these questions will determine a person's system of values and choice of a life style, and even the way he behaves toward himself and toward others.

7 America: A Self-Analysis

Our social critics by the very nature of their profession focus almost exclusively on the negative aspects of American life.

Do you also concentrate on the harsher realities of the world—the immoralities of injustice, starvation, death? Or do you, more optimistically, see America as moving toward peace and prosperity? In evaluating the success of the American way of life, one must take into consideration the victims of the American paradox—children starving in the midst of abundance, ghetto dwellers who don't have sanitary living conditions despite American technological prowess, and the martyrs of the 1960s whose desire to bring about valuable change led to hatred and death. A look at the analyses in this section may show how to draw a better blueprint for the future.

8 The Black Rage

The goal of the black slave was very modest: physical emancipation. The goals of the black man today are far more ambitious: social and economic independence, adequate housing, better education for his children—the same things most other Americans want.

There is a new black leadership. Its philosophy ranges from the peaceful integration advocated by the late Martin Luther King, Jr., to black separatism. Despite different viewpoints these leaders all agree on one thing—what they want has been earned by the simple fact of survival and American citizenship. Perhaps as a result of these new ideas, there is a noticeable change in the black's self-concept. He knows his beginnings, and is aware of what oppression has done to his race. But, even more important, he knows what he wants—and he wants it now.

9 The Arts

Men have always written poetry, drawn pictures, sung songs. But never before has there been such variety in art. Today you can have Bach or rock, a Campbell's soup can by Andy Warhol or a landscape by Andrew Wyeth. The world of the arts is growing larger every day. The man who wishes to be truly at home in this world rejects neither the old nor the new, but is willing to sample everything. He will find that art is not confined to museums or concert halls, that it exists in everything done with skill, imagination, and taste.

10 Developing a Life Style

One has only to look at the statistics on, say, the number of women who work outside the home, of people who own television sets, and of marriages that end in divorce to realize how much the life style of Americans has changed in this century. What effect have these changes had on the quality of life in our country? The authors of the following essays discuss, sometimes optimistically, sometimes pessimistically, the tremendous impact the new morality, the mass media, and the mechanical routine are having on all our lives.

Index

Guide to Rhetoric

1

WHY STUDENTS SEIZE POWER

Louis S. Levine

What are the causes of the current student unrest on college campuses across the United States? This article offers an explanation, as well as a warning to those adminis- *trators who would forcibly suppress campus rebellions. The author is a professor of psychology at San Francisco State College.*

1   Early in the morning of April 30, the week-long siege of Columbia University was ended. Police recaptured the five buildings held by activists, mostly students. More than 700 arrests were reported and approximately 150 persons were injured. Classes remained suspended and the division between students and administration widened.

2   The use of the police has intensified anti-administration attitudes. Many members of the faculty, previously aloof from the fray, are at this point highly critical of their administration. An official faculty committee composed of eight distinguished senior scholars and two junior members of the instructional staff was appointed to meet with representatives of the trustees, administration and students for the purpose of returning the university to operations as close to normal as possible.

3   As the substantive issues of this confrontation—the building of a gymnasium on a largely granite-covered little park used by the community, and the university's participation in the activities of the Institute for Defense Analysis—did not represent the beginning of the conflict, neither did the clearance of the buildings represent its end. True, the advantage of being able to command overwhelming force was demonstrated, but it is unlikely that this physical display will either resolve or limit the eventual outcome of the Columbia crisis.

4   As I write, the future course of the Columbia upheaval is in doubt, but the issues of war and peace present in this confrontation between students and college administration have been evident across the country in past campus crises, and they will increasingly become focal points of contention as the issues themselves intensify and as student militancy correspondingly increases. The following impressions, though expressed in general terms, derive from specific student-university confrontations that have occurred at various schools in the recent past.

5   The most significant point, which is not perceived by most faculties, administrations and boards of trustees or regents, is simply that students possess a great deal of power. If a very small percentage of students decides to employ that power, they can bring any academic institution to a halt. Further, there is in most communities a committed nonstudent minority which will line up with the students if the situation reaches crisis proportions. Given this fact of student power, and putting aside the issues of the means employed or the ends toward which the power is directed, several questions seem particularly relevant. Can university trustees, administrations and faculties be made to understand the degree of actual power that a small minority of students can mobilize? Must colleges and universities undergo crisis situations in order to develop appropriate policies and procedures for handling student-university confrontations? What issues complicate the resolution of campus crises?

6   It is possible that the degree of actual power that a minority of students can mobilize is underestimated or misperceived simply because students have not so behaved in the past. Although this may be partially true as far as the post-World War II population of students is concerned, a more inclusive explanation would have to cover several additional points. A critical consideration is that faculty, administration and students do not form monolithic groups. There seems to be a tendency on the part of all parties to a campus confrontation to perceive and treat one another as if they were homogeneous. Administrators or professors define their roles according to traditional functions; this role definition is one which increasing numbers of students concerned with Vietnam, the racial issue, and the economic and political scene reject as inappropriate and unrelated to their lives. Within that portion of the student population which may be termed disenchanted but not alienated, there are those committed to changing the system by working within it, those concerned with retribution for past and present wrongs, and those committed to revolution. These students are intellectually alert, highly critical, and ever ready to condemn the "Establishment." Faculty and administrators who see themselves as the dispensers of knowledge and the stimulators of rational inquiry, and who value a sense of detachment from the hurly-burly of the market place, lump the dissenters into such groups as "poor students," "neurotics," "undisciplined people" or "anarchists." They all fail to fit the old mold of the "good" (read docile) student.

7   The difficulties of changing one's style of perception are matched by the difficulties of changing one's style of professional life. Many faculty who have endeavored to reach the activists have done so in their own particular intellectual fashion and within their own role perceptions, and this has often resulted in considerable frustration. To these professors, the students may appear to lack knowledge or a capacity for logical thinking and rational analysis. Further, if the faculty member or

administrative official has contact with a member or members of a black student group, he may extrapolate his observations of those students to the members of Students for a Democratic Society, or vice versa, thus failing to differentiate among the dissenting groups. There is often an additional failure to see that many segments of opinion exist within each of the groups, in which case opinions as to who the students are and what they are tend to be both inaccurate and inadequate.

8   One of the serious misperceptions of dissenting students, at least at the leadership level, is the extent of their distrust of faculty and administration, and their disenchantment, to varying degrees, with conventional dialogue as a means to social change. This point was recently made by a high school student at a conference on "Students and Society" sponsored by the Center for the Study of Democratic Institutions, who stated that "dialogue assumes a common set of assumptions and goals; and in their absence, dialogue is only a way of avoiding change."

9   Although the range of student activist groups is wide and the differences between the objectives, tactics and rhetoric of black and white organizations are marked, they share a considerable interest in revolutionary strategy. Professors, on the other hand, even those in the relevant fields which have brought them into contact with the history of revolutionary events, have not had either experience in or knowledge of the tactics of confrontation. Many faculty and administrators think of dissenting students in terms of the 1963–64 civil rights movement; they now should be studying the writings of Frantz Fanon, Mao Tse-tung and Che Guevara.

10   The failure on the part of the faculty and the administration to appreciate the actual power which a small minority of students can mobilize leads directly to the need to formulate in advance procedures for negotiation whereby disputes can be resolved *before* they become actual showdowns. As long as a college president and his immediate supportive administrative staff believe that their students will never become militant, laying siege to buildings, disrupting classrooms, or holding administrative officers hostage, they are not likely to think seriously how they should respond to such uprisings. And yet the "business as usual" mechanisms of the university or college are poorly adapted to rapid decision making. Part of the reflective posture of the academic world is to "carefully study" problems that require either faculty recommendations or administrative decisions. The diversity among student groups is probably exceeded only by the divisions within any faculty. Hence, it is indeed a rare occasion when a faculty expresses its overwhelming support of a given position, as was the case at Berkeley in December, 1964, or at San Francisco State in December, 1967. But in both of these instances one important issue served to unify the faculty: groups outside the university were pressing to fragment or limit the traditional prerogatives of the institution. Often on occasions of direct

clash between student opinion and administrative policy, the faculty has lacked an apparatus for making its opinions known or its influence felt. Depending upon the matter at hand, faculty organization ranges from small units such as departments to the total faculty which is convened on special occasions for either academic or ceremonial purposes but which rarely operates as a legislative entity. Frequently, the pattern is for representative groups such as academic councils or senates to advise and counsel the administration. In its turn, the administration is often either restricted in fact, or believes itself restricted by the policies, procedures and past decisions of the board of regents or trustees. In this situation, the speed and cogency of the president's decision, when attempting to deal with a student confrontation, may be dependent not only upon his capacity to comprehend the nature of the situation—and of course on his courage—but also on his perception of his own relationship to his trustees.

11   Student activist groups that press for confrontation are well aware that the prolongation of actual disruption of the campus produces pressures that polarize the position of trustees, administration, faculty, students and members of the community. Student militants have learned well the dynamics of conflict. They understand that the initial or precipitating incidents either can be restricted or can be fanned out to include a host of related or unrelated grievances, and they can choose the method most advantageous to them. The militants will generally be quite clear about what constitutes the substance of their grievances and the tactics to be employed in pressing for confrontation. In some instances those confrontations, which place the administration in the most untenable position, may appear to be entirely tactical from the observer's frame of reference, but the militant's objective is to make clear the repressive and oppressive forces which a university can exert, usually through the local police, and this constitutes an end in itself because it can broaden the constituency of the militant groups. In this connection, the militants understand the distinctions between the political and mediator roles which may be performed on their behalf by sympathetic members of the faculty. The mediating efforts of the moderate or liberal, well-intentioned faculty interventionists may be summarily dismissed because they constitute an obstacle to violent confrontation.

12   Of the issues complicating the resolution of campus crises, some of the thorniest relate to the subsequent treatment of students who have disrupted the university. Although various patterns of faculty and student advisory boards and councils exist within many institutions, the actual responsibility for disciplinary action resides with the president, who may or may not be restricted by the trustees in the delegation of this authority to disciplinary committees composed of faculty, students and administrative staff.

13   Militant groups recognize that no matter what stipulations or con-

cessions are offered, they must inevitably hold out to the extent possible for total amnesty for all participants. At this point the nature of the conflict moves from substantive grievances into disputes over the operation of the university and past administrative decisions and procedures. And at this point, faculties and administrations that have been capriciously indifferent to the attitudes of students in the past will cite polls of students indicating that the majority supports punitive action against the dissenters. The hard-line, law and order position will be taken up by certain intellectuals on the faculty, the "jocks" and the trustees. Their rhetoric varies from the position that concession to the demands of the minority encourages further rebellion to the simple wish of the "jocks" and "freddies" to have a legitimatized chance to demonstrate their masculinity.

14   When the crisis approaches its peak, the president must formulate a plan to punish the offenders. The initial difficulty at this stage is to define the offender. If the criterion is to be a legal one and judged by the courts, what evidence is available to prosecute, and can actions such as suspension be taken by the university prior to court judgment without prejudicing the cases? If the definition is to be made within the university, the offense must still be specified. Is the student who enters a classroom while a lecture is going on and politely asks the instructor for permission to make a one-minute announcement guilty of "interfering with the normal processes of the university"? If the president takes a "soft" position, he risks the wrath not only of his board of trustees but also of many members of his student body, faculty and the community. This is an amount of pressure and force which few administrators are strong enough to resist.

15   The issue often requires a long-range perspective, wherein the president finds his position utterly untenable. Will a university that has failed to respond to the needs and interests of a significant minority of its students serve its own interests by taking a "hard line"? If outside police are called in and charges filed, the president has publicly acknowledged his incompetence and the incompetence of his institution to deal with its own students. If he does not, and the crisis is prolonged, there is a vivid possibility, particularly in urban centers and specifically when the issues relate to race or peace, that community support will flow in to assist the student activists. And if such outside assistance does come and violence occurs, the president will then be subject to the criticisms of those who equate law and order with justice.

16   The president who does call in outside force to clear a building or put down a demonstration violates the intellectual conscience of many within the academic community who may be sympathetic to the students' cause though in disagreement with their methods. The academic community—or at least a segment of it—will see the use of outside force as representing a failure in the power of reason, intellectual persuasion

and open dialogue. Sensitive to such concerns, the administration may call upon its faculty or some representative group or council for advice and may also ask for the consultative assistance of the local police. The territorial integrity of the university will usually be respected by the police who will, in effect, wait for the call, although they may take preliminary steps such as establishing command posts, communication centers, and drawing up their own strategies for dealing with the disturbance. But in the end, the critical decision of whether to call the police onto the campus and in force rests with the president. Given a disturbance that forces this question, one course of action will bring a president about as much criticism as another—he will not only lose either way but in most instances he will be unable even to lose gracefully.

17   The prolongation of siege states due to bickering over degrees of punishment can well be viewed as an effort to save dying institutions by knocking off the students who represent forces of change. Whether these changes are undesirable or offensive to some, or even if the ultimate judgment of history proves them wrong, to deny the presence of such social forces is to deny reality and thereby divert the university from one of its major endeavors.

18   What then is the reality? Or, more accurately, what are some of the realities reflected in the campus crises? The first and most obvious to everyone except the do-business-as-usual folks of the university and non-university world is that significant changes are occurring in a society which is being torn apart by its racism, its pursuit of an unpopular war, and its bureaucratic breakdown. The committed youth are not dropouts, but they see their professors as "copouts," who are often anti-ideological, and view dialogue as a convenient way to forestall action. Above all, the youth want action. They do not want to be patronized, lectured to, or ritualistically listened to; they want to be heard and they want a fast response. Lacking it, they will act, whether wisely or unwisely; they will use the power they have and, ultimately, they will move the university closer to what it should be—not a sheltered community of scholars detached from a dying world but rather a community of individuals seeking the truths that will, in fact as well as in words, set men free.

Discussion of Theme

1. What is student power? What can it accomplish? What harm can it do?
2. What were the substantive issues that triggered the Columbia student rebellion? What larger issues were actually behind the upheaval?
3. According to the author, what mistakes do faculty members make in trying to deal with rebelling students?
4. In a confrontation, where should the faculty's loyalty ultimately lie: with the administration or with the students?

5. According to the author, how can college administrators avoid campus disturbances, or at least minimize their unpleasant effects?

Discussion of Rhetoric
1. How would you describe the tone of this essay: calm and reasoned, or emotional and highly subjective? Is the tone appropriate to an analysis? What contributes to that tone or attitude?
2. What techniques does the author use to convey a sense of immediacy? Note, for example, the first sentence of paragraph 4.
3. This selection begins with a reference to the week-long siege of Columbia University. Why? Where does the author introduce his central thesis?
4. Is the title of the selection appropriate? Would you have chosen another? Why?

Writing Assignments
1. Describe the reforms you would like to see on your campus. Suggest ways of bringing them about.
2. If you do not believe that students should have the right to demonstrate or strike, present your arguments in a theme.
3. Levine suggests that much student unrest is caused by significant changes taking place in our society. Describe those changes and the impact they are having on your generation.
4. The author states that a college president "must formulate a plan to punish the offenders." Draw up such a plan.

Library Exploration
1. Who are Frantz Fanon, Herbert Marcuse, and Che Guevara? What influence have they had on today's militant students?
2. Report on the student uprisings at San Francisco State, including the role played by S. I. Hayakawa.
3. Who are the Students for a Democratic Society? What are their avowed principles? What part have they played in campus disruptions?

Vocabulary
substantive (3): real; essential
monolithic (6): structured as a single unit, like a huge stone block
homogeneous (6): alike in kind
prerogatives (10): rights
entity (10): being
cogency (10): the quality of being compelling or convincing because of sound argument
untenable (11): incapable of being held or maintained
constituency (11): body of supporters; membership
capriciously (13): by whim

2

THE PILL AND THE MODERN WOMAN

Robert Ostermann and Mark Arnold

The current population of the world will be doubled by the end of this century. The anticipated shortage of food and living space has already begun to worry our scientists. Many believe that the pill is the most promising method for curbing the population explosion.

1   In recent years two proposals, working hand in hand, appear to offer the best means of solving the bulging problems of the poor and over-populated nations. The first is to set up comprehensive birth-control campaigns to cut back their rising populations. At the same time they must develop natural resources, intensify economic growth, and promote the social welfare of their underprivileged masses.

2   The latter is a formidable task, as any student of United States foreign aid and development programs can readily testify. With the appearance of sophisticated contraceptives like the pill, the former has seized the imaginations of many experts.

3   The pill, however, contracts as well as expands the focus of birth-control possibilities. Because it is practically foolproof and used without impeding the sexual act in any way, the pill has brought out certain ironies, certain oppositions, latent from the start in birth control considered both as a philosophy and as a practice.

4   Draw back for a moment from the world scene. While the hourly increase of global population proceeds relentlessly on, a woman soon to be married is found sitting deep in thought.

5   She is pondering the consequences, for herself, of childbearing. She weighs them against the emotional, social, and economic advantages available to the childless female. The first looks like instant servitude to her; the second, like a world of expanding freedom from constraint.

6   What should she do?

7   The question does not delay her long. It's not new to her; it has come before her in one way or another since she attained puberty. In recent months, preparing for marriage, she has given it much thought.

8   She makes up her mind. She believes it will be to the interest of everyone concerned—herself, her future husband, the children she expects

one day to have—to postpone pregnancy for several years.

9   It only remains for her to decide how to do it. And that is no problem. It's a decision modern pharmaceutical science has made exceedingly easy. She'll use the pill. She knows from experience it is right for her.

10   So two images: That of the world with its population and its food production on a collision course and that of an informed young woman coolly choosing her reproductive career, with the means to make it stick.

11   They appear to have little in common. One has a humanitarian and global perspective; the other may be considered selfish and personal. One has a view to mankind and its betterment; the other, to the individual woman and her fulfilment as a whole person.

12   Opposing perspectives, it would seem. And in a sense they are. Yet the images mingle inextricably, join as well as separate, to form the birth-control environment of our time.

13   Without the first, governmental authorities all over the world would never be mobilized in the cause of controlling population. But they are being mobilized. Symbol of this is the U.N. General Assembly's endorsement of a 25-nation resolution calling on the U.N. and its specialized agencies to join the battle against uncontrolled population growth.

14   Without the second, there would probably be little progress in spreading the practice of birth control. Robert C. Cook, who heads the Population Reference Bureau, has stated the plain truth without equivocation: "I very much doubt whether any couple ever decided to reduce their fertility because it was in the national interest."

15   That is to say, a woman, who with the pill becomes complete custodian of birth control, will hardly use the medication unless she's persuaded it is in her self-interest to do so.

16   Evidence to support this contention can be found in the Scandinavian countries, long world leaders in openly promoting both birth control and liberal standards of sexual behavior.

17   Scandinavia has no population problem, no food problem, scant poverty. And birth control is almost a Scandinavian specialty. It is practiced by most adult women and is available on demand by adolescent girls without the consent of their parents. In Denmark, the law permits any 15- to 18-year-old boy or girl to go over parental authority in seeking contraceptive help from any clinic or doctor prepared to give it.

18   The explanation is that Scandinavian women, married and single, practice birth control for financial or personal reasons. The biggest reason, according to available data, is the desire of housewives to hold jobs outside the home.

19   It is no idle fancy to see the American woman in the example as the individual equivalent of deprived national populations in need of birth control. Her private contraceptive goals symbolize the com-

pelling requirements of whole populations: Economic security, self-improvement, practical liberation, and additional control over one's destiny.

20   The forms they may take for the American will be different. But in principle, there is agreement.

21   What the pill has done is reveal these two facets of birth control. Only one was visible before. Prior to the pill, birth control was a prerogative of the middle and upper classes. It had notably little appeal for anyone else, although in theory birth control was obviously more advantageous to the poor, who couldn't afford numerous children, than to the better situated person.

22   The trouble was that contraceptives weren't equal to the idea. Methods like the diaphragm, condom, chemical creams and jellies were poorly suited to the poor and ill-educated woman. They were expensive, troublesome, fallible, and their regular and effective use demanded sustained motivation.

23   So long as they were the only contraceptives, birth control remained reserved for the affluent public. And, historically, small families have proved to be the privilege of the more affluent social groups in society.

24   The pill has changed all this. By suppressing ovulation it is practically 100 per cent effective against involuntary conception. Its cost is decreasing all the time. The prescribed regimen of one pill a day for 20 days is easy to understand and simple to follow.

25   Perhaps the pill's greatest recommendation is the fact it does not intrude at the time of sexual intercourse.

26   To be sure, in a few women it causes temporary, unpleasant side effects like breakthrough bleeding and edema (excess fluid). But these usually vanish after several months' use. Other women, again a minority, having a history of cancer or thromboembolism (clotting) or liver disorders are prohibited from using the pill.

27   In the early years of the pill's history, it was generally thought the medication was unacceptable for controlling fertility among the woman of less developed countries. The argument was that their inexperience with medicine, a high incidence of illiteracy and ignorance, and a shortage of doctors to examine candidates for the pill made its use impractical.

28   For women in these circumstances, the intra-uterine device (IUD) seemed to be the ultimate answer. IUDs are small, variously shaped devices of metal or plastic. They are inserted by a physician into the uterine cavity, and by a mode of operation that is incompletely understood, they prevent pregnancy.

29   The IUD is permanently installed, is very inexpensive, and does not have to be replaced. Only an annual or semiannual checkup is recommended. Thus its advantages are clear.

30   But not even in its most popular form, the Lippes loop, invented by

Dr. Jack Lippes, is the IUD completely effective against pregnancy. From 2 to 7 women out of 100 can expect to become pregnant during the first year of use. That puts the IUD on a par with the condom and diaphragm, making it of questionable value where avoidance of pregnancy is imperative.

31   Moreover, IUDs are unsuitable for women who have not had children. They are also frequently expelled without knowledge of the fact, thus exposing the user to unexpected pregnancy.

32   Despite these limitations, and primarily for economic reasons, they are extensively used in several critically overpopulated countries. More than 1,000,000 loops have been placed in Indian women. Egyptian midwives are being paid a government bounty for every woman they persuade to have a loop inserted. Using primarily the loop, Korea has reduced its annual population growth rate of 3 per cent to 1.9 per cent.

33   In the meantime, pilot projects were testing the effectiveness of the pill among illiterate women having no familiarity with medicine. Would they, could they, take a pill a day for birth control?

34   The results were affirmative. In India, Puerto Rico, Malaysia, Mexico, Pakistan, and Ceylon, family-planning campaigns proved there was no cultural or literacy block to accepting pills when the programs were well-organized and conscientiously run.

35   The obstacles of higher cost and doctor shortages remain unanswered. Apparently both the pill and the IUD together will carry the burden of fertility control in the less developed countries with excessive population increases. Unless, for example, U.S. foreign aid funds could be used to purchase contraceptive devices in Agency for International Development family-planning programs.

36   This seems to be the direction in which AID policy is heading. "Key obstacles are being removed," says an AID official. "Soon we can get on with the job."

37   Any other radical change is likely to come only if some of the experimental contraceptives now being researched or tested were to prove themselves and be approved for public use by the Federal Food and Drug Administration.

38   At the moment, the most promising drug, for domestic as well as foreign use, takes the form of microdoses of progestin, one of the synthetic hormones now part of the pill compound for arresting ovulation. The progestin would probably be contained in a tiny plastic capsule that would then be injected under the skin, from which the hormone would seep into the body.

39   The advantage of this method is that one capsule may insure security from pregnancy for as long as 20 years, with fertility being restored by removing the capsule whenever the patient so wishes. Microdose therapy points in the direction most family-planning experts would like to see contraceptive development take, although researchers are also

hopeful it may be possible to immunize the female against male sperm cells or induce by chemical means a reversible sterility in the male.

40   This is all in the future, however, and speculation on contraceptive developments must be hedged by uncertainty. The drug companies are extremely cautious in speaking of products under consideration. It is quite likely that revolutionary contraceptives, unrelated to the present medication, are being devised by many pharmaceutical manufacturers.

41   The recent past contains significant hints to how revolutionary may be the future effect of these contraceptives on the growth of the United States population.

42   The pill received FDA approval in 1960. The ensuing years have seen the culmination of a remarkable reversal in the pattern of U.S. population increase. The growth rate has dropped sharply from a peak net gain in 1961 of 3,000,000 to about 2,160,000 in 1966.

43   Chiefly responsible for this has been the steady decline in the U.S. birth rate, which is measured in the number of births per year for every 1,000 women of childbearing age. The birth rate reached its maximum in 1957, dropping from the 122.9 of that year to the approximately 91 in early 1967. The actual number of annual births has dropped by 700,000 from the 1961 figure of 4,268,000.

44   It isn't clear yet how much influence on these changes the pill has had. The decision to start having children a little later in marriage became evident in the 1960s. In recent years, too, women have been getting married somewhat later than they used to; there are also longer intervals between children. None of this is directly attributable to the pill.

45   But Professor Norman B. Ryder, director of the University of Wisconsin's Population Research Center, points out that the decline in fertility definitely accelerated over the past two years, the period in which the numbers of women using the pill jumped from less than 4,000,000 to over 5,000,000.

46   Says Professor Ryder, who with Princeton sociologist Prof. Charles W. Westoff recently completed a study of national pill use, "The simultaneous acceleration in the adoption of oral contraception in this period is unlikely to be merely a coincidence."

47   On the basis of studies like Westoff-Ryder and of data being assembled by other population research centers, some family-planning experts are sounding optimistic about the progress in the intelligent control of U.S. population growth.

48   Others hesitate to draw even tentative conclusions. Their uncertainty is based on the anticipated increase in the population of young women of prime reproductive years, those from 20 to 29. In 1935 there were about 11,000,000 of them. By 1970 it is estimated they will number 15,500,000; by 1980, some 20,000,000.

49   Much depends upon the decisions of this group toward family plan-

ning. If these women continue to opt for fewer children, later in marriage, and more widely spaced, the birth rate will continue dropping. But behavior predictions are risky, and authorities are unwilling to say the downward trend will unquestionably proceed.

50 A number of astute observers challenge optimism full face. They insist it is imperative to know who uses contraceptives and who has the unwanted and unplanned births, otherwise broad population trends are misleading. They say contraception is still a privilege of the upper social groups, while the economically and socially deprived continue to bear children they don't want and can't adequately care for.

51 Most studies bear them out. Some of the figures run as high as 85 or 90 per cent, representing those women in the group studied whose last pregnancy was unplanned and unwanted. A survey made at the University of North Carolina Medical Center showed 82 per cent of the mothers in the last two lower social groups listed their last pregnancy as unwanted.

52 What concerns these critics is the high incidence of maternal and pediatric complications among these groups. More infants die before or shortly after birth to patients in deprived circumstances; 45 out of 1,000, current data indicate.

53 These women also experience a higher rate of premature births. And premature children, medical statistics show, have the highest incidence of cerebral palsy, mental retardation, blindness, deafness, and other sensory disorders that help arrest their development.

54 An ardent spokesman for the cause of fertility control among the deprived and indigent is Dr. Charles E. Flowers, head of the department of obstetrics and gynecology at Baylor University's prestigious college of medicine. Doctor Flowers is so convinced this is an imperative task he proposes giving incentives to welfare recipients, for example, to encourage them to use an appropriate method of family planning.

55 He recommends changes in the tax structure. "One possible solution," he says, "would be to limit the $600 income tax exemption to two children."

56 Remarking the appearance of a national guaranteed annual income on the welfare horizon, he says family planning should be included as one of the qualifying requirements participating clients must comply with.

57 "Happily," adds Doctor Flowers, "it is not now necessary to use any other method of coercion besides a financial reward." But his voice leans heavily on the phrase "now necessary."

58 The contest between these several views isn't likely to be resolved in the near future. More information is needed. It's an area of controversy where tempers rise rapidly, prejudices quickly show, and conclusions are leaped to with alarming rapidity and without sufficient evidence.

59   Right now, perhaps the best thing the United States has to offer its own deprived population and the needy populations of the world is that contraception can and does work, if conscientiously practiced. It can and does offer mastery over the reproductive side of life. The United States presents the largest demonstration that individual self-interest is the most effective method of moving a population group toward an appropriate goal.

60   The example does more. The United States is proof that a large society can make the change from "fertile" to "sterile" in a relatively short period.

61   The terms are applied to the United States by Dr. Andre Hellegers, internationally renowned gynecologist on the staff of Johns Hopkins Hospital in Baltimore, Md. He explains the fertile society as one in which decisions are made to interrupt fertility by using birth control. The emphasis is still on having children. Birth control is an option.

62   "In the sterile society," he says, "you choose to have children by ceasing to practice contraception. The United States is very near that condition today."

63   He adds, "There's all the difference in the world between the two ways of life."

64   The difference, in fact, is a revolution.

65   The test for the United States is whether the revolution can be successfully exported to regions that can benefit from it. That test is not one the United States has impressively passed in its efforts to export other aspects of the democratic revolution.

66   The critical observation is made by Dr. Karl Evang, head of Norway's health services and an old hand at family planning.

67   "America is very active but extremely naive," comments Doctor Evang. "The Americans seem to think that all you have to do is drop a load of contraceptives by parachute on a high birth-rate area, and the people will do the rest. So unrealistic."

68   And realism is a prerequisite of population control.

Discussion of Theme

1. According to the authors, why do women use the pill? Are those who use it motivated by selfish reasons?
2. What has been the pattern of U.S. population growth in the last decade? What is chiefly responsible for this pattern?
3. Has the use of the pill changed the old notion that contraception is a privilege of the middle and upper classes?
4. What is a "sterile" society? Is the United States becoming one?

Discussion of Rhetoric

1. Do the authors merely assume that their audience will agree with them? Do they make any effort to overcome the possible objections of those who might be opposed to the pill?

2. Note the use of short paragraphs. What is the overall effect of this device?
3. How would you characterize the tone of this selection? Do the authors use scare tactics? Or is their approach more reasoned? What kind of development is used to support their thesis?

Writing Assignments

1. Develop the following statement into a theme: "Increased use of the pill will encourage a breakdown in morality among young people in college."
2. What is our greatest threat: nuclear warfare, the population explosion, or the depletion of natural resources? Present your evidence in a theme.
3. If you are against the use of birth-control pills for religious or other reasons, give your views.
4. Should unmarried college students be given birth-control information by college health services?

Library Exploration

1. Some authorities on population growth differ with the authors of this article. You might be interested in reading their arguments.
2. What are some of the religious arguments against the use of the pill?
3. Investigate the population theories of Thomas Malthus, and their applicability to today's population problems.

Vocabulary

impeding (3): obstructing
latent (3): present but not visible or active
inextricably (12): entangled inseparably
equivocation (14): evasiveness; uncertainty; ambiguity
fallible (22): capable of error
opt (49): make a choice
astute (50): shrewd
indigent (54): needy; impoverished
prestigious (54): highly respected

3

BROTHERS IN THE ETERNAL COLD

Archibald MacLeish

Since the beginning of time, man's image of himself and his fellow men has been determined by his view of the earth. This short essay comments on a recent event that "may remake our image of mankind."

1   Men's conception of themselves and of each other has always depended on their notion of the earth. When the earth was the World— all the world there was—and the stars were lights in Dante's heaven, and the ground beneath men's feet roofed Hell, they saw themselves as creatures at the center of the universe, the sole, particular concern of God—and from that high place they ruled and killed and conquered as they pleased.

2   And when, centuries later, the earth was no longer the World but a small, wet spinning planet in the solar system of a minor star off at the edge of an inconsiderable galaxy in the immeasurable distances of space—when Dante's heaven had disappeared and there was no Hell (at least no Hell beneath the feet)—men began to see themselves not as God-directed actors at the center of a noble drama, but as helpless victims of a senseless farce where all the rest were helpless victims also, and millions could be killed in worldwide wars or in blasted cities or in concentration camps without a thought or reason but the reason— if we call it one—of force.

3   Now, in the last few hours, the notion may have changed again. For the first time in all of time, men have *seen* the earth: seen it not as continents or oceans from the little distance of a hundred miles or two or three, but seen it from the depths of space; seen it whole and round and beautiful and small, as even Dante—that "first imagination of Christendom"—had never dreamed of seeing it; as the 20th-century philosophers of absurdity and despair were incapable of guessing that it might be seen. And seeing it so, one question came to the minds of those who looked at it. "Is it inhabited?" they said to each other and laughed—and then they did not laugh. What came to their minds a hundred thousand miles and more into space—"halfway to the moon" they put it—what came to their minds was the life on that little, lonely,

floating planet, that tiny raft in the enormous, empty night. "Is it inhabited?"

4 The medieval notion of the earth put man at the center of everything. The nuclear notion of the earth put him nowhere—beyond the range of reason even—lost in absurdity and war. This latest notion may have other consequences. Formed as it was in the minds of heroic voyagers who were also men, it may remake our image of mankind. No longer that preposterous figure at the center, no longer that degraded and degrading victim off at the margins of reality and blind with blood, man may at last become himself.

5 To see the earth as it truly is, small and blue and beautiful in that eternal silence where it floats, is to see ourselves as riders on the earth together, brothers on that bright loveliness in the eternal cold— brothers who know now they are truly brothers.

Discussion of Theme
1. What does the author mean by "the nuclear notion of the earth?" Do you believe that it will be replaced by the "latest notion"?
2. MacLeish mentions several views men have taken of themselves and their surroundings. Which does he seem to advocate?
3. Why does MacLeish feel that "this latest notion" has removed from man the stigma of a "degraded and degrading victim off at the margins of reality and blind with blood"?
4. Does the author explain what he means by "man may at last become himself," or does he leave it to the reader to interpret his meaning? Is the meaning clear?

Discussion of Rhetoric
1. Who are the "brothers" MacLeish refers to in the title and in paragraph 5? How does the use of the word *brothers* relate to the theme and tone of this article?
2. Citing specific examples, comment on the structure of the sentences in this article.
3. Consider the tone and diction of this article. What do they tell us about the author's intentions?
4. How is the question "Is it inhabited?" important to the theme of this essay?
5. One of the notable characteristics of this article is its organization. Locate the thesis sentence, then distinguish and briefly summarize introduction, developmental points, and conclusion.
6. MacLeish arranges and develops the points of his essay sequentially. Why is this type of organization good for many topics? How effective is it in this case? If you felt it necessary, how would you rearrange the order of development?

Writing Assignments

1. Develop the following quotation into a theme or short story: "Is it inhabited?"
2. Discuss the cold war in an essay entitled "Enemies in the Eternal Cold."
3. Describe the earth as seen from an airplane, a space capsule, or from the moon.
4. If you have read Dante, compare his portrayal of heaven, earth, and hell with the ideas of these that are held by most informed persons today.

Library Exploration

Check the *Reader's Guide to Periodical Literature* for other recent essays on this topic. Report on two of them.

4

FOOTPRINTS ON THE MOON

John Noble Wilford

The author commends man's first landing on the moon as "a bold new extension of man's dominion over his environment."

1   On the desolate, lifeless landscape of the moon, a funny-looking vehicle squats motionless under the sun's glaring rays. On one of its four spindly legs is attached a small, stainless steel plaque which reads:

HERE MEN FROM THE PLANET EARTH
FIRST SET FOOT UPON THE MOON.
JULY 1969 A.D.
WE CAME IN PEACE FOR ALL MANKIND

2   The vehicle, the dispensable lower half of a lunar landing craft, is a monument to the historic event on July 20 when two American astronauts planted the first human footsteps on the earth's only satellite. The monument will remain there for ages, for without air the moon has no corrosion, without water it has no erosion.

3   The man who took the first step was Neil A. Armstrong, the 38-year-old civilian commander of the Apollo 11. As he reached the bottom of the landing craft's ladder and extended his booted left foot to touch the moon's powdery surface, he capsulized the momentous meaning of the moment: "That's one small step for man, one giant leap for mankind."

4   He was followed down the ladder minutes later by Edwin E. Aldrin, Jr., a 39-year-old Air Force colonel. For two hours and 21 minutes, the two men, cautiously at first and then boldly, capered about on the barren, rock-strewn lunar terrain. They tested their agility in the alien environment and took photographs. They erected scientific experiments and collected rock and soil samples. They set up a television camera so the whole world could watch. At one point Armstrong said to his colleague, "Isn't this fun?"

5   All the while the third member of the crew, Michael Collins, 38, an Air Force lieutenant colonel, piloted the Command Ship in lunar orbit 70 miles above the surface, waiting for the two explorers to rejoin him

for the trip back to earth. Altogether, the lunar visit lasted 21 hours and 37 minutes.

AN INCREDIBLE TRIUMPH

6   For the Apollo 11 crew, the successful 500,000-mile mission involving 88 separate steps was an incredible triumph of skill and courage. For the United States space team, from the other astronauts down to the technicians, it was the fulfillment of a decade of technological striving. For the world, it was the most dramatic demonstration of what man can do if he applies his mind and resources with single-minded determination. The moon, long the symbol of the impossible, was now within man's reach, the first port of call in the new age of spacefaring.

7   There have been other daring expeditions, of course. But Apollo 11 was different: a large proportion of mankind bore it witness. Through television and radio, literally hundreds of millions of people followed the activities aboard Columbia, the Command Ship, and Eagle, the landing craft—names chosen because, as Armstrong put it, they were "representative of the flight and the nation's hope." The television transmissions across the 238,000 miles from the moon were so clear and sharp, accentuating the deep shadows and bright sunlight, that they often created a sense of unreality.

8   Nor was Apollo 11 really a voyage of geographical discovery (its destination was known and had been photographed and probed by unmanned satellites) or an expedition of conquest (the 1967 space treaty, which was signed by the United States, stipulates that outer space, including the moon, "is not subject to national appropriation"). The space agency's primary objective was simply: "Perform a manned lunar landing and return."

9   Though the mission was accomplished almost without flaw, it was never without suspense and anxiety. The astronauts faced risks on the moon never before encountered by man. And, as with all space flights, chances of failure and disaster were ever present—the blast-off of the giant Saturn 5 rocket at Cape Kennedy, the entry of the spaceship into earth and lunar orbits, the never-before-attempted landing and lift-off from the moon, the link-up of Columbia and Eagle, the re-entry into the atmosphere, the splashdown. An error or malfunction of any of the millions of individual parts anywhere along the way could have ended the mission short of the goal. An equipment failure or accident on the moon could have left the astronauts stranded.

HEROES

10   But they made it. After eight days in space, they splashed down in the Pacific to a presidential greeting aboard the recovery carrier, the U.S.S. *Hornet*. They were the heroes of the nation and the world.

11   "This is the greatest week in the history of the world since the

Creation," a jubilant President Nixon told the space travelers. "As a result of what you've done, the world has never been closer together before."

12   The welcome was not the familiar red-carpet ceremony of space missions in which the returning astronauts walk across the deck of the carrier. The Apollo 11 crewmen were inside an isolation van and they conversed with Mr. Nixon by microphone. The astronauts were under quarantine as a precaution against the possibility that they brought back some deadly lunar organisms for which man has no immunity.

13   People everywhere, the important and the common, hailed the achievement. Perhaps never before had one event so captured the world's imagination and spirit of adventure. There were some grumbles about problems to be solved here on earth, but for days Apollo 11 monopolized the headlines, TV sets and radios, even in countries with Communist governments ordinarily hostile to the United States. The Soviet Union reported the mission at unprecedented length. "We rejoice at the success of the American astronauts," the government newspaper *Izvestia* said. Both Africans and Laplanders followed the mission on transistor radios.

14   Scores of heads of state and government sent President Nixon congratulatory messages praising the Apollo 11 crew for having added a new dimension to man's knowledge. Many shared the sentiment of Mrs. Golda Meir, Israel's premier, who hoped the demonstration of man's capacity might "open the way to that era of universal peace presaged by the prophets of old."

CULMINATION OF LONG EFFORT

15   Apollo 11 was the culmination of 12 years of effort since man discovered he could fly in space, and eight years of the Apollo program since President John F. Kennedy, concerned about Soviet space successes, committed the nation in 1961 to landing a man on the moon "before this decade is out." That commitment set in motion the greatest mobilization of men and resources ever undertaken for a peaceful project of science and exploration. The building of rockets and spacecraft required the concerted efforts of 20,000 industrial contractors, scores of university laboratories, and 400,000 people. In terms of money, the program cost $24 billion for Apollo, not counting the $392 million for the Mercury flights and the $1.3 billion for the Geminis—the two forerunner projects in which men proved they could live and work in space.

16   As the program gained momentum, it brought great changes to many rural regions and small towns where mills and abandoned war plants were converted to making such material as guidance instruments and booster rockets. Most of the activity was concentrated in the so-called "fertile crescent" stretching from Florida to Texas. At one end, en-

gineers erected a billion-dollar moonport on the sand around Cape
Canaveral; at the other, bulldozers cleared ranchlands outside Houston
for the complex flight control center, the heart of the system. And across
the globe, at remote spots and on ships, was strung a network of radar
stations to track the flights.

17   Though the program was carefully conceived and elaborately
planned, mistakes were made and accidents happened. The three
astronauts who were to make the first test flight of the Apollo Command
Ship—Virgil I. Grissom, Edward H. White and Roger B. Chaffee—
died in a fire that broke out in their cockpit during a launching-pad
rehearsal on January 27, 1967. The tragedy plunged the space team
into its gloomiest period, a time of self-doubt from which it took nearly
two years to recover.

18   Man's going to the moon sprang from political and technological considerations and even deeper, from the very roots of the human spirit.
One consideration was national security. Space was clearly connected
with development of rockets and instruments vital to defense. Another
was national prestige: the challenge to a great power to lead in an age
of technology. What moved the human spirit was, as Aldrin put it in a
reflective moment on the way home, "the insatiable curiosity of all mankind to explore the unknown" that had sent explorers to brave the
harshest conditions of this planet—to the poles, to the tops of mountains, to the loftiest balloon altitudes, to the deepest portions of the sea.
Then why not the moon?

19   There were critics who said that the Apollo program cost too much,
that the money and talent could be more usefully directed to fighting
disease and poverty, that it was a "childish stunt" to make a race out of
going to the moon and insisting on an artificial deadline. But by the time
of the lunar mission, thought turned to prospects that the astronauts
might bring back some clues to help solve the mysteries of the universe.

20   Whatever its impact on man and earth, the voyage of Apollo 11
marked a bold new extension of man's dominion over his environment.
It broke the bonds of his native planet and enabled him to reach another
world.

Discussion of Theme
1. President Nixon stated that "this [the week of the moon voyage] is
   the greatest week in the history of the world since the creation." Do
   you agree or disagree?
2. How would you have answered the critics who complained that the
   money spent on the Apollo program should have been used to fight
   poverty and disease?
3. What political considerations played a part in man's conquest of the
   moon?

4. In what sense did the voyage of Apollo 11 bring the peoples of the earth closer together? Was this true of earlier space missions?

Discussion of Rhetoric
1. Explain how personification is used in paragraph 1.
2. Many of the stories about the Apollo 11 mission were written in poetic language. Note the use of alliteration in paragraph 3 and other poetic devices elsewhere in the article.
3. Balanced sentences and phrases add rhythm to the article. Where have they been used to best effect?
4. Locate paragraphs where the author has used description to supplement narration. What do you notice about the kinds of description used?

Writing Assignments
1. Discuss the ways in which the astronauts' conquest of the moon was (or was not) a greater achievement than Columbus's voyage to the New World.
2. Write a theme about the way the moon landing affected romantic conceptions of the moon.

Library Exploration
Read some fictional accounts of voyages to the moon—perhaps by Jules Verne or Cyrano de Bergerac.

Vocabulary
presaged (14): foretold
insatiable (18): incapable of being satisfied
dominion (20): sovereignty; authority

5

"I AM THE NEW BLACK"

Thee Smith

In this essay, a young black student explains why he cannot accept the role he believes the white world has chosen for him. He wrote it when he was a student at Phillips Exeter Academy.

1   First of all, you should realize that you are white, and that I am black. . . . By and large, when I say that I am black, you picture one of two types of black men. But I refuse to be either; and if you listen as if I were one of them, you will never realize who and what I actually represent, and you will leave this place just as your fathers left it.

2   *I am the New Black.* I will neither babble about how much I love Jesus, nor entertain you with sparkling racial comedy. I will not eat with my fingers nor go out of my way to sit down at a dining hall table with you. I will not flunk out of this place, but neither will I participate in the childish fanaticism of raving with you about your math test, or your Phy Sci lab, or your grade in English. I want neither to be your enemy, nor your friend. I don't want your love, or your pity, or your guilt, or your fear. I demand only that you respect me. . . .

3   I, the New Black, am not exactly sure why I am here. . . . Last year I *did* know, without being told. Last year I was to eventually become a responsible American citizen. I felt that an investment had been made in me—not merely by this school but by your whole society—to provide a "safe," well-balanced, and responsible leadership for the black revolution. . . .

4   The fact that I once accepted your definition of my role as a black nauseates me. I see in your definition, and in my agreement, a continuation of what blacks in this country have been trying to do since the Civil War; a continuation of the efforts to teach blacks how to act "white," and at the same time teach them to deny the legitimacy of their own culture.

5   As the New Black, I shall not tolerate the teaching of other blacks to be industrious, puritanical, and relatively unemotional—as you are; for I feel that we, as human beings, have much more to lose by becoming white than by remaining true to ourselves, true to our culture, and true to our blackness. . . .

6   The problem, again, is you people. Our minority black middle class is willing and ready to prostitute itself before you, and you still cannot see *your* sickness inside them. The problem *is* racial. All men are *not* born equal. White *is* right. In a riot, *all* blacks are suspected of theft, and rape, and murder. . . .

7   I, the New Black, acknowledge my blackness, and the improbability of my ever becoming respected in your society by getting white. I, the New Black, not only accept but agree with your classification of all of us, regardless of class, as blacks. We have our blackness in common and we are united by your definition of what blacks in America are. . . . I am a black first, and an American when I can afford to be.

8   I am at Exeter, not to be like you, nor to prepare myself to enter your society as a Roy Wilkins or a James Meredith. This school's efforts to prepare me for that type of role in tomorrow's world are futile. That role no longer offers effective leadership for change, because it is based on the theory that a black leader should strive for assimilation of the black masses. Assimilation is no longer the solution, though. Civil rights, as a movement, is dying. My most effective role in tomorrow's society will be to lead the advancement of Black Power; and I, the New Black, dedicate my life to that role. . . .

9   We are at Exeter to obtain knowledge of ourselves, and when we become leaders, we will derive our strength not from your friendship, or your brains, or your money, but from ourselves.

Discussion of Theme

1. In the first paragraph, Smith states that " . . . when I say that I am black, you [whites] picture one of two types of black men." What are these two types?
2. The author tells his audience that if they ignore him, "you will leave this place [Exeter] just as your fathers left it." Explain this remark.
3. Why does the author reject what he considers the white man's definition of his role? What is his own conception of the black leader's role?
4. Should schools like Exeter continue to educate, and in some cases give scholarship funds to, black students who share Mr. Smith's views?

Discussion of Rhetoric

1. What is the author's relation to his audience? How does he stress it?
2. How would you describe his tone: angry? conciliatory? patronizing?
3. What is there about the sentence structure and diction that suggests this was originally a speech presented to the author's classmates?
4. Does this selection contain a statement of its central idea or thesis? If so, where is it stated? If not, phrase it in your own words.

Writing Assignments

1. Develop the following quotation, taken from this selection, into a theme: "The problem, again, is you people."
2. In an essay define Black Power.
3. Imagine you are a white classmate of Thee Smith; write a letter to him in response to this speech.

Library Exploration

1. Who are James Meredith and Roy Wilkins? Why do the New Blacks find them outdated or irrelevant? Investigate the events surrounding the enrollment of Meredith at the University of Mississippi, or the work of Roy Wilkins in civil-rights litigation.
2. Should colleges and universities establish black-studies departments? What steps have already been taken in this direction? Investigate the arguments of those who advocate separate programs for blacks, and present your recommendations, pro or con.
3. Who are the heroes of today's young black students? What qualities in these persons are admired and respected most?

Vocabulary

fanaticism (2): excessive zeal or enthusiasm
legitimacy (4): validity; legality
prostitute (6): debase
assimilation (8): absorption

6

INAUGURAL ADDRESS: SEARCH FOR PEACE

Richard M. Nixon

President Nixon delivered this address January 20, 1969.

1   Senator Dirksen, Mr. Chief Justice, Mr. Vice President, President Johnson, Vice President Humphrey, my fellow Americans and my fellow citizens of the world community: I ask you to share with me today the majesty of this moment. In the orderly transfer of power, we celebrate the unity that keeps us free.

2   Each moment in history is a fleeting time, precious and unique. But some stand out as moments of beginning, in which courses are set that shape decades or centuries.

3   This can be such a moment. Forces now are converging that make possible for the first time the hope that many of man's deepest aspirations can at last be realized.

4   The spiraling pace of change allows us to contemplate, within our own lifetime, advances that once would have taken centuries.

5   In throwing wide the horizons of space, we have discovered new horizons on earth.

6   For the first time, because the people of the world want peace and the leaders of the world are afraid of war, the times are on the side of peace.

7   Eight years from now America will celebrate its 200th anniversary as a nation. And within the lifetime of most people now living, mankind will celebrate that great new year which comes only once in a thousand years—the beginning of the third millennium.

8   What kind of a nation we will be, what kind of a world we will live in, whether we shape the future in the image of our hopes, is ours to determine by our actions and our choices.

9   The greatest honor history can bestow is the title of peacemaker. This honor now beckons America—the chance to help lead the world at last out of the valley of turmoil and on to that high ground of peace that man has dreamed of since the dawn of civilization.

10   If we succeed, generations to come will say of us now living that we mastered our moment, that we helped make the world safe for mankind.

11   This is our summons to greatness.

12   And I believe the American people are ready to answer this call.

13   The second third of this century has been a time of proud achievement. We have made enormous strides in science and industry and agriculture. We have shared our wealth more broadly than ever, we learned at last to manage a modern economy to assure its continued growth.

14   We have given freedom new reach, we have begun to make its promise real for black as well as for white.

15   We see the hope of tomorrow in the youth of today. I know America's youth. I believe in them. We can be proud that they are better educated, more committed, more passionately driven by conscience than any generation in our history.

16   No people has ever been so close to the achievement of a just and abundant society, or so possessed of the will to achieve it.

17   And because our strengths are so great, we can afford to appraise our weaknesses with candor and to approach them with hope.

18   Standing in this same place a third of a century ago, Franklin Delano Roosevelt addressed the nation ravaged by depression gripped in fear. He could say in surveying the nation's troubles: "They concern, thank God, only material things."

19   Our crisis today is in reverse.

20   We find ourselves rich in goods, but ragged in spirit, reaching with magnificent precision for the moon, but falling into raucous discord on earth.

21   We are caught in war, wanting peace. We're torn by division, wanting unity. We see around us empty lives, wanting fulfillment. We see tasks that need doing, waiting for hands to do them.

22   To a crisis of the spirit, we need an answer of the spirit.

23   And to find that answer, we need only look within ourselves.

24   When we listen to "the better angels of our nature," we find that they celebrate the simple things, the basic things, the basic things—such as goodness, decency, love, kindness.

25   Greatness comes in simple trappings.

26   The simple things are the ones most needed today if we are to surmount what divides us and cement what unites us. To lower our voices would be a simple thing.

27   In these difficult years, America has suffered from a fever of words; from inflated rhetoric that promises more than it can deliver; from angry rhetoric that fans discontents into hatreds; from bombastic rhetoric that postures instead of persuading.

28   We cannot learn from one another until we stop shouting at one another—until we speak quietly enough so that our words can be heard as well as our voices.

29   For its part, government will listen. We will strive to listen in new ways—to the voices of quiet anguish, the voices that speak without

words, the voices of the heart—to the injured voices, the anxious voices, the voices that have despaired of being heard.

30   Those who have been left out we will try to bring in. Those left behind, we will help to catch up.

31   For all our people, we will set as our goal the decent order that makes progress possible and our lives secure.

32   As we reach toward our hopes, our task is to build on what has gone before—not turning away from the old, but turning toward the new.

33   In this past third of a century, government has passed more laws, spent more money, initiated more programs, than in all our previous history.

34   In pursuing our goals of full employment, better housing, excellence in education; in rebuilding our cities and improving our rural areas; in protecting our environment, enhancing the quality of life—in all these and more, we will and must press urgently forward.

35   We shall plan now for the day when our wealth can be transferred from the destruction of war abroad to the urgent needs of our people at home.

36   The American dream does not come to those who fall asleep.

37   But we are approaching the limits of what government alone can do.

38   Our greatest need now is to reach beyond government, to enlist the legions of the concerned and the committed. What has to be done has to be done by government and people together or it will not be done at all. The lesson of past agony is that without the people we can do nothing; with the people we can do everything.

39   To match the magnitude of our talks, we need the energies of our people—enlisted not only in grand enterprises, but more importantly in those small splendid efforts that make headlines in the neighborhood newspaper instead of the national journal.

40   With these, we can build a great cathedral of the spirit—each of us raising it one stone at a time, as he reaches out to his neighbor, helping, caring, doing.

41   I do not offer a life of uninspiring ease. I do not call for a life of grim sacrifice. I ask you to join in a high adventure—one as rich as humanity itself, and exciting as the times we live in.

42   The essence of freedom is that each of us shares in the shaping of his own destiny. Until he has been part of a cause larger than himself, no man is truly whole.

43   The way to fulfillment is in the use of our talents; we achieve nobility in the spirit that inspires that use.

44   As we measure what can be done, we shall promise only what we know we can produce; but as we chart our goals we shall be lifted by our dreams.

45   No man can be fully free while his neighbor is not. To go forward at all is to go forward together.

46   This means black and white together, as one nation, not two. The laws have caught up with our conscience. What remains is to give life to what is in the law: to insure at last that as all are born equal in dignity before God, all are born equal in dignity before man.

47   As we learn to go forward together at home, let us also seek to go forward together with all mankind.

48   Let us take as our goal: where peace is unknown, make it welcome; where peace is fragile, make it strong; where peace is temporary, make it permanent.

49   After a period of confrontation, we are entering an era of negotiation. Let all nations know that during this Administration our lines of communication will be open.

50   We seek an open world—open to ideas, open to the exchange of goods and people, a world in which no people, great or small, will live in angry isolation.

51   We cannot expect to make everyone our friend, but we can try to make no one our enemy.

52   Those who would be our adversaries, we invite to a peaceful competition—not in conquering territory or extending dominion, but in enriching the life of man.

53   As we explore the reaches of space, let us go to the new worlds together—not as new worlds to be conquered, but as a new adventure to be shared.

54   And with those who are willing to join, let us cooperate to reduce the burden of arms, to strengthen the structure of peace, to lift up the poor and the hungry.

55   But to all those who would be tempted by weakness, let us leave no doubt that we will be as strong as we need to be for as long as we need to be.

56   Over the past 20 years, since I first came to this Capitol as a freshman Congressman, I have visited most of the nations of the world.

57   I have come to know the leaders of the world, the great forces, the hatreds, the fears that divide the world.

58   I know that peace does not come through wishing for it—that there is no substitute for days and even years of patient and prolonged diplomacy.

59   I also know the people of the world.

60   I have seen the hunger of a homeless child, the pain of a man wounded in battle, the grief of a mother who has lost her son. I know these have no ideology, no race.

61   I know America. I know the heart of America is good.

62   I speak from my own heart, and the heart of my country, the deep concern we have for those who suffer and those who sorrow.

63   I have taken an oath today in the presence of God and my countrymen. To uphold and defend the Constitution of the United States. And

to that oath, I now add this sacred commitment: I shall consecrate my office, my energies and all the wisdom I can summon, to the cause of peace among nations.

64 Let this message be heard by strong and weak alike.

65 The peace we seek—the peace we seek to win—is not victory over any other people, but the peace that comes with healing in its wings; with compassion for those who have suffered; with understanding for those who have opposed us; with the opportunity for all the peoples of this earth to choose their own destiny.

66 Only a few short weeks ago, we shared the glory of man's first sight of the world as God sees it, as a single sphere reflecting light in the darkness.

67 As Apollo astronauts flew over the moon's gray surface on Christmas Eve, they spoke to us of the beauty of earth and in that voice so clear across the lunar distance we heard them invoke God's blessing on its goodness.

68 In that moment, their view from the moon moved poet Archibald MacLeish to write: "To see the earth as it truly is, small and blue and beautiful in that eternal silence where it floats, is to see ourselves as riders on the earth together, brothers in that bright loveliness in the eternal cold—brothers who know now they are truly brothers."

69 In that moment of surpassing technological triumph, men turned their thoughts toward home and humanity—seeing in that far perspective that man's destiny on earth is not divisible; telling us that however far we reach into the cosmos our destiny lies not in the stars but on earth itself, in our own hands, in our own hearts.

70 We have endured a long night of the American spirit. But as our eyes catch the dimness of the first rays of dawn, let us not curse the remaining dark. Let us gather the light.

71 Our destiny offers not the cup of despair, but the chalice of opportunity. So let us seize it, not in fear, but in gladness—and "riders on the earth together," let us go forward, firm in our faith, steadfast in our purpose, cautious of the dangers; but sustained by our confidence in the will of God and the promise of man.

Discussion of Theme

1. What is "our summons to greatness"? What special challenges confront this generation of Americans?
2. In what sense are our problems today the reverse of those faced by the Depression generation?
3. What is Nixon's attitude toward other countries? Is he, for example, belligerent?
4. The President suggests that the "simple things" (paragraph 24) will help solve our problems. Do you agree? Does Nixon himself have the qualities he says will be useful?

5. Nixon is thought to be greatly admired by the average middle-class white citizen. What parts of this address might appeal particularly to this citizen? What parts might not?

Discussion of Rhetoric

1. How does Nixon achieve his informal, personal tone? Is this tone appropriate for such an occasion?
2. This address includes many words heavy with emotional overtones. Are they appropriate? Examine several for their effectiveness.
3. Notice the length and pattern of Nixon's sentences. What is there about the sentence structure that suggests this was an address?
4. Are there an introduction, body, and conclusion to this speech? If so, where are they?

Writing Assignments

1. Write a theme developing the following title: "America in the year 2000."
2. If you disagree with any of President Nixon's statements or conclusions, write a composition presenting your own views.
3. Develop the following sentence into a theme: "Greatness comes in simple trappings."

Library Exploration

1. Compare Nixon's inaugural address with John F. Kennedy's. How do they differ? What do the differences suggest about the men, as well as about their respective philosophies?
2. Read *Five Crises* by Richard Nixon, and report on the events that he regarded as crucial in his life.
3. Many political pundits believe there is a "new" Nixon. Investigate the part he played in the Alger Hiss trial of the early 1950s and the statements he has made on the threat of internal Communism. Report your findings.

Vocabulary

converging (3): coming together
millennium (7): period of a thousand years
candor (17): honesty; openness
bombastic (27): pretentious or pompous
dominion (52): political authority
consecrate (63): devote to a purpose with deep solemnity and dedication
compassion (65): sympathy
chalice (71): a drinking cup or goblet

7

NEXT—THE PLANETS

Arthur C. Clarke

With landing on the moon a reality, we can now start planning to explore the rest of the solar system. *A famous scientist (and science-fiction writer) tells us what we can expect to find.*

1   It has been said that history never repeats itself but that historical situations recur. To anyone, like myself, who has been involved in astronautical activities for over 30 years, there is a feeling of familiarity in some of the present arguments about the exploration of space. Like all revolutionary new ideas, the subject has had to pass through three stages, which may be summed up by these reactions: (1) "It's crazy—don't waste my time"; (2) "It's possible, but it's not worth doing"; (3) "I always said it was a good idea."

2   As far as orbital flights, and even journeys to the Moon, are concerned, we have made excellent progress through all of these stages, though it will be a few years yet before everyone is in category three. But where flights to the planets are involved, we are still almost where we were 30 years ago. True, there is much less complete skepticism—to that extent, history has *not* repeated itself—but there remains, despite all the events of the past decade, a widespread misunderstanding of the possible scale, importance and ultimate implications of travel to the planets.

3   Let us start by looking at some fundamentals, which are not as well known as they should be—even to space scientists. Forgetting all about rockets and today's astronautical techniques, consider the basic problem of lifting a man away from the Earth, purely in terms of the work done to move him against gravity. For a man of average mass, the energy requirement is about 1000 kilowatt-hours, which customers with a favorable tariff can purchase for ten dollars from their electric company. What may be called the basic cost of a one-way ticket to space is thus the modest sum of ten dollars.

4   For the smaller planets and all satellites—Mercury, Venus, Mars, Pluto, Moon, Titan, Ganymede, etc.—the exit fee is even less; you need only 50 cents' worth of energy to escape from the Moon. Giant planets such as Jupiter, Saturn, Uranus and Neptune are naturally a

much more expensive proposition. If you are ever stranded on Jupiter, you'll have to buy almost $300 worth of energy to get home. Make sure you take enough traveler's checks!

5   Of course, the planetary fields are only part of the story; work also has to be done traveling from orbit to orbit and thus moving up or down the enormous gravitational field of the Sun. But, by great good luck, the Solar System appears to have been designed for the convenience of space travelers: All the planets lie far out on the gentle slope of the solar field, where it merges into the endless plain of interstellar space. In this respect, the conventional map of the Solar System, showing the planets clustering round the Sun, is wholly misleading.

6   We can say, in fact, that the planets are 99 percent free of the Sun's gravitational field, so that the energy required for orbital transfers is quite small; usually, it is considerably less than that needed to escape from the planets themselves. In dollars and cents, the energy cost of transferring a man from the surface of the Earth to that of Mars is less than $20. Even for the worst possible case (surface of Jupiter to surface of Saturn), the pure energy cost is less than $1000.

7   Hardheaded rocket engineers may well consider that the above arguments, purporting to prove that space travel should be about a billion times cheaper than it is, have no relevance to the practical case—since, even today, the cost of the fuel is trivial, compared with the cost of the hardware. Most of the mountainous Saturn 5 standing on the pad can be bought for, quite literally, a few cents a pound; kerosene and liquid oxygen come cheap. The expensive items are the precision-shaped pieces of high-grade metals and all the little black boxes that are sold by the carat.

8   Although this is true, it is also, to a large extent, a consequence of our present immature, no-margin-for-error technology. Just ask yourself how expensive driving would be if a momentary engine failure were liable to write off your car—and yourself—and the fuel supply were so nicely calculated that you couldn't complete a mission if the parking meter you'd aimed at happened to be already occupied. This is roughly the situation for planetary travel today.

9   To imagine what it may one day become, let us look at the record of the past and see what lessons we can draw from the early history of aeronautics. Soon after the failure of Samuel Langley's "aerodrome" in 1903, the great astronomer Simon Newcomb wrote a famous essay, well worth rereading, that proved that heavier-than-air flight was impossible by means of known technology. The ink was hardly dry on the paper when a pair of bicycle mechanics irreverently threw grave doubt on the professor's conclusions. When informed of the embarrassing fact that the Wright brothers had just flown, Newcomb gamely replied: "Well, maybe a flying machine *can* be built. But it certainly couldn't carry a passenger as well as a pilot."

10   Now, I am not trying to poke fun at one of the greatest of American scientists. When you look at the Wright biplane, hanging up there in the Smithsonian Institution, Newcomb's attitude seems very reasonable, indeed; I wonder how many of us would have been prepared to dispute it in 1903.

11   Yet—and this is the really extraordinary point—there is a smooth line of development, without any major technological breakthroughs, from the Wright "flier" to the last of the great piston-engined aircraft, such as the DC-6. All the many-orders-of-magnitude improvement in performance came as a result of engineering advances that, in retrospect, seem completely straightforward and sometimes even trivial. Let us list the more important ones: variable-pitch airscrews, slots and flaps, retractable undercarriages, concrete runways, streamlining, and supercharging.

12   Not very spectacular, are they? Yet these things, together with steady improvements in materials and design, lifted much of the commerce of mankind into the air. For they had a synergistic effect on performance; their cumulative effect was much greater than could have been predicted by considering them individually. They did not merely add; they multiplied. All this took about 40 years. Then there was the second technological breakthrough—the advent of the jet engine—and a new cycle of development began.

13   Unless the record of the past is wholly misleading, we are going to see much the same sequence of events in space. As far as can be judged at the moment, the equivalent items of the table of aerospace progress may be: refueling in orbit, air-breathing boosters, reusable boosters, refueling on (or from) the Moon and lightweight materials (e.g., composites and fibers).

14   Probably the exploitation of these relatively conventional ideas will take somewhat less than the 40 years needed in the case of aircraft; their full impact should be felt by the turn of the century. Well before then, the next breakthrough or quantum jump in space technology should also have occurred, with the development of new propulsion systems—presumably fission-powered but, hopefully, using fusion as well, and with these, the Solar System will become an extension of the Earth—if we wish it to be.

15   It is at this point, however, that all analogy with the past breaks down; we can no longer draw meaningful parallels between aeronautics and astronautics. As soon as aircraft were shown to be practical, there were obvious and immensely important uses for them: military, commercial and scientific. They could be used to provide swifter connections between already highly developed communities—a state of affairs that almost certainly does not exist in the Solar System and may not for centuries to come.

16   It seems, therefore, that we may be involved in a peculiarly vicious

circle. Planetary exploration will not be really practical until we have developed a mature spaceship technology; but we won't have good spaceships until we have worthwhile places to send them—places, above all, with those adequate refueling and servicing facilities now sadly lacking elsewhere in the Solar System. How can we escape from this dilemma? Fortunately, there is one encouraging factor.

17   Almost all of the technology needed for long-range space travel will inevitably and automatically be developed during the exploration of *near* space. Even if we set our sights no higher than 1000 miles above the Earth, we would find that by the time we had perfected the high-thrust, high-performance surface-to-surface transports, the low-acceleration interorbital shuttles and the reliable, closed-cycle space-station ecologies, we would have proved out at least 90 percent of the technology needed for the exploration of the Solar System—and the most expensive 90 percent, at that.

18   Perhaps I had better deal here with those strange characters who think that space is the exclusive province of automatic, robot probes and that we should stay at home and watch TV, as God intended us to. This whole man-machine controversy will seem, in another couple of decades, to be a baffling mental aberration of the early space age.

19   I won't waste much time arguing with this viewpoint, as I hold these truths to be self-evident: (1) Unmanned spacecraft should be used whenever they can do a job more efficiently, cheaply and safely than manned vehicles; (2) Until we have automatons superior to human beings (by which time, all bets will be off), all really sophisticated space operations will demand human participation. I refer to such activities as assembling and servicing the giant applications satellites of the next decade and running orbital observatories, laboratories, hospitals and factories—projects for which there will be such obvious and overwhelming commercial and scientific benefits that no one will dispute them.

20   In particular, medium-sized telescopes outside the atmosphere—a mere couple of hundred miles above the Earth—will have an overwhelming impact on Solar System studies. The recent launching of OAO II—the initials stand for "Orbiting Astronomical Observatory"—was a promising beginning. Until the advent of radar and space probes, everything we knew about the planets had been painfully gathered, over a period of about a century and a half, by astronomers with inadequate instruments, hastily sketching details of a tiny, trembling disk glimpsed during moments of good sighting. Such moments—when the atmosphere is stable and the image undistorted—may add up to only a few hours in an entire lifetime of observing.

21   In these circumstances, it would be amazing if we had acquired any *reliable* knowledge about planetary conditions; it is safest to assume that we have not. We are still in the same position as the medieval cartogra-

phers, with their large areas of *"Terra Incognita"* and their "Here Be Dragons," except that we may have gone too far in the other direction— "Here Be *No* Dragons." Our ignorance is so great that we have no right to make either assumption.

22   As proof of this, let me remind you of some horrid shocks the astronomers have received recently, when things of which they were quite sure turned out to be simply not true. The most embarrassing example is the rotation of Mercury: Until a couple of years ago, everyone was perfectly certain that it always kept the same face toward the Sun, so that one side was eternally dark, the other eternally baked. But now, radar observations indicate that it turns on its axis every 59 days; it has sunrise and sunset, like any respectable world. Nature seems to have played a dirty trick on several generations of patient astronomers.

23   Einstein once said: "The good Lord is subtle, but He is not malicious." The case of Mercury casts some doubt on this dictum. And what about Venus? You can find, in the various reference books, rotation periods for Venus ranging all the way from 24 hours to the full value of the year, 225 days. But, as far as I know, not one astronomer ever suggested that Venus would present the extraordinary case of a planet with a day longer than its year. And, of course, it *would* be the one example we had no way of checking, until the advent of radar. Is this subtlety—or malice?

24   And look at the Moon. Five years ago, everyone was certain that its surface was either soft dust or hard lava. If the two schools of thought had been on speaking terms, they would at least have agreed that there were no alternatives. But then Luna 9 and Surveyor 1 landed—and what did they find? Good honest dirt.

25   These are by no means the only examples of recent shocks and surprises. There are the unexpectedly high temperature beneath the clouds of Venus, the craters of Mars, the gigantic radio emissions from Jupiter, the complex organic chemicals in certain meteors, the clear signs of extensive activity on the surface of the Moon. And now Mars seems to be turning inside out. The ancient, dried-up sea beds may be as much a myth as Dejah Thoris, Princess of Helium; for it looks as if the dark *Maria* are actually highlands, not lowlands, as we had always thought.

26   The negative point I am making is that we really know nothing about the planets. The positive one is that a tremendous amount of reconnaissance—the essential prelude to *manned* exploration—can be carried out from Earth orbit. It is probably no exaggeration to say that a good orbiting telescope could give us a view of Mars at least as clear as did Mariner 4. And it would be a view infinitely more valuable—a continuous coverage of the whole visible face, not a signal snapshot of a small percentage of the surface.

27   Nevertheless, there are many tasks that can best be carried out by unmanned spacecraft. Among these is one that, though of great scientific

value, is of even more profound psychological importance. I refer to the production of low-altitude oblique photographs. It is no disparagement of the wonderful Ranger, Luna and Surveyor coverage to remind you that what suddenly made the Moon a real place, and not merely an astronomical body up there in the sky, was the famous photograph of the Crater of Copernicus from Lunar Orbiter 2. When the newspapers called it the picture of the century, they were expressing a universally felt truth. This was the photograph that first proved to our emotions what our minds already knew but had never really believed—that Earth is not the only world. The first high-definition, oblique photos of Mars, Mercury and the satellites of the giant planets will have a similar impact, bringing our mental images of these places into sharp focus for the first time.

28   The old astronomical writers had a phrase that has gone out of fashion but that may well be revived: the plurality of worlds. Yet, of course, every world is itself a plurality. To realize this, one has only to ask: How long will it be before we have learned everything that can be known about the planet Earth? It will be quite a few centuries before terrestrial geology, oceanography and geophysics are closed, surprise-free subjects.

29   Consider the multitude of environments that exists here on Earth, from the summit of Everest to the depths of the Marianas Trench— from high noon in Death Valley to midnight at the South Pole. We may have equal variety on the other planets, with all that this implies for the existence of life. It is amazing how often this elementary fact is over-looked and how often a single observation or even a single extrapolation from a preliminary observation based on a provisional theory has been promptly applied to a whole world.

30   It is possible, of course, that the Earth has a greater variety of more complex environments than any other planet. Like a jet-age tourist "doing Europe" in a week, we may be able to wrap up Mars or Venus with a relatively small number of "landers." But I doubt it, if only for the reason that the whole history of astronomy teaches us to be cautious of any theory purporting to show that there is something special about the Earth. In their various ways, the other planets may have orders of complexity as great as ours. Even the Moon—which seemed a promising candidate for geophysical simplicity less than a decade ago—has already begun to unleash an avalanche of surprises.

31   The late Professor J. B. S. Haldane once remarked—and this should be called Haldane's Law—"The universe is not only stranger than we imagine, it is stranger than we *can* imagine." We will encounter the operation of this law more and more frequently as we move away from home. And as we prepare for this move, it is high time that we face up to one of the more shattering realities of the astronomical situation. For all practical purposes, we are still as geocentrically minded as if

Copernicus had never been born; to all of us, the Earth is the center, if not of the Universe, at least of the Solar System.

32   Well, I have news for you. There is really only one planet that matters; and that planet is not Earth but Jupiter. My esteemed colleague Isaac Asimov summed it up very well when he remarked: "The Solar System consists of Jupiter plus debris." Even spectacular Saturn doesn't count; it has less than a third of Jupiter's enormous mass—and Earth is a hundred times smaller than Saturn! Our planet is an unconsidered trifle, left over after the main building operations were completed. This is quite a blow to our pride, but there may be much worse to come, and it is wise to get ready for it. Jupiter may also be the *biological*, as well as the *physical*, center of gravity of the Solar System.

33   This, of course, represents a complete reversal of views within a couple of decades. Not long ago, it was customary to laugh at the naïve ideas of the early astronomers—Sir John Herschel, for example—who took it for granted that all the planets were teeming with life. This attitude is certainly overoptimistic; but it no longer seems as simpleminded as the opinion, to be found in the popular writings of the 1930s, that ours might be the only solar system and, hence, the only abode of life in the entire Galaxy.

34   The pendulum has, indeed, swung—perhaps for the last time; for in another few decades, we should know the truth. The discovery that Jupiter is quite warm and has precisely the type of atmosphere in which life is believed to have arisen on Earth may be the prelude to the most significant biological findings of this century. Carl Sagan and Jack Leonard put it well in their book *Planets*: "Recent work on the origin of life and the environment of Jupiter suggests that it may be more favorable to life than any other planet, not excepting the earth."

35   The extraordinary color changes in the Jovian atmosphere—in particular, the behavior of that Earth-sized, drifting apparition, the Great Red Spot—hint at the production of organic materials in enormous quantities. Where this happens, life may follow inevitably, given a sufficient lapse of time. To quote Isaac Asimov again: "If there are seas on Jupiter . . . think of the fishing." So that may explain the mysterious disappearances and reappearances of the Great Red Spot. It is, as Polonius agreed in a slightly different context, "very like a whale."

36   Contrary to popular thinking, gravity on Jupiter would not pose insurmountable difficulties. The Jovian gravity is only two and a half times Earth's—a condition to which even terrestrial animals (rats in centrifuges) have managed to adapt. The Jovian equivalent of fish, of course, couldn't care less about gravity, because it has virtually no effect in the marine environment.

37   Dr. James Edson, late of NASA, once remarked, "Jupiter is a problem for my grandchildren." I suspect that he may have been wildly optimis-

tic. The zoology of a world outweighing 300 Earths could be the full-time occupation of mankind of the next 1000 years.

38   It also appears that Venus, with its extremely dense, furnace-hot atmosphere, may be an almost equally severe yet equally promising challenge. There now seems little doubt that the planet's average temperature is around 700 degrees Fahrenheit; but this does not, as many have prematurely assumed, rule out all possibility of life—even life of the kind that exists on Earth.

39   There may be little mixing of the atmosphere and, hence, little exchange of heat between the poles and the equator on a planet that revolves as slowly as Venus. At high latitudes or great altitudes—and Venusian mountains have now been detected by radar—it may be cool enough for liquid water to exist. (Even on Earth, remember, the temperature difference between the hottest and the coldest points is almost 300 degrees.) What makes this more than idle specualtion is the exciting discovery, by the Russian space probe Venera IV, of oxygen in the planet's atmosphere. This extremely reactive gas combines with so many materials that it cannot occur in the free state—unless it is continuously renewed by vegetation. Free oxygen is an almost infallible indicator of life: If I may be allowed the modest cough of the minor prophet, I developed precisely this argument some years ago in a story of Venusian exploration, *Before Eden*.

40   On the other hand, it is also possible that we shall discover no trace of extraterrestrial life, past or present, on any of the planets. This would be a great disappointment; but even such a negative finding would give us a much sounder understanding of the conditions in which living creatures are likely to evolve; and this, in turn, would clarify our views on the distribution of life in the Universe as a whole. However, it seems much more probable that long before we can certify the Solar System as sterile, the communications engineers will have settled this ancient question—in the affirmative.

41   For that is what the exploration of space is really all about; and this is why many people are afraid of it, though they may give other reasons, even to themselves. It may be just as well that there are no contemporary higher civilizations in our immediate vicinity; the cultural shock of direct contact might be too great for us to survive. But by the time we have cut our teeth on the Solar System, we should be ready for such encounters. The challenge, in the Toynbeean sense of the word, should then bring forth the appropriate response.

42   Do not for a moment doubt that we shall one day head out for the stars—if, of course, the stars do not reach us first. I think I have read most of the arguments proving that interstellar travel is impossible. They are latter-day echoes of Professor Newcomb's paper on heavier-than-air flight. The logic and the mathematics are impeccable; the premises, wholly invalid. The more sophisticated are roughly equivalent to proving that dirigibles cannot break the sound barrier.

43   In the opening years of this century, the pioneers of astronautics were demonstrating that flight to the Moon and nearer planets was possible, though with great difficulty and expense, by means of chemical propellants. But even then, they were aware of the promise of nuclear energy and hoped that it would be the ultimate solution. They were right.

44   Today, it can likewise be shown that various conceivable, though currently quite impracticable, applications of nuclear and medical techniques could bring at least the closer stars within the range of exploration. And I would warn any skeptics who may point out the marginal nature of these techniques that, at this very moment, there are appearing simultaneously on the twin horizons of the infinitely large and the infinitely small, unmistakable signs of a breakthrough into a new order of creation. To quote some remarks made recently in my adopted country, Ceylon, by a Nobel laureate in physics, Professor C. F. Powell: "It seems to me that the evidence from astronomy and particle physics that I have described makes it possible that we are on the threshold of great and far-reaching discoveries. I have spoken of processes that, mass for mass, would be at least a thousand times more productive of energy than nuclear energy. . . . It seems that there are prodigious sources of energy in the interior regions of some galaxies, and possibly in the 'quasars,' far greater than those produced by the carbon cycle occurring in the stars . . . and we may one day learn how to employ them." And, if Professor Powell's surmise is correct, others may already have learned, on worlds older than ours. So it would be foolish, indeed, to assert that the stars must be forever beyond our reach.

45   More than half a century ago, the great Russian pioneer Tsiolkovsky wrote these moving and prophetic words: "The Earth is the cradle of the mind—but you cannot live in the cradle forever." Now, as we enter the second decade of the age of space, we can look still further into the future.

46   The Earth is, indeed, our cradle, which we are about to leave. And the Solar System will be our kindergarten.

Discussion of Theme
1. What is Mr. Clarke's attitude toward critics of our space program? Is he fair in his remarks?
2. Does the spirit of Simon Newcomb (paragraph 9) live on today? Give arguments, pro or con.
3. In what sense is Jupiter the only planet that counts? According to Clarke, how significant is our own planet in the solar system?
4. According to the author, why is it likely that life exists in other areas of the universe? What kind of life might it be?

Discussion of Rhetoric
1. What evidence is there that this essay was written for the layman, rather than for the scientist? Does Clarke talk down to his reader?

2. Reread the first sentences in paragraphs 3 and 9. What is their purpose? Where else does the author use this technique of paragraph development?

3. The author makes very good use of transitions, such as, "Let us start by looking at some fundamentals . . . " at the beginning of paragraph 3. Find other examples of this technique.

Writing Assignments

1. Write a theme in response to the following statement: "If God had intended us to fly, He would have given us wings."

2. If you disagree with Clarke's premise in this selection, write a rebuttal.

3. In a theme, give your opinion on the existence of U.F.O.s (Unidentified Flying Objects).

Library Exploration

1. If you found this article interesting, you would probably enjoy other works by Clarke. Read, for instance, *Before Eden*, one of his science-fiction stories.

2. What are the latest scientific theories about the existence of life on other planets? Investigate this topic and report your findings.

3. Find out what preparations, if any, our scientists have made for exploring other planets.

Vocabulary

synergistic (12): referring to the cooperative action of discrete agencies that produces a total effect greater than the sum of the efforts taken independently

fission (14): the breaking apart of atomic nuclei resulting in the release of large amounts of energy

fusion (14): the union of atomic nuclei resulting in the release of large amounts of energy

ecology (17): the relation between organisms and their environment

aberration (18): abnormality; deviation from standard behavior

cartographers (21): mapmakers

disparagement (27): belittling

extrapolation (29): inferring unknown data by expanding or projecting known data

geocentrically (31): in accordance with the notion that the earth is the center of the universe

centrifuges (36): machines that produce artificial gravity

impeccable (42): flawless; perfect

prodigious (44): enormous

quasars (44): celestial objects that resemble stars but emit blue and ultraviolet light and intense radio waves

8

THE
UNCERTAIN ROAD TO THE 21st CENTURY

Herman Kahn

A noted analyst of world affairs discusses some current trends in international politics and their pos- *sible implications for man's political and economic future.*

1   There are many reasons for believing that the world of tomorrow, 10 or 20 years from now, will be much different from the one we know today.

2   For example, there is the possibility of arms control which could make the world substantially safer. On the other hand, there may be dangerous nuclear proliferation, a breakdown of current security arrangements, or widespread revolutionary unrest in the so-called Third World. More hopefully, the current détente might not only continue but it might develop into some kind of entente—an "agreement" or new unity—between East and West Europe, or between the United States and the Soviet Union, or all four groups.

3   At the same time, China might develop rapidly and rise to true great power status. Non-Communist governments in South or Southeast Asia might collapse. There might also be a breakdown of the current political system in India because of economic or communal strains. Or there could be a European Political Community or even a United States of Europe. In any case, there will almost inevitably be a continuation of the Sino-Soviet split, further reemergence of Europe as an independent force and a further erosion of the Cold War and the bipolar international system.

4   While not all of the above are as likely as many observers have urged, I would argue that the range of serious possibilities is larger than the examples suggest. Other possibilities include: a China which is stagnating or even in a state of collapse: new and probably assertive roles for West Germany and Japan. Widespread racist or quasi-religious wars or other "irrational" violence in the recently decolonized areas; a "neo-isolationist" withdrawal of the United States and/or the Soviet Union from their intense participation in world affairs; and the emergence of what could be called a post-industrial culture in the currently developed nations.

5   All of these are likely enough *to be* seriously considered. But first let's
consider some other significant aspects of the present world which *are*
taken for granted.

6   Perhaps the most important is the growing belief by many in the
United States, Europe and Japan that we are entering a period of relative
stability, at least as far as wars threatening the homelands of the developed nations are concerned. The United States, of course, is currently
engaged in a rather large war in Southeast Asia, but despite this it is
much more difficult today to write a *plausible* scenario for escalation to
an all-out war than it was 10 years ago.

7   In part, this is because of such important political changes as the
revival in Europe and Japan of societies that are independent and
vigorous (but not so much so that they create threats on their own).
Large changes have also occurred in East Europe and in the Soviet
Union which seem to diminish the Sino-Soviet threat. There has also
been a better understanding on both sides of the Iron Curtain of the
motives and objectives of the opponent. There is the relative lack of
success of Communism in penetrating Africa and Latin America and
even South and Southeast Asia; this political strength of the underdeveloped areas against Communism is often combined with a relative
military weakness for offensive actions, which also, by and large, promote stability. Finally, there have also been a number of technical
developments and changes in strategic forces and doctrine which seem
to have reduced sharply the possibility of both premeditated and
accidental war.

8   Another stabilizing factor is the relatively small pressures toward
territorial expansion in North and South America, in Europe, and by
Japan and Russia in Asia. To a startling degree, these "old nations"
seem more or less satisfied with their current boundaries.

9   The German situation is not so stable, however, since reunification
with possible border adjustments might be peacefully or violently
accomplished. We should also admit the possibility of Chinese territorial aggression, of frontier changes in parts of Africa and Asia, and
of turmoil generally in the so-called "new nations."

10   One of the main reasons for the new attitude toward territorial expansion is that internal economic development now appears to be the
most efficient road to wealth and perhaps power. The postwar experiences of Japan, West Germany and other European countries
indicate that colonies are now economic liabilities and sources of political and military weakness rather than strength. Doubtless the pendulum of fashion has overshot, but this new attitude has important
effects.

11   An even more important factor is the likelihood of many "pluralistic
security communities" on the model of U.S.–Canadian relations in
which war (or even the threat of violence) is unthinkable. The term
"pluralistic security community" expresses more than just a willingness

to accept or live with current situations: it indicates a willingness to live with a much *deteriorated* situation, as well as a determination not to let situations deteriorate too far. Because of this, a pluralistic security community is an important step forward to peaceful political unification. Important, too, is the often neglected fact that trade no longer follows the flag. Thus West Germany, which hardly possesses a Navy, is the second largest trading nation in the world today.

12   Of course, even if the stability continues, military capabilities will remain important in international politics. However, as far as the "old nations" are concerned, the uses of such power are likely to be more sophisticated and subtle than in the 18th, 19th and early 20th centuries. In practice, most of the old and many of the new powers will have secure frontiers and access to world markets without much explicit need to enforce these rights.

13   This international context of seemingly great stability is most important in the consideration of the pressures on and roles of Japan and West Germany. Economically they are likely to be the third and fourth largest world powers and yet may be in very different positions in the international hierarchy in terms of political influence and military capability.

14   What will this hierarchy look like? Most probably there will be 10 "major" powers. The U.S. and USSR will continue to be considered superpowers; Japan, West Germany, France, China and the United Kingdom large powers; India, Italy, and Canada intermediate powers; and the next 120 nations small powers. The ranking is generally that of estimated GNP in the mid- and late 1970s, but the grouping is natural: the intermediate powers have at least twice the GNP of any of the small powers, the large powers about twice the GNP of the intermediate powers, and the superpowers more than three times the GNP of the large powers.

15   The chart on page 5 [here omitted] gives a reasonable projection of how the 10 largest nations may compare in GNP and population in the year 2000. The most likely projection, I would suggest, is that the United States, Japan and perhaps Canada will be toward the top of the indicated ellipse; the Soviet Union, West Germany, France and Italy in the middle; and the United Kingdom, China and India toward the bottom. Let us now consider some aspects of international relations in more detail.

16   There seem to be four kinds of typical and perhaps much exaggerated estimates of Communist China:

1. a tendency to overestimate the effectiveness of population—in effect, to multiply anything that happens in China by 750 million, as if the 600 million or so peasants (as distinguished from the 150 million or so urbanized Chinese) constitute an overwhelming economic, military, moral or political force.

2. a tendency to credit the Chinese with a nearly magical ability to

galvanize immediate revolutions not only in nearby regions but at great distances.

3. a tendency to assume perfect discipline in China (750 million "blue ants") and an inevitable and very successful industrial development in the next 35 years.

4. a tendency to size up Chinese leadership as wildly irrational and unlikely to be deterred even by credible and painful material or military threats. (It seems a fair statement that on Mondays, Wednesdays and Fridays the Chinese attempt to persuade us that they are crazy, and seven days a week the Soviets try to confirm this impression.)

17   Perhaps one source of these exaggerations is that many in the United States and Europe are looking for a new enemy to take the psychological and political role in internal politics formerly played by the Soviet Union. Yet almost all *expert* opinion in the U.S. seems agreed that China is today and may remain for the next decade or two rather weak in its ability to use offensive force (though its defensive capability may be large). Its large population is as likely to be a weakness as a strength. Its economic prospects are at best uncertain and perhaps poor. Its leaders, while rather inward-looking, chauvinistic and subject to biases, still seem to make and follow reasonable risk calculations. While they are likely to be as aggressive as practical and willing to run some risks, they are not likely to be wildly reckless. Indeed, in terms of their own values and goals, the Chinese leaders are probably less likely to be irrational on issues involving the risk of war than are many other leaders even in today's relatively conservative world.

18   In addition, the specter of Chinese mass armies fighting in India or Southeast Asia is unrealistic. It ignores the logistic constraints. Even within China, the population is no true gauge of the size of the armies Peking could recruit and equip. Available surpluses—in money, food and productive capacity—are small. Further, the Chinese Communists have and will continue to have internal problems of morale, discipline, authority, etc. The picture of a monolithic ant heap completely responsive to the desires of Mao is clearly wrong.

19   It is also important to note that Marshal Lin Piao's recent doctrinal statement on world revolution has been widely misunderstood. One is, of course, impressed by the very angry tone. However, what exactly was said is very weak. Lin Piao says, in effect, "We Chinese will help movements of national liberation, but not very much; you cannot depend on us but must do it on your own; if you don't, revolution will not work; outside help cannot be the decisive thing." Given that this was written in the context of the Vietnamese war one could scarcely imagine a more restrained declaration coming from China.

20   As time passes, the above points will become more widely understood and the Chinese will lose much of their present international charisma. Thus if they do better than many experts expect and average a growth rate of say 5 percent a year in GNP and about 2 percent a year in popula-

tion, they will become substantially richer by the end of the century. This would give them a GNP of about $400 billion but a per capita yearly income of only about $250. This performance, while in many ways an extraordinary achievement, would not be very impressive compared to many surrounding countries, let alone the United States and the Soviet Union. (Other Asian countries such as Taiwan, South Korea, Thailand, the Philippines and Malaysia are likely to grow much more rapidly in per capita income and, as discussed later, most important of all, Japan seems likely to grow much more rapidly in total GNP.)

21   In addition, the Chinese are likely to be technologically and economically even farther behind Japan than they are now. Thus, even if they continue their militant rhetoric, their influence will wane—in part because their extravagant claims and expectations are so obviously frustrated, and in part because Japan will overshadow them.

22   The Soviet Union is almost 50 years old. To some degree the system has evolved into an authoritarian rather than a totalitarian society, one that is in many ways successful, but also in many ways disillusioned. (To the great shock of traditional Marxists there is a good deal of intense discussion in both the Soviet Union and East Europe of the problem of alienation between man and job and man and society—a problem that was supposed to be solved with the abolition of capitalism.)

23   Though the party stays in absolute control, it allows modest dissent. This is done to reward or stimulate people, to act as a safety valve and corrective, and to reduce criticism from Western and Soviet intellectuals, whose views have increasingly significant impact upon Soviet publics. Eventually this relaxation may lead to other important political concessions, including legal tolerance of some degree of political opposition. The Soviets still believe in world revolution and support subversion in many places in the world, but with lessened intensity, confidence and enthusiasm.

24   There is a continuing erosion of the police-state and increasing "socialist legality." There is also an increasing embourgeoisement of the government, the managers and the masses. Nevertheless, the so-called "convergence phenomenon," the apparent and much publicized increasing similarities between Russia and the West, is likely to stop well short of parliamentary democracy.

25   The Chinese are likely to continue to compete with the Soviets for leadership of international Communism, emphasizing such current criticisms as the Soviet Union is:

1. capitulationist and revisionist (fearful of risking a confrontation with the U.S. and increasingly adopting capitalist practices),

2. counterrevolutionary (rich and no longer in sympathy with the poor),

3. not Afro-Asian (a predominantly white nation and therefore not to be trusted by the non-white peoples).

26   All of the charges sting—in part because they contain elements of

truth. Yet the Soviets continue to build bridges with Europe and the United States. It is unlikely, however, that this bridge-building, *contrary to surprisingly widespread expectations*, will soon get to the stage of firm alliance. Nevertheless, communism as a world movement (now to be written with a small *c*) is likely to lose even more of its traditional discipline and direction.

27   Germany is likely to remain divided—with East Germany likely to become a more legitimate and viable country with every year that passes. Eventually the Ulbricht regime will be replaced and the new regime may manage to acquire enough legitimacy and prestige so that it no longer needs Soviet bayonets. It could do this in part by making judicious internal concessions and in part by appealing to an increasing East German nationalism. Thus if the new regime successfully opposes the Soviets on a series of minor issues, its prestige will increase enormously.

28   While the East Germans and the Soviets will doubtless continue to pressure the United States and West Germany over various aspects of the Berlin question, all four countries are likely to be careful not to probe so deeply as to unbalance the situation, and to avoid incidents which could escalate into a serious confrontation.

29   In the meantime, the postwar political passivity of Bonn will increasingly be replaced by active and assertive policies. Germans who were young during World War II (by 1975 this is anyone under 50) will increasingly refuse to accept for themselves (or the German nation) any stigma. In East Germany nationalism may go even farther; indeed, East German national assertions are now a familiar, if carefully used theme. Thus one can find in East Germany many articles and books which point out that, "of course West Germany is rich; it had the Marshall Plan, other U.S. support and a capitalist system—furthermore its riches have been corrupting." They then point out that East Germany has also been successful—*and under Communism*. (They seem to take a wry satisfaction and considerable pride, as do many West Germans, in the ability of Germans to do so well even without foreign help and in a non-capitalist society.) This growing success may well have an unexpectedly great appeal to young people and others in West Germany. In any case, by the mid-70s the East Germans should have a well-developed position of being true Germans—austere, purposeful and disciplined—thus espousing a sort of charismatic "Prussian Socialism."

30   In the rest of Europe there is probably more distrust of a revived West Germany than fear of Soviet aggression. Most Europeans feel that Soviet aggression is perhaps permanently deterred. In addition they tend to accept the "new" Soviet Union as a more or less responsible power. As a result, the West Germans feel increasingly isolated and are unwilling to believe that they can satisfy their aspirations in the current

NATO framework. Of course the West Germans, partly as a result of their wartime and postwar experiences with the Soviets, partly because their country remains divided, and partly because they are on the firing line, are more preoccupied with the Soviet threat. As a result, United States and West German policies may remain in relatively close harmony: Washington and Bonn are the two capitals of the Western alliance which take the Soviet military threat most seriously (but, nonetheless, not very seriously).

31   On the other hand, it has become clear that the previous identity of interest between Washington and Bonn is now more illusory than real. Washington's current interests in avoiding nuclear war with the Soviets, and in articulating the increasing number of issues on which Soviet and American interests coincide, are moving West German aspirations to a lower priority. Thus Bonn's major official interest, to regain the "Soviet zone," conflicts with Washington and West Europe's willingness to accept a détente based on the status quo. While Bonn will doubtless go along with the détente, and perhaps gain much commercially in doing so, it may also become increasingly resentful and restless. This is clearly true of much of German youth who increasingly ask their elders, "What is being done about reunification?" (According to recent polls, 80 percent of the young West Germans think of this as the major issue facing West Germany today.) Ignoring the almost miraculous postwar recovery of West Germany, the younger generation often argues that the postwar policies are almost bankrupt since they do not seem to have brought reunification closer.

32   Meanwhile, as Moscow's hold slackens in the "satellites," East Germany may also become more independent. But there is a serious potential for trouble in both Germanys—through more or less popular revolt, competition or even collaboration. It is also possible that the situation will evolve peacefully or stabilize itself on the basis of a mutual but acceptable frustration.

33   Japan in 1966 was still the invisible nation of Asia. Like West Germany, the other major loser of World War II, Japan was characterized by great economic strength and political passivity. It is, however, a bigger country in population, has probably already surpassed West Germany in industrial production, is growing much more rapidly and, most important of all, is not held down by apprehensive allies and an overwhelming reunification problem. Thus Japan is likely to emerge in the 1970s as the true colossus of Asia—a further check on Chinese ambitions.

34   Partly because the Japanese are possibly the most achievement-oriented society in history, and partly because of their intense desire for prestige, their growth rates may well continue to be high, around 8 percent, for the rest of the century. At this rate they would double their GNP about every 8 or 9 years. Yet if there were a serious sustained

depression, it would probably disrupt the current political balance, making much more likely a sharp swing either to the right or to the left, or to some extremist group, such as the Soka Gakkai's Komeito, which falls outside these categories. However, things seem likely to go reasonably smoothly, and while there may be some anti-foreign and pro-traditional reaction against excessive "Americanization," this is likely to be limited in effect.

35   Some of the force of the Afro-Asian "revolution" has been spent and the future direction of this movement is now less clear. The revolution encompassed some elements that are exceedingly old—xenophobia, racial hatred, cultural exclusivism—and some elements that are new and even hyper-modern (for example, the "beat" quality of such Third World leaders as Castro and Lumumba). Among the newer elements are nationalism and Marxist ideology, both learned from Europe, though often in garbled form. But the ideological content of political movements in Afro-Asia is frequently exaggerated. While almost all Afro-Asian states describe themselves as "socialist" they are far removed from the political and economic system of the USSR or even Communist China. Their invocation of "socialism" is more a talismanic claim on modernity than an ideological commitment.

36   Of course, the mere fact that these movements called themselves socialist or Communist means that they often feel some identity with the Soviet Union or China, or both, and that they expect and often get aid from these countries. It is even possible that if they are in any way successful with their Afro-Asian socialism, they will attempt to deepen and continue this identity. But my prediction would be that Afro-Asian socialism will overwhelm the Marxist origins of these movements and any relationship to Chinese or Soviet Communism.

37   Since the middle of the 19th century, Latin America has been chronically anti-Yankee. This antipathy, stemming from both rational and irrational causes, was much strengthened by U.S. political and military intervention. The "irrational" causes were many, but a crucial one, which will presumably continue, is the simple necessity for Latins to distinguish themselves as a culture from the predominantly Protestant, commercial, aggressive North American civilization which might otherwise engulf them.

38   There are, however, some important new trends. Brazilians, Mexicans and Colombians, at least, seem now to have a kind of national self-confidence that makes them psychologically less dependent on the U.S. —either positively or negatively. This confidence is primarily based on their recent success in industrializing their countries but also on, respectively: (1) creating a new kind of society, (2) making a successful social revolution and (3) an ability to handle the North Americans. Thus, many Latin Americans—particularly the growing urbanized

commercial, technical and professional classes—no longer feel quite so overwhelmed or dominated by the colossus of the North. Further, the Christian Democrats (and other Democrats and Democratic-Leftists) are now leading a campaign for a new kind of relationship between the United States and Latin America involving more mutual respect and empathy.

39   Unlike much of Afro-Asia, where many of the problems seem overwhelming, most Latin American economic development problems seem either soluble or bearable. For one thing, the ratio of people to resources in Latin America is far more favorable. In contrast to Africa and much of Asia, Latin America is now capitalistic and technological, predominantly European in culture, and does not now suffer as much from the social disruptions of economic modernization.

40   However, the political conditions inhibiting parliamentary government and orderly development are still evident. Relatively violent and "illegal" changes of government are likely to persist; under Latin American conditions complex and subtle political systems—perhaps on the current Mexican model—may be more successful in maintaining a reasonable degree of order, liberty and development than parliamentary democracy.

41   In any case, with some luck or skill most of Latin America ought, by the end of the century, to achieve living standards comparable to or greater than Italy today (and with the same problem of unevenness, so that in the Latin American context the urban-rural problem replaces the Italian north-south disparities).

42   In the first decade after World War II the five principal victors either actually tested a nuclear device and then procured nuclear weapons or officially initiated programs with the intention of carrying them through to the test and procurement state (for this purpose we will consider Peking rather than Taiwan a victor of World War II). But, rather startlingly, in the next decade no country officially initiated a nuclear weapons program, though many initiated "peaceful" nuclear energy programs which give them an option on a military program. It is still possible that in the absence of immediate objective military pressures, this precedent will be continued and even strengthened and further proliferation prevented. But there are other possibilities.

43   If one examines the candidates for status as Nuclear Power No. 6, the most obvious ones are Israel, India, West Germany and Japan. The first two have, in effect, created a basis or option for such a program. The last two are now doing so.

44   However, it seems unlikely that either Israel or India will procure nuclear weapons, if only because the United States seems to have indicated that if they do, U.S. support will either be withdrawn or sharply cut, and they might be facing potential enemies alone.

45   In the absence of new developments West Germany, of course, is firmly precluded by political constraints arising out of the war (and some ambiguous treaty obligations) from going ahead on its own.

46   That leaves Japan. Most Japanese and observers of the Japanese do not think that Japan will become the sixth nuclear power. Informal polls taken at Japanese universities, and by the author, however, indicate that many Japanese expect Japan to be No. 8 to go nuclear, after India and West Germany. However, I would argue that it will become clear to the Japanese in the late '60s that India and West Germany will not be Nos. 6 and 7.

47   At the same time, the Japanese will almost certainly be increasingly assertive and self-confident in their own economic strength, desirous of increased prestige and independence, and concerned about their long-run security. Many Japanese will then argue that the easiest and most efficient route to these goals is to acquire nuclear weapons.

48   If Japan does try to be Nuclear Power No. 6, it seems quite plausible that West Germany will wish to follow suit. Credible military and political arguments could then openly be made for Germany's acquiring nuclear weapons. It is important to realize that once the "victors' monopoly" has been broken by one of the defeated powers of World War II, the other defeated powers will feel much less constrained by "war guilt." Bluntly, many in the West would be willing to tell the West Germans that they cannot revise the territorial results of World War II without going to war; but few would be willing to say, "Until you win a war you are politically second-class."

49   Assuming, then, that in four or five years Germany follows Japan; then the Italians will probably follow. If the Germans have sufficient political status to acquire nuclear weapons, they, too, out of self-respect, must also have them. One could also conjecture, then, that such countries as Sweden, Switzerland, Australia and India would soon no longer feel they are rocking the boat by achieving nuclear status. If this proliferation in fact occurred in the '70s and the '80s, then in the '90s, any one of 50 countries or so might have access to such weapons.

50   While this prospect is very frightening, it does not necessarily mean an inevitable cataclysmic nuclear war. Nor does it necessarily increase the likelihood of a nuclear war between the United States and the Soviet Union. Indeed, nuclear war between two relatively undeveloped nations or one developed and one undeveloped nation would be much more likely—and it does not by any means follow logically, or practically, that such a conflict would develop into a general holocaust. And even here, if proliferation continues, the attitudes about "first use," the risks of unsafe techniques, disproportionate response, etc., which now inhibit the United States and the Soviet Union, might inhibit the other nuclear states as well.

51   Despite such arguments, one cannot be confident that future effects

would not be cataclysmic. In fact, there is a surprising consensus among analysts, scholars, policy makers and men in the street in this respect. While they may be wrong, I share their judgment, at least in its less apocalyptic form, that proliferation is bad, and have discussed elsewhere ways to hinder it and deal with it if it occurs.

52 By the end of the century there will be nearly six billion people on earth, and about 20 percent of these should be living at a standard substantially better than the current American one. This achievement could result in the transition of these affluent societies to a new post-industrial culture, a transition which may be as dramatic and important as the 17th-century transition to an industrial culture. That is, if our assumptions about stability and economic growth rates (which range for most countries from 2 to 10 percent) hold, we should be entering a sort of new Augustan age. Conditions in the superdeveloped countries might by the year 2000 be as different from those in Europe in the early and mid-20th centuries as conditions in the early Roman Empire differed from those of the previous ancient world. We are all too familiar with lurid clichés about the decline of the Roman Empire, but for better than nine-tenths of the time, the first 200 years of the Roman Empire enjoyed almost unparalleled peace and prosperity. It should be noted that it also started as an "age of anxiety" and apprehension. It is often argued—and plausibly—that the "moral fiber" of the Romans degenerated during this period probably because of the lack of challenge, possibly because of other events or environmental factors. While the questions of cause and effect are complicated and inconclusive, there are some parallels between Roman times and ours.

53 Thus, it is interesting to note that when Augustus came to power the free citizens of Rome had 76 holidays a year. When Nero died, not quite a century later, they had 176 holidays a year. Similarly, in our own case, if productivity per hour goes up by 3 or 4 percent a year (or by a factor of three or four by the year 2000), as is expected by most experts, it is likely that not all of this increased productivity will be used to produce more. Paradoxically, increased productivity could also cause a general de-emphasis of private industry, which could come to occupy a relatively small portion of society's efforts and attentions. Thus Daniel Bell has suggested that the private firm will no longer be as important a source of innovation and prestige in this post-industrial culture, but that this role will increasingly be played by government, the professions, the not-for-profit educational and research institutions, foundations and other non-business organizations.

54 It would not be appropriate in an article on international relations to spend too much time on the domestic aspects of the post-industrial culture in the 20 percent or so of the world that may achieve this state. It is sufficient to mention that while there are exciting prospects for a humanistic and creative culture, there may be serious problems of

motivation, and of the use of leisure or even the possibility of a disastrous overreaction against work and achievement-oriented values. Projected to a national level, this overreaction could undercut the advancement of the national interest. Thus, some of these superdeveloped societies may have difficulty, in the long run, in international competition. But it seems more likely that, in spite of various internal strains and corrosive tendencies, enough citizens will continue—like the Roman stoics—to carry out the responsibilities of power.

55   A different aspect of this parallel which emphasizes international issues may also be worth mentioning. Here America plays the part of Rome, Europe of Greece, and the Soviet Union (or China) of Parthia, or Persia. There are indeed important similarities between the Greeks and the Europeans, on the one hand, and the Romans and the Americans on the other. Greece eagerly seized the opportunity for World Empire, but failed. The Romans—more or less against their will—were forced three times to intervene in the Greek world to prevent its domination by a single power. The first two times they withdrew after accomplishing this mission. The third time they stayed. Indeed, under the necessity (seemingly sincere) of protecting weak powers the Romans found it necessary to take over and administer about half of the area which had previously been conquered by the Greeks, leaving the other half to the Parthians, with whom they had an uneasy coexistence.

56   One problem of this post-industrial society which has no real counterpart in classical times—except possibly with some aspects of the free distribution of food to Roman citizens—might be an immense worldwide welfare program. Such a program would run the danger of being carried out with excessive bureaucratic harshness or with an unwise permissiveness that leads to an unintended worsening of the problems it is attempting to alleviate.

57   We have seen both these problems in current U.S. welfare programs and in our foreign aid programs. An important and not atypical example is the food-for-India program. The U.S. currently supplies half the wheat consumed in India (this takes about one-fourth the U.S. production). While the Indians have increased their food production by 50 percent in the last 15 years, most experts believe that with relatively minor changes in programs and government attitudes—particularly towards such things as fertilizer—food production could have been increased even faster. Furthermore, if the government had been willing to initiate harsh and therefore very unpopular measures (such as raising the price of food), production would have gone up even faster and India could have had food surpluses. But for various reasons even the mild and obvious measures were (and are) politically unpopular, especially since many Indians have come to think of the stream of food from the United States as a vested right and therefore feel under no

pressure to initiate such measures (and resent any direct pressure by the U.S. to do so).

58   The situation could get worse. For example, assume that in the year 2000 a minimum diet will cost roughly $100 (1965 dollars) a year (current food costs are less than $40 a year in India). Then if there are roughly three billion people in the underdeveloped world, $100 billion a year could furnish one-third of their food requirements. This would be about 2 or 3 percent of the expected U.S. GNP in the year 2000, and about one percent of the GNP of the developed portion of the world. Furthermore, there do not seem to be any serious bottlenecks or technical problems in converting these monetary calculations into actual production, provided that one makes reasonable preparations.

59   Assume now that the food-poor countries do not manage to increase their food production or reduce their population growth so as to maintain (or achieve) a balance and that this will be reasonably apparent in advance. Then, since it will be technologically and economically feasible for the developed nations to step in and prevent famine, many will feel there is a moral or political obligation for the affluent not only to do so, but to be prepared in advance to do so, since otherwise there may not be time to increase production drastically if there is a crop failure. One can agree with this and still be concerned that meeting this obligation, if done imprudently, could worsen the very problem it is trying to solve.

60   Thus we envision for the last third of the 20th century a condition in which such once vital questions as access to markets, frontier defense, and many other national security or economic issues are no longer dominating or immediate, at least for most of the industrialized nations of the world, in contrast to the new nations. Further, most nations— even the newer ones—will not feel under great pressure (or inducement) to expand aggressively and to grab available territories *now*—not even to prevent some other nations' grabbing them first or to balance previous grabs by even older nations. But within this framework, which is basically stable for the older nations, many important problems will arise or gestate—some of which could have disastrous consequences in the foreseeable, though even more long-range future.

61   The above picture is, of course, superficial and incomplete; it may also seem both too good and too bad to be true. Most thoughtful readers are also likely to feel that in addition to the many problems implicitly and explicitly set forth there will be some surprises even in the short run—some new trends or intense crises will arise well before the end of the 20th century and upset the delicate balance of forces. Many of the new nations will clearly be in turmoil, economic disparities and population pressures will increase, military technology will proliferate and increase in destructiveness, and there will be many occasions that will create at least some risks of war. Thus, to our crisis-prone expectations

the predictions for the old nations may seem implausibly evolutionary and crisis-free.

62   We can invent many scenarios in which we get into trouble—in fact, too many to discuss. We must also concede that any lengthy period without serious challenge does indeed tend to create its own particular tensions that can degenerate into or create disruptive forces.

63   Yet my feeling is that for the rest of the century, while surprises will surely occur as far as the old nations are concerned, these disruptive forces are likely to prove containable. While I scarcely like to be on record as arguing that the old nations—aside from their economic progress and the direct consequences of such progress—will change less in the final third of the 20th century than they did in either of the preceding thirds, I believe this is quite possible; thus the old nations may enjoy several decades of relatively stable and evolutionary change— much as the early Roman Empire did.

64   The above, of course, assumes continued care, vigilance and reasonably prudent policies by these nations. One obvious way in which the above "forecast" could turn out badly would be as a self-defeating prophecy, in which too much confidence led to complacency and carelessness. And this is surely one of the risks, but one which is more likely to be avoided by objective, careful and candid, even if uncertain analyses, than by warnings made for political or morale purposes.

65   Clearly our most important task is to understand current trends and policy alternatives well enough to avoid disasters, to preserve stability, and to make reasonable progress in the next few decades. But this is not sufficient: we must use this "breather," if we are lucky enough to have one, to lay a foundation for dealing with the immensely destructive forces that remain latent and may yet erupt. Difficult as it is to make useful estimates and to plan appropriate policies for such a task, there is a further contingency that should not be neglected: several decades of stability and economic growth could create unprecedented opportunities for improving the quality of life. It is not too soon to analyze economic, political and social aspects of the projected situation, so that we will not be caught unprepared for policy decisions that would enable us to exploit these opportunities for wise and constructive purposes.

Discussion of Theme

1. What is a pluralistic security community? Why is it likely to promote a more secure international situation?
2. What is Kahn's estimate of Red China's future role in world affairs? How accurate do you think he is? Do you see any evidence that would tend to weaken or contradict his arguments?
3. What are the goals of the Latin American countries? How much is the United States to blame for the anti-Yankee feeling in South America? Is this feeling changing?

4. Nuclear power can be harnessed for either productive or destructive ends. What use does the author predict it will be put to? Do you agree?

Discussion of Rhetoric

1. How would you describe the tone of this article? Is it personal or impersonal? What evidence can you offer to support your choice?
2. What is the purpose of paragraphs 1–5? 6–15? What are the other divisions of this essay?
3. Note the transitions and linking expressions in paragraph 2: *for example, on the other hand,* and *more hopefully.* Find other such transitions and linking expressions in paragraphs 3 and 4. In general, how do these words aid the reader's understanding?

Writing Assignments

1. What steps should be taken to prevent nuclear war? Should the larger powers try to keep small countries from developing nuclear weapons? What should the United States be doing?
2. Which poses the greatest danger: nuclear warfare, overpopulation, or depletion of our natural resources? Give supporting evidence.

Library Exploration

1. For a more detailed treatment of some of the issues raised in this article, read *On Thermonuclear War* by the same author.
2. In what respects have the U.S.S.R. and Communist China departed from the ideology of Marx? How do they differ from each other?

Vocabulary

proliferation (2): rapid growth
détente (2): a relaxation of tensions (as between nations)
galvanize (16): arouse; stimulate, excite
chauvinistic (17): blindly patriotic
logistic (18): of or relating to the procurement, maintenance, and transportation of equipment and personnel
charisma (20): personal magic or charm that excites followers
embourgeoisement (24): the process of becoming middle class
xenophobia (35): fear or hatred of foreigners
talismanic (35): of or relating to a small object, such as a charm, that produces apparently magical or miraculous effects
cataclysmic (50): descriptive of a momentous and violent event marked by overwhelming upheaval
holocaust (50): complete destruction, especially by fire
apocalyptic (51): forecasting imminent disaster or ultimate doom
gestate (60): grow or develop (prior to birth)
latent (65): present but not visible or active

9

OUR DAWNING ELECTRIC AGE

Herbert Marshall McLuhan

How will the Electric Age change our lives? McLuhan believes that the new technology will affect man's environment, his language, and even his concept of work.

1   I bring you greetings from the country of the DEW line, or early warning system. Canada carries perhaps a potential role as an early warning system. As the United States becomes a world environment, Canada might serve very well as an early warning system for culture and technology, and on many levels. But this is a whimsy.

2   We had a delightful story at lunch about the French actor who expressed the delight he had on the stage because of its permitting him to kiss ladies' hands. He said: "You know, you have to begin somewhere." The companion piece to that one is somewhat closer to my predicament—the mosquito in the nudist colony who said: "I don't know where to begin."

3   The world of humor, as a system of communications, is one that has occasionally interested people, and we live in a time when joke styles have changed very rapidly. I am told by my own children that the latest form of joke concerns the "Poles," and they gave me as an example: "Alexander Graham Kowalski—the first 'telephone Pole.'" This kind of humor is like the slightly older form of the elephant joke and the kind that the computer programmers enjoy—"What is purple and hums?" Of course, the answer is: "An electric grape." "And, why does it hum?" "It doesn't know the words." This kind of joke appeals enormously to youngsters today.

4   If you notice, the tendency in these kinds of jokes, or gags, is for the story line to be stripped off. They tend to be deprived of the old story line, and in its place you have a capsule, a compressed overlay, of stories. In fact, there are usually two stories in these little jokes, simultaneously. The older-fashioned jokes had a straight story line. Steve Allen has a theory that the funnyman is a man with a grievance. In French Canada there are a good many jokes going around these days that are by way of being grievance stories. One of them is this: A mouse being pursued around the house by the house cat, finally finds a little spot in the floor

to creep in and hide. After a while, everything seems quiet, until suddenly there is a kind of "Arf-Arf-Bow-Wow" noise and the mouse feels the dog must have frightened the cat away, so it pops up and the cat grabs it and chews it down. As he chews the mouse down, he says: "You know, it pays to be bilingual." That is the old kind of square joke with a story line around it.

5   The new stories tend to be much more compressed and on two levels at once, like the sort of *Finnegans Wake* phrase: "though he might have been more humble, there's no police like Holmes." That kind of compressed double-plot story is a very interesting development; and, if you notice, great successes like *My Fair Lady* usually have two plots. One of them is explicit. One is perfectly obvious, like the story of Liza Doolittle acquiring the King's English and becoming a great social success. But there is a subplot in *My Fair Lady* that is much more potent and much concealed. The subplot would seem to be "how to succeed in business without really trying."

6   The subplot is an environmental one—it includes everybody. The main plot, the little story about Liza Doolittle, appeals to a relatively small group and is not a new story. It is a Cinderella story. But the story of "how to succeed in business without really trying," or, in other words, how to become a huge success by sheer gimmickry, would seem to be the life story, the inside life story, of a very large proportion of the top executives of our world. In other words, *My Fair Lady* has this environmental subplot that is implicit and unverbalized, and that includes the audience. With the subplot, the audience goes right into action. With the main plot, they simply sit outside looking on.

7   There is a subplot in the famous Hathaway shirt advertisement of the baron with the black patch on his eye. The main plot is simply Hathaway shirts. The subplot, the one that really includes the whole audience, is the black patch which bespeaks the world of aristocratic intrigue, hunts for hidden treasure, and many other mysterious dimensions, all expressed instantaneously by the black patch. The subplot world, the sub-environment, is really that which includes the audience, and it is the power to effect this kind of inclusion that is the mystery of humor, and that explains the rapid change of humor styles—because one style joke will not accommodate a very large proportion of the audience from one period to another.

8   There is a new book by Jacques Ellul, the Frenchman. The book has recently been published in English. It is called *Propaganda*. Ellul's book has as a theme that propaganda is not ideology; it is not the Hathaway shirt story. It is rather the hidden, but complete, image of a social way of life that is embedded in the social technologies and social patterns, as it is embedded in, say, the English language. Ellul would say the action of the English language, the action of the French language—*that* is propaganda. That presents a total environmental image to men,

whereas the ideologies, the explicit verbalized messages, are relatively insignificant compared to this overall image. Ellul's theme in a word is this: Propaganda consists in using all the available means of one's society to create a way of life. Whatever that way may be, is propaganda —that is action that is total and invisible, and invincible.

9   This is another mysterious feature about the new and potent environment we now live in. The really total and saturating environments are invisible. The ones we notice are quite fragmentary and insignificant compared to the ones we don't see. The English language, for example, as it shapes our perceptions and all our habits of thought and feeling, is quite unperceived by the users of the English language. It becomes much more perceptible if we switch suddenly to French. But in the case of environments that are created by new technologies, while they are quite invisible in themselves, they do make visible the old environments. We can always see the Emperor's old clothes, but not his new ones.

10   I want to use this theme a little bit for our purposes here this afternoon. If the new environment is invisible, it does serve to make very visible the preceding environment. The obvious and simple illustration of that is the late show. On the late show on television we see old movies. They are very visible; they are very noticeable. Since television, the movie form has been reprocessed. The form of movie that once was environmental and invisible has been reprocessed into an art form, and, indeed, a highly valued art form. Indirectly, the new art films of our time have received an enormous amount of encouragement and impact from the television form. The television form has remained quite invisible—and will only become visible at the moment that television itself becomes the content of a new medium. The next medium, whatever it is—it may be the extension of consciousness—will include television as its content, not as its environment, and will transform television into an art form; but this process whereby every new technology creates an environment that translates the old or preceding technology into an art form, or into something exceedingly noticeable, affords so many fascinating examples I can only mention a few.

11   There is a wonderful book by Eric Havelock that I delight to refer to. Havelock, a year or so ago, published a book called *Preface to Plato*. It is a study of what happened in Greece before Plato. "Preface" means how did the Greeks educate each other before writing? What were the processes by which they educated their young people before Plato? He calls this process that preceded Plato "the tribal encyclopedia." The young memorized the poets. The poets were operative purveyors of practical wisdom and council. Homer, Hesiod and the rest actually provided the young people with models of perception and models of behavior and strategies for overcoming all sorts of difficulties and obstacles. The great Odysseus was above all a Greek hero because of his resourcefulness—his unfailing initiative and skill in every type of

opaque and threatening situation. Havelock describes this education that went on by the poets, the tribal encyclopedia, and then describes the advent of writing and the complete change that came over education as a result of that. With the coming of writing, education shifted from the memorizing of the tribal encyclopedia that made education a sort of "singing commercial." With writing came the classification of knowledge, the ideas, the categories; and Plato's detestation of the poets was mainly a rivalry with the old educational establishment which had naturally failed to come to grips with the new technology of the written word.

12   Havelock's book has a fascinating quality, because it really tells the story of what we are going through right now. We are playing that tape (the situation he describes) backward—the change from tribal man to individual man. As we move into the world of integral, computerized knowledge, mere classification becomes secondary and inadequate to the speeds with which data can now be processed. As data can be processed very rapidly we move literally into the world of pattern recognition, out of the world of mere data classification. One way of putting this is to say that our children today live in a world in which the environment itself is made of electric information. The environment of the young person today is typically and principally electrically fashioned information. The young person today is a data processor on a very large scale. Some people have estimated that the young person, the infant and the small child, growing up in our world today works harder than any child ever did in any previous human environment—only the work he has to perform is that of data processing. The small child in twentieth-century America does more data processing—more work— than any child in any previous culture in the history of the world, according to Jacques Ellul, among others. We haven't really cottoned on to the fact that our children work furiously, processing data in an electrically structured information world; and when these children enter a classroom—elementary school—they encounter a situation that is very bewildering to them. The youngster today, stepping out of his nursery or TV environment, goes to school and enters a world where the information is scarce but is ordered and structured by fragmented, classified patterns, subjects, schedules. He is utterly bewildered because he comes out of this intricate and complex integral world of electric information and goes into this nineteenth-century world of classified information that still characterizes the educational establishment. The educational establishment is a nineteenth-century world of classified data much like any factory set up with its inventories and assembly lines. The young today are baffled because of this extraordinary gap between these two worlds.

13   Paul Goodman has a book recording one aspect of the situation. It is titled *Growing Up Absurd*. To grow up today is to be absurd, because

we live in two worlds, and neither one of them inclines us to grow up. I have a friend who once pointed out to me something that struck me with great force. He said, "You know, the only work that royalty has to do is to grow up, and for a young prince or princess growing up and acquiring all the types of knowledge and language necessary for survival is a fantastically difficult job." It would seem that we have paradoxically created on a democratic scale a situation for royalty. Our youngsters today are mainly confronted with the problem of just growing up—that is our new work—and it is total. That is why it is not a job; it is a role. Growing up has become, in the age of electrically processed information, the major task of mankind. We still have our eyes fixed on the rearview mirror looking firmly and squarely at the job that is receding into the nineteenth-century past. The job that we feel we should have by rights belongs to the old mechanical technology of classified data and of fragmented tasks. Yet we are now surrounded by a new environment, of integrated tasks, integrated knowledge, and it demands pattern recognition. The kind of contrast between those two situations creates an absurdity that has launched the theater of the absurd. The theater of the absurd itself is postulated on this kind of dichotomy between these two cultures that never seem to get any closer together.

14   I have started then with the theme of the imperceptibility of new environments, and that what is perceptible in typical human situations is the old environment. It is plain that the content of Plato's work, of his new written form, was the old oral dialogue. The content of the print technology of the Renaissance was medieval writing. For two hundred years after printing there was hardly anything printed except medieval texts—think of poor Don Quixote! Don Quixote was the victim of the current Renaissance craze for medieval comic book or medieval romances. This went on for another century. What got printed in the main, for two centuries and more after the printing press, was the medieval tale, medieval Books of Hours, medieval liturgies and medieval philosophy. Shakespeare lived in the Renaissance world, and the content of Shakespeare's plays, as everybody knows, is medieval. His politics, and his world picture—the Elizabethan world picture—present a medieval world picture. They too looked back firmly and squarely at the receding medieval forms. But the Middle Ages were the late show for the Renaissance. By the nineteenth century the Renaissance had come into full view. As the industrial environment formed, this progressive time firmly and squarely confronted the Renaissance. The content of the nineteenth-century mind was the Renaissance; the content of the twentieth-century mind is the nineteenth century. We are obsessed with it. It is not as easy to banish that mirage as one might wish. But one of the most bizarre growths in this development occurred when railways and factories came in. The content of this new industrial, mechanical environment was the old agrarian world, and there was this

upsurge of awareness and delight in the old agrarian environment of arts and crafts—the pastoral world. This discovery of the receding age was called the "romantic movement."

15   The sudden discovery of nature was made possible by the railway and the factories that were so very different from nature. The romantic movement was a product of the mechanical age by way of a contrapuntal environment. It was not a repeat of the mechanical age; rather it was the content of the mechanical age, and the artists and poets turned to processing the old agrarian world into delightful landscapes and delightful pastoral poems. This was in turn altered by the rise of electric technology that went around the old mechanical world of a few decades ago. When the electric technology jacketed the machine world, when circuitry took over from the wheel, and the circuit went around the old factory, the machine became an art form. Abstract art, for example, is very much a result of the electric age going around the mechanical one.

16   In our time we can see that pop art consists in taking the outer environment and putting it in the art gallery, or indoors somewhere, suggesting that we have reached the stage where we have begun to process the environment itself as an art form. We may be catching up with ourselves. When we begin to deal with our actually existing new environment as an art form, we may be reaching that stage the planet itself seems to have reached. With satellite and electronic antennae as probes, the planet ceases in a way to be the human environment and becomes a satellite itself—a probe into space, creating new space and environments for the planet. If the planet itself has thus become the content of a new space created by its satellites, and its electronic extensions, if the planet has become the content and not the environment, then we can confidently expect to see the next few decades devoted to turning the planet into an art form. We will caress and shape and pattern every facet, every contour of this planet as if it were a work of art, just as surely as we put a new environment around it. Even as the Romantics began to deal with the old pastoral, agrarian world as an art form when machinery was new, so we will now begin to deal with the planet itself as a work of art.

17   I think the computer is admirably suited to the artistic programming of such an environment, of taking over the task of programming the environment itself as a work of art, instead of programming the content as a work of art. This situation suggests some considerable changes in the human state. It suggests that the role of art in the past has been not so much the making of environments as making of counterenvironments, or antienvironments. Flaubert, a hundred years ago, said: "Style is a way of seeing." Ever since that time the painters and artists have been quite conscious of their jobs as teaching people how to perceive the world they live in. "It is above all that you may see," said Conrad, apropos the meaning of his work. The training of perception upon the

otherwise unheeded environment became the basis of experimentation in what is called modern art and poetry. The artist, instead of expressing himself in various patterns and packages of message, turned his senses and the work of art to the business of probing the environment. The symbolists, for example, broke up the old romantic landscape into fragments that they used as probes to explore the urban and metropolitan environments. Then they turned to probing the inner life of man with the same verbal instruments in hand. Instead of using the verbal as a way of expression, they turned it inward for the purpose of exploring and discovering the contours of the inner life.

18   The psychiatrist took over the same pattern and began to erode the unconscious. If the unconscious has an important and irreplaceable function in human affairs, we had best look to it—it is being eroded at a furious pace; it is being invaded by dazzling investigations and insights; and we could quickly reach a stage in which we had no unconscious. This would be like dreaming awake. Such may well be the prophetic meaning of *Finnegans Wake* by James Joyce: his idea, among many others, that tribal man lived a dream and modern man is "back again Finnegan" into the cycle of the tribal involvement, but this time awake. This possibility that we are actively engaged in liquidating the unconscious for the first time in history, behooves us to pay some attention to how it is structured, and to what function it serves in human affairs. It may prove to be indispensable to sanity.

19   One overall consideration for our time and at a conference like this is to consider how, in the past, the environment was invisible in its operation upon us. Environments are not just containers, but are processes that change the content totally. New media are new environments. That is why the media are the message. One related consideration is that antienvironments, or counterenvironments created by the artist, are indispensable means of becoming aware of the environment in which we live and of the environments we create for ourselves technically. John Cage has a book called *Silence* in which, very early in the book, he explains that silence consists of all of the unintended noises of the environment. All the things that are going on all the time in any environment, but things that were never programmed or intended—that is silence. The unheeded world is silence. That is what James Joyce calls thunder in the *Wake*. In the *Wake* all the consequences of social change —all of the disturbances and metamorphoses resulting from technological change—create a vast environmental roar or thunder that is yet completely inaudible. It is like heat that in organic or other systems creates "noise." If the environment or process of change gets going at a clip consistent with electronic information movement, it becomes very easy to perceive social patterns for the first time in human history. In the pre-Electric Age patterns were imperceptible because change occurred just slowly enough to be invisible. Was it Bertrand Russell who

asked, if we were in a bath whose temperature rose half a degree an hour, how would we know when to scream? The pattern recognition that is quite impossible during processes of slow change, becomes quite easy when the same changes are speeded up even to movie or cinematic levels. So, the artist, as a creator of antienvironments, or counter-environments, created to permit perception of environments, has a very peculiar role in our society.

20   The artist as a maker of antienvironments becomes the enemy in society. He doesn't seem to be very well adjusted. He does not accept the environment with all its brainwashing functions with any passivity whatever; he just turns upon it and reflects his antienvironmental perceptions upon it. The artist, for the past century, has increasingly fused or merged with the criminal in popular estimation, as he has become antienvironmental. Since Baudelaire, the artist, the sleuth—the Sherlock Holmes type, the James Bond type, the Raymond Chandler-Marlow type—these men have turned a vision onto society that is very antienvironmental, very self-conscious, and the artist has mysteriously been hybridized with the criminal or the antisocial figure. By the same token, and I am just beginning to think about this while I stand here, crime has become obsessional in our society as a form of artistic expression. This is not lost on children. The delinquent child is often a very bright and keen, perceptive person. It is not lost on him that the kind of overwhelming, brainwashing forces of his environment really call for a little antisocial or artistic and exploratory activity. The child, by delinquent behavior, is aping the exploratory artist. Dostoevski was aware of this in *Crime and Punishment*. He saw the criminal as a sort of cross between the saint and the artist.

21   Our newspapers create an information environment, yet without crime as content we would not be able to perceive the environment. The newspapers have to have bad news, otherwise there would be only ads, or good news. Without bad news we could not discern the ground rules of the environment. This does not necessarily mean the environment is bad, but it means its operation upon us is total and ruthless. The environment is always the brainwasher, so that the well-adjusted person, by definition, has been brainwashed. He is adjusted. He's had it. There is a book by Erwin Straus recently that throws new light on Pavlov's operations (the Russian psychologist). He didn't get his conditioning effects by means of stimuli or signals to his experimental subjects. Rather he did it by environmental controls. He put them in environments in which there was no sound, in which the heat and other sensory controls were very carefully adjusted and maintained steadily. Pavlov discovered that if you tried to condition animals in an ordinary environment, it did not work. The environment is the real conditioner, not the stimulus or the content. So the Pavlov story needs to be turned around in order to be observed; but the role of crime as a way of per-

ceiving society is a mysterious one. I am not going to make any moral observations on it whatever. It has increasingly pushed the artist and the scientist into the role of being an enemy.

22   Let me resume a moment. We have, in the Electric Age, come suddenly to the end of the Neolithic Age. After a good many thousands of years of specialized habits and technology and fragmentary toolmaking, we discovered the electric circuits. It is the circuit that has ended the Neolithic Age. The Neolithic Age, just like its ultimate phase, the factory age in the nineteenth century, was dedicated to specialism, fragmentation, and extensions of this or that limb of man. With circuitry we have, instead of extensions of hand, or foot, or back, or arm, a kind of involvement of the whole nervous system, an extension of the nervous system itself, a most profoundly involving operation. The form and function of the telegraph press can help our observations here. One of the mysterious things about newspapers is that the items in them have no connection except the dateline. The only connecting factor in any newspaper is the dateline, and it is this date line that enables us to enter the world of the news, as it were, by going through the looking glass. Just as Alice in Wonderland went through the looking glass, when you enter the world of the telegraph or of the circuit, you really become involved in the information process. When you enter through the dateline, when you enter your newspaper, you begin to put together the news—you are producer. And this is a most important fact to understand about the electric time, for it is an age of decentralism. It is hard to face this. We still like to look in the rearview mirror. We still tend to think of the Electric Age as a mechanical age. It is in effect organic and totally decentralist. But the reader of the news, when he goes through his dateline apertures, enters the news world as a maker. There is no "meaning" in the news except what we make—there is no connection between any of the items except the instant dimension of electric circuitry. News items are like the parts of the symbolist structure. The reader is the cocreator, in a newspaper as in a detective story, in which the reader has to make the plot as he goes. The detective story was one of the very first anticipations of electric technology. Edgar Allan Poe was a considerable innovator in the matter of antienvironments for the Electric Age.

23   The newspaper is also very much like the world of the delightful films we have been seeing by Mr. Van Der Beek; the world of multiscreen projection is the world of the newspaper where umpteen news stories come at you without any connection, and without connected themes. So, what the new film is doing is stripping off the story line in favor of this mosaic pattern of simultaneous projection, which is very much in accordance with electric technology. It is the film world receiving its baptism by electricity. This hybridizing, this crossing of one technology with another, goes on all the time. The internal combustion

engine was a wedding of the old machine and the electric circuit. Perhaps the most startling and most upsetting electric innovation is coming in the matter of xerox and xerography.

24   Xerography is bringing a reign of terror into the world of publishing because it means that every reader can become both author and publisher. It totally decentralizes the long centralized publishing process. Authorship and readership alike can become production-oriented under xerography. Anybody can take any book apart, insert parts of other books and other materials of his own interest, and make his own book in a relatively fast time. Any teacher can take any ten textbooks on any subject and custom-make a different one by simply xeroxing a chapter from this one and a chapter from that one. The problem is copyrighting, and Congress is now pondering these problems—how to protect the old technology from the new technology by legislation. It will not succeed. There is no possible protection from technology except by technology. When you create a new environment with one phase of a technology, you have to create an antienvironment with the next. But xerography is electricity invading the world of typography, and it means a total revolution in this old sphere, or this old technology, a revolution that is being felt in the classroom itself.

25   I invite you to consider that perhaps the best way of estimating the impact of any new environmental technology is to notice what happens to the older technologies. You can never perceive the impact of any new technology directly, but it can be done in the manner of Perseus looking in the mirror at Medusa. It has to be done indirectly. You have to perceive the consequences of the new environment on the old environment before you know what the new environment is. You cannot tell what it is until you have seen it do things to the old one. The need, however, to understand the processes and changes brought about by new technology gets stronger as the technology does. Therefore, in terms of design or style or shaping of perception, a conference of this sort is very timely in bringing attention to the tremendous new role of design in shaping human perception. "Style is a way of seeing," as Flaubert put it.

26   We are engaged in Toronto in carrying out a unique experiment— it is far too big for us—we need a lot of help and a lot of collaboration. We are carrying out an experiment to establish what are the sensory thresholds of the entire population of Toronto. That is, we are attempting to measure, quantitatively, the levels at which the entire population prefers to set its visual, auditory, tactual, visceral and other senses as a matter of daily use and preference—how much light, how much heat, how much sound, how much movement—as a threshold level. Anything that alters a sensory threshold alters the outlook and experience of a whole society. The sensory thresholds change without warning or indications to the users thereof, for it is new technological environments

that shift these levels. We are concerned with what shifts occur in a sensory threshold when some new form comes in. What happens to our sensory lives with the advent of television, the motor car or radio? If we can establish this sort of knowledge quantitatively, we will have something that the computer can really bite into. A child is a genius till he is five because all his senses are in active interrelation. Then his senses shift. The computer will be in a position to carry out orchestrated programming for the sensory life of entire populations. It can be programmed in terms of their total needs, not just in terms of the messages they should be hearing, but in terms of the total experience as picked up and patterned by all the senses at once. For example, if you were to write an ideal sensory program for Indonesia or some area of the world that you wanted to leapfrog across a lot of old technology, this would be possible if you knew in the first place its present sensory thresholds and, second, if you had established what kind of sensory effect a given technology like radio or literacy had upon sensory life as a whole.

27   On this continent the sensory levels have changed drastically since television. This visual component in our lives has been dropped dramatically and the visceral, the kinetic, the auditory modes of response have shot up to compensate for the drop in the visual component of our culture. This sensory shift has changed the taste in design, in packaging, in every form of entertainment, as well as in every form of vehicle, food and in clothing.

28   The "Beatles" stare at us with eloquent messages of changed sensory modes for our whole population, and yet people merely think how whimsical, how bizarre, how grotesque. The Beatles are trying to tell us by the antienvironment they present just how we have changed and in what ways.

29   To repeat, and to make toward a conclusion, the effect of any new environment—every new technology creates a new environment just as the motor car does, as the railway did, or as radio and airplanes do—any new technology changes the whole human environment, and envelops and includes the old environments. It turns these old environments into "art forms"—old Model T's become precious art objects, as do old coach lamps, old anything. The world of Camp, for example, is the world of the nursery of thirty years ago being turned into a conscious art form. By simply taking into the shopwindow old toys, old ornaments, and the things Mom used to wear thirty years ago, you turn them into art forms and you have C-A-M-P, this mysterious new archetype.

30   The new environment is always creating new archetypes, new art forms, out of the old environment. This process can provide invaluable information for those who want to have some autonomy in controlling their destinies and their environments. I think we are rapidly moving toward a time when we might say, with full awareness of causes and effects: "In our present sensory condition, I don't think we could

properly accommodate two hundred more lines on TV." Color TV
will considerably change the whole sensory life of the public. It is a
much more tactual form than black and white. But what would happen
to the North American world if we did as the French and Germans have
done; if instead of four hundred and fifty lines on our television, we
were to put eight hundred? The results might be most gratifying to the
educational establishment. If we raised the visual intensity or the visual
component of the TV image, it might serve enormously to ease the
transition from the old mechanical age to the electronic age.

31   What would be the chances of getting an experimental study of such
a change in our time? I don't know. Lindegren would say the chances
were not good. Anything that is serious is out of bounds. I think it was
David Riesman who said no social scientist would ever study anything
important. To be scientific you must study the fragmental, the insignificant. How else can you give assurance of your precision and concentration? Perhaps this attitude explains why, in our world, we tend
to substitute moral indignation for observation. Moral vehemence is
proof positive of superior perception. For example, we now experience
simultaneously the dropout and the teach-in. The two forms are cor-
relative. They belong together. The teach-in represents an attempt to
shift education from instruction to discovery, from brainwashing students to brainwashing instructors. It is a big dramatic reversal. Vietnam,
as the content of the teach-in, is a very small, misleading Red Herring.
It really has nothing to do with the teach-in as such anymore than with
the dropout. The dropout represents a rejection of nineteenth-century
technology as manifested in our educational establishments. The teach-
in represents a creative effort to switch the educational process to
discovery, from package to probe. As with the Hawthorne experiment,
its strategy is to use the audience and the student body as work force—
one of the great things that is happening under electric conditions. As
the audience becomes participant, involved in the total electric drama,
it can become a major work force; and the classroom, as much as any
other place, can become a scene in which the audience can perform an
enormous amount of work.

32   The audience as work force has unlimited possibilities. Suppose
we were to brief fifty million people on some extremely difficult problems facing top-level scientists. Inevitably, some dozens, hundreds, of
the fifty million audience would see instantly through any type of opaque
problem, even on the highest scientific levels. Robert Oppenheimer
is fond of saying that "there are children playing in the street who could
solve some of my top problems in physics, because they have modes of
sensory perception that I lost long ago." There are enormous possibilities for using an audience as work force in scientific research, or any
other type of research. It is simply that we insist on beaming instruction
at them to participate in the action of discovery.

33   For example, when printing was new, it created what was known as the Public. In the sixteenth century and after, Montaigne's phrase, "*la publique*," came into use. The sixteenth century created the public as a new environment. This completely altered politics and altered all social arrangements in education, in work and in every other area. Electric circuitry did not create the public, it created the mass, meaning an environment of information that involved everybody in everybody. Now, to a man brought up in the environment of the public, the mass audience is a horror—it is a mess. In the same way, the public was a many-headed monster to a feudal aristocrat. He never bothered to study its structure any more than we study the mass. Circuitry brings people into relation with each other in total involvement which creates the possibility of dialogue and discovery on an enormous scale. The structure of the public had less of such possibility. The public consisted of fragmented separate individuals with separate points of view. The public was an additive structure. The mass audience is a quite different structure, enormously richer—enormously more capable of integrated creative activity than the old public was. All the old public could do was to enunciate private points of view which they clashed into each other furiously. At the present moment in Canada, if you want a DEW line warning, we are having an election in which no one is interested. There is no involvement because the old political forms do not permit participation. You simply register a fragmented, unrelated-to-anything vote. The population has dropped out of the political setup. Yet when these changing structures are studied they yield enormous meaning.

34   Let me suggest that it may be possible to write programs for changes, not only in consciousness but in unconsciousness in the future. One could write a kind of science fiction story of the future of consciousness, the future of the unconsciousness, "the future of an erosion." The future of consciousness is already assuming a very different pattern, a very different character. The future of the child is changing beneath our gaze. The small child was an invention of the seventeenth century, according to various historians like Philippe Arie; historically, the child came out of the seventeenth century, did not exist, so to speak, in Shakespeare's day. The child had, up until that time, been so completely merged in the adult world that there was nothing that could be called childhood in our sense at all. And so it is with the family, another seventeenth-century discovery. Suddenly today the child is merging with the total adult environment under electric information processing, and is disappearing from the scene as child.

35   The future of child may resemble the future of city. The city under conditions of very rapid movement takes on a totally new meaning. The motor car has served to destroy the city as it existed under the railway conditions. The future of city may be very much like a world's fair—

a place to show off new technology—not a place of work or residence whatever.

36   It is also fascinating to consider the future of language. We know right now some very important structural things about language that are new. The future of language will not be as a system of classified data or meanings. The future of language as a complex structure which can be learned without learning the words at all, is a possibility that the computer presents increasingly. A child does not learn language as a series of meanings of words. He learns language as he learns to walk, or to hear, or to see. He learns language as a way of feeling and exploring his environment. Therefore, he is totally involved. He learns very fast because of this enormous sensuous involvement and the resulting motivation. It will be possible in this generation, I hope, to program the environment in such a way that we can learn a second language as we learned our mother tongue, rapidly and totally, as a means of perception and of discovery. The future of language presents the possibility of a world without words, a wordless, intuitive world, like a technological extension of the action of consciousness.

37   I had a friend visiting from Harvard the other day who said: "You see, my generation does not have goals." (He is a young architect.) "We are not goal-oriented. We just want to know what is going on." Now that means not a point of view but total ecological awareness. I was reading aloud from *Finnegans Wake* for a moment, and he said: "When you take L.S.D., the whole world takes on a multidimensional and multisensuous character of discovery, and when I listened to *Finnegans Wake* I got the same experience as L.S.D." (Perhaps *Finnegan* would be safer, and also more rewarding.)

38   The point this person was making was that it is absurd to ask us to pursue fragmentary goals in an electric world that is organized integrally and totally. The young today reject goals—they want roles— R-O-L-E-S—that is, involvement. They want total involvement. They don't want fragmented, specialized goals, or jobs. Now that is not easy to explain or to prescribe for.

39   I have touched upon the future of language, the future of consciousness, the future of the city, the future, perhaps, finally, of work. As a form of organized human activity, work is undergoing the most drastic changes of all; and there is nobody in the world who knows more about this than the great man sitting down here in front of me who has had a most paralyzing, I am afraid, effect upon my endeavors this afternoon, Professor Buckminster Fuller. I thought of a phrase I came across recently, "Home is where you hang your head." Now, to have in front of me in an audience a man like Buckminster Fuller makes me feel terribly at home in that sense. I really feel shatteringly humble. I am grateful to you for your most genial attention. Thank you.

Discussion of Theme

1. How does McLuhan's Electric Age differ from the age in which your parents grew up?
2. What will bring about the new age he speaks of? What will be the role of the computer in such an age?
3. Why does McLuhan criticize education? Is it a fair criticism? Do the students who are protesting today seem to have these points in mind when they demand relevance in education?
4. Are we, as McLuhan claims, guiding ourselves with "our eyes fixed on the rear-view mirror"? Is this an apt metaphor?
5. What is the "new environment" he speaks of? In what sense is it "invisible"? How do artists and "antienvironments" help make it visible?

Discussion of Rhetoric

1. McLuhan has often been criticized for his lack of clarity. On the basis of this selection, do you think such attacks are justified? Are his ideas clearly set forth?
2. What is the purpose of the anecdotes and jokes in the opening paragraphs? How are they related to McLuhan's central idea?
3. This essay contains many outrageous statements, or "probes," as McLuhan calls them. What is their function? Locate several and comment on their effectiveness in furthering the author's thesis.
4. Is this selection organized in the conventional sense—that is, does it have a recognizable introduction, body, and conclusion? If so, where are these sections?
5. Describe McLuhan's sentence structure and diction: are they appropriate to his subject? Cite several instances of varied sentence patterns and levels of diction. For what purpose might he have done this?
6. McLuhan uses many literary references in this article. Do they add to the effectiveness of the article, or are they too obscure to be recognized by the average reader? Discuss, for example, his references to *Finnegan's Wake*.

Writing Assignments

1. "To grow up today is to be absurd, because we live in two worlds, and neither one of them inclines us to grow up." Keeping this quotation in mind, describe these two worlds and the obstacles in each that keep one from growing up.
2. In a theme, show how the "media are the message."
3. McLuhan says that the young today reject goals—they want roles and involvement. Develop this statement into a composition.

Library Exploration

1. McLuhan is the author of several books; if you found this essay interesting, you may want to read *The Gutenberg Galaxy* and *Understanding Media*.
2. Investigate the ideas of Buckminster Fuller or Jacques Ellul.

Vocabulary

opaque (11): hard to understand or explain

integral (12): integrated; formed of parts that together constitute a whole

postulated (13): dependent; based

dichotomy (13): division into two mutually exclusive or contradictory groups

contrapuntal (15): opposite, contrasting or complementary

apropos (17): concerning

apertures (22): openings

visceral (26): instinctive; originating, or seeming to originate, in the viscera—the internal organs of the body

archetype (29): original pattern or mold

ecological (37): environmental

10

THIS IS HOW COMPUTERS WORK

from *Changing Times*

The following article, written for the layman, explains how computers work, what they can do now, and what they may be able to do in the future.

1   Just as you've suspected, the computers are taking over. They're figuring bank balances, printing insurance notices, toting up utility bills, scanning your federal income tax return and maybe even writing your paycheck.

2   If you drive, computers probably picked your plate number; if you fly, they may have rummaged through thousands of choices for your airline seat reservation. If you do business with the VA or the Social Security Administration, computers regularly jog their electronic memories to keep your records current.

3   Readers of this magazine have hired computer services to help plan retirement income and appraise their budgets. And a large lending agency is testing a central computer with 1,500 terminals around the nation to see whether loans can be tailored to each customer's individual needs.

4   Besides processing vast amounts of data almost instantaneously, the nation's 50,000 computers guide missiles, satellites and space vehicles aloft, monitor the vital signs of critically ill patients, tell companies the best time and place to market new products, spot suspected criminals and stolen cars, help school kids learn, and predict traffic growth patterns and urban water requirements.

5   By the end of 1972, the value of the nation's production of general-purpose computers and related services, now nearing 15 billion dollars, is expected to more than double—a remarkable achievement when you consider that just 20 years ago serious men wondered whether there would ever be a need for more than a dozen or so of the machines.

YOU MAY BE USING ONE

6   Several thousand possible new applications have been cataloged for the computer, and more are on the way. Someday you may dial a central computer downtown for answers, or have one in the house to prepare

shopping lists, remind you of appointments, or even fill out your tax form from records you feed into it.

7   Does the idea of wrestling with computer complexities scare you? Relax. You've already been closer to a personalized computer than you suspect. The automatic washing machine and the telephone are computers of a sort.

8   They share the same fundamentals of operation—input, processing and output. In the washing machine the input is soiled clothes plus detergent; the processing is their washing; the output is clean clothes. For the telephone, input is the number you're calling; processing is the system's ability to find that number to open and close switches; and output is the completed connection to the person you dialed.

9   In a computer, input is a set of instructions—called a program—and data; processing is how the computer uses program and data to solve a problem (subtracting the amount of a withdrawal check from your bank balance, for example); output is the printed report of its solution (your new balance, or the answer to whatever other problem was fed into the computer).

10   Back to the washing machine; assume it is one with several cycles, giving you the option of washing flimsy items in cold water, shirts in warm water or flannels in hot water. Call these the "programs" of your washing machine. When you wash your clothes, you merely pick the program you want, either by pushing a button or turning a knob.

11   Now picture a computer with just three programs. One will add a number twice, multiply it three times and subtract it once. The second program will add a number four times, multiply it twice, subtract it three times and divide it once. The third will compare totals of the other two.

12   When you have some numbers you want to add, subtract, multiply, divide and compare, you simply put them into the computer, perhaps with a special typewriter. By turning a knob or pushing a button, you can pick which of the three programs you want.

13   For each program the programer must write the precise sequence of steps the machine is to perform in solving the problem.

HOW THE MACHINES DO IT

14   If the computer sounds to you like little more than an overgrown calculating machine, you are on the right track. It adds, subtracts, multiplies and divides. But it can do lengthy sequences of additions, subtractions, multiplications and divisions in vastly complex combinations. It has, in the course of a calculation, the ability to choose which of several steps to take next, depending on the way some foregoing step came out.

15   Essentially, though, it all boils down to arithmetic, and, fundamentally, the difference is between you adding two four-digit numbers

in ten seconds and a computer adding a million four-digit numbers in the same time.

16   A computer is asked to solve problems that are infinitely more complicated than anyone would assign to a platoon of even the brightest mathematicians with adding machines. When the television networks try to forecast the results of a Presidential election, for example, they feed into computers huge volumes of data from prior elections, which the machines compare almost instantly with the pattern of voting at the moment. In time, the mathematicians with the adding machines could do the same thing, but the election would be all over.

17   Computer calculations are only as accurate as the instructions and data going in. You can't blame the machine for an erroneous forecast or for disagreeing with another computer if its keepers have fed it poor data or programed it wrong, and you shouldn't laud it as a genius when it turns out to be right.

18   To understand the workings of a computer, imagine its five functions as rough equivalents of human sight, memory, analytical ability, nerve network and communication.

19   *Sight.* An input mechanism receives the program—orderly instructions of what to do together with the relevant data. These instructions are written by the programer in a code that the machine understands. Both instructions and data enter the computer via punched cards, magnetic tape, discs, or punched tape from the teletypewriter. The machine may recognize these as the presence or absence of punched holes detected by metal reading brushes, or as magnetic spots passing across photoelectric cells. This information in coded form is transferred to the memory.

20   *Memory.* In most modern computers this consists of thousands of tiny magnetized ferrite rings that store the input until successive arithmetical steps ask for it by means of a series of electric pulses.

21   *Analytical ability.* Analysis takes place in a part called the arithmetic unit, a network of circuits in which the additions are done. It is designed to convert patterns of pulses corresponding to individual numbers into new patterns of pulses corresponding to the results of the arithmetic procedure.

22   *Nerve network.* Another complex of circuits, controlling the whole process, fetches numbers in and out of the memory, channels pulses in the proper direction and guides the sequence of steps prescribed by the human programer.

23   *Communication.* The computer reports its results at lightning speed through an output mechanism, such as a typewriter, that converts pulses back to numbers and letters.

THE SECRET IS LANGUAGE

24   The computer is all the more remarkable because it does all this heady figuring with a rather simple language.

25   Most of us grew up using the decimal system, based on numbers one to ten and written with the aid of ten symbols, 0 to 9. It's the way we write checks, figure our income tax, or count change to pay the paper boy.

26   Not so the computer. Two symbols are all it needs, 0 and 1, a pairing the kids taking "new math" learn as "base two," or the binary system.

27   In the decimal system, as you know, the place values of digits signify ones, tens, hundreds, thousands and so on. In contrast, the binary system, using just the two figures, is based on the progression of the powers of 2. That is, the ones position of a binary number has the value of 1, the next position a value of 2, the next the value of 4, the next the value of 8 and so on, doubling each time as it goes.

28   Here is the way decimal numbers 0 to 9 look in binary:

| | Binary Place Value | | | |
Decimal	8	4	2	1
0	0	0	0	0
1	0	0	0	1
2	0	0	1	0
3	0	0	1	1
4	0	1	0	0
5	0	1	0	1
6	0	1	1	0
7	0	1	1	1
8	1	0	0	0
9	1	0	0	1

29   Although we figure in decimals, all calculations and manipulation of data in the computer are done in a binary language. Say the number to be fed into the computer is 265. In pure binary it would turn up as 100001001. Binary language can be coded; in one commonly used code the 265 would appear as 0010/0110/0101.

30   To the computer's electronic innards all this means is that the ones position corresponds to an "on" or "yes" position in the circuitry, the "0" corresponds to an "off" or "no" position. Our decimal number 265 shows up inside the computer simply as a pattern of electronic pulses. The positions represented by "1" are "on" and those represented by "0" are "off."

31   It seems like an involved way of doing things, but binary is perfect for the computer's yes-no language. The reason is that the electronic parts of a computer are essentially "bi-stable." A switch can be open or closed. A vacuum tube is on or off. Having just two stable conditions of operation, the computer needs only two symbols to work with, one to represent each condition. So its calculating centers are made to correspond only to the 1 and 0 of the binary system.

32   In the computer's memory are thousands of rings a few hundredths
of an inch in diameter called cores. Each core can be magnetized in one
direction to stand for 1 and magnetized in the other to stand for 0.
The memory holds any number by magnetizing groups of cores in
varying combinations of 1's and 0's. By representing letters as binary
numbers, the memory can remember words, too.

33   Actually, the first electronic computer, ENIAC was based on the
decimal system. Compared with some modern computers that are no
bigger than a jukebox, ENIAC required a bank of 100 vacuum tubes to
remember a ten-digit number, weighed 30 tons and covered 15,000
square feet of floor space.

WHAT'S NEW?

34   Early programers in the computer business had to put every instruction in binary numbers of "bits," a tedious chore to say the least.
With newer languages that have been developed, programers can now
write programs with something resembling English in a number of
situations. These shorthand languages have names like "Cobol" and
"Fortran."

35   In Cobol, for example, the programer can write out ADD DIVIDENDS
TO INCOME instead of writing the instructions as a series of 0's and 1's.
In a Fortran sentence he might even shorten it to something like:
INCO = DIV + INCO.

36   The Fortran or Cobol compiler program converts the program written in shorthand language to a program in binary. When the program
created by the compiler is run, its instructions tell it to add dividends to
income, where to find the right figures and where to put the results of the
addition. If the original income in the computer memory was $10,000,
and the dividend added was $15, then the original income is replaced
with $10,015 in the machine's memory.

37   Another innovation is time sharing, a system by which many people
in different places can use the same computer at the same time. On a
teletypewriter plugged into the computer by telephone lines a user may
need 30 seconds to think up and write out a question the computer can
answer in one second. Instead of frittering away the extra time, the
computer turns to the problems other users are posing.

38   Like a glutton for work, it hops from problem to problem, pausing a
split second on each, and going on as long as problems keep coming in.

39   Time sharing is growing by leaps and bounds. It's being used to test
computer programs, to let college students and teachers get full computer service from a single machine, and to reserve airline seats on a
coast to coast basis, just to name a few applications.

40   The ability of computers goes beyond highspeed arithmetic and into
analysis. When electrocardiograms are taken of normal hearts, for
example, the pulses can be converted into binary language and stored

in the machines as a pattern of how a healthy heart should beat. Using the model, doctors can rapidly screen ECG's for abnormalities.

41   More and more, computers are simulating real conditions, ranging from the inventory for a prospective chain store to a massive missile attack on the nation. Other computers play chess, write musical scores, analyze Shakespearean syntax, create a dubious kind of poetry. A limit to their versatility seems nowhere in sight.

42   Since man is in charge of the definition of thought, computers haven't yet been credited with "thinking." But as the ability of the machines to calculate nears the speed of light, and they proliferate in numbers and sophistication, the question might well be: "How long will man be in charge of the definition?"

Discussion of Theme
1. Some critics maintain that the computer has had a dehumanizing effect on our lives. Do you agree or disagree?
2. What role does the computer play in your own life? Has it made your life easier or more difficult?
3. When the author says that "it all boils down to arithmetic," what does he mean?
4. Reread the last paragraph of this essay. How would you answer the question the author poses there?

Discussion of Rhetoric
1. What purpose do the opening paragraphs serve?
2. What method does the author use to explain the basic functions of computers?
3. In paragraphs 18–23, the author discusses the five functions of computers. What is his method of development in doing so? Find other examples of such organizational devices.
4. Do you think the author was successful in his attempt to explain the computer to the layman? Could he have done a better job? Explain.

Writing Assignments
1. In your own words, describe the basic functions of a computer.
2. Write a paper describing some of the changes (other than those mentioned in this selection) that the computer could make in the average person's life in the next twenty years.
3. Have you heard computer-generated music or poetry? Do you believe that either might someday evolve into a new art form? Give arguments, pro or con.
4. The author of this selection has attempted to explain to the layman the workings of a very complex machine. Choose another difficult subject and explain it in terms that will be understood by your classmates.

Library Exploration
1. The origins of the modern computer can be traced far back into man's history. Investigate some of the early attempts to produce computers.
2. Examine several back issues of *Think*, the publication of the International Business Machine Corporation. What does this magazine have to say about new developments in computers, and their effects on our lives?

Vocabulary
appraise (3): estimate the value of
laud (17): praise
analytical (18): reasoning
ferrite (20): an iron compound
simulating (41): imitating (for a purpose)
proliferate (42): grow rapidly; multiply

11

THE VISION OF THE DEHUMANIZED SOCIETY OF A.D. 2000

Erich Fromm

A famed psychoanalyst makes a chilling prediction for the year 2000: it will mark the beginning of an era in which "man ceases to be human and becomes transformed into an unthinking and unfeeling machine."

1   What is the kind of society and the kind of man we might find in the year 2000, provided nuclear war has not destroyed the human race before then?

2   If people knew the likely course which American society will take, many if not most of them would be so horrified that they might take adequate measures to permit changing the course. If people are not aware of the direction in which they are going, they will awaken when it is too late and when their fate has been irrevocably sealed. Unfortunately, the vast majority are not aware of where they are going. They are not aware that the new society toward which they are moving is as radically different from Greek and Roman, medieval and traditional industrial societies as the agricultural society was from that of the food gatherers and hunters. Most people still think in the concepts of the society of the first Industrial Revolution. They see that we have more and better machines than man had fifty years ago and mark this down as progress. They believe that lack of direct political oppression is a manifestation of the achievement of personal freedom. Their vision of the year 2000 is that it will be the full realization of the aspirations of man since the end of the Middle Ages, and they do not see that the year 2000 may be not the fulfillment and happy culmination of a period in which man struggled for freedom and happiness, but the beginning of a period in which man ceases to be human and becomes transformed into an unthinking and unfeeling machine.

3   It is interesting to note that the dangers of the new dehumanized society were already clearly recognized by intuitive minds in the nineteenth century, and it adds to the impressiveness of their vision that they were people of opposite political camps.[1]

[1] Cf. the statements of Burckhardt, Proudhon, Baudelaire, Thoreau, Marx, Tolstoy quoted in *The Sane Society*, pp. 184 ff.

4   A conservative like Disraeli and a socialist like Marx were practically
of the same opinion concerning the danger to man that would arise
from the uncontrolled growth of production and consumption. They
both saw how man would become weakened by enslavement to the
machine and his own ever increasing cupidity. Disraeli thought the
solution could be found by containing the power of the new bourgeoisie;
Marx believed that a highly industrialized society could be transformed
into a humane one, in which man and not material goods were the goal
of all social efforts.[2] One of the most brilliant progressive thinkers of the
last century, John Stuart Mill, saw the problem with all clarity:

> I confess I am not charmed with the ideal of life held out by those
> who think that the normal state of human beings is that of strug-
> gling to get on; that the trampling, crushing, elbowing, and tread-
> ing on each other's heels, which form the existing type of social
> life, are the most desirable lot of human kind, or anything but the
> disagreeable symptoms of one of the phases of industrial pro-
> gress. . . . Most fitting, indeed, is it, that while riches are power,
> and to grow as rich as possible the universal object of ambition,
> the path to its attainment should be open to all, without favour or
> partiality. But the best state for human nature is that in which,
> while no one is poor, no one desires to be richer, nor has any
> reason to fear being thrust back by the efforts of others to push
> themselves forward.[3]

5   It seems that great minds a hundred years ago saw what would happen
today or tomorrow, while we to whom it is happening blind ourselves
in order not to be disturbed in our daily routine. It seems that liberals
and conservatives are equally blind in this respect. There are only few
writers of vision who have clearly seen the monster to which we are
giving birth. It is not Hobbes' *Leviathan*, but a Moloch, the all-
destructive idol, to which human life is to be sacrificed. This Moloch
has been described most imaginatively by Orwell and Aldous Huxley,
by a number of science-fiction writers who show more perspicacity than
most professional sociologists and psychologists.

6   I have already quoted Brzezinski's description of the technetronic
society, and only want to quote the following addition: "The largely
humanist-oriented, occasionally ideologically-minded intellectual-
dissenter . . . is rapidly being displaced either by experts and specialists
. . . or by the generalists-integrators, who become in effect house-
ideologues for those in power, providing overall intellectual integration
for disparate actions."[4]

---

[2] Cf. Erich Fromm, *Marx's Concept of Man* (New York: Ungar, 1961).
[3] *Principles of Political Economy* (London: Longmans, 1929; 1st Edition, 1848).
[4] "The Technetronic Society," p. 19.

7   A profound and brilliant picture of the new society has been given recently by one of the most outstanding humanists of our age, Lewis Mumford.[5] Future historians, if there are any, will consider his work to be one of the prophetic warnings of our time. Mumford gives new depth and perspective to the future by analyzing its roots in the past. The central phenomenon which connects past and future, as he sees it, he calls the "megamachine."

8   The "megamachine" is the totally organized and homogenized social system in which society as such functions like a machine and men like its parts. This kind of organization by total coordination, by "the constant increase of order, power, predictability and above all control," achieved almost miraculous technical results in early megamachines like the Egyptian and Mesopotamian societies, and it will find its fullest expression, with the help of modern technology, in the future of the technological society.

9   Mumford's concept of the megamachine helps to make clear certain recent phenomena. The first time the megamachine was used on a large scale in modern times was, it seems to me, in the Stalinist system of industrialization, and after that, in the system used by Chinese Communism. While Lenin and Trotsky still hoped that the Revolution would eventually lead to the mastery of society by the individual, as Marx had visualized, Stalin betrayed whatever was left of these hopes and sealed the betrayal by the physical extinction of all those in whom the hope might not have completely disappeared. Stalin could build his megamachine on the nucleus of a well-developed industrial sector, even though one far below those of countries like England or the United States. The Communist leaders in China were confronted with a different situation. They had no industrial nucleus to speak of. Their only capital was the physical energy and the passions and thoughts of 700 million people. They decided that by means of the complete coordination of this human material they could create the equivalent of the original accumulation of capital necessary to achieve a technical development which in a relatively short time would reach the level of that of the West. This total coordination had to be achieved by a mixture of force, personality cult, and indoctrination which is in contrast to the freedom and individualism Marx had foreseen as the essential elements of a socialist society. One must not forget, however, that the ideals of the overcoming of private egotism and of maximal consumption have remained elements in the Chinese system, at least thus far, although blended with totalitarianism, nationalism, and thought control, thus vitiating the humanist vision of Marx.

10   The insight into this radical break between the first phase of industrialization and the second Industrial Revolution, in which society itself

---

[5] Lewis Mumford, *The Myth of the Machine.*

becomes a vast machine, of which man is a living particle, is obscured by certain important differences between the megamachine of Egypt and that of the twentieth century. First of all, the labor of the live parts of the Egyptian machine was forced labor. The naked threat of death or starvation forced the Egyptian worker to carry out his task. Today, in the twentieth century, the worker in the most developed industrial countries, such as the United States, has a comfortable life— one which would have seemed like a life of undreamed-of luxury to his ancestor working a hundred years ago. He has, and in this point lies one of the errors of Marx, participated in the economic progress of capitalist society, profited from it, and, indeed, has a great deal more to lose than his chains.

11   The bureaucracy which directs the work is very different from the bureaucratic elite of the old megamachine. Its life is guided more or less by the same middle-class virtues that are valid for the worker; although its members are better paid than the worker, the difference in consumption is one of quantity rather than quality. Employers and workers smoke the same cigarettes and they ride in cars that look the same even though the better cars run more smoothly than the cheaper ones. They watch the same movies and the same television shows, and their wives use the same refrigerators.[6]

12   The managerial elite are also different from those of old in another respect: they are just as much appendages of the machine as those whom they command. They are just as alienated, or perhaps more so, just as anxious, or perhaps more so, as the worker in one of their factories. They are bored, like every one else, and use the same antidotes against boredom. They are not as the elites were of old—a culture-creating group. Although they spend a good deal of their money to further science and art, as a class they are as much consumers of this "cultural welfare" as its recipients. The culture-creating group lives on the fringes. They are creative scientists and artists, but it seems that, thus far, the most beautiful blossom of the twentieth-century society grows on the tree of science, and not on the tree of art.

Discussion of Theme

1. Is Fromm's vision of the future compatible with that of the other authors in this section? For example, could a society similar to the one Fromm envisions undertake exploration of the planets?
2. Fromm states that if people knew what course society would take, "they might take adequate measures to permit changing the course." Can you name any persons, groups, or agencies that are attempting to make such changes? What changes would you make?

---

[6] The fact that the underdeveloped sector of the population does not take part in this new style of life has been mentioned above.

3. What is a megamachine? How does it function? What other examples of megamachines can you cite?
4. Fromm tells us that today's superindustrialized society presents us with a series of problems which did not exist in the Egyptian "machine." What are these current problems? Why are they particularly difficult to cope with?

Discussion of Rhetoric
1. Where is the thesis of this article stated? How is it developed?
2. Does the author support his thesis with sound arguments?
3. Consider the tone of the opening paragraphs of this selection. What does it tell you about the author's attitude and intentions?
4. How are paragraphs 1–5 linked? What is Fromm attempting to do in these paragraphs?
5. This selection contains many allusions. Select four or five and show how they contribute to the meaning of the author's ideas.

Writing Assignments
1. In what way does the college or university contribute to the depersonalization that Fromm describes? What alterations or changes in the educational system would you make to counteract the trend toward depersonalization?
2. Develop the following sentence into a theme: "The most beautiful blossom of twentieth-century society grows on the tree of science, and not on the tree of art" (from paragraph 12). If you disagree with this idea, present contrary evidence to support your position.

Library Exploration
1. For other pessimistic views of the future, read either George Orwell's *1984* or Aldous Huxley's *Brave New World*.
2. Who is Lewis Mumford? What does he say about the future of society in *The Myth of the Machine*?

Vocabulary
irrevocably (2): beyond revocation or repeal
manifestation (2): that which makes evident or certain by showing or displaying
cupidity (4): greed
perspicacity (5): mental keenness
humanist (6): one who subscribes to a doctrine, attitude, or way of life that is centered on human interests or values
ideologues (6): theorists
disparate (6): dissimilar
vitiating (9): perverting, contaminating; making weak or ineffective
appendages (12): subordinate parts
antidotes (12): remedies

12

"I HAVE A DREAM..."

Martin Luther King, Jr.

This is the famous speech made by the civil rights leader at the 1963 march on Washington. In it the late *Dr. King describes his vision of future harmony between the black and white races.*

1   Five score years ago, a great American, in whose symbolic shadow we stand, signed the Emancipation Proclamation. This momentous decree came as a great beacon light of hope to millions of Negro slaves who had been seared in the flames of withering injustice. It came as a joyous daybreak to end the long night of captivity.

2   But one hundred years later, we must face the tragic fact that the Negro is still not free. One hundred years later, the life of the Negro is still sadly crippled by the manacles of segregation and the chains of discrimination. One hundred years later, the Negro lives on a lonely island of poverty in the midst of a vast ocean of material prosperity. One hundred years later, the Negro is still languished in the corners of American society and finds himself in exile in his own land. So we have come here today to dramatize an appalling condition.

3   In a sense we have come to our nation's Capital to cash a check. When the architects of our republic wrote the magnificent words of the Constitution and the Declaration of Independence, they were signing a promissory note to which every American was to fall heir. This note was a promise that all men would be guaranteed the unalienable rights of life, liberty, and the pursuit of happiness.

4   It is obvious today that America has defaulted on this promissory note insofar as her citizens of color are concerned. Instead of honoring this sacred obligation, America has given the Negro people a bad check; a check which has come back marked "insufficient funds." But we refuse to believe that the bank of justice is bankrupt. We refuse to believe that there are insufficient funds in the great vaults of opportunity of this nation. So we have come to cash this check—a check that will give us upon demand the riches of freedom and the security of justice. We have also come to this hallowed spot to remind America of the fierce urgency of *now*. This is no time to engage in the luxury of cooling off or to take the tranquilizing drug of gradualism. *Now* is the time to make real the

promises of Democracy. *Now* is the time to rise from the dark and desolate valley of segregation to the sunlit path of racial justice. *Now* is the time to open the doors of opportunity to all of God's children. *Now* is the time to lift our nation from the quicksands of racial injustice to the solid rock of brotherhood.

5   It would be fatal for the nation to overlook the urgency of the moment and to underestimate the determination of the Negro. This sweltering summer of the Negro's legitimate discontent will not pass until there is an invigorating autumn of freedom and equality. 1963 is not an end, but a beginning. Those who hope that the Negro needed to blow off steam and will now be content will have a rude awakening if the nation returns to business as usual. There will be neither rest nor tranquillity in America until the Negro is granted his citizenship rights. The whirlwinds of revolt will continue to shake the foundations of our nation until the bright day of justice emerges.

6   But there is something that I must say to my people who stand on the warm threshold which leads into the palace of justice. In the process of gaining our rightful place we must not be guilty of wrongful deeds. Let us not seek to satisfy our thirst for freedom by drinking from the cup of bitterness and hatred. We must forever conduct our struggle on the high plane of dignity and discipline. We must not allow our creative protest to degenerate into physical violence. Again and again we must rise to the majestic heights of meeting physical force with soul force. The marvelous new militancy which has engulfed the Negro community must not lead us to a distrust of all white people, for many of our white brothers, as evidenced by their presence here today, have come to realize that their destiny is tied up with our destiny and their freedom is inextricably bound to our freedom. We cannot walk alone.

7   And as we walk, we must make the pledge that we shall march ahead. We cannot turn back. There are those who are asking the devotees of civil rights, "When will you be satisfied?" We can never be satisfied as long as the Negro is the victim of the unspeakable horrors of police brutality. We can never be satisfied as long as our bodies, heavy with the fatigue of travel, cannot gain lodging in the motels of the highways and the hotels of the cities. We cannot be satisfied as long as the Negro's basic mobility is from a smaller ghetto to a larger one. We can never be satisfied as long as a Negro in Mississippi cannot vote and a Negro in New York believes he has nothing for which to vote. No, no, we are not satisfied, and we will not be satisfied until justice rolls down like waters and righteousness like a mighty stream.

8   I am not unmindful that some of you have come here out of great trials and tribulations. Some of you have come fresh from narrow jail cells. Some of you have come from areas where your quest for freedom left you battered by the storms of persecution and staggered by the winds of police brutality. You have been the veterans of creative suf-

fering. Continue to work with the faith that unearned suffering is redemptive.

9   Go back to Mississippi, go back to Alabama, go back to South Carolina, go back to Georgia, go back to Louisiana, go back to the slums and ghettos of our northern cities, knowing that somehow this situation can and will be changed. Let us not wallow in the valley of despair.

10   I say to you today, my friends, that in spite of the difficulties and frustrations of the moment I still have a dream. It is a dream deeply rooted in the American dream.

11   I have a dream that one day this nation will rise up and live out the true meaning of its creed: "We hold these truths to be self-evident; that all men are created equal."

12   I have a dream that one day on the red hills of Georgia the sons of former slaves and the sons of former slaveowners will be able to sit down together at the table of brotherhood.

13   I have a dream that one day even the State of Mississippi, a desert state sweltering with the heat of injustice and oppression, will be transformed into an oasis of freedom and justice.

14   I have a dream that my four little children will one day live in a nation where they will not be judged by the color of their skin but by the content of their character.

15   I have a dream today.

16   I have a dream that one day the state of Alabama, whose governor's lips are presently dripping with the words of interposition and nullification, will be transformed into a situation where little black boys and black girls will be able to join hands with little white boys and white girls and walk together as sisters and brothers.

17   I have a dream today.

18   I have a dream that one day every valley shall be exalted, every hill and mountain shall be made low, the rough places will be made plain, and the crooked places will be made straight, and the glory of the Lord shall be revealed, and all flesh shall see it together.

19   This is our hope. This is the faith with which I return to the South. With this faith we will be able to hew out of the mountain of despair a stone of hope. With this faith we will be able to transform the jangling discords of our nation into a beautiful symphony of brotherhood. With this faith we will be able to work together, to pray together, to struggle together, to go to jail together, to stand up for freedom together, knowing that we will be free one day.

20   This will be the day when all of God's children will be able to sing with new meaning

My country, 'tis of thee,
Sweet land of liberty,
Of thee I sing:

> Land where my fathers died,
> Land of the pilgrims' pride,
> From every mountain-side
> Let freedom ring.

21   And if America is to be a great nation this must become true. So let freedom ring from the prodigious hilltops of New Hampshire. Let freedom ring from the mighty mountains of New York. Let freedom ring from the heightening Alleghenies of Pennsylvania!

22   Let freedom ring from the snowcapped Rockies of Colorado!

23   Let freedom ring from the curvaceous peaks of California!

24   But not only that; let freedom ring from Stone Mountain of Georgia!

25   Let freedom ring from Lookout Mountain of Tennessee!

26   Let freedom ring from every hill and molehill of Mississippi. From every mountainside, let freedom ring.

27   When we let freedom ring, when we let it ring from every village and every hamlet, from every state and every city, we will be able to speed up that day when all of God's children, black men and white men, Jews and Gentiles, Protestants and Catholics, will be able to join hands and sing in the words of the old Negro spiritual, "Free at last! free at last! thank God almighty, we are free at last!"

Discussion of Theme

1. Who or what is casting the "symbolic shadow" that Dr. King refers to in the first sentence of his speech?
2. Why does he mention the Emancipation Proclamation?
3. In paragraph 5, Dr. King makes several statements about the Negro's determination to secure his rights as a citizen. Have subsequent events shown that Dr. King was right or wrong in his appraisal of the situation?
4. What does Dr. King mean by "creative suffering" (see paragraph 8)? Would this idea be endorsed by most black leaders today?
5. Do you think future historians will regard Dr. King's speech as a mere footnote to history or as one of our greatest speeches? Explain your view.
6. Have events since 1963 made Dr. King's vision of the future seem foolish and unrealistic or have they vindicated it?

Discussion of Rhetoric

1. Why do you think Dr. King opened his speech with "five score years ago" instead of the more usual "one hundred years ago"?
2. One of Dr. King's favorite rhetorical devices was the use of parallel structure. Find several examples in this speech. Why might he have used such a device? Is it effective? Why?

3. If you did not already know, would you be able to guess that this selection was originally given as a speech? Explain why or why not.
4. King relies heavily on figurative language in this speech; note, for instance, the metaphors ("check" and "promissory note") in paragraphs 3 and 4. Find other examples.

Writing Assignments

1. In a theme, briefly describe the contributions of Martin Luther King, Jr., to his country.
2. Develop the following title into a composition: "The March on Washington: An Assessment of Its Success."
3. What is your vision of America's future? Does it differ from Dr. King's? Describe it in a theme.

Library Exploration

1. The 1963 march on Washington received wide coverage in newspapers and magazines. Read some of the reports made at the time, and present the reaction that nonparticipants had to the march.
2. Dr. King was the author of several books and articles. If you enjoyed reading this speech, you may enjoy his other works.

Vocabulary

inextricably (6): as if entangled or tied together
interposition (16): the doctrine that an individual state may oppose any federal action that it believes encroaches on its sovereignty
nullification (16): failure of a state to aid in enforcement of federal laws within its limits
prodigious (21): enormous

13

WHY WE'RE AGAINST THE BIGGEES

James S. Kunen

The author of this article, a student at Columbia University, claims that a small group of powerful men (the "Biggees") control our daily lives and thoughts. In his view, today's youth—particularly the five million college students in the country—are rebelling against this control.

1   I have surveyed the opinions of the well-intentioned American middle class regarding Columbia. That is, I have spoken to my mother about it. She's been reading the *New Republic*, and is currently fond of saying that the Columbia rebellion was set up in advance by people who are not students at Columbia, and who do not have its interests at heart. This is entirely true.

2   The Columbia rebellion was set in motion by a nebulous group of outsiders who are variously known as the corporate power elite, the military-industrial complex, the Establishment. A friend of mine refers to them as the Biggees.

3   The Biggees are a small group of men. Little else about them is known. They are probably old. They possess wealth surpassing the bounds of imagination. They have no real needs or desires, but cultivate avarice as a sort of obsessive hobby. They sit in smoke-filled rooms, so it may be presumed that they smoke cigars. In the councils of the Biggees, one might hear decisions that one thought no one could make. Buy Uruguay. Sell Bolivia. Hold India. Pollute New York. The decisions are of incomprehensible variety, but they have in common the fact that they are swiftly implemented and invariably soak the Little Man.

4   Sometimes the Biggees slug it out with each other, as in the gold market, where they get down to the nitty-gritty of buying and selling *money* (a commerce that no one else can understand, let alone participate in), but more often they are after *our* coin.

5   The Biggees lie. They shout up and down that Vitalis has V_7, but they don't say what V_7 *is*. They say that Arrid stops wetness, but they don't explain why wetness should be stopped. (I can think of a lot of things that qualify for stoppage way ahead of wetness.) They lie about

little things like that, and big things like Vietnam, the ghetto, Democracy. It's all the same—truth in lending, truth in labeling, truth in
government; none of them exist.

6   The Biggees *control*. I read a sixth-grader's history paper about the
Spanish-American War. The young boy, having put away his Mattel
M-16 automatic rifle for the evening to do his homework, wrote that the
1898 war was fought by America to set the poor Cubans free from
tyranny. He added that America traditionally fights on the side of right
for justice and freedom and therefore always wins, "like in Vietnam
today." The Biggees have that kid right where they want him. They've
got his mind; when he's eighteen they'll take his body.

7   Look around you. The Biggees are everywhere. Look in your drive-
way. They build cars that dissociate in three years, and they make
everybody buy them, and they're in on the gas biz too, so you can forget
about mileage. And no one can make them change. You get organized
and ask them to please just put all bumpers at a standard level so maybe
a little less than 50,000 of us will die on the roads next year, but no,
they can't do it. They can't do it because it will *cost* to do it, and anyway,
if all bumpers were at the same height, then there wouldn't be any
choice, and that's what democracy's all about. If you didn't know that
that's what democracy's all about, there are frequent ads to remind
you. It seems, for instance, that in socialist countries there are only three
colors of lipstick, whereas capitalism provides forty.

8   And with these forty shades of lipstick the Biggees turn our women
into nauga-babes (vinyl girls) who in pre-fab sexiness sit tracing cheap
pictures in the air with cigarettes they never made up their minds to
start smoking. And, arguing about what to-do to do next, one of these
naugas might be heard to say, "It's a free country."

9   But it isn't a free country. You can't drop out of school because you'd
be drafted, and you have to study certain things to get a degree, and
you have to have a degree to make it, and you have to make it to get what
you want, and you can't even decide what you want, because it's all
programmed into you beforehand. You can *say* whatever you want,
but you won't be heard because the media control that, but if you do
manage to be heard, the People won't like it, because the people have
been told what to like. And if they don't like you, they might even kill
you, because the government endorses killing by exemplification.

10   All of which brings us to Columbia, because at Columbia we're all
together and we teach each other and feel strong. The Biggees are
killing people in Vietnam and keeping the blacks down at home, because
they have to keep some people at the bottom for their system to work,
or so they thought. Now they're finding out that the downs can really
screw them up bad, so they'd like to raise them just a bit, but that would
certainly cost, so for the moment they'll try to keep them down by
promising them rewards if they behave.

11 So here we all are at Columbia not comprehending this great money motivation because we didn't grow up in a depression and have always had coin and therefore don't value it as highly as we might. We're right at Harlem, so we see how it is. And we've got the draft right on us, so we know how that is. And we don't like it. We don't like it at all, because we've got a lot of life ahead of us and we're for it. Killing and dying just don't make it with us.

12 And lo and behold, right here at Columbia where all we young angries are seething, who should be president but Grayson Kirk, a Biggee if ever there was one. Consolidated Edison, IBM, Socony Mobil, Asia Foundation, I.D.A.—he's got an iron in every fire that's consuming us. And it turns out that Military Intelligence has offices at the university, and Electronic Research Laboratories is raking in about $5 million per annum on radar, and we're in the Institute for Defense Analysis in a big way, and the School of International Affairs is hitting it off really well with the CIA. All the while the university is systematically desiccating the integrated community of Morningside Heights, and has its eyes on land all the way over to Seventh Avenue, so that some fine day there'll be a nice white suburban buffer zone in the middle of Manhattan, which people will know, by the inevitable iron gates around it, to be Columbia.

13 Seeing all this, we decided to change it. Of course, if you don't like it you can leave, but if you leave you're going to run into something else you don't like, and you can't go on leaving forever because you'll run out of places to go. So we decided to change it. We petitioned, we demonstrated, we wrote letters, and we got nowhere. We weren't refused; we were ignored. So one day we went into the buildings, and one day somewhat later we were pulled out and arrested and many people were beaten. In the intervening days we were widely accused of having ourselves a good time in the buildings. We did have a good time. We had a good time because for six days we regulated our own lives and were free.

14 But Dr. Kirk and his associates saw that we were free and they knew of course that that sort of thing must not be permitted. They knew also that they could not deal with our demands, because that would mean a breakdown of their law and a violation of their order. So they called in the police. And they expressed regret that the police injured 150 people, and they really did regret it, because the brutal bust showed everybody how far the powerful will go to retain their power, how far they will go rather than answer a single question, rather than admit that questions can be asked.

15 As I write this and as you read it people are dying. So you see it isn't really a topic for suburban conversation or magazine articles. It's something that must be dealt with. That's what's happening at Columbia, not a revolution but a counterattack. We are fighting to recapture a school from business and war and rededicate it to learning and life.

Right now nobody controls Columbia, but if we get it, we will never give it back. And there are 5 million college students in the country watching us. And a lot of them have just about had it with the Biggees.

Discussion of Theme

1. Has the author convinced you that the Biggees control this country?
2. Kunen claims that the United States is not a free country. What evidence does he give for this assertion?
3. In paragraph 13, the author states that "if you don't like it you can leave, but if you leave you're going to run into something else you don't like." Do you agree? Is it sometimes wiser to do as certain draft resisters have done—leave the country rather than remain?
4. Is Kunen's criticism of the advertising industry fair? Reread paragraph 5, and consider its logic.

Discussion of Rhetoric

1. Describe the sentence structure (length, pattern) used in this essay. Note particularly the sentences in paragraphs 6, 7, and 9. What effect does the style have on the reader? Does it help or hinder the article's persuasiveness?
2. Can you find any instances of oversimplification in Kunen's argument? If you can, do you feel it has weakened his argument?
3. What does the phrase "well-intentioned" (paragraph 1) suggest about the tone of this article? Find other examples of the author's use of irony, understatement, and hyperbole.

Writing Assignments

1. Define "police brutality." Keeping your definition in mind, discuss whether you think police intervention on the campus is ever justified.
2. If you disagree with the central idea of this selection, write a rebuttal.

Library Exploration

1. Read newspaper accounts and magazine articles about the Columbia University riots in Spring 1968. Did the mass media, which the author believes are controlled by the "Biggees," show sympathy for the students?
2. Read Ralph Nader's book, *Unsafe at Any Speed*, and compare it with the claims made by Kunen in his statements in paragraph 7. Which author builds a better argument?

Vocabulary

nebulous (2): indistinct
avarice (3): greed
implemented (3): carried out
desiccating (12): drying up

14

I DON'T TRUST ANYONE UNDER 30

Cecelia Holland

The author of the following selection, a member of the under-thirty generation, criticizes her peers for their naïveté. In her opinion they have exaggerated their purity, their ideals, and their claim to "truth."

1   Militant, committed, articulate and radical, the generation under 30 claims to be the hope of the world. Our parents believe it. They contrast the purity of our motives and the energy of our commitments with their own corrupted morality and corroded traditions and decide that everything we say *must* be right. "Don't let the kids down," says an advertisement for Gene McCarthy. Not since the Children's Crusade in the early 13th century has an older generation entrusted so much of its salvation to the young. Not since the Renaissance have we wielded so much influence over our elders. (Did Cesare Borgia trust anybody over 30?).

2   Much of the work in the civil-rights crusade is done by people under 30 years of age. Almost all the protesters of the Vietnam war (and the great majority of those fighting in it) are under 30. There are very few hippies over 30, and the hippie movement stands out as the single most visible protest against the syndrome commonly called the American Way of Life. My generation is the most idealistic, the most dynamic and the most liberal in history; just ask us, we'll tell you. We're strong on freedom and long on love, and there are enough of us around to change the very definitions of the words to make these statements fact.

3   Are we strong on freedom? It would be hard to find a young person outside the South who isn't all for the Negro revolution. The freedom to protest the Vietnam war—to protest anything (except the protesters) —is as hallowed as the bones of a saint. Yet to hold a conservative viewpoint, however honestly, can only be a sign of cowardice. Anybody over 30 will ask first what your opinion is on the war. Anybody under 30 will automatically assume you're against it; if you aren't, you're a heretic.

4   Freedom and free speech should mean that anyone can hold any opinion he wants on the Negro or the war in Vietnam, as long as he doesn't try to enforce his views on anybody else. But our generation's

conception of freedom goes more like this: "Do your own thing and all will be well, as long as your own thing is certified pure by the rest of us."

5   But what if your own thing doesn't happen to conform to that of the hip world, the militant students, the nonstudents or any other faction? There are, after all, people in this world who manage to live entirely within the existing social structure, and who do so by choice. There are people who find it possible to go through life neither rebelling nor conforming. Are they all hypocrites? To the under-30 group, nonalignment is as abhorrent as slavish devotion to the *status quo.*

6   Let's face it, my generation is *not* strong on freedom. Basically, we simply want to do what we like, without being bothered by anything silly like antique conventions and laws. But why the devil can't we just say so and let it go at that? Why do we dress our preferences in the vestments of a quasi-religion?

7   Part of the reason, I suspect, is that we're still bound by at least one antique convention: doing things for the right reasons, the socially acceptable motives. We have a party line, certain things and opinions that must be professed under certain conditions. Deviation labels one unfit. Anybody who's ever ventured into the wilderness of conversation with more than one hip or militant student or political fanatic or fellow-traveler knows that there is a striking similarity, not only in the lines of argument taken on almost all subjects but in the words and slogans used, not only within each faction but across partisan lines. Doctrine has hardened into dogma. (I am a fellow-traveler with the "straights," which means that sometimes I'm self-consciously hip; and making the transition from one vernacular to the other is difficult enough to suggest that the differences are not merely linguistic. Hip-think doesn't require logic or clarity, which makes it easier, of course, to sound profound.)

8   The drug issue is a good example of our dogmatism. If you don't smoke or pop pills, you're narrow-minded, tradition-bound and a chicken. Your reasons for denying the Nirvana of drugs make no difference. There are people for whom "grass," "acid," "speed" and their relatives hold no interest, just as there are people who dislike roast beef. Usually they manage to commune with the infinite quite well without an interpreter. Yet these people are as square to the drug-user as the housewife who won't wear short skirts because the neighbors might talk.

9   What does love mean to the Love Generation? It can mean purging oneself of hatred and prejudice and welcoming everyone else as a brother, and it can mean preaching the gospel while pushing Methedrine. It can mean the L.A. Diggers, a group of well-off, sympathetic people who give runaway kids a place to stop and catch their breath, and it can mean the "rank sweat of an enseamèd bed." There's something of calf-love in all our uses of the word, and something else that's

just a little weird: The widely published off-campus living arrangements of college students like Barnard's Linda Leclair is another indication, with *Playboy* magazine and Ingmar Bergman, that sex is rapidly becoming a spectator sport. Why is it we can't love without announcing it to the world in infinite detail?

10   Love, as the song-makers know, is a private thing, and those who proclaim it in public tend to slip a little in the practice. Whatever the Columbia students were thinking about when they threw rocks, mailboxes and desks at the cops during their recent fit of self-expression, it wasn't love. If it was, it lost a lot in the translation.

11   Actually, when you cut out the preaching and look at the action, we're all sharpshooters—in the old sense—and our major target is that famous bogeyman, the world we never made. We think our parents made it—the hypocrisy, the prejudice, the materialism, the hatred, the uncertainty—and we know we have the answers for improving it. It takes the wisdom that comes with some age to realize that if the solution looks simple you probably don't understand the problem. And it takes the kind of minds we haven't got to realize that what you say means less than what you do.

12   The hip world isn't the whole of our generation, but it's a good microcosm. Its values and flaws characterize us all. The hippie drops out of society. But luckily for him, society sticks around, because the hippie is a parasite. The straight world supports him. Without this country's prosperity, there could be no hippies. They'd have nobody to bum from, nobody to give them easy jobs to tide them over the winter. There would be no leisure time in which to practice being hip, and no straight public to be titillated and fleeced. The hip world is neither self-supporting nor self-perpetuating, and it's hypocritical to claim that it is.

13   This kind of hypocrisy creeps into almost all our debunking of the Bad World. The institutions that create the atmosphere conducive to protest are inextricably bound up with the institutions we protest against. If it weren't for the Establishment, what would we fight against? And if we couldn't fight, who knows but—horrors—we might become Establishment ourselves? History is full of rebellious crusades that demolished the *status quo* and wound up becoming the *status quo* themselves.

14   To protect ourselves, we try to cover the deck with protests—prove our unimpeachable nobility by knocking everything in sight as ignoble. How well do we listen to what we say?

15   Materialism in this country has taken the odd turn of becoming a form of idealism: things put aside for tomorrow. Our parents live for tomorrow, in a thingy kind of way. They dream of the bright world ahead, a utopia which we find rather pathetic because we quit believing

in utopias a long time ago. We live for today. We grab what we can get, now. Tomorrow never comes anyway. And when it does, it's just like today. Actually we aren't even particularly cynical about it, just sad.

16   The deadly corollary to this kind of thinking is that what you have to work for isn't worth having. (A woman's magazine recently declared that the emphasis is on "roles, not goals," a decent square translation of "do your own thing.") We think knowledge that must be learned isn't valuable; only intuitive, revealed knowledge is worth while. The college "grind" is a pitiable figure. It's so much easier to fake your way through. College isn't a place where you learn; it's an object to be revolutionized. You don't find knowledge, it comes to you, complete with bright colors and dogs barking flowers.

17   If we work, we do just enough to survive. A job exists to keep one fed—we accept employment as a token reason for accepting a living. We're a generation of grasshoppers.

18   We love Marshall McLuhan because he makes it impossible, and therefore unnecessary, to think logically. Our passion for J. R. R. Tolkien is, I think, due not to the clear-cut moral position he espouses but to the blatantly mythological character of his books; they aren't about the real world, which makes them safe to handle. ("We can dig the morality, but we don't have to do anything about it, because we aren't mythological people," says my sister, who is 17.) The fads borrowed from Oriental and Indian cultures are deliberate archaisms. We long for the safe, still, dead worlds in which all values are only reflections of eternity. We don't like change, and we doubt we can cope with it, so we pretend it doesn't exist. Reality has become elusive, painful, a blind god that isn't dead but probably isn't human either, so we prefer ambiguity.

19   If we're grasshoppers, what about the ants? "Of course they're straight—they're parents." Nobody over 30 can possibly have access to the Truth. Actually, we don't dislike our parents so much as we resent them—their money-fever, their ability to muddle (and meddle in) almost everything and, above all, their timidity. J. Alfred Prufrocks, the batch of them. It's the lack of authority they display that revolts us, and their readiness to be fooled. If our parents were a bolder, tougher generation, we would be a meeker, sweeter pack of grasshoppers.

20   The harshness of our indictment of our parents stems from our essential innocence, and our innocence stems from ignorance. We're the best-educated generation around, judging by the number of years we spend in schools, but we really don't know much. Colleges insist on graduating students who can't write an intelligible English sentence, who don't speak three words of a foreign language, who have read neither Marx nor Keynes nor Freud nor Joyce, and who never will. It isn't necessarily the colleges' fault: The books and the professors are there, but we've lost the ability to take advantage of them. Nevertheless,

we feel ourselves entitled to hold an opinion on everything, whether we know anything about it or not. And we've discovered that the less we know about something, the easier it is to hold a strong opinion about it.

21   The Berkeley sit-in in defense of free speech was followed by the protest against the presence of a Navy recruiting booth on campus; many of the same students (and non-students) took part in both. Isn't this in some small, tinny way inconsistent? This may be an unfair parallel, but this kind of behavior reminds me of the U.S.S.R., where Benjamin Spock is considered a hero because he defies the United States Government; and where Soviet writers who publish anything in opposition to the Party are tried and punished as traitors.

22   Heaven preserve us from our own children.

Discussion of Theme

1. In paragraph 3, Miss Holland asks whether her generation is "strong on freedom." What is her answer? Her evidence?
2. According to the author, what are the current attitudes concerning love? What kinds of love does she mention? Do these concepts of love differ from yours?
3. Miss Holland says that "we've discovered that the less we know about something, the easier it is to hold a strong opinion about it." Do you believe this statement is a fair comment on today's young people? Their parents?

Discussion of Rhetoric

1. In this selection, Miss Holland uses both slang expressions and more formal, even scholarly, words. How does this variation in diction affect the tone of the article? Find examples of both kinds of diction.
2. Paragraphs 17 and 19 refer to youth as "grasshoppers" and parents as "ants." Why does the author use this analogy? Is it a good comparison?
3. Often the author gets her point across by making a statement, then offering contrary evidence, for example in paragraph 16 when she says "The college 'grind' is a pitiable figure." Find other examples of this device. How effective is it?
4. The introduction and conclusion of this selection are clearly set off from the body. Find them and determine how they are distinguished from the rest of the selection.
5. Describe the author's tone: is it, for example, one of outrage, good-natured chiding, or humor?

Writing Assignments

1. Define the phrase "Love Generation."
2. Are the colleges doing a good job of educating today's youth?
3. If you disagree with the author of this selection, write a rebuttal.

Library Exploration

1. Paragraph 18 refers to fads based on Oriental cultures. Investigate some of these fads, particularly those associated with hippy culture.
2. Look up the following names mentioned in this selection: James Joyce; Marshall McLuhan; John Maynard Keynes; Cesare Borgia.

Vocabulary

articulate (1): able to speak effectively

hallowed (3): sacred; holy

heretic (3): one who dissents from established beliefs or common opinion

abhorrent (5): detestable

partisan (7): pertaining to a group or party

vernacular (7): native speech or dialect (of a place or group)

Nirvana (8): paradise; salvation

microcosm (12): a world in miniature

blatantly (18): obviously

archaisms (18): things that belong to or have the characteristics of an earlier and often more primitive time

ambiguity (18): uncertainty

15

WHAT'S WRONG WITH "THE GRADUATE"

David Brinkley

In this short analysis of The Graduate, *a popular newscaster states that the only thing new about the Generation Gap is the phrase itself.*

1   One night at our house my son and several of his college-age friends found themselves in heated agreement. They thought *The Graduate* was absolutely the best movie they ever saw, and so I went to see it to find out what they liked so much.

2   Well, it was far from the best movie I ever saw and, except for a few minutes at the beginning, I thought it was pretty bad. But it seemed they liked it because it said about parents and elders what *they* would have said about us if they had made the movie themselves—that we are self-centered and materialistic, that we are licentious and deeply hypocritical about it, that we try to make them into walking advertisements for our own affluence, our own vanities draped around their necks like garlands of rancid marigolds.

3   These are harsh judgments. I wonder how often they are true.

4   In the movie, a boy named Benjamin comes home from college to find his parents have invited friends—their friends, not his—to a party where he is to be put on display and congratulated for his academic and athletic triumphs. It turns out these upper-middle-class, lower-middle-age friends, in their forced and alcoholic cheer, don't even know what his triumphs were, and are vastly interested in themselves and in him hardly at all.

5   There is a scene where the father, with unknowing brutality, *uses* Benjamin, browbeating him into a hideously embarrassing little performance, forcing him to come out to the swimming pool in a new skin-diving outfit, its price loudly announced, and then to make him flounder into the pool for the raucous amusement of the father's guests.

6   These episodes are shrewdly and effectively developed, and even though the picture thereafter stumbles into confusion, it persuades a college-age audience that Benjamin's furies are their furies.

7   With our black arts of communications and phrase-mongering, yet

another musty commonplace has now been made to appear a glittering
discovery because it is impaled on the point of a vivid phrase.

8   The enduring conflicts between parents and children have now, suddenly, been phrasemongered into something called The Generation
Gap.

9   A parent and a child are of two different orders of being. The age
difference is only the least of it. One gives, one gets. One is independent,
one dependent. One is experienced, one is not. One is looking toward
finishing his work, one has yet to begin. One has many responsibilities,
one has none. One grew up in depression and war, one in vast prosperity
and mainly in peace. One grew up with Franklin Roosevelt and Benny
Goodman, the other with Eisenhower, Kennedy and The Beatles. How
could they ever understand each other?

10   We knew all this before we knew the new phrase and before *The
Graduate* put up there on the screen a caricature of this classic conflict.

11   Parents as phony and cruel as these would never get, nor even deserve,
a son's understanding; and a son coming out of college as dumb,
awkward and inarticulately self-pitying as Benjamin would have trouble
holding theirs.

12   All that is new about The Generation Gap is the phrase itself. And,
in spite of the enthusiasm for it among the young, it seems to me *The
Graduate* only makes a few exaggerated points about familiar facts of
life and then slides off into the kind of frantic nonsense Mack Sennett
would have made if he had had the money.

Discussion of Theme

1. Do you agree with Brinkley's interpretation of *The Graduate*?
   Or do you feel that the movie (if you have seen it) had something
   important to say about today's youth and their parents?

2. What is the "musty commonplace" that Brinkley refers to in
   paragraph 7? What makes it appear to many of the young to be
   "a glittering discovery"?

3. How does Brinkley defend his generation? Does he specifically
   blame anyone, or anything, for the lack of communication between
   today's youth and their parents?

4. Is Brinkley in any way specially qualified to comment on *The
   Graduate* or the Generation Gap?

5. Do you agree with what Brinkley has to say about the Generation
   Gap? Or do you feel that he is perhaps too old to comment intelligently on the subject?

Discussion of Rhetoric

1. Brinkley's opinion of the movie is clearly stated in paragraph 2.
   How is this feeling developed in the rest of the essay?

2. What function does paragraph 7 serve in regard to the sections preceding and following it? Would it have been more effective structurally to have paragraphs 10 and 11 immediately following paragraph 6?
3. In paragraph 9, what rhetorical technique does the author use to make his point? Are his examples valid? Suggest other examples of your own.
4. What does the "new phrase" in paragraph 10 refer to? Would you change the reference to make its antecedent clearer?

Writing Assignments

1. Develop one variation of the following statement into a theme: "The child (parent) of today is (is not) misunderstood."
2. Present a well-considered and organized solution for closing the Generation Gap.
3. If you saw *The Graduate*, give your interpretation of it.
4. Defend or attack Brinkley's analysis of the Generation Gap.

Library Exploration

1. Read what other reviewers had to say about *The Graduate*, and compare their interpretations with that of Brinkley.
2. Read the novel *The Graduate* and compare it with the film. Which do you prefer?

Vocabulary

licentious (2): unrestrained (especially with respect to sexual matters)
hypocritical (2): falsely pretending to virtue
rancid: (2): stale; unpleasant or foul smelling
raucous (5): loud; harsh
phrase-mongering (7): the habitual use of fine-sounding but often empty phrases

16

TO ABOLISH CHILDREN

Karl Shapiro

The author of this article, a well-known American poet, is critical of America's overemphasis on youth-fulness and the resulting tolerance of infantilism.

1   Betrayal is an act of vengeance, obviously. But in an age of betrayal, when men of authority traduce their office and violate the trust placed in their hands, betrayal becomes the official morality. "Official morality" shortly becomes "public immorality"; whereupon the fabric of a society rots before one's eyes. In the years since the end of the Second World War, announced by the drop of the first Ultimate Weapon, the world has been stunned, horrified, and ultimately cajoled and won over to the official morality of America and its corollary of public immorality and anarchy. Hardly a leader, whether President, general, public-relations man, professor, publisher, or poet, can be held to be honorable in his intentions. Everywhere lies the hidden premise and the calculated betrayal, the secret and chauvinistic lie.

2   To what end? Who is the betrayer, and why? Who are the betrayed? In a pyramidal society, a hierarchy, one would know the answers. But in a jungle there are no answers, only cries of victory or death. In the modern American jungle there are no answers.

3   Must America give birth to fascism? Or can it survive its pristine Constitution? Both issues seem doubtful. Can the economic motive live with the mass monster it has created? Can the poor white who has sacrificed his brain to television, or the poor Negro who loots a TV set from the store, ever again cross the line from somnambulism to wakeful joy? Can only the modern artist discover beauty in the twentieth century?

4   The entire world has become aware of the pervasiveness of American violence. The Americans were the last to discover it. This is as it should be. A betrayed husband is the last to know his situation. America is shocked at itself; someone has handed it a mirror. Instead of the young and handsome heir of all the ages, with his bathing-beauty consort, winners of Olympic Games, we see the soft and rotten killer (almost Hemingway style) with his call-girl W.A.S.P. girl friend, wearing a tiny crucifix between her scientifically measured bosoms. Wars are staged

televised on the battlefield; all sports are openly and avowedly big business; all books sell according to the amount of money deposited for advertising; countries are bought and sold in the stock market like cattle. Not that any of this is particularly new. What is new is that it is all now *public* knowledge. And what is awesome is that nobody cares. Everyone wants a share of the rot, the *faisandage*. Ours is a gamy culture from top to bottom. Books about the gaminess are best sellers.

5   The goal of any writer or professor nowadays is to defend his—there is an old-fashioned word—honor. Can a writer write what he wants and in his manner? Can a teacher teach what he was hired to teach, in his own manner? Or must he give way to some form of blackmail from above or below, some Big Brother, who reinterprets his role for him. But we have heard enough of this structural mechanism from the time of Aldous Huxley, Orwell, McLuhan, and so forth.

6   At the bottom of the spectrum of betrayal are the "Movements," the pseudo-revolutionary insurrections without goals. The purest of these aim at simple theft and sabotage, such as occur during and after hurricanes. The more complicated are identified with civil rights and sex, freedom of drugs and pills of various forms, the right to unlimited travel vouchers and hospitalization. These are the heirs to the kingdom of Wall Street—the latest generation of betrayers and destroyers. This is the generation that uses the word Love as a synonym for Hate, that practices infantilism on a scale which has never been seen.

7   In between are the always-duped bourgeoisie, playing both ends against the middle. The bourgeois pays his children off to stay away, horrified at his mistake of educating these freewheeling organisms equipped with electric guitars.

8   Possibly because the economic structure has reached the saturation point, the old order of social development is defunct. The pattern roughly used to be: immigrant (or settler), bourgeois, professional man, and artist (or patron). The child enacts the pattern in reverse: the young man or woman aspires to be artist *first*, deploring professionalism and education itself, condemning the standards of safety of the bourgeois (while exploiting the material wealth of the bourgeois exchequer), and eventually achieving the role of pseudo-immigrant or "native." The Beats and Hippies are products of the American aesthetic which has always preached disaffiliation and single combat with the forces of nature and of society. All American dissident movements tend to fall apart as soon as they are organized. Each artist and pseudo-artist is his own Huckleberry Finn, a moral expatriate. All of our best artists have been recluses of one kind or another, Melville, Faulkner, Hemingway, Cummings. The American artist who does not shun the Center is suspect. The dissident, however, misunderstands the commitment of the artist and thinks of this commitment only in terms of rebellion. The failure of the masses of dissidents to evolve a politic is inherent in the national aesthetic of individualism. And because the dissidents offer

no organized threat to the existing order, the existing order continues
to consolidate its gains and to ignore the threat of blackmail. The dissidents simply supply additional dry rot to the cultural fabric. The burning and looting of slums signify the abysmal failure of imagination of the
would-be revolutionaries, who in fact have no goals. Their only goals
are pillage and revenge. The intellectual infantilism of the American
radical makes him a figure of fun or of affection (or disaffection, as the
case may be). The most one can say of an Allen Ginsberg or a Timothy
Leary or a LeRoi Jones is that they are sincere. Children are always
sincere.

9   Dissidence spread to the professoriat with the installation of artists
and writers on the campuses of the nation. (I am one of the writer-
professors who encouraged the moral-intellectual dropout philosophy
for about a decade.) It was easy and sometimes necessary to equate the
mass university with other forms of the bureaucratic organism, but the
vagueness of the issues involved and the failure to clarify them simply
added up to an abstract dissent. That a university can be a democracy
is patently absurd. The prattle about Free Speech at Berkeley which
thrilled the sophomores of all ages served simply to debase whatever
issues were at hand. Professors such as myself had already fought this
issue in the courts, and won. The campus rioters were betraying these
gains and taking a little private revenge on the side.

10   Vietnam itself is a falsified issue in the dissident "revolutions." The
war is one of the most evil adventures in our history and its evil effects
on the American character are incalculable, but the dissent is largely
hypocritical. The "Underground" did not raise its voice against the
Russian suppression of Hungary; it pursues a hands-off policy vis-à-vis
Castro, even to the endorsement of antique Marxist slogans; it does not
agitate for the overthrow of the last big brother of the Axis, Francisco
Franco. On the contrary, the dissidents are to be found disporting themselves as frequently in Spain as in other exotic places, pursuing their
careers and brushing up on the guitar. If it is laudable to avoid a draft,
it is despicable to moralize about it.

11   The importation of mysticism and pseudo-mysticism into the West
was an early stratagem of withdrawal from the known modes of communication. Mysticism is simultaneously an insult and a threat to
communal behavior. Mystical evidence is by definition hearsay and
inhibits communication. The conveniences of Zen and the Sutras to
the dissidents (who were rarely if ever "believers") were that they
opened the door to a counter-culture, one in which consciousness was
superseded by unconsciousness, and provisioned their minds with a
counter-literature. The literature of the Orient has never been and cannot be naturalized in the West, but the stratagem of the haiku, for
instance, is supposed to put the quietus on Western poetry.

12   But neither poetry nor any of the other arts are essential to the exist-

ence and furtherance of the "Movement," as its members refer to it with typical mystification. The Beat poets were the only dissidents who maintained even diplomatic relations with poetry, but their poetry was openly propaganda for the Movement. The plans of the primitive dissident platform were simple and narcissistic: pot, homosexuality, and doom-prophecy, a tame and almost Baptist program. The poetry lacked ambition to rise above these themes.

13 Because poetry was meaningless as a vehicle or an aesthetic to the Movement, the early Beat poetry took to the drum and trumpet (nineteenth-century symbols of slave revolt). The mixture of jazz and verse laid the groundwork for the dissident aesthetic: volume of noise, mass hypnotism, pure size, all canceled out the possibility of dialogue or even thought. Nor did hatred of the electronic world preclude the utmost exploitation of the amplifier. Herewith began the invasion of parks.

14 The deliberate and mischievous inversion of modes (anything "adult" was proscribed) opened a Pandora's box for the child mentality which would have driven Lewis Carroll to suicide. The wave of male and female hysterics with guitars and brotherhood lyrics turned into a mass industry, on the one hand, and, on the other, a generation of *révoltés* without goals. The dissident music is verbal—both the music and the language descend to levels of callousness and insensitivity heretofore unknown—but the contents are those of the infant banging its fists on the high chair. It is an amazing phenomenon that this art, pitched directly to the level of the five- or six-year-old, should also be the level of the college student. (Dissidence appears to taper off thereafter.) Dissident sartorial fashion also abolishes distinctions between the sexes; the not very subtle transvestism of the dissident costume situates the Movement in the years prior to puberty. The burlesque Edwardianism of The Beatles expresses a nostalgia for the age of aristocracy and unlimited wealth.

15 Throughout human history the fine arts have provided the nexus between intuitional insight and civilized hindsight. That is what the arts have been for. But at times when intuition usurps the more wakeful states of mind, the arts plunge into the playpen and the cry of "immediacy" fills the air. Immediacy (as in D. H. Lawrence's "immediate present" or the Zen Now!) cripples hindsight and deliberation and prevents criteria from coming into existence. The failure of the Beat community to create poetry or any of the other arts is the most significant fact about the Movement. The hidden aesthetic premise of the Movement is that art is evil and must be hamstrung. Only states of unconsciousness are valid: drug-states, violence in bed and on the street, secret languages, political nihilism. These are the *lingua franca* of the Movement.

16 The drug agitprop of the Movement is widely misinterpreted. The

Movement does not want drugs to be legalized for their own use; it wants to convert others to drugs. The drug propaganda is entirely evangelistic: take acid and you will be saved is the same message as Jesus Saves. The counter-violence of the police and the drug authorities is not so much opposed by the drug propagandists as it is courted. Legalization of the drugs would remove the thrill; without the official opposition and the melodrama of rebellion, LSD would be about as attractive as ice cream. But the uses of hallucinogenic materials also provide the necessary escape from creativity, from the action of writing a poem or painting a picture. If you have been to the artificial paradise, why write about it? There all the poems and paintings and music are ready-made. There everyone is a Michelangelo, a Mozart, and a Shakespeare. The Movement maintains its puritanical aversion to alcohol ("Scotch is for fathers"), for alcohol confers only a temporary non-activity upon the psyche. Hallucinogens show you the Promised Land.

17   As students of medieval and Oriental mysticism know, only about one in a hundred thousand mystics has ever recorded his or her "trip" in even mildly impressive prose or poetry. The jottings of drug takers are even less engaging. The taker of drugs may be trying to force the gates of the imagination, as perhaps was the case with Coleridge, but the mass movement for freedom of unconsciousness is clearly an aesthetic draft-dodge. The aesthetic arrogance of the drug user in any case lacks the substantiation of visible works. Pot-head, show me your book!

18   The nihilistic mind is a runaway horse. The Movement blots out literature without ever having cracked a book. Or rather, it burns all literature to the ground. The Movement cultivates cultural brain-washing; even advanced university students pretend to be ignorant of what they know. The fear of cultural infection and the demand for "immediacy" immunize their minds to any responses except to the latest fad or artifact. Their speech and writing degenerate into code (at the moment it is the underworld argot of the slum Negro, a genuine proletarian dialect for him which is, however, awkward and inap-plicable to well-wishers and fellow travelers). The Movement's adula-tion of the Negro slum-dweller or hero-victim leads it with characteristic naïveté to adopt his sub-language as a generalized medium of communi-cation. The very mystery of this language gives it credence: the terminology and metaphors of jazz, sex, drugs, double-speak, and revenge supply the necessary circuits of sympathy to the adolescent of the upper worlds. You dig?

19   The jazz put-on is a major form of cultural blackmail by the Move-ment. Anyone not "with" the jazz is a marked man. The hagiography of jazz is as immense as the Vatican Library. It is all phony, a conglom-eration of the Music Corporation of America and the masses of delayed and permanent adolescents. Jazz is only a minor facet of modern folk

music. What is beatified about jazz is that it is Negro. The Negro, as the most obvious victim of society since the latest massacre of the Jews, is thought to be universalizing about the human condition in jazz. Nothing could be further from reality. Negro jazz is—Negro jazz: charming, entertaining, hot, cool, abstract, evangelistic, white, black, blue, but never revolutionary. Negro jazz is masochistic, and that is precisely its failure and its appeal to the adolescent. What it lacks in content it makes up for in sentimentality, sexuality, and volume.

20   The blotting out of language in jazz lyrics, the accommodation by skillful musical improvisers to cranked-out dollar-making stanzas, many of them a half a century old, attests to the deliberate destruction of language as a medium. The nostalgia of the horn takes over; there is a vague reminiscence of language, unbelievably debased to begin with, whether it came from Tin Pan Alley or from Hollywood. The insistence on jazz, as taken over by the Movement, is the insistence on hysteria as a Way of Life. As such it appeals to the American joy in violence.

21   The Movement nominates Bob Dylan as great poet. The whining puerilities of this phenomenon are not to be taken lightly in the stock market or in the hearts of millions of children bursting with vitamins and cash. Is he the Leader?

22   The open release of violence is always a surprise to intellectuals. Rebellion without goals is the most fascinating spectacle of all. The Media intone with relentless stupidity: Why? Why? Congresses mourn. Whole cities are put to the torch while children dance and scream as at a jazz festival or an Ice Capade. Yet violence is inculcated by the elders and is exactly predictable. Violence is the answer to the question, Why?

23   It is quite natural and expectable in psycho-politics that Negro looters should espouse white genocide and Nazi anti-Semitism. It is quite natural that W.A.S.P. children in posh suburbs should play Nazi, instead of Cowboy and Indian. In a child society the only authentic emotion is hate. In Hippie language Hate is spelled Love; any four-letter word will suffice.

24   America is the child society *par excellence*, and possibly the only one ever politically arrived at. It is the society of all rights and no obligations, the society of deliberate wreckage and waste, the only society that ever raised gangsterism to the status of myth, and murder to the status of tragedy or politics. The American adulation of the child mentality leads to an industrialized hedonism, on the one hand, and a chauvinistic psychology of greed, on the other. In advertising, anyone over the age of twenty-one or twenty-five is portrayed as an idiot who has got behind in the science and commerce of rejuvenation. The "adult" is appealed to by an almost invisible Big Brother (Mad-Ave or the Executive in the White House) because the "adult" has made the mistake of legal and contractual obligation. Therefore he is an idiot. The costuming of the so-called radical population is a form of jeering: the beard is not only

a red flag with certain flickering political messages; it is also the ultimate taunt at the man in the suit. Arson, looting, and murder are also gentle reminders to the fathers that the tumbrels are rolling. (In many of my creative-writing classes the students sit in judgment on their parents and make specific judgments about which of the elders will be allowed to live. When they are confronted with the fact that the elders and the state are paying their way through education, the students snort and sneer at the stupidity of authorities.)

25   Humanities departments, notoriously the most deprived segment of the American university system, have been powerless to halt the invasion of the child psychosis in higher education. The effeminate backstairs aggressiveness of the Humanities gives way to the Creative Writing Gestalt. "Creative Writing" is to the Humanities as strychnine is to the horse. Any symptom of guilt discerned by the undergraduate on the part of its elders is parlayed into immediate sabotage—a sabotage which stops short of the curtailment of personal benefits, however. The gangsterism of the American youth mind makes it as easy a prey to the Marine recruiter as it does to the Creative Writing instructor. The goals are not education but theft, generally theft of scholarships and undeserved preferment. As American literature heroizes the outlaw, so the outlaw student gains advantage over his more serious companions; the style of contempt, the "cool," determines to a large extent the amount of loot acquired and the length of absolution from the institutions which threaten his freedom of operation.

26   The cultivation of Youth with a capital Y has kept the growth of the American mind off balance since perhaps the early nineteenth century. The trashy frontier mythology, hand-to-hand combat, Horatio Alger, Alger Hiss, spy psychology, advertising, Hell's Angels, Beats, Hippies, Beatles, dropouts, assassins, amnesiac mass murders, pseudo-mystics lately from Kyoto or Benares, C.I.A., Black Muslims and Black Nazis, these are all part and parcel of the American dream of Youth. The dream was dreamed by the fathers, now on the proscribed list.

27   As Negro anti-Semitism is Christian (the only political training the Negro was ever given was the flaming cross), so anti-adultism is American flag-waving in reverse. For this state of affairs there would seem to be no remedy. And indeed there is not. Should one suggest a program to slow down or stop the strangulation of American life by children, it might read:

1. Cut off all sources of economic supply to Youth except what they earn by physical or observable mental labor.
2. Deny all higher education except on absolute proof of ability. No student should be admitted to a college or university unless he or she has earned a scholarship or has otherwise demonstrated unusual ability. Public universities should be more stringent in this respect

than private, rich universities (the private school is unsupervisable).
3. Deny free travel privileges to children. For instance, raise the age minimum of drivers' licenses to thirty or forty. Deny foreign travel except to those who have been granted the privilege from their school.
4. Set aside a large land area for all dissidents to reside in, with ingress but no egress. As children think the world is their personal property, give them their acre of personal property. Keep them there.
5. Discourage the cowardice and intimidation of parents and "authorities" by reeducating them to the nature of the Yahoo. Encourage construction of housing, especially suburban housing, to delimit or exclude the child, and to suit the needs and requirements of adults.
6. Abolish the child. Deliberate the intelligent society in which the infant is loved and cared for and controlled until he is ready to be shipped to a place of education, should he be worthy. Consider two types of human beings: the infant and the adult. Destroy all concepts of the adolescent.

28   Whereupon his "literature" will wither away, his "music," his drugs, his revolutions and murders, his terrorism of everything he lacks the understanding and knowledge to comprehend.

29   The power shift lies in this direction. Man is an aesthetic animal. His greatest works are slashed to ribbons by "Youth" and will continue to be until Grown Man relinquishes his image of the advertised profile of Youth. As long as Grown Man apes Youth, he will remain the victim of his seed.

30   The American adult must battle "Youth" to the death. "Youth" is a figment of the American imagination which is destroying America itself.

Discussion of Theme

1. One of the charges made against today's rebellious youth is that its rebellion is aimed toward no particular goal, and that it is nihilistic. Do you think this is a valid charge? Before answering, consider the political activity on your own campus.
2. In paragraph 4, what image is presented of the modern American man and woman? Is it an accurate one?
3. Does Mr. Shapiro want us to take his proposals seriously (see paragraph 27)? Would you support any of them?
4. Do you believe that Mr. Shapiro is qualified to comment on American social problems? Why?

Discussion of Rhetoric

1. What does the tone of this article tell you about the author's attitude toward his subject?

2. Note the series of questions in paragraph 2. What is their purpose?
3. Does the author attempt to cover too much ground, or are the various topics dealt with adequately?

Writing Assignments

1. Develop the following statement, taken from this article, into a theme: "That a university can be a democracy is patently absurd."
2. Reread Shapiro's comments about Bob Dylan (paragraph 21). If you disagree with his opinion of popular music and musicians, write a rebuttal.

Library Exploration

1. Read some of the works of LeRoi Jones, who was mentioned in this article. Do you agree with Shapiro's estimate of them?
2. Karl Shapiro is a well-known American poet. Read some of his poems, which appear in several collections and in anthologies of modern American poetry.

Vocabulary

traduce (1): violate; betray
cajoled (1): deceived with soothing words or false promises
chauvinistic (1): blindly patriotic
pristine (3): pure; unspoiled
faisandage (4): corruption; decomposition
exchequer (8): funds; treasury
quietus (11): extinction or repression of activity
proscribed (14): forbidden
sartorial (14): pertaining to clothes
nexus (15): link
hagiography (19): a biography of saints or venerated persons
hedonism (24): the doctrine that pleasure is the chief good in life
tumbrels (24): carts for carrying condemned persons to the guillotine

17

IN PRAISE OF YOUNG REVOLUTIONARIES

John D. Rockefeller 3rd

In this piece (originally a speech), a member of the older generation, chairman of the foundation bearing *his family's name, examines the "youth revolution" and finds it worthy of respect.*

1   For some months, I have been engaged in the adventure of trying to understand a problem which, for want of a better term, has been called the "Youth Revolution." I found that young people will talk to an older person—even though they may regard him as a member of the Establishment—but only if they feel he is genuinely interested in them.

2   Every generation has had its gap. But it seems unmistakably clear to me that we are experiencing something much more than the age-old rebelliousness of youth. The ferment of today is deep and intense. Although the activists are a minority of young people, it is a larger and more vocal minority than ever before. The youth revolt is a world-wide phenomenon, occurring not only in the United States, but in a dozen other countries such as France, Mexico, Japan, and Czechoslovakia. There is a tenacity that was lacking in the past. Young people do not seem to be merely getting something out of their systems. Perhaps it is too early to tell, but I do not believe they will slip easily into the comforts of suburbia and the career, leaving behind their idealism and impulse for change.

3   How do we explain this phenomenon as it is occurring in the United States? There are many theories and no entirely satisfactory answers. The young people of today were born after the Depression and under a nuclear shadow. In an age of affluence and potential Armageddon, they are less concerned about material security and more concerned about basic human values. They feel that time is running out on the great problems—war, racial injustice, poverty. They dislike the impersonalism of large organizations and rapid technological change. Because of the influence of the mass media and the freedoms of our society, young people today learn faster and mature earlier. They become quickly aware—and deeply resentful—of the differences between what older people say and what they do. In short, the very accomplishments of our

generation—in technology, communications, affluence—have served to focus the attention of the young on what we have failed to accomplish.

4   I want to confess frankly that when I started my inquiry I was biased. My instincts told me that very much of what young people are doing and saying today basically makes sense and is good. I found this to be even more true than I had thought.

5   At the same time, I do not ignore the disturbing elements of the youth revolution. There are the far-left extremists who say that present society must be destroyed. Their challenge must be met. There are the truly alienated, the loners, and dropouts. They must be helped. There is the use of dangerous drugs. This must be stopped. Too often, while fighting for their beliefs, young people disregard the basic human values and rights which they are espousing. They frequently lack compassion. They are often contemptuous of those who do not fully agree with them. While crying out to be heard, they will shout down a speaker.

6   There is much to irritate and disturb the older generation. But I submit that we have let ourselves be distracted by the colorful fringes to the point where we miss the central meaning of today's youthful protest. I am convinced that not only is there tremendous vitality here, but that there is also great potential for good if we can only understand and respond positively. I believe this becomes evident if we examine how the youth revolution is manifested in three of the basic institutions of our society.

7   There is, first of all, the legal framework of society and its attendant issues of violence, social protest, justice, and respect for the law. A major factor distinguishing the current revolt from the past is the skill of young people in the tactics of social protest. They act in ways that would have been hard to imagine for the rebels of my generation. They have learned well from the civil rights movement of the 1950s and the Vietnam protests of the 1960s.

8   Yet, for the most part, young people attempt to work within normal channels to present their grievances and establish a dialogue. They have tried to work through the political system, their support of Senator McCarthy being the best example. It is they who have made the Peace Corps, VISTA, and the Teacher's Corps more than slogans. Many young people are preparing for long-term efforts to change society. For example, the law students of today are concerned less about trusts and estates and corporate law and more about how just the laws are, how poor people and black people can get a better break before the law.

9   But even as the majority of young people work constructively for change, it remains a fact that severe provocation and even violence have increased as forms of social protest. The protesters are fired by their sense of moral righteousness. They feel that they have learned from experience that it is necessary to be loud and demonstrative to get

results. It is this behavior that compels attention and strikes fear for the very stability of American society.

10   The nature of our response is crucial, for it has everything to do with whether there will continue to be violence and whether violence will pay. We must understand that social protest has an honorable history and has a rightful place in any enlightened society. We must remember that it was social protest that brought this nation into being.

11   At the same time, we must recognize that respect for law and the maintenance of order are essential for the protection of everyone in our society. Young people—anyone—who break the law as a form of protest must be prepared to pay the penalty and hope for ultimate vindication. But if we stop here we will have failed. The concept of law and order is meaningless without justice. We must be ready to re-examine our assumptions—and our laws. To do so, we must open channels of communication. We must have dialogue. If we do not—if we think the only answer is to suppress dissent—then the responsibility for violence hangs as heavily on us as it does on those who protest.

12   Many persons feel today that another of our fundamental institutions—the family—is in trouble. Much has been written and said about the permissive nature of the American family, which allegedly is responsible for many of the ills of today's youth. Yet criticism of American parents' "overpermissiveness" has been part of our society since the seventeenth-century Puritans. In his penetrating study of our country early in the nineteenth century, de Tocqueville commented about the domination of youth and their lack of respect for their elders. Even the authoritarian Victorian age was beset with youthful rebellion.

13   The family provides a framework and a set of guidelines for a child's growth and development toward adulthood. It is the parents' responsibility to give the child love, freely and warmly shared, and discipline, fairly but firmly administered, which in turn means time, attention, and interest devoted to the child. In this way, family life plays a major role in determining the stability of the child and the depth and solidarity of his values.

14   I cannot stress too strongly my belief that children learn much more from what their parents do than from what they say. Many young people state that while their parents talk about love, integrity, freedom, and fair play, their actions are heavily oriented toward materialistic security, comfort, and status. They repeatedly point out that they are not rejecting their parents themselves, but rather what they see as the hypocrisy of their parents' double-standard approach to important social values.

15   Again, it seems to me that the nature of our response is crucial. If I am right that the ferment of youth is potentially of enormous benefit to society, then we might ask: Would we really rather have apathetic and obedient copies of ourselves? More importantly, we might take

the criticisms of young people seriously and re-examine some of our basic assumptions. This, of course, is not easy. We are used to having our children listen to us, rather than our listening to them. Everyone likes to think that he has done reasonably well in life; it comes as a shock to find that our children believe differently. Change can be very difficult and threatening, especially when the pressure comes from the young. The temptation is to tune them out; it takes much more courage to listen.

16   When we turn to the third of our basic institutions—the church—we encounter a deep irony. Young people today are committed to values of love, human dignity, individual rights, and trust in one's fellowman. These are precisely the values of our Judeo-Christian heritage. The church has been the proponent of these values for centuries. Yet no institution in our society today suffers more from the sheer indifference of the young. By and large, they have dismissed the church as archaic, ineffective, and irrelevant. One young man told me: "There's a genuine religious revival going on, but the church is missing out on it." Another said: "The church could fill a great need in our society, if it would focus less on the divine and more on how to apply Christian teaching to today's world."

17   The problem again is that the young people perceive hypocrisy. They know the values that the church upholds, but they see too little in the way of action and results. Religion to many of them is Sunday-morning tedium instead of a guiding force and an inspiration. The older generation must examine its own behavior. The church is not an impersonal edifice, although all too often it seems that way. The church is what we have made it. Its dilemma is that while its mission should be the righting of wrongs and the active pursuit of the great Judeo-Christian values, we have instead made it for the most part a force for the status quo.

18   By and large, we are much more conservative as elders of the church than we are as parents. The minister who would remain a minister all too often must please a conservative laity, those who support the church financially. The result is that the church loses some of the finest members of the younger generation. If we have made this situation, we can also change it. Any dramatic reversal seems improbable. But the young people will come back gradually if the church becomes a place for searching inquiry, for social action; if more of the clergy become involved in today's problems and if the laity support them—and become involved, too.

19   There are common threads that run through all of these basic institutions of our society. The problem is not in our legal system, or the family, or the church. The problem lies in ourselves as people. The crucial issue is not the revolt of youth but the nature of our response to it. Broadly speaking, there are three possible responses. One is backlash and suppression. We caught frightening glimpses of what this would be

like in Chicago and Mexico City. If we choose this route, the only victors will be the small fringe of extremists who want to see our society destroyed. They are playing one of the oldest games, that of provocateurs. They want a backlash because they know that repression starts a vicious circle that inevitably leads to greater and greater explosions. If we are foolish enough to fall into this trap, then we will deserve what happens to us.

20   A much more likely response is apathy or muted hostility. We are resentful over the ingratitude and brashness of the young. We think if we cover our eyes and stop our ears their noise and fervor will go away. They don't understand how really complex everything is, we say. Being older, we believe we are wiser. We know that idealism is tempered by time and that realism sets in. Soon the young activists will pass the magic age of thirty, and eventually they will be stepping into our vacant shoes. We secretly enjoy thinking about what a tough time they will have explaining to their children why they did not solve all the problems of the world.

21   This response, or lack of it, basically avoids the issue or yields grudgingly in a kind of tokenism. It is not working very well, and if I am right that the youth revolt of today is something much more than the normal rebelliousness of the young, then it will not work at all in the long run. We will find ourselves constantly pushed toward the brink of backlash.

22   The greater tragedy will be the opportunity we will have lost. For we know all too well that time is running out on the great problems the world faces. It seems to me that we have a choice. By suppression or apathy, we can make the youth revolution into yet another problem—in which case the burden will become crushing. Or we can respond in positive ways so that the energy and idealism of youth can be a constructive force in helping to solve the world's great problems. The third possible response, then, is simply to be responsive—to trust our young people, to listen to them, to understand them, to let them know that we care deeply about them.

23   Instead of worrying about how to suppress the youth revolution, we of the older generation should be worrying about how to sustain it. The student activists are in many ways the elite of our young people. They perform a service in shaking us out of our complacency. We badly need their ability and fervor in these troubled and difficult times. The key to sustaining the energy and idealism of youth is more direct and effective action on the problems about which young people are concerned—the problems of our cities, of our environment, of racial injustice, of irrelevant and outmoded teachings, of overpopulation, of poverty, of war.

24   To achieve such action, we of the older generation must re-examine our attitudes, our assumptions, and our goals. We must take as seriously

as do the young the great Judeo-Christian values of our heritage. We must be as dedicated as they in fighting injustices and improving our laws. We must have a sense of responsibility, individually and collectively, for resolving the massive problems of our society. Secondly, we must revitalize our existing institutions whether they be in education, government, religion, business, or politics. They must be made more relevant to today's problems and have a greater sense of mission. At the same time, in support of the initiative of the young, new programs and institutions must be developed which can be effective in areas of pressing social need. Fresh approaches to meeting today's problems are essential.

25   A unique opportunity is before us to bring together our age and experience and money and organization with the energy and idealism and social consciousness of the young. Working together, almost anything is possible. If we follow this course, each of us will be involved personally and positively in the great drama of our times, rather than feeling like weary and impotent victims of imponderable forces. The antidote to despair is to be involved, to be imbued with the same spirit that fires the imagination and the efforts of the young. There is a VISTA slogan which captures this spirit: "If you're not part of the solution, you're part of the problem."

Discussion of Theme

1. Does Rockefeller believe that today's rebellion among youth is simply a repetition of similar revolts by previous generations? Does he give any examples to support his belief?
2. What elements does the author consider harmful in today's youth rebellion? What elements does he find constructive?
3. According to the author, what kinds of protest are valid? What kinds are not? Why?
4. Rockefeller discusses three possible reactions to youthful rebellion on the part of the older generation. Which does he believe to be the most intelligent? Do you agree? How do your own parents react to today's unrest among youth?
5. If Rockefeller had given his speech to a group of student radicals, how do you think his audience would have reacted to it?

Discussion of Rhetoric

1. The organization of this selection is clear; the author follows his introduction with a discussion of three basic institutions, considers three possible responses on the part of the older generation, and presents a conclusion. Find each of these divisions in the essay, and note the transition between each of them and the rest of the selection.

2. What is the author's relation with his audience? How do his choice of words and use of personal pronouns establish that relationship?
3. Can you see evidence that this selection was originally given as a speech? Consider, for example, the author's use of parallel structure, his diction, and sentence structure.

Writing Assignments

1. Develop the following statement into a theme: "There's a genuine religious revival going on, but the church is missing out on it."
2. Speculate on the role of the family fifty years from now; what changes (if any) do you foresee being made in its basic structure?
3. In the light of the VISTA slogan ("If you're not part of the solution, you're part of the problem"), present your approach to a contemporary social problem.

Library Exploration

Investigate the activities of volunteer groups such as the Peace Corps, VISTA, and the Teachers Corps. What is the purpose of each? What kinds of activity do they engage in? Who joins them? How effective are they?

Vocabulary

ferment (2): unrest; agitation
tenacity (2): determination; persistence
affluence (3): wealth
Armageddon (3): a final and totally destructive battle (from the battle foretold in the Book of Revelation)
espousing (5): supporting; advocating
vindication (11): justification
proponent (16): advocate; supporter
tedium (17): boredom
imbued (25): saturated; completely permeated

18

SALVATION ON THE CAMPUS:
Why Existentialism is Capturing the Students

J. Glenn Gray

The author of this article, a pro- *the popularity of existentialism on*
fessor of philosophy at Colorado *today's college campuses.*
College, examines the reasons for

1   "Our Tom looked like a bum when he came home for Christmas. His clothes were filthy, he was wearing a mandarin beard, and his hair hadn't been cut since September. Last fall we gave him permission to live alone off-campus and cook for himself. Now he has trench mouth, a bad case of athlete's foot, and some kind of mysterious virus."

2   Our neighbor was both exasperated and amused as she thus described her son, a senior at a famous Ivy League college. He is a superior student who had hitherto seemed anything but a beatnik. For years his parents have let him steer his own course and supported him financially at some sacrifice. What, then, is he rebelling against? Is this merely a ludicrous episode in his development or a sign of a severe disorder? His mother doesn't know.

3   Many other enlightened parents are equally perplexed by the bizarre actions of their college sons and daughters. Nor can professors and university administrators shed much light on the moods and motivations of students in the 'sixties. They have been baffled by the rioting at Berkeley last fall and other less publicized incidents elsewhere.

4   For today's student is a very different creature from his predecessors. In my own college days in the 'thirties, if I had come home at Christmas in Tom's condition, my parents would probably have had me committed to a different sort of institution. What lies behind the change?

5   For one thing, today's student is more affluent than we were, more comfortably housed, and better equipped with the materials of scholarship. But his college life is also more impersonal and competitive, less humane. It is harder for him to know his professors, the administration, or even his all too numerous fellow students. Learning is increasingly packaged and is sometimes referred to, shamelessly, as the "knowledge business." Knowledge itself expands at a rate that makes him feel like an imposter if he seeks to be broadly educated, and walls him off from others if he specializes. His professors are less attached to the institution where they teach and more to their disciplines. And they have less

time to give him or the college. In this situation, the traditional college spirit—of either the rah-rah variety or the community of learners—may seem to the students as outmoded as the raccoon coat and the hip flask.

6 If he has reached the age of reflection, today's student is seeking above all to differentiate himself from the crowd. Thirty years ago it was distinctive merely to be a college man. Now he must struggle to be more than a grade-point average, an anonymous statistic with a college and home address. Often he expresses this yearning for uniqueness in ways that parents, administrators, professors, and other outsiders consider illegitimate. Well publicized are the bearded, sloppily dressed students, defiant of even minimal administrative regulations, studious enough, but incontinent in their demands for alcoholic and sexual freedoms, fiercely insistent on leading their own lives.

7 Typical of this state of mind is a student's letter in a recent issue of our college newspaper. "The trouble is that they [administration and faculty] take it all as seriously as the rest of the piety we get about law and morality and the intellectual purpose of our existence. The most ironic thing on this campus is that they believe in their own hypocrisy. . . One of the reasons that administration and much of the faculty alike draw grotesque pictures of students is that they probably have never talked with one, not that they'd listen if they did. For years the same situations occur, the same opinions are given, the same pleas are voiced, and the same nothing happens."

8 The desire for self-definition often goes hand in hand with an inner need—more or less conscious—for a compelling authority to make freedom meaningful. In the 'thirties, economic pressures for existence and our opposition to the fascist menace rescued us from this dilemma. In the 'forties there was the war and, afterward, the threat of the Bomb to distract attention from inner conflicts. For some students in the 'sixties the civil-rights struggle has become a Cause—a clear-cut issue on which to act and to argue. But as yet this movement has not reached anything like the numbers nor hit with anything like the impact that we experienced with fascism, communism, the war, and the Bomb.

9 Lacking an embracing cause and a fervent ideology, the student's search for a durable purpose is likely to become aggressive, extremist, at times despairing. It can easily turn into preoccupation with subjective feelings and plain egotism. As André Gide has put it, "Each human being who has only himself for aim suffers from a horrible void." Paradoxical as it sounds, the real problem of our college youth is to discover some authority, both private and public, that will make possible authentic individuality.

THEIR FAVORITE REBEL

10 I have learned something about this search over the past fifteen years as one of the professors conducting a senior seminar called Freedom

and Authority. Before generalizing, perhaps I should say a word about Colorado College, where I teach philosophy. It is a fairly typical small, private liberal-arts institution, founded in 1874 by New England Congregationalists before Colorado was a state. It has long since cut loose from church ties, drifting—like Grinnell, Carleton, Pomona, and others—into secularism. Our students are drawn from many states; after Colorado, California and Illinois contribute the most.

11   We are not as selective as the Ivy League colleges nor as equalitarian as the state institutions. Since—like those of most private colleges— costs are high, our students come largely from upper-middle-class families. (Some are shockingly rich. A few years back when we banned automobiles for freshmen, a Texas girl wired our admissions committee, requesting in good faith that she be permitted to bring her private airplane.)

12   I was originally lured out here by a dean who painted an enticing picture of Back Bay Boston accents mixed with Western ranch drawls. But the percentage of students from ranches, farms, and the working class has steadily declined, and drawls are now rare. In sum, our students and their families are, economically and socially, very much like you who are reading this magazine. They represent an important— if not typical—sample of American college students.

13   Our Freedom and Authority seminar is a very freewheeling, wide-ranging course. Though we constantly change the readings, a few books have remained by nearly unanimous consent from the beginning. The first of these is Plato's account of the trial, imprisonment, and death of Socrates in the *Apology, Crito,* and end of *Phaedo.* These short dialogues, conveniently grouped in one paperback, are probably exerting a profounder influence on the campus today than such best-sellers as Golding, Salinger, and Baldwin, which bloom and fade in campus popularity.

14   Why does Socrates appeal to contemporary students? They respond to his fearless assertion of his right to determine his own conduct despite powerful opposition from the majority of his fellow citizens. The conflict between individual freedom and sociopolitical authority which he dramatizes expresses their own central dilemma. These students have outgrown the discipline of parents. In college, various authorities—the college administration, campus mores, and student cliques—vie for their allegiance. They are also uneasily conscious of the different standards of the professional and business worlds they are about to enter. The sensitive student, confused by these uncertain values, is thrilled when Socrates, the original rebel who became the "father" of philosophy, tells his fellow Athenians that he loves and cherishes them, but chooses to obey only his own vision of the right and good. Socrates' example can still engender a revolutionary fervor in youthful hearts. It was hardly an accident that the campus rebellions

at Berkeley and earlier at the University of Colorado were led by
philosophy majors.*

15   Less acceptable to my students than Socrates' idea of freedom is his
concept of authority, which leads him to refuse a proffered escape from
prison after he has been sentenced to death. He likens the laws of Athens
to parents, who must always be obeyed even if they chastise their
children unjustly. At this point, my students begin to protest, and their
identification with Socrates is broken. As one of them put it last fall,
"I can't imagine anything less comparable to my parents than the U.S.
government."

16   There are exceptions. One girl, for example, last November rec-
onciled the seeming contradictions in Socrates' philosophy in this
fashion: "In the *Apology* individual determination of conduct challenges
and defeats all other values, including Athenian law. However, the
reverse is not what happens in the *Crito*. Here, Athenian law is weighted
with his personal laws of conduct *against* a solitary value, his life. His
natural desire to flee for his life, not his individualism, is challenged
here. . . . As part of his personal conduct code, Socrates could not
destroy Athenian law simply because it was being used to destroy a
lesser value, his life on earth. 'To injure in turn when ill-treated' was
against his moral structure also, so that his personal conduct code
forced him to abide by Athenian law. Of the three values considered
in the *Apology* and the *Crito*, Socrates held individual determination
of conduct most important, Athenian law second, and his own life
least important."

17   All of us blessed her, a rank beginner in philosophy, for the kind of
insight that an unburdened mind often brings to a complex issue.
In the ensuing discussion, her classmates were intellectually persuaded
that Socrates' freedom was sustained by his lifelong membership in
the community of Athens. But how could his example be helpful
today? Since patriotism is hardly an operable emotion among contemporary students, Socratic freedom, though intellectually appealing,
does not in the end provide a satisfying answer. After all, Socrates was
an old man with secure roots in a small community, a situation quite
opposite to that of young people in our huge, fast-changing, incredibly
complex society.

"JUST LIKE MY OLD MAN"

18   As a contrast to Socrates, we study *The Death of Ivan Ilych,* Tolstoi's
powerful short story in which a modern man must face an agonizing

---

*Similarly, the unprecedented student demonstration at Yale in March was a protest
against the adminstration's failure to give tenure to an admired philosophy teacher.

death with no resources save the polite conventions of an artificial society. Slowly dying, daily more isolated and desperate, Ivan asks:

"Then what does it mean? Why? It can't be that life is so sense-less and horrible. But if it really has been so horrible and senseless, why must I die and die in agony? There is something wrong!

"Maybe I did not live as I ought to have done," it suddenly occurred to him. "But how could that be, when I did everything properly," he replied, and immediately dismissed from his mind this, the sole solution of all the riddles of life and death, as something quite impossible.

But he cannot dismiss these fears for long.

He lay on his back and began to pass his life in review in quite a new way. In the morning when he saw first his footman, then his wife, then his daughter, and then the doctor, their every word and movement confirmed to him the awful truth that had been revealed to him during the night. In them he saw himself— all that for which he had lived—and saw clearly that it was not real at all, but a terrible and huge deception which had hidden both life and death. This consciousness intensified his suffering tenfold.

19   In the end, Tolstoi rescues Ivan from utter meaninglessness and absurdity via his own (Tolstoi's) passionate faith in primitive Christianity. But this does little to alleviate the atmosphere of controlled terror and doom.

20   The story has a stunning impact on our students. If they find Socrates wholly admirable but a size larger than life, Ivan is all too human, the anonymous Everyman of our day, painfully contemporary. I have overheard more than one of my students breathe, "My God, he is just like my old man!" They do not identify with him for he is too much like adults they know and dislike—a portrait of what modern life may force them eventually to become. Though they hardly aspire to be heroes like Socrates, they desperately want to escape being victims like Ivan.

21   Ivan's "inauthentic" life has become a rich source for the Existentialists in their indictment of modern society. On the campus Existentialism—which is both a mood and a metaphysics—is compounded of anxiety about being lost in the crowd and the lack of closeness or intimacy with fellow students. Sometimes the despairing response to these feelings is sexual promiscuity; more often it is expressed in eccentric dress and flamboyant behavior. Such climates of opinion are contagious and often attract spurious reactions. These can be downright funny, as in the reported case of the student who used to telephone his girl friend and say, "Honey, I'm in the abyss again. How about going out for a beer?"

22   But in fact the underlying mood is quite different from the perennial depressions of late adolescence. These students are anxiously concerned with the problem of being themselves. Authenticity is the element of Existentialism that strikes the deepest note for them. The highest virtue is honesty with themselves and others while phoniness in whatever form is the greatest vice. "The thing that's wrong with this class," a senior burst out recently, "is that none of us is spontaneous. We're all trying to be so clever and to impress each other. I think we are simply afraid to be ourselves. I'm sick of my own pretending."

23   To be a genuine or authentic person is not primarily a moral matter, in the sense that older Americans think of morality. For Existentialists authenticity means freely choosing what is one's own in behavior, attitude, and mode of living, however singular these may appear to others. The kind of society we are building—or that is being built around us—is, for them, a major obstacle to the attainment of authentic individuality.

TRIGGERS OF SELF-DISCOVERY

24   The difficult art of becoming oneself can hardly be more than begun by the age of twenty-two or twenty-three. Hence the important question is: How long does the search continue? Graduates of our Freedom and Authority seminar often write to their old professors and many of them return to campus annually, from as far away as Pennsylvania and California. We hold an informal seminar with them at Homecoming, usually based on a book which we have assigned in advance.

25   Surprises about the future development of one's students are the rule for a college professor. But I am still disconcerted when the students I counted on fail me and the least promising prove to be "late bloomers."

26   In the last category is a pretty Connecticut girl who seemed quite unremarkable when she left my seminar section a couple of years ago and proceeded to a government job in Washington. Soon afterward an FBI agent came to my office for a routine loyalty check and I gave him the expected replies. But meanwhile someone denounced her as an associate of Communists at college, and she was subjected to a thorough investigation. She secured help from the American Civil Liberties Union, an organization she had first heard of in our course. The investigation ended harmlessly at a hearing where one government agent testified that she was "an innocuous person."

27   When she returned to campus last spring for a visit this characterization was much on her mind. "That agent was right," she told me. "Up till now I have been just that, an innocuous person, but I intend to be innocuous no longer." She asked me to support her application for law school, which she entered last fall. She had decided to become a defender of civil liberties in a private capacity, not to practice law. This winter she wrote me long letters displaying an unsuspected spirit and passion

and marking her as a person who has attained security of mind. She has already resolved not to take the loyalty oath required of members of the bar in the state where she is studying, to make a court case of the matter. She has also become a militant pacifist. It was apparently the description of her as "innocuous" that triggered all these responses— all dormant in her college days.

28   The death of President Kennedy had a similar transforming effect on another unlikely student whose undistinguished college career included a troubled progress through my Freedom and Authority course. He married and went to work for a national soap company where he was rising rapidly. But the Kennedy assassination disrupted his world. Soon afterward he wrote to me asking for "a philosopher's point of view." "I felt a strong sense of identity with him," he wrote, expressing a feeling widespread at that time. "Perhaps this is because he was young, or because we shared similar political views (weak and irresolute as mine are) or because he was an 'intellectual' President, or because . . . I felt guilty because of his murder, and I feel dead because of his death."

29   He had tried, he said, to cope with the disaster, to reason it through, but in vain. "I usually end up saying 'God damn,' with an incredulous shake of the head. Surely there must be more grief written in people's hearts than what is written on their faces. Aside from a few hours at the funeral, all seems to be normal with the people I see and know. But for me this one act has made all other acts irrelevant and trivial; it has displaced time with paranoia, good with evil, relative simplicity with incomprehensibility, and ideal with dirt."

30   He could no longer remain in the business world. Despite his wife and children, he decided to return to graduate school to prepare himself for work in international education. He is now immersed in the study of foreign languages and Existentialism. Wearing a heavy beard, he has lost all resemblance to the young executive of a year ago. For the first time in his life, he told me recently, he is truly "engaged" in discovering the meaning of existence through commitment to thought and action rather than middle-class drift.

31   These two cases are, of course, exceptions. Relatively few of our young alumni have made much progress toward attaining a distinctive individuality after leaving college. The demands of business and professional life on the men, of home-making and child-rearing on the women, tend either to halt the search or even to induce surrender to reigning values. It would seem that the very prosperity which permits college students to spend time pondering important issues of existence acts as a sedative in their early adulthood. Affluence, not religion, might be called the opiate of the 'sixties. The immediate requirements of making a living and getting ahead in the status race seem to dull the passions and despair which obsessed many of them in college. There is,

of course, nothing surprising in this. Many of us escape the need to give meaning to our existence through the age-old expedient of producing the next generation and letting them struggle with the problem.

THE APPEAL OF NOTHINGNESS

32   The Existentialist preoccupation with the Absurd, Nothingness, *Angst,* etc.—at least as metaphysical concepts—did not until recently have much of a grip on the English-speaking countries. When I first began teaching the leading Existentialists about 1950, interest in a Kierkegaard, Heidegger, or Sartre was likely to be a matter of either curiosity or fashion. Their very names were strange and most Americans had difficulty pronouncing the word Existentialism. In those years my colleagues frequently asked me to give a coffee-break explanation of the movement.

33   Now discussions are far more earnest and passionate. I conduct a Wednesday evening seminar on Existentialism at my home. Frequently I have to push the students out after several hours, if I am to simmer down and get any sleep that night. Often they continue heated arguments elsewhere till the small hours. In colleges all over America, courses dealing with Existentialists are currently very popular, to the disgust of the disciples of Language Analysis—an Oxford import—who once felt confident of dominating academic philosophy. The rapid availability of translations from German and French Existentialist writings and sales of large editions attest to the surprising new demand.

34   What accounts for it? Undeniably, there is a large element of the modish, for Americans have always been susceptible to philosophic imports from the Continent and England. (In philosophy, it has been said, we are still largely a colony of Europe.) I must also admit, rather shamefacedly, that even philosophy is not immune to the attraction of "the hottest thing in town." After the war it was Oxford Analysis, now it is Existentialism.

35   There is, however, much more to the matter. Existentialists draw their insights and inspiration from literature rather than science. They are concerned with the individual and with personal experience in an age that threatens to overwhelm individuality. This is why they attract so many American playwrights and novelists who have begun the process of Americanizing the European mood. Because the specific possibilities and frustrations of our everyday life are sharply different from those in France or Germany we were slow to accept the Existentialist mood and metaphysics. Now that our writers have succeeded in "translating" them into our American idiom, we are feeling their delayed impact.

36   The students I know best seem to have an intuitive grasp of what Heidegger and Sartre mean when they write of man's exposure to

Nothingness. In a few extreme cases Nothingness means a profound feeling of disengagement with American culture, if not Western civilization itself. Other students who say in the privacy of my office, "I am at the end of my rope," are feeling only a temporary despair, perhaps little more than the romantic storm and stress of late adolescence. Sometimes I respond with a gentle joshing, and refuse to take them too seriously. With others I am far from sure.

37   The latter group includes students who often do superb work in my classes but who are quite as likely to be on academic probation as on the Dean's list. (One of them recently spent three semesters in the near-failing and three in the excellent category.)

38   These are brilliant, alienated young people. Generally, they do not care for Karl Jaspers, the Existentialist who identifies himself most closely with conventional philosophy. They respond to the philosophers radically at odds with the whole tradition of modern culture. They want Kierkegaard's either-or—the leap of faith or gross sensuality; Sartre's good faith or self-deception; Heidegger's nearness to Being or nihilism.

39   The ablest student I ever taught at Colorado College was of this kind. He wrote better commentaries on these philosophers than are found in the published literature. His poems, which I alone was allowed to see, were also first-rate. But it was a trial to keep him in college from one semester to another. Again and again he would disappear into the mountains, by himself for days. My wife and I constantly feared his suicide. When he finally graduated I easily secured fellowships for him to three graduate schools. He turned down all of them and proceeded to wander over the country, supporting himself at odd jobs. In his college years I was, in effect, struggling with him for his very soul; it is now sadly clear that I lost.

TURNING INWARD

40   In an earlier day, before disillusionment with communism, some such students found release in action, in attachment to a utopian authority which gave them a feeling of belonging. For others, the crude menace of Hitler served to unite them with Western values. Today a few find a sense of belonging in Southern racism. Others in the civil-rights movement or in the Peace Corps with its opportunities for genuine service.

41   What these students need above all is action, not further study, yet how can I counsel them to give up their studies before the degree? To serve with any significance in our specialized society they will need more formal schooling than they have or want before they have "found" themselves. The plight of dropouts on the lower academic rungs is well known. Equally poignant is the problem of those at the top—

often even in graduate school—who do not know where they are headed nor whether they should stay in college at all.

42   Ironically, our technological society appears to widen the spheres of freedom while making it even harder to escape from the toils of "the system" as students call it. Students today travel far more than we did in the 'thirties and 'forties; learn and see more and participate in a much larger range of activities. At an early stage the choice of many different careers is open to them. But once they have chosen anything specific, whether it be a "major" or marriage, they are soon past the point of no return.

43   In this situation Existentialism appeals. Its deepest conviction is that through his choices each individual makes himself. Its emphasis is not only on the absurd character of social reality, in some cases, of the world as a whole, but also on Possibility. In an inner sense everyone determines his own course. He can choose to lead an authentic existence or choose to be lost in the crowd. If the overwhelming majority opt for the latter condition, this does not prevent the exceptional person from standing alone as an authentic "single one." To a man, Existentialists are against group activities. They never tire of reminding us that "existence" literally means to "stand out from".

44   "I have decided that I am simply different from all the others," a brilliant youth told me the other day, explaining how even his close friends saw no point whatever to his poetry. "I must think and write for myself from now on." Both resolution and pathos were in his voice.

WHAT, IF NOT ABSURD?

45   I doubt that Existentialist philosophy can ultimately satisfy the search for authority. So far, few of these thinkers have provided guidelines for social or political action, though all of them stress the necessity for individual commitment. However, for students who are not yet able or ready to act, Existentialism offers a great deal. At the least it presents an escape from the morass of conformity, *la dolce vita,* boredom, and the meaningless competitiveness in which they see so many of their elders caught.

46   Furthermore, those who go behind Sartre to the Danish and German originators of this movement discover a choice between an absurd or tragic view of human destiny. The absurd view is that existence is finally meaningless and futile, a defiant if admirable gesture in a void. The tragic conviction acknowledges the fragile and exposed character of individuality but discovers meaning and purpose in the individual's struggle to locate himself in nature and society. Though his personal life is of short duration, and subject to chance and misfortune while it lasts, his actions are of great importance in the moral sum of things. Tragedy links us to what has been in the history of our species and

binds us in faith to the future. It teaches that there are things worth living and dying for, ideas, ancestors, and descendants.

47   On the other hand, the metaphysical idea that "life is a tale told by an idiot, full of sound and fury, signifying nothing" can do none of these things. The conviction of absurdity cuts all ties to history and nature and with them the nerve of meaningful action. Which version of Existentialism will be accepted by students in the rest of the 'sixties?

48   The answer will be important. It has been a favorite taunt of European critics that in America there are no tragedies, only mistakes. The quality of current experience is rapidly dissipating any remaining truth in this ancient charge. Yet young people inevitably find it hard to learn the price in pain and suffering necessary to pay for the tragic vision. Falling into a persuasion of absurdity and meaninglessness is, on the surface at least, much easier. The polar choices again are between the life of Socrates and that of Ivan Ilych.

49   That the tragic and absurd should be competing for students' minds in the 'sixties is not surprising, when one remembers that many of their parents were fighting World War II while they were infants and that they have grown up in a world changing at an incredible pace. Indeed, were young people not constitutionally adaptable and pre-occupied with the immediate present, they would be in a much worse plight than they are. The wonder is that so many are sane and resilient.

RIFT BETWEEN GENERATIONS

50   Nevertheless, there has hardly been a time, in my experience, when students needed more attention and patient listening to by experienced professors than today. The pity is that so many of us retreat into research, government contracts, and sabbatical travel, leaving counsel and instruction to junior colleagues and graduate assistants. In so doing we deepen the rift between the generations and at the same time increase the sense of impersonality, discontinuity, and absence of community that makes college life less satisfactory in this decade than it used to be. What is needed are fewer books and articles by college professors and more cooperative search by teacher and taught for an authority upon which to base freedom and individuality.

51   After surviving so many turbulent decades of this century, some of us may feel a certain confidence that the present will prove no harder than the past has been. But we should remind ourselves that peace and affluence have their own perils as surely as do wars and depressions. Though our students increasingly come to us better prepared in the traditions of Western civilization, how many of them care more deeply about these traditions than did students in the bad old days? My pessimistic sense of catastrophe has lessened somewhat since 1960, but I find that deep uneasiness about the course of American higher

education has grown. Nowadays nearly everyone looks to education for salvation as once we looked to religion or to a political ideology. But before we succeed in building the great society, we shall need to resolve the doubt and bafflement about its validity and worth in the minds of those now in college who should serve as leaders. Many of the harassed young men and women I teach, at any rate, have not yet decided what sense, if any, their existence has.

Discussion of Theme

1. According to Gray, what is the state of mind of today's student? What are his chief problems?
2. Who is the favorite rebel among the students in the author's philosophy seminar? In what ways is this man's philosophy relevant today? In what ways is it not?
3. Who does the author present as an antithesis to Socrates? Why? Can you think of any other characters in nineteenth or twentieth century literature that the author could have chosen?
4. Do you believe that "the kind of society we are building [is] a major obstacle to the attainment of authentic individuality"?

Discussion of Rhetoric

1. What contributes to the warm and personal tone of this selection?
2. What is the purpose of the opening anecdote? How does it relate to the rest of the essay?
3. What method does Gray use to develop his thesis?

Writing Assignments

1. If you were teaching a seminar in "Freedom and Authority," what three books would you choose as central texts? Why?
2. Select one of the following quotations from the essay and develop it into a theme: "Each human being who has only himself for aim suffers from a horrible void." "The highest virtue is honesty . . . phoniness in whatever form is the greatest vice." "Many . . . young men and women . . . have not decided what sense, if any, their existence has."
3. Define alienation.
4. Define existentialism.

Library Exploration

1. Read some of the works by Plato mentioned in this essay. Are the ideas they contain relevant today?
2. If the philosophy of existentialism is of interest to you, read the works of some of the prominent existentialist writers, for example, Sartre, Heidegger, or Kierkegaard.

Vocabulary

affluent (5): wealthy

incontinent (6): unrestrained; uncontrolled

mores (14): customs

engender (14): produce

proffered (15): offered; tendered

alleviate (19): lessen

flamboyant (21): showy

authenticity (22): genuineness

innocuous (26): harmless

dormant (27): asleep

paranoia (29): excessive suspiciousness and distrust of others

expedient (31): means to an end

poignant (41): emotionally moving; touching

resilient (49): capable of recovering from or adjusting to change or
          misfortune

19

ON AIDING AND ABETTING:
The Anguish of Draft Counseling

Stephen Minot

This dialog between a teacher and a student points up some of the personal and philosophical problems faced by young men who refuse to serve in the armed forces and those who attempt to counsel them.

1   Any person who . . . knowingly counsels, aids, or abets another to refuse . . . service in the armed forces . . . shall be punished by imprisonment for not more than five years or a fine of not more than $10,000 or by both . . . .

Universal Military Training
and Service Act, Sec. 12

2   "I don't know about that Supreme Being bit. I mean, like I haven't seen my parish priest since I was about thirteen. He wasn't the type you could sit down and talk with. Besides, I don't think anyone talks all that straight anymore—not even my parents. But of course they wouldn't say so. It's not something you could discuss with them. You know, God's off bounds like sex and the drug scene. I remember once during my senior year in high school Mother asked me why I hadn't been to Mass for a year and I told her . . ."

3   The boy is talking too fast. It's his first session with me. He's sitting between me and the afternoon sun, which comes in through dirty windows. I am an assistant professor of English and am listening to this kid tell me about his version of God and his parish priest and his mother and I'm wondering, What the hell is a professor of English doing with all this personal information? What kind of crazy system is it that makes a student rehearse all this with me and then go on to testify before the five old men of his draft board and then be judged for sincerity and piety and sentenced to life or death? I'm wondering, What in hell is going on here?

4   "But I pray," he's telling me. "My parents don't know about that. They wouldn't understand. I mean, prayer to them is a social act. You know, a woman's got to have her best hat on—a man has to be in a suit and tie."

5   "What or whom do you pray *to*?" I ask, getting him back from the social commentary to the concern of the draft board. The question has to do with Series II on his Selective Service Form 150. He must answer the question, "Do you believe in a Supreme Being?" If he checks "No," he will be sent into the Army; if he checks "Yes" and defends his position to five old men, he may be allowed to serve two years in civilian work.

6   The boy is a pockmarked, crew-cut, nail-bitten specimen of manhood. He is the third counselee this afternoon and there are two more to come. It occurs to me that I have spent more time draft counseling today than I have teaching. I have spent more time listening to students today than I have to colleagues. I squirm in my seat and long for a cup of coffee in the faculty lounge and for casual conversation with some assistant professor about such major questions as the makeup of the curriculum committee or the identity of this year's commencement speaker. The lounge is well insulated against the sounds of the real world.

7   As the boy talks, he bends a paper clip back and forth and I wonder how long it will be before he breaks it. I am suddenly aware that he is quoting St. Thomas Aquinas. Good God, how many members of his board will have read Aquinas?

8   My mind wanders back to a Jewish student of mine who built an elaborate case for pacifism on the words of Spinoza. I would have given an A for the brief he presented to his board. It had sincerity and it had style and it was documented. I was six months younger then and I thought his statement was beautiful. But I should have known what would happen. The old men wouldn't even let him finish reading it. "Never mind all that," they told him in the middle of his oral presentation. "And who's this atheist professor of yours, this Spinoza?"

9   My student of the hour sits between me and the afternoon sun talking about Aquinas and I'm wondering if I should tell him about what another board did with Spinoza. Once again I'm walking that fence between optimism and realism.

10   "Can we say," I ask, "that your concern for moral values stems from your early religious training?"

11   "That's sort of a lie, isn't it?" He looks me in the eye and his pockmarked face is that of a contemporary. I have tried to move him too fast. I have given the hated parish priest of his childhood too good a rating. I wonder if I'm pushing the interview because I have two more students this afternoon, because I have a wife and two young boys waiting at home, because I'm thinking about a double Scotch on the rocks and some talk about the really important things in life like extending the lawn another fifty feet back into what is now woods to make room for baseball practice, and encouraging my wife to enter her paintings in a local art show.

12   "Is it really a lie?" I ask. "I mean, would you be here talking with me
this afternoon if you hadn't been exposed to moral concerns at an early
age?"

13   "I've got moral concern *in spite* of Father O'Brien."

14   "I think maybe there's a connection," I say—more for my own
integrity than from any hope of convincing him. "How about the
next question: Does your belief in a Supreme Being involve duties
which are superior to those arising from any human relation?"

15   So once again I have failed to convince a student of what to me is an
obvious cause-and-effect relation: the students who strike back hard
against their parents or church are usually the ones who were convinced
early in life that ethics are worth taking seriously. It will take, perhaps,
two more sessions before this boy can see that his hawkish priest and
militant parents were the ones from whom he, in the words of Form
150, "received the training and acquired the beliefs" that he now holds.

16   But we're on to his duty to the Supreme Being.

17   ". . . so maybe I really don't understand their question," he's
telling me. "I mean, like to me the Supreme Being is in all of us so it
isn't a matter of duty to *Him* or *it* being above those arising from
human relations, it's one and the same thing. I mean, that's the trouble
with their theology."

18   *Their* theology? What an incredible thought. I sit up straight and look
at this kid with new interest. The Selective Service has been defining a
State Religion? Of course! All these medieval questions contain
implied "right" or "wrong" responses in inquisitorial fashion. Put all
the "right" responses together and you have what the state demands as
minimal religious convictions. And the punishment for wrong convictions is ordeal by fire.

19   "I mean, to *their* way of thinking, God is up there and we're down
here and in between . . ."

20   Disappointed, I realize he didn't mean the theology of the draft
board. That was *my* theory. Once again I chastise myself for inventing
sophomoric theories when I should be listening to him, for Chrissake.

21   I'm as theory-prone as some of my too-intellectual students.
Last week (or was it last month?) a math major sitting in that same
chair was telling me how filling out the SS 150 would in effect involve
him in complicity since the SS (odd echo from *my* war) wanted above
all else to keep things moving smoothly. Anything he did to conform
with the law would aid them in their general purpose. They had
already reclassified him 1-A for failing to re-register as a student in the
fall.

22   I'd heard the argument before, of course, but I hadn't *confronted* it.
It was the difference between reading about "police action" and hearing
an ash club strike a boy's skull.

23   He was long-haired, that one, a regular Prince Valiant; and in three

years of college he'd earned all A's except for one B in, I think, economics.

24   His theory was tight and complex. Like chess. I've never mastered the game, but I can follow it.

25   "So you have two alternatives," I said to him.

26   "Three," he said to me. He was already two moves ahead of me. He had written off jail because, "They'd probably kill me and then where would I be?" An interesting question, that. I begged him not to pursue it on my time.

27   "Second option is Canada," I reminded him.

28   "Can't do," he said simply. "I couldn't live abroad. This is my country. Know what I mean? Like I'm American. This is where I'm at."

29   I made a note to tell the American Legion that the next time they asked me to address the national convention.

30   "I'm taking the third option," he told me. "Taking it on the lam."

31   Being an English professor I naturally wanted to play with *lam* and sacrificial *lambs* and the pedant within me clawed to be let loose. But then I thought of this honors student grubbing it for the next five or ten years.

32   "Like a killer," I said. "On the run."

33   "Yeh, man, like a killer."

34   He's dropped out of sight now with his record of A's and one B and no degree and no address and I recall his face now hesitantly, the way you resurrect friends who are dead.

35   But that was all weeks ago—perhaps months. I glance uneasily at the clock and realize that we are running twenty minutes behind. With two more conferences to go, I'll be late for supper. Another warmed-over meal. More apologies to the family. I try to steal a look at my engagement pad to see which ones are coming in—some take longer than others—but the kid has his eyes on my every move. I can't even yawn. There he is, still sitting there between me and the afternoon sun.

36   "Perhaps we can come back to that one," I say, and the seat of the chair suddenly feels hard at the prospect. "Let's tackle Number Five."

37   *Tackle?* Wrong verb. Number Five of Series II asks under what circumstances, if any, the applicants would use force. I listen to him begin with a tortured definition of force. I have heard several such that day and more than several that week. They always start abstract. I figure that if *I* can't make sense of them, what of the board?

38   They are not evil men, these board members, but they are busy with other things. They have not read recent court cases relating to classification appeals and some of them are not even familiar with the draft laws themselves. A student of mine was told that he would have to be either a Quaker or a Seventh Day Adventist to apply as a conscientious objector, a limitation which didn't apply even twenty years ago. It is

an awkward thing for a student to explain to his elders about the court cases which will affect his life. He must inform without appearing to lecture. He must make certain, for example, that they understand the Seeger case. That was in 1965 and the ruling held that "belief in a Supreme Being" is acceptable under the law if it "occupies a place . . . parallel to that filled by the orthodox belief in God of one who clearly qualifies for the exemption."

39 Whenever I review these cases my mind wanders in an undisciplined fashion, speculating on Roman courts which must have tangled with legal definitions of religious faith, and to Spanish courts centuries later.

40 Yet, oddly, it is not the medievalism which is the major threat facing this boy sitting here; it is the arbitrariness of the judgment which will be made of him. Here he is telling me about his view of the Supreme Being—or are we onto the use of force now?—and yet I know that his board will make its decision mainly on nonphilosophical grounds: on what their quota is that month, on whether the newspaper that morning reported another draft-card burning, on whether the previous applicant was surly or polite. Dare I tell this boy that much of their judgment will also be based on what he looks like and how he sounds? He has, of course, won points by being white, short-haired, and having an accent which is still more city than college; but he will lose points if he doesn't put on a tie and a clean shirt. As a general rule, cleanliness is more meaningful to them than Aquinas or Spinoza.

41 When I'm tired, I brood about these men and their power. It is easy to think the worst of them. I have to remind myself that they are unpaid, that they are busy, and they are old. I remember one board which had to resign *en masse* when it was ruled that members couldn't serve after age seventy-five. Many were originally selected during *my* war—over twenty-five years ago now. Often they confuse the two wars or place all wars in a single category. It is difficult for many of them to understand why these young men can't respond unquestioningly as most of us did when faced with the threat of Nazi Germany.

42 "So it seems to me," he's saying, "that one could practice *constraint* or *restraint* against those who are about to use *force* or *violence*, but the case of *coercion* is a more difficult one."

43 I am only half-listening to this parade of synonyms, but obviously I must hear him out. I have to remind myself that he is not just describing someone else's philosophy, he is constructing his own in my presence. He is trying to define himself. It occurs to me that some adults manage to get through a lifetime without being forced to tangle with the issues he is facing this afternoon.

44 Like this boy's parents, perhaps. Still, I don't know them and it would be unfair to prejudge them. Unfair and all too easy. Like the fraternity boy whose father was an Army officer with thirty-one years

of service behind him. I suffered preconfrontation pains with that boy
for weeks. And with good cause—but of course it was not the pattern
we had imagined. It was the mother in that case who went hysterical
and used the ultimate weapon—charged her son with homosexuality.
Shrieked it, in fact. This jolted the father into compassion, and the
two men had a heart-to-heart with each other for the first time in
their lives. How astounded they both must have been! And later the
father wrote a letter to his boy's board. He didn't defend pacifism, of
course, but he resoundingly defended his son in terms which sounded
almost military—courage, honor, self-respect. The boy is now teaching
in a ghetto school.

45   And will this one sitting before me now have the same opportunity?
All I know is that I cannot predict. My gaze passes beyond this student
and through the dirty, mullioned windows to the lawn outside where a
group of three seniors spin a frisbee in the spring air. The flying disk
moves slowly, an easy target, I'm thinking, like a helicopter. The one
nearest me, in a torn, dirty T-shirt and bare feet, makes a leap for the
frisbee and misses, falls, turning gracefully with a comic exaggeration
like a stunt man on *Combat*. Somehow he makes one complete revolution forward before he lands on the grass and goes limp, sprawled out,
arms and legs pointing in all directions. His classmates laugh.

46   "I don't really know what to say about force," my student is saying.
"How can I tell? I mean, I've never been in a situation where I even
had to hit a person. A shove, maybe." He tries a grin, perhaps wondering
if counseling sessions can afford such luxuries.

47   "Never murdered a roommate?" I ask, wide-eyed.

48   But enough of that. The time has come for a shift of pace. I sit up in
my seat and look at him hard. I feel my head clear.

49   "I'm going to ask you some specific questions," I say. The smile is
miles behind us now. "I don't want long, philosophical answers. Not
now. Tell me, what if Australia were attacked by China tomorrow
morning? Would you fight?"

50   "Well, I guess not. I mean . . ."

51   "Why not?"

52   "I haven't seen a war solve anything. I guess that's why not. I
mean, like we had to fight World War I and now we're fighting the
Civil War over and . . ."

53   "Chinese troops land in San Francisco. Would you fight?"

54   "Why Chinese? Do you really think . . .?"

55   "But *if*. Would you?"

56   "No." This comes out sharp. He's getting sore.

57   "Okay, now let's say you're married, happily married. And you
have two kids." He stiffens. He understands that I have become the
prosecutor. I'm playing dirty but he's not sure how to call foul. I'm
fully awake as I always am at this phase of the interview. "You're in

an isolated house in the country and three enemy soldiers break down your front door . . . ."

58   "Oh, come on now . . ."

59   "You have a loaded revolver in your hand."

60   He opens his mouth in protest but closes it again. He looks up at the ceiling, trying to escape, and then back at me. "I'm not talking about *your* life," I remind him. "I'm asking you about this wife and these two children. The soldiers are moving in on you. What do you do? Don't give me arguments—tell me what you'd *do*. You have to decide, you know. Even no action is a decision. So decide. Come on now."

61   "Damm it," he says like a pistol shot. "I'd do the wrong thing, that's what I'd do. I'd shoot. Hell yes, but don't you understand, *it would be the wrong thing.*"

62   I lean back in my seat, nodding, rubbing, rubbing my aching eyes with both hands. You'll make it, I'm thinking, you'll make it. CO or Canada or jail or wherever, you'll make it.

63   "Enough for today," I say. I stand up and for some reason I'm grinning and he's standing and smiling back at me. There is, of course, nothing whatever to laugh about. That's the joke we share.

Discussion of Theme

1. Do you believe that the young man in this article should have been deferred by his draft board? Why?

2. How did the student's "hawkish priest and militant parents" contribute to the formulation of his beliefs?

3. What legal risks does a draft counselor take? What personal and professional sacrifices may he be called on to make?

4. What are the implications of the Supreme Court decision in the Seeger case?

Discussion of Rhetoric

1. This selection is written in the form of a dialog between the author and a student. Would it have been more effective as straight exposition? Less? What are the advantages of the dialog technique?

2. Does the conclusion satisfy the needs of a dramatic scene? Would it have had greater dramatic impact if the exchange between the professor and his student had ended in a different way? What reason may the author have had for using this kind of conclusion?

3. What is the purpose of the references Minot makes to his private life at home?

Writing Assignments

1. Should the draft laws be revised and, if so, in what way?

2. React to the following statement: "Every man should serve in the armed services of his country."

Library Exploration
1. If possible, secure a copy of Selective Service Form 150. What kinds of questions does it ask? Do they cover all possible forms of conscientious objection?
2. Investigate the teachings of Gandhi, an advocate of nonviolence.
3. Who were Spinoza and St. Thomas Aquinas?

Vocabulary
   piety (3): reverence
   inquisitorial (18): in the manner of a court asking questions
   chastise (20): punish; reprimand
   pedant (31): one who parades his learning
   coercion (42): compulsion by force
   mullioned (45): divided by slender, vertical bars

20

STUDENTS, THE GOOD AND BAD

Art Buchwald

A famous—and very funny—newspaper columnist makes a satirical comment on the attitude of certain members of his generation toward campus rebellions.

1   It is generally agreed that the student unrest is world-wide these days. It doesn't matter if the students live in a permissive society or a totalitarian one—they're still raising Cain. And for that reason, those of us watching from the sidelines are divided as to whether the unrest is a good thing or a bad thing.

2   At the University Club the other day I was having a brandy and cigar with some very nice chaps when the question of student demonstrations came up.

3   "I see where they still haven't solved the problem at Columbia," Liverwhistle said.

4   "It's appalling, absolutely appalling," Cartwright sputtered.

5   "The students should all be booted out on their ears. You can't have a university if you're going to have children running around locking up the faculty."

6   Conrad said, "Did you see what's going on in Paris? The French students have tied up the city."

7   "AH, YES," said Cartwright. "One can't help admiring the French students' gumption. They've certainly put De Gaulle in his place."

8   "You have to respect their attitude," Liverwhistle said. "At least the students can see through De Gaulle, if the rest of the French people can't."

9   "I don't think things have cooled off at Stanford," Scarsdale commented. "They're still holding the administration building."

10   "If you ask me," said Cartwright, "it's a Communist plot. These things don't just happen. There's nothing the Commies wouldn't do to shut down the schools in this country. The only answer is force. It will make those radicals sing another tune."

11   "Did you read where the students in Czechoslovakia not only demonstrated, but caused the downfall of the Soviet-backed regime?"

12   "God bless them," said Conrad. "If we're ever going to see the end

of tyranny behind the Iron Curtain, it's going to be the students who accomplish it."

13   "I understand the same thing could happen in Poland," Liverwhistle said, "and perhaps even East Germany. They're a new breed, those students, and a credit to the human race."

14   "You know, of course," said Scarsdale, "that the administration completely collapsed at Northwestern and gave in to every demand of the students there."

15   Cartwright said, "My blood boiled when I read the story. Those damn kids don't know up from down and they're telling us how to run the country. I say we have to act now and act firmly. We ought to cut off all funds to any student who demonstrates or strikes against a university administration."

16   "The students in Franco's Spain have been agitating for a year now. No one knows how many are in jail," Conrad said.

17   "The poor kids," Liverwhistle said. "They're only trying to make a better world, and they're thrown in jail for it. I think we should get up a petition and send it to the Spanish ambassador."

18   "I see they're having another sit-in at Berkeley," Liverwhistle commented.

19   "They're always having a sit-in at Berkeley," Scarsdale said.

20   "I'll tell you what's wrong with the kids today. They've got too much money. They don't even appreciate what we've gone through to give them an education. All they talk about is freedom. What kind of freedom do they want?"

21   "It's the faculty," said Conrad. "They're the ones who egg the students on. Instead of jailing the students, they ought to lock up the faculty. Then we'd stop all this anarchy on campuses."

22   Cartwright, who was flipping through a newspaper, said, "It says here that the students in Communist China are thinking about having another Red Guard revolution."

23   "Great," said Liverwhistle. "Old Mao won't be able to take another one of those."

24   Cartwright agreed. "I must say one thing for the students abroad. They sure have a lot of class."

Discussion of Theme

1. What is the attitude of the club members toward foreign students who riot? What is their attitude toward American student rebels? In what way are they refusing to see what is happening in America?

2. What criticisms do these men make about American students who protest on college campuses? Is their criticism purely subjective, or do they offer any evidence to back up their statements?

3. Why are students in Iron Curtain countries praised for their rebellions? What are their general aims and goals?

4. If "the students abroad . . . sure have a lot of class," what can be said about American students?

Discussion of Rhetoric

1. What does Buchwald reveal about his attitude toward his characters when he refers to them as "chaps"?
2. What effect does the author achieve by using names like Liverwhistle, Cartwright, and Scarsdale?
3. Instead of writing down his thoughts about student riots in a straightforward manner, Buchwald creates a fictional dialog. Is this a more effective method of getting his point across? Why?

Writing Assignments

1. Choose another topic—military action, for example—and write about it in a dialog similar to Buchwald's.
2. Explain your ideas about the causes of the current wave of student unrest throughout the world.
3. Write a theme presenting other examples of inconsistency or hypocrisy you have observed.

Library Exploration

1. Read statements by student leaders in America and learn about the aims announced by the groups to which they belong.
2. If you enjoyed this article, read some more of Buchwald's newspaper columns. They have been collected in several books, including *How Much Is That in Dollars?* and *Have I Ever Lied to You?*

Vocabulary

totalitarian (1): authoritarian; despotic
anarchy (21): lawlessness or disorder due to the absence of governmental authority

21

TODAY'S YOUTH: A HOPEFUL GENERATION

Sen. Mark Hatfield

An outspoken critic of the war in Vietnam, Senator Hatfield (R., Oregon), offers qualified praise for today's impatient and idealistic youth. He calls them one of the most hopeful generations our nation has produced.

1   I suppose, technically, I left the classroom in 1956 when I resigned my position as dean of students at Willamette University in Salem, Oregon, to campaign for the office of Secretary of State. But I was never very far from the campus—physically or mentally. During my ten years in the state capitol I could always look out my office windows, across State Street, to the magnificent trees and historic buildings of the Willamette campus. I also tried to make as many trips as possible back across that street to talk with the students—sometimes in political science classes, sometimes in their residences, and occasionally before a more formal gathering of the whole student body.

2   Students have always been my favorite audience, and I have found that addressing them as a political figure is little different from facing them as a political science teacher. And the subject is not always different.

3   Whenever the speaking format permits, I pattern my speeches after the approach I used in the classroom. This approach was based on the premise that there are few absolutes, no final authorities to cite with which to crush the opposition, but instead room for interpolation and debate. In the classroom I would make as convincing an argument as I could in support of some political analysis and then immediately subject it to review by the students. Now when I appear before a student audience, I make a statement of my views on a given issue and then submit this view to the challenge of a question-and-answer period. As in the classroom, I want the stimulus of that challenge for the students as well as for myself.

4   But an even more important reason behind my preference for this speaking format over a declarative speech with no possibility for rebuttal is the opportunity it provides for the *exchange* of ideas. In office jargon, we often refer to my appearances before student audiences as "confrontations." This is exactly what I hope they will be, for it is in the

clash of ideas, the face-to-face collision of various points of view, that dogma is modified by tolerance and both the students and I are forced to maintain our perspective and to accommodate divergent views.

5   Students, and the faculty members who are usually present at such gatherings, are able skillfully to analyze and articulate views that oppose those I accept. By constantly exposing myself to this challenge I hope to help assure myself against the pitfall of positivism—the slide into arrogant self-assurance that never questions basic premises and that is never modified by changing events and circumstances. Effective debate and persuasion in the political arena require that the spokesmen of various views present these views honestly, but in their strongest and most convincing form. The protagonists, however, must not delude themselves with the smug assumption that they have a monopoly on the "truth." This leads them to propose simplistic solutions that are doomed to failure.

6   I schedule as many speaking engagements with students as possible in an effort to help maintain a dialogue between their generation and mine. Too often, I feel, adults make an insufficient effort to bridge the "generation gap." Either they become resentful of the attitudes and "antics of alienated youth" or they rather indifferently assume that young people will one day outgrow this "rebelliousness" and everything will be all right again. Instead of making an effort to communicate with the younger generation they often retire to nurse the wounds inflicted upon their egos by irreverent youth.

7   There have been many perceptive analyses of the causes of this alienation of young people. Some people see it as basically an exaggeration of youth's traditional rebellion against symbols of authority. But I believe it goes much deeper than this.

8   My generation also rejected authority, but, as one analyst, Lewis Yablonsky, put it, "The pre-World War II students . . . simply wanted a 'piece of the action.' " Today's students often reject "the action" entirely. They may disassociate themselves from society altogether and withdraw into apathy, or they may set out to alter society drastically and transform its values and priorities.

9   To today's young people the conventional forms of authority are shams. Adults, to whose wisdom youth is expected to defer, seem to have produced a dangerous and hate-filled world obsessed with goals and values youth finds repugnant. They reject the tyranny of the pay check, the job-house-mortgage-suburbia complex which they sum up as the "rat race." They are repulsed by an adult world that reveres material possessions, that is motivated by the search for status and the unrelenting compulsion to succeed. They resent the hypocrisy of an older generation that presents idealistic guideposts for the young at the same time it rejects them for itself, that self-righteously denies prejudice, at the same time it votes down open-housing laws.

10   Many young people reject the traditional authority of religious faith.

To them a personal relationship with God has been suffocated by "the institutionalized church." This idea was captured by a placard carried in a recent student demonstration which read, "Christ yes, Christianity no."

11   Finally, the authority of government has fallen into the chasm created by its own credibility gap. Youth, more than any other age group, has suffered the disillusionment of discovering that its government and its highest elected officials are not believable. Their loss of faith has been matched by their growing cynicism—not just toward the current Administration but toward our entire governmental system. They seriously question the validity of political processes that allow them few opportunities to make their views felt. They feel helpless and frustrated in attempting to influence governmental institutions effectively insulated from the desires of the people by a moat of bureaucratic red tape. Perhaps most important of all, young people resent the impersonalization of a government more preoccupied with producing institutional efficiency than with protecting human individuality. They resent a paternalistic government that assigns its citizens a number, categorizes them into groups, and then promises to provide for their corporate needs.

12   I once had a student point out to me a poem by W. H. Auden titled "The Unknown Citizen (To JS/07/M/378 This Marble Monument Is Erected by the State)."[1] The poem represented the final entry on the government's record of this unnamed citizen, listing numerous agencies' evaluation of his life. It began:

He was found by the Bureau of Statistics to be
One against whom there was no official complaint.
And all the reports on his conduct agree
That, in the modern sense of an old-fashioned word, he was a saint . . . .
. . . Both Producers Research and High-Grade Living declare
He was fully sensible to the advantages of the Installment Plan
And had every thing necessary to the Modern Man,
A phonograph, a radio, a car and a frigidaire. . . .
Our researchers into Public Opinion are content
That he held the proper opinions for the time of year;
When there was peace, he was for peace; when there was war, he went. . . .
Was he free? Was he happy? The question is absurd:
Had anything been wrong, we should certainly have heard.

13   Youth's alienation and rejection of traditional forms of authority have been magnified by the Vietnam war. On my many visits to college campuses, I have found this subject uppermost in the minds of students.

---

[1] Reprinted by permission of Random House, Inc. from *The Collected Poetry of W. H. Auden*, copyright 1945 by W. H. Auden and by permission of Faber and Faber Ltd. from *Collected Shorter Poems 1927–1957*.

They are extremely concerned with the morality and legitimacy of our involvement in Vietnam.

14   To me, the resentment that the war in Vietnam has bred into these young people is one of its most alarming effects. Nearly every day my mail includes a letter from some young man who must reconcile his duty to serve his conscience. I sympathize deeply with his torment. He must choose either to move to Canada, to declare himself a conscientious objector, or go to jail, or he must choose to kill men he does not hate, in a war he cannot justify, for a cause he does not believe in. Whatever course he chooses, he *resents* being forced to make such a decision.

15   Even more tragic are the letters I receive from parents of the young men who have given their lives in this confused and mixed-up war. Following is a representative letter:

Dear Sir:

First I wish to thank you for your letter of March 5, 1968, expressing sympathy for the death of our son in Vietnam. It helps to know men of your stature and position care enough to write.

The hardest part to take in this whole affair is the fact that he died in a war that *he* thought was wrong. He stated in his letters, "These people don't want us here. They don't do us any favors."

This is the first war where the parents are forced to send their sons food, rain gear, razor blades, toothbrushes, toothpaste, insect repellent, prescriptions for medicine to kill mites. There were so many things that a normal army makes sure its men have. If we hadn't sent them, he would have done without. I would estimate the cost to us at over $50 a month.

I wanted to write to you last fall, but when Bobby heard about it, he wrote, "Mom! Tell Dad don't do it. The word gets back here and they make it rough on us." From then on my hands were tied. Those bonds were cut by a Vietcong bullet on February 18. They can't make it rough on him any more.

If there is any information that we have that would aid in your fight against this mess we are in over there, we will send photocopies or help in any way we can.

It is with deepest respect that we thank you for what you have done and will continue to do to stop this needless and futile war.

Respectfully,
(names withheld)

16   I can't help contrasting the bitterness of many of today's young men about to be sent to Vietnam with the exhilaration my generation felt at the *privilege* of serving in World War II. We knew what we were

fighting for. We knew that the survival of the United States was at stake. And we knew that taking up arms was the only way to save our country. I was a student at Willamette when Pearl Harbor came and I remember, vividly, hearing President Roosevelt's war message to Congress on the radio in our fraternity house.

17   To a man, we marched down to the recruiting office to sign up, and we sincerely pitied those unable to join a service.

18   But today the young man often pitied by his peers is the young man who has been drafted to fight in Vietnam. Unfortunately, and un- justifiably, their reluctance to go to Vietnam is interpreted by an older generation—who fought with pride in Korea or World War II— as a lack of patriotism. This, on the whole, is not true. These young men who question our commitment in Vietnam are often motivated by the highest form of love for their country and the principles upon which it was founded. They honestly believe that the war in Vietnam does *not* serve the best interests of this nation and that it betrays its principles. It is not easy for them to go to Vietnam and aid a policy they feel harms their country. It is also extremely difficult for them to participate in a policy they believe to be morally wrong.

19   They view the purposes of the war as unjust. They reject the various justifications given by the Administration for our involvement in Vietnam as an inadequate and an insufficient basis on which to kill other men. Many also view the methods used in Vietnam as immoral. They are repulsed by the inadvertent but persistent killing and maiming of civilians by indiscriminant bombing of populated areas and by the use of such cruel and terrifying weapons as napalm. They find it im- possible morally to condone our "scorched earth" policies of leveling villages and chemically destroying vegetation and food crops—perhaps for generations to come.

20   Many of our nation's most idealistic young men are torn between their recognition of their duty to serve their country and their duty to apply an individual moral standard to the actions they perform. Early in 1968, I received a copy of a very moving letter written by a young man who had volunteered for service in the Army and had already served two of his four years. In the face of being transferred to Vietnam he had written to his commanding officer requesting that he be reduced to E-1 rank and "that all salaries, bonuses, and privileges, monetary or otherwise, granted to those serving in Vietnam be denied me." He continued:

> The above-requested action represents the only means by which I can simultaneously fulfill my responsibilities as a member of the armed forces and my responsibilities to my own conscience. The Nuremberg Principle existed, in fact, long before the Allies codified it at the end of the last war; for persons of any maturity whatever, the old moral soporific that "I was ordered to do it"

has never been effective—one cannot contradict one's own conscience without trauma and I, for one, do not intend to do so.

Whether or not a tribunal is ever actually convened to try Americans upon charges of war crimes or crimes against humanity in Vietnam, every man is tried in balance against his own values; if he does not measure up, he is lost—he could not even live with himself.

21   I also received correspondence from another American serviceman who had just returned from a year in Vietnam. Because of his outstanding service to his country in this conflict, he had been awarded the Bronze Star Medal. He sent me a copy of a letter he had written to his commanding officer in Vietnam rejecting this award:

> I recognize that the Army considers the medal a high honor, but to me it is a worthless memento, a scrap of ribbon, an object which stands for two years in the military where I was reduced to a common criminal and a participant in a war that lacks all reason.
>
> . . . The medal represents the insult and degradation I have received . . . as a human, thinking being who was told not to question any part of my value system, which has . . . been smashed by my participation in the wrecking of Vietnam.
>
> . . . Your medal is worthless and insulting. I cannot accept it. I will, instead, hope for peace in Vietnam which circumvents your military solutions, and then perhaps I can find something to be proud of.

22   In his letter to me this young man confessed: "I have felt guilty about my participation in the war. . . . I know that nothing will assuage that guilt."

23   These are the words not of "unpatriotic shirkers" but of highly idealistic and sensitive young men who are deeply tormented by the sacrifice of values that is demanded of them by their participation in a war they believe to be immoral.

24   My heart aches for the other young men who face the agony of choosing between their duty to their country and their duty to their consciences. And their fellow Americans must not be hasty to condemn the choice these young men—who genuinely face this dilemma— make. It is a very personal dilemma that each man must privately resolve on the basis of *his own* values, and the torment of this decision should not be heightened by the harsh judgment of someone who would have chosen a different course.

25   Unfortunately, this decision does not always remain the private problem that it should be. Out of feelings of guilt, frustration, and resentment, young men are sometimes prompted to burn draft cards, boo public speakers, and join in other forms of public protest that not

only harm their cause in opposing the war but incite others to question their motives and discredit the legitimacy of the dilemma they face. In the eyes of many people the burning of a draft card is a symbolic renunciation of the United States and the duty to serve one's country rather than an expression of frustration at being forced to compromise either this duty or the duty to one's conscience. This and other forms of public protest often generate more anger than sympathy; they alienate more people than they persuade and are therefore counter-productive.

26   For instance, when students boo Administration officials and prevent them from speaking, public sympathy lies with the speaker who was denied the right to be heard. I spoke on the Harvard and Stanford campuses within a short time after Secretary of Defense Robert McNamara (at Harvard) and Vice President Hubert Humphrey (at Stanford) had made attempts to present the Administration's Vietnam position. Instead of receiving a fair hearing they had received boos, hisses, and jeers.

27   When I appeared on these campuses shortly after those incidents, I opened my remarks by sharing with the students an experience I had had on the platform of the Republican National Convention in 1964. This was a convention hall dominated by extremists who were then in full cry against Governor Nelson Rockefeller. They moved against him with the full force of their venom, booing, and hooting, deriding him as he attempted to defend his civil rights position. I had never before witnessed such intolerance and viciousness. I came away from this experience with a greater appreciation for the democratic right, and *necessity*, for every man—whatever his views—to be heard. There is no difference in denying one man or another the right to be heard, I told the students. "I cannot condone discourtesy to the President of the United States, or the Vice President of the United States, or the Secretary of Defense, or *anyone*." Such conduct, I finished quietly was particularly reprehensible on academic campuses, the traditional guardians of our libertarian principles.

28   The shouting-down of speakers representing the Administration is not a reasonable way to oppose the President's Vietnam policies. Just like many other forms of protest, it is impotent to bring a solution of this conflict and betrays a sense of defeat that is not justified. The burning of draft cards, for instance, is a rather simplistic reaction to the Vietnam war and announces a despair about other possible approaches. Young people are understandably impatient; they want immediate solutions. And they are prone to opt for dramatic action in search for these solutions rather than undertake the slower, more arduous task of seeking them through accepted political processes.

29   Draft-card burning is not only a technique used to protest the war, but it is also used to express the rapidly growing dissatisfaction with

the draft system itself. Instead of setting fire to pieces of paper, draft protestors should "set fire" to, in the sense of energizing, legislation before Congress that would eliminate the Selective Service System and return military personnel recruitment to a volunteer basis. The first piece of legislation I sponsored in the U.S. Senate was a bill designed to upgrade the opportunities and rewards of military service in order to make this a career possibility attractive enough to generate the necessary number of volunteers. When hearings were held to explore suggested changes in the Selective Service System, there were no young men asking to testify and protest the inequities of the draft. There were no movements on college campuses supporting legislation designed to correct these inequities.

30   There are many symptoms and causes of the alienation of young people today. I only hope that the symptoms are temporary and that the causes are corrected. I am both concerned and encouraged by youth's questioning of the values of the world they are about to inherit. I am concerned that their frustration may lead some to despair and finally to withdrawal from productive roles in a society that does not share their values. I don't anticipate this as the general pattern, however, but believe that the idealism of today's younger generation will serve as the catalyst for change, for the remolding and redirection of our society to conform with the needs and values of individuals. As I told the 1967 graduating class during a commencement address at Willamette University: "I want to congratulate you on an excellent beginning as one of the most hopeful generations our nation has produced. I am excited about your enthusiasm; I am encouraged by your determination; and I am humbled by your idealism. I have no doubt that, if you retain these qualities, you will be the match for any burdens you inherit."

Discussion of Theme
1. What difference does Hatfield point out between the rebellious youth of a generation ago and the youth of today?
2. What public-speaking situation does Hatfield prefer? What part does he believe audiences should play in a lecture or debate? How can this relationship be valuable to both speaker and audience?
3. According to this article, what makes the war in Vietnam different from other wars? Why are young men troubled about fighting in this particular war?
4. What is the relation of Auden's poem (paragraph 12) to Senator Hatfield's thesis?

Discussion of Rhetoric
1. What does the author tell us about himself in the opening paragraphs? What relation with the reader is he trying to establish?

2. Paragraphs 1–8 comprise the introduction to this selection. How would you divide the rest of the essay into sections? What is the topic of each? How does the conclusion tie the whole article together?
3. Compare the tone of this article with that of Shapiro's article, also in this section. Which seems more sympathetic toward the younger generation? Which is more objective?

Writing Assignments

1. Define the expression *free speech*. Make clear any limitations you believe should be attached to this term.
2. Develop the following statement into a theme: "Christ, yes; Christianity, no."

Library Exploration

Look up accounts of the 1964 Republican National Convention and the 1968 Democratic National Convention. What was the atmosphere of each? Why were many viewers and participants upset by events at both conventions?

Vocabulary

interpolation (3): insertion of new material
condone (19): accept without protest or censure; overlook
soporific (20): something that tends to dull awareness or alertness
circumvents (21): checks or defeats, especially by ingenuity or
                  stratagem
assuage (22): ease
catalyst (30): someone or something that brings about a change,
               or accelerates change, but usually remains itself
               unchanged

22

PEACE IS THE ONLY THEME
OF WOODSTOCK FAIR

Bruce Cook

Four hundred thousand young peo-
ple converged on Bethel, New York,
for what promised to be the biggest
weekend of rock music ever. In an
age of so much violence, the theme
of the fair was peace.

1   It looked like a battlefield.

2   Not blood and shell, mind you, but all their attendant miseries
seemed to be spread out before me as I stood on a hill surveying the
devastation of the Woodstock Music and Art Fair. There were rain-
soaked tents in garbage-strewn encampments. Between them were great
patches of mud and pools of water through which the campers slipped
and sloshed on their way to answer calls of nature at temporary toilets.
Behind me, a little higher on the hill, the kids stood in long lines at the
food tents where already—this was just the second day of the three-
day "Aquarian Exposition"—supplies were running low.

3   And there to the left along the road from Highway 17-B flowed a
stream of newcomers, many of them mud-spattered and dressed in
what looked like hand-me-downs. They carried packs and bedrolls on
their backs and, occasionally, children in their arms. They looked like
war-weary refugees.

4   There must have been 250,000 of them then. Before the week end
was out that number would grow to an estimated 400,000. There have
been other music festivals—the Newport Jazz Festival, began as early
as 1954; 45,000 young people attended the Monterey, Calif., Pop
Festival in 1967; and 130,000 showed up earlier this year at the Atlantic
City, N.J., Pop Festival. But none of these approached the size of the
host that gathered here for what is becoming the newest fixture in the
style of life of Young America. Its program was conventionally advertised, of course, but by word of mouth the Woodstock event advertised
itself through the young people's grapevine; kids planned for weeks in
advance to come here. And when it was over, despite the travail, they
looked back on it, reminisced about it, with a mystic emotion.

5   They had come from all over the Eastern United States for what
promised to be the biggest week end of rock music ever put together.
("Why did I come?" said Lee Deckelnick of Oakhurst, N.J. "I saw

a program that said I could see 28 top groups for $18. That's why.")
Janis Joplin; Jefferson Airplane; Canned Heat; Iron Butterfly; Blood,
Sweat and Tears; and Indian sitar virtuoso Ravi Shankar were just a
few of the attractions that brought them in.

6   But was it really rock music alone that drew this army of young
people to the Woodstock festival? Remember, there were 400,000 of
them—this made an upstate New York cow pasture the third-largest
city (smaller than New York itself and Buffalo, larger than Rochester)
in the state for three days. And that was how the kids thought of it too.
Their city. "The only free city in the country," they were calling it.
The week-end population was also nearly equal to the number of U.S.
troops serving in Vietnam. The kids were also aware of that. The
affair had been advertised as "three days of peace and music." The
accent was on peace. But the appearance of the place was warlike.

7   This martial impression had grown steadily through the morning,
beginning with my first encounter with Max Yasgur, the Catskill
dairy farmer on whose 600-acre farm the Woodstock event was being
held. Stepping inside his office, I found the air charged with a sort of
battle urgency. "Listen," he was rasping into the phone, "I need that
skid tank of gas for the ambulances. I want you to meet me with a truck
at the command post." Pause. "I don't care about that. Even if we have
to put a hook on it and haul it over with a helicopter. I want that gas."
Mr. Yasgur hung up abruptly and turned his red-rimmed eyes to me.
He rubbed impatiently at his unshaven cheeks as I explained why I
wanted to speak with him, cutting me short in a moment with a wave
of his hand. "Maybe later," he said, "I'm sorry to be short with you
but I haven't been to bed since Tuesday. That's how busy we are."

8   Outside I cornered one of Mr. Yasgur's staff who was working closely
with the Woodstock people, and I asked him if perhaps something
had gone wrong in the planning for the fair. "No," he said, "not unless
you call having six to eight times the number you expected show up
for it. Water's short. Toilet facilities are overtaxed. The ambulances
are having a hard time getting through and are running low on gas.
And the 'copters can't fly in the rain. Anything else?"

9   Leaving the Yasgur office, I joined the long line of marchers moving
toward the site of the week-end rock-music festival. Cars were parked
tight for miles on either side of Highway 17-B, and inside them sexless
tangles of kids still slept, wet and exhausted from the night before.
All along the edge of the highway, and far out into the open fields,
tents were pitched; you could hear music from some—an alto saxo-
phone running the scale in one, an acoustic guitar thrumming away
in another, and innumerable portable radios filling the air with the
heavy sound of hard rock.

10   We marched. The New York state troopers were keeping open a

single middle lane through which passed ambulances, official cars, and trucks loaded with supplies. But in two lines on either side of the road went boys and girls, young men and women of every sort, from hard hippies to clean-jim types, from full beards, long hair, and body shirts to crew cuts and college windbreakers. They were a strangely silent bunch. Whether too weary from the trek to the music, which for some had begun 10 miles back, or too miserable from the rain, the kids bound for the Woodstock Fair were a silent, almost solemn bunch.

11   The Woodstock Music and Art Fair had been heavily promoted in the press, above- and underground, and on rock stations up and down the East Coast. Fair producers were thrown into a temporary tizzy earlier when plans to hold the event at Wallkill, N.Y., were over-turned by the local Town Council. And although the Bethel, N.Y. authorities had granted a permit for the Woodstock Fair to be held at Max Yasgur's farm, there was plenty of local opposition to it, which took the shape of a boycott of the dairyman's products.

12   Nevertheless, preparations moved ahead once the farm site was picked. The producers brought a crew three weeks before the opening, and its members worked around the clock building a 100-foot stage at the bottom of a natural bowl of some 80 acres in a pasture adjoining White Lake. By the time the appointed date—Aug. 15—rolled around, they were ready for an anticipated crowd of 50,000.

13   Far more than that number had shown up by the hour the fair was to begin. And so many more were on their way that main routes to Bethel were backed up bumper-to-bumper for miles. Halfway to New York City in that vast traffic jam was Sweetwater, the group that was to begin the program. Somehow word was communicated to the fair producers, and the group was airlifted in, instruments and all, by one of the fleet of helicopters that serviced the event. Arriving spectacularly, Sweetwater started the proceedings an hour late.

14   The night was still young and the program barely under way when the rain began. It came down steadily during Ravi Shankar's recital, and by the time young Arlo Guthrie had begun his set, it was pelting the crowd. The wind began to blow, the water began to sluice down the hill in rivulets, and before you knew it, the natural bowl had become a natural sink.

15   But that was one night. I, along with thousands of others, had run for what shelter I could find. Here I was, next morning, marching in as hopefully as the rest, confident that a bad beginning would mean a happy ending.

16   On the way in, I stopped to talk with officers at a mobile unit from the neighboring Dutchess County sheriff's police. "No problems here," said officer Bill Curtis. "Peace is the theme of the fair, and the kids

have really been sticking to it." He explained that his detachment was on loan to Sullivan County to reinforce local police should any trouble develop. But none did.

17   About the only business these officers had was with young campers who had become separated from their friends. Officer Charles Gesell, who had been exhaustedly sucking on a lime as I talked with his friend, said that the night before a girl six months pregnant had come in lost, chilled from the rain, and faint. She spent the night in the mobile unit and then found her friends. "She brought me back this lime," he said, "just as a sort of thank you."

18   Checking with the state police, I got the same story. "The kids in general have been very polite and well mannered," one of them told me. "Of course it's a monumental traffic problem that we've managed to handle pretty well using helicopters. But the kids haven't caused us any trouble. The only problems they're having are problems with themselves."

19   This last was a discreet reference to the drug problem. The security of the fair site was left up to the Woodstock people. As a result, there were practically no incidents of violence inside the gate. It was easy to see why. With no police, those in the crowd were totally free to do their own thing, whether this meant walking naked or rolling in the mud.

20   As a result, too, drugs were taken and marijuana smoked frequently and openly. Marijuana smoke hung over the place like an invisible smog; once you've smelled it, you will never ask why they call it "grass." It is also true there were tragic incidents of drug use during Woodstock's three days. One of the week end's two deaths was apparently caused by an overdose of heroin. And adverse reactions to LSD—"freak-outs," as they call them—were all too common, numbering nearly 100. I saw one pretty brunette wide-eyed and shrieking as her friends tried to calm her, and a blonde wandering blank and disoriented in ankle-deep mud.

21   A team of specialists in the treatment of psychotic episodes from psychedelic drugs was flown in from New York City. The team set up a treatment center in a special tent not far from the stage. From the loudspeaker came frequent admonitions to "leave the blue caps alone," and "with anything else, try a half tab before you take a whole dose just to be sure it's good stuff."

22   Such announcements came during between-the-acts intervals of what did indeed turn out to be a grand and glorious program of rock-pop music. Highlights of the week end? Folk-rocker Richie Havens was granted absolute attention and a standing ovation by the audience Friday night. Saturday night stretched on and on, so that when the sun came up Sunday morning Jefferson Airplane was just beginning the final set. The big hits of the evening, however, were San Francisco's Sly and the Family Stone with seven encores (about the only group

whose music moved the kids to get up and dance), and The Who, one of a number of English groups on hand, performing a two-hour set that included all their rock opera, *Tommy*. Sunday night? It was Jimi Hendrix hands down—but by that time the rain had come again, and the exodus had begun. Only the most loyal were on hand to hear.

23   Yet in a way the music was the least of it. You had the feeling looking around you, as kids wandered in and out of the audience, that for most of them just being there and sharing the same air with so many of their kind was enough. Tom O'Mallia of Youngstown, Ohio, says that the groups were fine, of course, "but I really loved the people. I think what's really great is seeing all those people gathering and getting along. They were really together."

24   Mere survival became a real problem for some. A few teeny boppers and some hard-core hippies had hitchhiked in with no money at all and no shelter for sleeping. (After all, this was the Age of Aquarius, wasn't it?) Many were outraged at the high prices charged at the concession stands and said they would go hungry rather than pay them. Some of these ate the high-protein gruel dished out by the Hog Farm, a New Mexico commune whose members served as staff and security for the fair.

25   Those who really saved the day were the residents of Bethel and surrounding Sullivan County. Disgusted by the few who took advantage of the situation and charged exorbitant prices for necessities— $1 a quart was not uncommon for drinking water early in the week end—citizens donated whole truckloads of food and drink to the stranded rock lovers.

26   "The greatest people in the world live right here in Sullivan County," said dairyman Max Yasgur when I nailed him down at last. "Many who were dead set against the fair worked hard to feed the kids and take care of them once they got here. When the chips were down, they showed what kind of people they are."

27   "We were afraid some of these Hell's Angels would come into town and wreck it," said one man who declined to give his name but said he was commander of the local American Legion post. "When we saw these kids weren't going to be like that, it was okay. They surprised us by being real good."

28   Once the weekend was over, however, many local residents voiced complaints. Mrs. Clarence Townsend says that the kids camped in the Townsends' alfalfa field without permission and ruined it. "They burned fenceposts and everything," she says. "The kids had to go somewhere, but not here. It never should have been held in a town this size." Richard Joyner, who worked in his store in Bethel through the week end, was appalled that "there was no law enforcement. I saw dope being sold right on the corner. It was awful for children to be exposed to this."

29   That wasn't the only problem for the Woodstock people, who lost
a great deal of money on the fair. Although advance ticket sales hit
$1,500,000, they made almost nothing at the gate because a lack of
security forces—New York's Commissioner Howard Leary withheld
the 300 off-duty New York City policemen who were to do the job—
made it impossible to hold people at the gate. "Everything was done,"
says coproducer Mel Lawrence, "for the safety and welfare of the
people in the audience."

30   "What happened was that this show transcended the limits of any
festival or entertainment. It was a phenomenon. I've worked on five
festivals before, and there was never anything like this. I guess it was a
combination of the right circumstances. But whatever it was, the
Woodstock Music and Art Fair took on a life of its own."

31   Yes, a phenomenon. But perhaps a phenomenon that has more to
do with mass psychology than with music appreciation. This is a point
on which men with strong opinions may indeed differ. Allen Ginsberg,
for instance, poet and guru to the young, sees such gatherings as this
one and the great San Francisco be-in of 1966 as basically religious
in nature. He compares them to the Hindu *Mela* convocations in which
the holy men of India—sometimes over a million of them—gather
together in one place periodically to trade rituals and enlist disciples.

32   Elias Canetti, on the other hand, the hermitic philosopher whose
Crowds and Power is the definitive work on the workings of the mass
mind, would be inclined to view the gathering at Bethel as a typical
example of an "open crowd," one whose real purpose and urge is simply
to *grow*. "In the crowd the individual feels that he is transcending the
limits of his own person. He has a sense of relief, for the distances are
removed which used to throw him back on himself and shut him in.
With the lifting of these burdens of distance he feels free; his freedom
is the crossing of these boundaries. He wants what is happening to him
to happen to others too; and he expects it to happen to them."

33   Or, as one of those disembodied voices on the public address system
put it to the crowd, "You are all part of the one big revolution." To
those of us who were there watching it all, puzzling, and comparing
notes, the Woodstock Music and Art Fair seemed a historical occasion,
all right, but one in the nature of a mass dropout, a new game for those
with time and money to play it. But to the kids there it may well seem
a revolution—which is, after all, a war of sorts.

34   People speak carelessly and often today of revolution, so perhaps it
would be best to be specific on a few conclusions carried away from that
week end:

35   The openness with which marijuana was smoked at the Woodstock Fair suggests that it may soon be legalized.

36   The prejudices, passions, and mass psychology of this generation may not alter appreciably as they grow older, and could even become dominant in American culture.

37   Such be-ins as the one at Bethel, whether with music or without, will become increasingly familiar as they are repeated summer after summer, year after year.

38 Will they always be so peaceful? That may depend on how others react. The kids here show no signs of changing their directions.

Discussion of Theme

1. One of the local citizens complained that "dope [was] being sold right on the corner. It was awful for children to be exposed to this." Do you agree or disagree?
2. The author writes that the Woodstock festival was "in the nature of a mass dropout, a new game for those with time and money to play it." Do you agree?
3. In what sense were those who attended the fair "all part of the one big revolution"?
4. What is the author's view of the festival? How can you tell?

Discussion of Rhetoric

1. The author uses the word *phenomenon* in describing the festival and then elaborates on it. Is this the usual use of the word? Is his use effective in communicating his meaning?
2. What is the effect of using the images of warfare and a battlefield to describe the festival? Is this consistent or inconsistent with the overall tone of the article?
3. Where does the conclusion of the article begin? How relevant is it to the rest of the article?

Writing Assignments

1. Describe a be-in or rock festival that you have attended.
2. Explain the meaning of the Aquarian age.

Library Exploration

For other impressions of the Woodstock Fair, read the special *Life* magazine edition or some other newspaper and magazine articles about it.

23

GRAMMAR FOR TODAY

Bergen Evans

*What determines "correct" Eng- professor of English at North-
lish? Usage, says the author, a western University.*

1   In 1747 Samuel Johnson issued a plan for a new dictionary of the
English language. It was supported by the most distinguished printers
of the day and was dedicated to the model of all correctness, Philip
Dormer Stanhope, Fourth Earl of Chesterfield. Such a book, it was
felt, was urgently needed to "fix" the language, to arrest its "corruption"
and "decay," a degenerative process which, then as now, was attributed
to the influence of "the vulgar" and which, then as now, it was a mark
of superiority and elegance to decry. And Mr. Johnson seemed the
man to write it. He had an enormous knowledge of Latin, deep piety,
and dogmatic convictions. He was also honest and intelligent, but the
effect of these lesser qualifications was not to show until later.

2   Oblig'd by hunger and request of friends, Mr. Johnson was willing
to assume the role of linguistic dictator. He was prepared to "fix" the
pronunciation of the language, "preserve the purity" of its idiom,
brand "impure" words with a "note of infamy," and secure the whole
"from being overrun by . . . low terms."

3   There were, however, a few reservations. Mr. Johnson felt it necessary to warn the oversanguine that "Language is the work of man, a
being from whom permanence and stability cannot be derived."
English "was not formed from heaven . . . but was produced by necessity and enlarged by accident." It had, indeed, been merely "thrown
together by negligence" and was in such a state of confusion that its very
syntax could no longer "be taught by general rules, but [only] by special
precedents."

In 1755 the *Dictionary* appeared. The noble patron had been given
a great deal more immortality than he had bargained for by the vigor
of the kick Johnson had applied to his backside as he booted him over-
board. And the *Plan* had been replaced by the *Preface*, a sadder but
very much wiser document.

5   Eight years of "sluggishly treading the track of the alphabet" had
taught Johnson that the hopes of "fixing" the language and preserving

its "purity" were but "the dreams of a poet doomed at last to wake a lexicographer." In "the boundless chaos of living speech," so copious and energetic in its disorder, he had found no guides except "experience and analogy." Irregularities were "inherent in the tongue" and could not be "dismissed or reformed" but must be permitted "to remain untouched." "Uniformity must be sacrificed to custom . . . in compliance with a numberless majority" and "general agreement." One of the pet projects of the age had been the establishment of an academy to regulate and improve style. "I hope," Johnson wrote in the Preface, that if "it should be established . . . the spirit of English liberty will hinder or destroy [it.]"

6   At the outset of the work he had flattered himself, he confessed, that he would reform abuses and put a stop to alterations. But he had soon discovered that "sounds are too volatile and subtle for legal restraints" and that "to enchain syllables and to lash the wind are equally undertakings of pride unwilling to measure its desires by its strength." For "the causes of change in language are as much superior to human resistance as the revolutions of the sky or the intumescence of the tide."

7   There had been an even more profound discovery: that grammarians and lexicographers "do not form, but register the language; do not teach men how they should think, but relate how they have hitherto expressed their thoughts." And with this statement Johnson ushered in the rational study of linguistics. He had entered on his task a medieval pedant. He emerged from it a modern scientist.

8   Of course his discoveries were not strikingly original. Horace had observed that use was the sole arbiter and norm of speech and Montaigne had said that he who would fight custom with grammar was a fool. Doubtless thousands of other people had at one time or another perceived and said the same thing. But Johnson introduced a new principle. Finding that he could not lay down rules, he gave actual examples to show meaning and form. He offered as authority illustrative quotations, and in so doing established that language is what usage makes it and that custom, in the long run, is the ultimate and only court of appeal in linguistic matters.

9   This principle, axiomatic today in grammar and lexicography, seems to exasperate a great many laymen who, apparently, find two hundred and five years too short a period in which to grasp a basic idea. They insist that there are absolute standards of correctness in speech and that these standards may be set forth in a few simple rules. To a man, they believe, of course, that they speak and write "correctly" and they are loud in their insistence that others imitate them.

10   It is useless to argue with such people because they are not, really, interested in language at all. They are interested solely in demonstrating their own superiority. Point out to them—as has been done hundreds of times—that forms which they regard as "corrupt,"

"incorrect," and "vulgar" have been used by Shakespeare, Milton, and the Bible and are used daily by 180 million Americans and accepted by the best linguists and lexicographers, and they will coolly say, "Well, if they differ from me, they're wrong."

11   But if usage is not the final determinant of speech, what is? Do the inhabitants of Italy, for example, speak corrupt Latin or good Italian? Is Spanish superior to French? Would the Breton fisherman speak better if he spoke Parisian French? Can one be more fluent in Outer Mongolian than in Inner Mongolian? One has only to ask such questions in relation to languages other than one's own, languages within which our particular snobberies and struggles for prestige have no stake, to see the absurdity of them.

12   The language that we do speak, if we are to accept the idea of "corruption" and "decay" in language, is a horribly decayed Anglo-Saxon, grotesquely corrupted by Norman French. Furthermore, since Standard English is a development of the London dialect of the fourteenth century, our speech, by true aristocratic standards, is woefully middle-class, commercial, and vulgar. And American speech is lower middle-class, reeking of counter and till. Where else on earth, for instance, would one find crime condemned because it didn't *pay*!

13   In more innocent days a great deal of time was spent in wondering what was the "original" language of mankind, the one spoken in Eden, the language of which all modern tongues were merely degenerate remnants. Hector Boethius tells us that James I of Scotland was so interested in this problem that he had two children reared with a deaf and dumb nurse on an island in order to see what language they would "naturally" speak. James thought it would be Hebrew, and in time, to his great satisfaction, it was reported that the children were speaking Hebrew!

14   Despite this experiment, however, few people today regard English as a corruption of Hebrew. But many seem to think it is a corruption of Latin and labor mightily to make it conform to this illusion. It is they and their confused followers who tell us that we can't say "I am mistaken" because translated into Latin this would mean "I am misunderstood," and we can't say "I have enjoyed myself" unless we are egotistical or worse.

15   It is largely to this group—most of whom couldn't read a line of Latin at sight if their lives depended on it—that we owe our widespread bewilderment concerning *who* and *whom*. In Latin the accusative or dative form would always be used, regardless of the word's position in the sentence, when the pronoun was the object of a verb or a preposition. But in English, for at least four hundred years, this simply hasn't been so. When the pronoun occurs at the beginning of a question, people who speak natural, fluent, literary English use the nominative, regardless. They say "Who did you give it to?" not "Whom did you give it to?" But the semiliterate, intimidated and bewildered,

are mouthing such ghastly utterances as a recent headline in a Chicago newspaper: WHOM'S HE KIDDING?

16 Another group seems to think that in its pure state English was a Laputan tongue, with logic as its guiding principle. Early members of this sect insisted that *unloose* could only mean "to tie up," and present members have compelled the gasoline industry to label its trucks *Flammable* under the disastrous insistence, apparently, that the old *Inflammable* could only mean "not burnable."

17 It is to them, in league with the Latinists, that we owe the bogy of the double negative. In all Teutonic languages a doubling of the negative merely emphasizes the negation. But we have been told for a century now that two negatives make a positive, though if they do and it's merely a matter of logic, then three negatives should make a negative again. So that if "It doesn't make no difference" is wrong merely because it includes two negatives, then "It doesn't never make no difference" ought to be right again. Both of these groups, in their theories at least, ignore our idiom. Yet idiom—those expressions which defy all logic but are the very essence of a tongue—plays a large part in English. We go to school and college, but we go to *the* university. We buy two dozen eggs but a couple *of* dozen. *Good and* can mean *very* ("I am good and mad!") and "a hot cup of coffee" means that the coffee, not the cup, is to be hot. It makes a world of difference to a condemned man whether his reprieve is *upheld* or *held up*.

18 There are thousands of such expressions in English. They are the "irregularities" which Johnson found "inherent in the tongue" and which his wisdom perceived could not and should not be removed. Indeed, it is in the recognition and use of these idioms that skillful use of English lies.

19 Many words in the form that is now mandatory were originally just mistakes, and many of these mistakes were forced into the language by eager ignoramuses determined to make it conform to some notion of their own. The *s* was put in island, for instance, in sheer pedantic ignorance. The second *r* doesn't belong in *trousers*, nor the *g* in *arraign*, nor the *t* in deviltry, nor the *n* in *passenger* and *messenger*. Nor, so far as English is concerned, does the first *c* in *arctic* which so many people twist their mouths so strenuously to pronounce.

20 And grammar is as "corrupted" as spelling or pronunciation. "You are" is as gross a solecism as "me am." It's recent, too; you won't find it in the Authorized Version of the Bible. *Lesser, nearer,* and *more* are grammatically on a par with *gooder*. *Crowed* is the equivalent of *knowed* or *growed*, and *caught* and *dug* (for *catched* and *digged*) are as "corrupt" as *squoze* for *squeezed* or *snoze* for *sneezed*.

21 Fortunately for our peace of mind most people are quite content to let English conform to English, and they are supported in their sanity by modern grammarians and linguists.

22   Scholars agree with Puttenham (1589) that a language is simply speech "fashioned to the common understanding and accepted by consent." They believe that the only "rules" that can be stated for a language are codified observations. They hold, that is, that language is the basis of grammar, not the other way round. They do not believe that any language can become "corrupted" by the linguistic habits of those who speak it. They do not believe that anyone who is a native speaker of a standard language will get into any linguistic trouble unless he is misled by snobbishness or timidity or vanity.

23   He may, of course, if his native language is English, speak a form of English that marks him as coming from a rural or an unread group. But if he doesn't mind being so marked, there's no reason why he should change. Johnson retained a Staffordshire burr in his speech all his life. And surely no one will deny that Robert Burns's rustic dialect was just as good as a form of speech as, and in his mouth infinitely better as a means of expression than, the "correct" English spoken by ten million of his southern contemporaries.

24   The trouble is that people are no longer willing to be rustic or provincial. They all want to speak like educated people, though they don't want to go to the trouble of becoming truly educated. They want to believe that a special form of socially acceptable and financially valuable speech can be mastered by following a few simple rules. And there is no lack of little books that offer to supply the rules and promise "correctness" if the rules are adhered to. But, of course, these offers are specious because you don't speak like an educated person unless you are an educated person, and the little books, if taken seriously, will not only leave the lack of education showing but will expose the pitiful yearning and the basic vulgarity as well, in such sentences as "Whom are you talking about?"

25   As a matter of fact, the educated man uses at least three languages. With his family and his close friends, on the ordinary, unimportant occasions of daily life, he speaks, much of the time, a monosyllabic sort of shorthand. On more important occasions and when dealing with strangers in his official or business relations, he has a more formal speech, more complete, less allusive, politely qualified, wisely reserved. In addition he has some acquaintance with the literary speech of his language. He understands this when he reads it, and often enjoys it, but he hesitates to use it. In times of emotional stress hot fragments of it may come out of him like lava, and in times of feigned emotion, as when giving a commencement address, cold, greasy gobbets of it will ooze forth.

26   The linguist differs from the amateur grammarian in recognizing all of these variations and gradations in the language. And he differs from the snob in doubting that the speech of any one small group among the language's more than 300 million daily users constitutes a model for all the rest to imitate.

27   The methods of the modern linguist can be illustrated by the question
of the grammatical number of *none*. Is it singular or plural? Should
one say "None of them is ready" or "None of them are ready"?

28   The prescriptive grammarians are emphatic that it should be singular. The Latinists point out that *nemo*, the Latin equivalent, is singular.
The logicians triumphantly point out that *none* can't be more than
one and hence can't be plural.

29   The linguist knows that he hears "None of them are ready" every
day, from people of all social positions, geographical areas, and degrees
of education. He also hears "None is." Furthermore, literature informs
him that both forms were used in the past. From Malory (1450) to
Milton (1650) he finds that *none* was treated as a singular three times
for every once that it was treated as a plural. That is, up to three
hundred years ago men usually said *None is*. From Milton to 1917,
none was used as a plural seven times for every four times it was used
as a singular. That is, in the past three hundred years men often said
None is, but they said *None are* almost twice as often. Since 1917,
however, there has been a noticeable increase in the use of the plural,
so much so that today *None are* is the preferred form.

30   The descriptive grammarian, therefore, says that while *None is*
may still be used, it is becoming increasing peculiar. This, of course,
will not be as useful to one who wants to be cultured in a hurry as a
short, emphatic permission or prohibition. But it has the advantage
of describing English as it is spoken and written here and now and
not as it ought to be spoken in some Cloud-Cuckoo-Land.

31   The descriptive grammarian believes that a child should be taught
English, but he would like to see the child taught the English actually
used by his educated contemporaries, not some pedantic, theoretical
English designed chiefly to mark the imagined superiority of the
designer.

32   He believes that a child should be taught the parts of speech, for
example. But the child should be told the truth—that these are functions of use, not some quality immutably inherent in this or that word.
Anyone, for instance, who tells a child—or anyone else—that *like* is
used in English only as a preposition has grossly misinformed him.
And anyone who complains that its use as a conjunction is a corruption
introduced by Winston cigarettes ought, in all fairness, to explain how
Shakespeare, Keats, and the translators of the Authorized Version of
the Bible came to be in the employ of the R. J. Reynolds Tobacco
Company.

33   Whether formal grammar can be taught to advantage before the
senior year of high school is doubtful; most studies—and many have
been made—indicate that it can't. But when it is taught, it should be
the grammar of today's English, not the obsolete grammar of yesterday's prescriptive grammarians. By that grammar, for instance,
please in the sentence "Please reply" is the verb and *reply* its object.

But by modern meaning *reply* is the verb, in the imperative, and *please* is merely a qualifying word meaning "no discourtesy intended," a mollifying or deimperatival adverb, or whatever you will, but not the verb.

34   This is a long way from saying "Anything goes," which is the charge that, with all the idiot repetition of a needle stuck in a groove, the uninformed ceaselessly chant against modern grammarians. But to assert that usage is the sole determinant in grammar, pronunciation, and meaning is *not* to say that anything goes. Custom is illogical and unreasonable, but it is also tyrannical. The least deviation from its dictates is usually punished with severity. And because this is so, children should be taught what the current and local customs in English are. They should not be taught that we speak a bastard Latin or a vocalized logic. And they should certainly be disabused of the stultifying illusion that after God had given Moses the Commandments He called him back and pressed on him a copy of Woolley's *Handbook of English Grammar.*

35   The grammarian does not see it as his function to "raise the standards" set by Franklin, Lincoln, Melville, Mark Twain, and hundreds of millions of other Americans. He is content to record what they said and say.

36   Insofar as he serves as a teacher, it is his business to point out the limits of the permissible, to indicate the confines within which the writer may exercise his choice, to report that which custom and practice have made acceptable. It is certainly not the business of the grammarian to impose his personal taste as the only norm of good English, to set forth his prejudices as the ideal standard which everyone should copy. That would be fatal. No one person's standards are broad enough for that.

Discussion of Theme

1. What was Samuel Johnson's original aim in writing his dictionary? How, in the course of his work, did this idea become modified?
2. What distinction is made by Evans between the "rational study of linguistics" and the approach of the strict grammarian?
3. What is the philosophy or attitude toward correctness of the groups of grammarians described in paragraphs 14–17? What kinds of difficulties does one encounter when using Latin or logic as the basis for English grammar?
4. Are linguists such as Evans advocates of "anything goes"? If not, what does he advocate?

Discussion of Rhetoric

1. How does the author's word choice in the opening paragraphs suggest his position?

2. What kind of picture of the traditional grammarians are we given in paragraphs 14–17? What is Evans's tone in this section?
3. Reread the last sentence in paragraph 32. How effective is it? Find other such instances of irony or allusion in this selection that give this tongue-in-cheek tone.
4. One of Evans's techniques is to juxtapose two sharply contrasting ideas or images. Find several examples of this device. Explain its purpose in each case.

Writing Assignments

1. Develop the following title into a theme: The Purpose of a Dictionary.
2. Give your own definition of "correct" English.
3. Comment on your experiences with grammar as a student of English.
4. If you disagree with Evans, defend your position.

Library Exploration

1. Look through some old grammar books and note their treatment of various grammatical taboos, such as beginning a sentence with a conjunction or ending a sentence with a preposition.
2. Compare the comments in a modern style book with the philosophy expressed in Evans's essay.

Vocabulary

infamy (2): disgrace; dishonor
oversanguine (3): excessively cheerful
copious (5): plentiful
inherent (5): part of the essential character
volatile (6): difficult to capture or hold permanently
intumescence (6): swelling
lexicographers (7): writers of dictionaries
pedant (7): a formalist
arbiter (8): judge
axiomatic (9): having the nature of a self-evident truth
Laputan (16): a reference to a flying island (in Swift's *Gulliver's Travels*) whose inhabitants were devoted to visionary projects
mandatory (19): required
solecism (20): an ungrammatical combination of words in a sentence
specious (24): having a false look of truth or genuineness
allusive (25): containing implied or indirect references
feigned (25): pretended
gobbets (25): lumps
immutably (32): in a way that cannot be changed
disabused (34): freed from error or fallacy; set right
stultifying (34): stupid, foolish, or absurd

24

LOGIC AND ILLOGIC

Bernard F. Huppe and Jack Kaminsky

What are the main obstacles to clear communication? The authors of this essay suggest that there are three: emotional arguments, faulty reasoning, and the misuse of language.

1   Some of the basic obstacles to obtaining and communicating reliable information will be discussed. These obstacles will be arranged, for utility and ease of reference, under three main headings: Emotional Argument, Faulty Reasoning, Misuse of Language.

EMOTIONAL ARGUMENT

2   *Argument Ad Hominem.* When someone attempts to argue by attacking the personal character of his opponent, he is making what is called an argument *ad hominem.* For example, in a discussion of higher wages, if the proponent of higher wages is a union official, his opponent may be strongly tempted to resort to the argument *ad hominem* by pointing out that the union official's argument must be discounted because he is an "interested party," a member of the union. But knowledge of a man's motives and attitudes has no bearing on the correctness of his argument, except in so far as it causes us to be much more careful in evaluating the argument. The question of whether a man is "right" or "wrong" does not depend on his occupation or his personality.

3   Very often the *ad hominem* argument is very vicious. Some people characteristically argue by making personal slurs against their opponents. They will say a particular person is wrong because he is a Jew or a Catholic, a Fascist or a Communist. Because name calling is frequently as effective as it is misleading, courts of law have strict rules to govern the attempts of lawyers to discredit witnesses in cross-examination. A lawyer may criticize the personal character of a witness only if such criticism is directly connected with the reliability of evidence. Thus the state of a man's eyesight would be highly relevant to his testimony concerning an accident he observed from a distance. But his marital status, for instance the fact that he had just married his fifth wife, would be totally irrelevant to the testimony.

4   A new dimension has been given to the *ad hominem* argument in

recent years through the popularization of discoveries in psychology. Now if a man argues for social security he is told that he argues this way because he has an "inferiority complex," or if he argues too strongly for free enterprise he has a "superiority complex." But it should be apparent that one does not answer an argument merely by pointing out that an individual has a "complex" of some kind. A scientist may have neurotic tendencies and may beat his wife, but these facts do not discredit his theories.

5   *Genetic Fallacy.* This fallacy involves the attempt to destroy the value of an argument by criticizing its origin. Thus, some have argued that religion is no more than a superstition because it originated out of superstition. But even if it is true that religious views resulted from superstition, this does not mean that such views are still to be equated with superstition. Even though chemistry originated in alchemy, chemistry is not therefore to be regarded as a prejudiced and superstitious study. Yet the appeal to "bad" origin is often sufficient to arouse enough emotion so that the real argument is obliterated.

6   The attempt to discredit an argument by reflecting on the proponent's background combines the *genetic fallacy* with the *ad hominem*. But because a man has grown up in a bad family and a worse environment, it does not follow that he himself is a bad human being nor does it follow that his arguments are false. Conversely a man who comes from a good family and a good environment does not always turn out to be a good human being.

7   In a more subtle way some social scientists have fallen into this fallacy by claiming that human beings are merely products of their environment. But a man may come from a very bad environment and still grow up to be a normal, healthy human being.

8   *Appeal to the People.* Because the public speaker or writer must gain the confidence of his audience if he is to make his point, he may often attempt to establish an atmosphere of friendliness. One of the ways in which he accomplishes this is by depicting himself as "one of the boys." The use of such expressions as "fellow citizens" or "friends and neighbors" is primarily an attempt to make an audience friendly and responsive. A similar purpose is served by such statements as "We're all Americans here and we all share one great ideal, etc.," or "I'm a fellow worker. You and I know how tough it is to earn a buck. My talk ain't fancy, but . . ." or "Because I am addressing a college-trained audience, I know that I can speak of difficult matters seriously." Generally, such appeals are not very dangerous. But when demagogues use them to stir up strong emotions, then the consequences can be disastrous. Lynch mobs have often been formed as a result of strong emotional appeal to group unity.

9   In its more subtle forms the appeal to the people occurs when we try to meet an argument by saying "it isn't natural" or "it isn't common sense." People once used to argue that flying machines were "not

natural" and "against common sense." But such criticisms are totally irrelevant to the argument.

10   *The Appeal to Pity.* The appeal to the people relies for its effect on the feeling of group unity. But a similar effect can be obtained when pity and sympathy are aroused. Lawyers will frequently use this means to defend a client. They have him wear shabby clothes, and then try to arouse the jury's sympathy by pointing out how he has suffered. Similarly, MacArthur's use of the refrain "Old soldiers never die; they just fade away" was designed to arouse sympathy and pity. In fact, anyone who argues by describing examples of personal persecution or martyrdom is appealing to pity and sympathy, rather than logic and evidence.

11   Appeals to the people and to pity can be important rhetorical devices, for in these ways effective speakers are able to arouse desired emotions. Unfortunately, effective speakers are not always effective thinkers, and only too often people have been led by demagogues who were effective persuaders but bad reasoners. Some congressmen have succeeded in getting their audience to weep with them and for them. They arouse reactions, not thought. But the *method of persuasion* and the *method of reasoning* must always be clearly differentiated.

12   *The Appeal to Authority.* This fallacy arises when we attempt to justify an idea by appealing to authority. Thus for many years people refused to accept the theory of evolution because it seemed to contradict the Bible and the Church Fathers. But the truth or falsity of a doctrine rests on the empirical and logical evidence that is given for it. Even the most scientifically attested hypothesis is not made acceptable merely because Einstein or some other scientist approves it; rather it is accepted because of the empirical evidence which attests to the reliability of the hypothesis. Einstein does not make the theory of relativity true, any more than a man of distinction makes a whisky good. On the contrary, Einstein would probably have been the first to claim that the theory is not based on his *word*, but rather on the evidence which anyone could obtain if he had the proper training in mathematics and the natural sciences.

13   Of course there is good reason to rely on authorities, but only when their views have been carefully examined to determine (1) whether they have based these views on verifiable fact and not merely subjective feelings, and (2) whether they are *really* authorities. The fact that a scientist is an expert in physics does not automatically make him an expert in political science. Eisenhower may be a great military general, but this does not qualify him to be an expert scientist.

14   *Appeal to Force.* The attempt to gain a point by threatening physical or other harm is an *appeal to force.* The appeal to force is resorted to more subtly when it is insinuated that a person may "lose his job" or "be reported to the authorities" because of his beliefs. It also occurs

when an argument is attacked as "dangerous." In such instances we try to *destroy* rather than *resolve* the argument.

15   An infamous example of the use of the appeal to force appears in Thucydides' account of the Athenian attempt to "persuade" the small island of Melos to join them.

> "You know," says the Athenian, "as well as we do, that, in the logic of human nature, Right only comes into question where there is a balance of power, while it is Might that determines what the strong extort and the weak concede . . . Your strongest weapons are hopes yet unrealized, while the weapons in your hand are somewhat inadequate for holding out against the forces already arrayed against you . . . Reflect . . . that you are taking a decision for your country . . . a country whose fate hangs upon a single decision right or wrong."   (Toynbee's translation.)

16   It is important to remember that appeals to force are rarely this obvious. Whenever there is a hidden threat to an opponent's social, economic, or political status, the appeal to force is being used.

FAULTY REASONING

17   *Faulty Generalization.* Any sweeping claim which is based on a very few selected instances is a faulty generalization. A statement such as "Foreigners just don't understand democracy" is usually based on hearsay or on one or two unfavorable encounters with foreigners. A fairly common type of faulty generalization rests on the acceptance of slogans, proverbs, or "tabloids." In the 1932 presidential election the Republicans told the nation to keep them in office because "You shouldn't change horses in the middle of the stream." The Democrats answered by saying "It's time for a new deal." In 1952 the slogans were reversed. People have often been told "never put off for tomorrow what you can do today," that is, when not told that "haste makes waste." Men who have associated with Communists are often regarded suspiciously because "birds of a feather flock together." The reply is, "You can't judge a book by its cover." Such slogans or proverbs are clever and often persuasive. But for the important purpose of deciding whether or not an argument is sound they are useless.

18   Sometimes a generalization is accepted as an unalterable truth. An argument against wartime censorship of the press on the basis of the statement, "Democracy can exist only as long as the press is free," ignores the fact that all generalizations hold only for specific circumstances and that this particular generalization might not hold under other circumstances. Even an important generalization such as "Thou shalt not kill" may have exceptions; soldiers are permitted to break this rule, and so are those who kill in self-defense.

19   *The Post Hoc Ergo Propter Hoc Fallacy.* (After this, therefore because of this.) This fallacy occurs when the cause of some occurrence
is attributed to an event that immediately preceded it, as when our
stomach-ache is attributed to the last meal eaten, a causal relationship
which might or might not be true. Sequence of events does not necessarily imply causal relationship. Yet people constantly think that,
because event X occurred immediately before event Y, therefore event
X is the *cause* of event Y. "I walked under a ladder; I failed the exam
I had immediately afterward; therefore walking under the ladder was
the cause of my failure." Superstitions are generally based on the
post hoc fallacy. Political success has frequently been based on the
argument: "See! Since I've been in office, things have gone well."

20   Newspapers sometimes make clever use of the *post hoc* fallacy. Thus
such headlines as MINERS STRIKE; REDS GAIN IN KOREA
may refer to two completely independent events. But linking the two
events in the same headline gives the impression to many readers that
the Communists are gaining in Korea *because* the miners are striking.

21   If something occurred just prior to an event it is not necessarily
the cause of the event. An infinite number of things all over the universe
occur the second before a given event. One of these may be the cause.
But much more knowledge is required than the simple fact that it
occurred a second or even a split second before the happening.

22   *Begging the Question—Circular Reasoning.* Begging the question, or
reasoning in circular fashion, consists in the mere reassertion of the
meaning of the premises in the conclusion. In its most obvious form
it can be seen in the argument: "John is a good man. Why? Because
he's good, that's why." In this example the conclusion "John is a good
man" does no more than repeat the premise.

23   Of course begging the question is usually not this obvious. Usually
the premise is repeated but in different words: "John is a good man.
Why? Because he is virtuous." But it should be apparent that "virtuous"
and "good" are synonymous and therefore the argument is circular.

24   Sometimes an argument is quite complex and then it is more difficult to check for circularity: "Freud claims that we are often
frustrated because our sex drives are blocked and they become blocked
because we are thwarted in our desires." The circularity here may be
difficult to discover until "frustrated" is seen to have the same meaning
as "thwarted in our desires."

25   *Special Pleading.* This fallacy occurs when a deliberate attempt is
made to "stack the cards" in favor of some given position. Politicians
are notoriously adept in employing this fallacy. They very often completely ignore or refuse to look for any evidence that could invalidate
their views. . . .

26   In a sense all of us are engaged in "special pleading." When we favor
some position we tend to minimize any data that criticize the position.

Lawyers are often concerned with *minimizing* unfavorable evidence. But only a dishonest lawyer would deliberately *ignore* such evidence.

27   *The Appeal to Ignorance.* This fallacy consists in an attempt to justify a belief even if there is no evidence for it. Thus people will sometimes be found to argue: "The occurrence of psychic phenomena is indeed a fact because no one has ever disproved it." But because something has never been proved *false*, it is not therefore to be considered true. The statement "A green-eyed elf sits on the other side of the moon" may not ever be disproved. But this does not mean that an elf does sit on the other side of the moon.

28   *Irrelevance.* This fallacy is probably the most frequently used. We start out by trying to prove one statement and then end up by trying to prove a different statement. Women sometimes argue in the following way:

> Mrs. X: But she's so stupid! Every time you ask her a question she has nothing to say. Furthermore, I know her I.Q. is very low.
> Mrs. Y: But wasn't that a nice blouse she was wearing?

29   In this example Mrs. X is trying to prove someone's stupidity. But Mrs. Y diverts the issue into another channel.

30   Examples abound in English themes, as in the following excerpt from a theme:

> In this paper I should like to comment on Ibsen's *Ghosts*. The play was very sincere and honest. Sincerity and honesty are two qualities that are praiseworthy. All people should be sincere and honest.

31   The student begins the theme by telling us he will discuss Ibsen's *Ghosts*. But he concludes by telling us that sincerity and honesty are good qualities.

32   *Imperfect Analogy.* Analogy is frequently a very compelling method of reasoning. For example, we might argue: "Conditions today are like conditions prior to World War II. Therefore, since war followed then, war will follow now." Similarly, Spengler argued that since conditions in modern Western civilization are just like those which were present during the decline of many ancient civilizations, Western civilization is also in the process of declining. But analogies of this kind can be satisfactory only if they compare two elements that have very few differences. We can argue that one tomato will be like all the others because one tomato is not different in any important respects from another, that is, tomatoes are generally considered to be homogeneous. But analogy is of little value in comparing civilizations. There are just as many important differences among civilizations as there are similarities. When we ignore differences and base analogy

on a few similarities, we are involved in the fallacy of imperfect analogy.

33   Unfortunately, analogy has found frequent use as a dangerous political weapon. At one time it was fashionable to argue that circular motion was natural because the earth revolved around the sun. Consequently, it was also natural for society to consist of a monarch around whom the rest of the nation revolved. Marxists have frequently argued that opposition of social classes is necessary in capitalistic societies by analogy with the opposition of physical forces in the universe.

34   However, analogy can sometimes serve a useful purpose in suggesting new and fruitful approaches to problems. The study of animal behavior has led to important clues concerning the principles motivating human behavior. The analogy between the flow of electricity through a wire and the flow of water through a tube served to stimulate the search for new and more complex properties of electricity. But such advantages of analogy must be weighed against the disadvantages.

MISUSE OF LANGUAGE

35   *Misuse of Metaphor.* The argument from analogy rests on presumed resemblances between otherwise unrelated events. Similar to analogy is *metaphor*, the use of a word to express a likeness. But whereas analogy usually rests upon a number of resemblances, metaphor utilizes only a limited number of resemblances. People are called "tigers," "angels," "wolves," "monsters," and so forth on the basis of one or two characteristics. Such metaphors are sometimes picturesque, sometimes clever, but very often they are misleading and confusing. They cause us to over-simplify our judgments of people and to attribute too much or too little to them. Calling a man a "tiger," for example, causes us to attribute to him many characteristics which he may not really possess— anger, hatred, ferocity, etc. Mark Twain's novel, *Pudd'nhead Wilson*, provides a good illustration. On the basis of one remark, Wilson, a promising young lawyer, new to a small town, was called "pudd'nhead." It took years for him to establish his practice because the townspeople judged him by the name he was given.

36   Metaphor, like analogy, is faulty only when it is misused, as it is in the following:

> Tree planting and similar *soft-headed quack remedies* would be in vogue. The dollar would be dishonest. The budget would be a national *laughing stock*. A spending *orgy* would be *gaining a momentum* which could hardly be checked. Class prejudice would be *rampant*. The treasury would have been *looted*.

37   The writer had misgivings about what would happen when Roosevelt became president of the United States in 1932, but notice that by his use of the italicized metaphors his misgivings are made to appear as if they related to actual events. Or, again, an editorial (1933) presents

the following highly emotional metaphorical warning:

> Whatever menace appears to these rights is a *dread specter* before the women of America of wrecked homes, wrecked lives, and a WRECKED FUTURE.

38   It is somewhat of a relief to discover that the warning was occasioned by a bill before Congress which would license interstate corporations!

39   A very glaring example of the misuse of metaphor is seen in the following:

> [Winston Churchill], the archbishop of torydom, came to tell us how we shall live. And what is the life he maps for us? An Anglo-American tyranny to ride roughshod over the globe. He said that it was against Communism that he wanted the armies and navies combined. The words are Churchill's but the plan is Hitler's. Churchill's own domain of plunder is ripping at the seams and he asks Americans to save it for him. We are to be the trigger men, we are to provide him billions of money to regain what the robber barons are losing. *(New Masses,* March 19, 1946.)

40   Notice how various pictorial phrases such as "archbishop of torydom," "domain of plunder," "ripping at the seams," "trigger men," and "robber barons" are able to convey the impression that Churchill is a criminal, trying to get us to join his "gang." The writing is colorful and vivid and serves to build up in our minds an association between Churchill and the "typical gangster." And, of course, this is precisely the association that the paragraph seeks to convey. But we are duped by metaphorical writing when we accept such writing as if it· were actually true.

41   *Hypostatization.* Not only may the unscrupulous writer take advantage of the normal uncritical response to metaphor, but he may also avail himself of a tendency in people to assume that abstract words refer to concrete entities. This tendency to speak of *democracy, justice, liberty,* as if they had reference to specific entities, is called *hypostatization.* The fallacy could be defined as a failure to distinguish between abstract and concrete words. The objects referred to by *table* and *chair* can be pointed to; the ideas represented by *justice* and *truth* cannot be pointed to. Examples of hypostatization can be found everywhere, as is suggested in the following list of slogans:

> The State can do no wrong.
> Nature decrees what is right.
> The Spirit of the Nation produces its art and literature.
> Science makes Progress.
> Democracy safeguards human liberty.

The effect of hypostatization is—like metaphor—to produce emotion.

A statement, "Justice triumphs over all," has emotional appeal. But it is too abstract to convey information about any specific situation.

42   *Semantic Ambiguity or Equivocation.* Almost all words are potentially ambiguous because almost all words have more than one meaning. Actually the meaning of a word is governed chiefly by the context in which it is found, as, for example, *bad* in the following sentences:

> Susie, don't be bad.
> He feels bad.
> She's not a bad number.
> That's too bad.
> It was a bad day at Black Rock.

43   When deliberately or mistakenly we use the same word with different meanings in the same context we are said to "equivocate." Equivocation causes trouble because of the habitually uncritical use of language. We tend to forget that a word has many meanings, so that meaning A which Mr. X has in mind may be very different from meaning B which Mr. Y has in mind, although both are using the same word.

> Mr. X: Don't you agree that *progress* is very important for a nation?
> Mr. Y: Yes, I agree with you.
> Several days later:
> Mr. X: to a friend: Mr. Y and I are in complete agreement. We both believe in *progress*, that is, that contemporary institutions should never be allowed to deteriorate. Therefore, I'm sure he will vote against a revision of the constitution.

44   This example is an instance of *apparent* agreement but *real* disagreement. The following is an instance of *real* agreement but *apparent* disagreement.

> Mr. X: I think you're wrong. Men are not *equal*. Some are stronger than others. Some have more intelligence.
> Mr. Y: You're wrong. They are *equal*. The law states that as far as the law is concerned each man is supposed to get *equal* treatment.
> Mr. X: Oh, I agree. I admit that every man is supposed to receive *equal* treatment in law courts. I thought you meant that all men have the same physical and intellectual abilities.

45   Equivocation can be used to make a point effectively, with no attempt at dishonesty, as with Benjamin Franklin's witty equivocation, "If we don't hang together, we'll hang separately." His equivocation served simply to enforce the grave reality behind his words. But equivocation is only too frequently used dishonestly. The communist dictatorship has developed a technique of equivocation which George

Orwell has satirized in *Animal Farm*, where he imagines an animal revolution led by the pigs. When the animals have triumphed, the pigs take the place of the old human masters, and the revolution which began with the slogan "All animals are *equal*" ends with the pigs proclaiming the equivocation, "All animals are *equal*. But some animals are more *equal* than others."

46   *Syntactic Ambiguity.* Not only words, but also the *structure of sentences* (syntax) may cause confusion. Ambiguity resulting from faulty sentence structure is termed *syntactic ambiguity*. Here are a few examples:

1. Horse shows increased profits.
2. State plan aids devastated area.
3. Out of gas she had to walk home.
4. With her enormous nose aimed toward the sky my mother rushed to the plane.

47   A subtle form of syntactic ambiguity is called the *complex question*. This question is usually so phrased that any answer to it is self-incriminating.

Mr. Jones: Have you stopped avoiding people you owe money to?
Mr. Smith: No.
Mr. Jones: Oh, so you're still avoiding them, you rascal.
Mr. Smith: I meant "yes."
Mr. Jones: Oh, so you've been avoiding them, just as I thought.

48   Some lawyers employ such techniques deliberately. A witness who is asked, "When did you buy the murder weapon?" cannot answer without admitting that he owned the weapon. Not only lawyers but politicians and editorial writers frequently employ the technique of the complex question. For example, during the Roosevelt-Truman administrations newspapers frequently made use of the complex question, "Are you going to stop this trend toward Socialism?" This was an unfair question because both the "yes" and "no" answer imply that such a trend existed. Writers of "letters to the editor" make use of the complex question, as in the following: "Are the financial resources of this government without a limit, that four billion dollars can be applied for purposes that will eventually damn the American people?" Any way this question is answered would involve damaging admissions.

49   Pause and emphasis can be used to make syntactic distinctions. The sentence "America without her security is lost" can give two different meanings, depending on punctuation or pauses in speech:

America, without her, security is lost.
America, without her security, is lost.

The meaning of almost any sentence is subject to alteration through emphasis. If after a dinner party someone said, "I enjoyed the dinner," he would not want to emphasize the I, "*I* enjoyed the dinner," because this might imply that the others had not. Emphasis on *dinner* might suggest that he *at least* found this part of the evening, *the dinner*, enjoyable. As he was leaving with his friends, he would not say, "*I* had a good time." Again the implication would be that the others had not enjoyed themselves. Mark Antony's funeral address in Shakespeare's *Julius Caesar* is a brilliant example of the way in which emphasis can be used to sway an audience.

Discussion of Theme

1. Why is the *ad hominem* argument so common? Can you cite examples of its use in political debate?
2. Why is the genetic fallacy often used when discussing racial and minority groups?
3. How are appeals to the people and appeals to pity similar? Can you give an example of each?
4. What are some advantages and disadvantages of using analogies in arguments? Why is false analogy a dangerous political weapon?

Discussion of Rhetoric

1. The authors use excerpts from newspapers and magazines as illustrations of logical fallacies. How effective are these? What impression do they give you of the authors' views?
2. How convincing are the examples taken from conversations and personal writings? Do they seem to be realistic representations? See, for example, the conversation in paragraph 28, or the essay excerpt in paragraph 30.

Writing Assignments

1. What are some valid uses of analogy and appeal to authority? Cite examples from your own experience.
2. Reread a recent essay you have written for one of your classes. What logical fallacies can you find in it? Rewrite any passages that contain errors in logic.

Library Exploration

Look up some of Lewis Carroll's exercises in logic. How do they illustrate some of the principles cited by the authors?

Vocabulary

proponent (2): supporter; advocate
genetic (5): basic to; inherent in the nature of
empirical (12): based on or derived from experience
rampant (36): widespread and unchecked

25

HOW TO WRITE AN "F" PAPER:
Fresh Advice for Students of Freshman English

Joseph C. Pattison

This short, humorous article cata-   *errors in composition made by*
logs some of the most common   *freshmen English students.*

1   Writing an "F" paper is admittedly not an easy task, but one can learn to do it by grasp of the principles to use. The thirteen below, if practiced at all diligently, should lead any student to that fortune in his writing.

2   OBSCURE THE IDEAS:

1. Select a topic that is big enough to let you wander around the main idea without ever being forced to state it precisely. If an assigned topic has been limited for you, take a detour that will allow you to amble away from it for a while.

2. Pad! Pad! Pad! Do not develop your ideas. Simply restate them in safe, spongy generalizations to avoid the need to find evidence to support what you say. Always point out repetition with the phrase, "As previously noted. . . ." Better yet, repeat word-for-word at least one or two of your statements.

3. Disorganize your discussion. For example, if you are using the time order to present your material, keep the reader alert by making a jump from the past to the present only to spring back into the past preparatory to a leap into the future preceding a return hop into the present just before the finish of the point about the past. Devise comparable strategems to use with such other principles for organizing a discussion as space, contrast, cause-effect, and climax.

4. Begin a new paragraph every sentence or two.

By generous use of white space, make the reader aware that he is looking at a page blank of sustained thought.

Like this.

3   MANGLE THE SENTENCES:

5. Fill all the areas of your sentences with deadwood. Incidentally, "the area of" will deaden almost any sentence, and it is particularly flat when displayed prominently at the beginning of a sentence.

6. Using fragments and run-on or comma-spliced sentences. Do not use a main subject and a main verb, for the reader will get the complete thought too easily. Just toss him part of the idea at a time, as in "Using fragments . . . ." To gain sentence variety, throw in an occasional run-on sentence thus the reader will have to read slowly and carefully to get the idea.

7. Your sentence order invert for statement of the least important matters. That will force the reader to be attentive to understand even the simplest points you make.

8. You, in the introduction, body, and conclusion of your paper, to show that you can contrive ornate, graceful sentences, should use involution. Frequent separation of subjects from verbs by insertion of involved phrases and clauses will prove that you know what can be done to a sentence.

4   SLOVENIZE THE DICTION:

9. Add the popular "-wise" and "-ize" endings to words. Say, "Timewise, it is fastest to go by U.S. 40," rather than simply, "It is fastest to go by U.S. 40." Choose "circularize" in preference to "circulate." Practice will smartenize your style.

10. Use vague words in place of precise ones. From the start, establish vagueness of tone by saying, "The thing is . . ." instead of, "The issue is. . . ." Make the reader be imaginative throughout his reading of your paper.

11. Employ lengthy Latinate locutions wherever possible. Shun the simplicity of style that comes from apt use of short, old, familiar words, especially those of Anglo-Saxon origin. Show that you can get the *maximum* (L.), not merely the *most* (AS.), from every word choice you make.

12. Inject humor into your writing by using the wrong word occasionally. Write "then" when you mean "than" or "to" when you mean "too." Every reader likes a laugh.

13. Find a "tried and true" phrase to use to clinch a point. It will have a comfortingly folksy sound for the reader. Best of all, since you want to end in a conversational and friendly way, sprinkle your conclusion with clichés. "Put a little frosting on the cake," as the saying goes.

5   Well, too ensconce this whole business in a nutshell, you, above all, an erudite discourse on nothing in the field of your topic should pen. Thereby gaining the reader's credence in what you say.

6   Suggestion-wise, one last thing: file-ize this list for handy reference the next time you a paper write.

Discussion of Theme

1. How many of these methods of obscuring ideas are you guilty of in your own writing? Were you aware of them before reading this essay?
2. How does one pad an essay? Give some examples of padded sentences from your own compositions.
3. Do you ever unknowingly "inject humor" into your compositions by misusing or misspelling simple words? What words seem to give you and your contemporaries the most trouble? Why?

Discussion of Rhetoric

1. The author says he wants to teach his readers how to write "F" papers. When do you learn that this is not his real intention?
2. In rule 6, Pattison advises "using fragments and run-on or comma-spliced sentences." Later, he tells his readers to "smartenize" their style. What is he really doing in each instance?
3. How many of the errors mentioned by Pattison can you find in the last two paragraphs of his essay?
4. How is irony used in this essay?

Writing Assignments

1. Write a theme addressed to a high school senior, titled "Things They Never Taught Me in High School English."
2. Develop the following title into a theme: "How to Write an 'A' Paper."

Library Exploration

Try to locate an essay or article which you believe Mr. Pattison would consider a successful "F" paper.

26

SOMETHING ABOUT ENGLISH

Paul Roberts

In 1500, English was a minor language, spoken by only a few people. Today it is spoken natively by over a quarter of a billion people and as a second language by many millions more. This selection outlines the fascinating history of the English language.

HISTORICAL BACKGROUNDS

1   No understanding of the English language can be very satisfactory without a notion of the history of the language. But we shall have to make do with just a notion. The history of English is long and complicated, and we can only hit the high spots.

2   The history of our language begins a little after A.D. 600. Everything before that is pre-history, which means that we can guess at it but can't prove much. For a thousand years or so before the birth of Christ our linguistic ancestors were savages wandering through the forests of northern Europe. Their language was a part of the Germanic branch of the Indo-European Family.

3   At the time of the Roman Empire—say, from the beginning of the Christian Era to around A.D. 400—the speakers of what was to become English were scattered along the northern coast of Europe. They spoke a dialect of Low German. More exactly, they spoke several different dialects, since they were several different tribes. The names given to the tribes who got to England are *Angles, Saxons,* and *Jutes.* For convenience, we can refer to them as Anglo-Saxons.

4   Their first contact with civilization was a rather thin acquaintance with the Roman Empire on whose borders they lived. Probably some of the Anglo-Saxons wandered into the Empire occasionally, and certainly Roman merchants and traders traveled among the tribes. At any rate, this period saw the first of our many borrowings from Latin. Such words as *kettle, wine, cheese, butter, cheap, plum, gem, bishop, church* were borrowed at this time. They show something of the relationship of the Anglo-Saxons with the Romans. The Anglo-Saxons were learning, getting their first taste of civilization.

5   They still had a long way to go, however, and their first step was to help smash the civilization they were learning from. In the fourth century the Roman power weakened badly. While the Goths were

pounding away at the Romans in the Mediterranean countries, their relatives, the Anglo-Saxons, began to attack Britain.

6 The Romans had been the ruling power in Britain since A.D. 43. They had subjugated the Celts whom they found living there and had succeeded in setting up a Roman administration. The Roman influence did not extend to the outlying parts of the British Isles. In Scotland, Wales, and Ireland the Celts remained free and wild, and they made periodic forays against the Romans in England. Among other defense measures, the Romans built the famous Roman Wall to ward off the tribes in the north.

7 Even in England the Roman power was thin. Latin did not become the language of the country as it did in Gaul and Spain. The mass of people continued to speak Celtic, with Latin and the Roman civilization it contained in use as a top dressing.

8 In the fourth century, troubles multiplied for the Romans in Britain. Not only did the untamed tribes of Scotland and Wales grow more and more restive, but the Anglo-Saxons began to make pirate raids on the eastern coast. Furthermore, there was growing difficulty everywhere in the Empire, and the legions in Britain were siphoned off to fight elsewhere. Finally, in A.D. 410, the last Roman ruler in England, bent on becoming emperor, left the islands and took the last of the legions with him. The Celts were left in possession of Britain but almost defenseless against the impending Anglo-Saxon attack.

9 Not much is surely known about the arrival of the Anglo-Saxons in England. According to the best early source, the eighth-century historian Bede, the Jutes came in 449 in response to a plea from the Celtic king, Vortigern, who wanted their help against the Picts attacking from the north. The Jutes subdued the Picts but then quarreled and fought with Vortigern, and, with reinforcements from the Continent, settled permanently in Kent. Somewhat later the Angles established themselves in eastern England and the Saxons in the south and west. Bede's account is plausible enough, and these were probably the main lines of the invasion.

10 We do know, however, that the Angles, Saxons, and Jutes were a long time securing themselves in England. Fighting went on for as long as a hundred years before the Celts in England were all killed, driven into Wales, or reduced to slavery. This is the period of King Arthur, who was not entirely mythological. He was a Romanized Celt, a general, though probably not a king. He had some success against the Anglo-Saxons, but it was only temporary. By 550 or so the Anglo-Saxons were firmly established. English was in England.

OLD ENGLISH

11 All this is pre-history, so far as the language is concerned. We have no record of the English language until after 600, when the Anglo-Saxons were converted to Christianity and learned the Latin alphabet.

The conversion began, to be precise, in the year 597 and was accomplished within thirty or forty years. The conversion was a great advance for the Anglo-Saxons, not only because of the spiritual benefits but because it reestablished contact with what remained of Roman civilization. This civilization didn't amount to much in the year 600, but it was certainly superior to anything in England up to that time.

12   It is customary to divide the history of the English language into three periods: Old English, Middle English, and Modern English. Old English runs from the earliest records—i.e., seventh century— to about 1100; Middle English from 1100 to 1450 or 1500; Modern English from 1500 to the present day. Sometimes Modern English is further divided into Early Modern, 1500–1700, and Late Modern, 1700 to the present.

13   When England came into history, it was divided into several more or less autonomous kingdoms, some of which at times exercised a certain amount of control over the others. In the century after the conversion the most advanced kingdom was Northumbria, the area between the Humber River and the Scottish border. By A.D. 700 the Northumbrians had developed a respectable civilization, the finest in Europe. It is sometimes called the Northumbrian Renaissance, and it was the first of the several renaissances through which Europe struggled upward out of the ruins of the Roman Empire. It was in this period that the best of the Old English literature was written, including the epic poem *Beowulf*.

14   In the eighth century, Northumbrian power declined, and the center of influence moved southward to Mercia, the kingdom of the Midlands. A century later the center shifted again, and Wessex, the country of the West Saxons, became the leading power. The most famous king of the West Saxons was Alfred the Great, who reigned in the second half of the ninth century, dying in 901. He was famous not only as a military man and administrator but also as a champion of learning. He founded and supported schools and translated or caused to be translated many books from Latin into English. At this time also much of the Northumbrian literature of two centuries earlier was copied in West Saxon. Indeed, the great bulk of Old English writing which has come down to us is in the West Saxon dialect of 900 or later.

15   In the military sphere, Alfred's great accomplishment was his successful opposition to the viking invasions. In the ninth and tenth centuries, the Norsemen emerged in their ships from their homelands in Denmark and the Scandinavian peninsula. They traveled far and attacked and plundered at will and almost with impunity. They ravaged Italy and Greece, settled in France, Russia, and Ireland, colonized Iceland and Greenland, and discovered America several centuries before Columbus. Nor did they overlook England.

16   After many years of hit-and-run raids, the Norsemen landed an

army on the east coast of England in the year 866. There was nothing much to oppose them except the Wessex power led by Alfred. The long struggle ended in 877 with a treaty by which a line was drawn roughly from the northwest of England to the southeast. On the eastern side of the line Norse rule was to prevail. This was called the Danelaw. The western side was to be governed by Wessex.

17   The linguistic result of all this was a considerable injection of Norse into the English language. Norse was at this time not so different from English as Norwegian or Danish is now. Probably speakers of English could understand, more or less, the language of the newcomers who had moved into eastern England. At any rate, there was considerable interchange and word borrowing. Examples of Norse words in the English language are *sky, give, law, egg, outlaw, leg, ugly, scant, sly, crawl, scowl, take, thrust.* There are hundreds more. We have even borrowed some pronouns from Norse—*they, their,* and *them.* These words were borrowed first by the eastern and northern dialects and then in the course of hundreds of years made their way into English generally.

18   It is supposed also—indeed, it must be true—that the Norsemen influenced the sound structure and the grammar of English. But this is hard to demonstrate in detail.

A SPECIMEN OF OLD ENGLISH

19   We may now have an example of Old English. The favorite illustration is the Lord's Prayer, since it needs no translation. This has come to us in several different versions. Here is one:

Fæder ure,
þu þe eart on heofonum,
si þin nama gehalgod.
Tobecume þin rice.
Gewurþe ðin willa on eorðan swa swa on heofonum.
Urne gedæghwamlican hlaf syle us to dæg.
And forgyf us ure gyltas, swa swa we forgyfað urum gyltendum.
And ne gelæd þu us on costnunge,
ac alys us of yfele. Soþlice.

20   Some of the differences between this and Modern English are merely differences in orthography. For instance, the sign *æ* is what Old English writers used for a vowel sound like that in modern *hat* or *and.* The *th* sounds of modern *thin* or *then* are represented in Old English by þ or ð. But of course there are many differences in sound too. *Ure* is the ancestor of modern *our,* but the first vowel was like that in *too* or *ooze. Hlaf* is modern *loaf;* we have dropped the *h* sound and changed the vowel, which in *hlaf* was pronounced something like the vowel in *father.* Old English had some sounds which we do not have. The sound represented by *y* does not occur in Modern English. If you pronounce the vowel in *bit* with your lips rounded, you may approach it.

21   In grammar, Old English was much more highly inflected than Modern English is. That is, there were more case endings for nouns, more person and number endings for verbs, a more complicated pronoun system, various endings for adjectives, and so on. Old English nouns had four cases—nominative, genitive, dative, accusative. Adjectives had five—all these and an instrumental case besides. Present-day English has only two cases for nouns—common case and possessive case. Adjectives now have no case system at all. On the other hand, we now use a more rigid word order and more structure words (prepositions, auxiliaries, and the like) to express relationships than Old English did.

22   Some of this grammar we can see in the Lord's Prayer. *Heofonum*, for instance, is a dative plural; the nominative singular was *heofon*. *Urne* is an accusative singular; the nominative is *ure*. In *urum glytendum* both words are dative plural. *Forgyfaþ* is the first person plural form of the verb. Word order is different: "urne gedæ ghwamlican hlaf syle us" in place of "Give us our daily bread." And so on.

23   In vocabulary Old English is quite different from Modern English. Most of the Old English words are what we may call native English: that is, words which have not been borrowed from other languages but which have been a part of English ever since English was a part of Indo-European. Old English did certainly contain borrowed words. We have seen that many borrowings were coming in from Norse. Rather large numbers had been borrowed from Latin, too. Some of these were taken while the Anglo-Saxons were still on the Continent (*cheese, butter, bishop, kettle*, etc.); a larger number came into English after the Conversion (*angel, candle, priest, martyr, radish, oyster, purple, school, spend*, etc.). But the great majority of Old English words were native English.

24   Now, on the contrary, the majority of words in English are borrowed, taken mostly from Latin and French. Of the words in *The American College Dictionary* only about 14 percent are native. Most of these, to be sure, are common, high-frequency words—*the, of, I, and, because, man, mother, road*, etc.; of the thousand most common words in English, some 62 percent are native English. Even so, the modern vocabulary is very much Latinized and Frenchified. The Old English vocabulary was not.

MIDDLE ENGLISH

25   Sometime between the years 1000 and 1200 various important changes took place in the structure of English, and Old English became Middle English. The political event which facilitated these changes was the Norman Conquest. The Normans, as the name shows, came originally from Scandinavia. In the early tenth century they established

themselves in northern France, adopted the French language, and developed a vigorous kingdom and a very passable civilization. In the year 1066, led by Duke William, they crossed the Channel and made themselves masters of England. For the next several hundred years, England was ruled by Kings whose first language was French.

26   One might wonder why, after the Norman Conquest, French did not become the national language, replacing English entirely. The reason is that the Conquest was not a national migration, as the earlier Anglo-Saxon invasion had been. Great numbers of Normans came to England, but they came as rulers and landlords. French became the language of the court, the language of the nobility, the language of polite society, the language of literature. But it did not replace English as the language of the people. There must always have been hundreds of towns and villages in which French was never heard except when visitors of high station passed through.

27   But English, though it survived as the national language, was profoundly changed after the Norman Conquest. Some of the changes— in sound structure and grammar—would no doubt have taken place whether there had been a Conquest or not. Even before 1066 the case system of English nouns and adjectives was becoming simplified; people came to rely more on word order and prepositions than on inflectional endings to communicate their meanings. The process was speeded up by sound changes which caused many of the endings to sound alike. But no doubt the Conquest facilitated the change. German, which didn't experience a Norman Conquest, is today rather highly inflected compared to its cousin English.

28   But it is in vocabulary that the effects of the Conquest are most obvious. French ceased, after a hundred years or so, to be the native language of very many people in England, but it continued—and continues still—to be a zealously cultivated second language, the mirror of elegance and civilization. When one spoke English, one introduced not only French ideas and French things but also their French names. This was not only easy but socially useful. To pepper one's conversation with French expressions was to show that one was well-bred, elegant, *au courant*. The last sentence shows that the process is not yet dead. By using *au courant* instead of, say, *abreast of things*, the writer indicates that he is no dull clod who knows only English but an elegant person aware of how things are done in *le haut monde*.

29   Thus French words came into English, all sorts of them. There were words to do with government: *parliament, majesty, treaty, alliance, tax, government*; church words: *parson, sermon, baptism, incense, crucifix, religion*; words for foods: *veal, beef, mutton, bacon, jelly, peach, lemon, cream, biscuit*; colors: *blue, scarlet, vermilion*; household words: *curtain, chair, lamp, towel, blanket, parlor*; play words: *dance, chess,*

music, leisure, conversation; literary words: *story, romance, poet, literary*; learned words: *study, logic, grammar, noun, surgeon, anatomy, stomach*; just ordinary words of all sorts: *nice, second, very, age, bucket, gentle, final, fault, flower, cry, count, sure, move, surprise, plain.*

30   All these and thousands more poured into the English vocabulary between 1100 and 1500 until at the end of that time many people must have had more French words than English at their command. This is not to say that English became French. English remained English in sound structure and in grammar, though these also felt the ripples of French influence. The very heart of the vocabulary, too, remained English. Most of the high-frequency words—the pronouns, the prepositions, the conjunctions, the auxiliaries, as well as a great many ordinary nouns and verbs and adjectives—were not replaced by borrowings.

31   Middle English, then, was still a Germanic language, but it differed from Old English in many ways. The sound system and the grammar changed a good deal. Speakers made less use of case systems and other inflectional devices and relied more on word order and structure words to express their meanings. This is often said to be a simplification, but it isn't really. Languages don't become simpler; they merely exchange one kind of complexity for another. Modern English is not a simple language, as any foreign speaker who tries to learn it will hasten to tell you.

32   For us Middle English is simpler than Old English just because it is closer to Modern English. It takes three or four months at least to learn to read Old English prose and more than that for poetry. But a week of good study should put one in touch with the Middle English poet Chaucer. Indeed, you may be able to make some sense of Chaucer straight off, though you would need instruction in pronunciation to make it sound like poetry. Here is a famous passage from the *General Prologue to the Canterbury Tales*, fourteenth century:

> Ther was also a nonne, a Prioresse,
> That of hir smyling was ful symple and coy,
> Hir gretteste oath was but by Seinte Loy,
> And she was cleped Madame Eglentyne.
> Ful wel she song the service dyvyne,
> Entuned in hir nose ful semely.
> And Frenshe she spak ful faire and fetisly,
> After the scole of Stratford-atte-Bowe,
> For Frenshe of Parys was to hir unknowe.

EARLY MODERN ENGLISH

33   Sometime between 1400 and 1600 English underwent a couple of sound changes which made the language of Shakespeare quite different

from that of Chaucer. Incidentally, these changes contributed much to the chaos in which English spelling now finds itself.

34   One change was the elimination of a vowel sound in certain unstressed positions at the end of words. For instance, the words *name, stone, wine, dance* were pronounced as two syllables by Chaucer but as just one by Shakespeare. The *e* in these words became, as we say, "silent." But it wasn't silent for Chaucer; it represented a vowel sound. So also the words *laughed, seemed, stored* would have been pronounced by Chaucer as two-syllable words. The change was an important one because it affected thousands of words and gave a different aspect to the whole language.

35   The other change is what is called the Great Vowel Shift. This was a systematic shifting of half a dozen vowels and diphthongs in stressed syllables. For instance, the word *name* had in Middle English a vowel something like that in the modern word *father*; *wine* had the vowel of modern *mean*; *he* was pronounced something like modern *hey*; *mouse* sounded like *moose*; *moon* had the vowel of *moan*. Again the shift was thorough-going and affected all the words in which these vowel sounds occurred. Since we still keep the Middle English system of spelling these words, the differences between Modern English and Middle English are often more real than apparent.

36   The vowel shift has meant also that we have come to use an entirely different set of symbols for representing vowel sounds than is used by writers of such languages as French, Italian, or Spanish, in which no such vowel shift occurred. If you come across a strange word—say, *bine*—in an English book, you will pronounce it according to the English system, with the vowel of *wine* or *dine*. But if you read *bine* in a French, Italian, or Spanish book, you will pronounce it with the vowel of *mean* or *seen*.

37   These two changes, then, produced the basic differences between Middle English and Modern English. But there were several other developments that had an effect upon the language. One was the invention of printing, an invention introduced into England by William Caxton in the year 1475. Where before books had been rare and costly, they suddenly became cheap and common. More and more people learned to read and write. This was the first of many advances in communication which have worked to unify languages and to arrest the development of dialect differences, though of course printing affects writing principally rather than speech. Among other things it hastened the standardization of spelling.

38   The period of Early Modern English—that is, the sixteenth and seventeenth centuries—was also the period of the English Renaissance, when people developed, on the one hand, a keen interest in the past and, on the other, a more daring and imaginative view of the future. New ideas multiplied, and new ideas meant new language. Englishmen had

grown accustomed to borrowing words from French as a result of the Norman Conquest; now they borrowed from Latin and Greek. As we have seen, English had been raiding Latin from Old English times and before, but now the floodgates really opened, and thousands of words from the classical languages poured in. *Pedestrian, bonus, anatomy, contradict, climax, dictionary, benefit, multiply, exist, paragraph, initiate, scene, inspire* are random examples. Probably the average educated American today has more words from French in his vocabulary than from native English sources, and more from Latin than from French.

39   The greatest writer of the Early Modern English period is of course Shakespeare, and the best-known book is the King James Version of the Bible, published in 1611. The Bible (if not Shakespeare) has made many features of Early Modern English perfectly familiar to many people down to present time, even though we do not use these features in present-day speech and writing. For instance, the old pronouns *thou* and *thee* have dropped out of use now, together with their verb forms, but they are still familiar to us in prayer and in Biblical quotation: "Whither thou goest, I will go." Such forms as *hath* and *doth* have been replaced by *has* and *does*; "Goes he hence tonight?" would now be "Is he going away tonight?"; Shakespeare's "Fie, on't, sirrah" would be "Nuts to that, Mac." Still, all these expressions linger with us because of the power of the works in which they occur.

40   It is not always realized, however, that considerable sound changes have taken place between Early Modern English and the English of the present day. Shakespearian actors putting on a play speak the words, properly enough, in their modern pronunciation. But it is very doubtful that this pronunciation would be understood at all by Shakespeare. In Shakespeare's time, the word *reason* was pronounced like modern *raisin*; *face* had the sound of modern *glass*; the *l* in *would, should, palm* was pronounced. In these points and a great many others the English language has moved a long way from what it was in 1600.

RECENT DEVELOPMENTS

41   The history of English since 1700 is filled with many movements and countermovements, of which we can notice only a couple. One of these is the vigorous attempt made in the eighteenth century, and the rather half-hearted attempts made since, to regulate and control the English language. Many people of the eighteenth century, not understanding very well the forces which govern language, proposed to polish and prune and restrict English, which they felt was proliferating too wildly. There was much talk of an academy which would rule on what people could and could not say and write. The academy never came into being, but the eighteenth century did succeed in establishing certain attitudes which, though they haven't had much

effect on the development of the language itself, have certainly changed the native speaker's feeling about the language.

42   In part a product of the wish to fix and establish the language was the development of the dictionary. The first English dictionary was published in 1603; it was a list of 2500 words briefly defined. Many others were published with gradual improvements until Samuel Johnson published his *English Dictionary* in 1755. This, steadily revised, dominated the field in England for nearly a hundred years. Meanwhile in America, Noah Webster published his dictionary in 1828, and before long dictionary publishing was a big business in this country. The last century has seen the publication of one great dictionary: the twelve-volume *Oxford English Dictionary*, compiled in the course of seventy-five years through the labors of many scholars. We have also, of course, numerous commercial dictionaries which are as good as the public wants them to be if not, indeed, rather better.

43   Another product of the eighteenth century was the invention of "English grammar." As English came to replace Latin as the language of scholarship it was felt that one should also be able to control and dissect it, parse and analyze it, as one could Latin. What happened in practice was that the grammatical description that applied to Latin was removed and superimposed on English. This was silly, because English is an entirely different kind of language, with its own forms and signals and ways of producing meaning. Nevertheless, English grammars on the Latin model were worked out and taught in the schools. In many schools they are still being taught. This activity is not often popular with school children, but it is sometimes an interesting and instructive exercise in logic. The principal harm in it is that it has tended to keep people from being interested in English and has obscured the real features of English structure.

44   But probably the most important force on the development of English in the modern period has been the tremendous expansion of English-speaking peoples. In 1500 English was a minor language, spoken by a few people on a small island. Now it is perhaps the greatest language of the world, spoken natively by over a quarter of a billion people and as a second language by many millions more. When we speak of English now, we must specify whether we mean American English, British English, Australian English, Indian English, or what, since the differences are considerable. The American cannot go to England or the Englishman to America confident that he will always understand and be understood. The Alabaman in Iowa or the Iowan in Alabama shows himself a foreigner every time he speaks. It is only because communication has become fast and easy that English in this period of its expansion has not broken into a dozen mutually unintelligible languages.

Discussion of Theme
1. Why does the history of the English language begin a little after A.D. 600?
2. Why is King Alfred an important figure in the history of the English language?
3. What are some of the important differences between Old English and Modern English? Between Middle English and Modern English?
4. How has Latin affected the teaching of English grammar? Does the author believe that this influence has been beneficial or harmful? Why?

Discussion of Rhetoric
1. How does Roberts organize his material in this selection? Why is this method particularly appropriate here?
2. Is Roberts writing for the linguist or the layman? How do you know?
3. This selection begins with an elaborate, lengthy introduction. Why? Where does it end? Is there a conclusion? If so, where does it begin?

Writing Assignments
1. Select one language that played a part in the development of English (Latin, Danish, French, etc.) and describe the way it has contributed to our vocabulary, grammar, or pronunciation.
2. Using the *Oxford English Dictionary*, make a study of the etymology of every word in a short passage from a newspaper article. What are the results in percentages?
3. Using specific examples, show why it is unwise to teach English as if it were similar in structure to Latin.

Library Exploration
If you find the history of language an interesting subject, you might enjoy reading one of the many histories of English that have been written. Among these are *A Structural History of English* by John Mist, *A Linguistic Introduction to the History of English* by Leonard Newmark and Morton Bloomfield, and *The Origins and Development of the English Language* by Thomas Pyles.

Vocabulary
restive (8): difficult to control
plausible (9): believable
autonomous (13): self-ruled; independent
impunity (15): freedom from punishment
orthography (20): spelling

27

CLICHÉS

Richard D. Altick

Everyone uses clichés; but the effective writer, as this essay points out, uses them sparingly and cau- tiously. As you read the following selection, notice which clichés you unwittingly use in your own writing.

1   The word *cliché* is French for stereotype, a metal plate cast from a page of type, which makes it possible for a printer who needs to produce more copies of a certain book to do so without the expensive and time-consuming labor of resetting all the type. Whenever he wants to re-issue a book, he simply puts the plates on the press and touches a button. In English usage, by a neat transfer of meaning, cliché means a ready-cast, or stereotyped, expression—a prefabricated phrase— which saves a writer or speaker the trouble of inventing a fresh new way of saying something.

2   Superficially it might seem that the cliché is an admirable device, for insofar as it economizes on time and effort, it is undoubtedly effi-cient. But good writing is not merely efficient: it is effective. Effective writing must be fresh. It must impress readers with the sincerity of the author. It must bear the marks of being written for a particular occasion. The big drawback of form letters is that they fail to meet these requirements of individuality and immediacy; and clichés are nothing but form letters in miniature. One who uses clichés is writing mechanically; his phrases smell of mimeograph ink.

3   Nor is fondness for the cliché a sign simply of indifference. It may be that a writer's affection for threadbare words is a clue to the quality of his thinking. In the first place, fresh new ideas by their very nature require fresh new language—they cannot be expressed in any other way. Ready-made language can be fitted only to ready-made thoughts. Again, since there is a demonstrable relationship between general intelligence and effective use of language, it is likely that a writer who fails to recognize stale terms when he uses them also fails to recognize stale ideas. Therefore, readers who can quickly detect hackneyed phraseology are forearmed against tired thinking. If, for instance, a man begins a letter to the editor or a luncheon-club address in this man-

ner: "The talk about the abolition of air pollution reminds me of what Mark Twain once said about the weather: everybody talks about it but nobody does anything about it"—the audience is entitled to wonder whether this could possibly be the preface to anything worth listening to. Is the writer or speaker not sufficiently intelligent to realize that the story about Mark Twain and the weather was a chestnut seventy years ago? Similarly with the speaker who must somehow drag in Ole Man River, who just keeps rolling along—and with the one who insists upon involving the hapless Topsy in his description of how a city or a business or a club, instead of developing according to a plan, just grew (or, as Topsy actually said, growed).

4   The willful or ignorant use of trite language, then, can expose a writer to suspicion of being intellectually as well as verbally imitative. A writer does not have to be a coiner of flamboyantly "original" phrases that might be welcomed in the "Picturesque Speech" department of the *Reader's Digest*; indeed, one can err almost as far in that direction as in the other. But readers have a right to expect that his style will unobtrusively provide traction for their minds rather than allow them to slide and skid on a slippery surface paved with well-worn phrases.

5   It would be pedantic, not to say foolish, to insist that good writers never, never use clichés; let him who has never sinned cast the first stone. But good writers, if they use clichés at all, use them with the utmost caution. In informal discourse, furthermore, clichés are almost indispensable. When we are relaxing with our friends, we do not want to be bothered to find new or at least unhackneyed ways of saying things; we rely upon our ready supply of clichés, and if we do not overdraw our account, no one thinks the worse of us. So long as we succeed in communicating the small, commonplace ideas we have in mind, no harm is done.

6   When does an expression become cliché? There can be no definite answer, because what is trite to one person may still be fresh to another. But a great many expressions are universally understood to be so threadbare as to be useless except in the most casual discourse. They have been loved not wisely but too well. A good practical test is this: If, when we are listening to a speaker, we can accurately anticipate the exact words he is going to use next, he is using clichés. "According to the report of earnings for last quarter, our company isn't yet in desperate _____ ("straits," we expect him to say, and lo and _____, he says it). There is, on the other hand, some ground for ("optimism," we correctly anticipate). But to be frank, I must lay it ("on the line": we win again). Let's put all our cards (yes, of course: "on the table"). We are locked in fierce ("competition") with no ("holds barred"). But we can learn to roll ("with the punches"). We have a lot of lost ground ("to recover") and it will be an uphill ("fight"—but "battle"

would serve him just as well) all the way (we can say it in unison with him). In the end, I am willing to bet my ("bottom dollar") and stake my ("reputation") on our emerging from the struggle ("victoriously")."

7   Similarly when we read: if we can read but half the words and yet know pretty certainly what the other half are, we are in the midst of dusty clichés. "He knew the layout of the place like ("the back of his hand"), but nevertheless shivers ("crept up his spine") and his hands were as cold ("as ice"). Though he was sober ("as a judge") his head ("whirled"). But he managed to keep ("an iron grip on himself"—though "a stiff upper lip" would have also suited the occasion) for he was filled with grim ("determination"). Secret Agent 3.1416 had his work ("cut out for him"). This was a mission on which he would either ("do or die")."

8   Clichés, in brief, are phrases that are self-completing, phrases whose words come in a sequence as predictable as the events in the formula plot of a second-rate spy-and-sex thriller. The degree to which a reader is aware of clichés depends directly upon the scope and sensitivity of his previous reading. If he has read widely, in both good books and bad, and has carefully observed authors' styles, he has probably become quite alert to trite language. Clichés to him are old but exceedingly tiresome acquaintances. But if a reader's experience of books and magazines has been limited, he will not recognize so many overripe expressions; in his eyes most clichés still have the dew on them.

9   Many (but by no means all) familiar clichés are figures of speech. Now a figure of speech is useful only so long as it makes an idea more vivid, enabling the reader to visualize an abstract concept in concrete terms. If the reader has become so accustomed to it that it no longer stimulates his imagination, it has no more value than a nonfigurative expression. And that is what has happened to many such images, which possibly were clever and appropriate long ago but now are almost lifeless. Some are similes (direct comparisons): *right as rain, hard as nails, patient as a saint (or Job), thick as thieves (or pea soup), black as the ace of spades (or night, or an eight ball), slow as molasses in January, soft as silk, green as grass, a voice like a foghorn, sold like hotcakes, a mind like a sieve* . . . Some are metaphors: *the fickle finger of fate, the long arm of the law (or coincidence), the salt of the earth, throw caution to the winds, nip a plot in the bud, burn one's bridges behind one, water over the dam, the lion's share, talk off the top of one's head, a face that would stop a clock, administer a tongue-lashing, reap the whirlwind, turn a cold shoulder, leap from the frying pan into the fire, till hell freezes over, a finger in the pie* . . .

10   The variety of clichés that have sprung from a single source—the desire to suggest a resemblance between some aspect of man's behavior and that of animals—is illustrated by this paragraph from a

leaflet issued periodically by the Columbia University Press. Occasionally we will omit a word to show how automatically the mind supplies
the missing element in a cliché:

11   "Man," says *The Columbia Encyclopedia*, "is distinguished from
other animals by his brain and his hands." But there the difference
would seem to end because he is chicken-livered, lion-hearted,
pigeon-toed. He is treacherous as a snake, sly as a fox, busy as a
_____, slippery as an _____, industrious as an ant, blind as a
bat, faithful as a dog, gentle as a lamb. He has clammy hands,
the ferocity of the tiger, the manners of a pig, the purpose of a
jellyfish. He gets drunk as an owl. He roars like a _____; he coos
like a dove. He is still as a mouse; he hops around like a sparrow.
He works like a horse. He is led like a sheep. He can fly like a
bird, run like a deer, drink like a _____, swim like a duck. He
is nervous as a cat. He sticks his head in the sand like an _____.
He acts like a dog in a manger. He is coltish and kittenish, and
stubborn as a _____. He plays possum. He gets hungry as a bear,
and wolfs his food. He has the memory of an elephant. He is
easily cowed. He gets thirsty as a camel. He is as strong as an
_____. He has a catlike walk, and a mousy manner. He parrots
everything he hears. He acts like a puppy, and is as playful as a
kitten. He struts like a rooster, and is as vain as a peacock. He is as
happy as a _____ and as sad as an owl. He has a whale of an
appetite. He has a beak for a nose, and arms like an ape. He has
the eyes of a _____ and the neck of a bull. He is as slow as a
tortoise. He chatters like a magpie. He has raven hair and the
shoulders of a buffalo. He's as dumb as an ox, and has the back
of an ox—he is even as big as an ox. He's a worm. His _____ is
cooked. He's crazy like a bedbug (or fox or coot). He's a rat. He's
a louse. Of course, he is cool as a cucumber, fresh as a _____,
red as a beet, etc.—but *The Columbia Encyclopedia* doesn't
suggest that he differs in any way from vegetables and other
flora, so we won't go into that.

12   One large category of clichés is composed of those which inflexibly
associate a particular descriptive adjective with a given noun. Such
stereotyped associations are exemplified by *hasty retreat, encyclopedic
learning, crashing bore, voracious reader, mad scramble, callow youth,
rude awakening, cruel blow.* Other common types of clichés include
verb and noun phrases. The former are typified by *add insult to _____,
arm to the _____, bite off more than _____, lead a charmed* (or *dog's)
life (or the life of Riley), come to the end of one's rope, _____ over
spilled _____, sign one's John Hancock, follow in the footsteps of, heave
a _____ of relief, lend a helping hand.* Among the noun phrases which
have outlasted their freshness (and therefore their usefulness) are
a fly in the _____, the tip of the tongue, the apple of his _____, a bull

in a china shop, hand in _____, *a labor of* _____, *the milk of* _____, *a pillar of the church, a dog in the manger.* Noun clichés often arrive and grow old and feeble as twins or even triplets: *leaps and* _____; *head and shoulders; kith and kin; short and* _____; *to all intents and* _____; *body and soul; part and parcel; bag and baggage;* _____ *and ruin; safe and* _____; *tired but happy; tooth and* _____; *lock,* _____ *and barrel; hop, skip, and jump; Tom,* _____, *and Harry; wine, women, and song;* _____, *wide and handsome; cease and desist, to have and to hold; race, creed, or national origin.*

13   Nowhere is the cliché more to be avoided than in descriptive and narrative writing, the whole success of which depends upon the freshness and exactness with which the writer communicates his impressions to the reader. A virtually certain mark of the inexperienced writer is his willingness to see his settings and characters through the eyes of someone else—to wit, the man who has used his clichés before him. "He walked with catlike tread" . . . "they were drenched by mountainous waves" . . . "the child was bubbling over with mirth" . . . "there was a blinding flash" . . . "he made a convulsive grab for the rope" . . . "they heard a rustle of leaves" . . . "the flowers nodded in the gentle breeze" . . . "the shadows were lengthening" . . . "he looked at her with a glassy stare." The only delight we can find in such writing is that of seeing old familiar faces. Surely we are allowed to participate in no new experience; we cannot see things from any new angle, or receive a fresh interpretation of their meaning. A "creative" writer who depends upon clichés is really not creating anything. He has a repertory of mere words and phrases, not genuine experience.

14   Whether we are aware of it or not, many of our trustiest clichés are derived from books which have had a great influence on our common speech. *To kill the fatted calf, cast thy bread upon the waters, my name is legion, covers a multitude of sins, the spirit is willing but the flesh is weak, the wages of sin, the blind lead the blind, the parting of the way, still small voice, voice crying in the wilderness*—all have their source in the Bible, even though in most cases their original biblical contexts have been forgotten. These phrases, originally so full of flavor and meaning, have lost much of their charm through unremitting use. Few people react to them as deeply as did those to whom the English Bible was a new and wonderful book, the phrases shining like coins from the mint.

15   The alert reader can watch clichés in the very process of being made. For example, words associated with atomic developments have quickly become standard clichés in all sorts of usages. The verb *to mushroom,* admittedly, was a fairly common cliché many years ago, when it meant "to grow as fast as mushrooms" or "to assume a mushroom shape" ("the suburbs of the city mushroomed," "the bullet mushroomed against the steel plate"). But once the typical ("awe-inspiring") cloud

produced by an atomic explosion was designated as mushroom-shaped, the cliché achieved new popularity and in the process lost its characteristic metaphorical suggestions. Today *mushrooming* is applied to everything from a dam under construction to a sudden burst of public sentiment on some issue. *Chain reaction*, originally a technical term in nuclear physics, now is an all too handy way of describing a series of events that are (or are supposed to be) causally connected, in the manner of a bowling ball knocking down the head pin, which in turn knocks down pins two and three, and so on. Observe also how the verb *to trigger*, first applied to the action of an atomic bomb in setting off the far greater explosion of the hydrogen bomb, has already become a tiresome cliché to describe any analogous action, no matter how remote the resemblance may be: "The protest of the home owners' delegation triggered a full-dress investigation by City Council"; "the heavy rains of the past three days triggered flood conditions." In such a fashion do clichés enter, in particular, the stock vocabulary of journalism.

Discussion of Theme

1. According to the author, when does an expression become a cliché?
2. How does Altick categorize clichés? What is the basis of his classification system?
3. How would you answer someone who claimed, "But clichés best describe what I want to say!"?
4. Some writers believe that a cliché expression, used appropriately, is less jarring than an original phrase that misses the mark. Do you agree?

Discussion of Rhetoric

1. What analogy is established by Altick in paragraph 2? Is it appropriate? In general, what is the function of analogies in exposition?
2. Why does Altick use clichés in his own writing? See, for example, the first sentence in paragraph 5.
3. How does the author use both extended definition and exemplification as methods of development in this article?
4. Where is the central thesis of the selection stated?

Writing Assignments

1. Select a sports story in a recent issue of a newspaper and rewrite it, omitting all clichés and hackneyed expressions.
2. Analyze the jargon of a particular organization or profession.
3. Using Altick's example of the overuse of clichés (paragraphs 6 and 7), construct a colorful but trite presentation of your own, using as many clichés as possible.

4. Trace the rise and fall of several expressions or words that have become clichés. Explain where they came from, why they were originally so popular, and how they achieved the status of cliché.

Library Exploration

1. For definitions of slang terms and slang that has become cliché, see *The Dictionary of American Slang.*
2. Read the "Picturesque Speech" department in back issues of *Reader's Digest.* Has the subject matter of the contributions changed through the years?

Vocabulary

hackneyed (3): trite or commonplace
pedantic (5): narrowly academic
repertory (13): collection
analogous (15): similar

28

WORDS AND BEHAVIOR

Aldous Huxley

Language, as this famous English *can be used for the suppression and*
novelist and essayist reminds us, *distortion of truth.*

1   Words form the thread on which we string our experiences. Without
them we should live spasmodically and intermittently. Hatred itself
is not so strong that animals will not forget it, if distracted, even in the
presence of the enemy. Watch a pair of cats, crouching on the brink
of a fight. Balefully the eyes glare; from far down in the throat of each
come bursts of a strange, strangled noise of defiance; as though animated
by a life of their own, the tails twitch and tremble. With aimed intensity
of loathing! Another moment and surely there must be an explosion.
But no; all of a sudden one of the two creatures turns away, hoists a
hind leg in a more than fascist salute and, with the same fixed and
focused attention as it had given a moment before to its enemy, begins
to make a lingual toilet. Animal love is as much at the mercy of distractions as animal hatred. The dumb creation lives a life made up of
discrete and mutually irrelevant episodes. Such as it is, the consistency
of human characters is due to the words upon which all human experiences are strung. We are purposeful because we can describe our
feelings in rememberable words, can justify and rationalize our desires
in terms of some kind of argument. Faced by an enemy we do not
allow an itch to distract us from our emotions; the mere word "enemy"
is enough to keep us reminded of our hatred, to convince us that we
do well to be angry. Similarly the word "love" bridges for us those
chasms of momentary indifference and boredom which gape from time
to time between even the most ardent lovers. Feeling and desire provide
us with our motive power; words give continuity to what we do and
to a considerable extent determine our direction. Inappropriate and
badly chosen words vitiate thought and lead to wrong or foolish
conduct. Most ignorances are vincible, and in the greater number of
cases stupidity is what the Buddha pronounced it to be, a sin. For,
consciously, or subconsciously, it is with deliberation that we do not
know or fail to understand—because incomprehension allows us, with
a good conscience, to evade unpleasant obligations and responsibilities,

because ignorance is the best excuse for going on doing what one likes, but ought not, to do. Our egotisms are incessantly fighting to preserve themselves, not only from external enemies, but also from the assaults of the other and better self with which they are so uncomfortably associated. Ignorance is egotism's most effective defense against that Dr. Jekyll in us who desires perfection; stupidity, its subtlest stratagem. If, as so often happens, we choose to give continuity to our experience by means of words which falsify the facts, this is because the falsification is somehow to our advantage as egotists.

2   Consider, for example, the case of war. War is enormously discreditable to those who order it to be waged and even to those who merely tolerate its existence. Furthermore, to developed sensibilities the facts of war are revolting and horrifying. To falsify these facts, and by so doing to make war seem less evil than it really is, and our own responsibility in tolerating war less heavy, is doubly to our advantage. By suppressing and distorting the truth, we protect our sensibilities and preserve our self-esteem. Now, language is, among other things, a device which men use for suppressing and distorting the truth. Finding the reality of war too unpleasant to contemplate, we create a verbal alternative to that reality, parallel with it, but in quality quite different from it. That which we contemplate thenceforward is not that to which we react emotionally and upon which we pass our moral judgment, is not war as it is in fact, but the fiction of war as it exists in our pleasantly falsifying verbiage. Our stupidity in using inappropriate language turns out, on analysis, to be the more refined cunning.

3   The most shocking fact about war is that its victims and its instruments are individual human beings, and that these individual human beings are condemned by the monstrous conventions of politics to murder or be murdered in quarrels not their own, to inflict upon the innocent and, innocent themselves of any crime against their enemies, to suffer cruelties of every kind.

4   The language of strategy and politics is designed, so far as it is possible, to conceal this fact, to make it appear as though wars were not fought by individuals drilled to murder one another in cold blood and without provocation, but either by impersonal and therefore wholly nonmoral and impassible forces, or else by personified abstractions.

5   Here are a few examples of the first kind of falsification. In place of "cavalrymen" or "foot-soldiers" military writers like to speak of "sabres" and "rifles." Here is a sentence from a description of the Battle of Marengo: "According to Victor's report, the French retreat was orderly; it is certain, at any rate, that the regiments held together, for the six thousand Austrian sabres found no opportunity to charge home." The battle is between sabres in line and muskets in échelon— a mere clash of ironmongery.

6   On other occasions there is no question of anything so vulgarly material as ironmongery. The battles are between Platonic ideas, between the abstractions of physics and mathematics. Forces interact; weights are flung into scales; masses are set in motion. Or else it is all a matter of geometry. Lines swing and sweep; are protracted or curved; pivot on a fixed point.

7   Alternatively the combatants are personal, in the sense that they are personifications. There is "the enemy," in the singular, making "his" plans, striking "his" blows. The attribution of personal characteristics to collectivities, to geographical expressions, to institutions, is a source, as we shall see, of endless confusions in political thought, of innumerable political mistakes and crimes. Personification in politics is an error which we make because it is to our advantage as egotists to be able to feel violently proud of our country and of ourselves as belonging to it, and to believe that all the misfortunes due to our own mistakes are really the work of the Foreigner. It is easier to feel violently toward a person than toward an abstraction; hence our habit of making political personifications. In some cases military personifications are merely special instances of political personifications. A particular collectivity, the army or the warring nation, is given the name and, along with the name, the attributes of a single person, in order that we may be able to love or hate it more intensely than we could do if we thought of it as what it really is: a number of diverse individuals. In other cases personification is used for the purpose of concealing the fundamental absurdity and monstrosity of war. What is absurd and monstrous about war is that men who have no personal quarrel should be trained to murder one another in cold blood. By personifying opposing armies or countries, we are able to think of war as a conflict between individuals. The same result is obtained by writing of war as though it were carried on exclusively by the generals in command and not by the private soldiers in their armies. ("Rennenkampf had pressed back von Schubert.") The implication in both cases is that war is indistinguishable from a bout of fisticuffs in a bar room. Whereas in reality it is profoundly different. A scrap between two individuals is forgivable; mass murder, deliberately organized, is a monstrous iniquity. We still choose to use war as an instrument of policy; and to comprehend the full wickedness and absurdity of war would therefore be inconvenient. For, once we understood, we should have to make some effort to get rid of the abominable thing. Accordingly, when we talk about war, we use a language which conceals or embellishes its reality. Ignoring the facts, so far as we possibly can, we imply that battles are not fought by soldiers, but by things, principles, allegories, personified collectivities, or (at the most human) by opposing commanders, pitched against one another in single combat. For the same reason, when we have to describe the processes and the results of

war, we employ a rich variety of euphemisms. Even the most violently patriotic and militaristic are reluctant to call a spade by its own name. To conceal their intentions even from themselves, they make use of picturesque metaphors. We find them, for example, clamoring for war planes numerous and powerful enough to go and "destroy the hornets in their nests"—in other words, to go and throw thermite, high explosives and vesicants upon the inhabitants of neighboring countries before they have time to come and do the same to us. And how reassuring is the language of historians and strategists! They write admiringly of those military geniuses who know "when to strike at the enemy's line" (a single combatant deranges the geometrical constructions of a personification); when to "turn the flank"; when to "execute an enveloping movement." As though they were engineers discussing the strength of materials and the distribution of stresses, they talk of abstract entities called "man power" and "fire power." They sum up the long-drawn sufferings and atrocities of trench warfare in the phrase, "a war of attrition"; the massacre and mangling of human beings is assimilated to the grinding of a lens.

8   A dangerously abstract word, which figures in all discussions about war, is "force." Those who believe in organizing collective security by means of military pacts against a possible aggressor are particularly fond of this word. "You cannot," they say, "have international justice unless you are prepared to impose it by force." "Peace-loving countries must unite to use force against aggressive dictatorships." "Democratic institutions must be protected, if need be, by force." And so on.

9   Now, the word "force," when used in reference to human relations, has no single, definite meaning. There is the "force" used by parents when, without resort to any kind of physical violence, they compel their children to act or refrain from acting in some particular way. There is the "force" used by attendants in an asylum when they try to prevent a maniac from hurting himself or others. There is the "force" used by the police when they control a crowd, and that other "force" which they used in a baton charge. And finally there is the "force" used in war. This, of course, varies with the technological devices at the disposal of the belligerents, with the policies they are pursuing; and with the particular circumstances of the war in question. But in general it may be said that, in war, "force" connotes violence and fraud used to the limit of the combatants' capacity.

10   Variations in quantity, if sufficiently great, produce variations in quality. The "force" that is war, particularly modern war, is very different from the "force" that is police action, and the use of the same abstract word to describe the two dissimilar processes is profoundly misleading. (Still more misleading, of course, is the explicit assimilation of a war, waged by allied League-of-Nations powers against an aggressor, to police action against a criminal. The first is the use of violence

and fraud without limit against innocent and guilty alike; the second is the use of strictly limited violence and a minimum of fraud exclusively against the guilty.)

11   Reality is a succession of concrete and particular situations. When we think about such situations we should use the particular and concrete words which apply to them. If we use abstract words which apply equally well (and equally badly) to other, quite dissimilar situations, it is certain that we shall think incorrectly.

12   Let us take the sentences quoted above and translate the abstract word "force" into language that will render (however inadequately) the concrete and particular realities of contemporary warfare.

13   "You cannot have international justice, unless you are prepared to impose it by force." Translated, this becomes: "You cannot have international justice unless you are prepared, with a view to imposing a just settlement, to drop thermite, high explosives and vesicants upon the inhabitants of foreign cities and to have thermite, high explosives and vesicants dropped in return upon the inhabitants of your cities." At the end of this proceeding, justice is to be imposed by the victorious party—that is, if there is a victorious party. It should be remarked that justice was to have been imposed by the victorious party at the end of the last war. But, unfortunately, after four years of fighting, the temper of the victors was such that they were quite incapable of making a just settlement. The Allies are reaping in Nazi Germany what they sowed at Versailles. The victors of the next war will have undergone intensive bombardments with thermite, high explosives and vesicants. Will their temper be better than that of the Allies in 1918? Will they be in a fitter state to make a just settlement? The answer, quite obviously, is: No. It is psychologically all but impossible that justice should be secured by the methods of contemporary warfare.

14   The next two sentences may be taken together. "Peace-loving countries must unit to use force against aggressive dictatorships. Democratic institutions must be protected, if need be, by force." Let us translate. "Peace-loving countries must unite to throw thermite, explosives and vesicants on the inhabitants of countries ruled by aggressive dictators. They must do this, and of course abide the consequences, in order to preserve peace and democratic institutions." Two questions immediately propound themselves. First, is it likely that peace can be secured by a process calculated to reduce the orderly life of our complicated societies to chaos? And, second, is it likely that democratic institutions will flourish in a state of chaos? Again, the answers are pretty clearly in the negative.

15   By using the abstract word "force," instead of terms which at least attempt to describe the realities of war as it is today, the preachers of collective security through military collaboration disguise from themselves and from others, not only the contemporary facts, but also the probable consequences of their favorite policy. The attempt to

secure justice, peace and democracy by "force" seems reasonable enough until we realize, first, that this noncommittal word stands, in the circumstances of our age, for activities which can hardly fail to result in social chaos; and second, that the consequences of social chaos are injustice, chronic warfare and tyranny. The moment we think in concrete and particular terms of the concrete and particular process called "modern war," we see that a policy which worked (or at least didn't result in complete disaster) in the past has no prospect whatever of working in the immediate future. The attempt to secure justice, peace and democracy by means of a "force," which means, at this particular moment of history, thermite, high explosives and vesicants, is about as reasonable as the attempt to put out a fire with a colorless liquid that happens to be, not water, but petrol.

16   What applies to "force" that is war applies in large measure to the "force" that is revolution. It seems inherently very unlikely that social justice and social peace can be secured by thermite, high explosives and vesicants. At first, it may be, the parties in a civil war would hesitate to use such instruments on their fellow-countrymen. But there can be little doubt that, if the conflict were prolonged (as it probably would be between the evenly balanced Right and Left of a highly industrialized society), the combatants would end by losing their scruples.

17   The alternatives confronting us seem to be plain enough. Either we invent and conscientiously employ a new technique for making revolutions and settling international disputes; or else we cling to the old technique and, using "force" (that is to say, thermite, high explosives and vesicants), destroy ourselves. Those who, for whatever motive, disguise the nature of the second alternative under inappropriate language, render the world a grave disservice. They lead us into one of the temptations we find it hardest to resist—the temptation to run away from reality, to pretend that facts are not what they are. Like Shelley (but without Shelley's acute awareness of what he was doing) we are perpetually weaving

> A shroud of talk to hide us from the sun
> Of this familiar life.

We protect our minds by an elaborate system of abstractions, ambiguities, metaphors and similes from the reality we do not wish to know too clearly; we lie to ourselves, in order that we may still have the excuse of ignorance, the alibi of stupidity and incomprehension, possessing which we can continue with a good conscience to commit and tolerate the most monstrous crimes:

> The poor wretch who has learned his only prayers
> From curses, who knows scarcely words enough
> To ask a blessing from his Heavenly Father,

Becomes a fluent phraseman, absolute
And technical in victories and defeats,
And all our dainty terms for fratricide;
Terms which we trundle smoothly o'er our tongues
Like mere abstractions, empty sounds to which
We join no meaning and attach no form!
As if the soldier died without a wound:
As if the fibers of this godlike frame
Were gored without a pang: as if the wretch
Who fell in battle, doing bloody deeds,
Passed off to Heaven translated and not killed;
As though he had no wife to pine for him,
No God to judge him.

18   The language we use about war is inappropriate, and its inappropriateness is designed to conceal a reality so odious that we do not wish to know it. The language we use about politics is also inappropriate; but here our mistake has a different purpose. Our principal aim in this case is to arouse and, having aroused, to rationalize and justify such intrinsically agreeable sentiments as pride and hatred, self-esteem and contempt for others. To achieve this end we speak about the facts of politics in words which more or less completely misrepresent them.

19   The concrete realities of politics are individual human beings, living together in national groups. Politicians—and to some extent we are all politicians—substitute abstractions for these concrete realities, and having done this, proceed to invest each abstraction with an appearance of concreteness by personifying it. For example, the concrete reality of which "Britain" is the abstraction consists of some forty-odd millions of diverse individuals living on an island off the west coast of Europe. The personification of this abstraction appears, in classical fancy-dress and holding a very large toasting fork, on the backside of our copper coinage; appears in verbal form, every time we talk about international politics. "Britain," the abstraction from forty millions of Britons, is endowed with thoughts, sensibilities and emotions, even with a sex—for, in spite of John Bull, the country is always a female.

20   Now, it is of course possible that "Britain" is more than a mere name—is an entity that possesses some kind of reality distinct from that of the individuals constituting the group to which the name is applied. But this entity, if it exists, is certainly not a young lady with a toasting fork; nor is it possible to believe (though some eminent philosophers have preached the doctrine) that it should possess anything in the nature of a personal will. One must agree with T. H. Green that "there can be nothing in a nation, however exalted its

mission, or in a society however perfectly organized, which is not in the persons composing the nation or the society . . . . We cannot suppose a national spirit and will to exist except as the spirit and will of individuals." But the moment we start resolutely thinking about our world in terms of individual persons we find ourselves at the same time thinking in terms of universality. "The great rational religions," writes Professor Whitehead, "are the outcome of the emergence of a religious consciousness that is universal, as distinguished from tribal, or even social. Because it is universal, it introduces the note of solitariness." (And he might have added that, because it is solitary, it introduces the note of universality.) "The reason of this connection between universality and solitude is that universality is a disconnection from immediate surroundings." And conversely the disconnection from immediate surroundings, particularly such social surrounding as the tribe or nation, the insistence on the person as the fundamental reality, leads to the conception of an all-embracing unity.

21   A nation, then, may be more than a mere abstraction, may possess some kind of real existence apart from its constituent members. But there is no reason to suppose that it is a person; indeed, there is every reason to suppose that it isn't. Those who speak as though it were a person (and some go further than this and speak as though it were a personal god) do so, because it is to their interest as egotists to make precisely this mistake.

22   In the case of the ruling class these interests are in part material. The personification of the nation as a sacred being, different from and superior to its constituent members, is merely (I quote the words of a great French jurist, Léon Duguit) "a way of imposing authority by making people believe it is an authority *de jure* and not merely *de facto*." By habitually talking of the nation as though it were a person with thoughts, feelings and a will of its own, the rulers of a country legitimate their own powers. Personification leads easily to deification; and where the nation is deified, its government ceases to be a mere convenience, like drains or a telephone system, and, partaking in the sacredness of the entity it represents, claims to give orders by divine right and demands the unquestioning obedience due to a god. Rulers seldom find it hard to recognize their friends. Hegel, the man who elaborated an inappropriate figure of speech into a complete philosophy of politics, was a favorite of the Prussian government. *"Es ist,"* he had written, *"es ist der Gang Gottes in der Welt, das der Staat ist."* The decoration bestowed on him by Frederick William III was richly deserved.

23   Unlike their rulers, the ruled have no material interest in using inappropriate language about states and nations. For them, the reward of being mistaken is psychological. The personified and deified nation becomes, in the minds of the individuals composing it, a kind of

enlargement of themselves. The superhuman qualities which belong to the young lady with the toasting fork, the young lady with plaits and a brass *soutien-gorge*, the young lady in a Phrygian bonnet, are claimed by individual Englishmen, Germans and Frenchmen as being, at least in part, their own. *Dulce et decorum est pro patria mori.* But there would be no need to die, no need of war, if it had not been even sweeter to boast and swagger for one's country, to hate, despise, swindle and bully for it. Loyalty to the personified nation, or to the personified class or party, justifies the loyal in indulging all those passions which good manners and the moral code do not allow them to display in their relations with their neighbors. The personified entity is a being, not only great and noble, but also insanely proud, vain and touchy; fiercely rapacious; a braggart; bound by no considerations of right and wrong. (Hegel condemned as hopelessly shallow all those who dared to apply ethical standards to the activities of nations. To condone and applaud every iniquity committed in the name of the State was to him a sign of philosophical profundity.) Identifying themselves with this god, individuals find relief from the constraints of ordinary social decency, feel themselves justified in giving rein, within duly prescribed limits, to their criminal proclivities. As a loyal nationalist or party-man, one can enjoy the luxury of behaving badly with a good conscience.

24   The evil passions are further justified by another linguistic error— the error of speaking about certain categories of persons as though they were mere embodied abstractions. Foreigners and those who disagree with us are not thought of as men and women like ourselves and our fellow-countrymen; they are thought of as representatives and, so to say, symbols of a class. In so far as they have any personality at all, it is the personality we mistakenly attribute to their class—a personality that is, by definition, intrinsically evil. We know that the harming or killing of men and women is wrong, and we are reluctant consciously to do what we know to be wrong. But when particular men and women are thought of merely as representatives of a class, which has previously been defined as evil and personified in the shape of a devil, then the reluctance to hurt or murder disappears. Brown, Jones and Robinson are no longer thought of as Brown, Jones and Robinson, but as heretics, gentiles, Yids, niggers, barbarians, Huns, communists, fascists, liberals—whichever the case may be. When they have been called such names and assimilated to the accursed class to which the names apply, Brown, Jones and Robinson cease to be conceived as what they really are—human persons—and become for the users of this fatally inappropriate language mere vermin or, worse, demons whom it is right and proper to destroy as thoroughly and as painfully as possible. Wherever persons are present, questions of morality arise. Rulers of nations and leaders of parties find morality embarrassing. That is why they take such pains to depersonalize their opponents. All propaganda

directed against an opposing group has but one aim: to substitute diabolical abstractions for concrete persons. The propagandist's purpose is to make one set of people forget that certain other sets of people are human. By robbing them of their personality, he puts them outside the pale of moral obligation. Mere symbols can have no rights — particularly when that of which they are symbolical is, by definition, evil.

25   Politics can become moral only on one condition: that its problems shall be spoken of and thought about exclusively in terms of concrete reality; that is to say, of persons. To depersonify human beings and to personify abstractions are complementary errors which lead, by an inexorable logic, to war between nations and to idolatrous worship of the State, with consequent governmental oppression. All current political thought is a mixture, in varying proportions, between thought in terms of concrete realities and thought in terms of depersonified symbols and personified abstractions. In the democratic countries the problems of internal politics are thought about mainly in terms of concrete reality; those of external politics, mainly in terms of abstractions and symbols. In dictatorial countries the proportion of concrete to abstract and symbolic thought is lower than in democratic countries. Dictators talk little of persons, much of personified abstractions, such as the Nation, the State, the Party, and much of depersonified symbols, such as Yids, Bolshies, Capitalists. The stupidity of politicians who talk about a world of persons as though it were not a world of persons is due in the main to self-interest. In a fictitious world of symbols and personified abstractions, rulers find that they can rule more effectively, and the ruled, that they can gratify instincts which the conventions of good manners and the imperatives of morality demand that they should repress. To think correctly is the condition of behaving well. It is also in itself a moral act; those who would think correctly must resist considerable temptations.

Discussion of Theme

1. Huxley's essay seems, at first, to be merely a rather general criticism of the way we use words to deceive ourselves and to falsify facts. Later, the essay evolves into a criticism of this process in two specific areas. What are they?

2. How does the language of politics deceive the public? Do we have a right to concrete expressions of truth in this area, or should we be protected from pain and unpleasantness? Consider, for example, the current practice in describing domestic disasters and battlefield statistics.

3. According to Huxley, why are personification and abstraction introduced into the language of politics? Is the result always detrimental?

4. What does Huxley suggest as an antidote to the abstractions and symbols of the vocabulary of politics?

Discussion of Rhetoric

1. Huxley contrasts certain aspects of feline and human behavior. Is the contrast effective?
2. Find the sentences in paragraph 7 which restate Huxley's thesis. How do they prepare us for the final section of the essay? Could they have been more effectively placed somewhere else?
3. Consider the last two sentences in paragraph 14. What is the name commonly given to questions of this sort? Why?

Writing Assignments

1. By analyzing a war report in a newspaper or news magazine, show how "words falsify facts."
2. To illustrate how a reader or hearer may misunderstand a communication phrased in abstract terms, describe an event or situation in concrete terms. Then describe the same event or situation in abstract terms. Huxley points out that there are many possible interpretations of an abstraction; now translate your abstract description back into a concrete one, but one that differs drastically from the one you started with.

Library Exploration

Read Stuart Chase's *The Tyranny of Words*.

Vocabulary

discrete (1): distinct; separate
vitiate (1): pervert
stratagem (1): a trick or scheme for gaining some end
verbiage (2): diction; wording
échelon (5): troops arranged in steplike formation
euphemisms (7): agreeable expressions used in place of ones that may offend
vesicants (7): substances that cause blistering
attrition (7): wearing down or away
de jure (22): by right or law
de facto (22): in fact
soutien-gorge (23): brassiere
rapacious (23): greedy
proclivities (23): tendencies or inclinations
inexorable (25): unyielding; relentless

29

THE CHICAGO POLICE RIOT

A Summary from the Walker Report

Millions of Americans watched with fascination and horror the violent clashes between police and citizens that took place in Chicago during the week of the 1968 Democratic National Convention. The following article, an excerpt from the report of the official commission created to investigate those events, summarizes the causes of the violence.

1   During the week of the Democratic National Convention, the Chicago police were the targets of mounting provocation by both word and act. It took the form of obscene epithets, and of rocks, sticks, bathroom tiles and even human feces hurled at police by demonstrators. Some of these acts had been planned; others were spontaneous or were themselves provoked by police action. Furthermore, the police had been put on edge by widely published threats of attempts to disrupt both the city and the Convention.

2   That was the nature of the provocation. The nature of the response was unrestrained and indiscriminate police violence on many occasions, particularly at night.

3   That violence was made all the more shocking by the fact that it was often inflicted upon persons who had broken no law, disobeyed no order, made no threat. These included peaceful demonstrators, onlookers, and large numbers of residents who were simply passing through, or happened to live in, the areas where confrontations were occurring.

4   Newsmen and photographers were singled out for assault, and their equipment deliberately damaged. Fundamental police training was ignored; and officers, when on the scene, were often unable to control their men. As one police officer put it: "What happened didn't have anything to do with police work."

5   The violence reached its culmination on Wednesday night.

6   A report prepared by an inspector from the Los Angeles Police Department, present as an official observer, while generally praising the police restraint he had observed in the parks during the week, said this about the events that night:

"There is no question but that many officers acted without restraint and exerted force beyond that necessary under the circumstances. The leadership at the point of conflict did little to prevent such conduct and the direct control of officers by first line supervisors was virtually non-existent."

7   He is referring to the police-crowd confrontation in front of the Conrad Hilton Hotel. Most Americans know about it, having seen the 17-minute sequence played and replayed on their television screens.

8   But most Americans do not know that the confrontation was followed by even more brutal incidents in the Loop side streets. Or that it had been preceded by comparable instances of indiscriminate police attacks on the North Side a few nights earlier when demonstrators were cleared from Lincoln Park and pushed into the streets and alleys of Old Town.

9   How did it start? With the emergence long before convention week of three factors which figured significantly in the outbreak of violence. These were: threats to the city; the city's response; and the conditioning of Chicago police to expect that violence against demonstrators, as against rioters, would be condoned by city officials.

10   The threats to the City were varied. Provocative and inflammatory statements, made in connection with activities planned for convention week, were published and widely disseminated. There were also intelligence reports from informants.

11   Some of this information was absurd, like the reported plan to contaminate the city's water supply with LSD. But some were serious; and both were strengthened by the authorities' lack of any mechanism for distinguishing one from the other.

12   The second factor—the city's response—matched, in numbers and logistics at least, the demonstrators' threats.

13   The city, fearful that the "leaders" would not be able to control their followers, attempted to discourage an inundation of demonstrators by not granting permits for marches and rallies and by making it quite clear that the "law" would be enforced.

14   Government—federal, state and local—moved to defend itself from the threats, both imaginary and real. The preparations were detailed and far ranging: from stationing firemen at each alarm box within a six block radius of the Amphitheatre to staging U.S. Army armored personnel carriers in Soldier Field under Secret Service control. Six thousand Regular Army troops in full field gear, equipped with rifles, flame throwers, and bazookas were airlifted to Chicago on Monday, August 26. About 6,000 Illinois National Guard troops had already been activated to assist the 12,000 member Chicago Police Force.

15   Of course, the Secret Service could never afford to ignore threats

of assassination of Presidential candidates. Neither could the city, against the background of riots in 1967 and 1968, ignore the ever-present threat of ghetto riots, possibly sparked by large numbers of demonstrators, during convention week.

16   The third factor emerged in the city's position regarding the riots following the death of Dr. Martin Luther King and the April 27th peace march to the Civic Center in Chicago.

17   The police were generally credited with restraint in handling the first riots—but Mayor Daley rebuked the Superintendent of Police. While it was later modified, his widely disseminated "shoot to kill arsonists and shoot to maim looters" order undoubtedly had an effect.

18   The effect on police became apparent several weeks later, when they attacked demonstrators, bystanders and media representatives at a Civic Center peace march. There were published criticisms—but the city's response was to ignore the police violence.

19   That was the background. On August 18, 1968, the advance contingent of demonstrators arrived in Chicago and established their base, as planned, in Lincoln Park on the city's Near North Side. Throughout the week, they were joined by others—some from the Chicago area, some from states as far away as New York and California. On the weekend before the convention began, there were about 2,000 demonstrators in Lincoln Park; the crowd grew to about 10,000 by Wednesday.

20   There were, of course, the hippies—the long hair and love beads, the calculated unwashedness, the flagrant banners, the open love-making and disdain for the constraints of conventional society. In dramatic effect, both visual and vocal, these dominated a crowd whose members actually differed widely in physical appearance, in motivation, in political affiliation, in philosophy. The crowd included Yippies come to "do their thing," youngsters working for a political candidate, professional people with dissenting political views, anarchists and determined revolutionaries, motorcycle gangs, black activists, young thugs, police and secret service undercover agents. There were demonstrators waving the Viet Cong flag and the red flag of revolution and there were the simply curious who came to watch and, in many cases, became willing or unwilling participants.

21   To characterize the crowd, then, as entirely hippie-Yippie, entirely "New Left," entirely anarchist, or entirely youthful political dissenters is both wrong and dangerous. The stereotyping that did occur helps to explain the emotional reaction of both police and public during and after the violence that occurred.

22   Despite the presence of some revolutionaries, the vast majority of the demonstrators were intent on expressing by peaceful means their dissent either from society generally or from the administration's policies in Vietnam.

23   Most of those intending to join the major protest demonstrations
scheduled during convention week did not plan to enter the Amphitheatre and disrupt the proceedings of the Democratic convention,
did not plan aggressive acts of physical provocation against the authorities, and did not plan to use rallies of demonstrators to stage an assault
against any person, institution, or place of business. But while it is
clear that most of the protesters in Chicago had no intention of initiating
violence, this is not to say that they did not expect it to develop.

24   It was the clearing of the demonstrators from Lincoln Park that led
directly to the violence: symbolically, it expressed the city's opposition
to the protesters; literally, it forced the protesters into confrontation
with police in Old Town and the adjacent neighborhoods.

25   The Old Town area near Lincoln Park was a scene of police ferocity
exceeding that shown on television on Wednesday night. From Sunday
night through Tuesday night, incidents of intense and indiscriminate
violence occurred in the streets after police had swept the park clear
of demonstrators.

26   Demonstrators attacked too. And they posed difficult problems for
police as they persisted in marching through the streets, blocking
traffic and intersections. But it was the police who forced them out of
the park and into the neighborhood. And on the part of the police
there was enough wild club swinging, enough cries of hatred, enough
gratuitous beating to make the conclusion inescapable that individual
policemen, and lots of them, committed violent acts far in excess of
the requisite force for crowd dispersal or arrest. To read dispassionately
the hundreds of statements describing at firsthand the events of Sunday
and Monday nights is to become convinced of the presence of what
can only be called a police riot.

27   Here is an eyewitness talking about Monday night:

> The demonstrators were forced out onto Clark Street and once
> again a traffic jam developed. Cars were stopped, the horns began
> to honk, people couldn't move, people got gassed inside their
> cars, people got stoned inside their cars, police were the objects
> of stones, and taunts, mostly taunts. As you must understand,
> most of the taunting of the police was verbal. There were stones
> thrown of course, but for the most part it was verbal. But there
> were stones being thrown and of course the police were responding
> with tear gas and clubs and every time they could get near enough
> to a demonstrator they hit him.
> But again you had this problem within—this really turned
> into a police problem. They pushed everybody out of the park,
> but this night there were a lot more people in the park than there
> had been during the previous night and Clark Street was just full
> of people and in addition now was full of gas because the police

were using gas on a much larger scale this night. So the police were faced with the task, which took them about an hour or so, of hitting people over the head and gassing them enough to get them out of Clark Street, which they did.

28   But police action was not confined to the necessary force, even in clearing the park:

29   A young man and his girl friend were both grabbed by officers. He screamed, "We're going, we're going," but they threw him into the pond. The officers grabbed the girl, knocked her to the ground, dragged her along the embankment and hit her with their batons on her head, arms, back and legs. The boy tried to scramble up the embankment to her, but police shoved him back in the water at least twice. He finally got to her and tried to pull her in the water, away from the police. He was clubbed on the head five or six times. An officer shouted, "Let's get the fucking bastards!" but the boy pulled her in the water and the police left.

30   Like the incident described above, much of the violence witnessed in Old Town that night seems malicious or mindless:

> There were pedestrians. People who were not part of the demonstration were coming out of a tavern to see what the demonstration was . . . and the officers indiscriminately started beating everybody on the street who was not a policeman.

31   Another scene:

> There was a group of about six police officers that moved in and started beating two youths. When one of the officers pulled back his nightstick to swing, one of the youths grabbed it from behind and started beating on the officer. At this point about ten officers left everybody else and ran after this youth, who turned down Wells and ran to the left.
>
> But the officers went to the right, picked up another youth, assuming he was the one they were chasing, and took him into an empty lot and beat him. And when they got him to the ground, they just kicked him ten times—the wrong youth, the innocent youth who had been standing there.

32   A federal legal official relates an experience on Tuesday evening.

> I then walked one block north where I met a group of 12–15 policemen. I showed them my identification and they permitted me to walk with them. The police walked one block west. Numerous people were watching us from their windows and balconies. The police yelled profanities at them, taunting them to come down where the police would beat them up. The police stopped a number of people on the street demanding identification. They

verbally abused each pedestrian and pushed one or two without hurting them. We walked back to Clark Street and began to walk north where the police stopped a number of people who appeared to be protesters, and ordered them out of the area in a very abusive way. One protester who was walking in the opposite direction was kneed in the groin by a policeman who was walking towards him. The boy fell to the ground and swore at the policeman who picked him up and threw him to the ground.We continued to walk toward the command post. A derelict who appeared to be very intoxicated, walked up to the policeman and mumbled something that was incoherent. The policeman pulled from his belt a tin container and sprayed its contents into the eyes of the derelict, who stumbled around and fell on his face.

33   It was on these nights that the police violence against media representatives reached its peak. Much of it was plainly deliberate. A newsman was pulled aside on Monday by a detective acquaintance of his who said: "The word is being passed to get newsmen." Individual newsmen were warned, "You take my picture tonight and I'm going to get you." Cries of "get the camera" preceded individual attacks on photographers.

34   A newspaper photographer describes Old Town on Monday at about 9:00 p.m.:

When the people arrived at the intersection of Wells and Division, they were not standing in the streets. Suddenly a column of policemen ran out from the alley. They were reinforcements. They were under control but there seemed to be no direction. One man was yelling, "Get them up on the sidewalks, turn them around." Very suddenly the police charged the people on the sidewalks and began beating their heads. A line of cameramen was 'trapped' along with the crowd along the sidewalks, and the police went down the line chopping away at the cameras.

A network cameraman reports that on the same night:

I just saw this guy coming at me with his nightstick and I had the camera up. The tip of his stick hit me right in the mouth, then I put my tongue up there and I noticed that my tooth was gone. I turned around then to try to leave and then this cop came up behind me with his stick and he jabbed me in the back.

All of a sudden these cops jumped out of the police cars and started just beating the hell out of people. And before anything else happened to me, I saw a man holding a Bell & Howell camera with big wide letters on it, saying "CBS." He apparently had been hit by a cop. And cops were standing around and there was blood streaming down his face. Another policeman was running after me and saying, "Get the fuck out of here." And I heard another guy scream, "Get their fucking cameras." And the next thing I know I was being hit on the head, and I think on the back, and I was just forced down on the ground at the corner of Division and Wells.

35 If the intent was to discourage coverage, it was successful in at least one case. A photographer from a news magazine says that finally, "I just stopped shooting, because every time you push the flash, they look at you and they are screaming about, 'Get the fucking photographers and get the film.'"

36 There is some explanation for the media-directed violence. Camera crews on at least two occasions did stage violence and fake injuries. Demonstrators did sometimes step up their activities for the benefit TV cameras. Newsmen and photographers' blinding lights did get in the way of police clearing streets, sweeping the park and dispersing demonstrators. Newsmen did, on occasion, disobey legitimate police orders to "move" or "clear the streets." News reporting of events did seem to the police to be anti-Chicago and anti-police.

37 But was the response appropriate to the provocation?

38 Out of 300 newsmen assigned to cover the parks and streets of Chicago during convention week, more than 60 (about 20%) were involved in incidents resulting in injury to themselves, damage to their equipment, or their arrest. Sixty-three newsmen were physically attacked by police; in 13 of these instances, photographic or recording equipment was intentionally damaged.

39 The violence did not end with either demonstrators or newsmen on the North Side on Sunday, Monday and Tuesday. It continued in Grant Park on Wednesday. It occurred on Michigan Avenue in front of the Conrad Hilton Hotel, as already described. A high-ranking Chicago police commander admits that on that occasion the police "got out of control." This same commander appears in one of the most vivid scenes of the entire week, trying desperately to keep individual policemen from beating demonstrators as he screams, "For Christ's sake, stop it!"

40 Thereafter, the violence continued on Michigan Avenue and on the side streets running into Chicago's Loop. A federal official describes how it began:

> I heard a 10-1 call [policeman in trouble] on either my radio or one of the other hand sets carried by men with me and then heard "Car 100—sweep." With a roar of motors, squads, vans and three-wheelers came from east, west and north into the block north of Jackson. The crowd scattered. A big group ran west on Jackson, with a group of blue shirted policemen in pursuit, beating at them with clubs. Some of the crowd would jump into door-

ways and the police would rout them out. The action was very tough. In my judgment, unnecessarily so. The police were hitting with a vengeance and quite obviously with relish. . . ."

41   What followed was a club-swinging melee. Police ranged the streets striking anyone they could catch. To be sure, demonstrators threw things at policemen and at police cars; but the weight of violence was overwhelmingly on the side of the police. A few examples will give the flavor of that night in Chicago:

42   "At the corner of Congress Plaza and Michigan," states a doctor, "was gathered a group of people, numbering between thirty and forty. They were trapped against a railing [along a ramp leading down from Michigan Avenue to an underground parking garage] by several policemen on motorcycles. The police charged the people on motorcycles and struck about a dozen of them, knocking several of them down. About twenty standing there jumped over the railing. On the other side of the railing was a three-to-four-foot drop. None of the people who were struck by the motorcycles appeared to be seriously injured. However, several of them were limping as if they had been run over on their feet."

43   A UPI reporter witnessed these attacks, too. He relates in his statement that one officer, "with a smile on his face and a fanatical look in his eyes, was standing on a three-wheel cycle, shouting, 'Wahoo, wahoo,' and trying to run down people on the sidewalk." The reporter says he was chased thirty feet by the cycle.

44   A priest who was in the crowd says he saw a "boy, about fourteen or fifteen, white, standing on top of an automobile yelling something which was unidentifiable. Suddenly a policeman pulled him down from the car and beat him to the ground by striking him three or four times with a nightstick. Other police joined in . . . and they eventually shoved him to a police van.

45   "A well-dressed woman saw this incident and spoke angrily to a nearby police captain. As she spoke, another policeman came up from behind her and sprayed something in her face with an aerosol can. He then clubbed her to the ground. He and two other policemen then dragged her along the ground to the same paddy wagon and threw her in."

46   "I ran west on Jackson," a witness states. "West of Wabash, a line of police stretching across both sidewalks and the street charged after the small group I was in. Many people were clubbed and maced as they ran. Some weren't demonstrators at all, but were just pedestrians who didn't know how to react to the charging officers yelling 'Police!' "

47   "A wave of police charged down Jackson," another witness relates. "Fleeing demonstrators were beaten indiscriminately and a temporary, makeshift first aid station was set up on the corner of State and Jackson.

Two men lay in pools of blood, their heads severely cut by clubs. A minister moved amongst the crowd, quieting them, brushing aside curious onlookers, and finally asked a policeman to call an ambulance, which he agreed to do . . ."

48   An Assistant U.S. Attorney later reported that "the demonstrators were running as fast as they could but were unable to get out of the way because of the crowds in front of them. I observed the police striking numerous individuals, perhaps 20 to 30. I saw three fall down and then overrun by the police. I observed two demonstrators who had multiple cuts on their heads. We assisted one who was in shock into a passer-by's car."

49   Police violence was a fact of convention week. Were the policemen who committed it a minority? It appears certain that they were—but one which has imposed some of the consequences of its actions on the majority, and certainly on their commanders. There has been no public condemnation of these violators of sound police procedures and common decency by either their commanding officers or city officials. Nor (at the time this Report is being completed—almost three months after the convention) has any disciplinary action been taken against most of them. That some policemen lost control of themselves under exceedingly provocative circumstances can perhaps be understood; but not condoned. If no action is taken against them, the effect can only be to discourage the majority of policemen who acted responsibly, and further weaken the bond between police and community.

50   Although the crowds were finally dispelled on the nights of violence in Chicago, the problems they represent have not been. Surely this is not the last time that a violent dissenting group will clash head-on with those whose duty it is to enforce the law. And the next time the whole world will still be watching.

Discussion of Theme

1. This study states, "Government—federal, state, and local—moved to defend itself from the threats, both imaginary and real." What were the imaginary threats, according to the authors? The real threats? Were the precautions taken by the Chicago police excessive?
2. Who were the demonstrators? Were they, for the most part, members of one particular group, or did they represent many groups and interests?
3. In what sense do the authors believe the police response to the news media was inappropriate to the provocation? What do they think was the reason for this response?
4. What conclusions are arrived at in this article? Could a similar situation develop at a future convention?

Discussion of Rhetoric

1. Some of the phrases and word choices indicate the authors' attitudes. Find examples of these. Is this an unbiased report? Is the language loaded with emotional overtones?
2. Examine the structure of the first sentence in paragraph 3. What rhetorical device is used? Find other places where this device is used.
3. How convincingly do the authors build their argument? What kinds of evidence do they use to support it?
4. Examine the last sentence of this essay. Is it an effective closing statement? What does it indicate about the authors' own views?

Writing Assignments

1. If you disagree with the conclusions of the Walker Report, present your views in a theme. Do not rely solely on opinion; you must cite evidence, as the authors of the Walker Report have done.
2. In a theme, outline your plan for preventing the occurrence at future conventions of the kind of events described in the Walker Report.
3. In general, are the police of our nation misunderstood? Or are many of them guilty of brutality? Give your views in a theme.

Library Exploration

The Chicago convention and its attendant violence were the subject of much discussion and writing. Read some of the news coverage of the convention and some articles analyzing the events of that week.

Vocabulary

epithets (1): disparaging or insulting names
disseminated (10): spread widely
inundation (13): flood
gratuitous (26): uncalled for
melee (41): brawl; free for all
condoned (49): accepted without protest or censure   . .

30

IS BREAKING THE LAW EVER JUSTIFIABLE?

Joseph L. Sax

Is strict adherence to the letter of the law necessary in all situations in order to avoid anarchy? The author, a professor of law at the University of Michigan, concludes that enforcement of the law must be guided by a sense of justice.

1   Nobody is opposed to civil disobedience; people simply want the laws that they deem important to be vigorously enforced and those they consider unfair to be ignored. Most motorists consider the idea of a speed trap outrageous, but rarely complain when policemen conceal themselves in public washrooms to ferret out homosexuals. The annual antics of American Legion conventioneers are viewed as harmless enough fun, but let political protestors go out in the streets and all the rigors of the law relating to trespass, obstruction of traffic, and disturbing the peace are suddenly remembered. . . .

2   Through the miracle of prosecutorial discretion—a device central to the operation of the legal system, but widely ignored in discussions of civil disobedience—criminality can be, and is, produced or ignored virtually at will by law enforcement officials. . . .

3   Justice Jackson once said that "a prosecutor has more control over life, liberty, and reputation than any other person in America . . . he can choose his defendant . . . a prosecutor stands a fair chance of finding at least a technical violation of some act on the part of almost anyone." No more profound statement was ever made about the legal system. . . .

4   In fact, no society could operate if it did not tolerate a great deal of technically or arguably illegal conduct on the ground that certain laws were obsolescent and others unwise as written or as applied to particular situations. A few weeks ago, newspapers carried the story of a man who had lured several boys to a mountain cabin, bound and then sexually abused them. One of the boys worked himself free, seized a rifle, and killed his abductor. The local prosecutor announced that no proceedings against the boy were contemplated, a result undoubtedly approved by every reader. Because the law of self-defense is so restrictive in permitting the use of deadly force, a technical case of murder might have been made out against the boy; the circumstances,

however, made clear that it would have been unjust to prosecute. It is not strict obedience to the law, but the sense of justice, which we require in the administration of the legal system.

5   The same breadth of discretion which produced justice in the case of the abducted boy can be turned toward less attractive ends, depending on the inclinations of those who are charged with administering the law. . . . Thus, the Southern oligarchs were not indicted for criminal conspiracy when they produced their massive resistance campaign against the school integration decision, or led the fight to stand in the schoolhouse door, while Dr. Spock and other war resisters were readily brought to trial under the umbrella of the vague and amorphous conspiracy doctrine.

6   No one who sat through the four weeks of trial in which Benjamin Spock, William Sloane Coffin, Mitchell Goodman, and Michael Ferber were convicted of conspiracy to abet violation of the draft law could have doubted that Judge Francis Ford was persuaded of the rightness of the government's case against them, or that the trial reflected his persuasion. . . . The possibilities for judicial management were most clearly illuminated by the way in which Judge Ford handled the question of the Vietnam war. A principal issue which the defense wished to raise was that the conduct of the Vietnam war violated international treaties governing such questions as the treatment of civilians and devastation of cities and towns. If the conduct of the war was illegal, the defendants argued, then to advocate refusal to participate in the war would be lawful, for it is not a crime to counsel one to refuse to do an illegal act. Moreover, even if the defendants were wrong about the legality of the war, they might have been found to have had a reasonable and good-faith belief in its illegality. Such a belief might itself have been sufficient to produce an acquittal under the legal precedents governing their case.

7   For each of these reasons it was tactically essential to the defendants that they be permitted to introduce evidence about the conduct of the war. . . . Had the judge permitted such evidence to be introduced, and had the jury been told that they might have acquitted upon finding the defendant's beliefs to be reasonable and held in good faith, the chances for acquittal would obviously have been vastly increased. . . .

8   The prosecutor failed to remind the jury of the extent to which their decision had been tied to a string that was tied to Francis Ford's inclinations, or that they wouldn't have been there at all had not some prosecutor decided that these five people, out of the thousands who had acted similarly, ought to be tried.

9   There is no answer to the question of whether Dr. Spock and his co-defendants violated "the law." It is not that law imposes no constraints upon a judge; it is simply that there is so much room for maneuver within those constraints that either of two conflicting results can

frequently be produced. Francis Ford presided over their conviction; another judge could have found a dozen cogent reasons, all supported by precedent and good legal logic, to have dismissed the indictment before the trial ever began. . . .

10   Since the law could have been used either to acquit or convict, the only truly relevant question is whether it was *just* that the law be used to convict. It is no easy task to make lawyers peek out from behind that supposedly value-free facade, "the law," and begin to talk about unjust laws and unjust administration of the law; but out they must come and face the reality of prosecutorial and judicial discretion. . . .

11   The first question is what social good is to be achieved by incarcerating men like Spock, Coffin, Goodman, and Ferber. They do not present the immediate danger to others of those who commit violent acts. Indeed, by advocating a form of passive resistance to governmental fiat, they operate at one of the least abrasive levels of conduct respecting an impact on the rights or property of others.

12   Moreover, the nature of their resistance is such that a layer of governmental decision is always imposed between their action and the prospect of harm to others. For example, it is clearly less intrusive for one opposed to school integration to boycott the schools than it is to stand in the doorway and prevent others from entering. And the boycott is very far removed from the acts of those who express their dissent by throwing a stone or a bomb. This is not to suggest that passive resistance should always be insulated from legal sanctions, but merely that the society's willingness to tolerate such conduct should be much greater than for direct action.

13   Another conventional rationale for incarceration is the desire to deter others similarly inclined. Where dissenting political activity is involved, history strongly suggests the inefficacy of such a response. One is hard-pressed to cite a political movement which has been suppressed through the jailing of its leaders. While it was said in the Spock-Coffin case that the prosecution was not directed at ideology, but rather at particular conduct, the record suggests the dubiousness of the distinction made by the government between thought and action.

14   The defendants were charged only with talking and publishing, collecting and returning some draft cards, and engaging in peaceful demonstrations. Even the government did not urge that any of this conduct in itself put a significant burden on the prosecution of its policies. The essence of the government's case was that the defendants' persuasiveness and prestige were an incitement to young men to resist the draft—not that their touching of draft cards, or any such formal acts, were at the heart of the danger which they supposedly posed to the state. Yet it was the formal act of participating in a draft card return which made the government's technical legal case against them. Upon

such sands is the difference between criminality and innocence built in "the law." A common sense inquiry into the justice of their prosecution makes it easy to see that it was their respectability, ideology, and forcefulness which were really at stake. Those elements are not likely to be amenable to incarceration.

15   It is also important to ask whether the society is likely to be affirmatively benefited by the defendants' acts. Here two considerations apply. Are they raising an important issue which ought to be confronted by the public, and are they raising it in as minimally abrasive a way as circumstances and the limitations of legal institutions permit? Certainly the former question can be answered affirmatively; the attempt to promote an investigation of the conduct of the Vietnam war in light of American treaty obligations is decidedly a matter of great public importance. And the inability to get that issue raised in any conventional proceeding, such as the formal committee of inquiry which defendant Marcus Raskin had been urging, invites some degree of tolerance for their unconventional conduct. This element of a constructive goal in their acts ought to weigh heavily in vindication of their conduct and distinguish it from activity which is limited to active obstruction of a matter adequately settled through some political or legal institution.

16   As one turns away from legalistic thinking about the problems of protest, it becomes apparent that no large, general formulae are going to resolve the infinitely varied issues which arise. In the common situation where a group of housewives block a bulldozer's path to protest the destruction of a park, for example, there are at least two good reasons to refrain from prosecution at the outset, though technically a conviction might easily be obtained for trespassing or the obstruction of traffic. Often such a maneuver is designed to inform the general public of an unknown situation and to promote more serious consideration by the appropriate public officials.

17   Certainly these are acceptable goals, and as a practical matter only newspaper publicity is likely to be an effective prod. Considering the tendency of the papers to ignore less dramatic moves and the generally minimal adverse impact on the project by a few days' obstruction, the ladies' tactic would seem an appropriate and tolerable means of promoting the political process. We ought not to balk at taking into account the reality that a neighborhood group is unlikely to be very effective in going through the more conventional channels used by established lobbies or that they are unlikely to have the means to produce a substantial paid advertising campaign.

18   Once having achieved appropriate attention, however, the social benefit of their protest is generally exhausted; having been prodded, the political process in an area such as this tends to be viable, and the public need not accommodate itself to perpetual obstruction. In fact,

this is precisely the way such matters are usually resolved; prosecutorial discretion is exercised to refrain from initiating a criminal prosecution at the early publicity stage of protest. We accommodate to a degree of civil disobedience whose social usefulness outweighs its detriments, and hang "the law" which says obstructing traffic is a crime.

19 Refusal to pay income taxes for reasons of political protest presents another variant of the problem. The device is a useful one, for the refusal to pay taxes is a serious act and the degree to which it is adopted on a particular issue can be a significant measure of the breadth and depth of public feeling on that issue. While a government cannot be expected simply to ignore the nonpayment of taxes, it has at its command an intermediate device whereby it can accommodate to both the positive and negative aspects of such refusals.

20 Where political protest is involved in the refusal, the government can refrain from criminal prosecution while going forward to recover the money due by attaching other assets of the taxpayer. This process involves some cost and inconvenience to the taxpayer, as it does to the government; yet from the point of view of both, the price thus paid is small considering the benefits of promoting vigorous interchange between them. Again, this is a device which the government seems to use with many tax protests; and again the rigors of the civil disobedience dilemma are resolved at the low visibility level of a discretionary decision.

21 As one moves on toward more overt direct action, such as the recent situation in which the Rev. Philip Berrigan poured blood over some draft board records in protest against the Vietnam war, the problem obviously becomes more difficult. Nonetheless, certain guidelines can be used to ask how accommodating we ought to be. Certainly it is relevant to weigh the symbolic content of the act against its adverse impact on the state. Where only a few records are defaced, and they are easily replaced or duplicated, and where the protest involves an issue as imminent in its impact on human life as war, it is reasonable to ask for a substantial degree of tolerance.

22 Whatever the statute relating to the destruction of government records might say, or however the free speech provision might be read by lawyers, it is the essence of a justly administered system that it be able to distinguish between an act with so little destructive impact and one in which whole sets of files were systematically destroyed. And even in such a case, consideration ought at least to be given to the moral differential between property destruction and the effort to preserve life from the ravages of war.

23 It is precisely these distinctions which the formal legal system seems to be so unwilling to consider, as evidenced by the Supreme Court decision this year upholding the conviction of a draft-card

burner; that, surely, was an act overwhelmingly of protest content, with only the most trivial justification of need for possession of Selective Service documents by individual registrants.

24   Both the draft-card burning case and that of Father Berrigan— in which sentences of six years were imposed—are illustrative of another element in the formal legal system produced by its unwillingness to recognize a certain tolerant flexibility as an essential of justice. This is the general refusal to review sentences.

25   It is fruitless to argue abstractly, as the debates over civil disobedience usually do, about whether Father Berrigan should have been convicted. The real issue is whether we ought to be willing in substantial measure to accommodate ourselves to such protests as his in recognition of their social value. There would be little to debate if Berrigan had been sentenced to a symbolic 30 days in jail; the injustice of his case is the extraordinarily vindictive nature of the sentence, by which he is classed with those who commit the most vicious crimes against the personal liberty of others.

26   Similarly irrelevant is the fear that every man will become a law unto himself. That is not the issue at all; no one in his right mind would suggest that a man should be exculpated from criminal responsibility simply because he thinks he ought to be. Rather, the issue is whether the public will be willing to tolerate *some* conduct that policemen, prosecutors, and judges think ought not to be tolerated.

27   The principal weapon available to implement a counterforce to such officials is an independent public unwilling to abdicate consideration of the justice with which the law is enforced. Where the criminal law is employed against political opponents of government, such independence is most urgently needed, lest self-interest affect the usual restraint through which justice and the law are harmonized.

28   A public less bedazzled by the mystique of "the law" and more willing to look through to the question of justness will inevitably be strengthened in its ability to impose upon public officials pressure to be less (or, as the case may be, more) vigorous in seeking to attribute criminality to particular kinds of conduct.

29   A substantial outcry by the press and general public against the Spock trial would have gone far to stifle the prospect of other such prosecutions; instead, we got the widespread response that "the law" left the government little choice but to proceed as it did. Sometimes more direct action may be required. Jurors may simply have to refuse to convict, or grand jurors to indict. An independent citizenry has ways.

30   Finally, it should be noted that at no point is it suggested that weight ought to be given to the fact that the actor is sincerely and conscientiously committed to his point of view. That issue is one of the typical red herrings thrust into ordinary civil disobedience debates.

As is often and correctly pointed out, one can be as sincere and con-scientious about exterminating the Jews as about ending the war in Vietnam. It is not sincerity that counts, but the justness of one's goals and the appropriateness of the means employed to reach them. The greatest danger of all is that an excessive focusing upon the legality of situations tends to blind one to the obligation to make humane judgments. . . .

31   A society which cares about itself requires a citizenry that is ready to see a moral difference between one who protests against the killing in a place such as Vietnam and one who protests to prevent black children from getting a decent education. To abdicate that responsi-bility is only to begin the march in law-abiding lockstep toward moral oblivion.

Discussion of Theme

1. What is prosecutorial discretion? Judicial discretion? How might both affect people who commit acts of civil disobedience?
2. Does the author believe that men like Spock and Coffin should be sent to prison? Do you agree with his conclusions?
3. What can society gain from civil protest? What can it lose?
4. Should the lawbreaker's sincerity have any bearing on the disposition of civil-disobedience cases? Should it be weighed by the judge in his deliberations?

Discussion of Rhetoric

1. This article was written by a professor of law. If his diction is an indication, is he writing for fellow lawyers or for educated laymen?
2. The author poses a question in his title. Does he answer it? If so, where? Or is the reader left to deduce the author's reply?
3. This essay has a clearly defined introduction and conclusion. Find these parts of the article, and indicate why they are distinct from the body of the essay.
4. In paragraphs 16, 17, 19, and 20, the author gives examples of other types of social protest, implying that they are analogous to the protests against the war in Vietnam. Are the analogies valid? Is their primary function to explain or to persuade?

Writing Assignments

1. Much discussion has taken place in recent years over the issue of "law and order." What does this expression mean to you?
2. Which would you ultimately follow: your conscience or the law? Explain your answer, using several hypothetical cases as examples.
3. What proposals could you make for the improvement of the American system of justice?

Library Exploration

Read the newspaper accounts of several war-protest trials, including that of Dr. Spock. Does the general opinion seem to be that justice was secured for the defendants?

Vocabulary

obsolescent (4): outmoded
oligarchs (5): members of a ruling clique
amorphous (5): without definite form or shape
cogent (9): compelling or convincing because of sound argument
incarcerating (11): imprisoning
fiat (11): an authoritative order or decree
abrasive (11): irritating
amenable (14): ready to submit or yield
viable (18): capable of growth and development; workable
imminent (21): about to happen
exculpated (26): freed from blame

31

WHAT POLICEMEN REALLY DO

Herman Goldstein

Most people think that the police-
man's job is to initiate criminal
prosecutions. The following article
makes it clear that this is only one
of his duties.

1   The police function in two worlds. They play an integral part, along with the prosecutor, the courts, and correctional agencies, in the operation of the criminal justice system. As the first agency in the system, their primary responsibility is to initiate a criminal action against those who violate the law.

2   This is a highly structured role, defined by statutes and court decisions and subjected to strict controls.

3   The second world is less easily defined. It comprises all aspects of police functioning that are unrelated to the processing of an accused person through the criminal system. Within this world, a police department seeks to prevent crimes, abates nuisances, resolves disputes, controls traffic and crowds, furnishes information, and provides a wide range of other miscellaneous services to the citizenry. In carrying out these functions, officers frequently make use of the authority which is theirs by virtue of their role in the criminal process—the first of their two worlds. Thus, the ability of a police officer to resolve a dispute and to eliminate a nuisance stems, in large measure, from widespread recognition of the fact that he has the authority to initiate criminal prosecutions. Indeed, in some situations, a police officer may actually exercise his authority—for example, by arresting an intoxicated person for safekeeping—even though he has no intention to initiate a criminal prosecution.

4   Police spend most of their time functioning in the second of these two worlds. . . . [Yet] police agencies are geared primarily to deal with crime. This is reflected in all aspects of their operations—in recruitment standards, in the content of training programs, in operating procedures and, perhaps most importantly, in the firm set of values and the rather narrow orientation which the police generally bring to the handling of those noncriminal matters that are included in the broad range of police functions. "Real" police work is viewed by police officers

as the investigation of criminal activity and the identification and apprehension of offenders. . . .

5   The manner in which the service role is performed is of special importance in molding citizen attitudes toward the police. Within the ghetto, the police are frequently called upon to handle domestic disputes, to assist in disciplining juveniles, and to arrange for the proper care of neglected children and of adults who are mentally or physically ill. In the ghetto more than in any other part of the city, they are the recipients of numerous complaints regarding such matters as lack of adequate heat, the presence of rats, and the accumulation of rubbish or garbage. And they are frequently presented with complicated personal problems of a legal, financial, and social nature that require disentangling.

6   A number of factors account for police involvement in such matters. Ghetto residents, lacking family ties and suffering the anonymity common to the ghetto, frequently do not have a circle of relatives or friends to whom to turn in time of need. Often new to the community and lacking education, they do not have the knowledge that would enable them to seek out governmental and private services. Moreover, they are not in a position to do battle on their own with their landlords, their employers, their merchants, or various governmental agencies.

7   Against this background, the police are recognized as the only agency of government that has a 24-hour-a-day, 7-day-a-week presence in the ghetto, that will usually respond quickly to a call for assistance, and that has sufficiently broad authority—whether-real or imagined— to permit effective action in resolving conflicts and in obtaining needed services.

8   The conditions under which the need for these social services develops are such that one could anticipate considerable difficulty in attempting to separate them from the police function. A social agency, for example, would have to make a substantial staff available around the clock if it were to approximate the built-in citywide capability of a police force to handle such requests. Moreover, there is no easy way to determine, in advance of responding to a call for assistance, whether the principal need is for one trained as a social worker or for one having the authority and training of a police officer. A telephone report of a minor family argument may, on response, require that a police officer intervene in a physical struggle—often involving a knife or other weapon.

9   While most police agencies currently respond to all such requests for help, the nature of the response is generally left to the individual officer. If he is inclined to be helpful, he will improvise a solution, drawing upon his past experience, his knowledge of available resources, and, perhaps most importantly, his imagination. The un-

interested officer, on the other hand, will seek to terminate the contact as soon as possible, once he has established that there is no substantial criminal involvement.

10   The absence of an organized, institutional response to situations that are noncriminal in nature is reflected at various points in the administration of a police force. For example, relatively little time is devoted to such matters in police training programs. In a recent study of police handling of domestic disturbances, it was found that one large metropolitan police force devoted only one hour of its 490-hour recruit training program to the handling of all kinds of disturbances— and this despite the fact that the teaching outline used for the one-hour session acknowledges that "disturbance calls outnumber any of the other type of calls that the officer receives." Similarly, traditional methods for measuring and rewarding the efficiency of both individual officers and organizational units place no positive value on the quality of the police response in other than crime-related situations.

11   There are, however, some indications of movement to improve that segment of police activity outside of the criminal process.

12   Among the earliest programs launched were those designed to establish increased contact between the police and identifiable leaders of the ghetto community. In their infancy, these programs suffered because of a failure to involve the "real" leaders and because of a frequent reluctance on the part of the police to make the effort a two-way dialogue. Now, in several cities, operating police personnel and representative members of the community are being brought together for an extended period of time in an effort to achieve greater mutual understanding. One of the first such programs was launched in 1967 in Grand Rapids, Mich., where police officers and citizens spend as much as 20 working days together over several months, with the guidance of a staff of social psychologists.

13   In a number of jurisdictions, the police have undertaken to respond to service needs by new programs of direct assistance and referral to other agencies. One of the most interesting efforts has been launched in New York City where an experimental program, the Family Crisis Intervention Project, has been initiated to explore the value of having specially trained officers respond to situations involving domestic disturbances. The officers seek initially to reduce tensions by talking to the involved parties. They then try to get enough information to determine if referral to another service agency will be helpful. All cases are followed up, both by reviewing the actions of the officers and by determining if the parties have sought out the assistance offered. In San Francisco, police are now assigned full time to assisting young men with police records to get jobs. And in Atlanta, officers are assigned to antipoverty centers to assist juveniles in obtaining available services. A general program of this kind has been established in Winston-Salem,

N.C., where a special unit provides direct assistance and referral to welfare and other agencies to meet a variety of citizen problems.

14   The desire to provide a more adequate response to complaints regarding a wide range of city government services has led to the creation in some cities of formal procedures by which the police process such complaints. In St. Louis and Baltimore, police man "storefront" offices where one of the primary duties is the receipt and funneling of grievances against various agencies. And in Chicago and several other cities, the police have instituted a program under which department employees ferret out situations that are commonly the subject of complaint and report them to the appropriate municipal agency.

15   The police are going beyond this in some cities, taking the initiative in identifying policies and practices of other governmental agencies which are in need of correction. For example, a few police departments have pressed other agencies to extend the operational hours of swimming pools on hot nights, to provide more adequate playground facilities, and to turn on fire hydrants for recreational purposes. A major difficulty is the lack of responsiveness on the part of agencies that do not feel the same sense of urgency as is felt by the police. . . .

16   While efforts such as these are significant, they hardly begin to fill the need. They touch upon but a few of the more obvious aspects of police functioning that require attention, leaving substantial areas unaffected. Moreover, where such programs do exist, they are of greatly varying quality. The National Advisory Commission on Civil Disorders, which reviewed these efforts as part of its over-all survey of "police-community relations programs," concluded that many were simply public relations ventures, designed primarily to improve the image of the police force in the community. Also, where the programs appear to have some real substance, they generally exist on very tenuous grounds—frequently involving but a small number of police officers who, organizationally, are isolated from others in their agency and who are frequently subject to being ostracized by their confreres.

17   Another major limitation is that each of the programs has been launched with obvious doubt as to its propriety; in all the programs with which I am familiar, the responsible officials have felt compelled to relate the value of the program to the agency's function in combating crime. Any improvement in citizen contact obviously serves in a very direct manner to improve the cooperation which the police can expect from the public in combating crime. This is a consideration of the utmost importance when one reflects upon the degree to which the police depend upon the public for assistance in reporting crimes and suspicious circumstances and in serving as witnesses and complaints in the prosecution of criminal cases. But if lasting improvements are to be made in that aspect of police functioning that is unrelated to crime,

they must be justified on their own merits rather than be rationalized on the basis of the relationship such improvements will have to those police efforts that more directly relate to crime. . . .

18   Although these programs are presently limited and tenuous, participation in them is bound to have some impact on the officers involved—just as the opportunity to work as a juvenile officer has served over the years to create a corps of individuals in a police agency committed to a substantially different set of values than is typically associated with the police. The potential impact would, of course, be greatly increased if a program were spread throughout a department as, for example, is now being proposed for the New York City Family Crisis Intervention Project. A series of such programs, involving large numbers of men, could over a period of time contribute significantly toward achieving the kind of change in police values, in operating policies, and in institutional goals that has frequently been cited as an essential prerequisite to improvement in the police field.

19   If a police administrator is committed to a broadening of both the police role and perspective, he could, in addition to launching new programs, undertake to institutionalize support for such programs by a number of changes in the administration of his force. He could, for example, work for revision of recruitment standards and processing techniques that frequently serve to screen out or at least discourage the programs and place a much greater emphasis upon those police responsibilities unrelated to crime. And he could undertake to modify the present reward structure so as to provide as much credit for exceptionally good judgment in the handling of a complex problem of human behavior as is presently accorded skill and physical courage in the apprehension of a dangerous offender.

20   It is apparent, at least for the immediate future, that there will be little progress along these lines. In the polarization of community attitudes that has taken place, the dominant pressure being exerted on the police demands that they engage only in those activities that contribute directly to maintaining "law and order." In the gross over-simplifications that accompany such reactions, all police efforts that do not conform to the stereotyped concept of the police role tend to be lumped together and characterized as "mollycoddling" or simple waste. . . .

21   Thus, even the more sensitive police administrators in larger American cities now find themselves confronted by an acute dilemma. . . . At a time when the need for new approaches is most critical, they are forced by weight of public opinion to revert to traditional methods. The current crisis has nevertheless afforded an opportunity for some much-needed experimentation which can be continued when and if current pressures subside.

Discussion of Theme

1. How do most people view policemen? Is this view different from the one popular a few years ago?
2. The policeman performs many functions that are not related to crime. What are they? Why are the police so often involved in matters that seem to be the province of some other social institution?
3. What are the chief problems facing policemen in the larger cities? Are steps being taken to solve them?
4. What is the author's attitude toward the kind of training most policemen are getting today? Is it effective preparation for the job they will have to do?

Discussion of Rhetoric

1. What topic unifies the first three paragraphs in this article? How does this section serve as the introduction?
2. Is the author sympathetic to the policeman's problems? How do you know?
3. Reread paragraph 21. What "signal" word suggests that the conclusion of the essay is at hand? Can you think of other such signal words or phrases? How are such words like traffic signals?

Writing Assignments

1. Use the following sentence as the basis for a well-organized theme: "If I were chief of police in my town, I would make several changes."
2. Why is the policeman often disliked or feared by the ghetto resident? How could this opinion be changed? Present your views in a composition.
3. If you are interested in law-enforcement work as a career, explain its attraction for you.

Library Exploration

What is the American Civil Liberties Union? Why is it looked upon with disfavor by many policemen?

Vocabulary

integral (1): necessary to the whole
abates (3): lessens or reduces
tenuous (16): flimsy; weak
ostracized (16): excluded or shunned
polarization (20): placing at opposite poles or ends; drawing
　　　　　　　　toward two separate points

32

ON CIVIL DISOBEDIENCE:
TWO STATEMENTS

William F. Buckley, Jr., and Noam Chomsky

The following statements on civil disobedience were made in response to questions concerning the difference between civil disobedience and *dissent, justification of an act of civil disobedience (especially in the case of Vietnam protests), and the limits of civil disobedience.*

WILLIAM F. BUCKLEY, JR.[1]

1   Of the two grounds for disobeying civil authorities, the first—that the United States is not legally at war because Congress hasn't gone through the drill specified by the Constitution—strikes me as particularly phony. To begin with, it is being used by gentlemen whose lives are scarcely lived in scriptural fidelity to the Constitution. If the head of the American Bar Association were to decline to support the Vietnam war on the ground of its shaky constitutional genealogy, that is one thing. But when the Constitution is suddenly discovered by Dwight Macdonald, one puts that down (or at least I put that down) to opportunism. It isn't that the question doesn't worry me, it does. A great deal of thought will have to go into the elision of general resolutions (like Tonkin) and all-out wars. But this isn't the moment for such reviews, any more than the dark days of the Civil War were appropriate for questioning Abraham Lincoln's use of his Presidential powers.

2   On the second ground, it ought to be the individual's right to refuse to go along with his community, but the community, not the individual, should specify the consequences. These, in an enlightened society, should vary according to the nature of the insubordination, and according as the insubordination is plausibly rooted in deep philosophical attachments. For instance, it seems to me right and obvious that a pacifist should be permitted to remain far from even those battlefields at which the safety of the pacifist is secured, and right, also, that young pacifists of draft age should be required to perform some duty or other, in some way commensurate with those performed by fellow citizens who are conscripted. But those others who ask to retain a personal veto over every activity of their Government, whether it is a

---

[1] Editor of *National Review* and author of *Up From Liberalism*.

war in Vietnam or the social or educational policies of a municipal administration, are asking for the kind of latitude which breaks the bonds of civil society.

3   That which is anarchic within me (which is very strong) tunes in strongly on the idea of a society in which people decide for themselves what taxes to pay, what rules to obey, when to cooperate and when not to with the civil authorities. But that which is reasonable within me, which I am glad to say most often prevails, recognizes that societies so structured do not exist, and cannot exist: an insight as ancient as Socrates's, so patiently explained to Crito. The indicated consequence for studied and aggravated civil disobedience seems to me to be obvious: deportation. Ideally, of course, a citizen whose disagreements with his country are organic and apparently unreconcilable should take the initiative and seek out more compatible countries.

NOAM CHOMSKY[2]

4   Although I feel that resistance to United States policy is justified—in fact, a moral necessity—I do not think that dissent should be abandoned. Critical analysis of American policy can extend opposition to this war and can help modify the intellectual and moral climate that made it possible. Government propaganda has shifted to a new position: American self-interest. Correspondingly, critical analysis can now be directed to such questions as these: Whose interest is served by this war? What motivates the hysterical claim that if we do not stand fast in Vietnam we shall have to fight in Hawaii and California?—"a frivolous insult to the United States Navy," as Walter Lippmann rightly comments. Would the richest and most powerful nation in the world be justified in imposing such suffering and destruction even if this were in its "self-interest?"

5   What justifies an act of civil disobedience is an intolerable evil. After the lesson of Dachau and Auschwitz, no person of conscience can believe that authority must always be obeyed. A line must be drawn somewhere. Beyond that line lies civil disobedience. It may be quite passive, a simple refusal to take part in Government-initiated violence. An example is refusal to pay war taxes; refusal to serve in Vietnam is a far more meaningful, far more courageous example. It may involve symbolic confrontation with the war-making apparatus, as in the Washington demonstrations, a confrontation that becomes civil disobedience when the participant stands his ground in the face of Government force. It may go well beyond such symbolic acts.

6   Each citizen must ask himself whether he wishes to take part in the annihilation of the people of Vietnam. He has a range of actions available to him. Docility and passive acquiescence is one possible course.

[2]Professor of linguistics at the Massachusetts Institute of Technology.

It is the course of full complicity in whatever the Government will do in his name.

7   The limits of civil disobedience must be determined by the extent of the evil that one confronts, and by considerations of tactical efficacy and moral principle. On grounds of principle and tactics, I think that civil disobedience should be entirely nonviolent, but space prevents a discussion of the reasons for and the consequences of this conclusion.

8   The final question posed is the crucial one. Those who defend American policy speak vaguely of Communist "aggression." Just when did this "aggression" take place? Was it in 1959, when Hanoi radio was urging that the leaders of the insurrection desist, when Diem spoke of having an Algerian war on his hands in the South while his agents were being parachuted into North Vietnam? Or was it perhaps in April, 1965, when North Vietnamese troops were first discovered in the South, two months after the bombing of North Vietnam began— 400 in guerrilla force of 140,000, at a time when more than 30,000 American troops were helping protect the Saigon Government from its own population?

9   Or is it now, when a vast American army of occupation has taken over the conduct of the war, with about as many South Korean mercenaries as there are North Vietnamese troops in the South?

10   Or does Hanoi's "aggression" consist in the sending of supplies and trained South Vietnamese cadres to the South? By these standards our aggression in the South has always been incomparably greater in scale, and we are engaged in such aggression in half the countries of the world. It is pointless to continue. If an objective observer were to listen to American voices speaking of aggression from Hanoi or of the necessity for *America* to contain *China's* aggressive expansionism, he would not challenge our arguments but would question our sanity.

11   American Government sources freely admit that United States military force was introduced to prevent a political, organizational, agit-prop victory by the N.F.L. (see Douglas Pike, "The Vietcong"). The terrible consequences of the use of American military might are apparent to anyone with eyes and ears. I will not try to describe what everyone knows. To use inadequate words to tell what we have done is an insult to the victims of our violence and our moral cowardice. Yes, civil disobedience is entirely justified in an effort to bring to a close the most disgraceful chapter in American history.

12   I'll finish with two quotes, each very true, from opposite extremes of the moral spectrum.

13   (1) "Naturally the common people don't want war . . . it is the leaders of the country who determine the policy, and it is always a simple matter to drag the people along, whether it is a democracy, or a Fascist dictatorship, or a parliament, or a Communist dictatorship. Voice or no voice, the people can always be brought to do the bidding of the leaders. That is easy. All you have to do is to

tell them that they are being attacked, and denounce the pacifists for lack of patriotism and exposing the country to danger. It works the same in every country."

14   (2) "Unjust laws and practices survive because men obey them and conform to them. This they do out of fear. There are things they dread more than the continuance of the evil."

15   The first quote is from Hermann Goering. Those who counsel civil disobedience are expressing their hope that it doesn't "work the same" in this country. The second quote is from A. J. Muste, paraphrasing Gandhi. These words have never been more appropriate than they are today.

Discussion of Theme
1. In Buckley's opinion, are there any valid grounds for disobeying civil authorities? Are his refutations of what he considers unacceptable grounds for civil disobedience sound (see paragraphs 1 and 2)? Is there an obvious bias in his summary of his opponents' arguments?
2. What justifies an act of civil disobedience, according to Chomsky? Can you cite examples that would fulfill his requirements for such an act?
3. According to Buckley, what two opposing forces are in every man? Does Chomsky show that he accepts this view of human nature?
4. Why does Chomsky include the quotation from Hermann Goering?

Discussion of Rhetoric
1. Compare the arguments of both writers. Which one relies more on reason, rather than emotion, in presenting his position? What evidence can you cite to support your answer?
2. Reread the first sentence of Buckley's essay. Comment on its structure, noting particularly the last word in the sentence.
3. What is the purpose of Chomsky's references to Dachau and Auschwitz?

Writing Assignments
1. Chomsky asks, "Whose interest is served by the war in Vietnam?" Answer his question in a theme.
2. What are some arguments for, or against, a volunteer army in place of a conscription army?

Vocabulary
elision (1): omission
commensurate (2): equal in measure or extent
docility (6): the quality or state of being easily led or managed
acquiescence (6): passive or tacit acceptance
efficacy (7): effectiveness

33

THE MEANING OF ETHICS

Philip Wheelwright

What makes a decision "right" or wrong"? What should determine our conduct: absolute norms, our consciences, or the particular situa- tion? *The following essay, written by a professor of philosophy, sets forth some tentative answers to these questions.*

> For you see, Callicles, our discussion is concerned with a matter in which even a man of slight intelligence must take the profoundest interest—namely, what course of life is best.—Socrates, in Plato's *Gorgias*

1   Man is the animal who can reflect. Like other animals, no doubt, he spends much of his time in merely reacting to the pressures and urgencies of his environment. But being a man he has moments also of conscious stock-taking, when he becomes aware not only of his world but of himself confronting his world, evaluating it, and making choices with regard to it. It is this ability to know himself and on the basis of self-knowledge to make evaluations and reflective choices that differentiates man from his subhuman cousins.

2   There are, as Aristotle has pointed out, two main ways in which man's power of reflection becomes active. They are called, in Aristotle's language, *theoretikos* and *praktikos* respectively; which is to say, thinking about what is actually the case and thinking about what had better be done. In English translation the words *contemplative* and *operative* probably come closest to Aristotle's intent. To think contemplatively is to ask oneself what *is*; to think operatively is to ask oneself what to *do*. These are the two modes of serious, one might even say of genuine thought—as distinguished from daydreams, emotional vaporizings, laryngeal chatter, and the repetition of clichés. To think seriously is to think either for the sake of knowing things as they are or for the sake of acting upon, and producing or helping to produce, things as they might be.

3   Although in practice the two types of thinking are much interrelated, it is operative thinking with which our present study is primarily concerned. Ethics, although it must be guided, limited, and qualified constantly by considerations of what is actually the case, is focused

upon questions of what should be done. The converse, however, does not follow. Not all questions about what should be done are ethical questions. Much of our operative thinking is given to more immediate needs—to means whereby some given end can be achieved. A person who deliberates as to the most effective way of making money, or of passing a course, or of winning a battle, or of achieving popularity, is thinking operatively, but if that is as far as his planning goes it cannot be called ethical. Such deliberations about adapting means to an end would acquire an ethical character only if some thought were given to the nature and value of the end itself. Ethics cannot dispense with questions of means, but neither can it stop there.

4   Accordingly, ethics may be defined as that branch of philosophy which is the systematic study of reflective choice, of the standards of right and wrong by which it is to be guided, and of the goods toward which it may ultimately be directed. The relation between the parts of this definition, particularly between standards of right and wrong on the one hand and ultimately desirable goods on the other, will be an important part of the forthcoming study.

THE NATURE OF MORAL DELIBERATION

5   The soundest approach to ethical method is through reflection on our experience of moral situations which from time to time we have had occasion to face, or through an imagined confrontation of situations which others have faced and which we can thus make sympathetically real to ourselves. For instance:

> Arthur Ames is a rising young district attorney engaged on his most important case. A prominent political boss has been murdered. Suspicion points at a certain ex-convict, known to have borne the politician a grudge. Aided by the newspapers, which have reported the murder in such a way as to persuade the public of the suspect's guilt, Ames feels certain that he can secure a conviction on the circumstantial evidence in his possession. If he succeeds in sending the man to the chair he will become a strong candidate for governor at the next election.
>
> During the course of the trial, however, he accidentally stumbles on some fresh evidence, known only to himself and capable of being destroyed if he chooses, which appears to establish the ex-convict's innocence. If this new evidence were to be introduced at the trial an acquittal would be practically certain. What ought the District Attorney do? Surrender the evidence to the defence, in order that, as a matter of fair play, the accused might be given every legitimate chance of establishing his innocence? But to do that will mean the loss of a case that has received enormous publicity; the District Attorney will lose the backing of the press; he will appear to have failed, and his political career may be

blocked. In that event not only will he himself suffer disappointment, but his ample plans for bestowing comforts on his family
and for giving his children the benefits of a superior education
may have to be curtailed. On the other hand, ought he to be
instrumental in sending a man to the chair for a crime that in all
probability he did not commit? And yet the ex-convict is a bad
lot; even if innocent in the present case he has doubtless committed many other crimes in which he has escaped detection. Is a
fellow like that worth the sacrifice of one's career? Still, there is
no proof that he has ever committed a crime punishable by death.
Until a man has been proved guilty he must be regarded, by sound
principle of American legal theory, as innocent. To conceal and
destroy the new evidence, then, is not that tantamount to rail-
roading an innocent man to the chair?

So District Attorney Ames reasons back and forth. He knows
that it is a widespread custom for a district attorney to conceal
evidence prejudicial to his side of a case. But is the custom,
particularly when a human life is at stake, morally right? A
district attorney is an agent of the government, and his chief aim
in that capacity should be to present his accusations in such a
way as to ensure for the accused not condemnation but justice.
The question, then, cannot be answered by appealing simply to
law or to legal practice. It is a moral one: *What is Arthur Ames'
duty? What ought he to do?*

Benjamin Bates has a friend who lies in a hospital, slowly
dying of a painful and incurable disease. Although there is no
hope of recovery, the disease sometimes permits its victim to
linger on for many months, in ever greater torment and with
threatened loss of sanity. The dying man, apprised of the outcome
and knowing that the hospital expenses are a severe drain on his
family's limited financial resources, decides that death had
better come at once. His physician, he knows, will not run the
risk of providing him with the necessary drug. There is only his
friend Bates to appeal to.

How shall Bates decide? Dare he be instrumental in hastening
another's death? Has he a moral right to be accessory to the taking
of a human life? Besides, suspicion would point his way, and his
honorable motives would not avert a charge of murder. On the
other hand, can he morally refuse to alleviate a friend's suffering
and the financial distress of a family when the means of doing so
are in his hands? To acquiesce and to refuse seem both somehow
in different ways wrong, yet one course or the other must be
chosen. *What ought Bates to do? Which way does his duty lie?*

In the city occupied by Crampton College a strike is declared by the employees of all the public-transit lines. Their wages have not been increased to meet the rising cost of living, and the justice of their grievance is rather widely admitted by neutral observers. The strike ties up business and causes much general inconvenience; except for the people who have cars of their own or can afford taxi fare, there is no way of getting from one part of the city to another. Labor being at this period scarce, an appeal is made by the mayor to college students to serve the community by acting in their spare time as motormen and drivers. The appeal is backed by a promise of lucrative wages and by the college administration's agreement to cooperate by permitting necessary absences from classes.

What ought the students of Crampton College to do? If they act as strikebreakers they aid in forcing the employees back to work on the corporation's own terms. Have they any right to interfere so drastically and one-sidedly in the lives and happiness of others? On the other hand, if they turn down the mayor's request the community will continue to suffer grave inconveniences until the fight is somehow settled. *What is the students' duty in the matter? What is the right course for them to follow?*

6   These three situations, although perhaps unusual in the severity of their challenge, offer examples of problems distinctively moral. When the act of moral deliberation implicit in each of them is fully carried out, certain characteristic phases can be discerned.

7   (i) *Examination and clarification of the alternatives.* What are the relevant possibilities of action in the situation confronting me? Am I clear about the nature of each? Have I clearly distinguished them from one another? And are they mutually exhaustive, or would a more attentive search reveal others? In the case of District Attorney Ames, for example, a third alternative might have been to make a private deal with the ex-convict by which, in exchange for his acquittal, the District Attorney would receive the profits from some lucrative racket of which the ex-convict had control. No doubt to a reputable public servant this line of conduct would be too repugnant for consideration; it exemplifies, nevertheless, the ever present logical possibility of going "between the horns"[1] of the original dilemma.

8   (ii) *Rational elaboration of consequences.* The next step is to think out the probable consequences of each of the alternatives in question. As this step involves predictions about a hypothetical future, the conclusions can have, at most, a high degree of probability, never certainty. The degree of probability is heightened according as there is found some precedent in past experience for each of the proposed

---

[1] I.e., finding a third alternative.

choices. Even if the present situation seems wholly new, analysis will always reveal *some* particulars for which analogies in past experience can be found or to which known laws of causal sequence are applicable. Such particulars will be dealt with partly by analogy (an act similar to the one now being deliberated about had on a previous occasion such and such consequences) and partly by the inductive-deductive method: appealing to general laws (deduction) which in turn have been built up as generalizations from observed particulars (induction). Mr. Ames, we may suppose, found the materials for this step in his professional knowledge of law and legal precedent, as well as in his more general knowledge of the policies of the press, the gullibility of its readers, and the high cost of domestic luxuries.

9   (iii) *Imaginative projection of the self into the predicted situation.* It is not enough to reason out the probable consequences of a choice. In a moral deliberation the chief interests involved are not scientific but human and practical. The only way to judge the comparative desirability of two possible futures is to live through them both in imagination. The third step, then, is to project oneself imaginatively into the future; i.e., establish a dramatic identification of the present self with that future self to which the now merely imagined experiences may become real. Few persons, unfortunately, are capable of an imaginative identification forceful enough to give the claims of the future self an even break. Present goods loom larger than future goods, and goods in the immediate future than goods that are remote. The trained ethical thinker must have a sound *temporal perspective*, the acquisition of which is to be sought by a frequent, orderly, and detailed exercise of the imagination with respect to not yet actual situations.

10   (iv) *Imaginative identification of the self with the points of view of those persons whom the proposed act will most seriously affect.* Whatever decision I make here and now, if of any importance, is likely to have consequences, in varying degrees, for persons other than myself. An important part of a moral inquiry is to envisage the results of a proposed act as they will appear to those other persons affected by them. I must undertake, then, a dramatic identification of my own self with the selves of other persons. The possibility of doing this is evident from a consideration of how anyone's dramatic imagination works in the reading of a novel or the witnessing of a play. If the persons in the novel or play are dramatically convincing it is not because their characters and actions have been established by logical proof, but because they are presented so as to provoke in the reader an impulse to project himself into the world of the novel or play, to identify himself with this and that character in it, to share their feelings and moods, to get their slant on things.

11   In most persons, even very benevolent ones, the social consciousness works by fits and starts. To examine fairly the needs and claims of

other selves is no less hard and is often harder than to perform a similar task with regard to one's own future self. Accordingly the ethical thinker must develop *social perspective*—that balanced appreciation of others' needs and claims which is the basis of justice.

12   In this fourth, as in the third step, the imaginative projection is to be carried out for each of the alternatives, according as their consequences shall have been predicted by Step ii.

13   (v) *Estimation and comparison of the values involved.* Implicit in the third and fourth steps is a recognition that certain values both positive and negative are latent in each of the hypothetical situations to which moral choice may lead. The values must be made explicit in order that they may be justly compared, for it is as a result of their comparison that a choice is to be made. To make values explicit is to give them a relatively abstract formulation; they still, however, derive concrete significance from their imagined exemplifications. District Attorney Ames, for example, might have envisaged his dilemma as a choice between family happiness and worldly success on the one hand as against professional honor on the other. Each of these is undoubtedly good, that is to say a value, but the values cannot be reduced to a common denominator. Family happiness enters as a factor into Benjamin Bates' dilemma no less than into that of Arthur Ames, but it stands to be affected in a different way and therefore, in spite of the identical words by which our linguistic poverty forces us to describe it, it does not mean the same thing. Family happiness may mean any number of things; so may success, and honor—although these different meanings have, of course, an intelligible bond of unity. Arthur Ames' task is to compare not just any family happiness with any professional honor but the particular exemplifications of each that enter into his problem. The comparison is not a simple calculation but an imaginative deliberation, in which the abstract values that serve as the logical ground of the comparison are continuous with, and interactive with, the concrete particulars that serve as its starting-point.

14   (vi) *Decision.* Comparison of the alternative future situations and the values embodied in each must terminate in a decision. Which of the possible situations do I deem it better to bring into existence? There are no rules for the making of this decision. I must simply decide as wisely and as fairly and as relevantly to the total comparison as I can. Every moral decision is a risk, for the way in which a person decides is a factor in determining the kind of self he is going to become.

15   (vii) *Action.* The probable means of carrying out the decision have been established by Step ii. The wished-for object or situation is an end; certain specific means toward the fulfillment of which lie here and now within my power. These conditions supply the premises for an ethical syllogism. When a certain end, x, is recognized as the best of the available alternatives, and when the achievement of it is seen to

be possible through a set of means, *a, b, c* . . . which lie within my power, then whichever of the means, *a, b, c* . . . is an action that can here and now be performed becomes at just this point my duty. If the deliberative process has been carried out forcefully and wisely it will have supplied a categorical answer to the question, What ought I to do?—even though the answer in some cases may be, Do nothing.

16   Naturally, not all experiences of moral deliberation and choice reveal these seven phases in a distinct, clear-cut way. Nor is the order here given always the actual order. Sometimes we may begin by deliberating about the relative merits of two ends, seeking the means simultaneously with this abstract inquiry, or after its completion. The foregoing analysis does, however, throw some light on the nature of a moral problem, and may be tested by applying it to the three cases described at the beginning of the chapter.

LOGICAL ANALYSIS OF A MORAL SITUATION

17   The usual sign of a moral question is the auxiliary verb, *ought*. Not every "ought," however, is a moral ought. There must be distinguished: (1) the logical "ought," as in "The balance ought to be $34 but I make it $29," "From the appearance of the sky I should say we ought to have snow tonight," "The story ought never to have had a happy ending"; (2) the prudential "ought," as in "If you want to avoid colds you ought to try Hydrolux Vapo-lite." These two uses of the word "ought" express, like the moral ought, propriety with respect to a certain end or standard. But unlike the moral ought, the ought in (1) does not refer directly to human conduct, and while the ought in (2) does have this reference, the imperative that it expresses is conditional on a wish. The imperative expressed by the moral ought is, on the contrary, unconditional: You ought to be honorable— not *if* you wish men to respect you; men's respect is a desirable adjunct of being honorable, but you ought to be honorable in any case. The moral ought is what Kant has called a categorical imperative. In being categorical it is distinguished from the prudential ought; in being an imperative, i.e., a call to action, it is distinguished also from the logical ought. It is the moral ought that is the subject-matter of ethics, and it is in this ethical sense, therefore, that the word "ought" will be used in the present volume. We may now consider the principal factors which the moral ought involves.

VALUE AND POSSIBILITY

18   The first factor to be noted in a moral situation is the *presence of value*. Whenever an inclination is felt, that toward which the inclination points is felt to have value. What is felt to have value need not on reflection be *judged* to have value. Judgment can correct our immediate

feelings of value, just as in an act of sense-perception judgment corrects and interprets the immediate sense-data. Inclination is thus not identical with value; but it is the psycho-physical basis of its presence.

19   To say that a value is present in an object is to declare that the object is *in some sense* good. We may therefore restate the first require-ment of a moral situation by saying that some things must be recog-nized as good; or, since good is a relative term, that *some things are recognized as better than others*. But if *a* is better than *b*, *b* is worse than *a*. It follows, then, that some things are *worse* than others, and the first requirement may therefore be restated as an ability to distinguish what is comparatively good from what is comparatively bad. What particular things are good, and what bad, is of course another question. The principle here laid down is simply that to a person who did not set a higher value on some things than on others there could be no moral problem. (Indeed, it is a little hard to see how such a person could have any *problems* at all.) A moral situation presupposes, then, as the first condition of its existence, the recognition of some values or other.

20   This primary characteristic of a moral situation defines ethics as a normative science. Ethics is not a science at all in the same way that the empirical sciences are so designated, and its methods are funda-mentally distinct. It shares, nevertheless, the larger meaning of science, for its subject-matter can be arranged systematically and certain guiding principles be found. But while such sciences as physics, psychology, economics, etc. are primarily concerned with the recording, predicting, and structuralizing of facts, ethics is concerned with facts only secondarily, only so far as they are morally evaluated or judged to be in some way relevant to the application of moral values. That skies are sunny in New Mexico is a fact; that many people are without lucra-tive employment is also a fact. Both are equally facts, but our valuations of them differ. It is such differences in valuation, such *normative* differences, that establish the basis of a moral situation.

21   A second element in any moral situation is the *presence of possible alternatives*. To evaluate anything as good is equivalent to declaring that it ought to be, or ought to persist. Ethics does not stop with the good, with what merely ought to *be*; it accepts this as but one element in the question, What ought to *be done*? To say that a person ought to do a thing implies a power on his part *to do or refrain from doing it*. We do not say that the President of the United States ought to put an immediate stop to all human suffering, for the President, however much he might desire such a consummation, has not the power of achieving it; the most we can say is that the President ought to take such steps as may lie within his power to move toward the goal. Nor, on the other hand, do we say, speaking accurately, that a man ought to obey the law of gravitation, for this is something that he must do

willy-nilly. Neither "must" nor "cannot" is in the strict sense compatible with "ought."

22 These two elements, the presence of value and the presence of possible alternatives in a moral situation, are intimately related, for in order that the alternatives may have moral significance some kind of value must be attached to each of them. In some cases the value of each alternative is assigned rationally. In other cases, the most familiar of which are those described as "battling with temptation," our rational judgment assigns value to only one of the alternatives; the other is merely *felt* to have value, as a result of our experiencing a strong inclination toward it. But in either type of situation there must be some value, whether deliberately judged or spontaneously felt, attached to both alternatives, in order that there may be a moral problem.

23 For example, there exist for me the possible alternatives of plucking a blade of grass or of not doing so, but the situation is not a moral one, for neither alternative has (on any likely occasion) any value. Or again, it lies in my power to go without my dinner. In this instance one of the alternatives (eating dinner) has value, the other (going without it) has probably none, so that again there is no moral problem. If, however, I judged that abstention from dinner would be a stoic discipline good for my character, or if by abstaining I could afford to attend a play that I wanted to see, or could devote the dinner hour to some work that needed to be done, the situation would be to this extent a moral one, for a value would be set on each of the alternatives. Indeed, the great difficulty of moral problems and the indecisiveness of much moral deliberation are due principally to this fact, that both of the alternatives with which our deliberation is concerned are in some manner valued and their values are often incommensurate.

MORAL INSIGHT

24 A moral situation, furthermore, must have a consequential character. Even where value and possibility are both present a situation may still be amoral—which is to say, it may be a situation to which ethical considerations do not properly apply. Choosing between different dishes on a restaurant menu provides a familiar example. If pot roast and sweetbreads are offered as alternative choices at the same price, the only thing that a diner would ordinarily have to consider is which one of them he would prefer. If his decision is not automatic, if he spends any time in deliberating over the choice, then he must evidently have set some value upon each of the two dishes, between which he regards himself as free to choose. Thus the first two conditions of a moral situation are met: there is a conflict between values, and a choice between them is possible. Nevertheless, the situation as it stands is not a moral one. The alternatives are considered simply as ends in

themselves; the values involved in the diner's choice will terminate in the enjoyment of what he has chosen, and the duration of that enjoyment will be short. Nothing of any significance will be entailed by his ordering one meat rather than the other. The situation is pretty much isolated from the main lines of his experience and his choices.

25   Even where no social relationships are immediately involved, a choice may have moral character, to the degree that it is significantly consequential. If a certain action promises a greater intensity of pleasure at the moment but appears likely to entail later pains or inconveniences of an important kind, moral insight into these future consequences is called for, and the situation is thus a moral one, although not in a social way. Whether consideration must be taken of the claims of other selves or only of one's own future self, in either case the choice is related to, and partly concerned with, something beyond the immediate result. Mechanical computation is not possible here as it is in the case of physical measurements, for there are no sets of physical units that can be compared. In a moral situation the difference between the competing values is at least partly one of kind, not merely of degree, and human interests and valuations are not manifold, so subject to continual growth and reconsideration, that the insights themselves have only a tenuous stability. What is required is an insight into the remoter values involved, and the probable embodiments they would take in relation to those affected. It is in the deepening and maturing of men's moral insights that the best index of human development is to be found.

26   The third requirement of a moral situation, then, has a double aspect. The choice must be consequential, and this may be seen from two sides. The alternatives are not simple ends-in-themselves terminating here and now; they involve values over and beyond the values of immediate enjoyment. And the agent by whom the choice is to be made must therefore have an imaginative grasp of the consequences, an imaginative insight into the nature of the values that are only hinted at in the immediate situation.

27   But is insight enough? Even when I fully comprehend that a certain course of action is both possible and the best one for me to undertake, is it guaranteed that I will therefore undertake it? We all know that it is not. The experience of temptation is familiar to everybody—the inward tension and struggle in which I perceive that one way of acting is the right way but am powerfully drawn towards some enticing but more limited good. Let us look at the nature of this kind of experience more closely.

THE GOOD AND THE RIGHT

28   What I want to do is frequently opposed to what I know I ought to do: i.e., the present good is often incompatible with what seems to be

right. As previously stated, there must be some inclination toward both of the alternatives with which any moral deliberation is concerned. This is the same thing as to say that both alternatives are felt or thought to be somehow good. But the qualities of the competing goods may be radically different. Say that I am tempted to sit drinking beer with friends when I know that I ought to be devoting the evening to my studies. There is an inclination to linger on; there is also an inclination, of another kind, to say good night and leave. The former inclination is strong and attractive but without rational sanction; whereas—

> Quite other is the prompting of the "ought." It is not so much a drive as an inner exhortation. It is not impulsive, but imperative. And what we experience is not ourselves impelled, but ourselves impelling, ourselves impelling ourselves, indeed ourselves impelling ourselves against impulse.[2]

The situation is a sufficiently familiar one. The strongest actual propensity at a given moment is toward a course of action contrary to the one toward which duty beckons. An effort is required to break away from the fascination of the immediate. The sense that such an effort is required, that it *can* be made, and that it would be better to make it because the result would be an eventually greater good, are conditions of a feeling of "ought."

29   The good and the right, though often specifically opposed, are related at bottom. Their actual conflicts are explained by a distinction within the meaning of "good"—between intrinsic and extrinsic goods. A good is called *intrinsic* when it is judged worthy of being sought for its own sake, i.e., when it is an end in itself; *extrinsic* or *instrumental* when it is sought as a means to some other good. The relation is a shifting one, for it is not always possible to distinguish sharply between the end and the means: what is an end from one point of view may be regarded as a means from another. Nevertheless we can say in general that the good of a surgical operation is extrinsic: it must be referred to the greater health that is to come. The enjoyment of a glass of wine is an intrinsic good, a "good in itself": the wine is not enjoyed for the sake of anything distinct from the enjoyment. Still other goods are at once intrinsic and extrinsic; an enjoyable *and* nourishing dinner, a refreshing *and* cleansing bath, and the like. Often the right course of action will consist in choosing some extrinsic good (say, diligent study) which is the only available means to the attainment of some important intrinsic good (say, a professional career). On such occasions the rightness of the action is founded on the good to which it leads, but to the agent it may not appear to partake

---

[2] Horace G. Wyatt, *The Art of Feeling*, pp. 169–170.

of any of the character of that remote good. Thus it happens that if the agent is tempted by some more immediate good (such as the pleasures of a lazy life) the conflict, which would be more rationally conceived as a conflict between two goods (present leisure vs. future career) acquires the appearance of a conflict between the present good (leisure) and the present right course of action (diligent study).

THE PARADOX OF VOLITION

30   Situations in which there is a genuine moral struggle, in which a temptation must be conquered by a putting forth of moral effort, are crucial for morality. The ultimate justification of a moral principle (and, indirectly, for any ethical theory) is the possibility that it can be made an effective force in moral struggles. William James describes the moral struggle as a situation in which "a rarer and more ideal impulse is called upon to neutralize others of a more instinctive and habitual kind"; in which "strongly explosive tendencies are checked, or strongly obstructive conditions overcome." He continues:

> We *feel*, in all hard cases of volition, as if the line taken, when the rarer and more ideal motives prevail, were the line of greater resistance, as if the line of coarser motivation were the more previous and easy one, even at the very moment when we refuse to follow it. He who under the surgeon's knife represses cries of pain, or he who exposes himself to social obloquy for duty's sake, feels as if he were following the line of greatest temporary resistance. . . .
>
> The ideal impulse appears . . . a still small voice which must be artificially reinforced to prevail. Effort is what reinforces it, making things seem as if, while the force of propensity were essentially a fixed quantity, the ideal force might be of various amount. But what determines the amount of the effort when, by its aid, an ideal motive becomes victorious over a great sensual resistance? The very greatness of the resistance itself. If the sensual propensity is small, the effort is small. The latter is *made great* by the presence of a great antagonist to overcome. And if a brief definition of ideal or moral action were required, none could be given which would better fit the appearances than this: *It is action in the line of greatest resistance.*[3]

31   In order to understand James' profoundly valid paradox we must avoid the popular tendency to explain a moral situation wholly by analogies drawn from the physical world. In those aspects of nature studied by physics and chemistry it is always the line of least, never of greater resistance that is followed. The universality of the physical

---

[3]William James, *The Principles of Psychology*, Vol. II, pp. 548–549.

law of least physical resistance, however, is due to the fact that it is not directly applicable to concrete experience, for in *concrete* experience no laws are applicable with unremitting exactitude. Physicists may be allowed to formulate their own laws by the methodology which their technical interests require. But scientific laws tell us nothing directly about moral experience. In this province everyone must be, to a large extent, his own observer. And what is a more assured fact of intro-spective observation than that in cases of moral struggle *we often can and sometimes do follow the path of greatest resistance?*

32   What we ought to do, however unappealing originally, can be made, by a concentration of purpose, what we want to do. Intelligence (or, as it has previously been called, insight) is the mediator. The reason why it may be *right for my present self* to forego the pleasure of a drinking party is that the sacrifice may promote *a good for my future self*: time for study, or a clear head for tomorrow morning, or money saved, or all three. What I choose is distinct from the greatest immediate satis-faction but not separate from all satisfaction whatever. I have put myself imaginatively in the place of my future self and am thus able to consider the good or the pleasure or the emotional satisfaction apart from, *abstracted* from (i.e., separated by the imagination from) the present experience. This abstractive ability of man is what marks him as rational, and, so far as it becomes effective in directing his conduct, as moral.

33   There is another way, too, in which man's abstractive ability shows itself: in the altruistic "ought." A person can recognize duties not only toward his own future self but toward other persons also.

> Here again intelligence is the mediator. Man is able to con-sider the good or the pleasure or the emotional satisfaction apart from the individual to be satisfied, apart not only from [the particular experience] but from the experiencer. If emotional satisfaction is the thing desired, it is so for B, C, D and others as well as for A. The happiness of others is just as much an end as my happiness and just as much to be sought after. The "ought" is the peculiar emotion which now enters to convert this intellectual achievement into conduct.[4]

By this abstractive process the Golden Rule of Jesus, "Do unto others as you would have them do unto you," and the less positive form of the same command, given half a millennium earlier by Confucius, "Refrain from doing to others what you would not have them do to yourself," can be realized as expressions of a binding obligation.

34   Right and wrong, then, are not hollow sounds nor is discussion about them an idle game. If we mean what we say in designating an

---

[4]Wyatt, *op. cit.*, p. 168.

action right or wrong, if we are doing more than mouthing a conventional formula, our judgment will in some manner affect our subsequent conduct. Ethics is not a pastime for the understanding alone. Ethical theory calls for moral practice, and the full meaning of ethics becomes intelligible only as we translate theories into moral principles that can be made effective forces in the struggle toward ideal ends.

THE SEARCH FOR A STANDARD

35   But how, it will be asked, is the particular character of right and wrong on any given occasion to be determined? How can one be sure that the development of moral insight (even if such an accomplishment were not in any case formidably difficult) will necessarily lead to a "right" judgment of where one's duties lie? Or, to shift the perspective, how can one be sure that one's moral insight is sufficiently developed? Superior intelligence is not always enough; it may be put at the service of evil ends. Satan, whatever his delinquencies, was no fool. What clear test, then, (so the popular quandary runs) can be applied to human conduct so as to determine on each occasion whether it is right or wrong; or (from a somewhat more mature point of view) so as to distinguish the higher of two contending values from the lower? Various criteria are proposed, such as the following.

36   (i) *Natural inclinations.* "Follow your impulses; do whatever gives you the most enjoyment"; people sometimes talk as if in these trite maxims they had discovered a significant moral truth. Actually they have done the contrary: they have denied that moral truth exists. If inclinations are the only standard of conduct, then there is no standard by which to choose between one inclination and another. Whatever inclination is strongest at any moment becomes for that reason right. Temptation becomes honorable by the sheer fact of being tempting. Evidently there is no moral standard offered here; there is merely a negation of moral standard.

37   Sometimes the claims of irrational impulse are bolstered by philosophical arguments based on the alleged facts of human nature. Such arguments will be examined more fully in Chapter 3; here it need only be remarked that human nature is too complex and mysterious to be reduced to any single set or type of facts. If it is a fact that men yield to impulse it is no less a fact that they can and sometimes do rationally redirect or halt their initial impulses. To overcome and remake one's nature is itself an expression of one's nature. That a man faced with alternatives can choose the harder course as against the easier is a supremely important fact, without which moral action would be powerless and moral judgment empty. But it is just this kind of *ideal fact* which the champions of impulse, instinct, and inclination as sufficient guides of life habitually overlook.

38   (ii) *Statute law.* The law of the land is a standard of right and wrong

from which no individual is wholly exempt. At the same time it is safe to say that no one obeys all the laws. In the first place, there are numerous laws on the statute books that have long ago become obsolete without ever having been annulled. To obey all the laws an individual would have to employ legal aid to find out what laws there are and exactly what they require in terms of conduct. Secondly, even among the laws that are known, some are held in higher respect than others. During the period when the eighteenth amendment to the Constitution was in force there were many so-called "law-abiding citizens" who had no scruples about buying a drink. Besides, it is a recognized right of an American citizen (by voting and in related ways) to seek to change the existing laws. There must, therefore, be some standard by which the goodness or badness of actual laws, as well as of proposed laws, can be judged.

39   (iii) *Public opinion* is in the long run more authoritative than statute law, for a law that lacks public support will not be obeyed and in the end will either be repealed or, as in the case of many "blue laws," ignored by common consent. Nevertheless, public opinion is often wrong. Its fallibility in particular cases is recognized even by those who accept it as a generally reliable guide. The vast majority of men think emotionally and gregariously. One of the chief tasks of education is admittedly to raise the standard of public opinion. There must be some higher standard, then, by which we can judge the state of public opinion at any time to be bad or good.

40   (iv) There are those who hold that the higher standard is furnished by *religious authority*. Such a view presupposes: (1) a belief in God, (2) a belief that God communicates His will either directly or indirectly to men, and (3) more particularly, a belief that one's own Church or sect or Holy Book is the channel through which God's will is revealed, as a check on the vagaries of one's individual conscience. Even if these beliefs can all be accepted without difficulty, questions of interpretation frequently arise. The Ten Commandments, for example, forbid stealing. Does this prohibition apply to the practice of ruining your business competitor by price-cutting, and so eventually pocketing his expected receipts? Does it apply to the practice of certain oil, mining, and lumber companies of wasting the country's (i.e., the American people's) natural resources for private gain? Since no clear definition of stealing receives universal consent, the divine command, though indubitably just and important, is subject to numerous ambiguities. Again, Christ's law of love is pretty clearly the keynote of his teaching. But Christians disagree widely on the method of applying that law to such socially urgent problems as war and labor relations.

41   (v) *Conscience* is a part of everyone's standard. Regardless of how we may explain it the existence of a "still small voice" that sometimes on

crucial occasions says "Do!" or "Refrain!" is an inescapable phenomenon. The voice of conscience often opposes itself to the inclinations
of the moment, sometimes to public opinion; and in fundamental
matters it may be, for the dedicated man, a higher court of appeal
than any outer law, secular or religious. Still, conscience is far from
infallible. It can and ought to be educated, and when a man relies on it
uncritically it may turn out to be but the prompting of self-interest
masquerading in holy dress.

42   (vi) Conscience then must be controlled, and revelation must be
interpreted, by *reason*. Very true. But that is not to say that reason is
the standard. Immanuel Kant is the outstanding example of a philosopher who tried to make it so, and as might have been expected, his
applications of his rationally established principles are quite as debatable
as those of any other moralist. If generosity is better than selfishness
that is not because it is more rational: some philosophers, in fact, have
held it to be less so. Rationality is a necessary aspect of ethics but not
its sufficient criterion. Ethics, in short, must be logical, but ethics is
not logic.

43   Evidently no isolated standard of right and wrong is proof against
attack. The function of ethics is not to provide a simple and sure rule
by which moral problems can be "solved." An active intelligence
revolts against whatever doctrine claims to utter the last word on any
matter. Especially is this true in ethics, where the conclusions sought
are of such intimate importance to each serious inquirer. Immediate
decisions will often have to be reached by appealing to some convenient rule of thumb or to some already developed habit or preference.
But it is an advantage of theories that they can be inquired into at
leisure. The task of theoretical ethics is not to lay down static norms
by which each new moral problem that arises can be decisively answered.
Its task is rather to develop a method suitable for the evaluation and
criticism of existing norms and for the exploration of new value
possibilities, in order that when moral decisions have henceforth to be
made their grounds may be more adequate and more worthy.

Discussion of Theme

1. What two kinds of serious thinking does Wheelwright describe?
   Which of the two is the study of ethics concerned with?
2. What factors are present in a moral situation, according to Wheelwright?
3. In what important way do the laws of physics differ from the "laws"
   of ethics?
4. When making an ethical choice, the individual is faced with a duty,
   according to Wheelwright. What is that duty? Apply his theory to
   a particular situation that might occur in your own life.
5. The author lists various criteria for determining right and wrong.
   What are they? Are all equally valid?

Discussion of Rhetoric

1. Why does Wheelwright use the personal pronoun *I* in the paragraphs that deal with the characteristic phases of moral deliberation?
2. The anecdotes in this article employ questions as rhetorical devices. Comment on the effectiveness—and the purpose—of each question.
3. To make his essay easier to follow, the author frequently divides and subdivides his topic. Find examples of this technique of classification.

Writing Assignments

1. Describe a moral decision you have made; present the alternatives and the processes of definition and decision that you went through.
2. If you disagree with Wheelwright—if you believe that there are absolute and unchanging moral laws which govern all situations —present your views in a theme.
3. Write a theme entitled "Is Mercy Killing Ethical?"
4. Present your answer to the following question: Are today's college students more moral than previous generations of students?

Library Exploration

1. For other statements on ethics, read some of the works of Plato, Aristotle, and Spinoza.
2. If you would like to read more of Philip Wheelwright's ideas, you might be interested in his *A Critical Introduction To Ethics*.

Vocabulary

tantamount (5): equivalent
acquiesce (5): accept or agree passively
lucrative (5): profitable
temporal (9): related to or dealing with time
envisage (10): visualize
syllogism (15): formal statement of deductive reasoning consisting of a major premise, a minor premise, and a conclusion
adjunct (17): something joined or added to another thing, but not necessarily a part of it
normative (20): relating to behavioral standards of a group
consummation (21): completion; fulfillment
incommensurate (23): lacking a common basis for comparison
manifold (25): many
exhortation (28): urging; advice; counsel
propensity (28): natural inclination
volition (30): exercise of the will
obloquy (30): condemnation; abuse
paradox (31): a statement that is seemingly contradictory or opposed to common sense and yet is perhaps true
altruistic (33): unselfish; interested in the welfare of others
vagaries (40): eccentric or unpredictable notions or actions

34

SHOULD GOD DIE?

Graham B. Blaine, Jr.

The author of this article, chief of psychiatry at the Harvard University Health Service, attacks the new morality and those theologians who espouse it. Their attempts to *"kill" God, he claims, "will seriously contribute to moral softness and irresolution in our young people."*

1   To me the greatest paradox of modern times is the attempted murder of God by some of those who were formerly His strongest supporters. We have always been faced with militant atheists and rationalist unbelievers, but never before have we seen ordained ministers rise against their God—and all He stands for—in the defiant fashion we now witness.

2   The image of God as an old man with flashing eyes and flowing beard is still held by very few, but God as a presence, whose guiding influence is communicated and explained to us by the ministers of His Church, is a powerful force in the lives of many. For the average young adult in today's world it can serve as an essential reinforcement for earlier moral standards learned at home, and as a continuing source of direction and inner strength. But religion can only have real meaning if it is the medium through which the word of God is transmitted. Without God, religion is merely a man-made philosophical framework. If God is destroyed, then with Him is destroyed the entire basis for traditional and absolute morality.

3   Parental example and control begin to become less effective with the start of adolescence, and as the adolescent moves on to college he looks almost entirely for example and advice to those whom he respects in his school and church community. He may need to challenge these individuals fairly brashly, but essentially he respects them for their consistency and firmness. Though he may openly disagree, inwardly he usually believes in them and with them.

4   Many of today's proponents of the New Morality, such as the Right Reverend John A. T. Robinson, the Bishop of Woolwich, and Joseph Fletcher, Professor of Social Ethics at the Episcopal Theological Seminary in Cambridge, Massachusetts, hold high positions in their churches and are not out of favor with the hierarchy, even though they

have blatantly contradicted the most basic tenets of Church doctrine. Perhaps these men cannot be defined as the original death-of-God theologians but, in denying the existence of an absolute system of ethics, they are essentially denying the existence of God.

5   The Reverend Fletcher, in his book, *Situation Ethics*, argues in favor of judging the right and wrong of every decision in the light of the total context in which this decision must be made. He is against prejudging a situation or entering any moral crisis with a previously determined set of values, no matter how much experience one may have had or what precepts one might have acquired from wise individuals. According to him, so long as one feels sure that no one will be hurt, anything goes. He states: "People are learning that we can have sex without love and love without sex; but if people do not believe it is wrong to have sex relations outside marriage, it isn't—unless they hurt themselves, their partners, or others." This would seem to give religious sanction to adultery as well as to premarital intercourse—so long as those who might be hurt by it do not find out about it. How easy it would be to convince oneself that such an act, in a particular situation, would be entirely harmless!

6   John A. T. Robinson is more subtle but equally permissive, when he says: "I recognize to the full that all of us, especially young people, have to have working rules. But my point is that when these are questioned as they are being questioned, the Christian is driven back to base them not on law ('Fornication is always wrong') but on love, on what deep concern for persons as whole persons, in their entire social context, really requires."

7   This seems to state that if some people object to some laws, then we should eliminate them and rely instead on one of our emotions (love), even though this emotion is usually characterized as blind, and leads often to biased or distorted judgment.

8   There *are* situations in which a law cannot be sensibly applied as written, but this does not seem a logical reason for eliminating it entirely. Joseph Fletcher describes four cases involving, respectively, prostitution, adultery, suicide, and mass homicide, which clearly demonstrate the impossibility of formulating a law that is right for every situation; but if his premise is correct, then because an ambulance or a fire engine must exceed the speed limit in order to save lives in special situations, we should have no speed laws. Perhaps love and, as Robinson says, "deep concern for people as whole persons in their entire social context" *would* keep everyone driving at a safe speed, but I doubt that any of us would be willing to count on it.

9   Theologians may readily argue among themselves about the logic or even the existence of absolute morality but, when they talk from the pulpit or write popular books, they may well do great harm if they promote new—and unproved—theories of ethics. A young adult, faced with many conflicting internal emotions and, at the same time,

vast numbers of external temptations and enticements, needs to know where he stands on important issues before he finds himself in a decision-making situation. At such a moment, there is usually no time to step back and view the entire context with coldly calculating calm. More often, reason has been submerged by passion, and decisions are made from the dictates of a conscience developed over the years as a result of training from Church and home, rather than a cool appraisal of the possibility of someone's being hurt by the action (or inaction) of the moment.

10   Why does a psychiatrist like myself get involved in matters of ethics, since his main job should be to treat the emotionally ill and, in the process, remain neutral and nonjudgmental? Professionally, a psychiatrist should try to understand and explain, rather than to criticize or punish. But in his job he needs to have limits not only clearly set but also firmly maintained by society. This is society's business. When a medical or psychiatric approach is adopted by others, it may do more harm than good to those in trouble. For example, a theological student who had been caught stealing—in fact, had a long history of it—was not reprimanded by his dean but was, instead, referred to a psychiatrist for help. When asked why he seemed so desultory about his treatment, he explained that he did not understand in what way he was ill. He still had the money he stole, he continued to be a student in good standing at the seminary, and he was able to chat with a psychiatrist when he wished to, at the school's expense. The rules were there, but they had no real meaning for him. In ignoring its obligation to make these rules clear by enforcing them, the theological school was contributing to the perpetuation of this student's illness rather than its resolution.

11   Some campus ministers, today, claim that students are no longer interested in traditional religion and that the concept of God has no meaning for them. They blame the emphasis on science, the popularity of existentialism, and the current college student's reliance on logic and rationalism, for what they see as the recent movement away from the Church. Their concern does not seem to be entirely warranted. Surveys have shown that college students profess more faith than seminarians, and it is also true that enthusiasm is still high on most campuses when religious leaders who follow traditional and orthodox patterns of belief appear.

12   I do not think that the situationists will succeed in murdering God. My fear, instead, is that, in their attempts to kill Him, His attackers will so maim and mutilate His image that they will seriously contribute to moral softness and irresolution in our young people, and that this, in turn, will have lasting ill effects upon them and their own children (both wanted and unwanted) in the years to come. Personally, I believe that God will prove to be indestructible.

Discussion of Theme

1. If God is destroyed, what do you think will furnish the basis for ethics and morality?
2. What are Dr. Blaine's reasons for counseling churchmen against a public debate over the death of God?
3. The author says that although students may question the morality they are taught by their elders, they basically agree with it. Would you and your friends agree with this statement?
4. What is the meaning of the last sentence in the article?
5. The author states that a psychiatrist's "main job should be to treat the emotionally ill and . . . remain neutral and nonjudgmental." Does he practice what he preaches?
6. After reading this selection, can you make any inferences about Dr. Blaine's view of human nature?
7. Should morality be absolute or relative?
8. In what way can there be a meaningful argument on this topic?

Discussion of Rhetoric

1. Has the author of this article fairly presented the viewpoint of the death-of-God theologians? How convincing is the author's "defense" of God? Is his appeal primarily to reason?
2. How valid is the analogy between the laws of the church and the laws governing cars?
3. What effect does the word *blatantly* have on the tone of paragraph 4?

Writing Assignments

1. Is religion the only basis for morality? Or can a person be ethical or moral without religious faith? Give your views in a theme.
2. Define sin.
3. Have you and your parents had disagreements over moral questions? Select a specific disagreement and analyze its causes and resolution.

Library Exploration

For a further treatment of Dr. Blaine's views, read his *Youth and the Hazards of Affluence*. For an opposing view, read *Situation Ethics* by Joseph Fletcher.

Vocabulary

paradox (1): something (a person, condition, or act) with seemingly contradictory qualities
rationalist (1): one who places reason above faith
proponents (4): supporters (of a particular view)
hierarchy (4): ranking of group leaders
desultory (10): lacking a definite plan or purpose; lacking in consistency

35

GOD IS DEAD IN GEORGIA

Anthony Towne

*The author of this mock obituary
records the death of a well-known
celebrity.*

1   God, creator of the universe, principal deity of the world's Jews,
ultimate reality of Christians, and most eminent of all divinities, died
late yesterday during major surgery undertaken to correct a massive
diminishing influence. His exact age is not known, but close friends
estimate that it greatly exceeded that of all other extant beings. While
he did not, in recent years, maintain any fixed abode, his house was said
to consist of many mansions.

2   The cause of death could not be immediately determined, pending
an autopsy, but the deity's surgeon, Thomas J. J. Altizer, 38, of Emory
University in Atlanta, indicated possible cardiac insufficiency. Assisting
Dr. Altizer in the unsuccessful surgery were Dr. Paul van Buren of
Temple University, Philadelphia; Dr. William Hamilton of Colgate-
Rochester, Rochester, N.Y.; and Dr. Gabriel Vahanian of Syracuse
University, Syracuse, N.Y.

3   Word of the death, long rumored, was officially disclosed to reporters
at five minutes before midnight after a full day of mounting anxiety
and the coming and going of ecclesiastical dignitaries and members
of the immediate family. At the bedside, when the end came, were, in
addition to the attending surgeons and several nurses, the Papal
Nuncio to the United States, representing His Holiness, Pope Paul VI,
Vicar of Christ on Earth and Supreme Pontiff of the Roman Catholic
Church; Iakovos, Archbishop of North and South America, rep-
resenting the Orthodox Churches; Dr. Eugene Carson Blake, Stated
Clerk of the Presbyterian Church in the U.S.A., representing the World
Council of Churches, predominantly a Protestant institution; Rabbi
Mark Tannenbaum of New York City, representing the tribes of
Israel, chosen people, according to their faith, of the deceased; The
Rev. William Moyers, Baptist minister, representing President John-
son; the 3rd Secretary of the Soviet embassy in Trinidad, representing
the Union of Soviet Socialist Republics; and a number of unidentified
curious bystanders.

4   Unable to be in Atlanta owing to the pressure of business at the second Vatican Council, now in session, the Pope, in Rome, said, in part: "We are deeply distressed for we have suffered an incalculable loss. The contributions of God to the Church cannot be measured, and it is difficult to imagine how we shall proceed without Him." Rumors swept through the Council, meeting under the great vaulted dome of St. Peter's, that, before adjourning the Council in December, the Pope will proclaim God a saint, an action, if taken, that would be wholly without precedent in the history of the Church. Several aged women were reported to have come forward with claims of miraculous cures due to God's intervention. One woman, a 103 year old Bulgarian peasant, is said to have conceived a son at the very instant God expired. Proof of miracles is a precondition for sanctification according to ancient tradition of the Roman Catholic faith.

5   In Johnson City, Texas, President Johnson, recuperating from his recent gall bladder surgery, was described by aides as "profoundly upset." He at once directed that all flags should be at half-staff until after the funeral. The First Lady and the two presidential daughters, Luci and Lynda, were understood to have wept openly. Luci, 18, the younger daughter, whose engagement has been lately rumored, is a convert to Roman Catholicism. It is assumed that the President and his family, including his cousin, Oriole, will attend the last rites, if the international situation permits. Both houses of Congress met in Washington at noon today and promptly adjourned after passing a joint resolution expressing "grief and great respect for the departed spiritual leader." Sen. Wayne Morse, Dem. of Oregon, objected on the grounds that the resolution violated the principle of separation of church and state, but he was overruled by Vice President Hubert Humphrey, who remarked that "this is not a time for partisan politics."

6   Plans for the deity's funeral are incomplete. Reliable sources suggested that extensive negotiations may be necessary in order to select a church for the services and an appropriate liturgy. Dr. Wilhelm Pauck, theologian, of Union Seminary in New York City proposed this morning that it would be "fitting and seemly" to inter the remains in the ultimate ground of all being, but it is not known whether that proposal is acceptable to the family. Funerals for divinities, common in ancient times, have been exceedingly rare in recent centuries, and it is understood that the family wishes to review details of earlier funerals before setting upon rites suitable for God.

7   (In New York, meanwhile, the stock market dropped sharply in early trading. Volume was heavy. One broker called it the most active market day since the assassination of President Kennedy, Nov. 22, 1963. The market rallied in late trading, after reports were received that Jesus—see 'Man in the News,' p. 36, col. 4—who survives, plans to assume a larger role in management of the universe.)

8   Reaction from the world's great and from the man in the street was

uniformly incredulous. "At least he's out of his misery," commented one housewife in an Elmira, N.Y., supermarket. "I can't believe it," said the Right Reverend Horace W. B. Donegan, Protestant Episcopal Bishop of New York, who only last week celebrated the 15th anniversary of his installation as Bishop. In Paris, President de Gaulle, in a 30 second appearance on national television, proclaimed: "God is dead! Long live the republic! Long live France!" Mrs. Jacqueline Kennedy, widow of the late President, was reported "in seclusion" in her Fifth Avenue apartment. "She's had about all she can take," a close friend of the Kennedy family said. News of the death was included in a one sentence statement, without comment, on the 3rd page of Pravda, official organ of the Soviet government. The passing of God has not been disclosed to the 800 million Chinese who live behind the bamboo curtain.

9   Public reaction in this country was perhaps summed up by an elderly retired streetcar conductor in Passaic, New Jersey, who said: "I never met him, of course. Never even saw him. But from what I heard I guess he was a real nice fellow. Tops." From Independence, Mo., former President Harry S. Truman, who received the news in his Kansas City barbershop, said: "I'm always sorry to hear somebody is dead. It's a damn shame." In Gettysburg, Pa., former President Dwight D. Eisenhower, released, through a military aide, the following statement: "Mrs. Eisenhower joins me in heartfelt sympathy to the family and many friends of the late God. He was, I always felt, a force for moral good in the universe. Those of us who were privileged to know him admired the probity of his character, the breadth of his compassion, the depth of his intellect. Generous almost to a fault, his many acts of kindness to America will never be forgotten. It is a very great loss indeed. He will be missed."

10   From Basel, Switzerland, came word that Dr. Karl Barth, venerable Protestant theologian, informed of the death of God, declared: "I don't know who died in Atlanta, but whoever he was he's an imposter." Dr. Barth, 79, with the late Paul Tillich, is widely regarded as the foremost theologian of the 20th Century.

11   (There have been unconfirmed reports that Jesus of Nazareth, 33, a carpenter and reputed son of God, who survives, will assume the authority, if not the title, of the deceased deity. Jesus, sometimes called the Christ, was himself a victim of death, having succumbed some 1932 years ago in Palestine, now the state of Israel, purportedly on orders of a Roman governor, Pontius Pilate, and at the behest of certain citizens of Jerusalem. This event, described by some as "deicide," has lately occupied the deliberations of the Vatican Council, who has solemnly exonerated the Jews generally of responsibility for the alleged crime. The case is complicated by the fact that Jesus, although he died, returned to life, and so may not have died at all. Diplomats around the world were speculating today on the place the resurrected

Jesus will occupy in the power vacuum created by the sudden passing of God.)

12   Dr. Altizer, God's surgeon, in an exclusive interview with the Times, stated this morning that the death was "not unexpected." "He had been ailing for some time," Dr. Altizer said, "and lived much longer than most of us thought possible." He noted that the death of God had, in fact, been prematurely announced in the last century by the famed German surgeon, Nietzsche. Nietzsche, who was insane the last ten years of his life, may have confused "certain symptoms of morbidity in the aged patient with actual death, a mistake any busy surgeon will occasionally make," Dr. Altizer suggested. "God was an excellent patient, compliant, cheerful, alert. Every comfort modern science could provide was made available to him. He did not suffer— he just, as it were, slipped out of our grasp." Dr. Altizer also disclosed that plans for a memorial to God have already been discussed informally, and it is likely a committee of eminent clergymen and laymen will soon be named to raise funds for use in "research into the causes of death in deities, an area of medicine many physicians consider has been too long neglected." Dr. Altizer indicated, finally, that he had personal confidence that Jesus, relieved of the burdens of divinity, would, in time, assume a position of great importance in the universe. "We have lost," he said, "a father, but we have gained a son."

13   (Next Sunday's New York Times will include, without extra charge, a 24-page full-color supplement with many photographs, reviewing the major events of God's long reign, the circumstances of his sudden and untimely death, and prospects for a godless future. The editors will be grateful for pertinent letters, photographs, visions, and the like.)

14   There has been as yet no statement from Jesus, but a close associate, the Holy Ghost, has urged prayer and good works. He also said that it is the wish of the family that in lieu of flowers contributions be made to the Building Fund of St. John the Divine in New York City so that the edifice may be finished.

Discussion of Theme

1. In paragraph 12 God's "surgeon" is quoted as saying that His death was "not unexpected." What comment is the author making about the current state of religion?
2. What institutions, ideas, and persons are satirized in this article?
3. Who are the individuals named in paragraph 2? Why would they be named in connection with the death of God?

Discussion of Rhetoric

1. What is parody? What is satire? How does the effectiveness of both depend on the reader's knowledge?

2. Does the tone of this article tell you anything about the author's attitude toward the death-of-God theologians?
3. Why is an obituary a likely vehicle for satire on this topic?
4. For what kind of readers was this selection written? Are there any groups it might offend?

Writing Assignments

1. Some critics have said this is the post-Christian age. Present evidence to support or refute this statement.
2. What is your attitude toward the ideas put forth by the theologians who have announced the death of God?
3. Select another idea or recent event and, in a similar vein, write a satirical account of it.

Library Exploration

1. For a more serious approach to theology, read some of the works of the philosophers and theologians mentioned in this article.
2. To appreciate the author's skill at parodying the *Times* style, you should read several obituaries in recent issues of that paper.

Vocabulary

extant (1): existing
venerable (10): worthy of respect because of age, character, and attainments
purportedly (11): reputedly; supposedly
exonerated (11): relieved of blame
compliant (12): yielding to the wishes of others
pertinent (13): relevant or applicable to the matter at hand

36

THE UNDERGROUND CHURCH

Paul Evans Kaylor

The author of this article, the Reverend Paul Evans Kaylor, believes that the institutional churches must recognize and try to understand the growing movement in Christianity often referred to as the Underground Church.

1   Recently, I was accused of being a conservative. This both irritated and puzzled me, primarily because I knew that in the matters of economics, war and peace, race relations, and morality, I was far to the left of my accusers, who as members of my class in Christian Ethics the previous year had distinguished themselves by a studied indifference to social reform. My consternation at the term "conservative"—or the misunderstanding of the term between us—was even greater than my irritation.

2   After a lengthy conversation, I discovered that I was being indicted on two counts: maintenance of good standing as a priest of the Episcopal Church, and employment as a chaplain and assistant professor of religion in their college. The fact of my long, if somewhat modest, involvement in the civil-rights movement, the peace movement, and in efforts directed toward political, educational, and church reform was irrelevant because of this association with these two established institutions. When I asked what I should do to "get with it" and move beyond what they described as "a fossilized condition of conservatism," I was told to take off my clerical collar, denounce the Establishment, and join them in the "Underground Church."

3   On Maundy Thursday last April, I joined with a group of upper-middle-class college students and faculty members for a fellowship meal to commemorate the Last Supper. We talked about the search for an appropriate response to the recent assassination of Martin Luther King, Jr. Dismissing the alternative of despair and "copping out," we formulated practical plans for immediate local action. The evening concluded with the sharing of bread and wine and the traditional passing of the Peace with the words: "The peace of the Lord be always with you." We left with renewed dedication to work for the transformation of society and the radical reform of the church. The next

day I asked one of the students who had been there what the experience had meant to him. He saw it as a gathering of the people of the "Underground" who share a realistic Christian commitment and hope for humanity.

4   In June I spent a holiday on the island of Maui in Hawaii. One evening I was invited by a bearded, barefoot young man and his girlfriend to join a discussion on the deck of a fishing boat. The participants would have been described as "hippies" by anyone of the well-scrubbed tourists staying at my hotel. They were disillusioned young men and women who had renounced conventional society for a simple and intensely personal style of life. I can only describe the long and subdued conversation as apocalyptic and mystical; any suggestions of creative action in society were discounted. On the walk back to the hotel, my young friend—a dropout from a Protestant seminary—informed me that he regarded this little band of alienated Jews, Roman Catholics, and Protestants as part of the "remnant" of the faithful, which he called the Underground Church.

5   On a weekend in August immediately after the publication of Pope Paul VI's 7,500-word encyclical on birth control, I visited Roman Catholic friends in a suburban New York community. A group of 30 persons—ranging in age from 16 through 40—were gathered for a home mass. At the conclusion of the simplified liturgy, the young priest, in a light-blue business suit and Brooks Brothers tie, lifted a goblet and said: "The blood of Christ." He sipped from the goblet and passed it around the table. After sharing the wine, the priest said: "The mass is over. Go in peace." The hostess then served coffee and cake and the group stayed far into the night discussing the crisis of authority in the Church—particularly the issue of birth control. The unanimous conclusion was that Pope Paul VI's encyclical was unwise and irrelevant to the faith which they shared. All of the couples said that they would follow their own conscience in this matter and would not consider themselves unfit to receive the sacraments of the Church by disobeying the teachings of the Pontiff. I was repeatedly amazed during the lengthy discussions of the specific issue of contraception, and the more general one of the authority of the papacy, to hear laymen—engineers, teachers, businessmen—intelligently cite not only contemporary social and psychological theory but also Scripture, St. Augustine, St. Thomas, and the documents of the councils of Trent, Vatican I, and Vatican II. This was not simply an angry gathering of uninformed rebels unwilling to accept an inconvenient ruling. They were sensitive, intelligent, committed seekers after truth. The young priest who had conducted the mass told me that he conducted two or three home masses, and discussions like this weekly. He called it the Underground Church.

6   These four diverse experiences reveal something of the extent of the

religious phenomenon first called the "Underground Church" by Malcolm Boyd, Episcopal priest, sometime night-club performer, and author, who has recently edited a book of essays with that title. They also indicate the wide-ranging meanings and expectations of the people who call themselves members of the Underground.

7   Despite the diversity of setting and conversation, these and the other manifestations of the movement I have attended have several characteristics in common: attendance of young people, mainly under 30; an ecumenical point of view; and rejection of the Establishment. Furthermore, with the exception of the group of alienated mystics on Maui, these occasions have all been marked by a profound concern for radical transformation of society. The attempt to recover the sense of awe and mystery in religious experience, coupled with the theme of withdrawal from society exhibited by the Maui community, is often found in the Underground. This theme has always been present in the Biblical religions (Christianity and Judaism). However, it was seldom dominant and it is of importance in the Underground only in those instances where Eastern religious thought or a drug subculture is influential. Far more characteristic for the Underground than this passive mysticism is the insistence on the essential solidarity and involvement of man with man in the elemental as well as complex texture of existence. Underlying all of this is an emphasis on community, but defined in a way which bears only small resemblance to the traditional Western emphasis on the necessity of a community for self-understanding, worship, and effective action in society. In the traditional syntax the concept is almost synonymous with the Church itself, with concise and established boundaries, and a given structure and membership. It is an institutional concept, with room for experiments *within* the defined structure, but none for changing its boundaries. This conception—the normative one for liberal Protestantism and the post-Vatican II Roman Catholic Church of Paul VI, as well as of more conservative bodies—is not violated by folk masses, the Liturgy in the vernacular, bureaucratic movements toward unity, and other minor experiments. By contrast, the Underground people see the Christian Community in a radically different manner. For them, the Christian Community itself *is* the experiment; as an experiment it is unfinished, and consequently it is not something one *does* experiments in or with.

8   Father George Hafner, a member of an experimental parish in Trenton, N.J., has written in a *Commonweal* series on "Underground Theology": "Since the world is in a state of continual flux, Christian communities must be continually experimenting with the emerging life-styles and thought patterns in order to discover how Jesus' mission can be continued in and through them. When the Christian Community stops being an experiment and thinks of itself as the Kingdom

which has come rather than the Kingdom which is coming, it ceases
to be the presence of the living Christ in the world and becomes a
community of idolators. For the mission of Christ can be discovered
only in the dialectical situation in which it is constantly validating
its authenticity by its contributions to the humanization of the world.
There are no other criteria for testing its vitality." (Italics mine.) This
properly distinguishes the Underground Church from the above-
ground or "Established" Church and affirms that this phenomenon
is something more than an avant-garde movement, or as one liberal
Churchman, firmly entrenched in the institution, has called it, "a little
bit of healthy revolution." By taking seriously the ancient Christian
teaching that "in Christ there is neither Gentile nor Jew," the Underground raises an issue so profound as to suggest dissolution of all
boundaries of previously known church organizations, theologies,
ethical theories, and world views. Seen in this light, the severe identity
and authority crises in the Western religious premise represent only
one aspect of the most important historical factor of the 20th-century:
world revolution. The specific revolutions—political, social, technological, economic, or moral—are all of one piece and must be considered as part of a transition in the history of mankind, which has
produced a new age qualitatively *and* quantitatively different from
past ages.

9   It has been called an age of "secularism" or "urbanism." In an urban
society men are related on a pragmatic and functional basis. The
individual's thinking and understanding of life arises from within his
experience of the world rather than from "outside," from supernatural
explanation or from technological conquest of nature. It is in principle
an open society which disregards tribal, caste, racial, and class boundaries. This is the antithesis of the world view of the previous period
when man's position was defined and contained by the concept of a
chain or ladder of being in which God, the source of being, is at the
top, the material world is at the bottom, and man is in the middle
receiving understanding from above and exercising control over the
world beneath him. The transition to the pragmatic and functional
understandings of the age of urbanism has not yet been completed,
and the violence of our time can be traced in part to resistance to this
essential thrust of the new society.

10   The generation gap, which is so often glibly explained as a "rejection
of middle-class values," is in reality a deep schism of consciousness
between those who are chronologically *and* spiritually under 30 and
the previous generations. This gulf between the younger generation,
who operate functionally and pragmatically, and those whose models
are based on a static and prescribed view of reality, is of such magnitude
that communication between the two is virtually impossible. Definitions of man's comprehension of himself, of time, of God, and of such

crucial questions as freedom, responsibility, and authority take radically
different forms for those on opposite sides of the schism.

11   In the churches this schism of consciousness is most apparent among
Roman Catholics. It had grown to gigantic proportions since Pope
John XXIII issued the call for Vatican Council II in December 1961,
and promised an *aggiornamento* ("updating") that would bring the
most ancient continuous institution of Western civilization into step
with the contemporary world. There has indeed been *aggiornamento*,
but it has not been of the orderly and predictable nature that Vatican
authorities, including many liberals, and the traditionalists envisioned.
For them, the forwarding of historical tradition, while renewing the
institutional church, is the primary hope and goal. The adherents of
the Underground are not concerned with the historical, institutional
church. Their radically secular perspective demands freedom to "do
their own thing" in the world. For them and those of other traditions
as well, their concern with religious experience and meaning is intense.
Equally intense is their rejection of the institutional forms in which it
has been embodied. For them, the message is more important than the
medium. The situation is as serious as was that of the 16th century
when the rupture of Christendom initially led by Luther and Calvin
got out of hand and led to what appeared to be a state of chaos in both
church and society. Although we no longer can speak meaningfully of
"Christendom," the parallels with earlier historical periods should
not be dismissed in attempts to understand the present.

12   The very term "underground" brings to mind other historical connotations which persons familiar with the conventional and highly
visible church find uncomfortable. (To the casual observer, it brings
to mind the equally disturbing image of the Hippie Underground.)
It recalls the early Christians barricaded in catacombs, confronting
the established civil and religious authority of the Roman Empire,
and the European underground during the Hitler era.

13   Despite persecution at the outset, by the early fourth century the
Christian movement had become the most influential force in the
social and political structure of the Empire. It provided the "cement"
of society rather than the prophetic and revolutionary force of the
earlier underground period. Subsequent church history has been
primarily social and institutional history. There have been instances
of a return to the earlier prophetic vision of opposition to the establishment, but most of the reform movements became institutionalized and,
therefore, drained of their prophetic impact.

14   The people of the Underground to whom I have spoken regard the
present movement as one of these instances of radical reform. The
realists among them do not expect the Underground to replace the
established churches and have no illusions about the eventual compromise of the movement. The very fact that a conference on the

Underground Church was called for last spring is evidence that the compromise and inevitable institutionalization is underway. (The incongruity of such an Establishment event as a conference on the campus of a large Roman Catholic college for those who oppose the present institutional nature and structure of the Church appears to be greater than it is. Students of history—particularly religious history—are aware that the movement from *ad-hoc* "spirit-led" groups to defined structure and form is the story of Western religion.) The hope—the intention—is to move the institutions away from mere self-perpetuation, self-service, and authoritarianism to active, meaningful involvement in, and creative influence on, the life-styles of individual men and the structures of society, and, like other such movements, to return Christianity to its original prophetic and revolutionary role.

15   The comparison of the movement to the underground groups that opposed the Nazi tyranny is also much to the point. This is not as obvious in the United States as in other areas of the world, such as the Communist nations of Poland, Czechoslovakia, and Red China, and also in Franco Spain and in the Latin-American countries where an alliance between the established church and totalitarian government demand the kind of obedience that the earliest Christians and the faithful in Hitler Germany rejected. It is in these places that the underground, in the form of genuine guerrilla action, is most vital.

16   What are we to say about the importance of the Underground Church movement? Certainly, it will not go away. The concerns for reconciliation, justice, and freedom as well as for relevant theology and meaningful worship must be reckoned with in any realistic appraisal of the religious situation. To be sure, the people of the Underground exhibit a naïve sense of history and express a frail sense of freedom and responsibility. But is this not a judgment upon those whom they have rejected as well as upon themselves? The institutional churches, allied as they have been with the oppressive forces of society at so many points, must recognize their culpability in the excesses of this movement as in the other rebellions of our era. As a member of the Establishment, which is repudiated and rejected by the younger generation and their adventurous allies of a riper age, I must admit culpability and try to learn from them in this difficult period of transition for mankind. Perhaps the gospel of revolution which they preach and practice is indeed the Truth and the only hope for man in a seemingly absurd world. This is not to advocate total acceptance of the extravagant search for a new religious style without offering criticism and attempting to find common grounds of meeting. It is simply to accept the importance of that which is.

17   I will not venture predictions about the future of religion at this Christmas Season, 1968. However, it is safe to say that the religious

situation will never be the same again for any of us. The revolutionary nature of the Christian gospel is a reality for vast numbers of people for the first time in centuries. The hope for "peace on earth, good will toward man" must be interpreted in connection with the emphasis of an aggressive and impatient generation on the saying of Jesus— "Do not think that I have come to bring peace on earth; I have not come to bring peace, but a sword." Perhaps this hard saying must be dealt with and accepted before the ancient hope associated with the Babe of Bethlehem can be realized on earth.

Discussion of Theme

1. How does the underground church differ from the institutional church? What are the goals of the new movement?
2. Why might the authorities of the Roman Catholic Church feel threatened by the underground church?
3. What characteristics do members of underground-church movements have in common?
4. How does the traditional church view the idea of the Christian in his community? How does the underground church view this concept?

Discussion of Rhetoric

1. Is the diction in this article appropriate or inappropriate to the subject matter? Are there too many terms used that are difficult for the layman to understand?
2. Find examples of the author's use of definition and analysis as structural devices.
3. Why does Father Kaylor include the biblical quote, "Do not think that I have come to bring peace on earth; I have not come to bring peace, but a sword"? What rhetorical devices are found in this quotation?
4. In what sense is the word "dialectical" (paragraph 8) used by Kaylor?

Writing Assignments

1. Is the underground-church movement a sign that Christianity is still a vital force in our society? Or does it indicate that God is indeed dead? Defend either view in a theme.
2. In "To Abolish Children," Karl Shapiro stated that the younger generation was trying to withdraw, to obliterate meaningful communication and dialogue. Compare this view with the one presented by Father Kaylor.
3. Senator Hatfield, in "Today's Youth: A Hopeful Generation," said that on the subject of religion the young people of today say, "Christ, yes; Christianity, no." If you agree with this view, state some of your reasons.

4. Describe some other underground movements. How do they compare with the underground-church movement in terms of methods and goals?

Library Exploration
1. Who were St. Augustine and St. Thomas?
2. If possible, read *The Underground Church* by Malcolm Boyd.
3. Find out what you can about Pope Paul VI's effect upon modern Catholic doctrine.
4. What are Vatican I and Vatican II?

Vocabulary
consternation (1): amazement; dismay
apocalyptic (4): forecasting imminent disaster or ultimate doom
encyclical (5): a papal letter to the bishops of the church
ecumenical (7): promoting worldwide Christian unity or cooperation
vernacular (7): native speech or dialect (of a place or group)
idolators (8): idol worshipers
secularism (9): indifference to or rejection of religion and religious
considerations
pragmatic (9): practical
antithesis (9): direct opposite
schism (10): division; discord
ad-hoc (14): for one particular purpose without consideration of
general application
culpability (16): the state of being guilty
repudiated (16): disowned; rejected as unauthorized or as having
no binding force

37

THE DECLINE OF RELIGION

William Barrett

*This essay examines the decline of
religious orthodoxy in Western
civilization.*

1   The central fact of modern history in the West—by which we mean
the long period from the end of the Middle Ages to the present—is
unquestionably the decline of religion. No doubt, the churches are
still very powerful organizations; there are millions of churchgoers all
over the world; and even the purely intellectual possibilities of religious
belief look better to churchmen now than in the bleak days of self-
confident nineteenth-century materialism. A few years ago there was
even considerable talk about a "religious revival," and some popular
and patriotic periodicals such as *Life* magazine gave a great deal of
space to it; but the talk has by now pretty much died down, the movement, if any, subsided, and the American public buys more automobiles and television sets than ever before. When *Life* magazine
promotes a revival of religion, one is only too painfully aware from the
nature of this publication that religion is considered as being in the
national interest; one could scarcely have a clearer indication of the
broader historical fact that in the modern world the nation-state, a
thoroughly secular institution, outranks any church.

2   The decline of religion in modern times means simply that religion
is no longer the uncontested center and ruler of man's life, and that the
church is no longer the final and unquestioned home and asylum of his
being. The deepest significance of this change does not even appear
principally at the purely intellectual level, in loss of belief, though this
loss due to the critical inroads of science has been a major historical
cause of the decline. The waning of religion is a much more concrete
and complex fact than a mere change in conscious outlook; it penetrates
the deepest strata of man's total psychic life. It is indeed one of the major
stages in man's psychic evolution—as Nietzsche, almost alone among
nineteenth-century philosophers, was to see. Religion to medieval man
was not so much a theological system as a solid psychological matrix
surrounding the individual's life from birth to death, sanctifying and

enclosing all its ordinary and extraordinary occasions in sacrament and ritual. The loss of the church was the loss of a whole system of symbols, images, dogmas, and rites which had the psychological validity of immediate experience, and within which hitherto the whole psychic life of Western man had been safely contained. In losing religion, man lost the concrete connection with a transcendent realm of being; he was set free to deal with this world in all its brute objectivity. But he was bound to feel homeless in such a world, which no longer answered the needs of his spirit. A home is the accepted framework which habitually contains our life. To lose one's psychic container is to be cast adrift, to become a wanderer upon the face of the earth. Henceforth, in seeking his own human completeness man would have to do for himself what he once had done for him, unconsciously, by the church, through the medium of its sacramental life. Naturally enough, man's feeling of homelessness did not make itself felt for some time; the Renaissance man was still enthralled by a new and powerful vision of mastery over the whole earth.

3   No believer, no matter how sincere, could possibly write the *Divine Comedy* today, even if he possessed a talent equal to Dante's. Visions and symbols do not have the immediate and overwhelming reality for us that they had for the medieval poet. In the *Divine Comedy* the whole of nature is merely a canvas upon which the religious symbol and image are painted. Western man has spent more than five hundred years—half a millennium—in stripping nature of these projections and turning it into a realm of neutral objects which his science may control. Thus it could hardly be expected that the religious image would have the same force for us as it did for Dante. This is simply a psychic fact within human history; psychic facts have just as much historical validity as the facts that we now, unlike the man of Dante's time, travel in airplanes and work in factories regulated by computing machines. A great work of art can never be repeated—the history of art shows us time and again that literal imitation leads to pastiche— because it springs from the human soul, which evolves like everything else in nature. This point must be insisted upon, contrary to the view of some of our more enthusiastic medievalists who picture the psychic containment of medieval man as a situation of human completeness to which we must return. History has never allowed man to return to the past in any total sense. And our psychological problems cannot be solved by a regression to a past state in which they had not yet been brought into being. On the other hand, enlightened and progressive thinkers are equally blind when they fail to recognize that every major step forward by mankind entails some loss, the sacrifice of an older security and the creation and heightening of new tensions. (We should bear this in mind against some of the criticisms of Existentialism as a philosophy that has unbearably heightened human tensions: it did not

create those tensions, which were already at work in the soul of modern man, but simply sought to give them philosophic expression, rather than evading them by pretending they were not there.)

4   It is far from true that the passage from the Middle Ages to modern times is the substitution of a rational for a religious outlook; on the contrary, the whole of medieval philosophy—as Whitehead has very aptly remarked—is one of "unbounded rationalism" in comparison with modern thought. Certainly, the difference between a St. Thomas Aquinas in the thirteenth century and a Kant at the end of the eighteenth century is conclusive on this point: For Aquinas the whole natural world, and particularly this natural world as it opens toward God as First Cause, was transparently accessible to human reason; while to Kant, writing at the bitter end of the century of Enlightenment, the limits of human reason had very radically shrunk. (Indeed, as we shall see later, the very meaning of human reason became altered in Kant.) But this "unbounded rationalism" of the medieval philosopher is altogether different from the untrammeled use later thinkers made of human reason, applying it like an acid solvent to all things human or divine. The rationalism of the medieval philosophers was contained by the mysteries of faith and dogma, which were altogether beyond the grasp of human reason, but were nevertheless powerfully real and meaningful to man as symbols that kept the vital circuit open between reason and emotion, between the rational and non-rational in the human psyche. Hence, this rationalism of the medieval philosophers does not end with the attenuated, bleak, or grim picture of man we find in the modern rationalists. Here, once again, the condition under which the philosopher creates his philosophy, like that under which the poet creates his poetry, has to do with deeper levels of his being— deeper than the merely conscious level of having or not having a rational point of view. We could not expect to produce a St. Thomas Aquinas, any more than a Dante, today. The total psychic condition of man—of which after all thinking is one of the manifestations—has evolved too radically. Which may be why present-day Thomists have on the whole remained singularly unconvincing to their contemporaries.

5   At the gateway that leads from the Middle Ages into the modern world stand Science (which later became the spirit of the Enlightenment), Protestantism, and Capitalism. At first glance, the spirit of Protestantism would seem to have very little to do with that of the New Science, since in matters religious Protestantism placed all the weight of its emphasis upon the irrational datum of faith, as against the imposing rational structures of medieval theology, and there is Luther's famous curse upon "the whore, Reason." In secular matters, however—and particularly in its relation toward nature—Protestantism fitted in very well with the New Science. By stripping away the wealth of images and symbols from medieval Christianity, Protestantism

unveiled nature as a realm of objects hostile to the spirit and to be conquered by puritan zeal and industry. Thus Protestantism, like science, helped carry forward that immense project of modern man: the despiritualization of nature, the emptying of it of all the symbolic images projected upon it by the human psyche. With Protestantism begins that long modern struggle, which reaches its culmination in the twentieth century, to strip man naked. To be sure, in all of this the aim was progress, and Protestantism did succeed in raising the religious consciousness to a higher level of individual sincerity, soul-searching, and strenuous inwardness. Man was impoverished in order to come face to face with his God and the severe and inexplicable demands of his faith; but in the process he was stripped of all the mediating rites and dogmas that could make this confrontation less dangerous to his psychic balance. Protestantism achieved a heightening of the religious consciousness, but at the same time severed this consciousness from the deep unconscious life of our total human nature. In this respect, its historical thrust runs parallel to that of the New Science and capitalism, since science was making the mythical and symbolic picture of nature disappear before the success of its own rational explanations, and capitalism was opening up the whole world as a field of operations for rationally planned enterprise.

6   Faith, for Protestantism, is nevertheless the irrational and numinous center of religion; Luther was saturated with the feeling of St. Paul that man of himself can do nothing and only God working in us can bring salvation. Here the inflation of human consciousness is radically denied, and the conscious mind is recognized as the mere instrument and plaything of a much greater unconscious force. Faith is an abyss that engulfs the rational nature of man. The Protestant doctrine of original sin is in all its severity a kind of compensatory recognition of those depths below the level of consciousness where the earnest soul demands to interrogate itself—except that those depths are cast into the outer darkness of depravity. So long as faith retained its intensity, however, the irrational elements of human nature were accorded recognition and a central place in the total human economy. But as the modern world moves onward, it becomes more and more secularized in every department of life; faith consequently becomes attenuated, and Protestant man begins to look more and more like a gaunt skeleton, a sculpture by Giacometti. A secular civilization leaves him more starkly naked than the iconoclasm of the Reformation had ever dreamed. The more severely he struggles to hold on to the primal face-to-face relation with God, the more tenuous this becomes, until in the end the relation to God Himself threatens to become a relation to Nothingness. In this sense Kierkegaard, in the middle of the nineteenth century, was the reckoning point of the whole Protestant Reformation that began three centuries earlier: He sees faith for the uncompromising and

desperate wager it is, if one takes it in all its Protestant strictness; and he cannot say, like his Catholic counterpart Pascal, "Stupefy yourself, take holy water, receive the sacraments, and in the end all shall be well"—for Protestant man has forsworn the sacraments and natural symbols of the soul as the snares and pomp of the devil. Some of Kierkegaard's books, such as *The Sickness Unto Death* and *The Concept of Dread*, are still frightening to our contemporaries and so are excused or merely passed over as the personal outpourings of a very melancholy temperament; yet they are the truthful record of what the Protestant soul must experience on the brink of the great Void. Protestant man is the beginning of the West's fateful encounter with Nothingness—an encounter that was long overdue and is perhaps only now in the twentieth century reaching its culmination.

Discussion of Theme
1. Do you agree with the author's appraisal (in paragraph 1) of the recent "religious revival" in this country?
2. In what way is religious belief a "psychic container"?
3. What, according to Barrett, are the three forces that stand "at the gateway" to the modern world? What has been their collective impact on modern man?
4. The author states that man is at "the beginning of the West's fateful encounter with Nothingness . . . ." Do you agree? Is this "encounter" inevitable?

Discussion of Rhetoric
1. Where is the central thesis of this article stated? Is this generally the best place for stating the main idea of an essay?
2. What method does Barrett use to develop his thesis? Is he convincing in his approach?

Writing Assignments
1. If you disagree with Barrett's thesis, write an essay entitled "The Growth of Religion."
2. Develop the following statement, taken from this selection, into a theme: "Every major step forward by mankind entails some loss."
3. If religion is truly dead, what will take its place as the basis of morality and ethics? Present your views in a theme.
4. Identify the following people: Dante; Nietzsche; St. Thomas; Kant; Kierkegaard.

Library Exploration
Read some of the works of the theologians and philosophers mentioned in this article. You might read, for example, *The Sickness unto Death* or *The Concept of Dread* by Kierkegaard.

Vocabulary

secular (1): worldly; not of the church

strata (2): layers

matrix (2): that which gives origin or form to a thing; or which
    serves to enclose it

transcendent (2): exceeding, or going beyond, the universe or
    material existence

pastiche (3): a literary, artistic, or musical work that imitates the
    style of previous work

untrammeled (4): unrestrained; free

attenuated (4): weakened

numinous (6): supernatural; mysterious

iconoclasm (6): attacking established beliefs or institutions

stupefy (6): make dull, stupid, or numb

38

THE VALUE OF PHILOSOPHY

Bertrand Russell

One of this century's greatest philosophers explores the values, uses, and limitations of philosophy.

1   Having now come to the end of our brief and very incomplete review of the problems of philosophy, it will be well to consider, in conclusion, what is the value of philosophy and why it ought to be studied. It is the more necessary to consider this question, in view of the fact that many men, under the influence of science or of practical affairs, are inclined to doubt whether philosophy is anything better than innocent but useless trifling, hair-splitting distinctions, and controversies on matters concerning which knowledge is impossible.

2   This view of philosophy appears to result, partly from a wrong conception of the ends of life, partly from a wrong conception of the kind of goods which philosophy strives to achieve. Physical science, through the medium of inventions, is useful to innumerable people who are wholly ignorant of it; thus the study of physical science is to be recommended, not only, or primarily, because of the effect on the student, but rather because of the effect on mankind in general. This utility does not belong to philosophy. If the study of philosophy has any value at all for others than students of philosophy, it must be only indirectly, through its effects upon the lives of those who study it. It is in these effects, therefore, if anywhere, that the value of philosophy must be primarily sought.

3   But further, if we are not to fail in our endeavour to determine the value of philosophy, we must first free our minds from the prejudices of what are wrongly called "practical" men. The "practical" man, as this word is often used, is one who recognizes only material needs, who realises that men must have food for the body, but is oblivious to the necessity of providing food for the mind. If all men were well off, if poverty and disease had been reduced to their lowest possible point, there would still remain much to be done to produce a valuable society; and even in the existing world the goods of the mind are at least as

important as the goods of the body. It is exclusively among the goods
of the mind that the value of philosophy is to be found; and only
those who are not indifferent to these goods can be persuaded that the
study of philosophy is not a waste of time.

4   Philosophy, like all other studies, aims primarily at knowledge.
The knowledge it aims at is the kind of knowledge which gives unity
and system to the body of the sciences, and the kind which results
from a critical examination of the grounds of our convictions, prejudices,
and beliefs. But it cannot be maintained that philosophy has had any
very great measure of success in its attempts to provide definite answers
to its questions. If you ask a mathematician, a mineralogist, a historian,
or any other man of learning, what definite body of truths has been
ascertained by his science, his answer will last as long as you are willing
to listen. But if you put the same question to a philosopher, he will,
if he is candid, have to confess that his study has not achieved positive
results such as have been achieved by other sciences. It is true that this
is partly accounted for by the fact that, as soon as definite knowledge
concerning any subject becomes possible, this subject ceases to be
called philosophy, and becomes a separate science. The whole study
of the heavens, which now belongs to astronomy, was once included
in philosophy; Newton's great work was called "the mathematical
principles of natural philosophy." Similarly, the study of the human
mind, which was, until very lately, a part of philosophy, has now been
separated from philosophy and has become the science of psychology.
Thus, to a great extent, the uncertainty of philosophy is more apparent
than real: those questions which are already capable of definite answers
are placed in the sciences, while those only to which, at present, no
definite answer can be given, remain to form the residue which is called
philosophy.

5   This is, however, only a part of the truth concerning the uncertainty
of philosophy. There are many questions—and among them those
that are of the profoundest interest to our spiritual life—which, so
far as we can see, must remain insoluble to the human intellect unless
its powers become of quite a different order from what they are now.
Has the universe any unity of plan or purpose, or is it a fortuitous concourse of atoms? Is consciousness a permanent part of the universe,
giving hope of indefinite growth in wisdom, or is it a transitory accident
on a small planet on which life must ultimately become impossible?
Are good and evil of importance to the universe or only to man? Such
questions are asked by philosophy, and variously answered by various
philosophers. But it would seem that, whether answers be otherwise
discoverable or not, the answers suggested by philosophy are none of
them demonstrably true. Yet, however slight may be the hope of discovering an answer, it is part of the business of philosophy to continue
the consideration of such questions, to make us aware of their im-

portance, to examine all the approaches to them, and to keep alive that speculative interest in the universe which is apt to be killed by confining ourselves to definitely ascertainable knowledge.

6   Many philosophers, it is true, have held that philosophy could establish the truth of certain answers to such fundamental questions. They have supposed that what is of most importance in religious beliefs could be proved by strict demonstration to be true. In order to judge of such attempts, it is necessary to take a survey of human knowledge, and to form an opinion as to its methods and its limitations. On such a subject it would be unwise to pronounce dogmatically; but if the investigations of our previous chapters have not led us astray, we shall be compelled to renounce the hope of finding philosophical proofs of religious beliefs. We cannot, therefore, include as part of the value of philosophy any definite set of answers to such questions. Hence, once more, the value of philosophy must not depend upon any supposed body of definitely ascertainable knowledge to be acquired by those who study it.

7   The value of philosophy is, in fact, to be sought largely in its very uncertainty. The man who has no tincture of philosophy goes through life imprisoned in the prejudices derived from common sense, from the habitual beliefs of his age or his nation, and from convictions which have grown up in his mind without the co-operation or consent of his deliberate reason. To such a man the world tends to become definite, finite, obvious; common objects rouse no questions, and unfamiliar possibilities are contemptuously rejected. As soon as we begin to philosophise, on the contrary, we find, as we saw in our opening chapters, that even the most everyday things lead to problems to which only very incomplete answers can be given. Philosophy, though unable to tell us with certainty what is the true answer to the doubts which it raises, is able to suggest many possibilities which enlarge our thoughts and free them from the tyranny of custom. Thus, while diminishing our feeling of certainty as to what things are, it greatly increases our knowledge as to what they may be; it removes the somewhat arrogant dogmatism of those who have never travelled into the region of liberating doubt, and it keeps alive our sense of wonder by showing familiar things in an unfamiliar aspect.

8   Apart from its utility in showing unsuspected possibilities, philosophy has a value—perhaps its chief value—through the greatness of the objects which it contemplates, and the freedom from narrow and personal aims resulting from this contemplation. The life of the instinctive man is shut up within the circle of his private interests: family and friends may be included, but the outer world is not regarded except as it may help or hinder what comes within the circle of instinctive wishes. In such a life there is something feverish and confined, in comparison with which the philosophic life is calm and

free. The private world of instinctive interests is a small one, set in the midst of a great and powerful world which must, sooner or later, lay our private world in ruins. Unless we can so enlarge our interests as to include the whole outer world, we remain like a garrison in a beleaguered fortress, knowing that the enemy prevents escape and that ultimate surrender is inevitable. In such a life there is no peace, but a constant strife between the insistence of desire and the powerlessness of will. In one way or another, if our life is to be great and free, we must escape this prison and this strife.

9   One way of escape is by philosophic contemplation. Philosophic contemplation does not, in its widest survey, divide the universe into two hostile camps—friends and foes, helpful and hostile, good and bad —it views the whole impartially. Philosophic contemplation when it is unalloyed, does not aim at proving that the rest of the universe is akin to man. All acquisition of knowledge is an enlargement of the Self, but this enlargement is best attained when it is not directly sought. It is obtained when the desire for knowledge is alone operative, by a study which does not wish in advance that its objects should have this or that character, but adapts the Self to the characters which it finds in its objects. This enlargement of Self is not obtained when, taking the Self as it is, we try to show that the world is so similar to this Self that knowledge of it is possible without any admission of what seems alien. The desire to prove this is a form of self-assertion, and like all self-assertion, it is an obstacle to the growth of Self which it desires, and of which the Self knows that it is capable. Self-assertion, in philosophic speculation as elsewhere, views the world as a means to its own ends; thus it makes the world of less account than Self, and the Self sets bounds to the greatness of its goods. In contemplation, on the contrary, we start from the not-Self, and through its greatness the boundaries of Self are enlarged; through the infinity of the universe the mind which contemplates it achieves some share in infinity.

10   For this reason greatness of soul is not fostered by those philosophies which assimilate the universe to Man. Knowledge is a form of union of Self and not-Self; like all union, it is impaired by dominion, and therefore by any attempt to force the universe into conformity with what we find in ourselves. There is a widespread philosophical tendency towards the view which tells us that man is the measure of all things, that truth is man-made, that space and time and the world of universals are properties of the mind, and that, if there be anything not created by the mind, it is unknowable and of no account for us. This view, if our previous discussions were correct, is untrue; but in addition to being untrue, it has the effect of robbing philosophic contemplation of all that gives it value, since it fetters contemplation to Self. What it calls knowledge is not a union with the not-Self, but a set of prejudices, habits, and desires, making an impenetrable veil

between us and the world beyond. The man who finds pleasure in such a theory of knowledge is like the man who never leaves the domestic circle for fear his word might not be law.

11   The true philosophic contemplation, on the contrary, finds its satisfaction in every enlargement of the not-Self, in everything that magnifies the objects contemplated, and thereby the subject contemplating. Everything, in contemplation, that is personal or private, everything that depends upon habit, self-interest, or desire, distorts the object, and hence impairs the union which the intellect seeks. By thus making a barrier between subject and object, such personal and private things become a prison to the intellect. The free intellect will see as God might see, with a *here* and *now*, without hopes and fears, without the trammels of customary beliefs and traditional prejudices, calmly, dispassionately, in the sole and exclusive desire of knowledge — knowledge as impersonal, as purely contemplative, as it is possible for man to attain. Hence also the free intellect will value more the abstract and universal knowledge into which the accidents of private history do not enter, than the knowledge brought by the senses, and dependent, as such knowledge must be, upon an exclusive and personal point of view and a body whose sense-organs distort as much as they reveal.

12   The mind which has become accustomed to the freedom and impartiality of philosophic contemplation will preserve something of the same freedom and impartiality in the world of action and emotion. It will view its purposes and desires as parts of the whole, with the absence of insistence that results from seeing them as infinitesimal fragments in a world of which all the rest is unaffected by any one man's deeds. The impartiality which, in contemplation, is the unalloyed desire for truth, is the very same quality of mind which, in action, is justice, and in emotion is that universal love which can be given to all, and not only to those who are judged useful or admirable. Thus contemplation enlarges not only the objects of our thoughts, but also the objects of our actions and our affections: it makes us citizens of the universe, not only of one walled city at war with all the rest. In this citizenship of the universe consists man's true freedom, and his liberation from the thraldom of narrow hopes and fears.

13   Thus, to sum up our discussion of the value of philosophy: Philosophy is to be studied, not for the sake of any definite answers to its questions, since no definite answers can, as a rule, be known to be true, but rather for the sake of the questions themselves; because these questions enlarge our conception of what is possible, enrich our intellectual imagination, and diminish the dogmatic assurance which closes the mind against speculation; but above all because, through the greatness of the universe which philosophy contemplates, the mind also is rendered great, and becomes capable of that union with the universe which constitutes its highest good.

Discussion of Theme

1. What, according to Russell, is a common—but erroneous—view of philosophy?
2. What distinction does the author make between science and philosophy?
3. What are the kinds of question that philosophy deals with? Can it completely answer these questions? If not, why is it worthwhile to raise them?

Discussion of Rhetoric

1. Although this selection was originally part of a longer work, it has the characteristics of a self-contained essay. Find the paragraphs that comprise the introduction, the body, and the conclusion. How is each clearly set off from the other parts of the essay?
2. Russell frequently uses long sentences. Note, for example, the last sentence of the essay. Are such sentences difficult to understand? Find several long sentences and examine each one for clarity.

Writing Assignments

1. In paragraph 5, Russell asks a series of questions. Select one of the questions and present your answer in a theme.
2. Define philosophy.
3. Do you have a personal philosophy? What contributed to its formulation? How does it affect your daily behavior? In a theme, present the main outlines of your philosophy.

Library Exploration

1. Bertrand Russell has written dozens of books, including an autobiography. Investigate some of his ideas as expressed in his writings.
2. Who are some other outstanding modern philosophers? What are their views on such issues as freedom, the will, the purpose and direction of life, and the meaning of truth?

Vocabulary

fortuitous (5): occurring by chance
concourse (5): a voluntary or spontaneous coming together
transitory (5): fleeting; temporary
tincture (7): trace
beleaguered (8): surrounded, as in a siege
unalloyed (9): pure
assimilate (10): adapt
dominion (10): external power or authority
fetters (10): shackles; confines
trammels (11): restraints
thraldom (12): slavery; bondage

39

MAN: THE NAKED APE

Desmond Morris

The origins of man—the "naked ape"—are examined in the following article. While this is not a direct philosophical commentary, *its conclusions—if accepted—force us to reexamine man's place in the scheme of things. The author is a British anthropologist.*

1   There is a label on a cage at a certain zoo that states simply, 'This animal is new to science'. Inside the cage there sits a small squirrel. It has black feet and it comes from Africa. No blackfooted squirrel has ever been found in that continent before. Nothing is known about it. It has no name.

2   For the zoologist it presents an immediate challenge. What is it about its way of life that has made it unique? How does it differ from the three hundred and sixty-six other living species of squirrels already known and described? Somehow, at some point in the evolution of the squirrel family, the ancestors of this animal must have split off from the rest and established themselves as an independent breeding population. What was it in the environment that made possible their isolation as a new form of life? The new trend must have started out in a small way, with a group of squirrels in one area becoming slightly changed and better adapted to the particular conditions there. But at this stage they would still be able to inter-breed with their relatives nearby. The new form would be at a slight advantage in its special region, but it would be no more than a race of the basic species and could be swamped out, reabsorbed into the mainstream at any point. If, as time passed, the new squirrels became more and more perfectly tuned-in to their particular environment, the moment would eventually arrive when it would be advantageous for them to become isolated from possible contamination by their neighbors. At this stage their social and sexual behaviour would undergo special modifications, making inter-breeding with other kinds of squirrels unlikely and eventually impossible. At first, their anatomy may have changed and become better at coping with the special food of the district, but later their mating calls and displays would also differ, ensuring that they attract only mates of the new type. At last, a new species would have

evolved, separate and discrete, a unique form of life, a three hundred and sixty-seventh kind of squirrel.

3   When we look at our unidentified squirrel in its zoo cage, we can only guess about these things. All we can be certain about is that the markings of its fur—its black feet—indicate that it is a new form. But these are only the symptoms, the rash that gives a doctor a clue about his patient's disease. To really understand this new species, we must use these clues only as a starting point, telling us there is something worth pursuing. We might try to guess at the animal's history, but that would be presumptuous and dangerous. Instead we will start humbly by giving it a simple and obvious label: we will call it the African black-footed squirrel. Now we must observe and record every aspect of its behaviour and structure and see how it differs from, or is similar to, other squirrels. Then, little by little, we can piece together its story.

4   The great advantage we have when studying such animals is that we ourselves are not black-footed squirrels—a fact which forces us into an attitude of humility that is becoming to proper scientific investigation. How different things are, how depressingly different, when we attempt to study the human animal. Even for the zoologist, who is used to calling an animal an animal, it is difficult to avoid the arrogance of subjective involvement. We can try to overcome this to some extent by deliberately and rather coyly approaching the human being as if he were another species, a strange form of life on the dissecting table, awaiting analysis. How can we begin?

5   As with the new squirrel, we can start by comparing him with other species that appear to be most closely related. From his teeth, his hands, his eyes and various other anatomical features, he is obviously a primate of some sort, but of a very odd kind. Just how odd becomes clear when we lay out in a long row the skins of the one hundred and ninety-two living species of monkeys and apes, and then try to insert a human pelt at a suitable point somewhere in this long series. Wherever we put it, it looks out of place. Eventually we are driven to position it right at one end of the row of skins, next to the hides of the tailless great apes such as the chimpanzee and the gorilla. Even here it is obtrusively different. The legs are too long, the arms are too short and the feet are rather strange. Clearly this species of primate has developed a special kind of locomotion which has modified its basic form. But there is another characteristic that cries out for attention: the skin is virtually naked. Except for conspicuous tufts of hair on the head, in the armpits and around the genitals, the skin surface is completely exposed. When compared with the other primate species, the contrast is dramatic. True, some species of monkeys and apes have small naked patches of skin on their rumps, their faces, or their chests, but nowhere amongst the other one hundred and ninety-two species is

there anything even approaching the human condition. At this point and without further investigation, it is justifiable to name this new species the 'naked ape'. It is a simple, descriptive name based on a simple observation, and it makes no special assumptions. Perhaps it will help us to keep a sense of proportion and maintain our objectivity.

6   Staring at this strange specimen and puzzling over the significance of its unique features, the zoologist now has to start making comparisons. Where else is nudity at a premium? The other primates are no help, so it means looking farther afield. A rapid survey of the whole range of the living mammals soon proves that they are remarkably attached to their protective, furry covering, and that very few of the 4,237 species in existence have seen fit to abandon it. Unlike their reptilian ancestors, mammals have acquired the great physiological advantage of being able to maintain a constant, high body temperature. This keeps the delicate machinery of the body processes tuned in for top performance. It is not a property to be endangered or discarded lightly. The temperature-controlling devices are of vital importance and the possession of a thick, hairy, insulating coat obviously plays a major role in preventing heat loss. In intense sunlight it will also prevent over-heating and damage to the skin from direct exposure to the sun's rays. If the hair has to go, then clearly there must be a very powerful reason for abolishing it. With few exceptions this drastic step has been taken only when mammals have launched themselves into an entirely new medium. The flying mammals, the bats, have been forced to denude their wings, but they have retained their furriness elsewhere and can hardly be counted as naked species. The burrowing mammals have in a few cases—the naked mole rat, the aardvark and the armadillo, for example—reduced their hairy covering. The aquatic mammals such as the whales, dolphins, porpoises, dugongs, manatees and hippopotamuses have also gone naked as part of a general stream-lining. But for all the more typical surface-dwelling mammals, whether scampering about on the ground or clambering around in the vegetation, a densely hairy hide is the basic rule. Apart from those abnormally heavy giants, the rhinos and the elephants (which have heating and cooling problems peculiar to themselves), the naked ape stands alone, marked off by his nudity from all the thousands of hairy, shaggy or furry land-dwelling mammalian species.

7   At this point the zoologist is forced to the conclusion that either he is dealing with a burrowing or an aquatic mammal, or there is something very odd, indeed unique, about the evolutionary history of the naked ape. Before setting out on a field trip to observe the animal in its present-day form, the first thing to do, then, is to dig back into its past and examine as closely as possible its immediate ancestors. Perhaps by examining the fossils and other remains and by taking a look at the closest living relatives, we shall be able to gain some sort of picture of

what happened as this new type of primate emerged and diverged from the family stock.

8   It would take too long to present here all the tiny fragments of evidence that have been painstakingly collected over the past century. Instead, we will assume that this task has been done and simply summarize the conclusions that can be drawn from it, combining the information available from the work of the fossil-hungry palaeontologists with the facts gathered by the patient ape-watching ethologists.

9   The primate groups, to which our naked ape belongs, arose originally from primitive insectivore stock. These early mammals were small, insignificant creatures, scuttling nervously around in the safety of the forests, while the reptile overlords were dominating the animal scene. Between eighty and fifty million years ago, following the collapse of the great age of reptiles, these little insect-eaters began to venture out into new territories. There they spread and grew into many strange shapes. Some became plant-eaters and burrowed under the ground for safety, or grew long, stilt-like legs with which to flee from their enemies. Others became long-clawed, sharp-toothed killers. Although the major reptiles had abdicated and left the scene, the open country was once again a battlefield.

10   Meanwhile, in the undergrowth, small feet were still clinging to the security of the forest vegetation. Progress was being made here, too. The early insect-eaters began to broaden their diet and conquer the digestive problems of devouring fruits, nuts, berries, buds and leaves. As they evolved into the lowliest forms of primates, their vision improved, the eyes coming forward to the front of the face and the hands developing as food-graspers. With three-dimensional vision, manipulating limbs and slowly enlarging brains, they came more and more to dominate their arboreal world.

11   Somewhere between twenty-five and thirty-five million years ago, these pre-monkeys had already started to evolve into monkeys proper. They were beginning to develop long, balancing tails and were increasing considerably in body size. Some were on their way to becoming leaf-eating specialists, but most were keeping to a broad, mixed diet. As time passed, some of these monkey-like creatures became bigger and heavier. Instead of scampering and leaping they switched to brachiating—swinging hand over hand along the underside of the branches. Their tails became obsolete. Their size, although making them more cumbersome in the trees, made them less wary of ground-level sorties.

12   Even so, at this stage—the ape phase—there was much to be said for keeping to the lush comfort and easy pickings of their forest of Eden. Only if the environment gave them a rude shove into the great open spaces would they be likely to move. Unlike the early mammalian explorers, they had become specialized in forest existence. Millions

of years of development had gone into perfecting this forest aristocracy, and if they left now they would have to compete with the (by this time) highly advanced ground-living herbivores and killers. And so there they stayed, munching their fruit and quietly minding their own business.

13   It should be stressed that this ape trend was for some reason taking place only in the Old World. Monkeys had evolved separately as advanced tree-dwellers in both the Old and the New World, but the American branch of the primates never made the ape grade. In the Old World, on the other hand, ancestral apes were spreading over a wide forest area from western Africa, at one extreme, to south-eastern Asia at the other. Today the remnants of this development can be seen in the African chimpanzees and gorillas and the Asian gibbons and orang-utans. Between these two extremities the world is now devoid of hairy apes. The lush forests have gone.

14   What happened to the early apes? We know that the climate began to work against them and that, by a point somewhere around fifteen million years ago, their forest strongholds had become seriously reduced in size. The ancestral apes were forced to do one of two things: either they had to cling on to what was left of their old forest homes, or, in an almost biblical sense, they had to face expulsion from the Garden. The ancestors of the chimpanzees, gorillas, gibbons and orangs stayed put, and their numbers have been slowly dwindling ever since. The ancestors of the only other surviving ape—the naked ape—struck out, left the forests, and threw themselves into competition with the already efficiently adapted ground-dwellers. It was a risky business, but in terms of evolutionary success it paid dividends.

15   The naked ape's success story from this point on is well known, but a brief summary will help, because it is vital to keep in mind the events which followed if we are to gain an objective understanding of the present-day behaviour of the species.

16   Faced with a new environment, our ancestors encountered a bleak prospect. They had to become either better killers than the old-time carnivores, or better grazers than the old-time herbivores. We know today that, in a sense, success has been won on both scores; but agriculture is only a few thousand years old, and we are dealing in millions of years. Specialized exploitation of the plant life of the open country was beyond the capacity of our early ancestors and had to await the development of advanced techniques of modern times. The digestive system necessary for a direct conquest of the grassland food supply was lacking. The fruit and nut diet of the forest could be adapted to a root and bulb diet at ground level, but the limitations were severe. Instead of lazily reaching out to the end of the branch for a luscious ripe fruit, the vegetable-seeking ground ape would be forced to scratch and scrape painstakingly in the hard earth for his precious food.

17   His old forest diet, however, was not all fruit and nut. Animal proteins were undoubtedly of great importance to him. He came originally, after all, from basic insectivore stock, and his ancient arboreal home had always been rich in insect life. Juicy bugs, eggs, young helpless nestlings, tree-frogs and small reptiles were all grist to his mill. What is more, they posed no great problems for his rather generalized digestive system. Down on the ground this source of food supply was by no means absent and there was nothing to stop him increasing this part of his diet. At first, he was no match for the professional killer of the carnivore world. Even a small mongoose, not to mention a big cat, could beat him to the kill. But young animals of all kinds, helpless ones or sick ones, were there for the taking, and the first step on the road to major meat-eating was an easy one. The really big prizes, however, were poised on long, stilt-like legs, ready to flee at a moment's notice at quite impossible speeds. The protein-laden ungulates were beyond his grasp.

18   This brings us to the last million or so years of the naked ape's ancestral history, and to a series of shattering and increasingly dramatic developments. Several things happened together, and it is important to realize this. All too often, when the story is told, the separate parts of it are spread out as if one major advance led to another, but this is misleading. The ancestral ground-apes already had large and high-quality brains. They had good eyes and efficient grasping hands. They inevitably, as primates, had some degree of social organization. With strong pressure on them to increase their prey-killing prowess, vital changes began to take place. They became more upright—fast, better runners. Their hands became freed from locomotion duties— strong, efficient weapon-holders. Their brains became more complex— brighter, quicker decision-makers. These things did not follow one another in a major, set sequence; they blossomed together, minute advances being made first in one quality and then in another, each urging the other on. A hunting ape, a killer ape, was in the making.

19   It could be argued that evolution might have favoured the less drastic step of developing a more typical cat- or dog-like killer, a kind of cat-ape or dog-ape, by the simple process of enlarging the teeth and nails into savage fang-like and claw-like weapons. But this would have put the ancestral ground-ape into direct competition with the already highly specialized cat and dog killers. It would have meant competing with them on their own terms, and the outcome would no doubt have been disastrous for the primates in question. (For all we know, this may actually have been tried and failed so badly that the evidence has not been found.) Instead, an entirely new approach was made, using artificial weapons instead of natural ones, and it worked.

20   From tool-using to tool-making was the next step, and alongside

this development went improved hunting techniques, not only in terms of weapons, but also in terms of social co-operation. The hunting apes were pack-hunters, and as their techniques of killing were improved, so were their methods of social organization. Wolves in a pack deploy themselves, but the hunting ape already had a much better brain than a wolf and could turn it to such problems as group communication and co-operation. Increasingly complex manoeuvres could be developed. The growth of the brain surged on.

21   Essentially this was a hunting-group of males. The females were too busy rearing the young to be able to play a major role in chasing and catching prey. As the complexity of the hunt increased and the forays became more prolonged, it became essential for the hunting ape to abandon the meandering, nomadic ways of its ancestors. A home base was necessary, a place to come back to with the spoils, where the females and young would be waiting and could share the food. This step, as we shall see in later chapters, has had profound effects on many aspects of the behaviour of even the most sophisticated naked apes of today.

22   So the hunting ape became a territorial ape. His whole sexual, parental and social pattern began to be affected. His old wandering, fruit-plucking way of life was fading rapidly. He had now really left his forest of Eden. He was an ape with responsibilities. He began to worry about the prehistoric equivalent of washing machines and refrigerators. He began to develop the home comforts—fire, food storage, artificial shelters. But this is where we must stop for the moment, for we are moving out of the realms of biology and into the realms of culture. The biological basis of these advanced steps lies in the development of a brain large and complex enough to enable the hunting ape to take them, but the exact form they assume is no longer a matter of specific genetic control. The forest ape that became a ground ape that became a hunting ape that became a territorial ape has become a cultural ape, and we must call a temporary halt.

Discussion of Theme
1. Why is the evolution of man so difficult to trace? What problems does the scientist encounter?
2. What is the author's purpose in calling man a "naked ape"?
3. What features of man are unique? What features does he share with primates?
4. Why do we use apes in laboratory experiments to learn about human behavior?

Discussion of Rhetoric
1. How is this essay organized (spatially, logically, chronologically)? Why is this a reasonable organizational pattern for this essay?

2. What evidence is there that Morris is writing for the layman?
3. What is the function of the opening anecdote about the blackfooted squirrel? How does it serve to introduce Morris's topic?

Writing Assignments

1. If you disagree with this presentation of man's history, write a rebuttal. Remember to give evidence and reasons, not merely opinion.
2. What is the importance of territory to man? Why hasn't it distinguished him from other animals? How has it affected his relationships with his fellow men?
3. Is man still changing? Will the next hundred thousand years bring radical changes in his physical, cultural, or social being? Use your imagination to speculate on some of the changes.

Library Exploration

1. If you are interested in the subject of evolution, examine some of the various theories that have been propounded.
2. Read *The Naked Ape*, from which this selection is taken. What other observations does Morris make in his book?
3. For an early, but fascinating, account of the propounding of the theory of evolution, read Charles Darwin's *Voyage of the Beagle*, in which he records his growing awareness of the evolutionary process.

Vocabulary

discrete (2): distinct
paleontologists (8): scientists who study fossil remains to learn more about the life of past geological periods
ethologists (8): scientists who study animal behavior
insectivore (9): insect-eating
arboreal (10): of or relating to a tree
cumbersome (11): clumsy
herbivores (12): plant-eating animals
carnivores (16): flesh-eating animals
ungulates (17): animals with hoofs
forays (21): expeditions in search of loot

40

THE GREAT SOCIETY IS A SICK SOCIETY

Sen. J. W. Fulbright

One of the most influential members of the United States Senate, and one of the most outspoken critics of *American foreign policy, offers his views on the state of the nation.*

1   Standing in the smoke and rubble of Detroit, a Negro veteran said: "I just got back from Vietnam a few months ago, but you know, I think the war is here."

2   There are in fact two wars going on. One is the war of power politics which our soldiers are fighting in the jungles of Southeast Asia. The other is a war for America's soul which is being fought in the streets of Newark and Detroit and in the halls of Congress, in churches and protest meetings and on college campuses, and in the hearts and minds of silent Americans from Maine to Hawaii. I believe that the two wars have something to do with each other, not in the direct, tangibly causal way that bureaucrats require as proof of a connection between two things, but in a subtler moral and qualitative way that is no less real for being intangible. Each of these wars might well be going on in the absence of the other, but neither, I suspect, standing alone, would seem so hopeless and demoralizing.

3   The connection between Vietnam and Detroit is in their conflicting and incompatible demands upon traditional American values. The one demands that they be set aside, the other that they be fulfilled. The one demands the acceptance by America of an imperial role in the world, or of what our policymakers like to call the "responsibilities of power," or of what I have called the "arrogance of power." The other demands freedom and social justice at home, an end to poverty, the fulfillment of our flawed democracy and an effort to create a role for ourselves in the world which is compatible with our traditional values. The question, it should be emphasized, is not whether it is *possible* to engage in traditional power politics abroad and at the same time to perfect democracy at home, but whether it is possible for *us Americans*, with our particular history and national character, to combine morally incompatible roles.

4   Administration officials tell us that we can indeed afford both Viet-

nam and the Great Society, and they produce impressive statistics of the gross national product to prove it. The statistics show financial capacity, but they do not show moral and psychological capacity. They do not show how a President preoccupied with bombing missions over North and South Vietnam can provide strong and consistent leadership for the renewal of our cities. They do not show how a Congress burdened with war costs and war measures, with emergency briefings and an endless series of dramatic appeals, with anxious constituents and a mounting anxiety of their own, can tend to the workaday business of studying social problems and legislating programs to meet them. Nor do the statistics tell how an anxious and puzzled people, bombarded by press and television with the bad news of American deaths in Vietnam, the "good news" of enemy deaths—and with vividly horrifying pictures to illustrate them—can be expected to support neighborhood antipoverty projects and national programs for urban renewal, employment and education. Anxiety about war does not breed compassion for one's neighbors nor do constant reminders of the cheapness of life abroad strengthen our faith in its sanctity at home. In these ways the war in Vietnam is poisoning and brutalizing our domestic life. Psychological incompatibility has proven to be more controlling than financial feasibility; and the Great Society has become a sick society.

5   When he visited America 100 years ago, Thomas Huxley wrote: "I cannot say that I am in the slightest degree impressed by your bigness, or your material resources, as such. Size is not grandeur, and territory does not make a nation. The great issue, about which hangs the terror of overhanging fate, is what are you going to do with all these things?"

6   The question is still with us, and we seem to have come to a time of historical crisis when its answer can no longer be deferred. Before the Second World War our world role was a potential role; we were important in the world for what we could do with our power, for the leadership we *might* provide, for the example we *might* set. Now the choices are almost gone: we are, almost, the world's self-appointed policeman; we are, almost, the world defender of the status quo. We are well on our way to becoming a traditional great power—an imperial nation if you will—engaged in the exercise of power for its own sake, exercising it to the limit of our capacity and beyond, filling every vacuum and extending the American "presence" to the farthest reaches of the earth. And, as with the great empires of the past, as the power grows, it is becoming an end in itself, separated except by ritual incantation from its initial motives, governed, it would seem, by its own mystique, power without philosophy or purpose.

7   That describes what we have almost become, but we have not become a traditional empire yet. The old values remain—the populism and

the optimism, the individualism and the roughhewn equality, the friendliness and the good humor, the inventiveness and the zest for life, the caring about people and the sympathy for the underdog, and the idea, which goes back to the American Revolution, that maybe —just maybe—we can set an example of democracy and human dignity for the world.

8   That is something which none of the great empires of the past has ever done, or tried to do, or wanted to do, but we were bold enough —or presumptuous enough—to think that we might be able to do it. And there are a great many Americans who still think we can do it, or at least they want to try.

9   That, I believe, is what all the hue and cry is about—the dissent in the Senate and the protest marches in the cities, the letters to the President from student leaders and former Peace Corps volunteers, the lonely searching of conscience by a student facing the draft and the letter to a Senator from a soldier in the field who can no longer accept the official explanations of why he has been sent to fight in the jungles of Vietnam. All believe that their country was cut out for something more ennobling than imperial destiny. Our youth are showing that they still believe in the American dream, and their protests attest to its continuing vitality.

10   There appeared in a recent issue of the journal Foreign Affairs a curious little article complaining about the failure of many American intellectuals to support what the author regards as America's unavoidable "imperial role" in the world. The article took my attention because it seems a faithful statement of the governing philosophy of American foreign policy while also suggesting how little the makers of that policy appreciate the significance of the issue between themselves and their critics. It is taken for granted—not set forth as a hypothesis to be proven—that any great power, in the author's words, "is entangled in a web of responsibilities from which there is no hope of escape," and that "there is no way the United States, as the world's mightiest power, can avoid such an imperial role. . . ." The author's displeasure with the "intellectuals" (he uses the word more or less to describe people who disagree with the Administration's policy) is that, in the face of this alleged historical inevitability, they are putting up a disruptive, irritating and futile resistance. They are doing this, he believes, because they are believers in "ideology"—the better word would be "values" or "ideals"—and this causes their thinking to be "irrelevant" to foreign policy.

11   Here, inadvertently, the writer puts his finger on the nub of the current crisis. The students and churchmen and professors who are protesting the Vietnam war do not accept the notion that foreign policy is a matter of expedients to which values are irrelevant. They reject this notion because they understand, as some of our policymakers do

not understand, that it is ultimately self-defeating to "fight fire with fire," that you cannot defend your values in a manner that does violence to those values without destroying the very thing you are trying to defend. They understand, as our policymakers do not, that when American soldiers are sent, in the name of freedom, to sustain corrupt dictators in a civil war, that when the Central Intelligence Agency subverts student organizations to engage in propaganda activities abroad, or when the Export-Import Bank is used by the Pentagon to finance secret arms sales abroad, damage—perhaps irreparable damage—is being done to the very values that are meant to be defended. The critics understand, as our policymakers do not, that, through the undemocratic expedients we have adopted for the defense of American democracy, we are weakening it to a degree that is beyond the resources of our bitterest enemies.

12   Nor do the dissenters accept the romantic view that a nation is powerless to choose the role it will play in the world, that some mystic force of history or destiny requires a powerful nation to be an imperial nation, dedicated to what Paul Goodman calls the "empty system of power," to the pursuit of power without purpose, philosophy or compassion. They do not accept the Hegelian concept of history as something out of control, as something that happens to us rather than something that we make. They do not accept the view that, because other great nations have pursued power for its own sake—a pursuit which invariably has ended in decline or disaster—America must do the same. They think we have some choice about our own future and that the best basis for exercising that choice is the values on which this republic was founded.

13   The critics of our current course also challenge the contention that the traditional methods of foreign policy are safe and prudent and realistic. They are understandably skeptical of their wise and experienced elders who, in the name of prudence, caution against any departure from the tried and true methods that have led in this century to Sarajevo, Munich and Dienbienphu. They think that the methods of the past have been tried and found wanting, and two world wars attest powerfully to their belief. Most of all, they think that, in this first era of human history in which man has acquired weapons which threaten his entire species with destruction, safety and prudence and realism require us to change the rules of a dangerous and discredited game, to try as we have never tried before to civilize and humanize international relations, not only for the sake of civilization and humanity but for the sake of survival.

14   Even the most ardent advocates of an imperial role for the United States would probably agree that the proper objective of our foreign policy is the fostering of a world environment in which we can, with reasonable security, devote our main energies to the realization of the

values of our own society. This does not require the adoption or imposition of these values on anybody, but it does require us so to conduct ourselves that our society does not seem hateful and repugnant to others.

15   At the present, much of the world is repelled by America and what America seems to stand for. Both in our foreign affairs and in our domestic life we convey an image of violence; I do not care very much about images as distinguished from the things they reflect, but this image is rooted in reality. Abroad we are engaged in a savage and unsuccessful war against poor people in a small and backward nation. At home—largely because of the neglect resulting from 25 years of preoccupation with foreign involvements—our cities are exploding in violent protest against generations of social injustice. America, which only a few years ago seemed to the world to be a model of democracy and social justice, has become a symbol of violence and undisciplined power.

16   "It is excellent," wrote Shakespeare, "to have a giant's strength; but it is tyrannous to use it like a giant." By using our power like a giant we are fostering a world environment which is, to put it mildly, uncongenial to our society. By our undisciplined use of physical power we have divested ourselves of a greater power: the power of example. How can we commend peaceful compromise to the Arabs and the Israelis when we are unwilling to suspend our relentless bombing of North Vietnam? How can we commend democratic social reform to Latin America when Newark, Detroit and Milwaukee are providing explosive evidence of our own inadequate efforts at democratic social reform? How can we commend the free enterprise system to Asians and Africans when in our own country it has produced vast, chaotic, noisy, dangerous and dirty urban complexes while poisoning the very air and land and water? There may come a time when Americans will again be able to commend their country as an example to the world and, more in hope than confidence, I retain my faith that there will; but to do so right at this moment would take more gall than I have.

17   Far from building a safe world environment for American values, our war in Vietnam and the domestic deterioration which it has aggravated are creating a most uncongenial world atmosphere for American ideas and values. The world has no need, in this age of nationalism and nuclear weapons, for a new imperial power, but there is a great need of moral leadership—by which I mean the leadership of decent example. That role could be ours but we have vacated the field, and all that has kept the Russians from filling it is their own lack of imagination.

18   At the same time, as we have noted, and of even greater fundamental importance, our purposeless and undisciplined use of power is causing

a profound controversy in our own society. This in a way is something to be proud of. We have sickened but not succumbed, and just as a healthy body fights disease, we are fighting the alien concept which is being thrust upon us, not by history but by our policymakers in the Department of State and the Pentagon. We are proving the strength of the American dream by resisting the dream of an imperial destiny. We are demonstrating the validity of our traditional values by the difficulty we are having in betraying them.

19   The principal defenders of these values are our remarkable younger generation, something of whose spirit is expressed in a letter which I received from an American soldier in Vietnam. Speaking of the phony propaganda on both sides, and then of the savagery of the war, of the people he describes as the "real casualties"—"the farmers and their families in the Delta mangled by air strikes, and the villagers here killed and burned out by our friendly Korean mercenaries"—this young soldier then asks ". . . whatever has become of our dream? Where is that America that opposed tyrannies at every turn, without inquiring first whether some particular forms of tyranny might be of use to us? Of the three rights which men have, the first, as I recall, was the right to life. How, then, have we come to be killing so many in such a dubious cause?"

20   While the death toll mounts in Vietnam, it is mounting too in the war at home. During a single week of July 1967, 164 Americans were killed and 2,100 were wounded in city riots in the United States. We are truly fighting a two-front war and doing badly in both. Each war feeds on the other and, although the President assures us that we have the resources to win both wars, in fact we are not winning either.

21   Together, the two wars have set in motion a process of deterioration in American society, and there is no question that each of the two crises is heightened by the impact of the other. Not only does the Vietnam war divert human and material resources from our festering cities; not only does it foster the conviction on the part of slum Negroes that their country is indifferent to their plight—in addition, the war feeds the idea of violence as a way of solving problems. If, as Mr. Rusk tells us, only the rain of bombs can bring Ho Chi Minh to reason, why should not the same principle apply at home? Why should not riots and snipers' bullets bring the white man to an awareness of the Negro's plight when peaceful programs for housing and jobs and training have been more rhetoric than reality? Ugly and shocking thoughts are in the American air, and they were forged in the Vietnam crucible. Black Power extremists talk of "wars of liberation" in the urban ghettos of America. A cartoon in a London newspaper showed the Negro soldiers in battle in Vietnam with one saying to the other: "This is going to be great training for civilian life."

22   The effect of domestic violence on the chances for peace in Vietnam

may turn out to be no less damaging than the impact of the war on events at home. With their limited knowledge of the United States, the Vietcong and the North Vietnamese may regard the urban riots as a harbinger of impending breakdown and eventual American withdrawal from Vietnam, warranting stepped-up warfare and an uncompromising position on negotiations. It is possible that the several opportunities to negotiate, which our Government has let pass, most recently last winter, could not now be retrieved. Some 18 months ago Gen. Maxwell Taylor said in testimony before the Senate Foreign Relations Committee that the war was being prolonged by domestic dissent. That dissent was based in part on apprehension as to the effects of the war on our domestic life. Now the war is being prolonged by the domestic deterioration which has in fact occurred, and it is doubtful that all of the war dissenters in America, even if they wanted to, as they certainly do not, could give the enemy a fraction of the aid and comfort that have been given him by Newark, Detroit and Milwaukee.

23   An unnecessary and immoral war deserves in its own right to be liquidated; when its effect in addition is the aggravation of grave problems and the corrosion of values in our own society, its liquidation under terms of reasonable and honorable compromise is doubly imperative. Our country is being awakened by a grotesque inversion of priorities, the effects of which are becoming clear to more and more Americans—in the Congress, in the press and in the country at large. Even The Washington Post, a newspaper which has obsequiously supported the Administration's policy in Vietnam, took note in a recent editorial of the "ugly image of a world policeman incapable of policing itself" as against the "absolute necessity of a sound domestic base for an effective foreign policy," and then commented: "We are confronted simultaneously with an urgent domestic crisis and an urgent foreign crisis and our commitments to both are clear. We should deal with both with all the energy and time and resources that may be required. But if the moment ever arises when we cannot deal adequately and effectively with both, there is no shame—and some considerable logic—in making it plain beyond a doubt that our first consideration and our first priority rests with the security of the stockade."

24   Commenting on the same problem of priorities, Mayor Cavanaugh of Detroit said:

25   "What will it profit this country if we, say, put our man on the moon by 1970 and at the same time you can't walk down Woodward Avenue in this city without some fear of violence?

26   "And we may be able to pacify every village in Vietnam, over a period of years, but what good does it do if we can't pacify the American cities?

27   "What I am saying . . . is that our priorities in this country are all

out of balance. . . . Maybe Detroit was a watershed this week in American history and it might well be that out of the ashes of this city comes the national resolve to do far more than anything we have done in the past."

28   Priorities are reflected in the things we spend money on. Far from being a dry accounting of bookkeepers, a nation's budget is full of moral implications; it tells what a society cares about and what it does not care about; it tells what its values are.

29   Here are a few statistics on America's values: Since 1946 we have spent over $1,578-billion through our regular national budget. Of this amount over $904-billion, or 57.29 per cent of the total, has gone for military power. By contrast, less than $96-billion, or 6.08 per cent, was spent on "social functions" including education, health, labor and welfare programs, housing and community development. The Administration's budget for fiscal year 1968 calls for almost $76-billion to be spent on the military and only $15-billion for "social functions."

30   I would not say that we have shown ourselves to value weapons five or ten times as much as we value domestic social needs, as the figures suggest; certainly much of our military spending has been necessitated by genuine requirements of national security. I think, however, that we have embraced the necessity with excessive enthusiasm, that the Congress has been all too willing to provide unlimited sums for the military and not really very reluctant at all to offset these costs to a very small degree by cutting away funds for the poverty program and urban renewal, for rent supplements for the poor and even for a program to help protect slum children from being bitten by rats. Twenty million dollars a year to eliminate rats—about 1/100th of the monthly cost of the war in Vietnam—would not eliminate slum riots; but, as correspondent Tom Wicker has written, "It would only suggest that somebody cared." The discrepancy of attitudes tells at least as much about our national values as the discrepancy of dollars.

31   While the country sickens for lack of moral leadership, a most remarkable younger generation has taken up the standard of American idealism. Unlike so many of their elders, they have perceived the fraud and sham in American life and are unequivocally rejecting it. Some, the hippies, have simply withdrawn; and while we may regret the loss of their energies and their sense of decency, we can hardly gainsay their evaluation of the state of society. Others of our youth are sardonic and skeptical, not, I think, because they do not want ideals but because they want the genuine article and will not tolerate fraud. Others—students who wrestle with their consciences about the draft, soldiers who wrestle with their consciences about the war, Peace Corps volunteers who strive to light the spark of human dignity

among the poor of India or Brazil and V.I.S.T.A. volunteers who try to do the same for our own poor in Harlem or Appalachia—are striving to keep alive the traditional values of American democracy.

32   They are not really radical, these young idealists, no more radical, that is, than Jefferson's idea of freedom, Lincoln's idea of equality or Wilson's idea of a peaceful community of nations. Some of them it is true, are taking what many regard as radical action, but they are doing it in defense of traditional values and in protest against the radical departure from those values embodied in the idea of an imperial destiny for America.

33   The focus of their protest is the war in Vietnam, and the measure of their integrity is the fortitude with which they refuse to be deceived about it. By striking contrast with the young Germans, who accepted the Nazi evil because the values of their society had disintegrated and they had no moral frame of reference, these young Americans are demonstrating the vitality of American values. They are demonstrating that, while their country is capable of acting falsely to itself, it cannot do so without internal disruption, without calling forth the regenerative counterforce of protest from Americans who are willing to act in defense of the principles they were brought up to believe in.

34   The spirit of this regenerative generation has been richly demonstrated to me in letters from student leaders, from former Peace Corps volunteers and from soldiers fighting in Vietnam. I quoted from one earlier. Another letter that is both striking and representative was written by an officer still in Vietnam. He wrote:

35   "For 11 years I was, before this war, a Regular commissioned officer—a professional military man in name and spirit; now—in name only. To fight well (as do the VC), a soldier must believe in his leadership. I, and many I have met, have lost faith in ours. Since I hold that duty to conscience is higher than duty to the Administration (not 'country' as cry the nationalists), I declined a promotion and have resigned my commission. I am to be discharged on my return, at which time I hope to contribute in some way to the search for peace in Vietnam."

36   Some years ago Archibald MacLeish characterized the American people as follows:

37   "Races didn't bother the Americans. They were something a lot better than any race. They were a People. They were the first self-constituted, self-declared, self-created People in the history of the world. And their manners were their own business. And so were their politics. And so, but 10 times so, were their souls."

38   Now the possession of their souls is being challenged by the false and dangerous dream of an imperial destiny. It may be that the challenge will succeed, that America will succumb to becoming a traditional empire and will reign for a time over what must surely be a moral

if not a physical wasteland, and then, like the great empires of the past, will decline or fall. Or it may be that the effort to create so grotesque an anachronism will go up in flames of nuclear holocaust. But if I had to bet my money on what is going to happen, I would bet on this younger generation—this generation of young men and women who reject the inhumanity of war in a poor and distant land, who reject the poverty and sham in their own country, who are telling their elders what their elders ought to have known—that the price of empire is America's soul and that the price is too high.

Discussion of Theme

1. Senator Fulbright speaks of two wars being fought by the United States. Who are the opponents? Why does the author believe that it is impossible to win both of these wars?
2. Fulbright states that we are becoming an imperialist nation. Does the United States resemble an empire? In what ways?
3. What reasons does the author give for viewing the protests of youth as an encouraging sign?
4. Does the United States lack moral leadership as the senator suggests?

Discussion of Rhetoric

1. What is the purpose of the opening anecdote? How does it set the mood for the rest of the essay?
2. How does Fulbright support his argument? Is he convincing? Are his examples appropriate? Note, for example, paragraph 5.
3. Senator Fulbright states a thesis, develops it, restates it, and supports it further. Find several instances of this technique. How useful is it in convincing you that he is right?
4. What kind of evidence does the author use to support his argument?
5. Describe the tone of this article. Is Fulbright, for example, bitter?

Writing Assignments

1. Develop the following quotation into a theme: "It is excellent to have a giant's strength; but it is tyrannous to use it like a giant."
2. Does anyone have the right to refuse to serve in the armed forces if he believes that his country is fighting an immoral war? Present your views in a theme.
3. Are there any projects—conservation, education, public health, for example—that you believe should receive a larger share of the available federal funds? Present your arguments in a theme.
4. Develop the following quotation into a theme: "They are not really radical, these young idealists, no more radical, that is, than Jefferson's idea of freedom, Lincoln's idea of equality, or Wilson's idea of a peaceful community of nations." If you disagree, present your opposing views clearly.

Library Exploration

1. How do such organizations as the Peace Corps and VISTA offer youth an opportunity to serve their country? Investigate these and similar groups.
2. Senator Fulbright has written several articles and books; you might enjoy reading some of these.

Vocabulary

tangibly (2): capable of being precisely realized by the mind
qualitative (2): of, relating to, or involving quality or kind
incantation (6): a spell; magical words
populism (7): the political and economic doctrines advocated by the Populist party, founded in 1891 primarily to represent agrarian interests and to advocate free coinage of silver and government control of monopolies
expedients (11): means to an end
succumbed (18): gave in (to); died
crucible (21): melting pot
harbinger (22): something that foreshadows what is to come
impending (22): imminent; about to occur
obsequiously (23): fawningly
gainsay (31): deny; dispute; contradict
anachronism (38): something that is chronologically out of place

41

DISPUTES IN THE SICK SOCIETY

Russell Baker

A well-known columnist takes a gentle poke at the breast-beating and self-recrimination indulged in by many white liberals today.

1   It used to be that when you went to parties the evening invariably declined into a series of disputes about which of the guests was the most neurotic.

2   "I'm twice as neurotic as you are," some 30-year-old would boast. "I still take my security blanket to the office."

3   To which another contender would snort, "Ha! Call that neurosis? I have a toenail fetish!"

4   Those were the good old days. With "Spellbound," Alfred Hitchcock had made schizophrenia socially alluring—the kind of thing that Gregory Peck might have—and anyone admitting that he suffered from mental normality was generally looked upon as a bore and possibly a social defective.

5   Nowadays, at least in the well-heeled, white, white-collar world, social boasting about one's frailties has to be done on the volcanic scale. In this world, social hypochondria has evolved into a hypochondriac society. In this perverse arrangement, one subtly proves himself a rare and noteworthy healthy figure by boasting about how greatly he is to blame for what is invariably called the "sick society."

6   Superiority—or social "health"—is established by proving that you realize that you are the most evil social force for miles around, and therefore, because you know the worst about yourself, are far ahead of your competitors on the road back to health.

7   Suppose, for example, Bob opens with, "I say this society is sick, and the reason it's sick is my own white racism."

8   Sam cannot let this pass unchallenged without conceding that he is a sicker white racist than Bob. "What white racism have you ever practiced?" Sam demands.

9   "I've acquiesced in de facto segregation," Bob retorts.

10   "Ha!" snorts Sam. "Call that racism? The other day I saw a graffiti on the wall. It said, 'Stokeley Carmichael eats watermelon,' and do you know what I did? I just smiled. Just smiled, that's all. That's racism,

buddy. That's the kind of sickness I'm pumping into the American bloodstream day after day."

11 "You two guys give me a pain," interrupts Mickey. "When I think of how I've lacked the guts to stand up against racism, I make myself sick. Just yesterday my mother said, 'That Mr. Poitier can come to my house for dinner any time, but not that Mr. Rap Brown.' And do you know what I didn't do? I didn't bust her right in her old nose. I'm a worse redneck than she is."

12 At this stage, Bob is threatened with the possibility of seeming to be the most tolerant racist in the room. He has to broaden the attack. "The sickness of racism is just a symptom of the broader sickness destroying the whole society," he counters. "And that results from the fact that people like me are rotten to the core with hypocrisy and immorality."

13 "I'll bet you're not half the hypocrite I am," says Sam.

14 "Oh yeah!" snarls Bob. "If I'm not a 100 per cent hypocritical four-flusher, how come I've never gone to jail, eh? Answer me that!"

15 "That's nothing," says Sam. "Look at my record for lily-livered toadying to a corrupt, immoral Establishment. I've never even had a traffic ticket."

16 Mickey, who once went to court for being caught in a horse parlor, is on the spot now and must recoup with another claim to superior swinishness.

17 "Hypocrisy and immorality," he says, "come about because people like us are incapable of loving. My boy was home from school last week and he said, 'Dad, you are an immoral, hypocritical racist who ought to be shot.'

18 "And what did I do? Did I respond with love? Did I say, 'you're right, Roland. Feel free to use my gun'? I did not. I'd lost the power to love. All I said was, 'If you were 20 pounds lighter, boy, I'd fan your tail.' I rejected my own son. I denied him the chance to do his own thing."

19 "That's nothing," snapped Bob. "I've got a boy in school, too. He's the kind of kid who doesn't even see that I deserve to be shot. Worse than that, he admires me. That's the kind of sickness I've spread in this world—teaching a boy to admire a corrupt, hypocritical racist who's over 30."

20 At this stage Bob is obviously the winner on points, and he signals his wife that it's time to go. "Great party," he says on the way home.

21 "How are you feeling?" asks his wife.

22 "Good."

23 Maybe the society really is sick.

Discussion of Theme

1. What new variation of an old party game is described in this article? Why is this particular variation so popular now?
2. Do you think this game is played everywhere in the country? By all kinds of people?
3. Are the speakers realistically portrayed or are they caricatures?
4. Look at the last sentence in this article. What observations have led Baker to this view?

Discussion of Rhetoric

1. Why does Baker use dialog? Is the conversation realistic?
2. What is irony? Satire? Does Baker use either in this piece?
3. How do we know what the author's own views are? At what point in the article does he let us know?

Writing Assignments

1. One of the characters in Baker's article says, "Hypocrisy and immorality come about because people like us are incapable of loving." Write a paper elaborating on this theme.
2. How guilty should we feel as individuals for the racism that exists in this nation? For example, should "white" churches give large sums of money to Negro organizations in payment for past injustices?
3. Underneath the humor, Baker is attacking some very basic weaknesses in our society. Depict those flaws, and suggest some remedies.

Library Exploration

For another comment on some games people play in our society, read *Games People Play* by Eric Berne. While not at exactly the same level, it, too, deals with forms of self-deception.

Vocabulary

hypochondria (5): a morbid anxiety about imagined ills
acquiesced (9): accepted; complied with (passively)
de facto (9): actual; in fact
graffiti (10): writings on walls or fences
toadying (15): fawning; playing up to
recoup (16): recover one's losses

42

CENSORSHIP: IS THE SKY THE LIMIT FOR BLUE MATERIAL?

Kevin Thomas

Should books and movies be subject to censorship? What is the state of censorship now, and what can be expected in the future? These are some of the questions considered in this article, written by a reporter familiar with the Hollywood scene.

1   In this era of increasing permissiveness many people are confused about the scope of the freedom of expression. To most of those who consider themselves enlightened the idea of censorship in any form is deplorable. In the next breath, however, many of those same people will reveal that they regard pornography as equally appalling. Still others fear that if some limits of candor aren't established, especially in regard to the stage and screen, that freedom of all forms of expression in our society could be endangered by the repressive effects of a Puritan backlash.

2   Over the past five years the U.S. Supreme Court has been attempting to resolve these contradicting attitudes by approving laws that could not stand when applied to adults but would be acceptable if applied only to children.

3   Last April, in the case of an upstate New York luncheonette operator convicted of selling four "girlie" magazines to a 16-year-old boy, the U.S. Supreme Court upheld the right of a state to regulate the sale of "harmful" books, magazines, photographs and similar published materials to minors. In a companion decision the justices voided a Dallas ordinance that classified pictures as to their suitability for young people. It was thrown out, however, because its wording was too vague, not because the principle of shielding youngsters was at issue.

A WORKABLE SOLUTION

4   The endorsement by Hollywood of that principle culminated last month with the Motion Picture Code's new rating system. Similarly, the month before that, Chief Postal Inspector Harry B. Montague stated that the Post Office had abandoned censorship as a weapon in the war against smut—but that its new goal was to keep advertisements for pornography out of the hands of children and young people.

5   Are we, then, at last heading toward a workable solution to a problem
that vexes all responsible parents? Or are there both forces at work
within human nature and larger issues of freedom of expression that
are yet to be reckoned with? What really is the state of censorship
right now, and what can we expect in the future? These are some of the
questions posed to attorney Stanley Fleishman, noted civil liberties
specialist who has successfully defended many of those accused as
pornographers. The bookseller or motion picture exhibitor accused of
purveying smut looks to Fleishman for salvation much as Hollywood
celebrities caught up in scandal used to rely upon the services of the
late Jerry Giesler.

6   Fleishman first went before the U.S. Supreme Court in 1957 to
defend David S. Alberts of Beverly Hills, who had been convicted on
charges of advertising and keeping for sale obscene books. He lost that
case, in a decision handed down at the same time to New York publisher
Samuel Roth, who had been convicted of sending obscene literature
through the mails.

7   It was at this time that the Supreme Court first held that obscenity is
not within the protection of the free speech and press provisions of the
First Amendment and has been confronted ever since with the question
of whether it is possible to punish the circulation of "obscene" materials
without doing violence to the Constitution.

8   "On the one hand it's unmistakable that enormous progress has
been made in a short time—it's been only 12 years since the Roth-
Alberts case. But on the other hand there are more criminal prosecutions
today than ever before except right after Ralph Ginzburg, the publisher
of Eros, was convicted of mailing obscene material," says Fleishman.

9   "It's been very close to a revolution for the freedom of the individual
to explore more freely his own sexuality and to express this in print.
Once you can say that it's all right for Henry Miller's works to be
contemplated in a civilized society just about all the barriers have fallen.
Once you can read Miller it takes away all the reasons for not being able
to read the same kind of descriptions of sex by lesser writers. If anything,
the better writer is more 'dangerous' because he's more effective.

10   "Those criminal prosecutions occur because so much frankness
makes those who'd preserve the status quo all the more nervous.
This is happening mostly at the low level of misdemeanors, of search-
and-seizure. In the small towns the retailer is virtually unprotected.
The greater the freedom, the greater the opposition to it.

11   "Nobody knows for sure what a Republican Administration is
going to do, but there's a growing belief that the Constitution protects
not merely the expression of ideas but all means of communication
between people."

12   In regard to this Fleishman has high praise for the California State
Supreme Court's recent decision (which reversed a 1965 conviction of a
San Pablo topless dancer on charges of indecent exposure and dis-

orderly conduct) that declared obscenity must be judged on uniform standards throughout the state and that judges and juries must be advised by expert testimony on the boundaries of indecency. (No guidelines were set for determining who would be the experts.)

13   "To my recollection this is the very broadest possible interpretation to the First Amendment ever made. It could apply to every kind of communication between people—big ideas, little ideas, emotions—everything. And it's getting tough for the prosecutor to get those 'expert' witnesses.

14   "What this means is that freedom is really indivisible—that you can't ban 'hateful' books about sex or politics or religions without jeopardizing every form of expression.

15   "For freedom you have to go to the top of the judicial pyramid. Juries are inclined to be hypocritical. A juror will see a stag show at the American Legion, yet vote a man guilty for putting out virtually the same thing. Without recourse to the appellate courts virtually everything of a controversial nature could be outlawed. Back in the McCarthy era a man connected with Purdue circulated a petition consisting only of the Declaration of Independence and the Bill of Rights as an experiment and could get scarcely anybody to sign it.

16   "Obscenity is a class concept—it's all right for us but not for them. It's easy to say something is 'utterly without redeeming social value,' but the question is 'For whom?' If a judge can identify with whatever is under question he'll see social value in it. But the perception of social value is pretty much limited to one's own class. After all, the wisest man seeing as far as he can see can only see a small part of life."

17   As a man who believes in the absolute freedom to discuss and portray anything of a sexual nature, Fleishman looks askance at the idea that that which may not be obscene to adults could be to minors.

18   "Adults always think anything dealing with sex is too much for kids. The fact of the matter is that adults are afraid of such material themselves. We're really displacing the old Victorian rationale that one must protect children *and women*. Women now demand equal sexual rights, and that creates enormous problems for many men. Women are my best jurors—you can reach them with the hypocrisy of sex laws.

19   "Adults are afraid of their children growing up and going away. We don't want to recognize that young people are sexual animals. It's all part of the attempt to protract the age of innocence as long as possible—far too long. At 18 a boy can be trained to kill, but one month before he's not supposed to look at Playboy magazine.

20   "The late Justice Curtis Bok was once asked if he would want his teen-age daughter to read 'God's Little Acre', and he replied that he'd rather she learned about the world through books that they could discuss together than from life. The notion that we can really make it better for our kids by protecting them from the seamy side of life is a fallacy.

21   "The only kids who grow up strong enough to live effectively, to grapple with strong problems, are those that haven't been over-protected. It's like raising a child in a glass house. When he finally goes outside he'll die of measles. Children should be exposed to all the crosscurrents that make up the world—not just the ones we wish it were made of."

22   Fleishman, however, says of the movies' new rating system: "It makes sense as an expediency. It was needed to head off a rash of laws that would have imposed impossible burdens upon the motion picture industry. There are more than 100,000 legislative bodies in America —city councils, aldermen, boards of supervisors—and they've all been wanting to get into the act. It would mean economic catastrophe.

23   "It's history repeating itself. When the Hayes Office was founded it was to head off a rash of legislation that would have crippled the industry. I think classification is bad, but it may be the lesser of two evils.

24   "I think we're going to learn an awful lot from Denmark's decision to abolish virtually all censorship. The way this came about is curious. They had prosecuted 'Fanny Hill' in the lower tribunals, where it was found obscene. When this was finally reversed they began to wonder whether if anything that went beyond 'Fanny Hill' was worth fighting over. A committee was appointed, studies were made, and it was decided that there were simply no adverse social effects from the free flow of sexually frank materials. Based on this report the experiment was made. As a result, the crime rate involving sex crimes has dropped drastically."

25   (In October, 1967, President Johnson created a Commission on Obscenity and Pornography to investigate the relationship of obscene or pornographic materials to anti-social behavior. Commission head William B. Lockhart, dean of the University of Minnesota Law School, asked at the outset for additional time beyond the January, 1970, deadline. According to Fleishman, the commission has "bogged down on an economic rock," and if it must resort to secondary sources in its studies he hopes it will draw upon Denmark's experience.)

26   What then, if anything, is to be done about pornography?

27   "A solution to the whole problem is to treat sex speech like any other—to bring it in harmony with all other forms of controversial speech. We couldn't suppress a political or religious speech because it went beyond 'customary candor.' It should be banned only if it can be proved to cause a clear and present danger to society.

28   "Whenever something new appears on the horizon the automatic reaction of society is fear and an attempt is made to crush it. When motion pictures came in people said certain things might be all right between hard covers but never on a screen. Now they're saying certain things are all right between hard covers but not in paperback. Almost all prosecutions are with paperbacks. When I was defending 'The Sex

Life of a Cop' in Grand Rapids it was supposed to be the obscene book par excellent. One week later the district attorney said he wondered how anybody could prosecute it, how could anybody get 40 years —one man 25 years, the other 15—and a total of $69,000 in fines. Less than 10 years ago everybody knew 'Lady Chatterley's Lover' was a terrible book."

29 As a crusader for freedom of expression, Fleishman and his wife earlier this year founded Censorship Today: A Review of the Continuing Fight for Free Speech. "I'd always say to my wife when I'd lose a case that we need a broader spreading of information. People don't really know what's going on in this area—about all these decisions that affect all of us."

30 With very little publicity Fleishman already has 600 subscribers. "Not too many yet but a very elite list, I can tell you. It's already in several Supreme Court libraries. In fact, it's in most of the important libraries across the country. All the motion picture and television studios have it. Book publishers and sellers, legislators subscribe.

31 "We're flesh and blood," Stanley Fleishman sums up philosophically. "Everybody, even the President of the United States, has to put either the left foot or the right foot into his pants. We're not very much and we're not here very long. We make too much of too little. One of the nice things is sex."

Discussion of Theme
1. Is the question asked in the title answered by the author, or is it to be answered by the reader?
2. How would Fleishman solve the problem of pornography? Do you agree with his proposed solution? How would you deal with pornography if you were a public official?
3. Is a preoccupation with pornography an illness?
4. How would you define social value?

Discussion of Rhetoric
1. How does the first paragraph of this article serve as an organizational framework for the rest of the essay?
2. How valid is Thomas's comparison of censorship with pornography? What is his own attitude toward pornography?
3. Most of Thomas's article is material quoted from Stanley Fleishman. Why? How does he introduce Fleishman?

Writing Assignments
1. Are there some restrictions you would place on the reading and viewing habits of your younger brothers or sisters or your children? Is this different from restrictions imposed from outside the family? Defend your views.

2. This article asserts that "at 18 a boy can be trained to kill, but one month before he's not supposed to look at Playboy magazine." If you find this attitude hypocritical or inconsistent, develop your ideas into a composition.
3. Define the term free speech.

Library Exploration

1. What laws concerning pornography have been passed by your state or local governing bodies? How effective are they?
2. What was the Hayes Office? What was its purpose? How effective was it?
3. Investigate several of the various lawsuits over the publication or sale of "obscene" books.

Vocabulary

candor (1): frankness
ordinance (3): law or decree
purveying (5): making available; supplying
protract (19): prolong
fallacy (20): false idea
expediency (22): means or methods that serve one's own interest or that give one a temporary advantage

43

THE DARK HEART OF AMERICAN HISTORY

Arthur Schlesinger, Jr.

We like to think of ourselves as a peaceful, tolerant, nation, but Arthur Schlesinger, Jr., sees and believes all of us should see the other strain in our tradition, which is a propensity for violence, both individual and collective.

1   The murders within five years of John F. Kennedy, Martin Luther King, Jr., and Robert F. Kennedy raise—or ought to raise—somber questions about the character of contemporary America. One such murder might be explained away as an isolated horror, unrelated to the inner life of our society. But the successive shootings, in a short time, of three men who greatly embodied the idealism of American life suggest not so much a fortuitous set of aberrations as an emerging pattern of response and action—a spreading and ominous belief in the efficacy of violence and the politics of the deed.

2   Yet, while each of these murders produced a genuine season of national mourning, none has produced a sustained season of national questioning. In every case, remorse has seemed to end, not as an incitement to self-examination, but as an escape from it. An orgy of sorrow and shame becomes an easy way of purging a bad conscience and returning as quickly as possible to business as usual.

3   "It would be . . . self-deceptive," President Johnson said after the shooting of Robert Kennedy, "to conclude from this act that our country is sick, that it has lost its balance, that it has lost its sense of direction, even its common decency. Two hundred million Americans did not strike down Robert Kennedy last night any more than they struck down John F. Kennedy in 1963 or Dr. Martin Luther King in April of this year."

4   I do not quarrel with these words. Of course two hundred million Americans did not strike down these men. Nor, in my judgment, is this a question of a "sick society" or of "collective guilt." I do not know what such phrases mean, but I am certain that they do not represent useful ways of thinking about our problem. Obviously most Americans are decent and God-fearing people. Obviously most

Americans were deeply and honestly appalled by these atrocities. Obviously most Americans rightly resent being told that they were "guilty" of crimes they neither willed nor wished.

5   Still, it is not enough to dismiss the ideas of a sick society and of collective guilt and suppose that such dismissal closes the question. For a problem remains—the problem of a contagion of political murder in the United States in the 1960s unparalleled in our own history and unequaled today anywhere in the world. If we minimize this problem, if we complacently say it is all the work of lunatics and foreigners, that nothing is wrong and that our society is beyond criticism, if we cry like Macbeth: "Thou canst not say I did it; never shake/ Thy gory locks at me," then we lose all hope of recovering control of the destructive impulse within. Then we will only continue the downward spiral of social decomposition and moral degradation.

6   Self-knowledge is the indispensable prelude to self-control; and self-knowledge, for a nation as well as for an individual, begins with history. We like to think of ourselves as a peaceful, tolerant, benign people who have always lived under a government of laws and not of men. And, indeed, respect for persons and for law has been one characteristic strain in the American tradition. Most Americans probably pay this respect most of their lives. Yet this is by no means the only strain in our tradition. For we also have been a violent people. When we refuse to acknowledge the existence of this other strain, we refuse to see our nation as it is.

7   We began, after all, as a people who killed red men and enslaved black men. No doubt we often did this with a Bible and a prayer book. But no nation, however righteous its professions, could act as we did without burying deep in itself—in its customs, its institutions, and its psyche—a propensity toward violence. However much we pretended that Indians and Negroes were subhuman, we really knew that they were God's children too.

8   Nor did we confine our violence to red men and black men. We gained our freedom, after all, through revolution. The first century after independence were years of incessant violence—wars, slave insurrections, Indian fighting, urban riots, murders, duels, beatings. Members of Congress went armed to the Senate and House. In his first notable speech, in January 1838, before the Young Men's Lyceum of Springfield, Illinois, Abraham Lincoln named internal violence as the supreme threat to American political institutions. He spoke of "the increasing disregard for law which pervades the country; the growing disposition to substitute the wild and furious passions, in lieu of the sober judgment of Courts; and the worse than savage mobs, for the executive ministers of justice." The danger to the American republic, he said, was not from foreign invasion:

At what point then is the approach of danger to be expected? I answer, if it ever reach us, it must spring up amongst us. It cannot come from abroad. If destruction be our lot, we must ourselves be its author and finisher. As a nation of freemen, we must live through all time, or die by suicide.

9   So the young Lincoln named the American peril—a peril he did not fear to locate within the American breast. Indeed, the sadness of America has been that our worst qualities have so often been the other face of our best. Our commitment to morality, our faith in experiment: these have been sources of America's greatness, but they have also led Americans into our error. For our moralists have sometimes condoned murder if the cause is deemed good; so Emerson and Thoreau applauded John Brown of Osawatomie. And our pragmatists have sometimes ignored the means if the result is what they want. Moralism and pragmatism have not provided infallible restraints on the destructive instinct.

10   America, Martin Luther King correctly said, has been "a schizophrenic personality, tragically divided against herself." The impulses of violence and civility continued after Lincoln to war within the American breast. The insensate bloodshed of the Civil War exhausted the national capacity for violence and left the nation emotionally and psychologically spent. For nearly a century after Appomattox, we appeared on the surface the tranquil and friendly people we still like to imagine ourselves to be. The amiability of that society no doubt exerted a restraining influence. There were still crazy individuals, filled with grievance, bitterness, and a potential for violence. But most of the people expended their sickness in fantasy; the Guiteaus and the Czolgoszs were the exception. These years of stability, a stability fitfully recaptured after the First World War, created the older generation's image of a "normal" America.

11   Yet even in the kindly years we did not wholly eradicate the propensity toward violence which history had hidden in the national unconscious. In certain moods, indeed, we prided ourselves on our violence; we almost considered it evidence of our virility. "Above all," cried Theodore Roosevelt, "let us shrink from no strife, moral or physical, within or without the nation, provided we are certain that the strife is justified." That fatal susceptibility always lurked under the surface, breaking out in Indian wars and vigilantism in the West, lynchings in the South, in labor riots and race riots and gang wars in the cities.

12   It is important to distinguish collective from individual violence— the work of mobs from the work of murderers; for the motive and the effect can be very different. There can, of course, be murder by a

mob. But not all mobs aim at murder. Collective violence—rioting against what were considered illegal British taxes in Boston in 1773, or dangerous Papist influence sixty years later, or inequitable draft laws in New York in 1863, or unfair labor practices in Chicago in 1937—is more characteristically directed at conditions than at individuals. In many cases (though by no means all), the aim has been to protest rather than protect the status quo; and the historian is obliged to concede that collective violence, including the recent riots in black ghettos, has often quickened the disposition of those in power to redress just grievances. Extralegal group action, for better or worse, has been part of the process of American democracy. Violence, for better or worse, *does* settle some questions, and for the better. Violence secured American independence, freed the slaves, and stopped Hitler.

13   But this has ordinarily been the violence of a society. The individual who plans violence is less likely to be concerned with reforming conditions than with punishing persons. On occasion the purpose is to protect the status quo by destroying men who symbolize or threaten social change (a tactic which the anarchists soon began to employ in reverse). A difference exists in psychic color and content between spontaneous mass convulsions and the premeditated killing of individuals. The first signifies an unstable society, the second, a murderous society. America has exhibited both forms of violence.

14   Now in the third quarter of the twentieth century, violence has broken out with new ferocity in our country. What has given our old propensity new life? Why does the fabric of American civility no longer exert restraint? What now incites crazy individuals to act out their murderous dreams? What is it about the climate of this decade that suddenly encourages—that for some evidently legitimatizes—the relish for hate and the resort to violence? Why, according to the Federal Bureau of Investigation, have assaults with a gun increased 77 per cent in the four years from 1964 through 1967?

15   We talk about the legacy of the frontier. No doubt, the frontier has bequeathed us a set of romantic obsessions about six-shooters and gun fighters. But why should this legacy suddenly reassert itself in the 1960s?

16   We talk about the tensions of industrial society. No doubt the ever-quickening pace of social change depletes and destroys the institutions which make for social stability. But this does not explain why Americans shoot and kill so many more Americans than Englishmen kill Englishmen or Japanese kill Japanese. England, Japan, and West Germany are, next to the United States, the most heavily industrialized countries in the world. Together they have a population of 214 million people. Among these 214 million, there are 135 gun murders a year. Among the 200 million people of the United States there are 6,500 gun murders a year—about *forty-eight times* as many.

17   We talk about the fears and antagonisms generated by racial conflict.

Unquestionably this has contributed to the recent increase in violence. The murders of Dr. King and Senator Kennedy seem directly traceable to ethnic hatreds. Whites and blacks alike are laying in arms, both sides invoking the needs of self-defense. Yet this explanation still does not tell us why in America today we are tending to convert political problems into military problems—problems of adjustment into problems of force.

18   The New Left tells us that we are a violent society because we are a capitalist society—that capitalism is itself institutionalized violence; and that life under capitalism inevitably deforms relations among men. This view would be more impressive if the greatest violence of man against man in this century had not taken place in noncapitalist societies—in Nazi Germany, in Stalinist Russia, in precapitalist Indonesia. The fact is that every form of society is in some sense institutionalized violence; man in society always gives up a measure of "liberty" and accepts a measure of authority.

19   We cannot escape that easily. It is not just that we were a frontier society or have become an industrial society or are a racist or a capitalist society; it is something more specific than that. Nor can we blame the situation on our gun laws, or the lack of them; though here possibly we are getting closer. There is no question, of course, that we need adequate federal gun laws. Statistics make it evident that gun controls have some effect. Sixty per cent of all murders in the United States are by firearms; and states with adequate laws—New Jersey, New York, Massachusetts, Rhode Island—have much lower rates of gun murder than states with no laws or weak ones—Texas, Mississippi, Louisiana, Nevada.

20   Still, however useful in making it harder for potential murderers to get guns, federal gun legislation deals with the symptoms and not with the causes of our trouble. We must go further to account for the resurgence in recent years of our historical propensity toward violence.

21   One reason surely for the enormous tolerance of violence in contemporary America is the fact that our country has now been more or less continuously at war for a generation. The experience of war over a long period devalues human life and habituates people to killing. And the war in which we are presently engaged is far more brutalizing than was the Second World War or the Korean War. It is more brutalizing because the destruction we have wrought in Vietnam is so wildly out of proportion to any demonstrated involvement of our national security or any rational assessment of our national interest. In the other wars we killed for need. In this war we are killing beyond need, and, as we do so, we corrupt our national life. When violence is legally sanctioned for a cause in which people see no moral purpose, this is an obvious stimulus to individuals to use violence for what they may maniacally consider moral purposes of their own.

22   A second reason for the climate of violence in the United States is

surely the zest with which the mass media, and especially television and films, dwell on violence. One must be clear about this. The mass media do *not* create violence. But they *reinforce* aggressive and destructive impulses, and they may well *teach* the morality as well as the methods of violence.

23   In recent years the movies and television have developed a pornography of violence far more demoralizing than the pornography of sex, which still seizes the primary attention of the guardians of civic virtue. Popular films of our day like *Rosemary's Baby* and *Bonnie and Clyde* imply a whole culture of human violation, psychological in one case, physical in the other. *Bonnie and Clyde*, indeed, was greatly admired for its blithe acceptance of the world of violence—an acceptance which almost became a celebration. Thus a student in a film course in San Francisco noted:

> There is a certain spirit that belongs to us. We the American people. It is pragmatic, rebellious, violent, joyous. It can create or kill. Everything about *Bonnie and Clyde* captures this spirit.
>
> John Brown was motivated by this spirit and it has scared the hell out of historians ever since. The Black Panthers have it. Cab drivers, musicians, used car salesmen and bus drivers understand it, but doctors, dentists and real estate salesmen don't.

24   Television is the most pervasive influence of all. The children of the electronic age sit hypnotized by the parade of killings, beatings, gunfights, knifings, maimings, brawls which flash incessantly across the tiny screen, and now in "living" color.

25   For a time, the television industry comforted itself with the theory that children listened to children's programs and that, if by any chance they saw programs for adults, violence would serve as a safety valve, offering a harmless outlet for pent-up aggressions: the more violence on the screen, the less in life. Alas, this turns out not to be necessarily so. As Dr. Wilbur Schramm, director of the Institute of Communication Research at Stanford has reported, children, even in the early elementary school years, view more programs designed for adults than for themselves; "above all, they prefer the more violent type of adult program including the Western, the adventure program, and the crime drama." Experiments show that such programs, far from serving as safety valves for aggression, attract children with high levels of aggression and stimulate them to seek overt means of acting out their aggressions. Evidence suggests that these programs work the same incitement on adults. And televiolence does more than condition emotion and behavior. It also may attenuate people's sense of reality. Men murdered on the television screen ordinarily spring to life after the episode is over: all death is therefore diminished. A child asked a man last June where he was headed in his car. "To Washington," he

said. "Why?" he asked. "To attend the funeral of Senator Kennedy." The child said, "Oh yeah—they shot him again." And such shooting may well condition the manner in which people approach the perplexities of existence. On television the hero too glibly resolves his problems by shooting somebody. The *Gunsmoke* ethos, however, is not necessarily the best way to deal with human or social complexity. It is hardly compatible with any kind of humane or libertarian democracy.

26   The problem of electronic violence raises difficult questions of prescription as well as of analysis. It would be fatal to restrain artistic exploration and portrayal, even of the most extreme and bitter aspects of human experience. No rational person wants to re-establish a reign of censorship or mobilize new Legions of Decency. Nor is there great gain in making the electronic media scapegoats for propensities which they reflect rather than create—propensities which spring from our history and our hearts.

27   Yet society retains a certain right of self-defense. Is it inconceivable that the television industry might work out forms of self-restraint? Beyond this, it should be noted that the networks and the stations do *not* own the airwaves; the nation does; and, if the industry cannot restrain itself, the Communications Act offers means, as yet unused, of democratic control.

28   We have a bad inheritance as far as violence is concerned; and in recent years war and television have given new vitality to the darkest strains in our national psyche. How can we master this horror in our souls before it rushes us on to ultimate disintegration?

29   There is not a problem of collective guilt, but there is a problem of collective responsibility. Certainly two hundred million Americans did not strike down John Kennedy or Martin Luther King or Robert Kennedy. But two hundred million Americans are plainly responsible for the character of a society that works on deranged men and incites them to depraved acts. There were Lee Harvey Oswalds and James Earl Rays and Sirhan Bishara Sirhans in America in the Thirties— angry, frustrated, alienated, resentful, marginal men in rootless, unstable cities like Dallas and Memphis and Los Angeles. But our society in the Thirties did not stimulate such men to compensate for their own failure by killing leaders the people loved.

30   Some of the young in their despair have come to feel that the answer to reason is unreason, the answer to violence, more violence; but these only hasten the plunge toward the abyss. The more intelligent disagree. They do not want America to beat its breast and go back to the golf course. *They do want America to recognize its responsibility.* They want us to tell it like it is—to confront the darkness in our past and the darkness in our present. They want us to realize that life is not solid and predictable but infinitely chancy, that violence is not the deviation but the ever-present possibility, that we can therefore never

rest in the effort to prevent unreason from rending the skin of
civility. They want our leaders to *talk* less about law and order and *do*
more about justice.

31   Perhaps the old in American society might now learn that sanctimony
is not a persuasive answer to anguish, and that we never cure ourselves
if we deny the existence of a disease. If they learn this, if they face up to
the schism in our national tradition, we all will have a better chance
of subduing the impulse of destruction and of fulfilling the vision of
Lincoln—that noble vision of a serene and decent society, united by
bonds of affection and mystic chords of memory, dedicated at last to
our highest ideals.

Discussion of Theme
1. Does Schlesinger agree with Fulbright that our society is sick?
   In what ways do they differ or agree?
2. According to the author, what accounts for the strain of violence
   in our national character?
3. Schlesinger mentions two forms of violence. How are they different?
4. What are the two reasons the author gives for the resurgence of
   violence in contemporary America?
5. Does the author hold out any hope for our society? Does he prescribe
   any remedies?

Discussion of Rhetoric
1. What arrangement or order determines the organization of this
   essay? What other patterns might have been used?
2. What kinds of evidence does the author present to support his
   thesis?
3. Why do you think Schlesinger wrote this article? To whom is it
   addressed?
4. Schlesinger uses a variety of sentence patterns. Examine several
   sentences and note the length, the position of subject and verb,
   and the methods used to subordinate ideas.

Writing Assignments
1. Does television viewing stimulate violence in children? Present
   your views in a theme.
2. Are stricter gun-control laws needed in this country?
3. Write a letter to the heads of the three major networks presenting
   your arguments for reducing the amount of violence on their
   shows.

Library Exploration
1. Study violence in other nations, and then present your own view on
   whether our country is the most violent.

2. Read Schlesinger's book, *Violence: America in the Sixties*, for other statements on this subject.

Vocabulary

fortuitous (1): occurring by chance
aberrations (1): deviations from what is right or normal
efficacy (1): effectiveness
benign (6): kind and gentle; humane
propensity (7): leaning; inclination
insurrections (8): uprisings
pragmatists (9): those who are concerned with the practical side
    of problems and affairs
insensate (10): senseless; brutal; inhuman
redress (12): set right; correct
depletes (16): weakens; exhausts
attenuate (25): weaken
sanctimony (31): assumed or hypocritical holiness
schism (31): division; rift

44

CONDITIONS OF LIFE
IN THE RACIAL GHETTO

The Kerner Report

The following excerpt from the presidential commission reveals, through statistics and other objec- *tive evidence, a chilling picture of hardship and misery in the ghetto.*

1   The conditions of life in the racial ghetto are strikingly different from those to which most Americans are accustomed—especially white, middle-class Americans. We believe it important to describe these conditions and their effect on the lives of people who cannot escape from the ghetto.

2   We have not attempted here to describe conditions relating to the fundamental problems of housing, education and welfare, which are treated in detail in later chapters.

I. CRIME AND INSECURITY

3   Nothing is more fundamental to the quality of life in any area than the sense of personal security of its residents, and nothing affects this more than crime.

4   In general, crime rates in large cities are much higher than in other areas of our country. Within such cities, crime rates are higher in disadvantaged Negro areas than anywhere else.

5   The most widely-used measure in crime is the number of "index crimes" (homicide, forcible rape, aggravated assault, robbery, burglary, grand larceny, and auto theft) in relation to population. In 1966, 1,754 such crimes were reported to police for every 100,000 Americans. In cities over 250,000, the rate was 3,153, and in cities over one million, it was 3,630—or more than double the national average. In suburban areas alone, including suburban cities, the rate was only 1,300, or just one-third the rate in the largest cities.

6   Within larger cities, personal and property insecurity has consistently been highest in the older neighborhoods encircling the downtown business district. In most cities, crime rates for many decades have been higher in these inner areas than anywhere else, except in downtown areas themselves where they are inflated by the small number of residents.

7   High crime rates have persisted in these inner areas even though the ethnic character of their residents continually changed. Poor immigrants used these areas as "entry port," then usually moved on to more desirable neighborhoods as soon as they acquired enough resources. Many "entry port" areas have now become racial ghettos.

8   The difference between crime rates in these disadvantaged neighborhoods and in other parts of the city is usually startling, as a comparison of crime rates in five police districts in Chicago for 1965 illustrates. Taking one high-income, all-white district at the periphery of the city, two very low-income, virtually all-Negro districts near the city core, both including numerous public housing projects, and two predominantly white districts, one with mainly lower-middle-income families, the other containing a mixture of very high-income and relatively low-income households, the table shows crime rates against persons and against property in these five districts, plus the number of patrolmen assigned to them per 100,000 residents, as follows:

Incidence of Index Crimes and Patrolmen Assignments per 100,000 Residents in 5 Chicago Police Districts, 1965

	High Income White District	Low-Middle-Income White District	Mixed High and Low-Income White District	Very Low Income Negro District No. 1	Very Low Income Negro District No. 2
Number					
Index crimes against persons	80	440	338	1,615	2,820
Index crimes against property	1,038	1,750	2,080	2,508	2,630
Patrolmen assigned	93	133	115	243	291

9   These data suggest the following conclusions:

Variations in the crime rate against persons within the city are extremely large. One very low-income Negro district had 35 times as many serious crimes against persons per 100,000 residents as did the high-income white district.

Variations in the crime rate against property are much smaller. The highest rate was only 2.5 times larger than the lowest.

Both income and race appear to affect crime rates: the lower the income in an area, the higher the crime rate there. Yet low-income Negro areas have significantly higher crime rates than low-income white areas. This reflects the high degree of social disorganization in Negro areas described in the previous chapter, as well as the fact that poor Negroes, as a group, have lower incomes than poor whites, as a group.

The presence of more police patrolmen per 100,000 residents does not necessarily offset high crime in certain parts of the city. Although the Chicago Police Department had assigned over three times as many patrolmen per 100,000 residents to the highest-crime area shown as to the lowest, crime rates in the highest-crime area for offenses against both persons and property combined were 4.9 times as high as in the lowest-crime area.

10   Because most middle-class Americans live in neighborhoods similar to the more crime-free district described above, they have little comprehension of the sense of insecurity that characterizes the ghetto resident. Moreover, official statistics normally greatly understate actual crime rates because the vast majority of crimes are not reported to the police. For example, a study conducted for the President's Crime Commission in three Washington, D.C. precincts showed that six times as many crimes were actually committed against persons and homes as were reported to the police. Other studies in Boston and Chicago indicated that about three times as many crimes were committed as were reported.

11   Two facts are crucial to understand the effects of high crime rates in racial ghettos: most of these crimes are committed by a small minority of the residents, and the principal victims are the residents themselves. Throughout the United States, the great majority of crimes committed by Negroes involve other Negroes as victims, just as most crimes committed by whites are against other whites. A special tabulation made by the Chicago Police Department for the President's Crime Commission indicated that over 85 percent of the crimes committed by Negroes between September 1965 and March 1966 involved Negro victims.

12   As a result, the majority of law-abiding citizens who live in disadvantaged Negro areas face much higher probabilities of being victimized than residents of most higher-income areas, including almost all suburbs. For nonwhites, the probability of suffering from any index crime except larceny is 78 percent higher than for whites. The probability of being raped is 3.7 times higher among nonwhite women, and the probability of being robbed is 3.5 times higher for nonwhites in general.

13   The problems associated with high crime rates generate widespread hostility toward the police in these neighborhoods for reasons described elsewhere in this Report. Thus, crime not only creates an atmosphere of insecurity and fear throughout Negro neighborhoods but also causes continuing attrition of the relationship between Negro residents and police. This bears a direct relationship to civil disorder.

14   There are reasons to expect the crime situation in these areas to become worse in the future. First, crime rates throughout the United States have been rising rapidly in recent years. The rate of index crimes against persons rose 37 percent from 1960 to 1966, and the rate of index crimes against property rose 50 percent. In the first nine months of 1967, the number of index crimes was up 16 percent over the same period in 1966 whereas the United States population rose about one percent. In cities of 250,000 to one million, index crime rose by over 20 percent, whereas it increased four percent in cities of over one million.[1]

15   Second, the number of police available to combat crime is rising much more slowly than the amount of crime. In 1966, there were about 20 percent more police employees in the United States than in 1960, and per capita expenditures for police rose from $15.29 in 1960 to $20.99 in 1966, a gain of 37 percent. But over the six-year period, the number of reported index crimes had jumped 62 percent. In spite of significant improvements in police efficiency, it is clear that police will be unable to cope with their expanding workload unless there is a dramatic increase in the resources allocated by society to this task.

16   Third, in the next decade the number of young Negroes aged 14 to 24 will increase rapidly, particularly in central cities. This group is responsible for a disproportionately high share of crimes in all parts of the nation. In 1966, persons under 25 years of age comprised the following proportions of those arrested for various major crimes: murder—37 percent; forcible rape—60 percent; robbery—71 percent; burglary—81 percent; larceny—about 75 percent; and auto theft— over 80 percent. For all index crimes together, the arrest rate for Negroes is about four times higher than that for whites. Yet the number of young Negroes aged 14 to 24 in central cities will rise about 63 percent from 1966 to 1975, as compared to only 32 percent for the total Negro population of central cities.[2]

II. HEALTH AND SANITATION CONDITIONS

17   The residents of the racial ghetto are significantly less healthy than most other Americans. They suffer from higher mortality rates, higher incidence of major diseases, and lower availability and utilization of medical services. They also experience higher admission rates to mental hospitals.

---

[1]The problem of interpreting and evaluating "rising" crime rates is complicated by the changing age distribution of the population, improvements in reporting methods, and the increasing willingness of victims to report crimes. Despite these complications, there is general agreement on the serious increase in the incidence of crime in the United States.

[2]Assuming those cities will experience the same proportion of total United States Negro population growth that they did from 1960 to 1966.

18   These conditions result from a number of factors.

19   *Poverty*. From the standpoint of health, poverty means deficient diets, lack of medical care, inadequate shelter and clothing, and often lack of awareness of potential health needs. As a result, about 30 percent of all families with incomes less than $2,000 per year suffer from chronic health conditions that adversely affect their employment —as compared with less than 8 percent of the families with incomes of $7,000 or more.

20   Poor families have the greatest need for financial assistance in meeting medical expenses. Only about 34 percent of families with incomes of less than $2,000 per year use health insurance benefits, as compared to nearly 90 percent of those with incomes of $7,000 or more.[3]

21   These factors are aggravated for Negroes when compared to whites for the simple reason that the proportion of persons in the United States who are poor is 3.5 times as high among Negroes (41 percent in 1966) as among whites (12 percent in 1966).

22   *Maternal Mortality*. Maternal mortality rates for nonwhite mothers are four times as high as those for white mothers. There has been a sharp decline in such rates since 1940, when 774 nonwhite and 320 white mothers died for each 100,000 live births. In 1965, only 84 nonwhite and 21 white mothers died per 100,000 live births—but the *relative* gap between nonwhites and whites actually increased.

23   *Infant Mortality*. Infant mortality rates among nonwhite babies are 58 percent higher than among whites for those under one month old, and almost three times as high among those from one month to one year old. This is true in spite of a large drop in infant mortality rates in both groups since 1940.

Number of Infants Who Died per 1,000 Live Births

Year	Less Than One Month Old		One Month to One Year Old	
	White	*Nonwhite*	*White*	*Nonwhite*
1940	27.2	39.7	16.0	34.1
1950	19.4	27.5	7.4	17.0
1960	17.2	26.9	5.7	16.4
1965	16.1	25.4	5.4	14.9

[3]Public programs of various kinds have been providing significant financial assistance for medical care in recent years. In 1964, over $1.1 billion was paid out by various governments for such aid. About 55 percent came from federal government agencies, 33 percent from states, and 12 percent from local governments. The biggest contributions were made by the Old Age Assistance program and the Medical Assistance for the Aged program. The enactment of Medicare in 1965 has significantly added to this flow of public assistance for medical aid. However, it is too early to evaluate the results upon health conditions among the poor.

24   *Life Expectancy.* To some extent because of infant mortality rates, life expectancy at birth was 6.9 years longer for whites (71.0 years) than for nonwhites (64.1 years) in 1965. Even in the prime working ages, life expectancy is significantly lower among nonwhites than among whites. In 1965, white persons 25 years old could expect to live an average of 48.6 more years; whereas nonwhites 25 years old could expect to live another 43.3 years, or 11 percent less. Similar but smaller discrepancies existed at all ages from 25 through 55, and these discrepancies actually became wider between 1960 and 1965.

25   *Lower Utilization of Health Services.* A fact that also contributes to poorer health conditions in the ghetto is that Negroes with incomes similar to those of whites spend less on medical services and visit medical specialists less often.

Income Group	Percent of Family Expenditures Spent for Medical Care 1960–61		Ratio White:
	White	*Nonwhite*	*Nonwhite*
Under $3,000	9	5	1.8:1
$3,000 to $7,499	7	5	1.4:1
$7,500 & over	6	4	1.5:1

26   Since the lowest income group contains a much larger proportion of nonwhite families than white families, the overall discrepancy in medical care spending between these two groups is very significant, as shown by the following table:

Health Expenses per Person per Year for the Period From July to December 1962

Income Racial Group	Total Medical	Expenses			
		Hospital	*Doctor*	*Dental*	*Medicine*
Under $2,000 per Family per Year:					
White	$130	$33	$41	$11	$32
Nonwhite	63	15	23	5	16
$10,000 and More per Family per Year:					
White	$179	$34	$61	$37	$31
Nonwhite	133	34	50	19	23

27   These data indicate that nonwhite families in the lower income group spent less than half as much per person on medical services as white families with similar incomes. This discrepancy sharply declines but is still significant in the higher income group, where total nonwhite

medical expenditures per person equal, on the average, 74.3 percent
of white expenditures.

28   Negroes spend less on medical care for several reasons. Negro
households generally are larger, requiring larger nonmedical expenses
for each household, and leaving less money for meeting medical
expenses. Thus lower expenditures per person would result even if
expenditures per household were the same. Negroes also often pay more
for certain other basic necessities such as food and consumer durables,
as is discussed in other sections of this Report. In addition, fewer
doctors, dentists, and medical facilities are conveniently available to
Negroes—especially to poor families—than to most whites. This is a
result both of geographic concentration of doctors in higher income
areas in large cities and of discrimination against Negroes by doctors
and hospitals. A survey in Cleveland indicated that there were 0.45
physicians per 1,000 people in poor neighborhoods, compared to 1.13
per 1,000 in nonpoverty areas. The result is fewer visits to physicians
and dentists.

Percent of Population Making One or More
Visits to Indicated Type of Medical
Specialist from July 1963 to June 1964

	Family Incomes of $2,000 to $3,999		Family Incomes of $7,000 to $9,999	
Type of Medical Specialist	*White*	*Nonwhite*	*White*	*Nonwhite*
Physician	64	56	70	64
Dentist	31	20	52	33

29   Although widespread use of health insurance has led many hospitals
to adopt nondiscriminatory policies, some private hospitals still refuse
to admit Negro patients or to accept doctors with Negro patients.
And many individual doctors still discriminate against Negro patients.
As a result, Negroes are more likely to be treated in hospital clinics
than whites, and they are less likely to receive personalized service.
This conclusion is confirmed by the following data:

Percent of All Visits to Physicians
from July 1963 to June 1964
Made in Indicated Ways

	Family Incomes of $2,000 to $3,999		Family Incomes of $7,000 to $9,999	
Type of Visit to Physician	*White*	*Nonwhite*	*White*	*Nonwhite*
In Physician's Office	68	56	73	66
Hospital clinic	17	35	7	16
Other (mainly telephone)	15	9	20	18
Total	100	100	100	100

30   *Environmental Factors.* Environmental conditions in disadvantaged Negro neighborhoods create further reasons for poor health conditions there. The level of sanitation is strikingly below that which is prevalent in most higher income areas. One simple reason is that residents lack proper storage facilities for food—adequate refrigerators, freezers, even garbage cans which are sometimes stolen as fast as landlords can replace them.

31   In many areas where garbage collection and other sanitation services are grossly inadequate—commonly in the poorer parts of our large cities, rats proliferate. It is estimated that in 1965, there were over 14,000 cases of rat-bite in the United States, mostly in such neighborhoods.

32   The importance of these conditions was outlined for the Commission as follows:[4]

> Sanitation Commissioners of New York City and Chicago both feel this [sanitation] to be an important community problem and report themselves as being under substantial pressure to improve conditions. *It must be concluded that slum sanitation is a serious problem in the minds of the urban poor and well merits, at least on that ground, the attention of the Commission.* A related problem, according to one Sanitation Commissioner, is the fact that residents of areas bordering on slums feel that sanitation and neighborhood cleanliness is a crucial issue, relating to the stability of their blocks and constituting an important psychological index of "how far gone" their area is.
>
> . . . There is no known study comparing sanitation services between slum and nonslum areas. The experts agree, however, that there are more services in the slums on a quantitative basis, although perhaps not on a per capita basis. In New York, for example, garbage pickups are supposedly scheduled for about six times a week in slums, compared to three times a week in other areas of the city; the comparable figures in Chicago are two-three times a week versus once a week.
>
> The point, therefore, is not the relative quantitative level of services, but the peculiarly intense needs of ghetto areas for sanitation services. This high demand is the product of numerous factors including: (1) higher population density; (2) lack of well managed buildings and adequate garbage services provided by landlords, number of receptacles, carrying to curbside, number of electric garbage disposals; (3) high relocation rates of tenants and businesses, producing heavy volume of bulk refuse left on streets and in buildings; (4) different uses of the streets—as outdoor living rooms in summer, recreation areas—producing

[4]Memorandum to the Commission dated November 16, 1967, from Robert Patricelli, Minority Counsel, Subcommittee on Employment Manpower and Poverty, U.S. Senate.

high visibility and sensitivity to garbage problems; (5) large
numbers of abandoned cars; (6) severe rodent and pest problems;
(7) traffic congestion blocking garbage collection; and (8) ob-
structed street cleaning and snow removal on crowded, car-
choked streets. Each of these elements adds to the problem and
suggests a different possible line of attack.

III. EXPLOITATION OF DISADVANTAGED CONSUMERS BY RETAIL MERCHANTS

33   Much of the violence in recent civil disorders has been directed at
stores and other commercial establishments in disadvantaged Negro
areas. In some cases, rioters focused on stores operated by white
merchants who, they apparently believed, had been charging exorbitant prices or selling inferior goods. Not all the violence against
these stores can be attributed to "revenge" for such practices. Yet it is
clear that many residents of disadvantaged Negro neighborhoods
believe they suffer constant abuses by local merchants.

34   Significant grievances concerning unfair commercial practices
affecting Negro consumers were found in 11 of the 20 cities studied by
the Commission. The fact that most of the merchants who operate
stores in almost every Negro area are white undoubtedly contributes
to the conclusion among Negroes that they are exploited by white
society.

35   It is difficult to assess the precise degree and extent of exploitation.
No systematic and reliable survey comparing consumer pricing and
credit practices in all-Negro and other neighborhoods has ever been
conducted on a nationwide basis. Differences in prices and credit
practices between white middle-income areas and Negro low-income
areas to some extent reflect differences in the real costs of serving these
two markets (such as differential losses from pilferage in supermarkets),
but the exact extent of these differential real costs has never been estimated accurately. Finally, an examination of exploitative consumer
practices must consider the particular structure and functions of the
low-income consumer durables market.

36   *Installment Buying.* This complex situation can best be understood
by first considering certain basic facts:

    Various cultural factors generate constant pressure on low-
    income families to buy many relatively expensive durable goods
    and display them in their homes. This pressure comes in part
    from continuous exposure to commercial advertising, especially
    on television. In January 1967, over 88 percent of all Negro
    households had TV sets. A 1961 study of 464 low-income families
    in New York City showed that 95 percent of these relatively poor
    families had TV sets.

    Many poor families have extremely low incomes, bad previous
    credit records, unstable sources of income, or other attributes
    which make it virtually impossible for them to buy merchandise

from established large national or local retail firms. These families lack enough savings to pay cash, and they cannot meet the standard credit requirements of established general merchants because they are too likely to fall behind in their payments.

Poor families in urban areas are far less mobile than others. A 1967 Chicago study of low-income Negro households indicated their low automobile ownership compelled them to patronize primarily local neighborhood merchants. These merchants typically provided smaller selection, poorer services, and higher prices than big national outlets. The 1961 New York study also indicated that families who shopped outside their own neighborhoods were far less likely to pay exorbitant prices.

Most low-income families are uneducated concerning the nature of credit purchase contracts, the legal rights and obligations of both buyers and sellers, sources of advice for consumers who are having difficulties with merchants, and the operation of the courts concerned with these matters. In contrast, merchants engaged in selling goods to them are very well informed.

In most states, the laws governing relations between consumers and merchants in effect offer protection only to informed, sophisticated parties with understanding of each other's rights and obligations. Consequently, these laws are little suited to protect the rights of most low-income consumers.

37   In this situation, exploitative practices flourish. Ghetto residents who want to buy relatively expensive goods cannot do so from standard retail outlets and are thus restricted to local stores. Forced to use credit, they have little understanding of the pitfalls of credit buying. But because they have unstable incomes and frequently fail to make payments, the cost to the merchants of serving them is significantly above that of serving middle-income consumers. Consequently, a special kind of merchant appears to sell them goods on terms designed to cover the high cost of doing business in ghetto neighborhoods.

38   Whether they actually gain higher profits, these merchants charge higher prices than those in other parts of the city to cover the greater credit risks and other higher operating costs inherent in neighborhood outlets. A recent study conducted by the Federal Trade Commission in Washington, D.C., illustrates this conclusion dramatically. The FTC identified a number of stores specializing in selling furniture and appliances to low-income households. About 92 percent of the sales of these stores were credit sales involving installment purchases, as compared to 27 percent of the sales in general retail outlets handling the same merchandise.

39   The median income annually of a sample of 486 customers of these stores was about $4,200, but one-third had annual incomes below $3,600, about 6 percent were receiving welfare payments, and another 76 percent were employed in the lowest paying occupations (service

workers, operatives, laborers, and domestics)—as compared to 36 percent of the total labor force in Washington in those occupations.

40   Definitely catering to a low-income group, these stores charged significantly higher prices than general merchandise outlets in the Washington area. According to testimony by Paul Rand Dixon, Chairman of the FTC, an item selling wholesale at $100 would retail on the average for $165 in a general merchandise store, and for $250 in a low-income specialty store. Thus, the customers of these outlets were paying an average price premium of about 52 percent.

41   While higher prices are not necessarily exploitative in themselves, many merchants in ghetto neighborhoods take advantage of their superior knowledge of credit buying by engaging in various exploitative tactics—high-pressure salesmanship, bait advertising, misrepresentation of prices, substitution of used goods for promised new ones, failure to notify consumers of legal actions against them, refusal to repair or replace substandard goods, exorbitant prices or credit charges, and use of shoddy merchandise. Such tactics affect a great many low-income consumers. In the New York study, 60 percent of all households had suffered from consumer problems (some of which were purely their own fault), about 43 percent had experienced serious exploitation, and 20 percent had experienced repossession, garnishment, or threat of garnishment.

42   *Garnishment.* Garnishment practices in many states allow creditors to deprive individuals of their wages through court action without hearing or trial. In about 20 states, the wages of an employee can be diverted to a creditor merely upon the latter's deposition, with no advance hearing where the employee can defend himself. He often receives no prior notice of such action and is usually unaware of the law's operation and too poor to hire legal defense. Moreover, consumers may find themselves still owing money on a sales contract even after the creditor has repossessed the goods. The New York study cited earlier in this chapter indicated that 20 percent of a sample of low-income families had been subject to legal action regarding consumer purchases. And the Federal Trade Commission study in Washington, D.C., showed that retailers specializing in credit sales of furniture and appliances to low-income consumers resorted to court action on the average for every $2,200 of sales. Since their average sale was for $207, this amounted to using the courts to collect from one of every 11 customers. In contrast, department stores in the same area used court action against approximately one of every 14,500 customers.[5]

43   *Variations in Food Prices.* Residents of low-income Negro neighborhoods frequently claim that they pay higher prices for food in local markets than wealthier white suburbanites and receive inferior quality

[5]Assuming their sales also averaged $207 per customer.

meat and produce. Statistically reliable information comparing prices and quality in these two kinds of areas is generally unavailable. The U.S. Bureau of Labor Statistics, studying food prices in six cities in 1966, compared prices of a standard list of 18 items in low-income areas and higher-income areas in each city. In a total of 180 stores, including independent and chain stores, and for items of the same type sold in the same types of stores, there were no significant differences in prices between low-income and high-income areas. However, stores in low-income areas were more likely to be small independents (which had somewhat higher prices), to sell low-quality produce and meat at any given price, and to be patronized by people who typically bought smaller-sized packages which are more expensive per unit of measure. In other words, many low-income consumers in fact pay higher prices, although the situation varies greatly from place to place.

44   Although these findings must be considered inconclusive, there are significant reasons to believe that poor households generally pay higher prices for the food they buy and receive lower quality food. Low-income consumers buy more food at local groceries because they are less mobile. Prices in these small stores are significantly higher than in major supermarkets because they cannot achieve economies of scale, and because real operating costs are higher in low-income Negro areas than in outlying suburbs. For instance, inventory "shrinkage" from pilfering and other causes is normally under 2 percent of sales, but can run twice as much in high-crime areas. Managers seek to make up for these added costs by charging higher prices for good quality food, or by substituting lower grades.

45   These practices do not necessarily involve "exploitation," but they are often perceived as exploitative and unfair by those who are aware of the price and quality differences involved, but unaware of operating costs. In addition, it is probable that genuinely exploitative pricing practices exist in some areas. In either case, differential food prices constitute another factor convincing urban Negroes in low-income neighborhoods that whites discriminate against them.

Discussion of Theme

1. What is the relation between crime and the ghetto? Why do most middle-class Americans have little comprehension of the sense of insecurity that characterizes the ghetto resident?
2. What are the differences in the kind of protection given a law-abiding citizen of the ghetto, and a law-abiding citizen of a middle-class neighborhood? What accounts for those differences?
3. Why do the authors of this report believe that the crime rate in the ghetto will increase in the future? Are any of the trends they mention reversible?

4. What is garnishment? How is it used by retailers? Why is it particularly unfair to the poor?
5. Is it easy to be productive or very concerned with legalities when you're constantly sick or underfed? Project some of the attitudes that might grow out of such a condition.

Discussion of Rhetoric
1. What is the tone of this article? Is it appropriate? Give reasons for your answers.
2. How do the writers of the report support their statements? How convincing are they in their documentation?
3. How is this selection organized? Does one segment follow logically from the next, or are the various parts interchangeable?

Writing Assignments
1. Develop the following statement into a theme: "Nothing is more fundamental to the quality of life in any area than the sense of personal security of its residents. . . ."
2. How are the poor exploited? Consider such areas as city sanitation services, health facilities, grocery prices, and police protection.
3. How true is the following statement: "The poor are always with us"? Should it be true?
4. Can you offer any long-range solutions to conditions in the ghetto as described by the report?

Library Exploration
1. Investigate the events that triggered a riot in a large metropolitan area (for example, in Watts).
2. What has the government done recently to improve life in the ghetto?
3. Read *The Fire Next Time* by James Baldwin for an insider's view of life in the ghetto.

Vocabulary
attrition (13): weakening; wearing down
allocated (15): designated or set apart (for a particular purpose)
proliferate (31): grow rapidly
pilferage (35): petty theft
deposition (42): testimony; declaration

45

FIVE MARTYRS IN A TIME
WITHOUT HEROES

Pete Hamill

Is ours an age without heroes? The author of the following selection thinks we prefer martyrs to heroes. He examines the impact on American youth of the deaths of five prominent men of action.

"Men reject their prophets and slay them, but they love their martyrs and honor those whom they have slain." Fedor Dostoevski

1   Ah, Dostoevski, old crapshooter, manic hack, wild and beautiful magician—you knew everything, didn't you? Poor America has become a nation infected with martyrdom and a lust for heroes. We are in terrible trouble because all of the heroes are dead. Consider the current crop. One was a Communist revolutionary. Two were sons of an Irish-American millionaire. The fourth was a black man who had been a drug addict and a pimp. An unlikely set of heroes for the American youth.

2   But there they are: Ché Guevara, John and Robert Kennedy, Malcolm X. You hear their names tumble from a thousand sets of lips. Their pictures, blown up into posters, adorn walls across the nation. Bookstores peddle their works. Dull, virtuous men use their names in vain. Four years after the death of Malcolm, young black kids in Watts and Cleveland wear orange sweat shirts bearing his likeness. Only months after Robert Kennedy is returned to the American earth, lesser men are squabbling for his political estate. In Bolivia, the Government totters and shakes as Ché's ghost prowls the *altiplano* and his diary goes into the hands of millions. Five years after Dallas, there are still men who have not fully recovered from the events of November 22, 1963.

3   There are no other heroes, except possibly the Beatles and Dylan. Who cheers Lyndon Johnson, Richard Nixon or Hubert Humphrey? Not the young. Who in public life today, except possibly Gene McCarthy, could end up enshrined on a campus wall? Hell, who is the heavyweight champion of the world? Who led the majors in homers last season? Who is leading the football leagues in rushing? No answers. There are no heroes; the real heroes are dead.

4   But why Ché? Or the Kennedy brothers? Or Malcolm?

5   The reasons are complicated, but there are some answers. First of all, all four were young: Ché was thirty-nine, as was Malcolm; John Kennedy was forty-eight, and Robert Kennedy was forty-three. That might be middle-aged by most people's standards, but compared to the Harrimans, the Eastlands, the Rusks, the chairmen of all the boards, the presidents of most of the universities, compared to most of the people who rule this earth, the martyrs were young.

6   Three of them were also dedicated to radical change. Malcolm X wanted to change the Negro himself from within by providing him with pride in his blackness and his history, and he wanted to change the black man's situation in the country, even if it meant something as radical as setting up a separate black nation within our borders. Ché Guevara wanted to change the terrible social conditions of Latin America, and the weapon he chose was guerrilla warfare; he had gone beyond compromise and ethereal notions about peaceful change; he knew the enemy would only respect force of arms and that took him to the mountains of Bolivia to die. Robert Kennedy had embarked on a political course whose ultimate objectives were as radical as anyone could hope for within the American system; he hoped to destroy much of the malaise and ugliness in American life, and instead, was destroyed himself. Only John F. Kennedy was cautious and somewhat con-servative. His death caused a different reaction: People cried for America, for promises that now would never be kept, for the abrupt end of a style we liked, and more than anything else, I suppose, because of a terrible sense of regret and remorse. For a few brief years America had been a young country again, and in a few seconds in Dallas, youth was over.

7   But what was common to all of these men was that they died at the proper moment. If Malcolm had lived and ended up as a director of the Ford Foundation or even a candidate for public office, his death would have been just that: a death. If John Kennedy had been reelected and served out another term, it would have meant relatively little for him to die later. (And it is odd to think of what his reputation might have been if he had lived and had become enmeshed in the Vietnam swamp even deeper, or if he would have become further enmeshed at all.) If Robert Kennedy had not tried to run for President in 1968 and still had been assassinated, it would have meant less than it did. If Ché Guevara had remained in Cuba to grow fat and sleek in a high govern-ment office and had died in some internecine feud, his face would not be looking out at us from all those campus walls.

8   The end of Martin Luther King might explain what I mean. King was undoubtedly a martyr; he was not shot by a civil libertarian or a group of people who believed in the rights of man, he was shot because he was a black leader and because some white people hated him. And yet, when the four-day televised orgy was over, when we had heard the freedom songs sung for the last time, when we heard "I have

a dream . . ." for the thirtieth time, when all the politicians and lawyers and friends and mourners had all gone home, King was buried only as a martyr; he did not become a hero. And he did not become a hero after death because his moment had passed. King was a man of the fifties. He believed in integration, in the possibility of white men and black men living together in harmony; he believed what the liberals believed. He was a fine, brave man; I knew him only slightly, but I could feel that in the most crucial matters—the affairs of the human heart—he was close to being a saint. But the time for saints was over. The last time I saw King he was sitting in a squalid little office on Chicago's South Side. He had tried to move his crusade into the North, and it wasn't working. You simply could not tell the Blackstone Rangers to turn the other cheek. They wanted headier wine, and King's Southern Christian nonviolence did not travel well. For the last two years of his life, King was a has-been; the country had been given its chance at nonviolence and had not seized it. Malcolm, who was an urban black man, had gotten his message across; Stokely Carmichael and Rap Brown were in the wings. So when the networks buried Martin Luther King, they were burying the 1950's. It was an old movie, and now that King is gone, no one invokes his name; his murder has just been added to our rhetoric.

9   I mention this because it seems crucial to me that when we discuss martyrs who become heroes, we must discuss the moment when death grabbed them. Ché, the two Kennedys, and Malcolm X all died, as they used to say, with their boots on. They knew what they wanted to do, they were taking the risks involved in accomplishing what they wanted to do, and they were killed doing it. Each seemed to be trying to go past their own history: Ché was trying to make a revolution that had worked on a small island work on a massive continent; Malcolm was trying to move out of the religious restrictiveness of the Muslims into a broader, more political position; John Kennedy seemed certain of reelection by a sweeping majority, a majority which would have assured him passage of legislation that his hairline victory in 1960 had kept from him; Robert Kennedy, after early indecision, was finally moving into combat with his own chosen enemies.

10   Each death, in retrospect, seemed inevitable. That was another reason why these martyrs acquired heroic stature: Heroes are nothing if they are not figures of myth. And heroes should have a proper sense of approaching doom.

11   "I know that societies often have killed the people who have helped to change those societies," Malcolm said. "And if I can die having brought any light, having exposed any meaningful truth that will help to destroy the racist cancer that is malignant in the body of America— then all of the credit is due to Allah. Only the mistakes have been mine."

12   John Kennedy had a cool, dry attitude about death, and yet he seemed to know that it could come to him at any moment, perhaps

because in the Pacific during the war and in a nearly fatal back operation in the 1950's, he had come close to dying. His favorite poem, according to Arthur M. Schlesinger Jr., was Alan Seeger's "I Have a Rendezvous With Death":[1]

> It may be he shall take my hand
> And lead me into his dark land
> And close my eyes and quench my breath . . .
>
> But I've a rendezvous with Death
> At midnight in some flaming town,
> When Spring trips north again this year,
> And I to my pledged word am true,
> I shall not fail that rendezvous.

13   Robert Kennedy's preoccupation with death was even stronger. He had seen it touch his family in a way that seems monstrous. His oldest brother, Joseph Jr., was killed in 1944 in a wartime flying mission over the English Channel. His sister, Kathleen, was killed in a plane crash after the war. His wife's parents were killed in a plane crash in 1955. His brother-in-law, George Skakel, and his closest friend, Dean Markham, were killed in a plane crash in September 1966. And of course, his brother John was assassinated. I remember sitting with Robert Kennedy during that brief euphoric primary campaign early this year. We were on a plane going to Denver. That day, nearly hysterical crowds in California had mauled him, and I asked him if he didn't worry that some nut would come out of nowhere and try to shoot him. It was something all of us who liked him worried about constantly.

14   Kennedy stared ahead for a while, his face cloudy. Then he said: "If it comes, it comes. What can you do to stop it?"

15   That attitude was what sent Kennedy into an almost frenetic kind of life. He climbed mountains, took risks on rivers, put his political reputation on the line by openly opposing a President from his own party. It was as if he knew he would never grow old and gray; he had to do it all, and quickly. One friend told British journalist Margaret Laing: "He doesn't believe any of them will live long. He thought after John's death and Teddy's crash that the family was doomed. He is still very fatalistic." Most Americans do not care to face the inevitability of death; the Kennedys had its reality thrust upon them.

16   Guevara was an even firmer believer that men must risk death if they are to accomplish anything. He was another son of the middle class who became a revolutionary and a Communist because he hated the injustice, the poverty and the suffering he saw among the masses of South America. He was a fatalist because he had seen men die in

---

[1] Lines from "I Have a Rendezvous With Death" are reprinted with the permission of Charles Scribner's Sons from *Poems* by Alan Seeger. Copyright ©1916; Charles Scribner's Sons; renewal copyright © 1944, Elsie Adams Seeger.

that struggle, first in Guatemala in 1954 when the CIA overthrew the leftist government of Jacobo Arbenz, and later in the fight for Cuba. In addition, he was constantly plagued with a severe case of asthma from age two and spent most of his life struggling to breathe; there were medicines and inhalators to ease his discomfort, but there were times when the fighting simply did not allow such luxuries. In his last battles, the medicines and the inhalator were gone, and for days his ragged band of followers carried him through the jungle on a litter.

17   He seemed to sense early that death would come to him, and yet he thought that risk was worth it. He could easily have stayed on in Havana, smoking good cigars and writing endless Marxist tracts that nobody would ever read. Instead, he threw that all aside and went back to the mountains.

18   "Wherever death may surprise us," he wrote, "it will be welcome, provided that this, our battle cry, reaches some receptive ear, that another hand reach out to take up weapons, and that other men come forward to intone our funeral dirge with the staccato of machine guns and new cries of battle and victory . . . . Each and every one of us will pay on demand his part of sacrifice . . . knowing that all together we are getting ever closer to the new man, whose figure is beginning to appear."

19   This is all very romantic, of course, but then heroes must be romantic, or they are nothing. It is easy for a Hubert Humphrey to talk about the necessity of war; he never fought in one; it is quite another thing when the same rhetoric comes from a man who is taking the risk himself. Of our four men, three were romantics (Malcolm, Ché, Bobby) because they believed that change was possible. Each was ironic about the time involved and pessimistic about the masses, as the Marxists like to call the rest of us, following his example. But they must have believed in change or they would not have bothered with the pain and the difficulty of trying to effect it. Robert Kennedy could easily have lived his life out on the beach at Cannes, oiling himself against the sun. Malcolm X would have made a superb gangster. Guevara could have died in bed. They chose instead to stay with the fight, and like most great gladiators, they were carried out on their shields.

20   These men were martyrs in the best sense of that word. *Webster's Third New International Dictionary* includes this definition: "One who sacrifices his life, station, or what is of great value for the sake of principle or to sustain a cause." But they became heroes in death, especially to the young because their work was not yet finished. Their example is being followed across America. Ché did not really die, and Malcolm lives. Ask anyone under thirty. And if you think that Robert Kennedy died in that pantry in Los Angeles, ask those politicians who will be brawling over his constituency for another ten years. Each man represented both an ideal and an idea, and no bullet can kill

either. The ideals are a living thing even though bullets have made their architects into a harvest for worms. Viva Ché, Viva Malcolm, Viva los Kennedys.

Discussion of Theme
1. The author claims that all of our heroes are dead. Do you agree or disagree?
2. What one thing did the four martyred heroes have in common?
3. Is the only good hero a dead hero?
4. How does Hamill distinguish between the deaths of the Kennedys, Ché, and Malcolm X on the one hand, and the death of Martin Luther King, Jr., on the other? How was King's death different?

Discussion of Rhetoric
1. How is the essay organized? Does the author consider each martyr individually or does he treat them together? Is he completely consistent in his treatment?
2. How is the introduction related to the conclusion of this essay?
3. Why does the poem quoted in paragraph 12 have a particular poignancy in this essay? Where else in the essay could the author have used it?

Writing Assignments
1. Define the following terms: martyr; hero.
2. Why is this an age without heroes? What (or who) has taken their place?
3. If you disagree with Hamill—if you believe that this is an age of heroes—write about your own hero, describing the qualities that make him outstanding.

Library Exploration
1. For a view of John Kennedy's notion of the hero, read his *Profiles in Courage*.
2. Read the works of one of the other men mentioned by Hamill. You might be interested in Malcolm X's autobiography or Ché Guevara's diary.

Vocabulary
altiplano (2): high tableland; plateau
ethereal (6): airy
malaise (6): a vague sense of moral or mental ill-being
internecine (7): relating to conflict within a group
euphoric (13): marked by an often unaccountable feeling of well-
                     being or elation

46

A TRIBUTE TO ROBERT F. KENNEDY

Sen. Edward M. Kennedy

This is the eulogy of Robert F. Kennedy, delivered at his funeral by his brother on June 8, 1968, at *St. Patrick's Cathedral in New York City.*

1   Your Eminences, your excellencies, Mr. President. In behalf of Mrs. Kennedy, her children, the parents and sisters of Robert Kennedy, I want to express what we feel to those who mourn with us today in this cathedral and around the world.

2   We loved him as a brother and as a father and as a son. From his parents and from his older brothers and sisters, Joe and Kathleen and Jack, he received an inspiration which he passed on to all of us.

3   He gave us strength in time of trouble, wisdom in time of uncertainty and sharing in time of happiness. He will always be by our side.

4   Love is not an easy feeling to put into words. Nor is loyalty or trust or joy. But he was all of these. He loved life completely and he lived it intensely.

5   A few years back Robert Kennedy wrote some words about his own father which expresses the way we in his family felt about him. He said of what his father meant to him, and I quote:

6   "What it really all adds up to is love. Not love as it is described with such facility in popular magazines, but the kind of love that is affection and respect, order and encouragement and support.

7   "Our awareness of this was an incalculable source of strength. And because real love is something unselfish and involves sacrifice and giving, we could not help but profit from it."

8   And he continued:

9   "Beneath it all he has tried to engender a social conscience. There were wrongs which needed attention, there were people who were poor and needed help, and we have a responsibility to them and this country.

10   "Through no virtues and accomplishments of our own, we have been fortunate enough to be born in the United States under the most comfortable condition. We therefore have a responsibility to others who are less well off."

11   That is what Robert Kennedy was given.

12   What he leaves to us is what he said, what he did and what he stood for.

13   A speech he made for the young people of South Africa on their day of affirmation in 1966 sums it up the best, and I would like to read it now.

14   "There is discrimination in this world and slavery and slaughter and starvation. Governments repress their people. Millions are trapped in poverty, while the nation grows rich and wealth is lavished on armaments everywhere.

15   "These are differing evils, but they are the common works of man. They reflect the imperfection of human justice, the inadequacy of human compassion, our lack of sensibility towards the suffering of our fellows.

16   "But we can perhaps remember, even if only for a time, that those who live with us are our brothers, that they share with us the same short moment of life, that they seek as we do nothing but the chance to live out their lives in purpose and happiness, winning what satisfaction and fulfillment they can.

17   "Surely this bond of common faith, this bond of common goals, can begin to teach us something. Surely we can learn at least to look at those around us as fellow men. And surely we can begin to work a little harder to bind up the wounds among us and to become in our own hearts brothers and countrymen once again.

18   "The answer is to rely on youth, not a time of life but a state of mind, a temper of the will, a quality of imagination, a predominance of courage over timidity, of the appetite for adventure over the love of ease. The cruelties and obstacles of this swiftly changing planet will not yield to the obsolete dogmas and outworn slogans; they cannot be moved by those who cling to a present that is already dying, who prefer the illusion of security to the excitement and danger that come with even the most peaceful progress.

19   "It is a revolutionary world which we live in, and this generation at home and around the world has had thrust upon it a greater burden of responsibility than any generation that has ever lived. Some believe there is nothing one man or one woman can do against the enormous array of the world's ills. Yet many of the world's great movements of thought and action have flowed from the work of a single man.

20   "A young monk began the Protestant Reformation. A young general extended an empire from Macedonia to the borders of the earth. A young woman reclaimed the territory of France, and it was a young Italian explorer who discovered the New World, and the 32-year-old Thomas Jefferson who explained that all men are created equal.

21   "These men moved the world, and so can we all. Few will have the greatness to bend history itself, but each of us can work to change a

small portion of events, and in the total of all those acts will be written the history of this generation.

22   "Each time a man stands for an ideal, or acts to improve the lot of others, or strikes out against injustice, he sends forth a tiny ripple of hope.

23   "And crossing each other from a million different centers of energy and daring, those ripples build a current that can sweep down the mightiest walls of oppression and resistance. Few are willing to brave the disapproval of their fellows, the censure of their colleagues, the wrath of their society. Moral courage is a rarer commodity than bravery in battle or great intelligence. Yet it is the one essential vital quality for those who seek to change a world that yields most painfully to change.

24   "And I believe that in this generation those with the courage to enter the moral conflict will find themselves with companions in every corner of the globe.

25   "For the fortunate among us there is the temptation to follow the easy and familiar paths of personal ambition and financial success so grandly spread before those who enjoy the privilege of education. But that is not the road history has marked out for us.

26   "Like it or not, we live in times of danger and uncertainty. But they are also more open to the creative energy of men than any other time in history. All of us will ultimately be judged and as the years pass, we will surely judge ourselves, on the effort we have contributed to building a new world society and the extent to which our ideals and goals have shaped that event.

27   "Our future may lie beyond our vision, but it is not completely beyond our control. It is the shaping impulse of America that neither faith nor nature nor the irresistible tides of history but the work of our own hands matched to reason and principle will determine our destiny."

28   There is pride in that, even arrogance, but there is also experience and truth, and in any event it is the only way we can live. That is the way he lived. That is what he leaves us.

29   My brother need not be idealized or enlarged in death beyond what he was in life. He should be remembered simply as a good and decent man who saw wrong and tried to right it, saw suffering and tried to heal it, saw war and tried to stop it.

30   Those of us who loved him and who take him to his rest today pray that what he was to us, and what he wished for others, will some day come to pass for all the world.

31   As he said many times, in many parts of this nation, to those he touched and who sought to touch him:

32   "Some men see things as they are and say why. I dream things that never were and say, why not."

Discussion of Theme

1. In what way did Robert Kennedy live life completely and intensely?
2. What qualities did Robert Kennedy and his father share?
3. Why was Robert Kennedy particularly attractive to minority groups?
4. Did Robert Kennedy have moral courage? Explain.
5. What is Robert Kennedy's legacy to his fellow men?

Discussion of Rhetoric

1. Nineteen out of the thirty-two paragraphs in this eulogy are quotations from the speeches of Robert Kennedy. Why are they appropriate?
2. Several historical figures are referred to in this eulogy. Who are they? Why did Kennedy choose these particular figures?
3. Explain the unusual power of this eulogy. Find examples of parallel structure, a favorite Kennedy device.

Writing Assignments

1. Analyze Robert Kennedy's popularity with the young and with minority groups.
2. Would Kennedy have made a good president? Support your statements wherever possible.

Library Exploration

Read some of the speeches made by Robert Kennedy during his campaign for the Democratic nomination for president. What were his programs and goals?

Vocabulary

facility (6): ease
incalculable (7): beyond measure
engender (9): produce
censure (23): strong disapproval

47

THE CHICANO REBELLION

Roy Bongartz

Only recently has the rest of America become aware of the plight of the Mexican-American. This *article explores the aspirations and expectations of the Chicano.*

1   Now it's the Mexican Americans—Chicanos, they are called in California—who are appearing on the scene of protest, with a self-evalution that breaks radically away from the old, degrading stereotype of fatalistic loafer asleep under a sombrero. These young Chicanos are wide-awake, and when something happens, they intend to be the ones who make it happen. Militant Chicano student organizations are active throughout California, not only in colleges but in high schools as well, and they are growing in the rest of the Southwest: the Mexican-American Student Association, United Mexican-American Students, Mexican-American Student Confederation. They all make a central demand for courses in Mexican-American studies, such as are now available at San Francisco State College, Sacramento State College, California State College in Los Angeles, San Fernando Valley College and the University of California at Berkeley.

2   Teaching the course at Berkeley is Octavio I. Romano, an anthropologist, born in Mexico and raised in California, who wants to destroy the myth of the passive Mexican. He points out that Mexican Americans have been the main figures in the labor movement in the Southwest, that they published the first Western underground newspapers, that they have pushed through bilingual education in two states, that they clinched the victory for John F. Kennedy, that they have a strong influence on the Spanish language that extends into Mexico itself, even that they originated driftwood sculpture.

3   Romano's most energetic attacks are aimed at sociologists who are preserving stale anti-Mexican prejudices in the academic jargon of scholarly works. In place of "the Mexican is lazy," the academic (in this case Celia Heller) writes: "The combination of stress on work and rational use of time forms little or no part of the Mexican-American socialization process." Instead of saying that you can't tell them apart, she writes: "They exhibit a marked lack of internal differentiation." Referring to this and other writers of Chicano studies, including

William Madsen, Ruth Tuck, Lyle Saunders, Florence Kluckhohn, Fred L. Strodbeck, Julian Samora and Richard Lamanna, Romano says: "Contemporary social scientists [are] busily perpetuating the very same opinions of Mexican culture that were current during the Mexican-American War. These opinions were, and are, pernicious, vicious, misleading, degrading and brainwashing."

4   Romano has some new ideas on how to give a college course. For one, students will think up a subject and assign it as a term paper to the instructor, then grade the paper and discuss it in class. Students' own papers must be presented in three versions—one in academic style, one in a "journal" style for possible publication in a Chicano review, and the last a newspaper version to be submitted to a local paper. Students writing the papers for publication will work directly with the editors. Members of the course may take a third of class time to address their colleagues on any relevant subject. It is Romano's hope that by using students' own ideas and writings the course may improve and grow in the future. Sacramento State is already planning a four-year program leading to a B.A. in Mexican-American studies.

5   But the Mexican Americans at Berkeley have not confined themselves to the classroom. A number of Romano's students are among the hundred-odd members of a student group called Quinto Sol, some of whom two years ago marched in upon hearings of the U.S. Civil Rights Commission in San Francisco to protest the exclusion of Mexican Americans from a program designed to recruit college students from minority groups. They also attacked the commission for having but one Mexican American on its staff of 350, yelling "Practice what you preach!" at commission members until police threw them out. Quinto Sol members invaded and occupied the office of the university president at Berkeley to protest the purchase of California grapes by the university cafeteria—student groups all solidly support the nation-wide grape boycott led by César Chavez and the United Farm Workers. The Chicanos were forcibly removed from the office and eleven of them were jailed.

6   Says one Quinto Sol leader, Nick Vaca, 24, a graduate student and an editor of a sharp new quarterly review called *El Grito* (The Cry): "The message our group wants to give is that the Mexican American is not docile. That idea of the 'sleeping giant' is an insult—it's that same old peon taking his siesta under his hat. Mexican Americans are not an *emerging* people. We're already here!" Bill Vega, 24, and John Carrillo, 27, who, along with Professor Romano, also help edit the review, agree that the Chicano is here; but they add ruefully that he is here in very few numbers at Berkeley—some 200 out of an enrollment of 25,000. Though they do not want to deny the Negro *his* chance, they have been forced to vie with him for benefits from the Educational Opportunity Program, whereby colleges recruit a certain number of minority students who cannot satisfy the regular academic entrance

requirements and lack the money for college. Even though there are nearly twice as many Mexican Americans as Negroes in California, blacks in the Berkeley Opportunity Program outnumber Chicanos 9 to 1. The average Chicano has an 8th-grade education; the average Negro has ten and a half years of school (Anglos, 12.1 years) in California. Chicanos earn less money than Negroes; that is, less than anybody else in the state.

7   A little more than two years ago a conference was held in Berkeley to enable Mexican-American high school students from the Bay area who were interested in college to meet counselors from all the colleges in the state; the idea was to help them pick a school and find out how to go about getting admitted. Nearly 2,000 Chicanos applied to attend the conference, which had to be limited to 600 from lack of space. Two counselors showed up, only Mills College and Contra Costa bothering to send anybody. "We're facing a monumental indifference to the Mexican American," says Romano. "And they blame the kid in the *barrio* for being 'non-goal-oriented.'"

8   In the continuous political free-for-all at Sather Gate, Berkeley students wearing great Walt Disney pig heads rush a group of sign carriers in a noontime skit lampooning police attacks on militants over at San Francisco State. But Chicanos and their problems are invisible. *El Grito* is aware that Berkeley students are supposed to be radicals, but notes that they give Chicanos very little support. They don't back the grape boycott; they don't demand increased Chicano student enrollment. The editors believe that the Anglos are moved by self-interest and that the Mexican-American cause doesn't fit the pattern.

9   Chicanos have only a toehold at Berkeley, but they are more numerous at some other colleges. At San Jose City College, for example, the Mexican-American Student Confederation (MASC) recently organized a Mexican Week for both students and townspeople. It provided an art show, film festival, discussions, a show of regional Mexican clothing, a *charreado* (football match), and a horse show put on by Los Charros de la Plata Aspada (Silver Spurs). The climax was a talk by an old Mexican revolutionary who had fought with Pancho Villa and Zapata. Says one MASC member, Manuel Madrid, 23, "Our main goal is to orient the Chicano to *think* Chicano so as to achieve equal status with other groups, not to emulate the Anglo. A decade ago, the idea was that the Mexican American wanted to be totally assimilated into the American culture. But not now."

10   A Mexican-American counselor named Angelo Atondo is on the scene at San Jose City College as a direct result of Chicano student agitation. "The attitudes of Mexican Americans toward themselves has completely changed since I graduated from college in 1956," he says. "We never spoke Spanish. We would have been stared at. There was a silent taboo against Spanish." He explains that San Jose is an "open door" college, with a two-year program that can lead to

continued studies at one of the state colleges or can give a diploma in a wide variety of vocational fields, mostly technical. "A student can get in here even if he had straight Ds in high school," says Atondo. "We salvage many students that way."

11   One student who dropped out of high school is Lee Polanco, now 31, a qualified electrician who bitterly recalls answering a help-wanted ad by telephone, being invited for an interview, and then, because he's a Chicano, being greeted with: "What do *you* want? Get out of here!" Polanco, director of campus activities in MASC, is studying social sciences. "We found that the colleges were paying attention to the blacks because they were militant, so we started to get as militant as the blacks," he says. His friend Manuel Madrid adds, "I hope we don't have to get as militant as the blacks. But if we have to, we will."

12   Polanco points out that the 12,000 students at San Jose, some 1,200 are Mexican American, while 200 are black. But four courses are offered in black studies, and only one in a Mexican-American subject. Naturally the Chicanos want to adjust the balance. "We're being ignored," says Madrid, "but we want to work with the blacks."

13   Besides getting a counselor assigned to the college, the Chicanos succeeded in having a committee from their group screen the professor who teaches the one Mexican culture course; they even got some money from the administration for their Mexican Week. In addition to demanding more Chicano-oriented courses, including one in Spanish for the Spanish-speaking, they want free buses to town and back. Going beyond their own issues, they have held a vigil of sympathy for students at Mexico City who were killed or injured there by troops last year.

14   Manuel Madrid also dropped out of high school from discouragement. "The white kids knew you weren't like them. Talking Spanish was a 'no-no.' It gave us an inferiority complex." One of the most encouraging things about Madrid and other dropouts now in college is their concern for the young coming up behind them. They go out to the high schools to talk with Chicano students and encourage them to stay in school, and they intend to have MASC make this a part of its official program. Madrid, who may well realize that he's on his way, still says, "Let's get a little uncomfortable about our friends back there."

15   But these days there is much less apathy among the friends back in high school. Thirteen East Los Angeles Chicanos were arrested last May for organizing a boycott of their schools to protest intolerable conditions. In Livingston, fifty-three Chicanos skipped their high school classes on Mexican Independence Day, demanding it be made an official holiday. They also wanted the schools to hire Mexican teachers and counselors, and to offer courses in Mexican and black history. They wanted the double lunch periods ended—white kids at the first; black and brown at the second. Police picked up the truants,

although at harvest time, when the big local farms need extra help, the compulsory attendance law is ignored.

16   At Fremont High School, in Oakland, students demonstrated for weeks to demand a Chicano student union, and Mexican-American entertainment and speakers at assemblies. A Chicano group called Los Carnales at Redwood High in Visalia made twenty-one demands on the principal, including Mexican food in the cafeteria, mandatory attendance by all teachers at classes in black and Mexican culture, and a rule to keep police, probation and parole officers off the school grounds.

17   Though nothing enrages the young Chicanos more than to be called "emerging," the facts are not only that their political awareness (like that of all young people) has become greatly sharpened of late but also that their presence as an intellectual force is for the first time establishing itself. *Bronze*, a new militant paper at San Jose, deals with problems that haunt Mexican Americans. Writes Luis Valdez: "This is a society largely hostile to our cultural values. There is no poetry about the United States. No depth, no faith, no allowance for human contrariness. No soul, no *mariachi*, no chili sauce, no *pulque*, no mysticism, no *chigaderas*." Valdez sees a gloomy future for Mexican Americans who lose their identity in the cities: "They have solved their Mexican contradictions with a pungent dose of Americanism, and are more concerned with status, money and bad breath than with their ultimate destiny." But he does not despair altogether. "There will always be *raza* [the race, the people] in this country. There are millions more where we came from." Manuel Madrid says that the 50,000 immigrants who arrive every year from Mexico "give us all a shot in the arm."

18   Another student describes the strains of holding to a clear identity: "Sometimes you have to go to a Mexican show or a Mexican bar and be by yourself, to remind yourself of what you are. And then you . . . begin to see that you are becoming something that you are not and you know it. I had to relearn how it is to be a Mexican and what it is like for so many Mexicans to be poor in San Jose. *Hijo*, I was so dumb that I used to be proud to have Mexicans die in the war. I used to be so dumb that I used to think in college how beautiful it would be to pick *fruta* again and watch *la raza* work against the rays of the sun, that is how stupid I used to be."

19   A number of newspapers have formed the Chicano Press Association, which includes *El Malcriado* in Delano, *La Raza, Carta Editorial* and *Inside Eastside* in Los Angeles, *El Gallo* in Denver, *El Papel* in Albuquerque, *Inferno* in San Antonio and *Compass* in Houston. A note in *El Grito* says they are all "very relevant to Mexican Americans, Spanish Americans, Chicanos, Hispanos, Spanish-Speaking Latin Americans, Mexican-Latin Spanish Speakers, greasers, spics and bandits." (One of *El Grito*'s favorite targets is the way some *Tío Tomás*

Mexicans try to dissociate themselves from *la raza* by using fancy group names: "a vacuous ethnic taxonomy," *El Grito* calls it.)

20   By far the most impressive evidence of intellectual liveliness among Chicano students is to be found in the pages of *El Grito*, named for the famous "cry" of the Mexican Revolution. It grew out of publication by Quinto Sol, the Berkeley student group, of articles attacking social scientists; these were called The Mexican-American Liberation Papers, and were priced at $2 for students, $15 for federal agencies, $500 for governors of states and $15,000 for the President of the United States. *El Grito* first appeared in the fall of 1967, after the editors had each contributed $50 to $100 to pay the printing bill; it has been solvent ever since. The journal threatens its readers: "Subscribe now, or La Llorona will get you" (she's the witch who grabs bad Mexican children). The journal has been much helped financially by the fact that several of the Mexican-American college courses use it—900 copies, for example, go to San Jose State. But at Berkeley itself enthusiasm remains low; a mailing of 300 fliers brought in but one subscription. "Publishing in Berkeley is a real hang-up," the editors say.

21   The editors want to explore relationships between Chicanos and Mexico. They believe they can see philosophies of life that are very different here and in Mexico. They say the United States has a nationalistic ideology that develops "self-interest groups through a combination of political and religious affiliation." The Mexican idea, in their view, is much broader—people tackling moral problems as world-wide concerns, not just Mexican. The editors have published some work, and want to carry more, from the Mexican *nueva ola*— new wave—currently being produced by a café clique in Guadalajara.

22   Chicanos accuse both Jews and Negroes of nationalism. Writes Nick Vaca, "After viewing the effects of the nationalistic fervor in Israel, it is not surprising to note that it has been the Jewish merchant who has exploited and continues to exploit Negroes in the ghettos. . . ." Vaca is no more friendly toward the black, who, he writes, "is systematically 'putting down' his 'brown brother.' " The Chicanos were especially angered by a black teacher's remark: "While blacks were out protesting, Mexican Americans were sitting at home before their television sets, eating beans." Chicanos have much warmer feelings toward the smaller ethnic groups—American Indians, Filipinos, Hawaiians, Samoans and Koreans, and include them in demands for a fair share of educational opportunity.

23   A more encouraging aspect of *El Grito*'s point of view is its concern about aspects of American society that affect everybody. For example, they would like to do away with commercials in television and radio news broadcasts: "When a people have to wait for news of the world, for news of their country, and even of their own community, while mascara is peddled, then that people have lost the right to be called

civilized." The editors would also put an end to Congressional hearings on local social problems: "It seems absurd, as we do today, to elect a man to Washington only to have him return to find out what problems exist. . . . People are electing representatives who do not know what is going on, and who then, at taxpayers, expense, must return in order to find out." *El Grito* also favors having the length of military service determined by income, and in wartime would draft industry, so that workers and management receive soldiers' pay.

24   The journal runs thoroughgoing pieces on the use of Mexican national workers in the border areas, which *El Grito* calls the Mexican-Dixon line, and one of its contributors has offered the pertinent suggestion that U.S. aid to Mexico should go mainly to raising Mexican income, along the border, and "not, as is happening now, to lowering the American to present Mexican levels." A joint border authority would take over the economics of these international communities. The journal prints some of its material in Spanish, and derides such continuing tenets as that of Theodore Roosevelt, who said: "We have room for but one language here, and that is the English language, for we intend to see that the crucible turns our people out as Americans, of American nationality, and not as dwellers in a polyglot boarding house." The editors point out that many people "speak English somewhat colorfully," and suggest Lyndon Johnson, May West, Zsa Zsa Gabor, Wernher von Braun, Lawrence Welk, Everett Dirksen and George Jessel.

25   Excellent graphic work, both drawings and photographs, enliven the pages of *El Grito*. The clash-and-blend flavor of Mexican-American life is expressed in a renewed tradition of bilingual poetry in which lines of Spanish alternate with lines of English. They do not translate each other, but move the thought along in the two tongues.

26   Mexican Americans everywhere in the Southwest are feeling their oats, not only in traditional labor-movement unity but now also as students, writers, artists, teachers—as thinkers. A bilingual poem by John J. Martinez, a mathematics major at Berkeley, sounds the note:

> brown power!
> qué?
> Together we must . . .
> Si!
> The problem . . .
> qué?
> It's your fault . . .
> who?
> I mean . . .
> qué?
> brown power!
> testing, testing, testing
> uno, dos, tres . . .

Discussion of Theme

1. What is the stereotyped image of the Mexican-American? What kind of image is projected in this selection?
2. Is Romano's criticism of sociologists justified (see paragraphs 2 and 3)?
3. What can the colleges do to help the Mexican-American secure his rights? Do they share the blame for his condition today?
4. According to Bongartz, what is the most serious obstacle in the path of the Mexican-American? How do you think it can be removed?
5. What does the poem at the end of this article say about the feelings of young Mexican-Americans today?
6. Is the Chicanos' goal a realistic one? Can they—or any other group—achieve equal status in our society without sacrificing their political or ethnic integrity?

Discussion of Rhetoric

1. Is Bongartz' argument strengthened or weakened by the use of particular quotes? Does he let the spokesmen of the cause speak for themselves, or does he interpret their statements?
2. What is the purpose of referring to the efforts of blacks to secure justice? Does this strengthen the Mexican-Americans' case?
3. Are his examples and samplings sufficient, or is Bongartz guilty of generalizing? Has this essay modified your attitudes on this topic?
4. How is the poem at the end of the article used? Is it effective?

Writing Assignments

1. Should only standard English be taught in the public schools, or should dialectal variations and foreign languages be encouraged?
2. What contributions have men like Chavez and Tejerine made to the Chicano's fight for equal status?
3. What are some common notions Anglos have about Chicanos? In what ways are they true or false?
4. Reread the quotation by Theodore Roosevelt (paragraph 24) and present your reaction to it.

Library Exploration

1. What are some of the contributions Mexican-Americans have made to this country?
2. Read one or more of the underground newspapers mentioned in this article and report your findings.
3. The *barrio* has recently been the subject of many sociological studies. Locate and read two of these.

Vocabulary

pernicious (3): highly destructive or injurious
emulate (9): strive to equal or excel
mandatory (16): required
pungent (17): having a stinging or biting quality (esp. of odors)
vacuous (19): stupid; inane
taxonomy (19): a system of classification
crucible (24): melting pot
polyglot (24): one who speaks or writes many languages

48

THE FIRE NOW

Eldridge Cleaver

A prominent member of the Black Panther organization explains the shift in leadership in the black *movement—and what this shift will mean for white America.*

1   A reassessment of national black leadership has been in order since the assassination of Malcolm X. The assassination of Martin Luther King makes such a reassessment inevitable. With the death of King, an entire era of leadership with a distinct style and philosophy, spanning some fifty years, draws to a final and decisive close. A new black leadership with its own distinct style and philosophy, which has always been there, waiting in the wings and consciously kept out of the lime-light, will now come into its own, to center stage. Nothing can stop this leadership from taking over because it is based on charisma, has the allegiance and support of the black masses, is conscious of its self and its position, and is prepared to shoot its way to power if the need arises.

2   It is futile and suicidal for white America to greet this new leadership with a political ostrich response. What white America had better do is find out what these leaders want for black people and then set out to discover the quickest possible way to fulfill their demands. The alternative is war, pure and simple, and not just a race war, which in itself would destroy this country, but a guerrilla war which will amount to a second civil war, with thousands of white new-John-Browns fighting on the side of the blacks, plunging America into the depths of its most desperate nightmare, on the way to realizing the American Dream.

3   When the NAACP was founded in 1911, it vowed, in its preamble, that until black people were invested with full political, economic and social rights, it would never cease to assail the ears of white America with its protests. Protest as the new posture of blacks toward white America was on its way in, and was destined to dominate the black struggle for the next fifty years. On its way out was the era of begging and supplication, rooted in slavery and the plantation, personified in

the genuflecting leadership of Booker T. Washington; chief amongst its myriad treasonous acts was giving black acquiescence to the Southern racist policy of segregation, in Booker T.'s notorious sell-out speech at the Atlantic Exposition in 1896. In the same historic breath, the U.S. Supreme Court made segregation the law of the land when it approved the Separate But Equal doctrine in the case of Plessy v. Ferguson.

4   Dissenting from this confluence of racist ideology, black submission and judicial certification, W. E. B. DuBois led the protest that was institutionalized in the founding of the NAACP; this held sway until 1954, when the U.S. Supreme Court, recognizing that the racist ideology no longer had the necessary allegiance of black leadership, reversed itself and declared Separate But Equal, i.e., segregation, unconstitutional. Black protest leadership, which was born to combat segregation, did not know that when it heard, with universal jubilation throughout its ranks, Chief Justice Earl Warren pronounce the death penalty upon that institution, it was, in fact, listening to its own death knell. There was to be, however, a period of transition between the new outmoded protest leadership and a new prevailing leadership that had not yet defined itself.

5   The transitional leadership was supplied by Martin Luther King and Malcolm X, and Malcolm X, at his death, had laid the foundation of the new leadership that would succeed both him and King. Martin Luther King was a transitional figure, a curious melange of protest and revolutionary activism. He embodied the first ideological strain in its fullest flower; he contained only a smidgin of the latter. He seemed to be saying to white America: If you don't listen to what I am saying, then you are going to have to deal with what I am doing. As far as the willingness of the white power structure to deal with black leadership goes, Martin Luther King, and the type of leadership he personified, held sway from the launching of the Montgomery Bus Boycott in 1956 down to our own day, when the vestigial remains of leadership from King's transitional era are still frantically trying to cling to power. In reality their leadership is just as dead as that of the lieutenants of Booker T. Washington at the end of their era.

6   The difference between Martin Luther King and Malcolm X as transitional leaders between the era of protest and our era of revolutionary activism, is that King's leadership was based on the black bourgeoisie and Malcolm's leadership was based on the black masses. In the vernacular of the ghetto, King had House Nigger Power and Malcolm had Field Nigger Power. What we have now entered, then, is an era in which Field Nigger Power and the grievances and goals of the Field Nigger—and the leadership of Field Niggers—will dominate the black movement for justice in America.

FIELD NIGGERS, MOLOTOV COCKTAILS AND GUNS

7   Malcolm X used to tell a little story that points up the difference in perspective and perceived self-interest between the House Nigger and the Field Nigger. The House Nigger was close to the slavemaster. He ate better food, wore better clothes, and didn't have to work as hard as the Field Nigger. He knew that he was better off than his brothers, the Field Niggers, who were kept cooped up in the slave quarters, had only a subsistence diet this side of garbage, and had to work hard "from can't see in the morning until can't see at night." When the slavemaster's house caught on fire, the House Nigger, even more upset and concerned than the slavemaster himself, came running up to say: "Master, master, *our* house is on fire! What shall *we* do?" On the other hand, the Field Nigger, viewing the conflagration from the distance of the slave quarters, hoped for a wind to come along and fan the flames into an all-consuming inferno.

8   The kernel of truth contained in that story has remained constant from the prison plantations of slavery's South to the prison ghettos of oppression's North, and the urban black, lacking the patience of his forefathers who prayed for a high wind, has opted in favor of the molotov cocktail.

9   The Black Muslims were the first organization of any significance in our history to understand and harness the volcanic passions of the molotov cocktail-tosser. This organization, which was a transitional organization, rooted in the black masses, based on a protest philosophy with a pinch of revolutionary activism thrown in, made the major contribution of redirecting the dialogue between black leadership and the white power structure, changing it into a dialogue between black leadership and the black masses. This was a necessary by-product of the Muslims' bid to organize black people, because Elijah Muhammad and Malcolm X, in order to get their points across, had to talk over the heads of protest leaders to make themselves heard by the black masses.

10   Standing toe to toe with the protest leaders, Malcolm and Elijah, talking over their heads, exposed these leaders for what they were, and these leaders, helping to prove the Muslims' point by talking even louder than before, were talking over Malcolm and Elijah's heads— but not to the black masses. They were still chatting with Charlie, a note of desperation having slipped into their tone to be sure. But essentially, what they were saying to Charlie now was that if Charlie didn't listen to them, fund their picayune programs, then he was going to be faced with Malcolm and Elijah.

11   (Now, in the wake of King's death, chatting with Charlie has been driven to the ludicrous, asinine length of Whitney Young pleading to Henry Ford, Rockefeller and George Meany to lead a white folk's

march on Washington to prove to blacks that all white folks aren't killers of the dream. The only salutory result of this bankrupt, ridiculous proposal, as far as the black masses are concerned, is that in singling out these three sterling figures, Young brushed them with his Judas kiss of death, identifying for the black masses three of their most culpable oppressors in the spheres of Big Fat Industry, Big Fat Finance and Big Fat Labor. Maybe all whites aren't killers of the dream, as Young suggests, but his three pals are exploiters of oppressed people, both home and abroad.)

12   When black leaders stopped chatting with Charlie and started cutting it up with the brothers on the block, a decisive juncture had been reached and blacks had seized control of their own destiny. A full ideological debate ensued. The consensus of this debate was given to the world on a Mississippi dusty road, when young Stokely Carmichael leaped from obscure anonymity and shouted, with a roar of thunder, WE WANT BLACK POWER! How to get it was the only question as far as the black people were concerned.

13   There have been a lot of simple answers to this question, which is by no means a simple one. Black Power, whatever the form of its implementation, has to solve the question of massive unemployment and underemployment, massive bad housing, massive inferior education. It must also deal with the massive problems of institutionalized white racism manifested in subtle forms of discrimination that result in blacks being denied equal access to and use of existing public accommodations and services. From access to medical facilities through the injustices suffered by blacks in the courts, to the pervasive problem of racist, repressive police practices, Black Power has to come up with solutions.

14   If the experience of other colonized people is relevant, then the answers given by Huey P. Newton, leader of the Black Panther Party, have to be dealt with. The only real power that black people in America have, argues Huey, is the power to destroy America. We must organize this destructive potential, he goes on, then we can say to the power structure that if black people don't get their political desires and needs satisfied, we will inflict a political consequence upon the system. This is a rejection of the Chamber of Commerce's *laissez faire* myth of the market place that argues to blacks that if they go out and hustle, get themselves educated, learn skills (pull yourself up by your own bootstraps, etc., etc., *ad nauseam*), the American Free Enterprise System will do the rest, that if you don't become President, you are sure at least to make a million bucks. In the age of automation and cybernation, the marketplace has been abolished by the computer. We must make a frontal attack upon the system as a whole, Huey says. We need a redistribution of wealth in America. The form of ownership of the means of production is no longer functional. It is time for the present, non-

functional system to be abolished and replaced by a functional, humanistic system that can guarantee a good life for everybody. Everyman is entitled to the best and highest standard of living that the present-day level of technological development is capable of delivering. Every human being is entitled to live. If men must work in order to get the necessities of living, then every man capable of working is entitled to a job. If a man is incapable of working because of a physical inability, then society is responsible for taking care of him for as long as the physical inability exists, for life if necessary. If the businessmen who now control the economic system are incapable of fulfilling the needs of society, then the economic system must be taken out of their hands and rearranged; then the people can appoint administrators to run the economy who can deliver. That is the eternal right of a free people.

15   The viability of the Black Panther Party's approach to solving problems is testified to by the fact that it has engineered two remarkable feats which constitute the foundation for a revolutionary movement that overlooks nothing, is afraid of nothing and is able to resolve the major contradiction of our time. On the one hand, the Black Panther Party cemented a working coalition with the predominantly white Peace and Freedom Party. On the other hand, it effected a merger with SNCC. This is the key center of the eye of the storm, because whether they know it or not, whether they like it or not, neither white radicals nor black radicals are going to get very far by themselves, one without the other. In order for a real change to be brought about in America, we have to create machinery that is capable of moving in two different directions at the same time, machinery the two wings of which are capable of communicating with each other. The Black Panther Party, through its coalition with the Peace and Freedom Party and its merger with SNCC, has been the vector of communication between the most important vortexes of black and white radicalism in America. Any black leadership in our era with national ambitions has to embody this functional flexibility without sacrificing its integrity or its rock-bottom allegiance to the black masses.

16   Stokely Carmichael is Prime Minister of the Black Panther Party. Rap Brown is its Minister of Justice. James Foreman is its Minister of Foreign Affairs, and George Ware is its Field Marshal. At the same time, Huey Newton, Minister of Defense of the Black Panther Party, is running for Congress on the Peace and Freedom Party ticket. The Black Panther Party's nomination for President of the United States, running on the Peace and Freedom Party ticket, is Robert F. Williams, the black leader in exile in the People's Republic of China. Williams picked up the gun against white racism as far back as 1959. If the Black Panther Party succeeds in getting the Peace and Freedom Party to see the wisdom of picking Williams as its Presidential candidate, then

a bid for the new national black leadership will begin to come into sharper focus. And America will be astounded by this fact: not only will this leadership bear a charismatic relationship to the black masses, but it also will exercise charismatic leadership upon the white masses as well, and it will reach down into the bowels of this nation, amongst its poor, dispossessed and alienated, and it will set aflame a revolutionary wave of change that will give America a birth of freedom that it has known hitherto only in the dreams of its boldest dreamers. And it will kill, once and for all, all the killers of the dream.

Discussion of Theme
1. According to Cleaver, what are the phases through which black leadership has passed? What leaders exemplify the various phases, including the most recent transitional phase?
2. Explain the significance of the anecdote about field niggers and house niggers. Which group does Cleaver identify with?
3. What are the American myths that Cleaver rejects? How sound is his reasoning?
4. What future does Cleaver see for this country? Is he bent on its destruction as some have claimed?

Discussion of Rhetoric
1. Diction in this article is generally quite formal, but occasionally the author uses informal, colloquial phrases. Find examples of the latter.
2. What is the unifying element in paragraphs 3–6? How does it relate to the thesis presented in the first two paragraphs?
3. Explain the use of parentheses in paragraph 11.

Writing Assignments
1. Is separation of the races—perhaps into two nations within our borders—a sensible solution to our racial crisis? Give your views in a theme.
2. Are Cleaver and James Forman effective leaders? Assess their effectiveness in a composition.
3. Develop the following quotation into a theme: "The new black leadership will kill, once and for all, all the killers of the American dream."
4. Define black power.

Library Exploration
1. Read the history of the National Association for the Advancement of Colored People. How has the philosophy of black leadership changed since the organization of the NAACP in 1911?

2. Eldridge Cleaver is the author of *Soul on Ice*, written while he was in jail. If you enjoyed this article, you may also enjoy reading his book.
3. Identify Booker T. Washington, W. E. B. DuBois, Malcolm X, and Elijah Muhammad.

Vocabulary

charisma (1): personal magic or charm
myriad (3): innumerable; many
confluence (4): a coming together
mélange (5): mixture
vestigial (5): pertaining to traces of something no longer present
vernacular (6): native speech or dialect
conflagration (7): great fire
opted (8): made a choice
picayune (10): petty
salutary (11): wholesome; beneficial
culpable (11): guilty
pervasive (13): spread throughout
ad nauseam (14): to the point of becoming sickening
viability (15): capability of growing or developing; workability
vector (15): line
vortexes (15): whirlpools

49

BLACK RAGE

William H. Grier and Price M. Cobbs

*Two black psychiatrists examine
the psychological consequences of
white oppression of blacks.*

1   History may well show that of all the men who lived during our fateful century none illustrated the breadth or the grand potential of man so magnificently as did Malcolm X. If, in future chronicles, America is regarded as the major nation of our day, and the rise of darker people from bondage as the major event, then no figure has appeared thus far who captures the spirit of our times as does Malcolm.

2   Malcolm is an authentic hero, indeed the only universal black hero. In his unrelenting opposition to the viciousness in America, he fired the imagination of black men all over the world.

3   If this black nobleman is a hero to black people in the United States and if his life reflects their aspirations, there can be no doubt of the universality of black rage.

4   Malcolm responded to his position in his world and to his blackness in the manner of so many black boys. He turned to crime. He was saved by a religious sect given to a strange, unhistorical explanation of the origin of black people and even stranger solutions to their problems. He rose to power in that group and outgrew it.

5   Feeding on his own strength, growing in response to his own commands, limited by no creed, he became a citizen of the world and an advocate of all oppressed people no matter their color or belief. Anticipating his death by an assassin, he distilled, in a book, the essence of his genius, his life. His autobiography thus is a legacy and, together with his speeches, illustrates the thrusting growth of the man—his evolution, rapid, propulsive, toward the man he might have been had he lived.

6   The essence of Malcolm X was growth, change, and a seeking after truth.

7   Alarmed white people saw him first as an eccentric and later as a dangerous radical—a revolutionary without troops who threatened to stir black people to riot and civil disobedience. Publicly, they treated

him as a joke; privately, they were afraid of him.

8   After his death he was recognized by black people as the "black shining prince" and recordings of his speeches became treasured things. His autobiography was studîed, his life marveled at. Out of this belated admiration came the philosophical basis for black activism and indeed the thrust of Black Power itself, away from integration and civil rights and into the "black bag."

9   Unlike Malcolm, however, the philosophical underpinnings of the new black militancy were static. They remained encased within the ideas of revolution and black nationhood, ideas Malcolm had outgrown by the time of his death. His stature has made even his earliest statements gospel and men now find themselves willing to die for words which in retrospect are only milestones in the growth of a fantastic man.

10   Many black men who today preach blackness seem headed blindly toward self-destruction, uncritical of anything "black" and damning the white man for diabolical wickedness. For a philosophical base they have turned to the words of Malcolm's youth.

11   This perversion of Malcolm's intellectual position will not, we submit, be held against him by history.

12   Malcolm's meaning for us lies in his fearless demand for truth and his evolution from a petty criminal to an international statesman—accomplished by a black man against odds of terrible magnitude—in America. His message was his life, not his words, and Malcolm knew it.

13   Black Power activism—thrust by default temporarily at the head of a powerful movement—is a conception that contributes in a significant way to the strength and unity of that movement but is unable to provide the mature vision for the mighty works ahead. It will pass and leave black people in this country prouder, stronger, more determined, but in need of grander princes with clearer vision.

14   We believe that the black masses will rise with a simple and eloquent demand to which new leaders must give tongue. They will say to America simply: "GET OFF OUR BACKS!"

15   The problem will be so simply defined.

16   What is the problem?

17   *The white man has crushed all but the life from blacks from the time they came to these shores to this very day.*

18   What is the solution?

19   *Get off their backs.*

20   How?

21   *By simply doing it—now.*

22   This is no oversimplification. Greater changes than this in the relations of peoples have taken place before. The nation would benefit tremendously. Such a change might bring about a closer examination

of our relations with foreign countries, a reconsideration of economic policies, and a re-examination if not a redefinition of nationhood. It might in fact be the only change which can prevent a degenerative decline from a powerful nation to a feeble, third-class, ex-colonialist country existing at the indulgences of stronger powers.

23   In spite of the profound shifts in power throughout the world in the past thirty years, the United States seems to have a domestic objective of "business as usual," with no change needed or in fact wanted.

24   All the nasty problems are overseas. At home the search is for bigger profits and smaller costs, better education and lower taxes, more vacation and less work, more for me and less for you. Problems at home are to be talked away, reasoned into nonexistence, and put to one side while we continue the great American game of greed.

25   There is, however, an inevitability built into the natural order of things. Cause and effect are in fact joined, and if you build a sufficient cause then not all the talk or all the tears in God's creation can prevent the effect from presenting itself one morning as the now ripened fruit of your labors.

26   America began building a cause when black men were first sold into bondage. When the first black mother killed her newborn rather than have him grow into a slave. When the first black man slew himself rather than submit to an organized system of man's feeding upon another's flesh. America had well begun a cause when all the rebels were either slain or broken and the nation set to the task of refining the system of slavery so that the maximum labor might be extracted from it.

27   The system achieved such refinement that the capital loss involved when a slave woman aborted could be set against the gain to be expected from forcing her into brutish labor while she was with child.

28   America began building a potent cause in its infancy as a nation.

29   It developed a way of life, an American ethos, a national life style which included the assumption that blacks are inferior and were born to hew wood and draw water. Newcomers to this land (if white) were immediately made to feel welcome and, among the bounty available, were given blacks to feel superior to. They were required to despise and depreciate them, abuse and exploit them, and one can only imagine how munificent this land must have seemed to the European—a land with built-in scapegoats.

30   The hatred of blacks has been so deeply bound up with being an American that it has been one of the first things new Americans learn and one of the last things old Americans forget. Such feelings have been elevated to a position of national character, so that individuals now no longer feel personal guilt or responsibility for the oppression of black people. The nation has incorporated this oppression into itself in the form of folkways and storied traditions, leaving the individual

free to shrug his shoulders and say only: "That's our way of life."

31   This way of life is a heavy debt indeed, and one trembles for the debtor when payment comes due.

32   America has waxed rich and powerful in large measure on the backs of black laborers. It has become a violent, pitiless nation, hard and calculating, whose moments of generosity are only brief intervals in a ferocious narrative of life, bearing a ferocity and an aggression so strange in this tiny world where men die if they do not live together.

33   With the passing of the need for black laborers, black people have become useless; they are a drug on the market. There are not enough menial jobs. They live in a nation which has evolved a work force of skilled and semi-skilled workmen. A nation which chooses simultaneously to exclude all black men from this favored labor force and to deny them the one thing America has offered every other group— unlimited growth with a ceiling set only by one's native gifts.

34   The facts, however obfuscated, are simple. Since the demise of slavery black people have been expendable in a cruel and impatient land. The damage done to black people has been beyond reckoning. Only now are we beginning to sense the bridle placed on black children by a nation which does not want them to grow into mature human beings.

35   The most idealistic social reformer of our time, Martin Luther King, was not slain by one man; his murder grew out of that large body of violent bigotry America has always nurtured—that body of thinking which screams for the blood of the radical, or the conservative, or the villain, or the saint. To the extent that he stood in the way of bigotry, his life was in jeopardy, his saintly persuasion notwithstanding. To the extent that he was black and was calling America to account, his days were numbered by the nation he sought to save.

36   Men and women, even children, have been slain for no other earthly reason than their blackness. Property and goods have been stolen and the victims then harried and punished for their poverty. But such viciousness can at least be measured or counted.

37   Black men, however, have been so hurt in their manhood that they are now unsure and uneasy as they teach their sons to be men. Women have been so humiliated and used that they may regard womanhood as a curse and flee from it. Such pain, so deep, and such real jeopardy, that the fundamental protective function of the family has been denied. These injuries we have no way to measure.

38   Black men have stood so long in such peculiar jeopardy in America that a *black norm* has developed—a suspiciousness of one's environment which is necessary for survival. Black people, to a degree that approaches paranoia, must be ever alert to danger from their white fellow citizens. It is a cultural phenomenon peculiar to black Americans. And it is a posture so close to paranoid thinking that the mental dis-

order into which black people most frequently fall is paranoid psychosis.

39   Can we say that white men have driven black men mad?

> An educated black woman had worked in an integrated setting for fifteen years. Compliant and deferential, she had earned promotions and pay increases by hard work and excellence. At no time had she been involved in black activism, and her only participation in the movement had been a yearly contribution to the N.A.A.C.P.
>
> During a lull in the racial turmoil she sought psychiatric treatment. She explained that she had lately become alarmed at waves of rage that swept over her as she talked to white people or at times even as she looked at them. In view of her past history of compliance and passivity, she felt that something was wrong with her. If her controls slipped she might embarrass herself or lose her job.

> A black man, a professional, had been a "nice guy" all his life. He was a hard-working non-militant who avoided discussions of race with his white colleagues. He smiled if their comments were harsh and remained unresponsive to racist statements. Lately he has experienced almost uncontrollable anger toward his white co-workers, and although he still manages to keep his feelings to himself, he confides that blacks and whites have been lying to each other. There is hatred and violence between them and he feels trapped. He too fears for himself if his controls should slip.

40   If these educated recipients of the white man's bounty find it hard to control their rage, what of their less fortunate kinsman who has less to protect, less to lose, and more scars to show for his journey in this land?

41   The tone of the preceding chapters has been mournful, painful, desolate, as we have described the psychological consequences of white oppression of blacks. The centuries of senseless cruelty and the permeation of the black man's character with the conviction of his own hatefulness and inferiority tell a sorry tale.

42   This dismal tone has been deliberate. It has been an attempt to evoke a certain quality of depression and hopelessness in the reader and to stir these feelings. These are the most common feelings tasted by black people in America.

43   The horror carries the endorsement of centuries and the entire lifespan of a nation. It is a way of life which reaches back to the beginnings of recorded time. And all the bestiality, wherever it occurs and however long it has been happening, is narrowed, focused, and refined to shine into a black child's eyes when he views his world. All that

has ever happened to black men and women he sees in the victims closest to him, his parents.

44 A life is an eternity and throughout all that eternity a black child has breathed the foul air of cruelty. He has grown up to find that his spirit was crushed before he knew there was need of it. His ambitions, even in their forming, showed him to have set his hand against his own. This is the desolation of black life in America.

45 Depression and grief are hatred turned on the self. It is instructive to pursue the relevance of this truth to the condition of black Americans.

46 Black people have shown a genius for surviving under the most deadly circumstances. They have survived because of their close attention to reality. A black dreamer would have a short life in Mississippi. They are of necessity bound to reality, chained to the facts of the times; historically the penalty for misjudging a situation involving white men has been death. The preoccupation with religion has been a willing adoption of fantasy to prod an otherwise reluctant mind to face another day.

47 We will even play tricks on ourselves if it helps us stay alive.

48 The psychological devices used to survive are reminiscent of the years of slavery, and it is no coincidence. The same devices are used because black men face the same danger now as then.

49 The grief and depression caused by the condition of black men in America is an unpopular reality to the sufferers. They would rather see themselves in a more heroic posture and chide a disconsolate brother. They would like to point to their achievements (which in fact have been staggering); they would rather point to virtue (which has been shown in magnificent form by some blacks); they would point to bravery, fidelity, prudence, brilliance, creativity, all of which dark men have shown in abundance. But the overriding experience of the black American has been grief and sorrow and no man can change that fact.

50 His grief has been realistic and appropriate. What people have so earned a period of mourning?

51 We want to emphasize yet again the depth of the grief for slain sons and ravished daughters, how deep and lingering it is.

52 If the depth of this sorrow is felt, we can then consider what can be made of this emotion.

53 As grief lifts and the sufferer moves toward health, the hatred he had turned on himself is redirected toward his tormentors, and the fury of his attack on the one who caused him pain is in direct proportion to the depth of his grief. When the mourner lashes out in anger, it is a relief to those who love him, for they know he has now returned to health.

54 Observe that the amount of rage the oppressed turns on his tormentor is a direct function of the depth of his grief, and consider the intensity of black men's grief.

55 Slip for a moment into the soul of a black girl whose womanhood is blighted, not because she is ugly, but because she is black and by definition all blacks are ugly.

56 Become for a moment a black citizen of Birmingham, Alabama, and try to understand his grief and dismay when innocent children are slain while they worship, for no other reason than that they are black.

57 Imagine how an impoverished mother feels as she watches the light of creativity snuffed out in her children by schools which dull the mind and environs which rot the soul.

58 For a moment make yourself the black father whose son went innocently to war and there was slain—for whom, for what?

59 For a moment be any black person, anywhere, and you will feel the waves of hopelessness that engulfed black men and women when Martin Luther King was murdered. All black people understood the tide of anarchy that followed his death.

60 It is the transformation of *this* quantum of grief into aggression of which we now speak. As a sapling bent low stores energy for a violent backswing, blacks bent double by oppression have stored energy which will be released in the form of rage—black rage, apocalyptic and final.

61 White Americans have developed a high skill in the art of misunderstanding black people. It must have seemed to slaveholders that slavery would last through all eternity, for surely their misunderstanding of black bondsmen suggested it. If the slaves were eventually to be released from bondage, what could be the purpose of creating the fiction of their subhumanity?

62 It must have seemed to white men during the period 1865 to 1945 that black men would always be a passive, compliant lot. If not, why would they have stoked the flames of hatred with such deliberately barbarous treatment?

63 White Americans today deal with "racial incidents" from summer to summer as if such minor turbulence will always remain minor and one need only keep the blacks busy till fall to have made it through another troubled season.

64 Today it is the young men who are fighting the battles, and, for now, their elders, though they have given their approval, have not joined in. The time seems near, however, for the full range of the black masses to put down the broom and buckle on the sword. And it grows nearer day by day. Now we see skirmishes, sputtering erratically, evidence if you will that the young men are in a warlike mood. But evidence as well that the elders are watching closely and may soon join the battle.

65 Even these minor flurries have alarmed the country and have resulted in a spate of generally senseless programs designed to give *temporary summer jobs*! More interesting in its long-range prospects has been the apparent eagerness to draft black men for military service. If in fact this is a deliberate design to place black men in uniform in

order to get them off the street, it may be the most curious "instant cure" for a serious disease this nation has yet attempted. Young black men are learning the most modern techniques for killing—techniques which may be used against *any* enemy.

66   But it is all speculation. The issue finally rests with the black masses. When the servile men and women stand up, we had all better duck.

67   We should ask what is likely to galvanize the masses into aggression against the whites.

Will it be some grotesque atrocity against black people which at last causes one-tenth of the nation to rise up in indignation and crush the monstrosity?

Will it be the example of black people outside the United States who have gained dignity through their own liberation movement?

Will it be by the heroic action of a small group of blacks which by its wisdom and courage commands action in a way that cannot be denied?

Or will it be by blacks, finally and in an unpredictable way, simply getting fed up with the bumbling stupid racism of this country? Fired not so much by any one incident as by the gradual accretion of stupidity into fixtures of national policy.

68   All are possible, or any one, or something yet unthought. It seems certain only that on the course the nation now is headed it will happen.

69   One might consider the possibility that, if the national direction remains unchanged, such a conflagration simply might *not* come about. Might not black people remain where they are, as they did for a hundred years during slavery?

70   Such seems truly inconceivable. Not because blacks are so naturally warlike or rebellious, but because they are filled with such grief, such sorrow, such bitterness, and such hatred. It seems now delicately poised, not yet risen to the flash point, but rising rapidly nonetheless. No matter what repressive measures are invoked against the blacks, they will never swallow their rage and go back to blind hopelessness.

71   If existing oppressions and humiliating disenfranchisements are to be lifted, they will have to be lifted most speedily, or catastrophe will follow.

72   For there are no more psychological tricks blacks can play upon themselves to make it possible to exist in dreadful circumstances. No more lies can they tell themselves. No more dreams to fix on. No more opiates to dull the pain. No more patience. No more thought. No more reason. Only a welling tide risen out of all those terrible years of grief, now a tidal wave of fury and rage, and all black, black as night.

Discussion of Theme

1. Do you agree with the authors that history may show that Malcolm X is the man who captured the spirit of our times? If not, who would your choice be?
2. The authors ask, "Can we say that white men have driven black men mad"? What is their answer to the question? Do you agree?
3. What accounts for the "black rage" the authors refer to? How is it shown?

Discussion of Rhetoric

1. Why was Malcolm X discussed at the beginning of this article? What is he a symbol of?
2. Comment on the paragraph structure and sentence variety in paragraphs 15–21.
3. Compare the description in paragraph 39 of the feelings of black persons with that in paragraphs 55–59. Which is more emotional? Which is more effective? Why?
4. Comment on the tone of this article. What effect do you think words like conflagration (paragraph 69) and catastrophe (paragraph 71) have on the reader?

Writing Assignments

1. The following statements are often heard. Select one and answer it. (1) "I want to stop being referred to as 'they' and I want what everybody else wants." (2) "What the hell do they [the blacks] want anyway?" (3) "Every other ethnic group has made it up the ladder on its own. Why can't the blacks do likewise?"
2. If you were president of the United States, what would you do to ease racial tension? Present your course of action in a theme.
3. Who in your opinion is the more admirable black: Malcolm X or Martin Luther King, Jr.? Why? Give your reasons in a theme.

Library Exploration

Read other chapters from *Black Rage*.

Vocabulary

ethos (29): underlying and distinctive character of a people
obfuscated (34): confused; made obscure
paranoia (38): excessive suspiciousness and distrust of others
deferential (39): very respectful
disconsolate (49): hopelessly sad
quantum (60): amount; quantity
apocalyptic (60): forecasting imminent disaster or ultimate doom

50

THOUGHTS ON BLACK POWER

Norman Mailer

A famous American novelist examines divergent attitudes within the Black Power movement, believing that they foreshadow the shape of future wars and revolutions.

> "You don't even know who you are," Reginald had said. "You don't even know, the white devil has hidden it from you, that you are of a race of people of ancient civilizations, and riches in gold and kings. You don't even know your true family name, you wouldn't recognize your true language if you heard it. You have been cut off by the devil white man from all true knowledge of your own kind. You have been a victim of the evil of the devil white man ever since he murdered and raped and stole you from your native land in the seeds of your forefathers. . . ."
>
> *The Autobiography of Malcolm X*

1   In not too many years, we will travel to the moon, and on the trip, the language will be familiar. We have not had our education for nothing—all those sanitized hours of orientation via high school, commercials, corporations and mass media have given us one expectation: no matter how beautiful, insane, dangerous, sacrilegious, explosive, holy or damned a new venture may be, count on it fellow Americans, the language will be familiar. Are you going in for a serious operation, voting on the political future of the country, buying insurance, discussing nuclear disarmament or taking a trip to the moon? You can depend on the one great American certainty—the public vocabulary of the discussion will suggest the same relation to the resources of the English language that a loaf of big-bakery bread in plastic bag and wax bears to the secret heart of wheat and butter and eggs and yeast.

2   Your trip to the moon will not deal needlessly with the vibrations of the heavens (now that man dares to enter eschatology) nor the metaphysical rifts in the philosophical firmament; no poets will pluck a stringed instrument to conjure with the pale shades of the white lady as you move along toward the lunar space. Rather, a voice will emerge

from the loudspeaker, "This is your pilot. On our starboard bow at four o'clock directly below, you can pick out a little doojigger of land down there like a vermiform appendix, and that, as we say good-bye to the Pacific Coast, is Baja California. The spot of light at the nub, that little bitty illumination like the probe bulb in a cystoscope or comparable medical instrument is Ensenada, which the guidebooks call a jeweled resort."

3   Good-bye to earth, hello the moon! We will skip the technological dividend in the navigator's voice as he delivers us to that space station which will probably look like a breeding between a modern convention hall and the computer room at CBS. Plus the packaged air in the space suits when the tourists, after two days of acclimation in air-sealed moon motels, take their first reconnoiter outside in the white moon dust while their good American bowels accommodate to relative weightlessness.

4   All right, bright fellow, the reader now may say—what does all this have to do with Black Power? And the author, while adept at dancing in the interstices of a metaphor, is going to come back nonetheless straight and fast with this remark—our American mass-media language is not any more equipped to get into a discussion of Black Power than it is ready to serve as interpreter en route to the moon. The American language has become a conveyer belt to carry each new American generation into its ordained position in the American scene, which is to say the corporate technological world. It can deal with external descriptions of everything which enters or leaves a man, it can measure the movements of that man, it can predict until such moment as it is wrong what the man will do next, but it cannot give a spiritual preparation for our trip to the moon any more than it can talk to us about death, or the inner experiences of real sex, real danger, real dread. Or Black Power.

5   If the preface has not been amusing, cease at once to read, for what follows will be worse: the technological American is programmed to live with answers, which is why his trip to the moon will be needlessly God-awful; the subject of Black Power opens nothing but questions, precisely those unendurable questions which speak of premature awakenings and the hour of the wolf. But let us start with something comfortable, something we all know, and may encounter with relaxation, for the matter is familiar:

> . . . think of that black slave man filled with fear and dread, hearing the screams of his wife, his mother, his daughter being *taken*—in the barn, the kitchen, in the bushes! . . . *Think* of hearing wives, mothers, daughters, being *raped*! And you were too filled with *fear* of the rapist to do anything about it! . . . Turn around and look at each other, brothers and sisters, and *think*

of this! You and me, polluted all these colors—and this devil
has the arrogance and the gall to think we, his victims, should
love him!

The Autobiography of Malcolm X

6   "Okay," you say, "I know that, I know that already. I didn't do it.
My great-grandfather didn't even do it. He was a crazy Swede. He
never even saw a black skin. And now for Crysake, the girls in Sweden
are crazy about Floyd Patterson. I don't care, I say more power to him.
All right," goes the dialogue of this splendid American now holding up
a hand, "all right, I know about collective responsibility. If some
Scotch-Irish planter wanted to tomcat in the magnolias, then I'll
agree it's easier for me than for the victim to discern subtle differences
between one kind of WASP and another, I'll buy my part of the ancestral curse for that Scotch-Irish stud's particular night of pleasure,
maybe I'm guilty of something myself, but there are limits, man.
All right, we never gave the Negro a fair chance, and now we want to,
we're willing to put up with a reasonable amount of disadvantage,
in fact, discomfort, outright inequality and inefficiency. I'll hire
Negroes who are not as equipped in the productive scheme of things
as whites; that doesn't mean we have to pay iota for iota on every
endless misdemeanor of the past and suffer a vomit bag of bad manners
to boot. Look, every student of revolution can tell you that the danger
comes from giving the oppressed their first liberties. A poor man who
wins a crazy bet always squanders it. The point, buddy, is that the
present must forgive the past, there must be forgiveness for old sins,
or else progress is impossible." And there is the key to the first door;
progress depends upon anesthetizing the past. What if, says Black
Power, we are not interested in progress, not your progress with
packaged food for soul food, smog for air, hypodermics for roots,
air conditioning for breeze—what if we think we have gotten strong
by living without progress and your social engineering, what if we
think that an insult to the blood is never to be forgotten because it
keeps your life alive and reminds you to meditate before you urinate.
Who are you to say that spooks don't live behind the left ear and
ha'nts behind the right? Whitey, you smoke so much you can't smell,
taste, or kiss—your breath is too bad. If you don't have a gun, I can
poke you and run—you'll never catch me. I'm alive 'cause I keep alive
the curse you put in my blood. Primitive people don't forget. If
they do, they turn out no better than the civilized and the sick. Who
are you, Whitey, to tell me to drop my curse, and join your line of
traffic going to work? I'd rather keep myself in shape and work out
the curse, natural style. There's always white women, ahem! Unless
we decide they're too full of your devil's disease, hypocritical pus-
filled old white blood, and so we stay black with black, and repay the

curse by drawing blood. That's the life-giving way to repay a curse."

7   "Why must you talk this way?" says the splendid American. "Can't you see that there are whites and whites, whites I do not begin to control? They wish to destroy you. They agree with your values. They are primitive whites. They think in blood for blood. In a war, they will kill you, and they will kill me."

8   "Well, daddy, I'm just putting you on. Didn't you ever hear of the hereafter? That's where it will all work out, there where us Blacks are the angels and honkies is the flunky. Now, let me take you by the tail, white cat, long enough to see that I want some more of these handouts, see, these homey horse balls and government aid."

9   The splendid American has just been left in the mire of a put-on and throwaway. How is he to know if this is spring mud or the muck of the worst Negro Hades?

10   The native's relaxation takes precisely the form of a muscular orgy in which the most acute aggressivity and the most impelling violence are canalised, transformed and conjured away. . . . At certain times on certain days, men and women come together at a given place, and there, under the solemn eye of the tribe, fling themselves into a seemingly unorganized pantomime, which is in reality extremely systematic, in which by various means— shakes of the head, bending of the spinal column, throwing of the whole body backwards—may be deciphered as in an open book the huge effort of a community to exorcise itself, to liberate itself . . . in reality your purpose in coming together is to allow the accumulated libido, the hampered aggressivity to dissolve as in a volcanic eruption. Symbolic killings, fantastic rites, imaginary mass murders—all must be brought out. The evil humours are undammed, and flow away with a din as of molten lava. . . .   Frantz Fanon—*The Wretched of the Earth*

11   Here is the lesson learned by the struggles of present-day colonial countries to obtain their independence: a war of liberation converts the energies of criminality, assassination, religious orgy, voodoo and the dance into the determined artful phalanxes of bold guerrilla armies. A sense of brotherhood comes to replace the hitherto murderous clan relations of the natives. Once, that propensity to murder each other had proved effective in keeping the peace—for the settler. Now, these violent sentiments turn against the whites who constrain them. Just as the natives upon a time made good servants and workers for the whites, while reserving the worst of their characters for each other, now they looked to serve each other, to cleanse the furies of their exploited lives in open rude defiance against the authority.

12   This is the conventional explanation offered by any revolutionary spokesman for the Third World—that new world which may or may

not emerge triumphant in Latin America, Asia and Africa. It is a powerful argument, an uplifting argument, it stirs the blood of anyone who has ever had a revolutionary passion, for the faith of the revolutionary (if he is revolutionary enough to have faith) is that the repressed blood of mankind is ultimately good and noble blood. Its goodness may be glimpsed in the emotions of its release. If a sense of brotherhood animates the inner life of guerrilla armies, then it does not matter how violent they are to their foe. That violence safeguards the sanctity of their new family relations.

13   If this is the holy paradigm of the colonial revolutionary, its beauty has been confirmed in places, denied in others. While the struggles of the NLF and the North Vietnamese finally proved impressive even to the most gung ho Marine officers in Southeast Asia, the horrors of the war in Biafra go far toward proving the opposite. The suspicion remains that beneath the rhetoric of revolution, another war, quite separate from a revolutionary war, is also being waged, and the forces of revolution in the world are as divided by this concealed war as the civilized powers who would restrain them. It is as if one war goes on between the privileged and the oppressed to determine how the productive wealth of civilization will be divided; the other war, the seed contained within this first war, derives from a notion that the wealth of civilization is not wealth but a corporate productive poisoning of the wellsprings, avatars and conduits of nature; the power of civilization is therefore equal to the destruction of life itself. It is, of course, a perspective open to the wealthy as well as to the poor— not every mill owner who kills the fish in his local rivers with the wastes from his factory is opposed to protecting our wilderness preserve, not at all, some even serve on the State Conservation Committee. And our First Lady would try to keep billboards from defacing those new highways which amputate the ecology through which they pass. Of course, her husband helped to build those highways. But then the rich, unless altogether elegant, are inevitably comic. It is in the worldwide militancy of the underprivileged, undernourished and exploited that the potential horror of this future war (concealed beneath the present war) will make itself most evident. For the armies of the impoverished, unknown to themselves, are already divided. Once victorious over the wealthy West—if ever!—they could only have a new war. It would take place between those forces on their side who are programmatic, scientific, more or less Socialist, and near maniac in their desire to bring technological culture at the fastest possible rate into every backward land, and those more traditional and/or primitive forces in the revolution of the Third World who reject not only the exploitation of the Western world but reject the West as well, in toto, as a philosophy, a culture, a technique, as a way indeed of even attempting to solve the problems of man himself.

14   Of these colonial forces, black, brown and yellow, which look to overthrow the economic and social tyrannies of the white man, there is no force in Africa, Asia, or Latin America which we need think of as being any more essentially colonial in stance than the American Negro. Consider these remarks in *The Wretched of the Earth* about the situation of colonials:

15   "The colonial world is a world cut in two. The dividing line, the frontiers are shown by barracks and police stations." (Of this, it may be said that Harlem is as separate from New York as East Berlin from West Berlin.)

16   ". . . if, in fact, my life is worth as much as the settler's, his glance no longer shrivels me up nor freezes me, and his voice no longer turns me into stone. I am no longer on tenterhooks in his presence; in fact, I don't give a damn for him. Not only does his presence no longer trouble me, but I am already preparing such efficient ambushes for him that soon there will be no way out but that of flight." (Now, whites flee the subways in New York.) ". . . there is no colonial power today which is capable of adopting the only form of contest which has a chance of succeeding, namely, the prolonged establishment of large forces of occupation." (How many divisions of paratroops would it take to occupy Chicago's South Side?)

17   The American Negro is of course not synonymous with Black Power. For every Black militant, there are ten Negroes who live quietly beside him in the slums, resigned for the most part to the lessons, the action and the treadmill of the slums. As many again have chosen to integrate. They live now like Negroid Whites in mixed neighborhoods, suburbs, factories, obtaining their partial peace within the white dream. But no American Negro is contemptuous of Black Power. Like the accusing finger in the dream, it is the rarest nerve in their head, the frightening pulse in their heart, equal in emotional weight to that passion which many a noble nun sought to conquer on a cold stone floor. Black Power obviously derives from a heritage of anger which makes the American Negro one man finally with the African, the Algerian and even the Vietcong—he would become schizophrenic if he tried to suppress his fury over the mutilations of the past.

18   The confrontation of Black Power with American life gives us then not only an opportunity to comprehend some of the forces and some of the style of that war now smoldering between the global rich and the global poor, between the culture of the past and the intuitions of the future, but—since Black Power has more intimate, everyday knowledge of what it is like to live in an advanced technological society than any other guerrilla force on earth—the division of attitudes within Black Power has more to tell us about the shape of future wars and revolutions than any other militant force in the world. Technological man in his terminal diseases, dying of air he can no longer breathe, of packaged

food he can just about digest, of plastic clothing his skin can hardly bear and of static before which his spirit has near expired, stands at one end of revolutionary ambition—at the other is an inchoate glimpse of a world now visited only by the primitive and the drug-ridden, a world where technology shatters before magic and electronic communication is surpassed by the psychic telegraphy of animal mood.

19   Most of the literature of Black Power is interested entirely, or so it would seem, in immediate political objectives of the most concrete sort. Back in 1923, Marcus Garvey, father of the Back-to-Africa movement, might have written, "When Europe was inhabited by a race of cannibals, a race of savages, naked men, heathens and pagans, Africa was peopled with a race of cultured black men, who were masters in art, science and literature, men who were cultured and refined; men who, it was said, were like the gods," but the present leaders of Black Power are concerned with political mandate and economic clout right here. Floyd McKissick of CORE: the Black Power Movement seeks to win power in a half-dozen ways. These are:
  1. The growth of Black *political* power.
  2. The building of Black *economic* power.
  3. The improvement of the *self-image* of Black people.
  4. The development of Black *leadership*.
  5. The attainment of *Federal law enforcement*.
  6. The mobilization of Black *consumer power*.

20   These demands present nothing exceptional. On their face, they are not so different from manifestos by the NAACP or planks by the Democratic party. A debater with the skill of William F. Buckley or Richard Nixon could stay afloat for hours on the life-saving claim that there is nothing in these six points antithetical to conservatives. Indeed, there is not. Not on the face. For example, here is Adam Clayton Powell, a politician most respected by Black Power militants, on some of these points. Political power: "Where we are 20% of the voters, we should command 20% of the jobs, judgeships, commissionerships, and all political appointments." Economic power: "Rather than a race primarily of consumers and stock boys, we must become a race of producers and stockbrokers." Leadership: "Black communities . . . must neither tolerate nor accept outside leadership— black or white." Federal law enforcement: "The battle against segregation in America's public school systems must become a national effort, instead of the present regional skirmish that now exists." Even consumer protest groups to stand watch on the quality of goods sold in a slum neighborhood are hardly revolutionary, more an implementation of good conservative buying practices. *Consumers Digest* is not yet at the barricades.

21   Indeed, which American institution of power is ready to argue with these six points? They are so rational! The power of the technological

society is shared by the corporations, the military, the mass media, the trade unions and the Government. It is to the interest of each to have a society which is *rational*, even as a machine is rational. When a machine breaks down, the cause can be discovered; in fact, the cause must be capable of being discovered or we are not dealing with a machine. So the pleasure of working with machines is that malfunctions are correctable; satisfaction is guaranteed by the application of work, knowledge and reason. Hence, any race problem is anathema to power groups in the technological society, because the subject of race is irrational. At the very least, race problems seem to have the property of repelling reason. Still, the tendency of modern society to shape men for function in society like parts of a machine grows more powerful all the time. So we have the paradox of a conservative capitalistic democracy, profoundly entrenched in racial prejudice (and hitherto profoundly attracted to racial exploitation) now transformed into the most developed technological society in the world. The old prejudices of the men who wield power have become therefore inefficient before the needs of the social machine—so inefficient, in fact, that prejudiced as many of them still are, they consider it a measure of their responsibility to shed prejudice. (We must by now move outside the center of power before we can even find Gen. Curtis LeMay.)

22   So the question may well be posed: if the demands formally presented by Black Power advocates like McKissick and Powell are thus rational, and indeed finally fit the requirements of the technological society, why then does Black Power inspire so much fear, distrust, terror, horror and even outright revulsion among the best liberal descendants of the beautiful old Eleanor Roosevelt bag and portmanteau? And the answer is that an intellectual shell game has been played up to here. We have not covered McKissick's six points, only five. The sixth (point number three) was "The improvement of the *self-image* of Black people." It is here that sheer Black hell busts loose. A technological society can deal comfortably with people who are mature, integrated, goal-oriented, flexible, responsive, group-responsive, etc., etc.—the word we cannot leave out is white or white-oriented. The technological society is not able to deal with the self-image of separate peoples and races if the development of their self-image produces personalities of an explosive individuality. We do not substitute sticks of dynamite for the teeth of a gear and assume we still have an automotive transmission.

23   McKissick covers his third point, of course: "Negro history, art, music and other aspects of Black culture . . . make Black people aware of their contributions to the American heritage and to world civilization." Powell bastes the goose with orotundities of rhetorical gravy "We must give our children a sense of pride in being black. The glory of our past and the dignity of our present must lead the way to

the power of our future." Amen. We have been conducted around the point.

24   Perhaps the clue is that political Right and political Left are meaningless terms when applied conventionally to Black Power. If we are to use them at all (and it is a matter of real convenience), then we might call the more or less rational programmatic and recognizably political arm of Black Power, presented by McKissick and Powell, as the Right Wing, since their program can conceivably be attached to the programs of the technological society, whether Democrat or Republican. The straight-out political demands of this kind of Black Power not only can be integrated (at least on paper) into the needs of the technological society, but must be, because—we would repeat—an exploited class creates disruption and therefore irrationality in a social machine; efforts to solve exploitation and disruption become mandatory for the power groups. If this last sentence sounds vaguely Marxist in cadence, the accident is near. What characterizes technological societies is that they tend to become more and more like one another. So America and the Soviet will yet have interchangeable parts, or at least be no more different than a four-door Ford from a two-door Chevrolet. It may thus be noticed that what we are calling the Right Wing of Black Power—the technological wing—is in the conventional sense interested in moving to the left. Indeed, after the Blacks attain equality—so goes the unspoken assumption—America will be able to progress toward a rational society of racial participation, etc., etc. What then is the Left Wing of Black Power? Say, let us go back to Africa, back to Garvey.

25   We must understand that we are *replacing* a dying culture, and we must be prepared to do this, and be absolutely conscious of what we are replacing it with. We are sons and daughters of the most ancient societies on this planet. . . . No movement shaped or contained by Western culture will ever benefit Black people. Black power must be the actual force and beauty and wisdom of Blackness . . . reordering the world.

                                                                     LeRoi Jones

26   Are you ready to enter the vision of the Black Left? It is profoundly anti-technological. Jump into it all at once. Here are a few remarks by Ron Karenga:

27   "The fact that we are Black is our ultimate reality. We were Black before we were born.

28   "The white boy is engaged in the worship of technology; we must not sell our souls for money and machines. We must free ourselves culturally before we proceed politically.

29   "Revolution to us is the creation of an alternative . . . we are not here to be taught by the world, but to teach the world."

30   We have left the splendid American far behind. He is a straight-punching all-out truth-sayer; he believes in speaking his mind; but if LeRoi Jones—insults, absolute rejection and consummate bad-mouthing—is not too much for him, then Karenga will be his finish. Karenga obviously believes that in the root is the answer to where the last growth went wrong—so he believes in the wisdom of the blood, and blood-wisdom went out for the splendid American after reading *Lady Chatterley's Lover* in sophomore year. Life is hard enough to see straight without founding your philosophy on a metaphor.

31   Nonetheless the mystique of Black Power remains. Any mystique which has men ready to die for it is never without political force. The Left Wing of Black Power speaks across the void to the most powerful conservative passions—for any real conservatism is founded on regard for the animal, the oak and the field; it has instinctive detestation of science, of the creation-by-machine. Conservatism is a body of traditions which once served as the philosophical home of society. If the traditions are now withered in the hum of electronics; if the traditions have become almost hopelessly inadequate to meet the computed moves of the technological society; if conservatism has become the grumbling of the epicure at bad food, bad air, bad manners; if conservatism lost the future because it enjoyed the greed of its privileged position to that point where the exploited depths stirred in righteous rage; if the conservatives and their traditions failed because they violated the balance of society, exploited the poor too savagely and searched for justice not nearly enough; if finally the balance between property rights and the rights of men gave at last too much to the land and too little to the living blood, still conservatism and tradition had one last Herculean strength: they were of the marrow, they partook of primitive wisdom. The tradition had been founded on some half-remembered sense of primitive perception, and so was close to life and the sense of life. Tradition had appropriated the graceful movements with which primitive strangers and friends might meet in the depth of a mood, all animal in their awareness: lo! the stranger bows before the intense presence of the monarch or the chief, and the movement is later engraved upon a code of ceremony. So tradition was once a key to the primitive life still breathing within us, a key too large, idiosyncratic and unmanageable for the quick shuttles of the electronic. Standing before technology, tradition began to die, and air turned to smog. But the black man, living a life on the fringe of technological society, exploited by it, poisoned by it, half-rejected by it, gulping prison air in the fluorescent nightmare of shabby garish electric ghettos, uprooted centuries ago from his native Africa, his instincts living ergo like nerves in the limbo of an amputated limb, had thereby an experience unique to modern man—he was forced to live at one and the same time in the

old primitive jungle of the slums, and the hygienic surrealistic landscape of the technological society. And as he began to arise from his exploitation, he discovered that the culture which had saved him owed more to the wit and telepathy of the jungle than the value and programs of the West. His dance had taught him more than writs and torts, his music was sweeter than Shakespeare or Bach (since music had never been a luxury to him but a need), prison had given him a culture deeper than libraries in the grove, and violence had produced an economy of personal relations as negotiable as money. The American Black had survived—of all the peoples of the Western World, he was the only one in the near seven decades of the twentieth century to have undergone the cruel weeding of real survival. So it was possible his manhood had improved while the manhood of others was being leached. He had at any rate a vision. It was that he was black, beautiful and secretly superior —he had therefore the potentiality to conceive and create a new culture (perchance a new civilization), richer, wiser, deeper, more beautiful and profound than any he had seen. (And conceivably more demanding, more torrential, more tyrannical.) But he would not know until he had power for himself. He would not know if he could provide a wiser science, subtler schooling, deeper medicine, richer victual and deeper view of creation until he had the power. So while some (the ones the Blacks called Negroes) looked to integrate into the super-suburbs of technology land (and find, was their hope, a little peace for the kids), so others dreamed of a future world which their primitive lore and sophisticated attainments might now bring. And because they were proud and loved their vision, they were warriors as well, and had a mystique which saw the cooking of food as good or bad for the soul. And taste gave the hint. That was the Left of Black Power, a movement as mysterious, dedicated, instinctive and conceivably bewitched as a gathering of Templars for the next Crusade. Soon their public fury might fall upon the fact that civilization was a trap, and therefore their wrath might be double, for they had been employed to build civilization, had received none of its gains, and yet, being allowed to enter now, now, this late, could be doomed with the rest. What a thought!

32   When the *canaille roturière* took the liberty of beheading the high
        noblesse, it was done less, perhaps, to inherit their goods than to
        inherit their ancestors.   Heinrich Heine

33   But I am a white American, more or less, and writing for an audience
      of Americans, white and Negro in the main. So the splendid American
      would remind me that my thoughts are romantic projections, hypotheses unverifiable by any discipline, no more legitimate for discussion
      than melody. What, he might ask, would you do with the concrete
      problem before us. . . .

34   You mean: not jobs, not schools, not votes, not production, not consumption. . . .

35   No, he said hoarsely, law and order.

36   Well, the man who sings the melody is not normally consulted for the by-laws of the Arranger's Union.

37   Crap and craparoola, said the splendid American, what it all comes down to is: how do you keep the peace?

38   I do not know. If they try to keep it by force—we will not have to wait so very long before there are Vietnams in our own cities. A race which arrives at a vision must test that vision by deeds.

39   Then what would you do?

40   If I were king?

41   We are a republic and will never support a king.

42   Ah, if I were a man who had a simple audience with Richard Milhous Nixon, I would try to say, "Remember when all else has failed, that honest hatred searches for responsibility. I would look to encourage not merely new funding for businessmen who are Black, but Black schools with their own teachers and their own texts, Black solutions to Black housing where the opportunity might be given to rebuild one's own slum room by room, personal idiosyncrasy next to mad neighbor's style, floor by floor, not block by block; I would try to recognize that an area of a city where whites fear to go at night belongs by all existential— which is to say natural—law to the Blacks, and would respect the fact, and so would encourage Black local self-government as in a separate city with a Black sanitation department run by themselves, a Black fire department, a funding for a Black concert hall, and most of all a Black police force responsible only to this city within our city and Black courts of justice for their own. There will be no peace short of the point where the Black man can measure his new superiorities and inferiorities against our own."

43   You are absolutely right but for one detail, said the splendid American. What will you do when they complain about the smog *our* factories push into *their* air?

44   Oh, I said, the Blacks are so evil their factories will push worse air back. And thus we went on arguing into the night. Yes, the times are that atrocious you can hardly catch your breath. "Confronted by outstanding merit in another, there is no way of saving one's ego except by love."

45   Goethe is not the worst way to say goodnight.

Discussion of Theme

1. What does Mailer mean when he says (paragraph 6) that "progress depends upon anesthetizing the past"?

2. Are Mailer's sympathies ultimately with the black radicals or the black moderates?

3. Do you approve or disapprove of Mailer's suggestions for keeping peace in the cities (see paragraph 42)?

Discussion of Rhetoric

1. What function do the quotations scattered throughout this essay serve? Note particularly those by Malcom X and Frantz Fanon.
2. Find some very long and some very short paragraphs in this essay. After analyzing them carefully, see if you can decide why critics agree there is no "ideal" paragraph length.
3. Explain the relationship of the last sentence of this essay to the rest of the selection.

Writing Assignments

1. What evils in our society is Mailer attacking? Do you see them in a similar light? If so, present your argument, together with your remedy for their cure. Be specific; don't make vague charges.
2. If you disagree with Mailer's article, write a rebuttal to it.
3. Define the following terms: radical; reactionary; New Left.

Library Exploration

1. Who is Norman Mailer? What has he written? What part did he play recently in New York City politics?
2. Identify Marcus Garvey, Frantz Fanon, and LeRoi Jones. What contribution did each make to black progress?

Vocabulary

eschatology (2): the branch of theology that treats of death and the future state of the soul

metaphysical (2): dealing with phenomena having no physical basis

interstices (4): spaces between

exorcise (10): get rid of something unpleasant, troublesome, or menacing

phalanxes (11): bodies of troops in close array

paradigm (13): pattern; example

avatars (13:) embodiments (usually in a person) of some concept or philosophy

conduits (13): channels through which electricity or fluids flow

inchoate (18): imperfectly formed; unfinished

anathema (21): something cursed or disliked

orotundities (23): pomposities

mandatory (24): required; obligatory

torts (31): civil wrongs

canaille roturière (32): the mob; rabble

noblesse (32): nobility

51

MY DUNGEON SHOOK:
Letter to My Nephew on the 100th Anniversary
of the Emancipation

James Baldwin

In this brief, moving letter to his nephew and namesake, a famous black novelist and essayist expresses his feelings about the white world.

Dear James:

1   I have begun this letter five times and torn it up five times. I keep seeing your face, which is also the face of your father and my brother. Like him, you are tough, dark, vulnerable, moody—with a very definite tendency to sound truculent because you want no one to think you are soft. You may be like your grandfather in this, I don't know, but certainly both you and your father resemble him very much physically. Well, he is dead, he never saw you, and he had a terrible life; he was defeated long before he died because, at the bottom of his heart, he really believed what white people said about him. This is one of the reasons that he became so holy. I am sure that your father has told you something about all that. Neither you nor your father exhibit any tendency towards holiness: you really *are* of another era, part of what happened when the Negro left the land and came into what the late E. Franklin Frazier called "the cities of destruction." You can only be destroyed by believing that you really are what the white world calls a *nigger*. I tell you this because I love you, and please don't you ever forget it.

2   I have known both of you all your lives, have carried your Daddy in my arms and on my shoulders, kissed and spanked him and watched him learn to walk. I don't know if you've known anybody from that far back; if you've loved anybody that long, first as an infant, then as a child, then as a man, you gain a strange perspective on time and human pain and effort. Other people cannot see what I see whenever I look into your father's face, for behind your father's face as it is today are all those other faces which were his. Let him laugh and I see a cellar your father does not remember and a house he does not remember and I hear in his present laughter his laughter as a child. Let him curse and I remember him falling down the cellar steps,

and howling, and I remember, with pain, his tears, which my hand or your grandmother's so easily wiped away. But no one's hand can wipe away those tears he sheds invisibly today, which one hears in his laughter and in his speech and in his songs. I know what the world has done to my brother and how narrowly he has survived it. And I know, which is much worse, and this is the crime of which I accuse my country and my countrymen, and for which neither I nor time nor history will ever forgive them, that they have destroyed and are destroying hundreds of thousands of lives and do not know it and do not want to know it. One can be, indeed one must strive to become, tough and philosophical concerning destruction and death, for this is what most of mankind has been best at since we have heard of man. (But remember: *most* of mankind is not *all* of mankind.) But it is not permissible that the authors of devastation should also be innocent. It is the innocence which constitutes the crime.

3   Now, my dear namesake, these innocent and well-meaning people, your countrymen, have caused you to be born under conditions not very far removed from those described for us by Charles Dickens in the London of more than a hundred years ago. (I hear the chorus of the innocents screaming, "No! This is not true! How *bitter* you are!"— but I am writing this letter to *you*, to try to tell you something about how to handle *them*, for most of them do not really know that you exist. I *know* the conditions under which you were born, for I was there. Your countrymen were *not* there, and haven't made it yet. Your grandmother was also there, and no one has ever accused her of being bitter. I suggest that the innocents check with her. She isn't hard to find. Your countrymen don't know that *she* exists, either, though she has been working for them all their lives.)

4   Well, you were born, here you came, something like fifteen years ago; and though your father and mother and grandmother, looking about the streets through which they were carrying you, staring at the walls into which they brought you, had every reason to be heavy-hearted, yet they were not. For here you were, Big James, named for me—you were a big baby, I was not—here you were: to be loved. To be loved, baby, hard, at once, and forever, to strengthen you against the loveless world. Remember that: I know how black it looks today, for you. It looked bad that day, too, yes, we were trembling. We have not stopped trembling yet, but if we had not loved each other none of us would have survived. And now you must survive because we love you, and for the sake of your children and your children's children.

5   This innocent country set you down in a ghetto in which, in fact, it intended that you should perish. Let me spell out precisely what I mean by that, for the heart of the matter is here, and the root of my dispute with my country. You were born where you were born and

faced the future that you faced because you were black and *for no other reason*. The limits of your ambition were, thus, expected to be set forever. You were born into a society which spelled out with brutal clarity, and in as many ways as possible, that you were a worthless human being. You were not expected to aspire to excellence: you were expected to make peace with mediocrity. Wherever you have turned, James, in your short time on this earth, you have been told where you could go and what you could do (and *how* you could do it) and where you could live and whom you could marry. I know your countrymen do not agree with me about this, and I hear them saying, "You exaggerate." They do not know Harlem, and I do. So do you. Take no one's word for anything, including mine—but trust your experience. Know whence you came. If you know whence you came, there is really no limit to where you can go. The details and symbols of your life have been deliberately constructed to make you believe what white people say about you. Please try to remember that what they believe, as well as what they do and cause you to endure, does not testify to your inferiority but to their inhumanity and fear. Please try to be clear, dear James, through the storm which rages about your youthful head today, about the reality which lies behind the words *acceptance* and *integration*. There is no reason for you to try to become like white people and there is no basis whatever for their impertinent assumption that *they* must accept *you*. The really terrible thing, old buddy, is that *you* must accept *them*. And I mean that very seriously. You must accept them and accept them with love. For these innocent people have no other hope. They are, in effect, still trapped in a history which they do not understand; and until they understand it, they cannot be released from it. They have had to believe for many years, and for innumerable reasons, that black men are inferior to white men. Many of them, indeed, know better, but, as you will discover, people find it very difficult to act on what they know. To act is to be committed, and to be committed is to be in danger. In this case, the danger, in the minds of most white Americans, is the loss of their identity. Try to imagine how you would feel if you woke up one morning to find the sun shining and all the stars aflame. You would be frightened because it is out of the order of nature. Any upheaval in the universe is terrifying because it so profoundly attacks one's sense of one's own reality. Well, the black man has functioned in the white man's world as a fixed star, as an immovable pillar: and as he moves out of his place, heaven and earth are shaken to their foundations. You, don't be afraid. I said that it was intended that you should perish in the ghetto, perish by never being allowed to go behind the white man's definitions, by never being allowed to spell your proper name. You have, and many of us have, defeated this intention; and, by a terrible law, a terrible paradox, those innocents who believed that your imprisonment made them safe

are losing their grasp of reality. But these men are your brothers—
your lost, younger brothers. And if the word *integration* means anything,
this is what it means: that we, with love, shall force our brothers to see
themselves as they are, to cease fleeing from reality and begin to change
it. For this is your home, my friend, do not be driven from it; great
men have done great things here, and will again, and we can make
America what America must become. It will be hard, James, but you
come from sturdy, peasant stock, men who picked cotton and dammed
rivers and built railroads, and, in the teeth of the most terrifying odds,
achieved an unassailable and monumental dignity. You come from a
long line of great poets, some of the greatest poets since Homer. One
of them said, *The very time I thought I was lost, My dungeon shook
and my chains fell off.*

6   You know, and I know, that the country is celebrating one hundred
years of freedom one hundred years too soon. We cannot be free until
they are free. God bless you, James, and Godspeed.

Your uncle,

James

Discussion of Theme
1. What difference does Baldwin say exists between the men of his
   brother's and nephew's era and those of his grandfather's?
2. What does Baldwin mean when he says, "It is the innocence which
   constitutes the crime" (last line of paragraph 2)?
3. Who are the "innocents" Baldwin refers to? Do such innocents
   exist today?
4. What is the meaning of Baldwin's remark, "We cannot be free
   until they are free"?

Discussion of Rhetoric
1. Comment on the tone and diction of this article.
2. Is Baldwin writing only to his nephew, or does he have a wider
   audience in mind?
3. Explain the analogy Baldwin makes between the black man and a
   fixed star (paragraph 5). Is it apt?

Writing Assignments
1. What hope can be held out to a black child in the ghetto? How can
   he believe in the American dream?
2. Develop the following statement into a theme: "The country is
   celebrating one hundred years of freedom one hundred years too
   soon."
3. Develop the following title into a theme: "Letter from the White
   Ghetto."

Library Exploration

Read *The Fire Next Time*, from which this letter was taken, or one of Baldwin's essays, novels, or short stories.

Vocabulary

vulnerable (1): capable of being hurt
truculent (1): quarrelsome
unassailable (5): not open to doubt or attack

52

MESSAGE TO THE GRASS ROOTS

Malcolm X

*One of the great black leaders of
our time addresses his people on
the subject of black revolution.*

1   We want to have just an off-the-cuff chat between you and me, us.
We want to talk right down to earth in a language that everybody here
can easily understand. We all agree tonight, all of the speakers have
agreed, that America has a very serious problem. Not only does America
have a very serious problem, but our people have a very serious
problem. America's problem is us. We're her problem. The only
reason she has a problem is she doesn't want us here. And every time
you look at yourself, be you black, brown, red or yellow, a so-called
Negro, you represent a person who poses such a serious problem for
America because you're not wanted. Once you face this as a fact, then
you can start plotting a course that will make you appear intelligent,
instead of unintelligent.

2   What you and I need to do is learn to forget our differences. When
we come together, we don't come together as Baptists or Methodists.
You don't catch hell because you're a Baptist, and you don't catch hell
because you're a Methodist. You don't catch hell because you're a
Methodist or Baptist, you don't catch hell because you're a Democrat
or a Republican, you don't catch hell because you're a Mason or an
Elk, and you sure don't catch hell because you're an American; because
if you were an American, you wouldn't catch hell. You catch hell
because you're a black man. You catch hell, all of us catch hell, for the
same reason.

3   So we're all black people, so-called Negroes, second-class citizens,
ex-slaves. You're nothing but an ex-slave. You don't like to be told
that. But what else are you? You are ex-slaves. You didn't come here
on the "Mayflower." You came here on a slave ship. In chains, like
a horse, or a cow, or a chicken. And you were brought here by the
people who came here on the "Mayflower," you were brought here
by the so-called Pilgrims, or Founding Fathers. They were the ones
who brought you here.

4   We have a common enemy. We have this in common: We have a common oppressor, a common exploiter, and a common discriminator. But once we all realize that we have a common enemy, then we unite— on the basis of what we have in common. And what we have foremost in common is that enemy—the white man. He's an enemy to all of us. I know some of you all think that some of them aren't enemies. Time will tell.

5   In Bandung back in, I think, 1954, was the first unity meeting in centuries of black people. And once you study what happened at the Bandung conference, and the results of the Bandung conference, it actually serves as a model for the same procedure you and I can use to get our problems solved. At Bandung all the nations came together, the dark nations from Africa and Asia. Some of them were Buddhists, some of them were Muslims, some of them were Christians, some were Confucianists, some were atheists. Despite their religious differences, they came together. Some were communists, some were socialists, some were capitalists—despite their economic and political differences, they came together. All of them were black, brown, red or yellow.

6   The number-one thing that was not allowed to attend the Bandung conference was the white man. He couldn't come. Once they excluded the white man, they found that they could get together. Once they kept him out, everybody else fell right in and fell in line. This is the thing that you and I have to understand. And these people who came together didn't have nuclear weapons, they didn't have jet planes, they didn't have all of the heavy armaments that the white man has. But they had unity.

7   They were able to submerge their little petty differences and agree on one thing: That there one African came from Kenya and was being colonized by the Englishman, and another African came from the Congo and was being colonized by the Belgian, and another African came from Guinea and was being colonized by the French, and another came from Angola and was being colonized by the Portuguese. When they came to the Bandung conference, they looked at the Portuguese, and at the Frenchman, and at the Englishman, and at the Dutchman, and learned or realized the one thing that all of them had in common— they were all from Europe, they were all Europeans, blond, blue-eyed and white skins. They began to recognize who their enemy was. The same man that was colonizing our people in Kenya was colonizing our people in the Congo. The same one in the Congo was colonizing our people in South Africa, and in Southern Rhodesia, and in Burma, and in India, and in Afghanistan, and in Pakistan. They realized all over the world where the dark man was being oppressed, he was being oppressed by the white man; where the dark man was being exploited, he was being exploited by the white man. So they got together on this basis—that they had a common enemy.

8   And when you and I here in Detroit and in Michigan and in America who have been awakened today look around us, we too realize here in America we all have a common enemy, whether he's in Georgia or Michigan, whether he's in California or New York. He's the same man—blue eyes and blond hair and pale skin—the same man. So what we have to do is what they did. They agreed to stop quarreling among themselves. Any little spat that they had, they'd settle it among themselves, go into a huddle—don't let the enemy know that you've got a disagreement.

9   Instead of airing our differences in public, we have to realize we're all the same family. And when you have a family squabble, you don't get out on the sidewalk. If you do, everybody calls you uncouth, unrefined, uncivilized, savage. If you don't make it at home, you settle it at home; you get in the closet, argue it out behind closed doors, and then when you come out on the street, you pose a common front, a united front. And this is what we need to do in the community, and in the city, and in the state. We need to stop airing our differences in front of the white man, put the white man out of our meetings, and then sit down and talk shop with each other. That's what we've got to do.

10   I would like to make a few comments concerning the difference between the black revolution and the Negro revolution. Are they both the same? And if they're not, what is the difference? What is the difference between a black revolution and a Negro revolution? First, what is a revolution? Sometimes I'm inclined to believe that many of our people are using this word "revolution" loosely, without taking careful consideration of what this word actually means, and what its historic characteristics are. When you study the historic nature of revolutions, the motive of a revolution, the objective of a revolution, the result of a revolution, and the methods used in a revolution, you may change words. You may devise another program, you may change your goal and you may change your mind.

11   Look at the American Revolution in 1776. That revolution was for what? For land. Why did they want land? Independence. How was it carried out? Bloodshed. Number one, it was based on land, the basis of independence. And the only way they could get it was bloodshed. The French Revolution—what was it based on? The landless against the landlord. What was it for? Land. How did they get it? Bloodshed. Was no love lost, was no compromise, was no negotiation. I'm telling you—you don't know what a revolution is. Because when you find out what it is, you'll get back in the alley, you'll get out of the way.

12   The Russian Revolution—what was it based on? Land; the landless against the landlord. How did they bring it about? Bloodshed. You haven't got a revolution that doesn't involve bloodshed. And you're afraid to bleed. I said, you're afraid to bleed.

13   As long as the white man sent you to Korea, you bled. He sent you to Germany, you bled. He sent you to the South Pacific to fight the Japanese, you bled. You bleed for white people, but when it comes to seeing your own churches being bombed and little black girls murdered, you haven't got any blood. You bleed when the white man says bleed; you bite when the white man says bite; and you bark when the white man says bark. I hate to say this about us, but it's true. How are you going to be nonviolent in Mississippi, as violent as you were in Korea? How can you justify being nonviolent in Mississippi and Alabama, when your churches are being bombed, and your little girls are being murdered, and at the same time you are going to get violent with Hitler, and Tojo, and somebody else you don't even know?

14   If violence is wrong in America, violence is wrong abroad. If it is wrong to be violent defending black women and black children and black babies and black men, then it is wrong for America to draft us and make us violent abroad in defense of her. And if it is right for America to draft us, and teach us how to be violent in defense of her, then it is right for you and me to do whatever is necessary to defend our own people right here in this country.

15   The Chinese Revolution—they wanted land. They threw the British out, along with the Uncle Tom Chinese. Yes, they did. They set a good example. When I was in prison, I read an article—don't be shocked when I say that I was in prison. You're still in prison. That's what America means: prison. When I was in prison, I read an article in *Life* magazine showing a little Chinese girl, nine years old; her father was on his hands and knees and she was pulling the trigger because he was an Uncle Tom Chinaman. When they had the revolution over there, they took a whole generation of Uncle Toms and just wiped them out. And within ten years that little girl became a full-grown woman. No more Toms in China. And today it's one of the toughest, roughest, most feared countries on this earth—by the white man. Because there are no Uncle Toms over there.

16   Of all our studies, history is best qualified to reward our research. And when you see that you've got problems, all you have to do is examine the historic method used all over the world by others who have problems similar to yours. Once you see how they got theirs straight, then you know how you can get yours straight. There's been a revolution, a black revolution, going on in Africa. In Kenya, the Mau Mau were revolutionary; they were the ones who brought the word "Uhuru" to the fore. The Mau Mau, they were revolutionary, they believed in scorched earth, they knocked everything aside that got in their way, and their revolution also was based on land, a desire for land. In Algeria, the northern part of Africa, a revolution took place. The Algerians were revolutionists, they wanted land. France

offered to let them be integrated into France. They told France to hell with France, they wanted some land, not some France. And they engaged in a bloody battle.

17   So I cite these various revolutions, brothers and sisters, to show you that you don't have a peaceful revolution. You don't have a turn-the-other-cheek revolution. There's no such thing as a nonviolent revolution. The only kind of revolution that is nonviolent is the Negro revolution. The only revolution in which the goal is loving your enemy is the Negro revolution. It's the only revolution in which the goal is a desegregated lunch counter, a desegregated theater, a desegregated park, and a desegregated public toilet; you can sit down next to white folks— on the toilet. That's no revolution. Revolution is based on land. Land is the basis of all independence. Land is the basis of freedom, justice, and equality.

18   The white man knows what a revolution is. He knows that the black revolution is world-wide in scope and in nature. The black revolution is sweeping Asia, is sweeping Africa, is rearing its head in Latin America. The Cuban Revolution—that's a revolution. They overturned the system. Revolution is in Asia, revolution is in Africa, and the white man is screaming because he sees revolution in Latin America. How do you think he'll react to you when you learn what a real revolution is? You don't know what a revolution is. If you did, you wouldn't use that word.

19   Revolution is bloody, revolution is hostile, revolution knows no compromise, revolution overturns and destroys everything that gets in its way. And you, sitting around here like a knot on the wall, saying, "I'm going to love these folks no matter how much they hate me." No, you need a revolution. Whoever heard of a revolution where they lock arms, as Rev. Cleage was pointing out beautifully, singing "We Shall Overcome"? You don't do that in a revolution. You don't do any singing, you're too busy swinging. It's based on land. A revolutionary wants land so he can set up his own nation, an independent nation. These Negroes aren't asking for any nation—they're trying to crawl back on the plantation.

20   When you want a nation, that's called nationalism. When the white man became involved in a revolution in this country against England, what was it for? He wanted this land so he could set up another white nation. That's white nationalism. The American Revolution was white nationalism. The French Revolution was white nationalism. The Russian Revolution too—yes, it was—white nationalism. You don't think so? Why do you think Khrushchev and Mao can't get their heads together? White nationalism. All the revolutions that are going on in Asia and Africa today are based on what?—black nationalism. A revolutionary is a black nationalist. He wants a nation. I was reading

some beautiful words by Rev. Cleage, pointing out why he couldn't get together with someone else in the city because all of them were afraid of being identified with black nationalism. If you're afraid of black nationalism, you're afraid of revolution. And if you love revolution, you love black nationalism.

21   To understand this, you have to go back to what the young brother here referred to as the house Negro and the field Negro back during slavery. There were two kinds of slaves, the house Negro and the field Negro. The house Negroes—they lived in the house with master, they dressed pretty good, they ate good because they ate his food— what he left. They lived in the attic or the basement, but still they lived near the master; and they loved the master more than the master loved himself. They would give their life to save the master's house— quicker than the master would. If the master said, "We got a good house here," the house Negro would say, "Yeah, we got a good house here." Whenever the master said "we," he said "we." That's how you can tell a house Negro.

22   If the master's house caught on fire, the house Negro would fight harder to put the blaze out than the master would. If the master got sick, the house Negro would say, "What's the matter, boss, *we* sick?" *We* sick! He identified himself with his master, more than his master identified with himself. And if you came to the house Negro and said, "Let's run away, let's escape, let's separate," the house Negro would look at you and say, "Man, you crazy. What you mean, separate? Where is there a better house than this? Where can I wear better clothes than this? Where can I eat better food than this?" That was that house Negro. In those days he was called a "house nigger." And that's what we call them today, because we've still got some house niggers running around here.

23   This modern house Negro loves his master. He wants to live near him. He'll pay three times as much as the house is worth just to live near his master, and then brag about "I'm the only Negro out here." "I'm the only one on my job." "I'm the only one in this school." You're nothing but a house Negro. And if someone comes to you right now and says, "Let's separate," you say the same thing that the house Negro said on the plantation. "What you mean, separate? From America, this good white man? Where you going to get a better job than you get here?" I mean, this is what you say. "I ain't left nothing in Africa," that's what you say. Why, you left your mind in Africa.

24   On that same plantation, there was the field Negro. The field Negroes —those were the masses. There were always more Negroes in the field than there were Negroes in the house. The Negro in the field caught hell. He ate leftovers. In the house they ate high up on the hog. The Negro in the field didn't get anything but what was left of the insides

of the hog. They call it "chitt'lings" nowadays. In those days they called them what they were—guts. That's what you were—gut-eaters. And some of you are still gut-eaters.

25   The field Negro was beaten from morning to night; he lived in a shack, in a hut; he wore old, castoff clothes. He hated his master. I say he hated his master. He was intelligent. That house Negro loved his master, but that field Negro—remember, they were in the majority, and they hated the master. When the house caught on fire, he didn't try to put it out; that field Negro prayed for a wind, for a breeze. When the master got sick, the field Negro prayed that he'd die. If someone came to the field Negro and said, "Let's separate, let's run," he didn't say "Where we going?" He'd say, "Any place is better than here." You've got field Negroes in America today. I'm a field Negro. The masses are the field Negroes. When they see this man's house on fire, you don't hear the little Negroes talking about "*our* government is in trouble." They say, "*The* government is in trouble." Imagine a Negro: "*Our* government"! I even heard one say "*our* astronauts." They won't even let him near the plant—and "*our* astronauts"! "*Our* Navy"—that's a Negro that is out of his mind, a Negro that is out of his mind.

26   Just as the slavemaster of that day used Tom, the house Negro, to keep the field Negroes in check, the same old slavemaster today has Negroes who are nothing but modern Uncle Toms, twentieth-century Uncle Toms, to keep you and me in check, to keep us under control, keep us passive and peaceful and nonviolent. That's Tom making you nonviolent. It's like when you go to the dentist, and the man's going to take your tooth. You're going to fight him when he starts pulling. So he squirts some stuff in your jaw called novocaine, to make you think they're not doing anything to you. So you sit there and because you've got all of that novocaine in your jaw, you suffer—peacefully. Blood running all down your jaw, and you don't know what's happening. Because someone has taught you to suffer—peacefully.

27   The white man does the same thing to you in the street, when he wants to put knots on your head and take advantage of you and not have to be afraid of your fighting back. To keep you from fighting back, he gets these old religious Uncle Toms to teach you and me, just like novocaine, to suffer peacefully. Don't stop suffering—just suffer peacefully. As Rev. Cleage pointed out, they say you should let your blood flow in the streets. This is a shame. You know he's a Christian preacher. If it's a shame to him, you know what it is to me.

28   There is nothing in our book, the Koran, that teaches us to suffer peacefully. Our religion teaches us to be intelligent. Be peaceful, be courteous, obey the law, respect everyone; but if someone puts his hand on you, send him to the cemetery. That's a good religion. In fact, that's that old-time religion. That's the one that Ma and Pa

used to talk about: an eye for an eye, and a tooth for a tooth, and a head for a head, and a life for a life. That's a good religion. And nobody resents that kind of religion being taught but a wolf, who intends to make you his meal.

29   This is the way it is with the white man in America. He's a wolf— and you're sheep. Any time a shepherd, a pastor, teaches you and me not to run from the white man and, at the same time, teaches us not to fight the white man, he's a traitor to you and me. Don't lay down a life all by itself. No, preserve your life, it's the best thing you've got. And if you've got to give it up, let it be even-steven.

30   The slavemaster took Tom and dressed him well, fed him well and even gave him a little education—a *little* education; gave him a long coat and a top hat and made all the other slaves look up to him. Then he used Tom to control them. The same strategy that was used in those days is used today, by the same white man. He takes a Negro, a so-called Negro, and makes him prominent, builds him up, publicizes him, makes him a celebrity. And then he becomes a spokesman for Negroes— and a Negro leader.

31   I would like to mention just one other thing quickly, and that is the method that the white man uses, how the white man uses the "big guns," or Negro leaders, against the Negro revolution. They are not a part of the Negro revolution. They are used against the Negro revolution.

32   When Martin Luther King failed to desegregate Albany, Georgia, the civil-rights struggle in America reached its low point. King became bankrupt almost, as a leader. The Southern Christian Leadership Conference was in financial trouble; and it was in trouble, period, with the people when they failed to desegregate Albany, Georgia. Other Negro civil-rights leaders of so-called national stature became fallen idols. As they became fallen idols, began to lose their prestige and influence, local Negro leaders began to stir up the masses. In Cambridge, Maryland, Gloria Richardson; in Danville, Virginia, and other parts of the country, local leaders began to stir up our people at the grass-roots level. This was never done by these Negroes of national stature. They control you, but they have never incited you or excited you. They control you, they contain you, they have kept you on the plantation.

33   As soon as King failed in Birmingham, Negroes took to the streets. King went out to California to a big rally and raised I don't know how many thousands of dollars. He came to Detroit and had a march and raised some more thousands of dollars. And recall, right after that Roy Wilkins attacked King. He accused King and CORE [Congress Of Racial Equality] of starting trouble everywhere and then making the NAACP [National Association for the Advancement of Colored People] get them out of jail and spend a lot of money; they accused King and CORE of raising all the money and not paying it back.

This happened; I've got it in documented evidence in the newspaper. Roy started attacking King, and King started attacking Roy, and Farmer started attacking both of them. And as these Negroes of national stature began to attack each other, they began to lose their control of the Negro masses.

34   The Negroes were out there in the streets. They were talking about how they were going to march on Washington. Right at that time Birmingham had exploded, and the Negroes in Birmingham— remember, they also exploded. They began to stab the crackers in the back and bust them up 'side their head—yes, they did. That's when Kennedy sent in the troops, down in Birmingham. After that, Kennedy got on the television and said "this is a moral issue." That's when he said he was going to put out a civil-rights bill. And when he mentioned civil-rights bill and the Southern crackers started talking about how they were going to boycott or filibuster it, then the Negroes started talking—about what? That they were going to march on Washington, march on the Senate, march on the White House, march on the Congress, and tie it up, bring it to a halt, not let the government proceed. They even said they were going out to the airport and lay down on the runway and not let any airplanes land. I'm telling you what they said. That was revolution. That was revolution. That was the black revolution.

35   It was the grass roots out there in the street. It scared the white man to death, scared the white power structure in Washington, D.C., to death; I was there. When they found out that this black steamroller was going to come down on the capital, they called in Wilkins, they called in Randolph, they called in these national Negro leaders that you respect and told them, "Call it off." Kennedy said, "Look, you all are letting this thing go too far." And Old Tom said, "Boss, I can't stop it, because I didn't start it." I'm telling you what they said. They said, "I'm not even in it, much less at the head of it." They said, "These Negroes are doing things on their own. They're running ahead of us." And that old shrewd fox, he said, "If you all aren't in it, I'll put you in it. I'll put you at the head of it. I'll endorse it. I'll welcome it. I'll help it. I'll join it."

36   A matter of hours went by. They had a meeting at the Carlyle Hotel in New York City. The Carlyle Hotel is owned by the Kennedy family; that's the hotel Kennedy spent the night at, two nights ago; it belongs to his family. A philanthropic society headed by a white man named Stephen Currier called all the top civil-rights leaders together at the Carlyle Hotel. And he told them, "By you all fighting each other, you are destroying the civil-rights movement. And since you're fighting over money from white liberals, let us set up what is known as the Council for United Civil Rights Leadership. Let's form this council, and all the civil-rights organizations will belong to it, and we'll use it for fund-raising purposes." Let me show you how tricky the white man

is. As soon as they got it formed, they elected Whitney Young as its chairman, and who do you think became the co-chairman? Stephen Currier, the white man, a millionaire. Powell was talking about it down at Cobo Hall today. This is what he was talking about. Powell knows it happened. Randolph knows it happened. Wilkins knows it happened. King knows it happened. Every one of that Big Six—they know it happened.

37   Once they formed it, with the white man over it, he promised them and gave them $800,000 to split up among the Big Six; and told them that after the march was over, they'd give them $700,000 more. A million and a half dollars—split up between leaders that you have been following, going to jail for, crying crocodile tears for. And they're nothing but Frank James and Jesse James and the what-do-you-call-'em brothers.

38   As soon as they got the setup organized, the white man made available to them top public-relations experts; opened the news media across the country at their disposal, which then began to project these Big Six as the leaders of the march. Originally they weren't even in the march. You were talking this march talk on Hastings Street, you were talking march talk on Lenox Avenue, and on Fillmore Street, and on Central Avenue, and 32nd Street and 63rd Street. That's where the march talk was being talked. But the white man put the Big Six at the head of it; made them the march. They became the march. They took it over. And the first move they made after they took it over, they invited Walter Reuther, a white man; they invited a priest, a rabbi, and an old white preacher, yes, an old white preacher. The same white element that put Kennedy into power—labor, the Catholics, the Jews, and liberal Protestants; the same clique that put Kennedy in power, joined the march on Washington.

39   It's just like when you've got some coffee that's too black, which means it's too strong. What do you do? You integrate it with cream, you make it weak. But if you pour too much cream in it, you won't even know you ever had coffee. It used to be hot, it becomes cool. It used to be strong, it becomes weak. It used to wake you up, now it puts you to sleep. This is what they did with the march on Washington. They joined it. They didn't integrate it, they infiltrated it. They joined it, became a part of it, took it over. And as they took it over, it lost its militancy. It ceased to be angry, it ceased to be hot, it ceased to be uncompromising. Why, it even ceased to be a march. It became a picnic, a circus. Nothing but a circus, with clowns and all. You had one right here in Detroit—I saw it on television—with clowns leading it, white clowns and black clowns. I know you don't like what I'm saying, but I'm going to tell you anyway. Because I can prove what I'm saying. If you think I'm telling you wrong, you bring me Martin Luther King and A. Philip Randolph and James Farmer and those other three, and see if they'll deny it over a microphone.

40   No, it was a sellout. It was a takeover. When James Baldwin came
in from Paris, they wouldn't let him talk, because they couldn't make
him go by the script. Burt Lancaster read the speech that Baldwin
was supposed to make: they wouldn't let Baldwin get up there, because
they know Baldwin is liable to say anything. They controlled it so
tight, they told those Negroes what time to hit town, how to come,
where to stop, what signs to carry, what song to sing, what speech they
could make, and what speech they couldn't make; and then told them
to get out of town by sundown. And every one of those Toms was out
of town by sundown. Now I know you don't like my saying this. But
I can back it up. It was a circus, a performance that beat anything
Hollywood could ever do, the performance of the year. Reuther and
those other three devils should get an Academy Award for the best
actors because they acted like they really loved Negroes and fooled a
whole lot of Negroes. And the six Negro leaders should get an award
too, for the best supporting cast.

Discussion of Theme
1. What is the real basis of unity among black people, according to
   Malcolm X? What or who is the common enemy?
2. Why does Malcolm say that the Negro Revolution is not a true
   revolution? Why do you think he makes fun of the concept?
3. What is Malcolm X's attitude toward violence?
4. Why, according to the author, must white blood be shed? Do you
   agree?
5. What seems to be the purpose of this speech?

Discussion of Rhetoric
1. How formal is Malcolm X's style? Does it fit his audience?
2. Was your reaction to this article conditioned by *what* was said, or
   by *how* it was said?
3. Notice the repetition of the word *problem* in the first paragraph.
   Is this effective, or merely monotonous?
4. To what effect does Malcolm X use humor? Is there evidence he
   is at times having a private laugh at either himself or his audience?
5. Consider two analogies made by the speaker, one in paragraph 26
   and one in paragraph 39. Are they equally effective? Explain.
6. Are there any weaknesses in Malcolm's argument?

Writing Assignments
1. Many black—and white—radical leaders have said that there will
   be violence in this country until the races have achieved mutual

understanding or accord. Do you agree? Give your views in a theme.
2. Many people regard Malcolm X as a hero or saint; others regard him as a demagogue. What is your own view?
3. What are the arguments for (or against) a black separatist movement?

Library Exploration
Read *The Autobiography of Malcolm X* to learn more about this leader and his ideas.

Vocabulary
uncouth (9): ill-mannered
Uhuru (16): freedom (Swahili)
philanthropic (36): devoted to efforts to promote human welfare

53

THIS IS THE LOOSE-PAINT GENERATION

Douglas M. Davis

Painters of the loose-paint generation have moved away from conceptual, object-like art forms toward expressive, more intuitive ones. Once again, they take pride in the act of painting.

1   The new painting proves the old adage: The more things change, the more they stay the same. A great many young painters are now embarking on a path that is "new" in certain physical ways. But the central idea behind what they do is familiar, by now almost traditional, if not precisely "old." They all come round to expressing it, sooner or later, while discussing their work, each man in his own terms. What they mean as a group is what Tom Holland, a young Californian, means when he says: "I don't have a very intellectual approach. . . . I take a material for what it is. I let each painting make its own demands."

2   In their eyes, in other words, painting is as much a physical act as an intellectual act. This is precisely the position that grounded that most important—and American—of postwar art movements, known as abstract expressionism. A movement that has been under relentless attack throughout the past decade, by artists, critics, and the lay public. In the face of it all, however, in the face of Pop, Op, Minimal Art, and everything related to it, "AE," in one limited but important sense, is back.

3   A whole new generation of artists in their 20s and early 30s is looking back to those days, and to its heroes, with reverence. They speak in awed terms not of Barnett Newman and Donald Judd and Frank Stella, their precursors, but of Jackson Pollock, Willem De Kooning, Clifford Still, Adolph Gottlieb, Jules Olitski, Morris Louis, and Helen Frankenthaler. Along with the awe comes a definite sense of release, joy, and exuberance. After a decade of "cool," carefully planned art, it is all right once again to "let go," to enjoy the physical act of applying paint to canvas as the moment or the mood dictates.

4   "We're freeing ourselves," says Linda Benglis, a New York artist, "from the idea that painting has to be an idea. There are lots of painters working with sprays now, totally involved in nothing more than the intensity of spraying. They're going wild."

'GREENBERG'S GLIMPSES'

5   She adds, quite significantly: "We're no longer involved with
Greenberg's glimpses." By "Greenberg," she means Clement Greenberg, the influential critic who put abstract expressionism, and particularly Jackson Pollock, on the map. Throughout the 1950s, however,
Mr. Greenberg moved toward a far more rigorous, logically oriented
view of art. His comments tended to deprecate the place of illusion in
painting, as well as "self-expression" or the evidence of the painterly
process—such as the brush stroke—on the surface of the canvas.
Quality painting began, he seemed to say, with a recognition that the
canvas is a flat, two-dimensional object, nothing more.

6   Then came *Post-Painterly Abstraction*, a show organized by Mr.
Greenberg at the Los Angeles County Museum in 1959. This show, a
triumphant expression of Mr. Greenberg's new line, set the stage for
the next decade in American art. Barely a brush stroke showed in
Post-Painterly Abstraction; the surfaces were smooth and flat, as if
the pigment had been applied by machine, not hand. More important,
these painters organized color largely in geometric terms, through
stripes, triangles, and circles. The results looked more like objects
than paintings in the sense of abstract impressionism. It wasn't long
before the swing from canvas to objects became complete, first in the
shaped canvases of Frank Stella, then in the three-dimensional object
sculpture of Donald Judd and countless other painters.

7   Now they march in reverse. Now the old Greenbergian laws are
being openly flouted. "This is the loose-paint generation," says
Sam Gilliam, a Washington, D.C., painter. "Sure my paintings suggest
other things," says Linda Benglish, striking directly at the law against
illusion, "but they're not just about being objects." "I agree with
Ezra Pound," says Brice Marden, a New Yorker. "He said poems come
from feelings. Emotion is the lasting thing in art." And Dan Christensen, a New York painter out of Kansas City, takes the final step. When
reminded that the turn to sculpture came during the 1960s because
of a dissatisfaction with the quiet, almost effete qualities of painting,
he replies: "That's right. I'm decorative, like Matisse. A painting
can't overwhelm you, like light shows or movies. You just look at them,
that's all. But that's pleasure, isn't it?"

NO PERMANENT REVOLUTION

8   Not that the new painting's break with the work preceding it should
be overstressed, as it has been by commentators eager to see the history
of art as a kind of permanent revolution, one style rising to obliterate
the other. In fact the major difference between this work and classic
AE are certain habits, forms, and ideas directly derived from the
Greenberg-Stella-Judd axis. There is still alive in American painting
a certain distaste for "self-expression," a certain devotion to large,

monochromatic fields of color, a certain hard, intellectual edge to theory.

9   These characteristics are especially strong in three of the younger artists whose work represents a kind of middle ground between the old "cool," if you will, and the new "warm": Robert Huot, Brice Marden, and Richard Tuttle. Mr. Huot in particular is engaged in a kind of devastating play with the Greenbergian ideology, rather than frontal assault. *Orange Boon*, a huge painting, twelve feet long, curves, at one end, into the wall, "eliminating," as he says, "the candy box structure." Another way of looking at it, of course, is to see it as a deadpan, literal realization of Mr. Greenberg's insistence on flatness.

10   A number of painters have played with the same motif, some by covering their canvases with smooth, deadpan fields of white paint. Mr. Huot goes a step further, by stretching a translucent nylon surface across his frame. "The nylon took the painting's clothes off," he says, "and let the wall show through. The next thing to do was paint on the wall." Which Mr. Huot now does, using one solid color, usually blue, in galleries, homes of his friends, anywhere he can find a "canvas." He has begun as well to make "paintings" out of shadows cast on a wall, and I-beams projecting from the wall, painted on the underside with brass in acrylic resin.

11   "Painters have been too much involved with making objects," he says. "That's a cop-out: They're not fat enough to be decent objects. I decided to eliminate the object and just get back to painting itself."

12   Despite his breakthroughs, Robert Huot is still a basically conceptual artist, as much in the Greenberg-Judd tradition as outside it. Brice Marden is a step further away. Like Mr. Huot, he works with large, monochromatic areas of color, but the closer you get to his paintings the more painterly activity you find, as well as complexity. He applies the pigment with a brush, though the result is a smooth, fine surface that appears to be sprayed. He draws upon this surface with a knife, however, creating tiny lines that appear to be accidental scratches—when you see them. A moment's reflection reminds you that they have to be intentional, as is the even more tell-tale bottom edge of the canvas, which is anything but smooth: It reveals a series of random drips, in the old abstract-expressionist manner, a series Mr. Marden makes way for by leaving the bottom line unprimed, allowing the paint above it to drip down.

THE GENERATION GAP

13   Why? Mr. Marden's answer goes to the heart of the main difference between his generation and the one that preceded him. "The dripped edge keeps the painting from looking mechanical," he says. "When you see it, you know the work was done by hand, with a brush. And the

scratches, they keep the painting coarse. Also more complicated. The farther away you are, the more you think it's an object, not a surface. As you get closer, you change your mind. I'm beginning to work with color in that way, too, putting on a gray, for example, that under certain conditions shows up green, so you aren't sure about the color at all. These aren't quick paintings. But art isn't fast, I think."

14   Barnett Newman once said, speaking about the cool, monochromatic works that started Minimal Art: "The impact had to be total, immediate, at once." Brice Marden clearly has an opposite goal in mind, even though he continues to work within the context of a Newmanesque color field. He wants his work to have another tone, in part, which he gets at by using the adjective "coarse." It is a bit strong, but it points in the right direction. The new painting has in common a certain looseness or roughness, an informality that directly challenges the traditional art and the formality of the art that followed Newman.

15   In this sense, it is related to what has been called "Soft Sculpture" and "Process Art." The relationship varies greatly in degree, however, and must not be oversimplified. In a painter like Richard Tuttle, the relationship is extremely close. Mr. Tuttle often has been grouped in certain museum shows with "process" artists who work in three dimensions—with Alan Saret, for example, who makes sculpture out of scrappy, informal groupings of chicken wire; with Richard Serra, who mixes long blocks of lead with pieces of tin, or splashes liquid lead against a wall; and with Barry Le Va, who freely scatters metal filings about the floor. All these are done in the name of sculpture, however, and all are derived from the freewheeling use of "soft" materials like vinyl and felt in the earlier work of sculptors Claes Oldenburg and Robert Morris.

16   What Richard Tuttle has done is to take a canvas off its stretcher, dye it, and leave to the gallery or the collector the decision about where to put it. Most often they decide to tack it up on a wall, as they did, much to his dismay, at the Corcoran Biennial, held last winter in Washington, D.C. "I was upset when I saw the works there," he recalls. "But I decided that if I want the determination of this work to be made by others, I have to abide by their decisions. What I'm trying to do is to make a work that can go anywhere, that you can hold in your hand, if you like. I want to make a painting like a poem, and a poem can go anywhere."

17   Wherever you put it, a Tuttle painting is still a painting, and he still thinks of himself as a painter. His slim, flimsy pieces of cloth—"like the wall"—he says, "but not the wall"—are fetchingly dyed as well in bright pinks, greens, and blues, sensual delights despite themselves. More importantly, they are made the way they appear to be made,

as an act rather than a plan. "My color is so intuitive I forget what my pieces look like until I see them hung in the gallery," he says. "More than that I can't bring myself to do."

18   There are touches of Mr. Tuttle's determined informality throughout the new painting, but the results, in the main, are more sensuous than either he, Mr. Marden, or Mr. Huot yet allow. The real warmth begins to show in a painter like Tom Holland, the Californian. "My roots are back in abstract expressionism," he admits, right off. "Painting is an experience with me, and it's always unplanned. Basically because I studied at Berkeley under David Park, whose attitude toward oil has always influenced me, though he was a figurative painter. I used to watch him buy oil in quarts and gallons and smear it on the canvas with his hands, then attack with brushes."

19   This strong physical tie with the materials of painting is still in Tom Holland, though he no longer works either with oil or with canvas. He turned to glass fiber two years ago, in the search for what he calls a "slick" material. At first he cut the glass fiber into rough, gridlike formats, upon which he applied epoxy paint—in mixtures, forms, and colors that were equally rough, presenting a surface almost De Kooning-like. Across these early Hollands were occasionally stretched long, loose chains and rings of color, the whole construction hanging with supreme insouciance from the wall. His paint now, always, is epoxy. "Glass fiber is indestructible," he says, "and epoxy is the only thing that will stick to it. Epoxy feels like a real material, and you can mix any combination you want. You can wash my painting, shove it, bend it, and it stays the same. I usually dry brush twelve layers of color, one over another, until I get the rough appearance I want."

A SHEET OF COLOR

20   The new Holland paintings are slimmer and smoother. The form is a kind of envelope, into which he inserts strips of colored glass fiber, so that the painting appears to be nothing more than a sheet of color, more like a traditional painting. He is very insistent upon this point for everything he has done, including the object-like grid paintings. "I build the piece beforehand," he says, "but then the problem is putting something on it that dominates it. I'm not involved with decorating an object, but making a painting."

21   Which means, in Tom Holland's eyes, that the act of application, whatever the material, is the important act. This may well be the major —perhaps only—distinction between painting and sculpture in a time when the two frequently converge. The "warmer" you get in the new painting, the more crucial that act of application becomes. For Sam Gilliam, a native Mississippian who now works in Washington, it is clearly everything. He applies paint—acrylic paint—in unconventional ways, to say the least. At first he was an orthodox "color painter"

in the geometrical Washington tradition of Kenneth Noland, Gene Davis, and Tom Downing. Of late his canvases have begun to take on the freer, more expressive forms characteristic of the late Morris Louis, the first of the color painters. Like Louis, Mr. Gilliam pours the quick-drying acrylics onto his canvases, which are normally laid out unstretched across the floor. He will brush and sponge the colors, too, in order to achieve certain patterns and forms of color.

22   About two years ago, however, Mr. Gilliam went even further in the pursuit of freedom. He began to fold his canvases while they were still wet, so that the colors rub and smear each other, creating a complex, run-together effect. In his latest shows, moreover, he has moved in the same direction as Richard Tuttle, by hanging his canvas unstretched. There are major differences, though between the effect of a loose, floppy Tuttle and a similar Gilliam. The latter's are far larger: *Swing*, exhibited recently at the Jefferson Place Gallery in Washington is almost 30 feet long; it is hung very much like a huge piece of drapery on rawhide thongs, not on the wall. The viewer "enters" a Gilliam almost as he would enter a room.

23   Finally, there is an unabashed sensuality about Mr. Gilliam's work. He works with bright, striking acrylic colors, that, because of their smooth, staining qualities, call attention to themselves as colors not as surface. Frequently Mr. Gilliam will apply flecks of thin gold pigment over his canvas, making it dance with a kind of light all its own. Or he will hang a particularly radiant painting in front of a window, so that the painting appears lighted from inside itself. On stretcher or off, a Gilliam painting is much more than "loose paint," his own term. Like a Louis or a De Kooning it is a strongly sensual experience.

24   It is this willingness to return to the strength of traditional painting—to the creation of colorful, complicated, and pleasing surfaces—that best isolates the new painting, not only from Minimal Art, but from process sculptures like the Messrs. Serra, Saret, Le Va, Morris, and Oldenburg. The new painting to put it another way, is not afraid to be "pretty" in orthodox terms. It is no accident that Brice Marden refers to himself as a "very traditional painter," and asks: "Why not paint like everybody else has painted?" Dan Christensen, who lives and works in New York, talks much the same way. "I'm a traditional painter. I don't think I've made anything new at all. Noland's format may be more radical, but he's just making pictures too. I'm an armchair artist, like Matisse. Painting is for pleasure. It's like listening to music, that's all."

25   Mr. Christensen is one of the many artists now "going wild" with spray cans, to borrow Linda Benglis' words. Until two years ago he worked with a brush, creating hard-edge, geometrical forms. "I was making very close value paintings," he says, "with two or three colors. I started to spray because I could 'dust' two or three colors onto a

surface without seeming to separate them with a brush stroke. Then I got into the spray itself."

26   The recent Christensen paintings betray the evidence of how they are made. The edges of the new forms are soft and hazy; the forms themselves are circular and swooping, as if they had been sprayed in a graceful, spraying motion. They all have a filmy quality, as though you are looking at them through a kind of haze or filter. This results from the Christensen method: He begins by wetting his canvas with a detergentlike substance, then spraying over it, the combination producing a "soapy" color. He works on several paintings at once, on huge strips of canvas spread upon the floor. Each day he concentrates on a single color, spraying a little on each picture. He applies as many as ten coats of paint to his large paintings, which end by presenting an ocean of colors, some piled deeply upon each other.

MAKING MORE DECISIONS

27   Needless to say, he has discarded careful planning in the process, but not completely to avoid control. "In some ways, you find yourself making more decisions, not less, this way," he says. "I used to work from one clear plan. Now I have to make a new plan each step of the way." William Pettet, another of the "wild" sprayers, feels the same way. "I try to let my structure grow out of the paintings themselves," he says. "But as I interact with the colors, I do so with all the knowledge that is built into me, a knowledge of what painting has been in the past."

28   The work of Mr. Pettet, a Californian moved to New York, has often been compared with Jules Olitski's, which took spray painting into large, open forms during the early 1960s. But in fact he was first influenced on the West Coast by Billy Al Bengston, who sprayed but in a way that made the process indistinguishable in the finished product. "There are some spray paintings," Dan Christensen says, "where you can't tell whether the brush or the spray was involved." The contribution of Messrs. Olitski, Christensen, and Pettet has been to exploit the spray fully. Mr. Pettet began in 1965 with dry sprays, lots of air mixed with the pigment, on dry canvas. Then he tried saturating his canvas with water tension breaker, spreading it across a large table, and spraying "wet" colors upon it. Finally, he discovered that after the application, he could "paint," in effect, with "air"—by spraying from an empty can and moving the wet colors around by the force of the spray alone.

29   The result can only be described as "clouds" of soft, misty colors. They are not so bright as an Olitski, less structured than a Christensen, but beautiful. "The remarkable thing about a spray gun," says Mr. Pettet, "is that it attacks the surface very delicately. I can put a wet

color on top of a wet color without disturbing it at all. Also, I can spray large areas of space in a short time, without stopping to load a brush, you might say. The spray allows me to stay with the whole canvas over a much longer period."

PAINTING WITH FLAME

30   If William Pettet paints with air, Linda Benglis does so with flame, among other things. She works with many innovative mixtures, one of which combines pigment, wax, and resin, on a masonite surface. After the mixture hardens, she uses flame to "move" the colors around. "I'm fascinated with the way the colors melt and dissolve," she says. "It marbleizes the image, when you're through. They're also very intense, sensuous paintings, which disturbs some people."

31   Even more disturbing, for some, are her "floor" paintings, made by pouring a mixture of pigment and liquid rubber on the floor. She uses bright, sharply defined colors, that, though they occasionally run into and over each other, remain sharply defined in the final product. The mixture is self-vulcanizing and hardens after three weeks: The pigment thus turns into its own medium. Although a Benglis painting demands to be left where it began—on the floor, not the wall—she insists that it is primarily a painting. "I like the idea of floating these very colorful images on the floor, and suspending them there. It is in no sense an object. If anything, it's an image."

32   Miss Benglis and her seven colleagues are by no means the only artists involved in this new direction. They are allied in various ways with countless painters both their own age and beyond. The work of Larry Poons and Michael Goldberg, both in their 40s, to mention just two names, has been crucial to the new painting. The change in Mr. Poon's work, away from carefully constructed canvases toward looser, freer structures, has been especially influential. But taken as a group, the eight fairly represent a strong, coherent tendency in American art today, a tendency that, despite its variety and contradiction, means one inescapable thing: Painting—the act of applying one material onto another—is alive once more. Only time can indicate whether this fact represents a renaissance rather than a reaction, for the new painting must yet prove itself over the long esthetic run, must prove in particular that its loose, physical methodology can produce work that will stand as well as Barnett Newman's say, or Willem De Kooning's.

33   For the moment, however, these younger artists are changing the habits of a decade. In lofts, colleges, and art schools throughout the country, an old pleasure is being rediscovered, a pleasure that William Pettet best defines when he talks about why he prefers painting to sculpture: "Sculpture takes a great deal of forethought and complica-

tion. The directness and simplicity of a roll and canvas and a bottle of paint really appeals to me. It's easy to paint. People are doing it every Sunday. I like to think about that."

Discussion of Theme

1. Explain the following statements. "Painting is as much a physical act as an intellectual act" (paragraph 2). "Quality painting began, he [Greenberg] seemed to say, with a recognition that the canvas is a flat, two-dimensional object, nothing more" (paragraph 5).
2. How is the new painting different from the style of painting that preceded it? How is it similar?
3. What is Process Art? Soft Sculpture?

Discussion of Rhetoric

1. For whom was this article written: artists, interested laymen, or the general public?
2. Is this article primarily exposition or is the author trying to influence the reader's opinion? To what extent does he use description to support his statements?
3. What are some of the ways Mr. Davis uses comparison and contrast?
4. Many articles on art are difficult to read because they contain jargon or specialized language. Find examples of each in this article.

Writing Assignments

1. What kind of art do you prefer? Name several artists whose work is of the kind you like; describe and evaluate their painting.
2. What constitutes beauty? Is it truly in the eye of the beholder?
3. Should everyone be required to take an art-appreciation course in college? Give your views in a theme.

Library Exploration

1. Find and study reproductions of the works of Jackson Pollock, Willem de Kooning, and Helen Frankenthaler.
2. What are AE, Pop art, Op art, and Minimal art?

Vocabulary

precursors (3): forerunners; predecessors
deprecate (5): depreciate; represent as of little value
flouted (7): scorned
effete (7): weak; decadent
axis (8): alliance
insouciance (19): nonchalance; lighthearted unconcern

54

NOTES ON CAMP

Susan Sontag

The following discourse on the character and characteristics of Camp was written by the person who made the term famous.

1   Many things in the world have not been named; and many things, even if they have been named, have never been described. One of these is the sensibility—unmistakably modern, a variant of sophistication but hardly identical with it—that goes by the cult name of "Camp."

2   A sensibility (as distinct from an idea) is one of the hardest things to talk about; but there are special reasons why Camp, in particular, has never been discussed. It is not a natural mode of sensibility, if there be any such. Indeed the essence of Camp is its love of the unnatural: of artifice and exaggeration. And Camp is esoteric—something of a private code, a badge of identity even, among small urban cliques. Apart from a lazy two-page sketch in Christopher Isherwood's novel *The World in the Evening* (1954), it has hardly broken into print. To talk about Camp is therefore to betray it. If the betrayal can be defended, it will be for the edification it provides, or the dignity of the conflict it resolves. For myself, I plead the goal of self-edification, and the goad of a sharp conflict in my own sensibility. I am strongly drawn to Camp, and almost as strongly offended by it. That is why I want to talk about it, and why I can. For no one who wholeheartedly shares in a given sensibility can analyze it; he can only, whatever his intention, exhibit it. To name a sensibility, to draw its contours and to recount its history, requires a deep sympathy modified by revulsion.

3   Though I am speaking about sensibility only—and about a sensibility that, among other things, converts the serious into the frivolous— these are grave matters. Most people think of sensibility or taste as the realm of purely subjective preferences, those mysterious attractions, mainly sensual, that have not been brought under the sovereignty of reason. They *allow* that considerations of taste play a part in their reactions to people and to works of art. But this attitude is naïve. And even worse. To patronize the faculty of taste is to patronize oneself. For taste governs every free—as opposed to rote—human response. Nothing is more decisive. There is taste in people, visual taste, taste in

emotion—and there is taste in acts, taste in morality. Intelligence, as well, is really a kind of taste: taste in ideas. (One of the facts to be reckoned with is that taste tends to develop very unevenly. It's rare that the same person has good visual taste *and* good taste in people *and* taste in ideas.)

4   Taste has no system and no proofs. But there is something like a logic of taste: the consistent sensibility which underlies and gives rise to a certain taste. A sensibility is almost, but not quite, ineffable. Any sensibility which can be crammed into the mold of a system, or handled with the rough tools of proof, is no longer a sensibility at all. It has hardened into an idea. . . .

5   To snare a sensibility in words, especially one that is alive and power-ful,[1] one must be tentative and nimble. The form of jottings, rather than an essay (with its claim to a linear, consecutive argument), seemed more appropriate for getting down something of this particular fugitive sensibility. It's embarrassing to be solemn and treatise-like about Camp. One runs the risk of having, oneself, produced a very inferior piece of Camp.

6   These notes are for Oscar Wilde.

"One should either be a work of art, or wear a work of art."
                                    —*Phrases & Philosophies for the Use of the Young*

7   1. To start very generally: Camp is a certain mode of aestheticism. It is *one* way of seeing the world as an aesthetic phenomenon. That way, the way of Camp, is not in terms of beauty, but in terms of the degree of artifice, of stylization.

8   2. To emphasize style is to slight content, or to introduce an attitude which is neutral with respect to content. It goes without saying that the Camp sensibility is disengaged, depoliticized—or at least apolitical.

9   3. Not only is there a Camp vision, a Camp way of looking at things. Camp is as well a quality discoverable in objects and the behavior of persons. There are "campy" movies, clothes, furniture, popular songs, novels, people, buildings. . . . This distinction is important. True, the Camp eye has the power to transform experience. But not everything can be seen as Camp. It's not *all* in the eye of the beholder.

10   4. Random examples of items which are part of the canon of Camp:

> *Zuleika Dobson*
> Tiffany lamps
> Scopitone films

[1]The sensibility of an era is not only its most decisive, but also its most perishable, aspect. One may capture the ideas (intellectual history) and the behavior (social history) of an epoch without ever touching upon the sensibility or taste which informed those ideas, that behavior. Rare are those historical studies—like Huizinga on the late Middle Ages, Febvre on 16th-century France—which do tell us something about the sensibility of the period.

The Brown Derby restaurant on Sunset Boulevard in LA
The Enquirer, headlines and stories
Aubrey Beardsley drawings
Swan Lake
Bellini's operas
Visconti's direction of *Salome* and *'Tis Pity She's a Whore*
certain turn-of-the-century picture postcards
Schoedsack's *King Kong*
the Cuban pop singer La Lupe
Lynn Ward's novel in woodcuts, *God's Man*
the old Flash Gordon comics
women's clothes of the twenties (feather boas, fringed and beaded dresses, etc.)
the novels of Ronald Firbank and Ivy Compton-Burnett
stag movies seen without lust

11   5. Camp taste has an affinity for certain arts rather than others. Clothes, furniture, all the elements of visual décor, for instance, make up a large part of Camp. For Camp art is often decorative art, emphasizing texture, sensuous surface, and style at the expense of content. Concert music, though, because it is contentless, is rarely Camp. It offers no opportunity, say, for a contrast between silly or extravagant content and rich form. . . . Sometimes whole art forms become saturated with Camp. Classical ballet, opera, movies have seemed so for a long time. In the last two years, popular music (post rock-'n'-roll, what the French call *yé yé*) has been annexed. And movie criticism (like lists of "The 10 Best Bad Movies I Have Seen") is probably the greatest popularizer of Camp taste today, because most people still go to the movies in a high-spirited and unpretentious way.

12   6. There is a sense in which it is correct to say: "It's too good to be Camp." Or "too important," not marginal enough. (More on this later.) Thus, the personality and many of the works of Jean Cocteau are Camp, but not those of André Gide; the operas of Richard Strauss, but not those of Wagner; concoctions of Tin Pan Alley and Liverpool, but not jazz. Many examples of Camp are things which, from a "serious" point of view, are either bad art or kitsch. Not all, though. Not only is Camp not necessarily bad art, but some art which can be approached as Camp (example: the major films of Louis Feuillade) merits the most serious admiration and study.

"The more we study Art, the less we care for Nature."
          — *The Decay of Lying*

13   7. All Camp objects, and persons, contain a large element of artifice. Nothing in nature can be campy. . . . Rural Camp is still man-made, and most campy objects are urban. (Yet, they often have a serenity—

or a naïveté—which is the equivalent of pastoral. A great deal of Camp suggests Empson's phrase, "urban pastoral.")

14   8. Camp is a vision of the world in terms of style—but a particular kind of style. It is the love of the exaggerated, the "off," of things-being-what-they-are-not. The best example is in Art Nouveau, the most typical and fully developed Camp style. Art Nouveau objects, typically, convert one thing into something else: the lighting fixtures in the form of flowering plants, the living room which is really a grotto. A remarkable example, the Paris Métro entrances designed by Hector Guimard in the late 1890s in the shape of cast-iron orchid stalks.

15   9. As a taste in persons, Camp responds particularly to the markedly attenuated and to the strongly exaggerated. The androgyne is certainly one of the great images of Camp sensibility. Examples: the swooning, slim, sinuous figures of pre-Raphaelite painting and poetry; the thin, flowing, sexless bodies in Art Nouveau prints and posters, presented in relief on lamps and ashtrays; the haunting androgynous vacancy behind the perfect beauty of Greta Garbo. Here, Camp taste draws on a mostly unacknowledged truth of taste: the most refined form of sexual attractiveness (as well as the most refined form of sexual pleasure) consists in going against the grain of one's sex. What is most beautiful in virile men is something feminine; what is most beautiful in feminine women is something masculine. . . . Allied to the Camp taste for the androgynous is something that seems quite different but isn't: a relish for the exaggeration of sexual characteristics and personality mannerisms. For obvious reasons, the best examples that can be cited are movie stars. The corny flamboyant femaleness of Jayne Mansfield, Gina Lollobrigida, Jane Russell, Virginia Mayo; the exaggerated he-man-ness of Steve Reeves, Victor Mature. The great stylists of tempera-ment and mannerism, like Bette Davis, Barbara Stanwyck, Tallulah Bankhead, Edwige Feuillière.

16   10. Camp sees everything in quotation marks. It's not a lamp, but a "lamp"; not a woman, but a "woman." To perceive Camp in objects and persons is to understand Being-as-Playing-a-Role. It is the farthest extension, in sensibility, of the metaphor of life as theater.

17   11. Camp is the triumph of the epicene style. (The convertibility of "man" and "woman," "person" and "thing.") But all style, that is, artifice, is, ultimately, epicene. Life is not stylish. Neither is nature.

18   12. The question isn't, "Why travesty, impersonation, theat-ricality?" The question is, rather, "When does travesty, impersonation, theatricality acquire the special flavor of Camp?" Why is the atmo-sphere of Shakespeare's comedies (*As You Like It*, etc.) not epicene, while that of *Der Rosenkavalier* is?

19   13. The dividing line seems to fall in the 18th century; there the

origins of Camp taste are to be found (Gothic novels, Chinoiserie, caricature, artificial ruins, and so forth.) But the relation to nature was quite different then. In the 18th century, people of taste either patronized nature (Strawberry Hill) or attempted to remake it into something artificial (Versailles). They also indefatigably patronized the past. Today's Camp taste effaces nature, or else contradicts it outright. And the relation of Camp taste to the past is extremely sentimental.

20   14. A pocket history of Camp might, of course, begin farther back— with the mannerist artists like Pontormo, Rosso, and Caravaggio, or the extraordinarily theatrical painting of Georges de La Tour, or Euphuism (Lyly, etc.) in literature. Still, the soundest starting point seems to be the late 17th and early 18th century, because of that period's extraordinary feeling for artifice, for surface, for symmetry; its taste for the picturesque and the thrilling, its elegant conventions for representing instant feeling and the total presence of character— the epigram and the rhymed couplet (in words), the flourish (in gesture and in music). The late 17th and early 18th century is the great period of Camp: Pope, Congreve, Walpole, etc., but not Swift; les précieux in France; the rococo churches of Munich; Pergolesi. Somewhat later: much of Mozart. But in the 19th century, what had been distributed throughout all of high culture now becomes a special taste; it takes on overtones of the acute, the esoteric, the perverse. Confining the story to England alone, we see Camp continuing wanly through 19th-century aestheticism (Burne-Jones, Pater, Ruskin, Tennyson), emerging full-blown with the Art Nouveau movement in the visual and decorative arts, and finding its conscious ideologists in such "wits" as Wilde and Firbank.

21   15. Of course, to say all these things are Camp is not to argue they are simply that. A full analysis of Art Nouveau, for instance, would scarcely equate it with Camp. But such an analysis cannot ignore what in Art Nouveau allows it to be experienced as Camp. Art Nouveau is full of "content," even of a political-moral sort; it was a revolutionary movement in the arts, spurred on by a utopian vision (somewhere between William Morris and the Bauhaus group) of an organic politics and taste. Yet there is also a feature of the Art Nouveau objects which suggests a disengaged, unserious, "aesthete's" vision. This tells us something important about Art Nouveau—and about what the lens of Camp, which blocks out content, is.

22   16. Thus, the Camp sensibility is one that is alive to a double sense in which some things can be taken. But this is not the familiar split-level construction of a literal meaning, on the one hand, and a symbolic meaning, on the other. It is the difference, rather, between the thing as meaning something, anything, and the thing as pure artifice.

23   17. This comes out clearly in the vulgar use of the word Camp as a verb, "to camp," something that people do. To camp is a mode of seduction—one which employs flamboyant mannerisms susceptible of a double interpretation; gestures full of duplicity, with a witty meaning for cognoscenti, and another, more impersonal, for outsiders. Equally and by extension, when the word becomes a noun, when a person or a thing is "a camp," a duplicity is involved. Behind the "straight" public sense in which something can be taken, one has found a private zany experience of the thing.

"To be natural is such a very difficult pose to keep up."

—An Ideal Husband

24   18. One must distinguish between naïve and deliberate Camp. Pure Camp is always naïve. Camp which knows itself to be Camp ("camping") is usually less satisfying.

25   19. The pure examples of Camp are unintentional; they are dead serious. The Art Nouveau craftsman who makes a lamp with a snake coiled around it is not kidding, nor is he trying to be charming. He is saying, in all earnestness: Violà! the Orient! Genuine Camp— for instance, the numbers devised for the Warner Brothers musicals of the early thirties (*42nd Street*; *The Golddiggers of 1933*; . . . *of 1935*; . . . *of 1937*; etc.) by Busby Berkeley—does not *mean* to be funny. Camping—say, the plays of Noel Coward—does. It seems unlikely that much of the traditional opera repertoire could be such satisfying Camp if the melodramatic absurdities of most opera plots had not been taken seriously by their composers. One doesn't need to know the artist's private intentions. The work tells all. (Compare a typical 19th-century opera with Samuel Barber's *Vanessa*, a piece of manufactured, calculated Camp, and the difference is clear.)

26   20. Probably, intending to be campy is always harmful. The perfection of *Trouble in Paradise* and *The Maltese Falcon*, among the greatest Camp movies ever made, comes from the effortless smooth way in which tone is maintained. This is not so with such famous would-be Camp films of the fifties as *All About Eve* and *Beat the Devil*. These more recent movies have their fine moments, but the first is so slick and the second so hysterical; they want so badly to be campy that they're continually losing the beat. . . . Perhaps, though, it is not so much a question of the unintended effect versus the conscious intention, as of the delicate relation between parody and self-parody in Camp. The films of Hitchcock are a showcase for this problem. When self-parody lacks ebullience but instead reveals (even sporadically) a contempt for one's themes and one's materials—as in *To Catch a Thief*, *Rear Window*, *North by Northwest*—the results are forced and heavy-handed, rarely Camp. Successful Camp—a movie like Carné's *Drôle de Drame*; the film performances of Mae West and

Edward Everett Horton; portions of the Goon Show—even when it reveals self-parody, reeks of self-love.

27   21. So, again, Camp rests on innocence. That means Camp discloses innocence, but also, when it can, corrupts it. Objects, being objects, don't change when they are singled out by the Camp vision. Persons, however, respond to their audiences. Persons begin "camping": Mae West, Bea Lillie, La Lupe, Tallulah Bankhead in *Lifeboat*, Bette Davis in *All About Eve*. (Persons can even be induced to camp without knowing it. Consider the way Fellini got Anita Ekberg to parody herself in *La Dolce Vita*.)

28   22. Considered a little less strictly, Camp is either completely naïve or else wholly conscious (when one plays at being campy). An example of the latter: Wilde's epigrams themselves.

"It's absurd to divide people into good and bad. People are either charming or tedious."
                                                      —*Lady Windemere's Fan*

29   23. In naïve, or pure, Camp, the essential element is seriousness, a seriousness that fails. Of course, not all seriousness that fails can be redeemed as Camp. Only that which has the proper mixture of the exaggerated, the fantastic, the passionate, and the naïve.

30   24. When something is just bad (rather than Camp), it's often because it is too mediocre in its ambition. The artist hasn't attempted to do anything really outlandish. ("It's too much," "It's too fantastic," "It's not to be believed," are standard phrases of Camp enthusiasm.)

31   25. The hallmark of Camp is the spirit of extravagance. Camp is a woman walking around in a dress made of three million feathers. Camp is the paintings of Carlo Crivelli, with their real jewels and *trompe-l'oeil* insects and cracks in the masonry. Camp is the outrageous aestheticism of Sternberg's six American movies with Dietrich, all six, but especially the last, *The Devil Is a Woman*. . . . In Camp there is often something *démesuré* in the quality of the ambition, not only in the style of the work itself. Gaudí's lurid and beautiful buildings in Barcelona are Camp not only because of their style but because they reveal—most notably in the Cathedral of the Sagrada Familia—the ambition on the part of one man to do what it takes a generation, a whole culture to accomplish.

32   26. Camp is art that proposes itself seriously, but cannot be taken altogether seriously because it is "too much." *Titus Andronicus* and *Strange Interlude* are almost Camp, or could be played as Camp. The public manner and rhetoric of de Gaulle, often, are pure Camp.

33   27. A work can come close to Camp, but not make it, because it succeeds. Eisenstein's films are seldom Camp because, despite all exaggeration, they do succeed (dramatically) without surplus. If

they were a little more "off," they could be great Camp—particularly *Ivan the Terrible I & II*. The same for Blake's drawings and paintings, weird and mannered as they are. They aren't Camp; though Art Nouveau, influenced by Blake, is.

34   What is extravagant in an inconsistent or an unpassionate way is not Camp. Neither can anything be Camp that does not seem to spring from an irrepressible, a virtually uncontrolled sensibility. Without passion, one gets pseudo-Camp—what is merely decorative, safe, in a word, chic. On the barren edge of Camp lie a number of attractive things: the sleek fantasies of Dali, the haute couture preciosity of Albicocco's *The Girl with the Golden Eyes*. But the two things— Camp and preciosity—must not be confused.

35   28. Again, Camp is the attempt to do something extraordinary. But extraordinary in the sense, often, of being special, glamorous. (The curved line, the extravagant gesture.) Not extraordinary merely in the sense of effort. Ripley's Believe-It-Or-Not items are rarely campy. These items, either natural oddities (the two-headed rooster, the egg-plant in the shape of a cross) or else the products of immense labor (the man who walked from here to China on his hands, the woman who engraved the New Testament on the head of a pin), lack the visual reward—the glamour, the theatricality—that marks off certain extravagances as Camp.

36   29. The reason a movie like *On the Beach*, books like *Winesburg, Ohio* and *For Whom the Bell Tolls* are bad to the point of being laugh-able, but not bad to the point of being enjoyable, is that they are too dogged and pretentious. They lack fantasy. There is Camp in such bad movies as *The Prodigal* and *Samson and Delilah*, the series of Italian color spectacles featuring the super-hero Maciste, numerous Japanese science fiction films (*Rodan, The Mysterians, The H-Man*) because, in their relative unpretentiousness and vulgarity, they are more ex-treme and irresponsible in their fantasy—and therefore touching and quite enjoyable.

37   30. Of course, the canon of Camp can change. Time has a great deal to do with it. Time may enhance what seems simply dogged or lacking in fantasy now because we are too close to it, because it resembles too closely our own everyday fantasies, the fantastic nature of which we don't perceive. We are better able to enjoy a fantasy as fantasy when it is not our own.

38   31. This is why so many of the objects prized by Camp taste are old-fashioned, out-of-date, *démodé*. It's not a love of the old as such. It's simply that the process of aging or deterioration provides the necessary detachment—or arouses a necessary sympathy. When the theme is important, and contemporary, the failure of a work of art may make us indignant. Time can change that. Time liberates the

work of art from moral relevance, delivering it over to the Camp sensibility. . . . Another effect: time contrasts the sphere of banality. (Banality is, strictly speaking, always a category of the contemporary.) What was banal can, with the passage of time, become fantastic. Many people who listen with delight to the style of Rudy Vallee revived by the English pop group, The Temperance Seven, would have been driven up the wall by Rudy Vallee in his heyday.

39 Thus, things are campy, not when they become old—but when we become less involved in them, and can enjoy, instead of be frustrated by, the failure of the attempt. But the effect of time is unpredictable. Maybe Method Acting (James Dean, Rod Steiger, Warren Beatty) will seem as Camp some day as Ruby Keeler's does now—or as Sarah Bernhardt's does, in the films she made at the end of her career. And maybe not.

40 32. Camp is the glorification of "character." The statement is of no importance—except, of course, to the person (Loie Fuller, Gaudí, Cecil B. De Mille, Crivelli, de Gaulle, etc.) who makes it. What the Camp eye appreciates is the unity, the force of the person. In every move the aging Martha Graham makes she's being Martha Graham, etc., etc. . . . This is clear in the case of the great serious idol of Camp taste, Greta Garbo. Garbo's incompetence (at the least, lack of depth) as an *actress* enhances her beauty. She's always herself.

41 33. What Camp taste responds to is "instant character" (this is, of course, very 18th century); and, conversely, what it is not stirred by is the sense of the development of character. Character is understood as a state of continual incandescence—a person being one, very intense thing. This attitude toward character is a key element of the theatricalization of experience embodied in the Camp sensibility. And it helps account for the fact that opera and ballet are experienced as such rich treasures of Camp, for neither of these forms can easily do justice to the complexity of human nature. Wherever there is development of character, Camp is reduced. Among operas, for example, *La Traviata* (which has some small development of character) is less campy than *Il Trovatore* (which has none).

"Life is too important a thing ever to talk seriously about it."

—Vera, or The Nihilists

42 34. Camp taste turns its back on the good-bad axis of ordinary aesthetic judgment. Camp doesn't reverse things. It doesn't argue that the good is bad, or the bad is good. What it does is to offer for art (and life) a different—a supplementary—set of standards.

43 35. Ordinarily we value a work of art because of the seriousness and dignity of what it achieves. We value it because it succeeds—in being what it is and, presumably, in fulfilling the intention that lies behind it. We assume a proper, that is to say, straightforward relation between

intention and performance. By such standards, we appraise *The Iliad*, Aristophanes' plays, The Art of the Fugue, *Middlemarch*, the paintings of Rembrandt, Chartres, the poetry of Donne, *The Divine Comedy*, Beethoven's quartets, and—among people—Socrates, Jesus, St. Francis, Napoleon, Savonarola. In short, the pantheon of high culture: truth, beauty, and seriousness.

44   36. But there are other creative sensibilities besides the seriousness (both tragic and comic) of high culture and of the high style of evaluating people. And one cheats oneself, as a human being, if one has *respect* only for the style of high culture, whatever else one may do or feel on the sly.

45   For instance, there is the kind of seriousness whose trademark is anguish, cruelty, derangement. Here we do accept a disparity between intention and result. I am speaking, obviously, of a style of personal existence as well as of a style in art; but the examples had best come from art. Think of Bosch, Sade, Rimbaud, Jarry, Kafka, Artaud, think of most of the important works of art of the 20th century, that is, art whose goal is not that of creating harmonies but of overstraining the medium and introducing more and more violent, and unresolvable, subject-matter. This sensibility also insists on the principle that an *oeuvre* in the old sense (again, in art, but also in life) is not possible. Only "fragments" are possible. . . . Clearly, different standards apply here than to traditional high culture. Something is good not because it is achieved, but because another kind of truth about the human situation, another experience of what it is to be human—in short, another valid sensibility—is being revealed.

46   And third among the great creative sensibilities is Camp: the sensibility of failed seriousness, of the theatricalization of experience. Camp refuses both the harmonies of traditional seriousness, and the risks of fully identifying with extreme states of feeling.

47   37. The first sensibility, that of high culture, is basically moralistic. The second sensibility, that of extreme states of feeling, represented in much contemporary "avant-garde" art, gains power by a tension between moral and aesthetic passion. The third, Camp, is wholly aesthetic.

48   38. Camp is the consistently aesthetic experience of the world. It incarnates a victory of "style" over "content," "aesthetics" over "morality," of irony over tragedy.

49   39. Camp and tragedy are antitheses. There is seriousness in Camp (seriousness in the degree of the artist's involvement) and, often, pathos. The excruciating is also one of the tonalities of Camp; it is the quality of excruciation in much of Henry James (for instance, *The Europeans*, *The Awkward Age*, *The Wings of the Dove*) that is responsible for the large element of Camp in his writings. But there is never, never tragedy.

50   40. Style is everything. Genet's ideas, for instance, are very Camp. Genet's statement that "the only criterion of an act is its elegance"[2] is virtually interchangeable, as a statement, with Wilde's "in matters of great importance, the vital element is not sincerity, but style." But what counts, finally, is the style in which ideas are held. The ideas about morality and politics in, say, *Lady Windemere's Fan* and in *Major Barbara* are Camp, but not just because of the nature of the ideas themselves. It is those ideas, held in a special playful way. The Camp ideas in *Our Lady of the Flowers* are maintained too grimly, and the writing itself is too successfully elevated and serious, for Genet's books to be Camp.

51   41. The whole point of Camp is to dethrone the serious. Camp is playful, anti-serious. More precisely, Camp involves a new, more complex relation to "the serious." One can be serious about the frivolous, frivolous about the serious.

52   42. One is drawn to Camp when one realizes that "sincerity" is not enough. Sincerity can be simple philistinism, intellectual narrowness.

53   43. The traditional means for going beyond straight seriousness— irony, satire—seem feeble today, inadequate to the culturally over- saturated medium in which contemporary sensibility is schooled. Camp introduces a new standard: artifice as an ideal, theatricality.

54   44. Camp proposes a comic vision of the world. But not a bitter or polemical comedy. If tragedy is an experience of hyperinvolvement, comedy is an experience of underinvolvement, of detachment.

"I adore simple pleasures, they are the last refuge of the complex."
                                                            —*A Woman of No Importance*

55   45. Detachment is the prerogative of an elite; and as the dandy is the 19th century's surrogate for the aristocrat in matters of culture, so Camp is the modern dandyism. Camp is the answer to the problem: how to be a dandy in the age of mass culture.

56   46. The dandy was overbred. His posture was disdain, or else *ennui*. He sought rare sensations, undefiled by mass appreciation. (Models: *Des Esseintes* in Huysmans' *À Rebours, Marius the Epicurean,* Valéry's *Monsieur Teste.*) He was dedicated to "good taste."

57   The connoisseur of Camp has found more ingenious pleasures. Not in Latin poetry and rare wines and velvet jackets, but in the coarsest, commonest pleasures, in the arts of the masses. Mere use does not defile the objects of his pleasure, since he learns to possess them in a rare way. Camp—Dandyism in the age of mass culture—

---

[2]Sartre's gloss on this in *Saint Genet* is: "Elegance is the quality of conduct which transforms the greatest amount of being into appearing."

makes no distinction between the unique object and the mass-produced object. Camp taste transcends the nausea of the replica.

58   47. Wilde himself is a transitional figure. The man who, when he first came to London, sported a velvet beret, lace shirts, velveteen knee-breeches and black silk stockings, could never depart too far in his life from the pleasures of the old-style dandy; this conservatism is reflected in *The Picture of Dorian Gray*. But many of his attitudes suggest something more modern. It was Wilde who formulated an important element of the Camp sensibility—the equivalence of all objects—when he announced his intention of "living up" to his blue-and-white china, or declared that a doorknob could be as admirable as a painting. When he proclaimed the importance of the necktie, the boutonniere, the chair, Wilde was anticipating the democratic *esprit* of Camp.

59   48. The old-style dandy hated vulgarity. The new-style dandy, the lover of Camp, appreciates vulgarity. Where the dandy would be continually offended or bored, the connoisseur of Camp is continually amused, delighted. The dandy held a perfumed handkerchief to his nostrils and was liable to swoon; the connoisseur of Camp sniffs the stink and prides himself on his strong nerves.

60   49. It is a feat, of course. A feat goaded on, in the last analysis, by the threat of boredom. The relation between boredom and Camp taste cannot be overestimated. Camp taste is by its nature possible only in affluent societies, in societies or circles capable of experiencing the psychopathology of affluence.

"What is abnormal in Life stands in normal relations to Art. It is the only thing in Life that stands in normal relations to Art."
                         —*A Few Maxims for the Instruction of the Over-Educated*

61   50. Aristocracy is a position vis-à-vis culture (as well as vis-à-vis power), and the history of Camp taste is part of the history of snob taste. But since no authentic aristocrats in the old sense exist today to sponsor special tastes, who is the bearer of this taste? Answer: an improvised self-elected class, mainly homosexuals, who constitute themselves as aristocrats of taste.

62   51. The peculiar relation between Camp taste and homosexuality has to be explained. While it's not true that Camp taste *is* homosexual taste, there is no doubt a peculiar affinity and overlap. Not all liberals are Jews, but Jews have shown a peculiar affinity for liberal and re-formist causes. So, not all homosexuals have Camp taste. But homo-sexuals, by and large, constitute the vanguard—and the most articulate audience—of Camp. (The analogy is not frivolously chosen. Jews and homosexuals are the outstanding creative minorities in contemporary urban culture. Creative, that is, in the truest sense: they are creators of sensibilities. The two pioneering forces of modern sensibility are

Jewish moral seriousness and homosexual aestheticism and irony.)

63   52. The reason for the flourishing of the aristocratic posture among homosexuals also seems to parallel the Jewish case. For every sensibility is self-serving to the group that promotes it. Jewish liberalism is a gesture of self-legitimization. So is Camp taste, which definitely has something propagandistic about it. Needless to say, the propaganda operates in exactly the opposite direction. The Jews pinned their hopes for integrating into modern society on promoting the moral sense. Homosexuals have pinned their integration into society on promoting the aesthetic sense. Camp is a solvent of morality. It neutralizes moral indignation, sponsors playfulness.

64   53. Nevertheless, even though homosexuals have been its vanguard, Camp taste is much more than homosexual taste. Obviously, its metaphor of life as theater is peculiarly suited as a justification and projection of a certain aspect of the situation of homosexuals. (The Camp insistence on not being "serious," on playing, also connects with the homosexual's desire to remain youthful.) Yet one feels that if homosexuals hadn't more or less invented Camp, someone else would. For the aristocratic posture with relation to culture cannot die, though it may persist only in increasingly arbitrary and ingenious ways. Camp is (to repeat) the relation to style in a time in which the adoption of style—as such—has become altogether questionable. (In the modern era, each new style, unless frankly anachronistic, has come on the scene as an anti-style.)

"One must have a heart of stone to read the death of Little Nell without laughing."

—In conversation

65   54. The experiences of Camp are based on the great discovery that the sensibility of high culture has no monopoly upon refinement. Camp asserts that good taste is not simply good taste; that there exists, indeed, a good taste of bad taste. (Genet talks about this in *Our Lady of the Flowers*.) The discovery of the good taste of bad taste can be very liberating. The man who insists on high and serious pleasures is depriving himself of pleasure; he continually restricts what he can enjoy; in the constant exercise of his good taste he will eventually price himself out of the market, so to speak. Here Camp taste supervenes upon good taste as a daring and witty hedonism. It makes the man of good taste cheerful, where before he ran the risk of being chronically frustrated. It is good for the digestion.

66   55. Camp taste is, above all, a mode of enjoyment, of appreciation—not judgment. Camp is generous. It wants to enjoy. It only seems like malice, cynicism. (Or, if it is cynicism, it's not a ruthless but a sweet cynicism.) Camp taste doesn't propose that it is in bad taste to be serious; it doesn't sneer at someone who succeeds in being seriously dramatic. What it does is to find the success in certain passionate failures.

67   56. Camp taste is a kind of love, love for human nature. It relishes, rather than judges, the little triumphs and awkward intensities of "character." . . . Camp taste identifies with what it is enjoying. People who share this sensibility are not laughing at the thing they label as "a camp," they're enjoying it. Camp is a *tender* feeling.

68   (Here, one may compare Camp with much of Pop Art, which—when it is not just Camp—embodies an attitude that is related, but still very different. Pop Art is more flat and more dry, more serious, more detached, ultimately nihilistic.)

69   57. Camp taste nourishes itself on the love that has gone into certain objects and personal styles. The absence of this love is the reason why such kitsch items as *Peyton Place* (the book) and the Tishman Building aren't Camp.

70   58. The ultimate Camp statement: it's good *because* it's awful. . . . Of course, one can't always say that. Only under certain conditions, those which I've tried to sketch in these notes.

Discussion of Theme
1. Explain Miss Sontag's statement, "The essence of Camp is its love of the unnatural."
2. The list of Camp items in paragraph 10 could be expanded indefinitely. What movies, persons, or objects would you add to the list? Why?
3. What is the difference between naive and deliberate Camp? Cite an example of each.
4. Why are so many of the objects declared to be Camp products of past eras?

Discussion of Rhetoric
1. Describe the audience Miss Sontag is writing for. What clues are given in the essay?
2. Miss Sontag entitles her article "Notes . . ." and within the selection refers to it as "jottings." Is the article that informal, or is there actually a structure and an organization?
3. What function do the quotations from Oscar Wilde serve in this essay? What do they contribute to its tone?

Writing Assignments
1. Define (with background and examples) one of the following terms: chic; dandyism; kitsch.
2. Describe several objects or people you regard as Camp.
3. Which of today's popular television programs are Camp?
4. If you disagree with Miss Sontag in her designation of a particular person or object as Camp, write a rebuttal or defense.

Library Exploration

1. Read another of Miss Sontag's critical studies. Many are collected in her *Against Interpretation*.
2. Read a biography of either Aubrey Beardsley or Oscar Wilde. What influence did either have on the artistic taste of his contemporaries?

Vocabulary

sensibility (1): feeling; awareness of and responsiveness toward something

esoteric (2): understood by only a few

edification (2): enlightenment

ineffable (4): incapable of being expressed in words

aestheticism (7): concentration on or cultivation of beauty (especially in the arts)

attenuated (15): refined; rarefied

androgyne (15): one who has characteristics of both sexes

epicene (17): sexless

euphuism (20): artificial elegance of language

les précieux (20): extremely or excessively refined persons

cognoscenti (23): those who have (or claim to have) special knowledge

ebullience (26): exuberance; enthusiastic expression of thoughts and feelings

démesuré (31): (literally, beyond measure) out of proportion; excessive

preciosity (34): fastidious or excessive refinement

démodé (38): (literally, beyond fashion) out of fashion

incandescence (41): glow; light given off by heat

oeuvre (45): (literally, work) a substantial body of work constituting the lifework of a composer, artist, or writer

antitheses (49): direct opposites

philistinism (52): insensitivity (to artistic and intellectual values)

polemical (54): characterized by argument and controversy

surrogate (55): substitute

ennui (56): boredom

boutonniere (58): flower worn in a buttonhole

vis-à-vis (61): (literally, face to face) in relation to

anachronistic (64): chronologically out of place

hedonism (65): the doctrine that pleasure or happiness is the sole or chief good in life

nihilistic (68): destructive (because it denies intrinsic meaning and value in life)

kitsch (69): artistic or literary work characterized by sentimentality, sensationalism, or slickness

55

THE HIDDEN TREND IN PSYCHOANALYSIS

Herbert Marcuse

One of the leading contemporary philosophers, often identified with the New Left, discusses Freud's *concepts of man's development and their relation to the state of modern man and his civilization.*

1   The concept of man that emerges from Freudian theory is the most irrefutable indictment of Western civilization—and at the same time the most unshakable defense of this civilization. According to Freud, the history of man is the history of his repression. Culture constrains not only his societal but also his biological existence, not only parts of the human being but his instinctual structure itself. However, such constraint is the very precondition of progress. Left free to pursue their natural objectives, the basic instincts of man would be incompatible with all lasting association and preservation: they would destroy even where they unite. The uncontrolled Eros is just as fatal as his deadly counterpart, the death instinct. Their destructive force derives from the fact that they strive for a gratification which culture cannot grant: gratification as such and as an end in itself, at any moment. The instincts must therefore be deflected from their goal, inhibited in their aim. Civilization begins when the primary objective—namely, integral satisfaction of needs—is effectively renounced.

2   The vicissitudes of the instincts are the vicissitudes of the mental apparatus in civilization. The animal drives become human instincts under the influence of the external reality. Their original "location" in the organism and their basic direction remain the same, but their objectives and their manifestations are subject to change. All psychoanalytic concepts (sublimation, identification, projection, repression, introjection) connote the mutability of the instincts. But the reality which shapes the instincts as well as their needs and satisfaction is a socio-historical world. The animal man becomes a human being only through a fundamental transformation of his nature, affecting not only the instinctual aims but also the instinctual "values"—that is, the principles that govern the attainment of the aims. The change in the governing value system may be tentatively defined as follows:

from:	to:
immediate satisfaction	delayed satisfaction
pleasure	restraint of pleasure
joy (play)	toil (work)
receptiveness	productiveness
absence of repression	security

3   Freud described this change as the transformation of the *pleasure principle* into the *reality principle*. The interpretation of the "mental apparatus" in terms of these two principles is basic to Freud's theory and remains so in spite of all modifications of the dualistic conception. It corresponds largely (but not entirely) to the distinction between unconscious and conscious processes. The individual exists, as it were, in two different dimensions, characterized by different mental processes and principles. The difference between these two dimensions is a genetic-historical as well as structural one: the unconscious, ruled by the pleasure principle, comprises "the older, primary processes, the residues of a phase of development in which they were the only kind of mental processes." They strive for nothing but for "gaining pleasure; from any operation which might arouse unpleasantness ('pain') mental activity draws back."[1] But the unrestrained pleasure principle comes into conflict with the natural and human environment. The individual comes to the traumatic realization that full and painless gratification of his needs is impossible. And after this experience of disappointment, a new principle of mental functioning gains ascendancy. The reality principle supersedes the pleasure principle: man learns to give up momentary, uncertain, and destructive pleasure for delayed, restrained, but "assured" pleasure.[2] Because of this lasting gain through renunciation and restraint, according to Freud, the reality principle "safeguards" rather than "dethrones," "modifies" rather than denies, the pleasure principle.

4   However, the psychoanalytic interpretation reveals that the reality principle enforces a change not only in the form and timing of pleasure but in its very substance. The adjustment of pleasure to the reality principle implies the subjugation and diversion of the destructive force of instinctual gratification, of its incompatibility with the established societal norms and relations, and, by that token, implies the transubstantiation of pleasure itself.

5   With the establishment of the reality principle, the human being which, under the pleasure principle, has been hardly more than a

---

[1]"Formulations Regarding the Two Principles in Mental Functioning," in *Collected Papers* (London: Hogarth Press, 1950), IV, 14. Quotations are used by permission of the publisher.

[2]*Ibid.*, p. 18.

bundle of animal drives, has become an organized ego. It strives for "what is useful" and what can be obtained without damage to itself and to its vital environment. Under the reality principle, the human being develops the function of *reason*: it learns to "test" the reality, to distinguish between good and bad, true and false, useful and harmful. Man acquires the faculties of attention, memory, and judgment. He becomes a conscious, thinking *subject*, geared to a rationality which is imposed upon him from outside. Only one mode of thought-activity is "split off" from the new organization of the mental apparatus and remains free from the rule of the reality principle: *phantasy* is "protected from cultural alterations" and stays committed to the pleasure principle. Otherwise, the mental apparatus is effectively subordinated to the reality principle. The function of "motor discharge," which, under the supremacy of the pleasure principle, had "served to unburden the mental apparatus of accretions of stimuli," is now employed in the "appropriate alteration of reality": it is converted into *action*.[3]

6   The scope of man's desires and the instrumentalities for their gratification are thus immeasurably increased, and his ability to alter reality consciously in accordance with "what is useful" seems to promise a gradual removal of extraneous barriers to his gratification. However, neither his desires nor his alteration of reality are henceforth his own: they are now "organized" by his society. And this "organization" represses and transubstantiates his original instinctual needs. If absence from repression is the archetype of freedom, then civilization is the struggle against this freedom.

7   The replacement of the pleasure principle by the reality principle is the great traumatic event in the development of man—in the development of the genus (phylogenesis) as well as of the individual (ontogenesis). According to Freud, this event is not unique but recurs throughout the history of mankind and of every individual. Phylogenetically, it occurs first in the *primal horde,* when the *primal father* monopolizes power and pleasure and enforces renunciation on the part of the sons. Ontogenetically, it occurs during the period of early childhood, and submission to the reality principle is enforced by the parents and other educators. But, both on the generic and on the individual level, submission is continuously reproduced. The rule of the primal father is followed, after the first rebellion, by the rule of the sons, and the brother clan develops into institutionalized social and political domination. The reality principle materializes in a system of institutions. And the individual, growing up within such a system, learns the requirements of the reality principle as those of law and order, and transmits them to the next generation.

---

[3] *Ibid.,* p. 16.

8   The fact that the reality principle has to be re-established continually in the development of man indicates that its triumph over the pleasure principle is never complete and never secure. In the Freudian conception, civilization does not once and for all terminate a "state of nature." What civilization masters and represses—the claim of the pleasure principle—continues to exist in civilization itself. The unconscious retains the objectives of the defeated pleasure principle. Turned back by the external reality or even unable to reach it, the full force of the pleasure principle not only survives in the unconscious but also affects in manifold ways the very reality which has superseded the pleasure principle. The *return of the repressed* makes up the tabooed and subterranean history of civilization. And the exploration of this history reveals not only the secret of the individual but also that of civilization. Freud's individual psychology is in its very essense social psychology. Repression is an historical phenomenon. The effective subjugation of the instincts to repressive controls is imposed not by nature but by man. The primal father, as the archetype of domination, initiates the chain reaction of enslavement, rebellion, and reinforced domination which marks the history of civilization. But ever since the first, prehistoric restoration of domination following the first rebellion, repression from without has been supported by repression from within: the unfree individual introjects his masters and their commands into his own mental apparatus. The struggle against freedom reproduces itself in the psyche of man, as the self-repression of the repressed individual, and his self-repression in turn sustains his masters and their institutions. It is this mental dynamic which Freud unfolds as the dynamic of civilization.

9   According to Freud, the repressive modification of the instincts under the reality principle is enforced and sustained by the "eternal primordial struggle for existence, . . . persisting to the present day." Scarcity (*Lebensnot*, Ananke) teaches men that they cannot freely gratify their instinctual impulses, that they cannot live under the pleasure principle. Society's motive in enforcing the decisive modification of the instinctual structure is thus "economic; since it has not means enough to support life for its members without work on their part, it must see to it that the number of these members is restricted and their energies directed away from sexual activities on to their work."[4]

10   This conception is as old as civilization and has always provided the most effective rationalization for repression. To a considerable extent, Freud's theory partakes of this rationalization: Freud considers the "primordial struggle for existence" as "eternal" and therefore believes that the pleasure principle and the reality principle are "eternally"

---

[4] *A General Introduction to Psychoanalysis* (New York: Garden City Publishing Co., 1943), p. 273.

antagonistic. The notion that a non-repressive civilization is impossible is a cornerstone of Freudian theory. However, his theory contains elements that break through this rationalization; they shatter the predominant tradition of Western thought and even suggest its reversal. His work is characterized by an uncomprising insistence on showing up the repressive content of the highest values and achievements of culture. In so far as he does this, he denies the equation of reason with repression on which the ideology of culture is built. Freud's metapsychology is an ever-renewed attempt to uncover, and to question, the terrible necessity of the inner connection between civilization and barbarism, progress and suffering, freedom and unhappiness—a connection which reveals itself ultimately as that between Eros and Thanatos. Freud questions culture not from a romanticist or utopian point of view, but on the ground of the suffering and misery which its implementation involves. Cultural freedom thus appears in the light of unfreedom, and cultural progress in the light of constraint. Culture is not thereby refuted: unfreedom and constraint are the price that must be paid.

11   But as Freud exposes their scope and their depth, he upholds the tabooed aspirations of humanity: the claim for a state where freedom and necessity coincide. Whatever liberty exists in the realm of the developed consciousness, and in the world it has created, is only derivative, compromised freedom, gained at the expense of the full satisfaction of needs. And in so far as the full satisfaction of needs is happiness, freedom in civilization is essentially antagonistic to happiness: it involves the repressive modification *(sublimation)* of happiness. Conversely, the unconscious, the deepest and oldest layer of the mental personality, *is* the drive for integral gratification, which is absence of want and repression. As such it is the immediate identity of necessity and freedom. According to Freud's conception the equation of freedom and happiness tabooed by the conscious is upheld by the unconscious. Its truth, although repelled by consciousness, continues to haunt the mind; it preserves the memory of past stages of individual development at which integral gratification is obtained. And the past continues to claim the future: it generates the wish that the paradise be recreated on the basis of the achievements of civilization.

12   If memory moves into the center of psychoanalysis as a decisive mode of *cognition*, this is far more than a therapeutic device; the therapeutic role of memory derives from the *truth value* of memory. Its truth value lies in the specific function of memory to preserve .promises and potentialities which are betrayed and even outlawed by the mature, civilized individual, but which had once been fulfilled in his dim past and which are never entirely forgotten. The reality principle restrains the cognitive function of memory—its commitment to the past experience of happiness which spurns the desire for its

conscious recreation. The psychoanalytic liberation of memory explodes the rationality of the repressed individual. As cognition gives away to re-cognition, the forbidden images and impulses of childhood begin to tell the truth that reason denies. Regression assumes a progressive function. The rediscovered past yields critical standards which are tabooed by the present. Moreover, the restoration of memory is accompanied by the restoration of the cognitive content of phantasy. Psychoanalytic theory removes these mental faculties from the non-committal sphere of daydreaming and fiction and recaptures their strict truths. The weight of these discoveries must eventually shatter the framework in which they were made and confined. The liberation of the past does not end in its reconciliation with the present. Against the self-imposed restraint of the discoverer, the orientation on the past tends toward an orientation on the future. The *recherche du temps perdu* becomes the vehicle of future liberation.[5]

13   The subsequent discussion will be focused on this hidden trend in psychoanalysis.

14   Freud's analysis of the development of the repressive mental apparatus proceeds on two levels:

> (a) Ontogenetic: the growth of the repressed individual from early infancy to his conscious societal existence.
>
> (b) Phylogenetic: the growth of repressive civilization from the primal horde to the fully constituted civilized state.

15   The two levels are continually interrelated. This interrelation is epitomized in Freud's notion of the return of the repressed in history: the individual re-experiences and re-enacts the great traumatic events in the development of the genus, and the instinctual dynamic reflects throughout the conflict between individual and genus (between particular and universal) as well as the various solutions of this conflict.

Discussion of Theme

1. In what sense has the history of mankind been affected by repression?
2. Do you believe that man's instincts are incompatible with society's needs? Cite some specific examples to support your belief.
3. What is the pleasure principle? The reality principle? In what way are they evident in society? Should either be thwarted or redirected?
4. In what way does the psychoanalytic liberation of memory also free man?

---

[5] Ernest G. Schachtel's paper "On Memory and Childhood Amnesia" gives the only adequate psychoanalytic interpretation of the function of memory at the individual as well as societal level. The paper is entirely focused on the explosive force of memory, and its control and "conventionalization" by society. It is, in my view, one of the few real contributions to the philosophy of psychoanalysis. Schachtel's paper is in *A Study of Interpersonal Relations*, edited by Patrick Mullahy (New York: Hermitage Press, 1950), pp. 3–49.

Discussion of Rhetoric

1. Notice the variety of sentence structure in this selection. Select a paragraph and analyze the structure of its sentences, particularly with respect to length, subject-verb patterns, the use of subordinating elements, and parallelism.
2. What hints are contained in the article that it is the first chapter in a book? What sort of audience would this book appeal to?
3. How would you characterize Marcuse's style: clear, difficult, bewildering, direct?

Writing Assignments

1. Develop the following statement by Marcuse into a theme: "The individual, growing up within such a system, learns the requirements of the reality principle as those of law and order and transmits them to the next generation."
2. How important is fantasy to children? Do television programs and comic books encourage the development of imagination? Are they harmful? Present your views in a theme.
3. Develop the following title into a composition: "The Pleasure Principle and the Reality Principle in Action."

Library Exploration

1. Read more about the two principles mentioned here in *A General Introduction to Psychoanalysis* by Sigmund Freud.
2. Read Marcuse's book *Eros and Civilization*, which presents in greater detail the ideas outlined in this selection.

Vocabulary

irrefutable (1): undeniable
vicissitudes (2): changes; ups and downs
introjection (2): the unconscious incorporation of ideas or attitudes
        into one's personality
mutability (2): changeability
ascendancy (3): dominance
transubstantiation (4): the changing of one substance into another
accretions (5): accumulations; extraneous additions
archetype (6): original pattern or model
primordial (9): fundamental; original; primitive
Eros (10): the pleasure-directed life instincts
Thanatos (10): instinctual desire for death
cognition (12): the act or process of knowing (including both
        awareness and judgment)
epitomized (15): typically represented; ideally expressed

56

MARSHALL McLUHAN
AND THE TECHNOLOGICAL EMBRACE

Michael J. Arlen

Marshall McLuhan has exerted a tremendous influence on our age. Some of his key ideas are discussed, *in less-than-reverent tones, in the following article.*

1   Marshall McLuhan, who, as just about everybody ought to know by now, is the Canadian agricultural expert and author of *The Romance of Wheat*—No. I am mistaken. Marshall McLuhan, who, as just about everybody ought to know by now, is the Canadian communications whizbang and author of a number of books about media, was on TV the other Sunday afternoon, on one of the new *NBC Experiment in Television* programs, and although McLuhan didn't say anything he hasn't said before (actually, he almost never says anything he hasn't said before, although sometimes he says it differently, and very reassuring is this note of constancy in a world gone mad), it was a mighty hippy, moderny, zim-zam-zap performance all the same, complete with the full Pop ritual of flashy, splashy lighting, electronic sound, fancy cutting, zooms, lots of stop action—in fact, the whole art-director's kit of exciting-visual-effects: go-go girls zazzing away but as if the film ran sidewise (why do they never show go-go girls dancing straight up, the way their mothers would want them to?), and, toward the end, a cute little bit of I-can-be-as-cool-as-you-are-buddy contemporary graphics showing an H-bomb exploding in the shape of an exclamation point as the narrator intoned, "The hydrogen bomb is history's exclamation point." (Once, I remember, McLuhan was pleased to describe a hydrogen-bomb explosion as "information," which goes to show you the sort of pressure the dictionary-revision people have to work under.) It was a snappy show, really. Interesting. But, for all its snap and flash, it was awfully reverential in tone— reverential toward McLuhan and reverential, more especially, toward the whole idea of modernism and technology. I don't know that it was supposed to work out that way. I don't know that McLuhanism is supposed to work out that way. Now and then, McLuhan will waft out to us a sentence ("There is absolutely no inevitability as long as there is a willingness to contemplate what is happening") that gives the impression, or maybe gives *him* the impression, that he is making

some sort of evaluative confrontation of the onrush of technology. But a sentence like that doesn't ever appear to be connected to anything else, to any other thought—to any other sentence, even—and when you get right down to cases, it seems to me, the confrontation turns out to be largely illusory, turns out to be instead an almost bland embrace. The NBC program provided a fairly broad embrace, as these things go. "The electric age is having a profound effect on us," intoned the narrator, paraphrasing McLuhan. "We are in a period of fantastic change . . . that is coming about at fantastic speed. Your life is changing dramatically! You are numb to it!" And: "The walls of your rooms are coming down. It is becoming a simple matter to wire and pick out of your homes your private, once solely personal life and record it. Bugging is the new means for gathering information." And: "The family circle has widened, Mom and Dad! The world-pool of information constantly pouring in on your closely knit family is influencing them a lot more than you think." Well, okay. But it all sounds rather too much like the revival preacher, who doesn't really tell you anything about hellfire you didn't know before but who tells it to you more forcefully, with all the right, meliorative vogue words ("fantastic change . . . fantastic speed . . . dramatically . . . numb"), and so makes you feel appropriately important and guilty in the process. In this instance, McLuhan tells us, the fire next time will be technological and lit by an electric circuit, but, having told us that, the preacher seems content to take up the collection and walk out of the church, leaving us with happy, flagellated expressions and a vague sense of having been in touch with an important truth—if we could only remember what it was.

2   For myself, I'm not so sure about McLuhan's truths. He has this Big Idea, which he pushes, about the effects on Western man of the alphabet, movable type, print—how this visual-mental dependence on little letters all in a row, lines of type, *lines*, one word right after another, has created in man a linear response to the world, has created specialization, compartmentalization, civilization even, mass production, and sundry other evils. It's an interesting idea, all right, and there's a lot of substance to it, but, in the first place, it seems plain foolish to try to rest the full breadth and weight of man's linear sense of order on a single factor even as large as the alphabet and print. Art, after all, imitates life, and life is surely, among other things, intrinsically geometric. Nature is geometric. Trees, tides, plants, planets don't move psychedelically, they move geometrically, and as long as nature exists in any recognizable form the paths of force and tension and, consequently, the order that man intuitively responds to will in the main be linear too. In the second place, it seems worse than plain foolish to be so modernistically airy about man's sense of logic. McLuhan seems to have the idea that man's dependence on print has been constricting and unnatural and has resulted in an imbalance

of the senses, and that, with the disappearance of print and the concomitant rise of electronic information-feeding technology, man will
once again come into a fuller life of the senses. "Television . . . reintegrates the human senses, thereby making books obsolete" is one of
the ways he put it that afternoon. Oh, boy, some life of the senses is my
thought for the week, with Brother and Sis upstairs in the kids' communication room watching "Uncle Don's Visit to the Fulton Fish
Market," which they can't smell, and Mom and Dad curled up on
Acrilan grass in Dad's windowless information center, holding hands
and watching a twenty-four-hour weather program. In any case, just
because an electronic circuit looks circular, or sounds circular, and
just because the hippy teen-agers that McLuhan admires so much
(by gosh, fellows, I admire them, too) go floating about absorbing
sense impressions and otherwise having a fine old time, doesn't seem
to me much of a reason for supposing that we're going to start wanting
to do without logic—intuitive, deductive, analytical, linear, call it
what you will. After all, logic, brains, intellect, sustained formal
thought are how we splendid, wonderful people got to be so splendid
and wonderful in the first place, and when a philosopher-king like
McLuhan starts saying things like "The way you react to them [tele-
vision and computers] is what is important, not what is in them or on
them," it's hard to forget that the first thing that boring old Gutenberg
printed was the Bible and the first thing television gave us was Uncle
Miltie—and, on present evidence, there doesn't seem to be any very
pressing basis for tossing out the first because of the second. McLuhan
is so cheery and accommodating to the hard bewilderments of technology. I don't know, maybe he worries like hell about them, but he
comes on cheery and accommodating. ("There is nothing sterile
about television, except in the eye of the beholder.") I guess if you live
here and now, you might as well enjoy it. Still, there's an appalling
inevitability to this onrush of technology, and since much of it is
likely to bring secondary effects that will just as inevitably diminish
the possibilities of natural human life, I don't really see that you're
doing much of anything when you toss up a line like "The new electronic interdependence re-creates the world in the image of a global
village," or "We have begun again to structure the primordial feeling,"
or "Our new environment compels commitment and participation,"
and leave it hanging. I don't really see that you're doing much of
anything except, possibly, trying to ride with the winners.

3   It seems a pity, because McLuhan is an original man. A lot of people,
I know, are down on him these days, because he's been so much in the
public eye (all those cover stories; even *Family Circle* had something
on him this month, in which it referred to McLuhan as "the most
sought-after dinner guest of our time in New York") and because,
they say, he's inconsistent, which he is, and often wrong, which he is,
and unfunny, which he certainly is, and even (they say) unoriginal.

The thing is, about fifteen years ago, when McLuhan—then, as now, a teacher of undergraduate English courses—began writing about print and communications and media, he didn't claim to be entirely original. Most of these notions about print and type and Western man had been written about for a number of years by a number of people (even though the editors of *Life* may not have been reading them then). What McLuhan did that *was* original was to put them together in a new way and add a sort of twist of his own that gave them relevance— and expansiveness. One got a feeling, in reading those earlier books, of rooms being opened up. But that was a while ago. These days, I get the feeling, especially watching McLuhan on something like the NBC show, which was content to present his views pretty much at face value (as, indeed, most of the mass magazines have been), that, for all his talk about how he's mainly an investigator, a prober, how he's interested in getting people to think about their environment, the principal result of what he writes and speaks—partly because of what he says, partly because of how he says it—has been to diminish discussion. When he touches something ("The technology of the railway created the myth of a green-pasture world of innocence." "Pop Art simply tells you the only art form left for you today is your own natural environment"), he seems to do it in such a way that although there's often substance or interest in his thought, the effect is somehow to close the subject off, to leave it in the end (despite the aphoristic crackle) more dead than alive. At least, it's odd that for all the talk of controversy surrounding his work, most people trying to come to grips with it, in conversation or in print, rarely ever seem to do much more than helplessly paraphrase what he's already said. On the NBC program that afternoon, he appeared sometimes in darkness, sometimes in light, sometimes with a red light flickering on his face. He appeared, disappeared. Sentences hung in the air. Print. Electronics. Technology. The alphabet. Western man. Life. Death. Pop Art. The motorcar. The Beatles. Gutenberg. Civilization. Quite some time ago, Archimedes said, "Give me a lever long enough, and a place to stand, and I will move the world." McLuhan seems to be intent on moving the world, all right, and thinks he has found the lever— "the clash between print and electric technologies." But the lever keeps bending, and it's hard to find a place to stand. At least, he hasn't found one yet, which is perhaps why he keeps skittering all over the place. Maybe, one day, he'll settle for something less.

Discussion of Theme
1. Why does the author object to McLuhan's "truths"?
2. Do you agree with McLuhan that books are becoming obsolete? If so, what do you think will replace them?

3. If you wanted information on a particular subject, would you rather obtain it by listening to a good lecture or reading a good book? Explain.
4. In what sense does "television . . . reintegrate the human senses?"

Discussion of Rhetoric

1. What does the tone of the selection tell you about the author's attitudes toward his subject and audience? What does it tell you about his intentions?
2. Comment on the paragraph structure of this selection. Should the paragraphs have been divided into shorter units? How does the author develop his paragraphs?
3. Why is slang used in this essay? Is it appropriate?
4. The author refers to "vogue words" (toward the end of paragraph 1). What do they add to a piece of writing or to a conversation?

Writing Assignments

1. In a theme, point out ways that the criticisms in this article could be applied to the selection by McLuhan in this anthology.
2. Develop the following statement into a theme: "Television reintegrates the human senses, thereby making books obsolete."

Library Exploration

1. Read one of McLuhan's books; among them are *Understanding Media*, *The Mechanical Bride*, and *The Medium Is the Message*.
2. McLuhan has been the subject of many studies. Read one of them and react to it. Does it give you another view of his work?

Vocabulary

meliorative (1): improving
flagellated (1): whipped; beaten
concomitant (2): accompanying; at the same time
primordial (2): fundamental; original; primitive
aphoristic (3): having the characteristics of an aphorism, that is, a short and often ingenious statement of a truth or sentiment

57

TELEVISION AND REALITY

Neil Compton

A Canadian professor of English and of racial issues in American discusses the treatment of violence television programing.

1   "Television *as* Reality" might almost have been a better title for this article. The last five horrific years have clearly demonstrated, if demonstration was necessary, that television is no longer a secondary and contingent factor in American life, but part of the very fabric of corporate existence. That the TV versions of some major events have come to seem more authentic than the unmediated occurrences themselves is due, not merely to repetition and ubiquity, but also to the awesome credibility of whatever is transmitted by that unblinking and apparently dispassionate electronic eye. Yet common sense is surely right (whatever philosophers or communications theorists may say) to urge us to be worried about the distortion of reality (or our sense of it) that results from the unavoidable selectivity of the medium. Nowadays, complaints tend to center around television's evident preoccupation with violence, and its "white, racist bias." Opinions may and do differ about the significance and justice of these charges, but not even Marshall McLuhan (I like to think) would dismiss them as totally irrelevant.

2   Even if public indignation and ritualistic self-incrimination by television executives and producers did not invite comment, a review of the past few months could hardly avoid trying to come to grips with this subject. The triumphs of Eugene McCarthy, the Têt offensive, the decision of the President not to seek re-election, the death and burial of Martin Luther King and Robert Kennedy, and the eruption into riot of scores of American cities were all phenomena which either could not have happened at all before the video age, or would have happened in a very different way. To have ignored all this in favor of such interesting but less urgent topics as the motherless family in serial drama and situation comedy, or the clash of cultures in *Celebrity Billiards*, would have been easier than trying to come to grips with what I suspect are insoluble problems. Nonetheless, it would have been a dereliction of duty.

3   Does American television deliberately and cynically exploit violence for profit? The charge has been frequently made, and seems to be striking home, because all the networks have recently made pious resolutions to change their ways. (Whether any real reformation will take place may be doubted.) Being an old-fashioned, rather bourgeois soul, I find the cult of violence in contemporary culture (whether high or low) both repellent and boring, and I have minimal respect for the intelligence and good faith of those who control commercial television. Nevertheless, I think they deserve to be defended against this particular charge.

4   The fact is that violence in popular art is nothing new. The Scottish border ballads, much of the Elizabethan drama, Smollett's novels, and Gothic horror tales, all in their different ways testify to this enduring human fascination. In the 20th century, the United States media certainly have no monopoly in this field: no American series ever exploited death and torture with such kinky and inhuman stylishness as *The Avengers*, made in Britain. Oddly enough, the admirers of Steed and Mrs. Peel include many who would be the first to complain of sadism in such American series as *The Untouchables* or *Wild, Wild West*. Of course, *The Avengers* is viewed by these sophisticates as an elegant send-up. Perhaps they believe that, to paraphrase Burke, violence itself loses half its evil by losing all its grossness.

5   H. Rap Brown struck to the heart of the matter in his notorious remark (made on camera) that "Violence is as American as cherry pie." The point is that there is nothing specifically American about cherry pie, though the U.S. probably leads the world in the production and consumption of this delicacy. So with violence. American culture has no monopoly in the sanction of domestic (not to mention international) aggressiveness, but it also has no serious rival among the advanced nations of the world. In a country which is engaged in a savage and highly visible war and where some sixty-five hundred citizens were murdered last year, it is asking too much to expect that popular art should be irradiated with the values of brotherhood, sweetness, and light. One can sympathize with the motives that prompt Dr. Frederic Wertham's crusade against media violence, and share his dismay at the findings of a survey which showed that in one week on the television channels of a large American city, there were 7,887 acts and 1,087 threats of violence, without agreeing with him that to attack these symptoms is the best way to cure the communal disease. In any case, the most casual and fragmented (and therefore the most obscene) images of violence are to be found these days on the news shows, and one assumes that Dr. Wertham is not trying to clean *them* up.

6   If they prove anything, these horrific statistics indicate that the cult of violence is based upon something far more serious than the

desire of a few cynical men to get rich by pandering to base appetites. Video mayhem on that scale could not be the product of rational calculation. Something much more sinister and atavistic must be involved. The tragic truth seems to be that the greatest popular myth of 20th-century America has become not merely irrelevant (in which case it would cease to be popular and fade away) but lethal and neurotic. The Western and its urban counterpart, the crime thriller, incarnate virtually all the most dangerous tendencies of man in 20th-century mass society: contempt for legal authority or due process, the glorification of alienation, the resort to individual violence, and racist attitudes towards Indians, Mexicans, or urban minority groups. If it were practical, there might be something to be said for banning these genres from the television screen.

7   Since it is not practical, and since getting rid of the programs would not get rid of the public attitudes to which they appeal, the enlightened solution is to use the myth creatively in the service of a less antisocial vision. This, I take it, was the fumbling and half-conscious intention of a movie which has been quite savagely attacked for its exploitation of violence, *Bonnie and Clyde*. This picture beautifully combined a nostalgic, pastoral evocation of smalltown life in the South and Midwest during the 30's with a realistic emphasis upon its physical and emotional poverty. It explained why this environment produced minor desperadoes like Clyde Barrow and why they became heroic figures to many an ostensibly respectable American. Though the audience was encouraged to identify with the almost innocent euphoria of Bonnie and Clyde at the start of their criminal career ("We rob banks!"), the sinister consequences of their violence, both for their victims and themselves, is made increasingly explicit until its climax in the gruesome ambush which ends their lives and the picture. Our ambiguous feelings about the protagonists seem to me to be exactly appropriate to the dramatic situation. Was it luck or genius that inspired the choice of a story with this particular setting in space and time? Bonnie and Clyde are heirs to the territory and much of the glamorous tradition of the Western outlaw, but their lifestyle and their technological sophistication resemble those of the urban gangster; at the same time, they are not, like the cowboy, cut off from us by temporal remoteness or, like the mob leader, by penthouse affluence. Hence, the astonishing mythic force of the picture. Of course, since this is a commercial product of the Hollywood studios, *Bonnie and Clyde* does not consistently maintain its own highest standards: in particular the theme of Clyde's impotence is handled with all the subtlety and insight of a sophomore psychologist.

8   To Dr. Wertham, of course, Bonnie and Clyde is no more than the sum total of its violent episodes, but I hope that I have indicated some of the ways in which the film provides a model that television producers

might emulate—if only they were allowed to think in terms of worthier aims than a top-ten rating. In any case, the statistical approach to media violence can be very misleading: how can we compare the enemies of CONTROL dying like flies at the end of a *Get Smart* episode with a single savage beating in (say) *Gunsmoke*, the camera up close from below and focused on the sadistic twitch at the corners of the assailant's mouth? It is well known that a violent argument between husband and wife in a domestic drama can be more disturbing to juvenile viewers than half a dozen shootings in a typical Western which, though exciting, does not dramatize a situation with which they closely identify.

9   That this generalization applies to adults as well as to children is suggested by the fact that the most disturbing programs dealing with the racial conflicts of the past few months have not been those which showed cities burning, police and rioters battling, or even the distended bellies of starving Southern children—dreadful though these spectacles were. The greatest and most salutary shocks to white complacency and self-confidence were applied by purely verbal confrontations between leaders of the black and white communities. One of these was staged during the inaugural program of the Public Broadcasting Laboratory, but I was not able to see it. However, I was an astonished witness of "Civil Rights—What Next?" (NET, April. Producer: R. D. Squier) in which three angry blacks in a New York studio overwhelmed three rather feeble and inadequate whites in Washington with an eloquent torrent of argument and invective. While Floyd McKissick of CORE, James Foreman of SNCC, and Hosea Williams of SCLC kept pouring it on, the unfortunate Washingtonians seemed incapable of reply. They tried to talk against the flow of verbiage, but had trouble concentrating while the sound from New York kept dinning into their earpieces at a volume quite loud enough to be audible to viewers. In desperation, audio from New York was cut off for a few minutes to give the whites a chance to blurt out a few lame words. Then back to New York where it became immediately apparent that the black rhetoric had continued unabated all through this little hiatus.

10   At the end, the hapless moderator concluded that "to expose racial problems in this country is to exacerbate them." One saw what he meant, even while disagreeing.

11   Since NET programs have only recently become visible in Montreal, and this was one of the earliest I was able to see, I at first attributed the lack of control over this debate to a low budget and inadequate technical facilities. However, something rather similar happened on a commercial network program, "Newark—the Anatomy of a Riot" (ABC, July. Producer: Ernest Pendrell), in the series *Time for Americans*. Here a number of citizens, black and white, demonstrated that Newark is a

long way from either agreeing on the causes of last year's outbreak or taking the kind of action that will prevent a recurrence. The babble of bitter talk between white merchants and black community leaders made it painfully clear that what one participant called the "tragic dance" of hate and suspicion will not soon be ended in Newark. Other programs in the same six-part series were equally depressing: "Bias and the Mass Media" featured two hour-long discussions. On the first, Harry Belafonte, Lena Horne, Larry Neal, and Dr. Alvin Poussaint delivered a choric denunciation of white-owned media, concluding that they "will not permit the people to understand." There was such unanimity and so little direction or discipline to the discussion that the program became boring. So did its successor the following week, though for different reasons. Here, the impassioned common sense of Norman Cousins of the *Saturday Review* and Edward P. Morgan of NET shone fitfully amidst the ponderous evasiveness of a gaggle of top media brass.

12   "Prejudice and the Police" was at once more dramatic and more sinister. This program confronted nine members of the Houston police force with an equal number of citizens, mostly black or Mexican. It was one of a number of similar group sessions organized by the city to enable police and public to engage in face-to-face discussion. The chief obstacle to dialogue was the truculent defensiveness of the police. To a man, they refused to admit that there was substance to complaints of violence and lack of respect put forward, with great moderation and charity, by the colored citizens. Only the example of the endlessly patient group leaders added an element of hope to this ugly little vignette of life in Texas. With their admirably American faith in the sure triumph of reason and good will if people can be made to level with each other, they carried on with discussion, psychodrama, and role reversal as though oblivious to the policemen's sullen self-righteousness.

13   Whatever may happen on the city streets, this is certainly proving to be a long hot summer for this kind of confrontation on television. As though responding to the urging of some unseen prompter, all the networks have scheduled a total of about two dozen specials devoted wholly or in part to the racial crisis. Cynics may observe that summer is a period of low ratings and panel shows are cheap to produce; optimists might retort that prime time is prime time, and low budgets may have unintended advantages. The underproduced rawness and untidiness of human relations on the programs I have been describing is much closer to the reality of black-white interaction than a more disciplined format would suggest.

14   But even this kind of program involves its own characteristic form of distortion. Black audiences may watch (if they do) for the pleasure of seeing the white establishment being outtalked or unmasked, but

they do not learn anything about their situation that they did not know before. It is the white audience that is being enlightened and informed. Blackness is not taken for granted as part of the kaleidoscopic variety of American life, but exposed as a problem, a threat to the status quo. In other words, these well-intentioned and wholly admirable programs cannot avoid defining normality (and hence, by extension, "reality") in terms of whiteness.

15   So far as the media are concerned, there are two possible cures for this intolerable social disease. Both are being tried this year, in timid, experimental doses, though they are ultimately incompatible with one another. Either of them, if seriously attempted, would involve a more radical reform of current practice than anything now being dreamed of at NBC or CBS.

16   The first alternative is to make darkness visible throughout the media. I well remember my surprise at the racial variety in the streets of New York, upon my first visit three years ago: Hollywood's version of American reality tended to suppress that little detail. Things have improved somewhat since then, and there are apparently plans afoot to enrich the racial mix on both programs and commercials this autumn. However, there are limits to what can be accomplished along these lines. So long as Bill Cosby cannot lay a hand on a white chick in *I Spy*, his visibility tends to emphasize his inferior status. Furthermore, television's view of life tends to be not merely lilywhite, but even more fervently bourgeois. One can imagine network executives coming to accept a kind of *café-au-lait* consciousness, but not the matriarchal, proletarian values of the great black ghettos.

17   A more promising alternative would be to establish black-owned and operated outlets in large cities. This is a project that might interest the Ford Foundation, which has shown a willingness to support relatively radical experiments in the field of public communications. However, it is doubtful whether the Foundation would be prepared to tolerate the inevitably heterodox political, social, and sexual orientation of such stations. Local white communities would presumably be even less sympathetic. Yet this kind of facility is a necessity for any minority which wishes to maintain its identity in the modern world.

18   In the meantime, a few small experiments in programming by and for black people are under way. National Educational Television leads the way with two regular series. *History of the Negro People* is a series of half-hour programs devoted to uncovering the heritage, African and American, of black culture; and *Black Journal* (editor: Louis Potter) is a moderately lively hour-long weekly magazine-type show which seems to be hitting its stride after an understandably shaky start.

19   *Of Black America* (CBS), a rather lavish series of documentaries and panel discussions, was not produced by or exclusively for black viewers

but it has managed so far to avoid acquiring too whitish an aura. The first program, "Black History: Lost, Strayed, or Stolen" (Producers: Andrew Rooney and Perry Wolf), narrated by Bill Cosby, was a masterpiece of research, editing, and cool, hip commentary. The use of old and new film clips to illustrate prejudice and stereotypes was both hilarious and appalling. "The Black Soldier" (Producer: Peter Poor), though limited by its thirty-minute format, used old drawings and still photos very effectively, the camera zooming in to single out the "invisible" black faces among the armies of a dozen American wars. Other programs in the series (not yet over) have not been quite so successful. Nevertheless, *Of Black America* at its best demonstrates what superlative resources of intelligence, public spirit, and style CBS News can marshal when it wants to and is given the chance. What a pity the parent organization displays so few of the same qualities. But then intelligence, public spirit, and style have limited value to a business whose main purpose is to sell soap, cars, and cheese.

Discussion of Theme
1. As the author suggests, would "Television *as* Reality" have been a better title for this article?
2. What is Professor Compton's response to the charges that American television consciously and cynically exploits violence for profit? Do you agree with him?
3. What is twentieth century America's greatest popular myth? Has it become "lethal and neurotic"? Are any of the more positive aspects of this myth exploited on television?
4. According to the author, how successful has television been in handling racial issues?

Discussion of Rhetoric
1. What are the two main themes in this essay? How are they tied together?
2. An interesting quality of this essay is its specificity—its use of names and dates. Does this quality strengthen the author's argument? Or does it detract from it?

Writing Assignments
1. Should the depiction of violence on television be subject to regulation or censorship? If so, how should it be regulated—and by whom?
2. In the main, has television made a positive or negative contribution to the education of the young in this country?
3. Describe your favorite television program, explaining clearly why you enjoy it. For example, do you watch it to be entertained or educated or both?

Library Exploration

Who is Dr. Frederic Wertham? Read articles about him in your library and report on his theories concerning violence on television.

Vocabulary

contingent (1): dependent on or conditioned by something else
ubiquity (1): the condition of being in a number of places at once
dereliction (2): neglect
atavistic (6): marked by reversion to a primitive type
ostensibly (7): seemingly
euphoria (7): an often unaccountable feeling of well-being or elation
temporal (7): related to or dealing with time
emulate (8): strive to equal or excel
salutary (9): wholesome; beneficial
invective (9): insulting or abusive speech
hiatus (9): interruption
exacerbate (10): make more violent, bitter, or severe
truculent (12): quarrelsome
matriarchal (16): of a society where the mother is head of the family unit
proletarian (16): of the working class
heterodox (17): different from or contrary to accepted beliefs or standards

58

THE NOW MOVIE

Anthony Schillaci

Young people have been instrumental in changing the movie into an "environmental art." This article examines the cinematic ferment that has resulted and the impact it is making on our culture.

1   The better we understand how young people view film, the more we have to revise our notion of what film is. Seen through young eyes, film is destroying conventions almost as quickly as they can be formulated. Whether the favored director is "young" like Richard Lester, Roman Polanski, and Arthur Penn, or "old" like Kubrick, Fellini, and Buñuel, he must be a practicing cinematic anarchist to catch the eye of the young. If we're looking for the young audience between sixteen and twenty-four, which accounts for 48 per cent of the box office today, we will find they're on a trip, whether in a Yellow Submarine or on a Space Odyssey. A brief prayer muttered for Rosemary's Baby and they're careening down a dirt road with Bonnie and Clyde, the exhaust spitting banjo sounds, or sitting next to The Graduate as he races across the Bay Bridge after his love. The company they keep is fast; Belle de Jour, Petulia, and Joanna are not exactly a sedentary crowd. Hyped up on large doses of *Rowan and Martin's Laugh-In*, and *Mission: Impossible*, they are ready for anything that an evolving film idiom can throw on the screen. And what moves them must have the pace, novelty, style, and spontaneity of a television commercial.

2   All of this sounds as if the script is by McLuhan. Nevertheless, it is borne out by the experience of teaching contemporary film to university juniors and seniors, staging film festivals for late teens and early adults, and talking to literally hundreds of people about movies. The phenomenon may be interesting, and even verifiable, but what makes it important is its significance for the future of film art. The young have discovered that film is an environment which you put on, demanding a different kind of structure, a different mode of attention than any other art. Their hunger is for mind-expanding experience and simultaneity, and their art is film.

3   Occasionally a young director gives us a glimpse of the new world of film as environmental art. The optical exercise known as *Flicker*

came on like a karate chop to the eyes at Lincoln Center's Film Seminar three years ago. One half-hour of white light flashing at varied frequency, accompanied by a deafening sound track designed to infuriate, describes the screen, but not what happened to the audience. As strangers turned to ask if it was a put-on, if they had forgotten to put film in the projector, they noticed that the flickering light fragmented their motions, stylizing them like the actions of a silent movie. In minutes, the entire audience was on its feet, acting out spontaneous pantomines for one another, no one looking at the flashing screen. The happening precipitated by *Flicker* could be called the film of the future, but it was actually an anti-environment that gives us an insight into the past. By abstracting totally from content, the director demonstrated that the film is in the audience which acts out personal and public dramas as the screen turns it on. The delight of this experience opened up the notion of film as an environmental art.

4   Critics have noted the trend which leaves story line and character development strewn along the highways of film history like the corpses in Godard's *Weekend*. The same critics have not, in general, recognized that the growing option for nonlinear, unstructured experiences that leave out sequence, motivation, and "argument" is a vote for film as environment. Young people turn to film for a time-space environment in which beautiful things happen to them. The screen has, in a sense, less and less to do with what explodes in the audience. This new scene could mean either that film is plunging toward irrelevant stimulation, or that there is a new and unprecedented level of participation and involvement in young audiences. I prefer to think the latter is the case. Young people want to talk about Ben's hang-up, why Rosemary stayed with the baby, or what it feels like to be in the electronic hands of a computer like Hal. They do not forget the film the minute they walk out of the theater.

5   The attention given the new style of film goes beyond stimulation to real involvement. A generation with eyes fixed on the rearview mirror tended to give film the same attention required for reading— that is, turning off all the senses except the eyes. Film became almost as private as reading, and little reaction to the total audience was experienced. As the Hollywood dream factory cranked out self-contained worlds of fantasy, audiences entered them with confidence that nothing even vaguely related to real life would trouble their reveries. As long as one came and left in the middle of the film, it was relatively non-involving as environment. When television brought the image into the living room, people gave it "movie attention," hushing everyone who entered the sacred presence of the tube as they would a film patron who talked during a movie. One was not allowed to speak, even during commercials. It took post-literate man to teach us how to use television as environment, as a moving image on the wall to which one may give

total or peripheral attention as he wishes. The child who had TV as a baby-sitter does not turn off all his senses, but walks about the room carrying on a multiplicity of actions and relationships, his attention a special reward for the cleverness of the pitchman, or the skill of the artist. He is king, and not captive. As McLuhan would put it, he is not an audience, he *gives* an audience to the screen.

6   The new multisensory involvement with film as total environment has been primary in destroying literary values in film. Their decline is not merely farewell to an understandable but unwelcome dependence; it means the emergence of a new identity for film. The diminished role of dialogue is a case in point. The difference between *Star Trek* and *Mission: Impossible* marks the trend toward self-explanatory images that need no dialogue. Take an audio tape of these two popular TV shows, as we did in a recent study, and it will reveal that while *Mission: Impossible* is completely unintelligible without images, *Star Trek* is simply an illustrated radio serial, complete on the level of sound. It has all the characteristics of radio's golden age: actions explained, immediate identification of character by voice alone, and even organ music to squeeze the proper emotion or end the episode. Like *Star Trek*, the old film was frequently a talking picture (emphasis on the adjective), thereby confirming McLuhan's contention that technologically "radio married the movies." The marriage of dependence, however, has gone on the rocks, and not by a return to silent films but a new turning to foreign ones. It was the films of Fellini and Bergman, with their subtitles, that convinced us there had been too many words. Approximately one-third of the dialogue is omitted in subtitled versions of these films, with no discernible damage—and some improvement—of the original.

7   More than dialogue, however, has been jettisoned. Other literary values, such as sequential narrative, dramatic choice, and plot are in a state of advanced atrophy, rapidly becoming vestigial organs on the body of film art as young people have their say. *Petulia* has no "story," unless one laboriously pieces together the interaction between the delightful arch-kook and the newly divorced surgeon, in which case it is nothing more than an encounter. The story line wouldn't make a ripple if it were not scrambled and fragmented into an experience that explodes from a free-floating present into both past and future simultaneously. *Petulia* is like some views of the universe which represent the ancient past of events whose light is just now reaching us simultaneously with the future of our galaxy, returning from the curve of outer space. Many films succeed by virtue of what they leave out. *2001: A Space Odyssey* is such a film, its muted understatement creating gaps in the action that invite our inquiry. Only a square viewer wants to know where the black monolith came from and where it is going. For most of the young viewers to whom I have spoken,

it is just there. *Last Year at Marienbad* made the clock as limply shapeless as one of Salvador Dali's watches, while *8-1/2* came to life on the strength of free associations eagerly grasped by young audiences. The effect of such films is a series of open-ended impressions, freely evoked and enjoyed, strongly inviting inquiry and involvement. In short, film is freed to work as environment, something which does not simply contain, but shapes people, tilting the balance of their faculties, radically altering their perceptions, and ultimately their views of self and all reality. Perhaps one sense of the symptomatic word "grooving," which applies to both sight and sound environments, is that a new mode of attention—multisensory, total, and simultaneous—has arrived. When you "groove," you do not analyze, follow an argument, or separate sensations; rather, you are massaged into a feeling of heightened life and consciousness.

8   If young people look at film this way, it is in spite of the school, a fact which says once more with emphasis that education is taking place outside the classroom walls. The "discovery" that television commercials are the most exciting and creative part of today's programming is old news to the young. Commercials are a crash course in speed-viewing, their intensified sensations challenging the viewer to synthesize impressions at an ever increasing rate. The result is short films like one produced at UCLA, presenting 3,000 years of art in three minutes. *God Is Dog Spelled Backwards* takes you from the cave paintings of Lascaux to the latest abstractions, with some images remaining on the screen a mere twenty-fourth of a second! The young experience the film, however, not as confusing, but as exuberantly and audaciously alive. They feel joy of recognition, exhilaration at the intense concentration necessary (one blink encompasses a century of art), and awe at the 180-second review of every aspect of the human condition. Intended as a put-on, the film becomes a three-minute commercial for man. This hunger for overload is fed by the television commercial, with its nervous jump cuts demolishing continuity, and its lazy dissolves blurring time-space boundaries. Whether the young are viewing film "through" television, or simply through their increased capacity for information and sensation (a skill which makes most schooling a bore), the result is the same—film becomes the primary environment in which the hunger to know through experience is satisfied.

9   Hidden within this unarticulated preference of the young is a quiet tribute to film as the art that humanizes change. In its beginnings, the cinema was celebrated as the art that mirrored reality in its functional dynamism. And although the early vision predictably gave way to misuse of the medium, today the significance of the filmic experience of change stubbornly emerges again. Instead of prematurely stabilizing change, film celebrates it. The cinema can inject life into historical

events by the photo-scan, in which camera movement and editing liberate the vitality of images from the past. *City of Gold*, a short documentary by the National Film Board of Canada, takes us by zoom and cut into the very life of the Klondike gold rush, enabling us to savor the past as an experience.

10   Education increasingly means developing the ability to live humanly in the technological culture by changing with it. Film is forever spinning out intensifications of the environment which make it visible and livable. The ability to control motion through its coordinates of time and space makes film a creative agent in change. Not only does film reflect the time-space continuum of contemporary physics, but it can manipulate artistically those dimensions of motion which we find most problematic. The actuality of the medium, its here-and-now impact, reflects how completely the present tense has swallowed up both past and future. Freudian psychology dissolves history by making the past something we live; accelerated change warps the future by bringing it so close that we can't conceive it as "ahead" of us. An art which creates its own space, and can move time forward and back, can humanize change by conditioning us to live comfortably immersed in its fluctuations.

11   On the level of form, then, perhaps the young are tuned in to film for "telling it like it is" in a sense deeper than that of fidelity to the event. It is film's accurate reflection of a society and of human life totally in flux that makes it the liberating art of the time. We live our lives more like Guido in *8-1/2*—spinners of fantasies, victims of events, the products of mysterious associations—than we do like Maria in *The Sound of Music*, with a strange destiny guiding our every step. Instead of resisting change and bottling it, film intensifies the experience of change, humanizing it in the process. What makes the ending of *The Graduate* "true" to young people is not that Ben has rescued his girl from the Establishment, but that he did it without a complete plan for the future. The film may fail under analysis, but it is extraordinarily coherent as experience, as I learned in conversations about it with the young. The same accurate reflection of the day may be said of the deep space relativity of *2001*, the frantic pace of *Petulia*, or the melodramatic plotting of *Rosemary's Baby*. Whether this limitless capacity for change within the creative limits of art has sober implications for the future raises the next (and larger) questions of what young people look for and get out of film.

12   When the question of film content is raised, the example of *Flicker* and other films cited may seem to indicate that young people favor as little substance as possible in their film experiences. A casual glance at popular drive-in fare would confirm this opinion quickly. Nevertheless, their attitude toward "what films are about" evidences a young, developing sensitivity to challenging comments on what it means to

be human. The young are digging the strong humanism of the current film renaissance and allowing its currents to carry them to a level deeper than that reached by previous generations. One might almost say that young people are going to the film-maker's work for values that they have looked for in vain from the social, political, or religious establishments. This reaction, which has made film modern man's morality play, has not been carefully analyzed, but the present state of evidence invites our inquiry.

13   As far as the "point" of films is concerned, young people will resist a packaged view, but will welcome a problematic one. The cry, "Please, I'd rather do it myself!" should be taken to heart by the film-maker. It is better to use understatement in order to score a personal discovery by the viewer. Such a discovery of an idea is a major part of our delight in the experience of film art. A frequent answer to a recent survey question indicated that a young man takes his girl to the movies so that they will have something important to talk about. It is not a matter of pitting film discussion against "making out," but of recognizing that a rare and precious revelation of self to the other is often occasioned by a good film. The young feel this experience as growth, expanded vitality, more integral possession of one's self with the consequent freedom to go out to others more easily and more effectively.

14   Very little of the business of being human happens by instinct, and so we need every form of education that enlightens or accelerates that process. While young people do not go to films for an instant humanization course, a strong part of the pleasure they take in excellent films does just this. Whether through a connaturality of the medium described earlier, or because of a freer viewpoint, young audiences frequently get more out of films than their mentors. It is not so much a matter of seeing more films, but of seeing more in a film. The film-as-escape attitude belongs to an age when the young were not yet born; and the film-as-threat syndrome has little meaning for the sixteen to twenty-four group, simply because they are free from their elders' hang-ups. A typical irrelevance that causes youthful wonder is the elderly matron's complaint that *Bonnie and Clyde* would teach bad driving habits to the young.

15   The performance of youthful audiences in discussions of contemporary film indicates their freedom from the judgmental screen which blurs so many films for other generations. In speaking of *Bonnie and Clyde*, late high school kids and young adults do not dwell upon the career of crime or the irregularity of the sexual relationship, but upon other things. The development of their love fascinates young people, because Clyde shows he knows Bonnie better than she knows herself. Although he resists her aggressive sexual advances, he knows and appreciates her as a person. It is the sincerity of their growing love that overcomes his impotence, and the relationship between this

achievement and their diminished interest in crime is not lost on the young audience. The reversal of the "sleep together now, get acquainted later" approach is significant here. These are only a few of the nuances that sensitive ears and eyes pick up beneath the gunfire and banjo-plucking. Similarly, out of the chaotic impressions of *Petulia*, patterns are perceived. Young people note the contrasts between Petulia's kooky, chaotic life, and the over-controlled precision of the surgeon's existence. The drama is that they both come away a little different for their encounter. Instead of a stale moral judgment on their actions, one finds open-ended receptivity to the personal development of the characters.

16   Youth in search of identity is often presented as a ridiculous spectacle, a generation of Kierkegaards plaintively asking each other: "Who am I?" Nevertheless, the quest is real and is couched in terms of a hunger for experience. SDS or LSD, McCarthy buttons or yippie fashions, it is all experimentation in identity, trying on experiences to see if they fit. The plea is to stop the world, not so that they can get off, but so they can get a handle on it. To grasp each experience, to suck it dry of substance, and to grow in that process is behind the desire to be "turned on." But of all the lurid and bizarre routes taken by young people, the one that draws least comment is that of the film experience. More people have had their minds expanded by films than by LSD. Just as all art nudges man into the sublime and vicarious experience of the whole range of the human condition, film does so with a uniquely characteristic totality and involvement.

17   Ben, *The Graduate,* is suffocating under his parents' aspirations, a form of drowning which every young person has felt in some way. But the film mirrors their alientation in filmic terms, by changes in focus, by the metaphors of conveyor belt sidewalk and swimming pool, better than any moralist could say it. The satirical portraits of the parents may be broad and unsubtle, but the predicament is real and compelling. This is why the young demand no assurances that Ben and the girl will live happily ever after; it is enough that he jarred himself loose from the sick apathy and languid sexual experimentation with Mrs. Robinson to go after one thing, one person that he wanted for himself, and not for others. Incidentally, those who are not busy judging the morality of the hotel scenes will note that sex doesn't communicate without love. Some may even note that Ben is using sex to strike at his parents—not a bad thing for the young (or their parents) to know.

18   Emotional maturity is never painless and seldom permanent, but it can become a bonus from viewing good films because it occurs there not as taught but experienced. Values communicated by film are interiorized and become a part of oneself, not simply an extension of the womb that parents and educators use to shield the young from the

world. Colin Smith, in *The Loneliness of the Long Distance Runner*, IS youth, not because he did it to the Establishment, but because he is trying to be his own man and not sweat his guts out for another. The profound point of learning who you are in the experience of freedom, as Colin did in running, is not lost on the young who think about this film a little. Some speak of Col's tragedy as a failure to realize he could have won the race for himself, and not for the governor of the Borstal. Self-destruction through spite, the pitfalls of a self-justifying freedom, and the sterility of bland protest are real problems that emerge from the film. The values that appeal most are the invisible ones that move a person to act because "it's me" (part of one's identity), and not because of "them." Because they have become an object of discovery and not of imposition, such values tend to make morality indistinguishable from self-awareness.

19   It should be made clear, however, that it is not merely the content, but the mode of involvement in the film experience that makes its humanism effective. In terms of "message," much of contemporary film reflects the social and human concerns that Bob Dylan, the Beatles, Simon and Garfunkel, and Joan Baez communicate. But the words of their songs often conceal the radical nature of the music in which they appear. The direct emotional appeal of the sound of "Eleanor Rigby," "Give a Damn," "I Am a Rock," or "Mr. Businessman" communicates before we have the words deciphered. Films with honest human concern, similarly, change audiences as much by their style as their message. *Elvira Madigan's* overpowering portrait of a hopeless love, *A Thousand Clowns'* image of nonconformity, *Zorba's* vitality, and *Morgan's* tragedy are not so much the content of the images as the outcome of their cinematic logic. If these films change us, it is because we have done it to ourselves by opening ourselves to their experiences.

20   Expo 67 audiences were charmed by the Czech Kinoautomat in which their vote determined the course of comic events in a film. Once again, we find here not a peek into the future, but an insight into all film experience. In one way or another, we vote on each film's progress. The passive way is to patronize dishonest or cynical films, for our box-office ballot determines the selection of properties for years to come. We have been voting this way for superficial emotions, sterile plots, and happy endings for a generation. But we vote more actively and subtly by willing the very direction of a film through identification with the character, or absorption into the action. The viewer makes a private or social commitment in film experience. He invests a portion of himself in the action, and if he is changed, it is because he has activated his own dreams. What happens on the screen, as in the case of *Flicker*, is the catalyst for the value systems, emotional responses, and the indirect actions which are the byproducts of a good film. Film invites young people to be part of the action by

making the relationships which take the work beyond a mere succession of images. The reason why young people grow through their art is that they supply the associations that merely begin on the screen but do not end there. When parents and educators become aware of this, their own efforts at fostering maturity may be less frantic, and more effective.

21   It is not only the films that please and delight which appeal to the young, but also those which trouble and accuse by bringing our fears into the open. The new audience for documentary films highlights a new way of looking at film as an escape *into* reality. From *The War Game* to *Warrendale*, from *The Titicut Follies* to *Battle of Algiers*, young audiences are relishing the film's ability to document the present in terms of strong social relevance. *Portrait of Jason* is more than a voyeuristic peek into the psyche of a male whore; it is a metaphor for the black man's history in America, and this is what young people see in that film. Even the most strident dissenters will appreciate the ambiguities of *The Anderson Platoon*, which leaves us without anyone to hate, because it is not about Marines and Vietcong, but about men like ourselves. In these as in other films, the social content is intimately wed to the film experience, and together they form a new outlook. Ultimately, we may have to change our views on what film art is about.

22   The foregoing analysis of how young people look at film will appear to some to constitute a simplistic eulogy to youth. For this reason, we may temper our optimisim by a hard look at real problems with this generation. There is a desperate need for education. Although they cannot all be structured, none of the better youthful attitudes or responses described came about by chance. Mere screening of films, for example, whether they be classics or trash, does little good. Colleges can become places where the young are taught hypocrisy, being told they "should" like Fellini, Bergman, Antonioni, or Godard. They can accept these film-makers just as uncritically as their parents adulated movie stars. Unless there is encouragement to reflect on film experience, its impact can be minimal and fleeting. Most of the responses I have mentioned came from students who were well into the habit of discussing film. These discussions are best when they flow from the natural desire we have to communicate our feelings about a film. Nonverbalization, the reluctance to betray by treacherous abstractions the ineffable experience of the film, arises at this point. Real as it is, there must be found some middle ground between a suffocatingly detailed dissection of a film, and the noncommunicative exclamation, "like WOW!" Reflecting on one's experience is an integral part of making that experience part of one's self. Furthermore, one can see an almost immediate carry-over to other film experiences from each film discussed.

23   A problem more crucial than lack of reflection is the poverty of

critical perspective. The young can plunge into their personal version of the *auteur* theory and make a fad or fetish out of certain films and directors. Roman Polanski has made some bad films, that is, films which do not reflect his own experience and feelings honestly as did *Knife in the Water*. Fascinating as *Rosemary's Baby* is, it suffers from an uncertain relationship of the director to his work. Some directors are adulated for peripheral or irrelevant reasons. Joseph Losey is a good film-maker, not because of a cynical preoccupation with evil, but because, like Hitchcock and Pinter, he makes us less certain of our virtue. And Buñuel, far from being a cheerful anarchist attacking church and society with abandon, is a careful surgeon, excising with camera the growths of degenerate myth on the cancerous culture.

24   In their own work, young people can celebrate bad film-making as "honest" and voyeuristic films as "mature." Criticism of poor films is not "putting down" the director for doing his own thing, especially if his thing is trite, dishonest, or so personal that it has no meaning accessible to others. Criticism means taking a stand on the basis of who you are. The current preference of spoof over satire is not just another instance of cool over hot, but is symptomatic of a noncritical stance. *Dr. Strangelove* makes comic absurdity out of the cold war from a certain conviction about what mature political action should be. The *Laugh-In* has no convictions but a lot of opinions. If it is accused of favoring an idea or cause, it will refute the charge by ridiculing what it holds. The cynical, sophisticated noninvolvement of the "won't vote" movement in the recent election has its counterpart in film viewing.

25   A question that should perhaps have been asked earlier is: Why should we be concerned with asking how young people look at film? Tired reasons, citing *Time's* Man of the Year, the under-twenty-five generation, or the youth-quake menace of *Wild in the Streets* (they'll be taking over!) are not appropriate here. Anyone who is interested in the direction taken by cinema, and its continued vitality in the current renaissance of the art, will have to take the young into account as the major shaping force on the medium. If the age group from sixteen to twenty-four accounts for 48 per cent of the box office, it means that this eight-year period determines the success or failure of most films. Fortunately, there has not yet appeared a formula for capturing this audience. *Variety* described the youth market as a booby trap for the industry, citing the surprise success of sleepers such as *Bonnie and Clyde* and *The Graduate*, as well as the supposed youth-appeal failures (*Half a Sixpence, Poor Cow, Here We Go Round the Mulberry Bush*). The list may suggest a higher level of young taste than producers are willing to admit. In any case, if the young have influenced the medium this far, we cannot ignore the fact. It is for this reason that we are encouraged to speculate on the future in the form of two

developments revolutionizing the young approach to film: student film-making and multi-media experiences.

26   More and more, the answer to how young people look at film is "through the lens of a camera." In coming years, it will be youth as film-maker, and not simply as audience, that will spur the evolution of the cinema. Students want a piece of the action, whether in running a university, the country, or the world; in terms of our question, this means making films. There is a strong resonance between film-making and the increasingly sophisticated film experience. Young people delighted by a television commercial are tempted to say: "I could do that!" Considering the cost and artistry of some commercials, this is a pretty naïve statement, but it doesn't stop the young from taking out their father's Super-8 or buying an old Bolex to tell their story on film. Today, anyone can make a film. Although Robert Flaherty's longed-for parousia, when film is as cheap as paper, has not yet arrived, the art has come into the reach of almost everyone. The Young Film-Makers Conference held by Fordham University last February drew 1,200 people, 740 of them student film-makers below college age. On a few weeks' notice, some 120 films were submitted for screening. Kids flew in from Richmond, California, and bussed in from Louisville, Kentucky, with twenty-seven states and Canada represented. Numbers, however, do not tell the story. One of the notable directors and actors present sized up the scene by saying: "My God, I'm standing here in the middle of a revolution!" It was the quality of the films that caused Eli Wallach to remark, only half in jest, that some day he'd be working for one of these film-makers. The young look at film as potential or actual film-makers, and this fact raises participation to an unprecedented critical level. The phenomenon also removes the last residue of passive audience participation from the Golden Forties box-office bonanza.

27   Foolhardy though it may be, one can predict that the new interest in film will take the direction of multi-media experimentation. Expo 67, it seems, is *now*. Our new and growing capacity to absorb images and synthesize sounds demands a simultaneity that cannot be met by traditional forms of film-making. The response so far has been the halfhearted multiple screens of *The Thomas Crown Affair*, not part of the conception of the film, but inserted as fancy dressing. The object of multiple images is not so much to condense actions as to create an environment such as the Ontario pavilion film, *A Place to Stand*. My own students have begun to relegate location shots such as street scenes or mood sequences to peripheral attention on side screens and walls, while the action takes place on the main screen.

28   It is symptomatic that the staged novelty of the Electric Circus is giving way to a new and interesting experiment in Greenwich Village, Cerebrum—where for a modest fee parties can set up their own media

platforms equipped with projectors, tape recorders, and lights to stage their own happening. The idea being developed here is central to multi-media art, that is, the orchestration of contemporary media instruments. Young people are not afraid to carry a running projector around, spraying the images on walls and ceilings for distortions which communicate. An older generation is inclined to think of the media hardware as "machines" to be screwed to the floor or locked in a booth while they "produce" images and sounds. The young, in contrast, recognize this hardware as part of the information environment of electronic technology, and they use it accordingly. Spontaneity, the chance synchronization, overload that leads to breakthrough—these are all part of the excitement that draws people to media rather than film alone.

29   The young look at film is a revolutionary one, motivated more by love of the medium than hatred of the Establishment. In a sense, the new taste is liberating film for a free exploration of its potential, especially in the area of humanizing change. The hunger for a relativity of time and space will extend to morality, producing films that explore problems rather than package solutions. Nevertheless, the very intensity of young involvement gives promise of profound changes in the youth audience as people themselves to the reality of the medium. Whether as young film-maker or multi-media entrepreneur, the young will have their say. If we take the time to cultivate their perspective, we may learn an interesting view of the future of media, and a fascinating way to stay alive.

Discussion of Theme

1. How is the younger generation responsible for the kind of films we see today?
2. What is an environmental art? In what sense is film an environmental art form?
3. Why does the author believe that the film is the great liberating art of our time? Do you agree?
4. The author believes that the values learned from films become more a part of oneself than those learned from parents and educators. Why? Do you agree?

Discussion of Rhetoric

1. To what age group is Schillaci making his appeal? What rhetorical devices does he employ to capture that group?
2. Note the concluding sentence of the essay. Explain the phrase "to stay alive" as he uses it. How does this concluding sentence relate to the rest of the essay?
3. How is this essay organized: from the general to the specific, or vice versa? Why?

4. Are *movie* and *film* two words that mean the same thing? Or do do they have different connotations? Explain.

Writing Assignments

1. Describe a commercial that you regard as particularly effective. Analyze the reasons for its effectiveness.
2. Why do you go to the movies?
3. Develop the following statement into a theme: "Social morality is, to a large extent, shaped by movie morality."
4. Compare the work of a European film maker—for example, Ingmar Bergman or Jean-Luc Godard—with that of a contemporary American director—for example, Mike Nichols (*Virginia Woolf* and *The Graduate*) or Arthur Penn (*Bonnie and Clyde*).

Library Exploration

1. Investigate the various attempts that have been made to censor or regulate movies.
2. What determines whether a novel or story will be bought by Hollywood? After it is bought, what are the next steps required to make it into a movie? (You might consult a textbook in creative writing for insight into this process).

Vocabulary

simultaneity (2): the presentation of different views of the same object in one work of art
peripheral (5): located away from the center or central position
jettisoned (7): discarded
sequential (7): following in order
atrophy (7): decrease in size or wasting away
audaciously (8): boldly
connaturality (14): being of the same nature
nuances (15): subtle distinctions or qualities
vicarious (16): felt through imaginative participation in the experience of another
catalyst (20): someone or something that brings about a change in other persons or things, but usually remains itself unchanged
eulogy (22): formal tribute or praise
adulated (22): admired excessively or slavishly
ineffable (22): incapable of being expressed in words
excising (23): cutting out
voyeuristic (24): appealing to a voyeur (Peeping Tom)
parousia (26): Second Coming; vision of an ideal future

59

THE MECHANICAL ROUTINE

Lewis Mumford

A well-known American social critic and philosopher describes the characteristics of our machine-age civilization and explains why the machine has not brought us greater social and material benefits.

1   Let the reader examine for himself the part played by mechanical routine and mechanical apparatus in his day, from the alarm-clock that wakes him to the radio program that puts him to sleep. Instead of adding to his burden by recapitulating it, I purpose to summarize the results of his investigations, and analyze the consequences.

2   The first characteristic of modern machine civilization is its temporal regularity. From the moment of waking, the rhythm of the day is punctuated by the clock. Irrespective of strain or fatigue, despite reluctance or apathy, the household rises close to its set hour. Tardiness in rising is penalized by extra haste in eating breakfast or in walking to catch the train: in the long run, it may even mean the loss of a job or of advancement in business. Breakfast, lunch, dinner, occur at regular hours and are of definitely limited duration: a million people perform these functions within a very narrow band of time, and only minor provisions are made for those who would have food outside this regular schedule. As the scale of industrial organization grows, the punctuality and regularity of the mechanical régime tend to increase with it: the time-clock enters automatically to regulate the entrance and exit of the worker, while an irregular worker—tempted by the trout in spring streams or ducks on salt meadows—finds that these impulses are as unfavorably treated as habitual drunkenness: if he would retain them, he must remain attached to the less routinized provinces of agriculture. "The refractory tempers of work-people accustomed to irregular paroxysms of diligence," of which Ure wrote a century ago with such pious horror, have indeed been tamed.

3   Under capitalism time-keeping is not merely a means of co-ordinating and interrelating complicated functions: it is also like money an independent commodity with a value of its own. The schoolteacher, the lawyer, even the doctor with his schedule of operations conform their functions to a timetable almost as rigorous as that of the locomotive

engineer. In the case of childbirth, patience rather than instrumentation is one of the chief requirements for a successful normal delivery and one of the major safeguards against infection in a difficult one. Here the mechanical interference of the obstetrician, eager to resume his rounds, has apparently been largely responsible for the current discreditable record of American physicians, utilizing the most sanitary hospital equipment, in comparison with midwives who do not attempt brusquely to hasten the processes of nature. While regularity in certain physical functions, like eating and eliminating, may in fact assist in maintaining health, in other matters, like play, sexual intercourse, and other forms of recreation the strength of the impulse itself is pulsating rather than evenly recurrent: here habits fostered by the clock or the calendar may lead to dullness and decay.

4   Hence the existence of a machine civilization, completely timed and scheduled and regulated, does not necessarily guarantee maximum efficiency in any sense. Time-keeping establishes a useful point of reference, and is invaluable for co-ordinating diverse groups and functions which lack any other common frame of activity. In the practice of an individual's vocation such regularity may greatly assist concentration and economize effort. But to make it arbitrarily rule over human functions is to reduce existence itself to mere time-serving and to spread the shades of the prison house over too large an area of human conduct. The regularity that produces apathy and atrophy—that *acedia* which was the bane of monastic existence, as it is likewise of the army—is as wasteful as the irregularity that produces disorder and confusion. To utilize the accidental, the unpredictable, the fitful is as necessary, even in terms of economy, as to utilize the regular: activites which exclude the operations of chance impulses forfeit some of the advantages of regularity.

5   In short: mechanical time is not an absolute. And a population trained to keep a mechanical time routine at whatever sacrifice to health, convenience, and organic felicity may well suffer from the strain of that discipline and find life impossible without the most strenuous compensations. The fact that sexual intercourse in a modern city is limited, for workers in all grades and departments, to the fatigued hours of the day may add to the efficiency of the working life only by a too-heavy sacrifice in personal and organic relations. Not the least of the blessings promised by the shortening of working hours is the opportunity to carry into bodily play the vigor that has hitherto been exhausted in the service of machines.

6   Next to mechanical regularity, one notes the fact that a good part of the mechanical elements in the day are attempts to counteract the effects of lengthening time and space distance. The refrigeration of eggs, for example, is an effort to space their distribution more uniformly than the hen herself is capable of doing: the pasteurization of milk

is an attempt to counteract the effect of the time consumed in completing the chain between the cow and the remote consumer. The accompanying pieces of mechanical apparatus do nothing to improve the product itself: refrigeration merely halts the process of decomposition, while pasteurization actually robs the milk of some of its value as nutriment. Where it is possible to distribute the population closer to the rural centers where milk and butter and green vegetables are grown, the elaborate mechanical apparatus for counteracting time and space distances may to a large degree be diminished.

7   One might multiply such examples from many departments; they point to a fact about the machine that has not been generally recognized by those quaint apologists for machine-capitalism who look upon every extra expenditure of horsepower and every fresh piece of mechanical apparatus as an automatic net gain in efficiency. In *The Instinct of Workmanship* Veblen has indeed wondered whether the typewriter, the telephone, and the automobile, though creditable technological achievements "have not wasted more effort and substance than they have saved," whether they are not to be credited with an appreciable economic loss, because they have increased the pace and the volume of correspondence and communication and travel out of all proportion to the real need. And Mr. Bertrand Russell has noted that each improvement in locomotion has increased the area over which people are compelled to move: so that a person who would have had to spend half an hour to walk to work a century ago must still spend half an hour to reach his destination, because the contrivance that would have enabled him to save time had he remained in his original situation now—by driving him to a more distant residential area—effectually cancels out the gain.

8   One further effect of our closer time co-ordination and our instantaneous communication must be noted here: broken time and broken attention. The difficulties of transport and communication before 1850 automatically acted as a selective screen, which permitted no more stimuli to reach a person than he could handle: a certain urgency was necessary before one received a call from a long distance or was compelled to make a journey oneself: this condition of slow physical locomotion kept intercourse down to a human scale, and under definite control. Nowadays this screen has vanished: the remote is as close as the near; the ephemeral is as emphatic as the durable. While the tempo of the day has been quickened by instantaneous communication the rhythm of the day has been broken: the radio, the telephone, the daily newspaper clamor for attention, and amid the host of stimuli to which people are subjected, it becomes more and more difficult to absorb and cope with any one part of the environment, to say nothing of dealing with it as a whole. The common man is as subject to these interruptions as the scholar or the man of affairs, and even the weekly

period of cessation from familiar tasks and contemplative reverie, which was one of the great contributions of Western religion to the discipline of the personal life, has become an ever remoter possibility. These mechanical aids to efficiency and cooperation and intelligence have been mercilessly exploited, through commercial and political pressure: but so far—since unregulated and undisciplined—they have been obstacles to the very ends they affect to further. We have multiplied the mechanical demands without multiplying in any degree our human capacities for registering and reacting intelligently to them. With the successive demands of the outside world so frequent and so imperative, without any respect to their real importance, the inner world becomes progressively meager and formless: instead of active selection there is passive absorption ending in the state happily described by Victor Branford as "addled subjectivity."

9   One of the by-products of the development of mechanical devices and mechanical standards has been the nullification of skill. What has taken place here within the factory has also taken place in the final utilization of its products. The safety razor, for example, has changed the operation of shaving from a hazardous one, best left to a trained barber, to a rapid commonplace of the day which even the most inept males can perform. The automobile has transformed engine-driving from the specialized task of the locomotive engineer to the occupation of millions of amateurs. The camera has in part transformed the artful reproductions of the wood engraver to a relatively simple photo-chemical process in which anyone can acquire at least the rudiments. As in manufacture the human function first becomes specialized, then mechanized, and finally automatic or at least semi-automatic.

10   When the last stage is reached, the function again takes on some of its original non-specialized character: photography helps recultivate the eye, the telephone the voice, the radio the ear, just as the motor car has restored some of the manual and operative skills that the machine was banishing from other departments of existence at the same time that it has given to the driver a sense of power and autonomous direction— a feeling of firm command in the midst of potentially constant danger— that had been taken away from him in other departments of life by the machine. So, too, mechanization, by lessening the need for domestic service, has increased the amount of personal autonomy and personal participation in the household. In short, mechanization creates new occasions for human effort; and on the whole the effects are more educative than were the semi-automatic services of slaves and menials in the older civilizations. For the mechanical nullification of skill can take place only up to a certain point. It is only when one has completely lost the power of discrimination that a standardized canned soup can, without further preparation, take the place of a home-cooked one, or when one has lost prudence completely that a four-wheel brake can

serve instead of a good driver. Inventions like these increase the province and multiply the interests of the amateur. When automatism becomes general and the benefits of mechanization are socialized, men will be back once more in the Edenlike state in which they have existed in regions of natural increment, like the South Seas: the ritual of leisure will replace the ritual of work, and work itself will become a kind of game. That is, in fact, the ideal goal of a completely mechanized and automatized system of power production: the elimination of work: the universal achievement of leisure. In his discussion of slavery Aristotle said that when the shuttle wove by itself and the plectrum played by itself chief workmen would not need helpers nor masters slaves. At the time he wrote, he believed that he was establishing the eternal validity of slavery; but for us today he was in reality justifying the existence of the machine. Work, it is true, is the constant form of man's interaction with his environment, if by work one means the sum total of exertions necessary to maintain life; and lack of work usually means an impairment of function and a breakdown in organic relationship that leads to substitute forms of work, such as invalidism and neurosis. But work in the form of unwilling drudgery or of that sedentary routine which, as Mr. Alfred Zimmern reminds us, the Athenians so properly despised—work in these degrading forms is the true province of machines. Instead of reducing human beings to work-mechanisms, we can now transfer the main part of burden to automatic machines. This potentiality, still so far from effective achievement for mankind at large, is perhaps the largest justification of the mechanical developments of the last thousand years.

11   From the social standpoint, one final characterization of the machine, perhaps the most important of all, must be noted: the machine imposes the necessity for collective effort and widens its range. To the extent that men have escaped the control of nature they must submit to the control of society. As in a serial operation every part must function smoothly and be geared to the right speed in order to ensure the effective working of the process as a whole, so in society at large there must be a close articulation between all its elements. Individual self-sufficiency is another way of saying technological crudeness: as our technics becomes more refined it becomes impossible to work the machine without large-scale collective cooperation, and in the long run a high technics is possible only on a basis of worldwide trade and intellectual intercourse. The machine has broken down the relative isolation—never complete even in the most primitive societies—of the handcraft period: it has intensified the need for collective effort and collective order. The efforts to achieve collective participation have been fumbling and empirical: so for the most part, people are conscious of the necessity in the form of limitations upon personal freedom and initiative—limitations like the automatic traffic signals of a congested

center, or like the red-tape in a large commercial organization. The collective nature of the machine process demands a special enlargement of the imagination and a special education in order to keep the collective demand itself from becoming an act of external regimentation. To the extent that the collective discipline becomes effective and the various groups in society are worked into a nicely interlocking organization, special provisions must be made for isolated and anarchic elements that are not included in such a wide-reaching collectivism—elements that cannot without danger be ignored or repressed. But to abandon the social collectivism imposed by modern technics means to return to nature and be at the mercy of natural forces.

12   The regularization of time, the increase in mechanical power, the multiplication of goods, the contraction of time and space, the standardization of performance and product, the transfer of skill to automata, and the increase of collective interdependence—these, then, are the chief characteristics of our machine civilization. They are the basis of the particular forms of life and modes of expression that distinguish Western Civilization, at least in degree, from the various earlier civilizations that preceded it.

13   In the translation of technical improvements into social processes, however, the machine has undergone a perversion: instead of being utilized as an instrument of life, it has tended to become an absolute. Power and social control, once exercised chiefly by military groups who had conquered and seized the land, have gone since the seventeenth century to those who have organized and controlled and owned the machine. The machine has been valued because—it increased the employment of machines. And such employment was the source of profits, power, and wealth to the new ruling classes, benefits which had hitherto gone to traders or to those who monopolized the land. Jungles and tropical islands were invaded during the nineteenth century for the purpose of making new converts to the machine: explorers like Stanley endured incredible tortures and hardships in order to bring the benefits of the machine to inaccessible regions tapped by the Congo: insulated countries like Japan were entered forcibly at the point of the gun in order to make way for the trader: natives in Africa and the Americas were saddled with false debts or malicious taxes in order to give them an incentive to work and to consume in the machine fashion—and thus to supply an outlet for the goods of America and Europe, or to ensure the regular gathering of rubber and lac.

14   The injunction to use machines was so imperative, from the standpoint of those who owned them and whose means and place in society depended upon them, that it placed upon the worker a special burden, the duty to consume machine-products, while it placed upon the manufacturer and the engineer the duty of inventing products weak enough and shoddy enough—like the safety razor blade or the common

run of American woolens—to lend themselves to rapid replacement. The great heresy to the machine was to believe in an institution or a habit of action or a system of ideas that would lessen this service to the machines: for under capitalist direction the aim of mechanism is not to save labor but to eliminate all labor except that which can be channeled at a profit through the factory.

15 At the beginning, the machine was an attempt to substitute quantity for value in the calculus of life. Between the conception of the machine and its utilization, as Krannhals points out, a necessary psychological and social process was skipped: the stage of evaluation. Thus a steam turbine may contribute thousands of horsepower, and a speedboat may achieve speed: but these facts, which perhaps satisfy the engineer, do not necessarily integrate them in society. Railroads may be quicker than canalboats, and a gas lamp may be brighter than a candle: but it is only in terms of human purpose and in relation to a human and social scheme of values that speed or brightness have any meaning. If one wishes to absorb the scenery, the slow motion of a canalboat may be preferable to the fast motion of a motor car: and if one wishes to appreciate the mysterious darkness and the strange forms of a natural cave, it is better to penetrate it with uncertain steps, with the aid of a torch or a lantern, than to descend into it by means of an elevator, as in the famous caves of Virginia, and to have the mystery entirely erased by a grand display of electric lights—a commercialized perversion that puts the whole spectacle upon the low dramatic level of a cockney amusement park.

16 Because the process of social evaluation was largely absent among the people who developed the machine in the eighteenth and nineteenth centuries the machine raced like an engine without a governor, tending to overheat its own bearings and lower its efficiency without any compensatory gain. This left the process of evaluation to groups who remained outside the machine milieu, and who unfortunately often lacked the knowledge and the understanding that would have made their criticisms more pertinent.

17 The important thing to bear in mind is that the failure to evaluate the machine and to integrate it in society as a whole was not due simply to defects in distributing income, to errors of management, to the greed and narrow-mindedness of the industrial leaders: it was also due to a weakness of the entire philosophy upon which the new techniques and inventions were grounded. The leaders and enterprisers of the period believed that they had avoided the necessity for introducing values, except those which were automatically recorded in profits and prices. They believed that the problem of justly distributing goods could be sidetracked by creating an abundance of them: that the problem of applying one's energies wisely could be cancelled out simply by multiplying them: in short, that most of the difficulties that had hitherto

vexed mankind had a mathematical or mechanical—that is a quantitative
—solution. The belief that values could be dispensed with constituted
the new system of values. Values, divorced from the current processes
of life, remained the concern of those who reacted against the machine.
Meanwhile, the current processes justified themselves solely in terms
of quantity production and cash results. When the machine as a whole
overspeeded and purchasing power failed to keep pace with dishonest
overcapitalization and exorbitant profits—then the whole machine
went suddenly into reverse, stripped its gears, and came to a standstill:
a humiliating failure, a dire social loss.

18   One is confronted, then, by the fact that the machine is ambivalent.
It is both an instrument of liberation and one of repression. It has
economized human energy and it has misdirected it. It has created a
wide framework of order and it has produced muddle and chaos. It
has nobly served human purposes and it has distorted and denied them.

Discussion of Theme

1. What are the chief characteristics of a machine civilization? Does
   the United States have all of them?
2. What is time-keeping? Why does Mumford criticize it?
3. Who, according to the author, has profited most from the machine?
4. According to the author, why are faster travel and communication
   not necessarily an advantage?
5. Which would you prefer to submit to—the control of nature or the
   control of society?
6. According to the author, what groups have been traditionally most
   concerned about the values of the machine age?

Discussion of Rhetoric

1. This essay is developed chiefly by argumentation. The central
   thesis is found in paragraph 14. How does Mumford support it?
   What is the function of the first thirteen paragraphs?
2. What sentence serves as a transition to paragraph 4? How does it
   link the preceding section?
3. What is the author's attitude or tone throughout this essay? Does
   it change in the last paragraph?

Writing Assignments

1. If you disagree with Mumford's assessment of our machine
   civilization, write a rebuttal. Support your opinion with facts.
2. Develop the following statement: "Power machines have given a
   sort of license to social inefficiency."
3. React to the following notion: Some technological achievements
   may have "wasted more effort and substance than they have saved."

Library Exploration

Examine the ideas of Thorstein Veblen on the machine age.

Vocabulary

recapitulating (1): repeating briefly

temporal (2): related to or dealing with time

refractory (2): stubborn

paroxysms (2): sudden attacks

atrophy (4): wasting away

acedia (4): spiritual apathy; sloth

ephemeral (8): transient; temporary

plectrum (10): a small thin pick (as of ivory or metal) used to pluck the strings of a musical instrument

empirical (11): based on or derived from observation or experience

lac (13): a resinous substance used chiefly in the form of shellac

60

OF HAPPINESS AND OF DESPAIR
WE HAVE NO MEASURE

Ernest van den Haag

The author of the following essay discusses the depersonalizing effects of mass culture. "All mass media," he states, " . . . alienate people from *personal experience and, though appearing to offset it, intensify their moral isolation from each other, from reality and from themselves."*

> "non ridere non lugere, neque destestari; sed intelligere." — *Spinoza*

1   How is the mass market formed on which popular culture is sold and perpetuated? In the first place, individual taste has become uneconomic for the purchaser and for the seller, and this effectively stunts its growth. People are prepared accordingly throughout the educational process. Group acceptance, shared taste, takes the place of authority and of individual moral and aesthetic judgment and standards. But people often move from group to group. Any taste therefore that cannot be sloughed off—an individual taste, not easily divided from the person in whom it dwells—becomes an obstacle to adaptation. Success is hindered by a discriminating personal taste which expresses or continues an individual personality, and success is fostered by an unselective appetite.

2   Numerous precautions are taken, beginning in nursery school (itself hardly an individualizing institution) to avoid elaboration of personal discernment and to instill fear of separation from the group. Group acceptance is stressed through formal and informal popularity contests, teamwork, and polling. Education altogether stresses group instruction. For instance, the size of his classes and the class average, not the qualities of individual pupils, are often considered the measure of the teacher. The student himself is so much treated as part of a group that, except in higher education (which is only partly immune), he may be automatically promoted with his group regardless of individual achievement or variation. Finally, the surviving individual talent is instructed not to cultivate, but to share, itself. The writer gives a writing course, the scholar lectures and writes popularizations, the beauty models or appears on TV, and the singer deserts the concert hall for the juke box.

3   The aggregate effect of advertising is to bring about wide sharing of

tastes. The actual social function of advertising is *not* to mold taste in any particular way, nor to debase it. This goes for manufacturers, publishers and movie-makers too. They are quite content to produce and advertise what people want—be it T. S. Eliot or Edgar Guest, Kierkegaard or Norman Vincent Peale, "September Morn" or mobiles. It does not matter what people want to buy as long as they want to buy enough of the same thing to make mass production possible. Advertising helps to unify taste, to de-individualize it and thus to make mass production possible.

4   There is no evidence to support conspiracy theories which hold that wicked capitalists, through advertising and mass media, deliberately (or stupidly) debauch the originally good, natural taste of the masses. Mass production—capitalist or socialist—demands unified taste; efficiency (or profitableness) is dependent only on its being shared by sizeable groups.

5   Can one say anything about mass tastes beyond saying that they are widely shared? Are they homogenized on the "lowest common denominator"? There seems to be no good reason to assume that the lowest tastes are most widespread. One may say something of the sort about some crowds united temporarily by crude common appetites at the expense of reason, restraint and refinement. But why consider consumers a crowd? Even the fare offered by the entertainment media is usually consumed by people separately or in very small groups. (Except for movies, but movie-goers are isolated from each other though they are together.)

6   Producers have no interest in lowering taste or in catering to low rather than high taste. They seek to provide for a *modal* average of tastes which through advertising they try to make as congruent with the *mean* average as possible. Neither average can be identical with the "lowest common denominator."

7   Yet in one sense consumers are treated as a crowd: their individual tastes are not catered to. The mass-produced article need not aim low, but it must aim at an average of tastes. In satisfying all (or at least many) individual tastes in some respects, it violates each in other respects. For there are—so far—no average persons having average tastes. Averages are but statistical composites. A mass-produced article, while reflecting nearly everybody's taste to some extent, is unlikely to embody anybody's taste fully. This is one source of the sense of violation which is rationalized vaguely in theories about deliberate debasement of taste.

8   The sense of violation springs from the same thwarting of individuality that makes prostitution (or promiscuity) psychologically offensive. The cost of cheap and easy availability, of mass production, is wide appeal; and the cost of wide appeal is de-individualization of the relationship between those who cater and those who are catered to; and of the relationship of both to the object of the transaction. By using each other indiscriminately as impersonal instruments (the seller for

profit, the buyer for sensation—or, in promiscuity, both parties for sensation and relief of anxiety) the prostitute and her client sacrifice to seemingly more urgent demands the self which, in order to grow, needs continuity, discrimination and completeness in relationships. Though profit and sensation can be achieved by depersonalization, the satisfaction ultimately sought cannot be, for the very part of personality in which it is felt—the individual self—is stunted and atrophied, at least if de-individualization continues long enough and is comprehensive. Ultimately, the sense of violation too is numbed.

9   Now, the depersonalizing effects of the mass production of some things—say, electric clocks—may be minor as far as consumers are concerned and more than offset by the advantages of cheapness. The same cannot be said for mass entertainment or education. And though some individuals may, society cannot have one without the other. The effects of mass production on people as producers and consumers are likely to be cumulative. Besides, even goods that seem purely utilitarian include elements of non-utilitarian, of aesthetic and psychic (e.g., prestige) appeal. Indeed, less than half of consumer expenditure goes for the satisfaction of simple biological needs. (More, perhaps, in the lowest income groups, and much less still in the higher ones.) Distinctions of this kind are necessarily hazy, but if cigarettes, newspapers, television, drinks, shaving lotion or lipstick, the prestige location of one's apartment, the fashionableness of one's clothing, etc., are taken to satisfy nonbiological needs—and we can do without them biologically—then we are motivated by psychic needs in spending most of our money. This, of course, is not in itself objectionable—except that the processes by which many of these needs now arise and are stilled bring to mind the processes by which bread is now mass produced.

10   In milling and baking, bread is deprived of any taste whatever and of all vitamins. Some of the vitamins are then added again (taste is provided by advertising). Quite similarly with all mass-produced articles. They can no more express the individual taste of producers than that of consumers. They become impersonal objects, however pseudo-personalized. Producers and consumers go through the mass production mill to come out homogenized and de-characterized—only it does not seem possible to reinject the individualities which have been ground out, the way the vitamins are added to enrich bread. The "human relations" industry tries to do just that and it doubtlessly supplies a demand and can be helpful, just as chemical sedatives or stimulants can be. But it seems unlikely that any assembly line— including one manned by human relations counselors—can give more than the illusion of individuality.

11   To produce more, people work under de-individualizing conditions and are rewarded by high income and leisure. Thus they can and do consume more. But as consumers, they must once more rid themselves

of individual tastes. The benefits of mass production are reaped only by matching de-individualizing work with equally de-individualizing consumption. The more discontinuous income earning and spending become physically, the more continuous they seem to become psychologically. Failure to repress individual personality in or after working hours is costly; in the end the production of standardized things by persons demands also the production of standardized persons.

12   In a material sense, this assembly-line shaping, packaging and distributing of persons, of life, occurs already. Most people perch unsteadily in mass-produced, impermanent dwellings throughout their lives. They are born in hospitals, fed in cafeterias, married in hotels. After terminal care, they die in hospitals, are shelved briefly in funeral homes, and are finally incinerated. On each of these occasions— and how many others?—efficiency and economy are obtained and individuality and continuity stripped off. If one lives and dies discontinuously and promiscuously in anonymous surroundings, it becomes hard to identify with anything, even the self, and uneconomic to be attached to anything, even one's own individuality. The rhythm of individual life loses autonomy, spontaneity, and distinction when it is tied into a stream of traffic and carried along according to the speed of the road, as we are, in going to work, or play, or in doing anything. Traffic lights signal when to stop and go, and much as we seem to be driving we are driven. To stop spontaneously, to exclaim, *Verweile doch Du bist so schoen* (Stay, for you are beautiful), may not lose the modern Faust his soul—but it will cause a traffic jam.

13   One motive for delinquency—a way of getting out of line—is, possibly, a preference for occasional prison terms to imprisonment by routine. Crime, by its ultimate irrationality, may protest against the subordination of individual spontaneity to social efficiency. Three further reactions to anonymity may be noted:

> 1. The prestige of histrionics has risen. We long to impersonate, to get a name—better a pseudonym than to remain nameless; better a borrowed character than none; better to impersonate than never to feel like a person. The wish to be oneself does not occur, for the only self known is empty and must be filled from the outside.
>
> 2. The attempt to become "interesting" (no doubt unconsciously to become interested) by buying a ready-made individuality, through "sending for," "enrolling in," or "reading up on" something, or "going places."
>
> 3. Impersonal and abstract things and utilitarian relationships are cozily "personalized" as though to offset the depersonalization of individual life.

14   De-individualization, however, should not be viewed as a grim, deliberate, or coercive process. It is induced gradually by economic

rewards and not experienced as de-individualization at all, though the symptoms are demonstrable. Most of the people who are nourished with homogenized pap never had solid food on which to cut their teeth. They feel vaguely restless and dissatisfied, but do not know what they are pining for and could not masticate or digest it if they had it. The cooks are kept busy ransacking all the recipes the world has ever known to prepare new dishes. But the texture is always the same, always mushy, for the materials are always strained, blended, beaten, heated, and cooled until it is.

15   Let us briefly tour the institutional kitchens where "recreation" is cooked up—movies, radio, television.

16   Mass media cannot afford to step on anyone's toes, and this implies a number of restrictions which, though less significant than the positive prescriptions, are not negligible. We can forebear rehearsing tiresome minutiae—forbidden words, topics, situations, actions; but the countless dangerous associations mass media must avoid deserve some scrutiny.

17   No religious, racial, occupational, national, economic, political, etc., group can be offended. Hence: Can an evil man be Jewish? Left-handed? Pipesmoking? Can he perish in an airplane accident? Can a villain have any qualities shared with non-villains and a hero have disapproved traits? In short, can either be human? The playwright or script writer may not mean to say that Jews are evil or all evil men left-handed, or all pipesmokers; he may not intend to advocate bigamy or to suggest that airplanes are dangerous or that we ought to be atheists. Joseph Conrad did not intend *The Nigger of the Narcissus* as an anti-Negro tract, any more than Shakespeare intended *Othello* as a tract against handkerchiefs (in favor of Kleenex?). No matter. There is a danger that the play will be so understood. In Shylock and Fagin, Shakespeare and Dickens created individuals, experiences, and ideas and, unlike copywriters or propagandists, did not intend them as instructions on how to act and think. Yet the groups that press restrictions on mass media are not wrong. For the audience tends to react as though such instruction had been received.

18   The audience of mass media always expects to be sold goods, stereotypes, and recipes for living—a new vitamin for that tired, listless feeling, or a new line for romance. And the audience is usually right: the same actress who just implored a soap-opera husband not to leave her and the kids turns and implores one and all in identically sincere and personal tones to buy insurance or perfume. The small boy's heroes admonish him to get mommy to buy this or that (and even if the heroes didn't, someone will sell Davy Crockett caps to the small boy). In many breakfast and news shows, advertising recommendations are deliberately mixed in with "actual" expressions of opinion. Even

non-professionals—society leaders, well-known novelists, successful and "average" common men—ringingly declare their profound personal convictions on brands of soap, or beer, or God: "This I believe." The line dividing views and characters presented as fiction and as "real" becomes hazy and the audience necessarily muddled about separating advertisements, pleas, and recipes from art. In such a context, the audience cannot receive art as individual experience and perspective on experience. Art becomes irrelevant. It is not perceived in its own terms, but first reduced to, then accepted or rejected as, a series of rules and opinions on what to expect or do.

19   The idea that something must be sold is held by the media managers as fervently as it is held by the audience. It transcends the commercial motives which begot it. Thus public or educational stations, which do not accept commercial advertising, spend nearly as much time on (non-commercial) attempts to sell something as do commercial ones. They sell themselves or their program, or next week's offering— anything at all, as long as something is sold: "please listen again tomorrow," "please send for our booklet," "please do this or don't do that"—the listener must always be hectored, sold on or wheedled into something.

20   How, then, could the audience see that a character such as Shylock simply is? A character in the audience's experience always exists for a purpose; a character is invented to sell something, a point of view, or a product, or himself. It is never an end in itself. Hence the audience always asks, Should we buy his line?, and it is nearly impossible to present something without suggesting by implication that it be bought. Art, like love, can be experienced only as a personal, continuous, cumulative relationship. Else art becomes entertainment—dull entertainment often—just as love is reduced to sex or prestige. Not that art should not be entertaining; but it is no more deliberately aimed at entertainment than love is. Art (and love) must be felt; they cannot be manufactured by someone to suit the taste of someone else. Yet mass-media fare is prepared for consumers devoted to amusement, not, as art (and love) must be, devoted to the work (or person) itself.

21   The circumstances which permit the experience of art are rare in our society anyway and they cannot be expected in the audience of mass media. That audience is dispersed and heterogeneous, and though it listens often, it does so incidentally and intermittently and poised to leave if not immediately enthralled and kept amused. Such an audience is captured by loud, broad, and easy charms, by advertising posters, by copywriter's prose. And the conditions and conditioning of the audience demand a mad mixture of important and trivial matters, atom bombs, hit tunes, symphonies, B.O., sob stories, hotcha girls, round tables and jokes. It jells into one thing: diversion. Hence what art is presented is

received as entertainment or propaganda. Shylock would be understood as an anti-Semitic stereotype. The mass media may as well fit their offerings to the audience which they address and, knowing the limitations of that audience, they would be irresponsible to disregard the kind of understanding and misunderstanding their offerings will meet. They must omit, therefore, all human experience likely to be misunderstood—all experience and expression, the meaning of which is not obvious and approved. Which is to say that the mass media cannot touch the experiences that art, philosophy and literature deal with: relevant and significant human experience presented in relevant and significant form. For if it is such, it is new, doubtful, difficult, perhaps offensive, at any rate easily misunderstood. Art is not concerned with making the obvious and approved more obvious and approved; it is precisely after this point that art begins and the mass media stop.

22   When attempting to be serious, the mass media must rig up pseudo-problems and solve them by cliché. They cannot touch real problems or real solutions. Plots are packed with actions which obscure the vagueness and irrelevance of meanings and solutions. Similarly, to replace actual individuality, each character and situation is tricked up with numerous identifying details and mannerisms. The more realistic the characteristics, the less real the character usually, or the situation, and the less revealing. Literal realism cannot replace relevance. Mass media inveigh against sin and against all evils accepted as such. But they cannot question things not acknowledged as evil or appear to support things felt as evil. Even *Rigoletto*, were it a modern work, could not be broadcast since crime and immorality pay and the ending is unhappy for everybody but the villain.

23   Combating legal censorship, organized group pressures, and advertising agencies is gallantly romantic—and as quixotic as man's rage against his own mirrored image. These agencies are interested only in presenting what is wanted and in preventing what might offend people. They are nuisances perhaps, but things could not be very different without them. Policemen do not create the law, though becoming the target of the few who would defy it.

24   The very nature of mass media excludes art, and requires surrogation by popular culture. Though the Hays production code applies only to movies, its basic rule states a principle which all mass media must follow: "Correct standards of life, subject only to the requirements of drama and entertainment" must be upheld. Doubtless "correct standards" are those standards most of the audience is likely to believe correct. They authorize whatever does not upset or offend the audience, and nothing else. "Correct standards of life" must exclude art (except occasional classics). For art is bound to differ from the accepted, that is, the customary moral and aesthetic view, at least as it takes shape in the

audience's mind. Art is always a fresh vision of the world, a new experience or creation of life. If it does not break, or develop, or renew in significant aspects the traditional, customary, accepted aesthetic and moral standards, if it merely repeats without creating, it is not art. If it does, it is incompatible with the "correct standards of life" which must control mass media.

25   Mass media thus never can question man's fate where it is questionable; they cannot sow doubt about an accepted style of life, or an approved major principle. To be sure, mass media often feature challenges to this and that, and clashes of opinion. These are part of our accepted style of life, as long as challenges do not defy anything but sin and evil in the accepted places and manner. The mass media must hold up "correct standards of life" whereas art must create, not uphold views. When filmed or broadcast, the visions of the playwright or novelist cannot deviate from the accepted "correct standards" and they must be entertaining. They must conform to the taste of the audience; they cannot form it. Virtue must triumph entertainingly— virtue as the audience sees it.

26   The poets, Shelly thought, are "the unacknowledged legislators of the world." Shelley's poets wrote for a few who would take the trouble to understand them. They addressed an audience that knew and shared the common traditions they were developing. High culture was cultivated in special institutions—courts, monasteries, churches, universities—by people who devoted their lives to the development of its traditions, and were neither isolated nor surrounded by masses wishing to be entertained. (Besides, there were no means of addressing a mass.) There was no need and no temptation for the artist to do anything but to create in his own terms. Poets, painters, or philosophers lived in and were of the group for whom they produced, as did most people, were they peasants, artisans or artists. The relations between producers of culture and consumers were so personal (as were the relations between producers and consumers generally) that one can hardly speak of an impersonal market in which one sold, the other bought.

27   In both high and folk culture, each bounded an autonomous universe—court or village—relied on the particular cultivators and inventors of its arts and sciences no less than the latter relied on their patrons. Each region or court depended on its musicians as it depended on its craftsmen, and vice versa. The mutual personal dependence had disadvantages and advantages, as has any close relationship. Michelangelo or Beethoven depended on irksome individual patrons more than they would today. On the other hand, whatever the patrons' tastes or demands, they were individual and not average tastes or demands. Folk culture grew without professional help. High culture

was cultivated like an orchard or garden. But both folk and high cultures grew from within the groups they distinguished and remained within them.

28   High culture was entirely dominated by people with more than average prestige, power and income—by the elite as a group, who also dominated politics and society in general. This group determined what was to be produced, culturally and otherwise; and they took their toll often by oppression and spoliation of the mass of people whom they ruled.

29   With the development of industry, the elite as a group lost its power. The great mass of consumers now determines what is to be produced. Elite status, leadership in any form, is achieved and kept today by catering to the masses, not by plundering or oppressing them. The nobleman may have become rich by robbing (taking from) his peasants. But the industrialist becomes a millionaire by selling to (exchanging with) farmers. And his business is helped by giving his customers, via television, the entertainers they want. These in turn reach elite status by appealing to the masses. So do politicians.

30   The elite no longer determines what is produced, any more than it dominates society in other respects. Rather, the elite becomes the elite by producing the goods that sell, the goods that cater to an average of tastes. With respect to culture, the elite neither imposes any taste nor cultivates one of its own. It markets and helps homogenize and distribute popular culture—that which appeals to an average of tastes—through the mass media. The changes in income distribution, mobility and communication, the economics of mass production already discussed, have caused the power of individual consumers to wane. But the power of consumers as a group has risen and that of producers as a group has dwindled.

31   With the invention of mass media, a mass market for culture became possible. The economics yielded by the mass production of automobiles became available in the mass production of entertainment. Producers of popular culture supply this new mass market. Popular culture does not *grow* within a group. It is manufactured by one group—in Hollywood or in New York—for sale to an anonymous mass market. The product must meet an average of tastes and it loses in spontaneity and individuality what it gains in accessibility and cheapness. The creators of popular culture are not a sovereign group of "unacknowledged legislators." They work for Hooper ratings to give people what they want. Above all, they are salesmen; they sell entertainment and produce with sales in mind. The creators of high culture are no longer insulated from the demands of the mass market by an educated elite, as they still were during the nineteenth century (and there are no stable, isolated communities in which folk culture could grow). They do not create for or have personal relationships with patrons whom they can lead as a

man may lead in a conversation. A personal tutor is much more dependent on a few persons than a television lecturer. But his influence on his pupil is also much greater than the influence of any one television lecturer on any one pupil.

32   Today's movie producer, singer, or writer is less dependent on the taste of an individual customer, or village, or court, than was the artist of yore; but he does depend far more on the average of tastes, and he can influence it far less. He need not cater to any individual taste —not even his own. He caters to an impersonal market. He is not involved in a conversation. He is like a speaker addressing a mass meeting and attempting to curry its favor.

33   All mass media in the end alienate people from personal experience and, though appearing to offset it, intensify their moral isolation from each other, from reality and from themselves. One may turn to the mass media when lonely or bored. But mass media, once they become a habit, impair the capacity for meaningful experience. Though more diffuse and not as gripping, the habit feeds on itself, establishing a vicious circle as addictions do.

34   The mass media do not physically replace individual activities and contacts—excursions, travel, parties, etc. But they impinge on all. The portable radio is taken everywhere—from seashore to mountaintop —and everywhere it isolates the bearer from his surroundings, from other people, and from himself. Most people escape being by themselves at any time by voluntarily tuning in on something or somebody. Anyway, it is nearly beyond the power of individuals to escape broadcasts. Music and public announcements are piped into restaurants, bars, shops, cafes, and lobbies, into public means of transportation, and even taxis. You can turn off your radio but not your neighbor's, nor can you silence his portable or the set at the restaurant. Fortunately, most persons do not seem to miss privacy, the cost of which is even more beyond the average income than the cost of individuality.

35   People are never quite in one place or group without at the same time, singly or collectively, gravitating somewhere else, abstracted, if not transported by the mass media. The incessant announcements, arpeggios, croonings, sobs, bellows, brayings and jingles draw to some faraway world at large and by weakening community with immediate surroundings make people lonely even when in a crowd and crowded even when alone.

36   We have already stressed that mass media must offer homogenized fare to meet an average of tastes. Further, whatever the quality of the offerings, the very fact that one after the other is absorbed continuously, indiscriminately and casually, trivializes all. Even the most profound of experiences, articulated too often on the same level, is reduced to a cliché. The impact of each of the offerings of mass media is thus weakened by the next one. But the impact of the stream of all mass-

media offerings is cumulative and strong. It lessens people's capacity to experience life itself.

37   Sometimes it is argued that the audience confuses actuality with mass-media fiction and reacts to the characters and situations that appear in soap operas or comic strips as though they were real. For instance, wedding presents are sent to fictional couples. It seems more likely, however, that the audience prefers to invest fiction with reality —as a person might prefer to dream—without actually confusing it with reality. After all, even the kids know that Hopalong Cassidy is an actor and the adults know that "I Love Lucy" is fiction. Both, however, may attempt to live the fiction because they prefer it to their own lives. The significant effect is not the (quite limited) investment of fiction with reality, but the de-realization of life lived in largely fictitious terms. Art can deepen the perception of reality. But popular culture veils it, diverts from it, and becomes an obstacle to experiencing it. It is not so much an escape from life but an invasion of life first, and ultimately evasion altogether.

38   Parents, well knowing that mass media can absorb energy, often lighten the strain that the attempts of their children to reach for activity and direct experience would impose; they allow some energy to be absorbed by the vicarious experience of the television screen. Before television, the cradle was rocked, or poppy juice given, to inhibit the initiative and motility of small children. Television, unlike these physical sedatives, tranquillizes by means of substitute gratifications. Manufactured activities and plots are offered to still the child's hunger for experiencing life. They effectively neutralize initiative and channel imagination. But the early introduction of de-individualized characters and situations and early homogenization of taste on a diet of meaningless activity hardly foster development. Perhaps poppy juice, offering no models in which to cast the imagination, was better.

39   The homogenizing effect of comic books or television, the fact that they neither express nor appeal to individuality, seems far more injurious to the child's mind and character than the violence they feature, though it is the latter that is often blamed for juvenile delinquency. The blame is misplaced. Violence is not new to life or fiction. It waxed large in ancient fables, fairy tales, and in tragedies from Sophocles to Shakespeare.

40   Mom always knew that "her boy could not have thought of it," that the other boys must have seduced him. The belief that viewing or reading about violence persuades children to engage in it is Mom's ancient conviction disguised as psychiatry. Children are quite spontaneously bloodthirsty and need both direct and fantasy outlets for violence. What is wrong with the violence of the mass media is not that it is violence, but that it is not art—that it is meaningless violence which thrills but does not gratify. The violence of the desire for life and meaning is displaced and appears as a desire for meaningless violence. But

the violence which is ceaselessly supplied cannot ultimately gratify it because it does not meet the repressed desire.

41   We have hinted that the gratifications offered by popular culture are spurious and unsatisfactory. Let us summarize these hints now, and then try to make explicit the psychological effects we implied before.

42   While immensely augmenting our comforts, our conveniences and our leisure, and disproportionately raising the real income of the poor, industry has also impoverished life. Mass production and consumption, mobility, the homogenization of taste and finally of society were among the costs of higher productivity. They de-individualized life and drained each of our ends of meaning as we achieved it. Pursuit thus became boundless. The increased leisure time would hang heavy on our hands, were it not for the mass media which help us kill it. They inexorably exclude art and anything of significance when it cannot be reduced to mass entertainment, but they divert us from the passage of the time they keep us from filling. They also tend to draw into the mass market talents and works that might otherwise produce new visions and they abstract much of the capacity to experience art or life directly and deeply. What they do, however, is what people demand.

43   We scrutinized the causes, the effects and the general characteristics of popular culture and found them unavoidable in a mass-production economy. But we have hardly touched on the contents of popular culture. Some work on this subject has been done and much remains. Limitations of scope also restricted us from stressing the many material advantages of industrialism. We do not intend to deny them. Finally, prophecy too is beyond our means. True, extrapolation of present trends makes a dismal picture. But there is comfort in the fact that no extrapolation has ever predicted the future correctly. Elements can be forecast, but only prophets can do more (and they are unreliable, or hard to interpret). History has always had surprises up its sleeves— it would be most surprising if it changed its ways. Our ignorance here leaves the rosy as well as the grim possibilities open for the future. But this does not allow us to avert our gaze from the present and from the outlook it affords. Neither is cheerful.

44   The gist of any culture is an ethos which gives meaning to the lives of those who dwell in it. If this be the purport of popular culture, it is foiled. We have suggested how it comes to grief in various aspects. What makes popular culture as a whole so disconcerting is best set forth now by exploring the relationship among diversion, art and boredom.

45   Freud thought of art as a diversion, "an illusion in contrast to reality," a "substitute gratification" like a dream. In this he fully shared what was and still is the popular view of art. It is a correct view—of popular "art," of pseudo-art produced to meet the demand for diversion. But it is a mistaken, reductive definition of art.

46   Freud finds the "dreamwork" attempting to hide or disguise the

dreamer's true wishes and fears so that they may not alarm his consciousness. The "substitute gratification" produced by the dreamwork, mainly by displacements, helps the dreamer continue sleeping. However, one major function of art is precisely to undo this dreamwork, to see through disguises, to reveal to our consciousness the true nature of our wishes and fears. The dreamwork covers, to protect sleep. Art discovers and attempts to awaken the sleeper. Whereas the dreamwork tries to aid repression, the work of art intensifies and deepens perception and experience of the world and of the self. It attempts to pluck the heart of the mystery, to show where "the action lies in its true nature."

47   Though dreams and art both may disregard literal reality, they do so to answer opposite needs. The dream may ignore reality to keep the sleeper's eyes closed. Art transcends immediate reality to encompass wider views, penetrate into deeper experience and lead to a fuller confrontation of man's predicament. The dreamwork even tries to cover upsetting basic impulses with harmless immediate reality. Art, in contrast, ignores the immediate only to uncover the essential. Artistic revelation need not be concerned with outer or with social reality. It may be purely aesthetic. But it can never be an illusion if it is art. Far from distracting from reality, art is a form of reality which strips life of the fortuitous to lay bare its essentials and permit us to experience them.

48   In popular culture, however, "art" is all that Freud said art is, and no more. Like the dreamwork, popular culture distorts human experience to draw "substitute gratifications" or reassurances from it. Like the dreamwork, it presents "an illusion in contrast to reality." For this reason, popular "art" falls short of satisfaction. And all of popular culture leaves one vaguely discontented because, like popular art, it is only a "substitute gratification"; like a dream, it distracts from life and from real gratification.

49   Substitute gratifications are uneconomic, as Freud often stressed. They do not in the end gratify as much, and they cost more psychologically than the real gratifications which they shut out. This is why sublimation and realistic control are to be preferred to substitution and repression. That is why reality is to be preferred to illusion, full experience to symptomatic displacements and defense mechanisms. Yet substitute gratifications, habitually resorted to, incapacitate the individual for real ones. In part they cause or strengthen internalized hindrances to real and gratifying experience; in part they are longed for because internal barriers have already blocked real gratification of the original impulses.

50   Though the specific role it plays varies with the influence of other formative factors in the life of each individual, popular culture must be counted among the baffling variety of causes and effects of defense mechanisms and repressions. It may do much damage, or do none at all,

or be the only relief possible, however deficient. But whenever popular culture plays a major role in life significant repressions have taken (or are taking) place. Popular culture supplants those gratifications, which are no longer sought because of the repression of the original impulses. But it is a substitute and spurious. It founders and cannot succeed because neither desire nor gratification are true. "Nought's had, all's spent/where desire is got without content."

51   It may seem paradoxical to describe popular culture in terms of repression. Far from repressed, it strikes one as uninhibited. Yet the seeming paradox disappears if we assume that the uproarious din, the raucous noise and the shouting are attempts to drown the shriek of unused capacities, of repressed individuality, as it is bent into futility.

52   Repression bars impulses from awareness without satisfying them. This damming up always generates a feeling of futility and apathy or, in defense against it, an agitated need for action. The former may be called listless, the latter restless boredom. They may alternate and they may enter consciousness only through anxiety and a sense of meaninglessness, fatigue and nonfulfillment. Sometimes there is such a general numbing of the eagerness too often turned aside that only a dull feeling of dreariness and emptiness remains. More often, there is an insatiable longing for things to happen. The external world is to supply these events to fill the emptiness. Yet the bored person cannot designate what would satisfy a craving as ceaseless as it is vague. It is not satisfied by any event supplied.

53   The yearning for diversion to which popular culture caters cannot be sated by diversion "whereof a little more than a little is by much too much," because no displaced craving can be satisfied by catering to it in its displaced form. Only when it becomes possible to experience the desire in its true form and to dispense with the internalized processes that balked and displaced it does actual gratification become possible. Diversion at most, through weariness and fatigue, can numb and distract anxiety.

54   For instance, in many popular movies the tear ducts are massaged and thrills are produced by mechanized assaults on the centers of sensation. We are diverted temporarily and in the end perhaps drained—but not gratified. Direct manipulation of sensations can produce increases and discharges of tension, as does masturbation, but it is a substitute. It does not involve the whole individual as an individual, it does not involve reality but counterfeits it. Sensations directly stimulated and discharged without being intensified and completed through feelings sifted and acknowledged by the intellect are debasing because they do not involve the whole individual in his relation to reality. When one becomes inured to bypassing reality and individuality in favor of meaningless excitement, ultimate gratification becomes impossible.

55   Once fundamental impulses are thwarted beyond retrieving, once they are so deeply repressed that no awareness is left of their aims,

once the desire for a meaningful life has been lost as well as the capacity to create it, only a void remains. Life fades into tedium when the barrier between impulses and aims is so high that neither penetrates into consciousness and no sublimation whatever takes place. Diversion, however frantic, can overwhelm temporarily but not ultimately relieve the boredom which oozes from nonfulfillment.

56   Though the bored person hungers for things to happen to him, the disheartening fact is that when they do he empties them of the very meaning he unconsciously yearns for by using them as distractions. In popular culture even the second coming would become just another barren "thrill" to be watched on television till Milton Berle comes on. No distraction can cure boredom, just as the company so unceasingly pursued cannot stave off loneliness. The bored person is lonely for himself, not, as he thinks, for others. He misses the individuality, the capacity for experience from which he is debarred. No distraction can restore it. Hence he goes unrelieved and insatiable.

57   The popular demand for "inside" stories, for vicarious sharing of the private lives of "personalities" rests on the craving for private life —even someone else's—of those who are dimly aware of having none whatever, or at least no life that holds their interest. The attempts to allay boredom are as assiduous as they are unavailing. Countless books pretend to teach by general rules and devices what cannot be learned by devices and rules. Individual personalities cannot be mass produced (with happiness thrown in or your money back). Nevertheless, the message of much popular culture is "you, too, can be happy" if you only buy this car or that hair tonic; you will be thrilled, you will have adventure, romance, popularity—you will no longer be lonely and left out if you follow this formula. And success, happiness or at least freedom from anxiety is also the burden of popular religion, as unchristian in these its aims as it is in its means. From Dale Carnegie to Normal Vincent Peale to Harry and Bonaro Overstreet only the vocabulary changes. The principle remains the same. The formula is well illustrated in the following.

Warm Smile Is an Attribute of Charm
For this, train the upper lip by this method:
1. Stretch the upper lip down over the teeth. Say "Mo-o-o-o."
2. Hold the lip between the teeth and smile.
3. Purse the lips, pull them downward and grin.
4. Let the lower jaw fall and try to touch your nose with your upper lip.
    Months of daily practice are necessary to eliminate strain from the new way of smiling, but it, too, can become as natural as all beguiling smiles must be.   [*Indianapolis News.*]

58   Whatever the formula, nothing can be more tiresome than the tireless, cheerless pursuit of pleasure. Days go slowly when they are empty; one cannot tell one from the other. And yet the years go fast. When time is endlessly killed, one lives in an endless present until time ends without ever having passed, leaving a person who never lived to exclaim, "I wasted time and now doth time waste me."

59   To the Christian, despair is a sin not because there is anything to be hoped for in this life, but because to despair is to lack faith in redemption from it—in the life everlasting. As for the pleasures of this life, they are not worth pursuing. Lancelot Andrewes described them: ". . . though they fade not of themselves yet to us they fade. We are hungry and we eat. Eat we not till that fades and we are as weary of our fulness as we were of our fasting? We are weary and we rest. Rest we not till that fades and we are as weary of our rest as ever we were of our weariness?" Our bodies and minds themselves fade as do their pleasures. The insults of time are spared to none of us. Such is the human predicament.

60   In *Civilization and Its Discontents*, Freud pointed to the additional burdens that civilization imposes on human beings. They, too, are inevitable, for civilization, despite its cost, eases the total burden we bear.

61   A little more than a hundred years ago, Henry David Thoreau wrote in *Walden*: "The mass of men lead lives of quiet desperation. . . . A stereotyped but unconscious despair is concealed even under what are called the games and amusements of mankind." Despair, we find, is no longer quiet. Popular culture tries to exorcise it with much clanging and banging. Perhaps it takes more noise to drone it out. Perhaps we are less willing to face it. But whether wrapped in popular culture, we are less happy than our quieter ancestors, or the natives of Bali, must remain an open question despite all romanticizing. (Nor do we have a feasible alternative to popular culture. Besides, a proposal for "the mass of men" would be unlikely to affect the substance of popular culture. And counsel to individuals must be individual.)

62   There have been periods happier and others more desperate than ours. But we don't know which. And even an assertion as reasonable as this is a conjecture like any comparison of today's bliss with yesterday's. The happiness felt in disparate groups, in disparate periods and places cannot be measured and compared. Our contention is simply that by distracting from the human predicament and blocking individuation and experience, popular culture impoverishes life without leading to contentment. But whether "the mass of men" felt better or worse without the mass-production techniques of which popular culture is an ineluctable part, we shall never know. Of happiness and of despair, we have no measure.

Discussion of Theme

1. What are "group acceptance" and "shared taste" as the author uses these terms? How do they affect us?
2. What is the relationship between standardized goods and standardized people? Can you cite examples that agree with van den Haag's observations?
3. In what way can modern man be said to have become anonymous? What, according to the author, are four possible reactions to the anonymity and standardization of his life? Have you ever reacted similarly?
4. How do "high culture" and "folk culture" differ from today's "popular culture"? How has the relation between producer and consumer changed? What has been the effect of this change?

Discussion of Rhetoric

1. How does the title of this article tie in with the thesis? With the last paragraph? Is it apt?
2. Van den Haag uses a combination of generalizations followed by specific examples. Find several instances of this technique. Why is it effective? Can one write effectively employing only generalizations?
3. What is the tone of this article? Is the author's attitude toward his subject objective and neutral or is it subjective and emotional?

Writing Assignments

1. Many have criticized mass education in this country. In a theme, defend the American public-school system, and show its effectiveness.
2. Select a paragraph or two from this essay and paraphrase it. Be careful not to change the meaning of the original passage; merely put it in your own words.
3. Define culture.
4. What is an educated man? Give your views in a theme.

Library Exploration

1. For an interesting companion view to this article, read *Civilization and Its Discontents* by Sigmund Freud.
2. Many articles and books have been written in recent years analyzing culture and taste in this country. You might be interested in comparing van den Haag's conclusions with those of other writers.

Vocabulary

debauch (4): corrupt
modal (6): most common; typical
congruent (6): coincident; corresponding
atrophied (8): wasted away or decreased in size from lack of use

histrionics (13): deliberate expression of emotion for effect
masticate (14): chew
hectored (19): harassed, bullied, or intimidated
inveigh (22): protest bitterly or complain vehemently
quixotic (23): hopelessly romantic
surrogation (24): substitution
impinge (34): touch (upon); infringe
motility (38): mobility
spurious (41): false
inexorably (42): relentlessly; unyieldingly
extrapolation (43): inferring unknown data by expanding or pro-
                jecting known data
fortuitous (47): occurring by chance
inured (54): accustomed to
assiduous (57): marked by sustained devotion to work
exorcise (61): get rid of
ineluctable (62): inescapable; inevitable

61

DON'T SEND JOHNNY TO COLLEGE

Hugh Kenner

An English professor says that most of the students now in American colleges should not be there, and proposes a solution that he believes will make the college experience more rewarding for both the gifted and the not-so-gifted student.

1   Johnny goes by the official title of "student." Yet Johnny's is the face every professor would prefer to see anywhere but in his classroom where it blocks with its dreary smile, or its stoical yawn, the educational process on which we are proud to spend annually billions of dollars. By his sheer inert numbers he is making the common pursuit of professors and students—real students—impossible.

2   No one, least of all his professor, wills Johnny an injustice. Even the dean of students, whose lot he renders abysmal, finds it impossible not to like him, though some miraculous multiplication of loafers and fish sends Johnnies in an endless column trooping past the dean's receptionist, to stammer out their tale of dragging grades and just not digging the stuff.

3   Johnnies by the thousand, by the hundred thousand, clutter up every college in the land, where they long ago acquired a numerical majority. If you have a teenager in your home, thinking of college, the chances are you have Johnny. On behalf of my 400,000 colleagues in the academic profession, I'd be grateful if you'd keep him home.

4   Though Johnny is by definition multitudinous and anonymous, bits of Johnnyism stick in every teacher's mind. I remember the set neon smile that greeted me class after class for three whole weeks from a front-row seat just next to the door. The smile's owner and operator— let's call her Jonnie—never said a word, never took a note, never turned a page in her copy of *Gulliver's Travels*. Then, the day after I assigned a paper, the smile was gone, and so was she, apparently for good.

5   A month later, having heard that I would welcome some explanation, Jonnie turned up in my office, smiling. No, she couldn't do papers at all, not at all. Then what, pray, had brought her to a university, where, as everyone knows, one does papers? Well, she had enrolled on the

advice of her psychiatrist. He had said the College Experience would be good therapy. Unwilling to monkey with therapy, I referred her, smile and all, to the dean. I've forgotten what he decided. There are so many Johnnies and Jonnies.

6   And there is no end to what their mentors and counselors, not to say psychiatrists, expect a university to do. Teach Johnny to behave like a gentleman. Prevent his simultaneous presence with Jonnie in parked cars after 10 P.M. Help him (her) get to know girls (boys). Improve his work habits. Open his mind (he has nothing but prejudices). Shut his mouth (he does nothing but talk). Tighten his morals. Loosen his imagination. Spread beneath his slack chin the incredible banquet of Western Civilization. And discharge him fit to earn a better living, make a better marriage and digest (Lord help him) *The New York Times*.

7   The parents and mentors who expect all this expect it not of the college but of the College Experience, which is turning, accordingly, into the experience of living in a whole cityful of Johnnies. (I've just been told by a Sunday supplement that within 35 years many colleges with enrollments of 100,000 to 200,000 will have become cities in their own right.)

8   Johnny (Jonnie) expects none of the wonders of the College Experience, except *in re* girls (boys). Johnny is amiably devoid of expectations. One might say that he goes where he's shoved. One might affirm with more tact that he lends himself amiably to the College Experience, having no better plans. That is what marks him as Johnny, not as a student. A student has a vocation for study. But there's really nothing that Johnny comes to campus burning to learn about.

9   "Real education," wrote Ezra Pound 30 years ago, "must ultimately be limited to men who INSIST on knowing; the rest is mere sheep-herding."

10   The mind that insists on knowing is (alas) not to be identified by tests, which explains why, despite the well-publicized vigilance of admissions officers, the number of campus Johnnies keeps rising. A mind that insists on knowing has begun to focus its energies by the time it has been in the world 16 years. By 17 or 18—the age of a college freshman—it has learned the taste of knowledge and the sensation of reaching for more. It may spell erratically, if it is served (like Yeats) by a deficient visual memory. It may calculate imperfectly, if it is (like Einstein) more at home with concepts than with operations. There may be strange gaps in its information, since a young mind cannot be everywhere at once.

11   But what it does not know it will encounter with pleasure. And it *must* learn, as a cat must eat. It may not yet know where its need for knowledge is meant to be satisfied. It may tack about, sails taut, without regard for curricular symmetry, changing majors perhaps more than once. But its tireless curiosity is unmistakable. In time, if all goes well,

it will accept training, and the lifelong responsibilities of keeping itself trained.

12   But Johnny has no such appetite, no such momentum. When Johnny applies his brand-new ball-point to his first blue book, each sentence comes out smudged with his unmistakable pawprint. "Newspaper comics are good because they put a rosy glow on the grayish realities of the mind": There you have Johnny ingenuously expressing the state of *his* mind—a gray place which Pogo can occasionally animate, and a place of Good Things and Bad Things where Pogo is a Good Thing.

13   "The three main groups of people are the well-educated, semi-educated, and semiuneducated." There is all mankind characterized (a feat that taxed Aristotle), complete with a category for Johnny himself; he never forgets himself.

14   I am not inventing these examples. A colleague of mine gleaned a dozen like them in a single afternoon, from freshman themes at a university that accepts only the top one-eighth of the high-school crop. What they illustrate isn't primarily the "inability to express oneself," i.e., technical difficulties with the English language. What they illustrate is something deeper, probably irremediable; a happy willingness to emulate the motions of thought, since a teacher is standing there expecting such motions, along with a nearly total want of experience of what the process of thinking feels like.

15   "And this is why we should have no prejudice against Negroes and other lower races." That mind, we may say with some confidence, doesn't insist upon knowing. It doesn't know even its own most blatant contradictions. "To analyze this theory, it can be broken down into two parts: men and women." That's what men and women are, for the nonce—they are the parts of Johnny's theory. "The result is a ridiculous fiasco under which the roof falls in." It is indeed, and one does not know whether to marvel more at the oppressive weight of that fiasco, crashing through the roof like a half-ton bear, or at the innocent ease with which Johnny, supposing ideas to be weightless, pats them to and fro like bubbles.

16   But examples don't define a problem which by its very nature arises out of sheer multitudinousness. The amiable dumbbell has for decades been a part of campus folklore, like the absentminded professor. It is when you multiply him by a million that he grows ominous, swamping the campus as with creeping molasses. His uncle of 40 years ago, Joe College, had no more interest in learning than Johnny has, but none of Johnny's baleful power. With a certain talent for grotesque stylization, he conducted his entertaining ballet of raccoon coats, hip flasks, and whiffenpoofery, while the business of the academy, a considerably more modest business than today, went on.

17   What has created the Johnny problem isn't some freakish meta-

morphosis of Joe College into numberless protozoa, but rather the nearly universal conviction that everybody ought to spend four years at college if it can possibly be managed.

18   Johnny's parents, needless to say, believe this. His state legislator, despite the fantastic costs, tries to believe it, since his constituents seem to. The prospective employer believes it: let Johnny check "none" when the personnel blank inquires after "college record," and Johnny will be lucky to be issued a pick and shovel, let alone a sample kit. Even the college, caught in competitions for funds (which tend to hinge on enrollments), has come to believe it believes it.

19   Meanwhile B.A.'s grow so common that employers who once demanded them now demand M.A.'s, and the Master's requirement in some fields (not just the academic) has been upgraded to the Ph.D. In the years since Robert M. Hutchins sardonically proposed that we achieve our desires with less trouble by granting every American citizen a B.A. at birth, we have moved closer and closer to a utopia in which everyone receives it at 21, in return for doing classroom time. One already hears talk of attendance being compulsory through age 20. In California, where problems tend to surface before New England need worry about them, the state population rose 50 percent in one decade, and the college population 82 percent. It grows easy to forsee the day when 50 percent of the population of California (and, after a suitable time lag, of Massachusetts, of New York, of Illinois and, yes of Montana) will be employed at teaching the other 50 percent, perhaps changing ends at the half.

20   Clearly something has got to bust, and no one doubts what: the idea of a university. As an institution for (in Thomas Jefferson's words) "the instruction of those who will come after us," it's already being trampled out of recognizable existence by hordes of Johnnies.

21   The real student, struggling against suffocation of the soul, draws back, or beefs about how "the class" is holding things up, or starts feeling superior (and energy expended in nourishing a feeling of superiority is wholly lost). At worst, from being eager he turns merely "sensitive," and allows his zeal to be leached away. He is deprived, and can rightfully resent being deprived, of the kind of company he deserves to expect at a place where, often at considerable sacrifice, he has elected to invest four years of his life.

22   The professors suffer too. For one thing, they are coming off the production line too rapidly (though the harried trustees, looking wildly around at teaching machines and television hookups say "Not rapidly enough!"). Since there's no way of growing scholars at a pace keyed to the amoebalike increase of Johnnies, substitutes have begun to be manufactured. As real students are swamped by Johnnies, real professors must coexist with a swarm of Johnny-professors.

23   And like the real students, the real professors grow obsessed with

futility, and unless they succeed, as some do, in isolating themselves with advanced students, fall victim to the real occupational hazard of the profession: an inability to believe that anybody can be taught anything. I once heard of a man who was so startled by the discovery of a real student that, lest she slip over his horizon, he divorced his wife and married her. I don't believe that story, but it's indicative; the professor who told it to me found it believable.

24   There's no doubt that as a nation we settle for only the side effects and the fringe benefits of what we invest in universities: the products of physics labs and research stations, and the economic advantages, to which our economy has been attuned ever since the G.I. Bill, of keeping several million young people off the labor market as long as possible. We are getting even this, though, at the price of a colossal wastage of time and spirit—the time and spirit of the real students on whose behalf the system in allegedly being run. If by the year 2000, as President Clark Kerr of California expects, educational institutions will be the largest single force in the economy, and if attendance to the age of 20 is compulsory, as Dr. Dwayne Orton of I.B.M. expects, why then the economy will in the lifetime of most of us have begun devoting its principal energies to the maintenance of huge concentration camps for keeping Johnnies by the multimillion agreeably idle.

25   So do we kick out Johnny? Alas, things will never be that simple again. Our social and economic system has come to depend on Johnny, B.A., in ways that can probably never be unstitched. Moreover, the College Experience probably *is* the most important event in the lives of most of the people who undergo it, even of the hundreds of thousands who learn very little. It is their time of access to the intellectual traffic patterns that define the quality of American life. A Kansan and a Georgian who have both been to college—merely been there—will have more to say to one another than a Vermonter who has and a Vermonter who hasn't. The College Experience is our folk ritual for inducting our adolescents into the 20th century. As part of our established religion, it must be treated as immune from curtailment.

26   Very well, then: the College Experience for Johnny, in his Johnny-classrooms. But let us, in the name of sanity, allow the real students to have *their* version of the College Experience. That means either separate-but-equal facilities, or (better, I think) some college equivalent of the two-track high schools that already exist.

27   One way of arranging a two-track college with minimum disruption is to permit only the real students to pursue majors. The University of Toronto has been doing that for more than half a century. Two decades ago I was one of a group of 40 freshman English majors there. In the sophomore year there were 20 of us, in the junior year 10; there the ruthless cutting stopped. But the missing 30 were not slung out of

school. All but a few hopeless cases were "permitted," as the official formula had it, "to transfer to the pass course," which meant that, if they wanted to stay on at college, they abandoned the major and enrolled in "pass arts."

28   Pass arts was a three-year humanities mixture, leading to the degree of B.A. And it wasn't a ghetto for dropouts; many students enrolled in it to start with. Its degree satisfied employers, parents, and the Ontario College of Education. It satisfied Johnny just fine. It gave the university all the advantages of bigness, as the quality of the library testified. It wasn't conducive to snobbery or segregation; every honor student took a couple of pass courses a year, in subjects peripheral to his major.

29   It was, in short, a two-track system, with the tracks parallel, and with means for switching laggards onto the slow track.

30   Everyone, we agree, should have access to all the education he can absorb. Everyone who can absorb education deserves, I would add, a chance to absorb it, free from the distracting tramp of the million-footed Johnny. As colleges now operate, the idea that everybody should be sent to them is nonsense. The only hope is to start operating them differently, detached from the dogma that Johnny is by birthright a student. He needs, in fact, explicit treatment as a nonstudent. There's no inherent reason why the nation's universities shouldn't make special curricular arrangements for several million nonstudents, any more than there's an inherent reason why one of the nation's universities shouldn't be the world's largest purveyor of white mice. (One of them is.)

Discussion of Theme
1. Is Kenner's representation of the typical college student a fair one?
2. The author compares the questing mind to the mind of Johnny. What differences does he point out?
3. Is the anecdote in paragraph 23 believable? Why did Kenner include it?
4. Is the author's proposed solution to the Johnny problem an intelligent one? Will it solve all the problems mentioned in the first part of the article?

Discussion of Rhetoric
1. What do the tone and diction of this article tell you about the kind of audience the author was speaking to?
2. How does Kenner establish his competency? Does he make clear his qualifications to write on this subject?
3. Consider the analogies in paragraph 11. Are they apt?
4. Is there a concession in the concluding paragraph of Kenner's essay? Does he contradict himself?

5. In one of the opening paragraphs, the author makes a playful allusion to a passage in a famous work. Can you find the allusion?

Writing Assignments

1. Develop the following statement into a theme: "Most girls who attend college are really looking for a husband."
2. Should everyone go to college today? Develop your views on this topic.
3. If you were in a position of authority, what changes would you make in higher education? Be specific.
4. If you disagree with Kenner's essay, write a rebuttal supporting your views with evidence.

Library Exploration

Has American education declined in quality since World War II? Some critics think so. Read several articles on this subject.

Vocabulary

stoical (1): without passion or interest
abysmal (2): immeasurably hopeless or wretched
mentor (6): trusted counselor or guide
nonce (15): present occasion
fiasco (15): complete failure
metamorphosis (17): change
sardonically (19): bitterly
purveyor (30): supplier

62

THE CHANGING PLACE OF WOMEN
IN AMERICA

Carl N. Degler

The role of the American woman has changed drastically since the frontier days. This article discusses the feminist movement in America, as well as its sociological implications.

1   If feminism is defined as the belief that women are human beings and entitled to the same opportunities for self-expression as men, then America has harbored a feminist bias from the beginning. In both the eighteenth and nineteenth centuries foreign travelers remarked on the freedom for women in America. "A paradise for women," one eighteenth-century German called America, and toward the close of the nineteenth century Lord Bryce wrote that in the United States "it is easier for women to find a career, to obtain work of an intellectual as of a commercial kind, than in any part of Europe."

2   Certainly the long history of a frontier in America helps to account for this feminist bias. In a society being carved out of a wilderness, women were active and important contributors to the process of settlement and civilization. Moreover, because women have been scarce in America they have been highly valued. During almost the whole of the colonial period men outnumbered women, and even in the nineteenth century women remained scarce in the West. As late as 1865, for example, there were three men for each women in· California; in Colorado the ratio was as high as 20 to 1. Such disparities in the sex ratio undoubtedly account for the West's favorable attitude toward women as in an Oregon law of 1850 that granted land to single women and, even more significant for the time, to married women; or in the willingness of western territories like Wyoming (1869) and Utah (1870) to grant the suffrage to women long before other regions where the sex ratio was more nearly equal.

3   Another measure of women's high esteem in American society was the rapidity with which the doors of higher education opened to women. Even without counting forerunners like Oberlin College, which admitted women in 1837, the bars against women came down faster and earlier in America than anywhere. The breakthrough came during the Civil War era, when women's colleges like Elmira, Vassar

and Smith were founded, and universities like Michigan and Cornell became coeducational. The process was later and slower in Europe. Girton College, Cambridge, for example, which opened in 1869, was the sole English institution of higher education available to women until London University accorded women full privileges in 1879. Heidelberg, which was the first German university to accept women, did not do so until 1900. More striking was the fact that at its opening Girton provided six places for young women; Vassar alone, when it opened in 1865, counted some 350 students in residence. Another indication of the American feminist bias was that at the end of the century girls outnumbered boys among high school graduates.

4   But if the frontier experience of America helped to create a vague feminist bias that accorded women more privileges than in settled Europe, the really potent force changing women's place had little to do with the frontier or the newness of the country. It was the industrial revolution that provided the impetus to women's aspirations for equality of opportunity; it was the industrial revolution that carried through the first stage in the changing position of women—the removal of legal and customary barriers to women's full participation in the activities of the world.

5   Today it is axiomatic that men work outside the home. But before the industrial revolution of the nineteenth century, the great majority of men and women were co-workers on the land and in the home. Women worked in the fields when the chores of the home and child-rearing permitted, so that there was not only close association between work and home for both sexes, but even a certain amount of overlap in the sexual division of labor. The coming of machine production changed all that. For a time, it is true, many unmarried women and children— the surplus labor of the day—were the mainstay of the new factory system, but that was only temporary. By the middle of the nineteenth century the bulk of industrial labor was male. The coming of the factory and the city thus wholly changed the nature of men's work. For the first time in history, work for most men was something done outside the family, psychologically as well as physically separated from the home.

6   The same industrial process that separated work and home also provided the opportunities for women to follow men out of the home. For that reason the feminist movement, both socially and intellectually, was a direct consequence of the industrial changes of the nineteenth century. Furthermore, just as the new industrial system was reshaping the rural men who came under its influence, so it reshaped the nature of women.

7   The process began with the home, which in the early years of industrialization, was still the site of most women's work. Because of

high land values, the city home was smaller than the farm house, and with less work for children, the size of the urban family was smaller than the rural. Moreover, in the city work in the home changed. Machines in factories now performed many of the tasks that had long been women's. In truth, the feminist movement began not when women felt a desire for men's jobs, but when men in factories began to take away women's traditional work. Factory-produced clothing, commercial laundries, prepared foods (e.g. prepared cereals, canned vegetables, condensed milk, bakery bread) were already available in the years after the Civil War. Toward the end of the century an advanced feminist like Charlotte Perkins Gilman, impressed by the accelerating exodus of women's chores from the middle-class home, predicted that the whole kitchen would soon be gone. She was wrong there, but even today the flight continues with precooked and frozen foods, TV dinners, cake mixes, special packaging for easy disposal, diaper services and the like.

8   Middle-class women were the main beneficiaries of the lightening of the chores of the home; few working-class or immigrant women could as yet take advantage of the new services and products. These middle-class women became the bone and sinew of the feminist movement, which was almost entirely an urban affair. They joined the women's clubs, organized the temperance crusades and marched in the suffrage parades. With an increasing amount of time available to them in the city, and imbued with the historic American value of work, they sought to do good. And there was much to be done in the raw, sometimes savage, urban environment of the late nineteenth century. For example, public playgrounds in the United States began in Boston only in the 1880's, when two public-spirited middle-class women caused a cartload of sand to be piled on an empty lot and set the neighborhood children loose upon it. Many a city and small town at the turn of the century owed its public library or its park to the dedicated work of women's clubs. The venerable giant redwood trees of northern California survive today because clubwomen of San Francisco and nearby towns successfully campaigned in 1900 to save them from being cut down for lumber. The saloon and prostitution were two other prevalent urban blights that prompted study and action by women's organizations.

9   More important than women's opposition to social evils was the widening of women's knowledge and concerns that inevitably accompanied it. What began as a simple effort to rid the community of a threat to its purity often turned into a discovery of the economic exploitation that drove young working girls into brothels and harried working men into saloons. Frances Willard for example, while head of the Women's Christian Temperance Union, broadened the WCTU's reform interests far beyond the liquor question, causing it to advocate

protective legislation for working women, kindergartens and training programs for young working girls. Jane Addams, at Hull-House in Chicago's slums, quickly learned what historians have only recently discovered, that it was the urban boss's undeniable services to the immigrants that were the true sources of his great political power and the real secret of his successful survival of municipal reform campaigns.

10   The most direct way in which industrialization altered the social function of women was by providing work for women outside the home. Production by machine, of course, widened enormously the uses to which women's labor could be put once physical strength was no longer a consideration. And toward the end of the century, as business enterprises grew and record-keeping, communications and public relations expanded, new opportunities for women opened up in business offices. The telephone operator, the typist, the clerical worker and the stenographer now took places beside the seamstress, the cotton mill operator and the teacher.

11   As workers outside the home, women buried the Victorian stereotype of the lady under a mountain of reality. After all, it was difficult to argue that women as a sex were weak, timid, incompetent, fragile vessels of spirituality when thousands of them could be seen trudging to work in the early hours of the day in any city of the nation. Nor could a girl who worked in a factory or office help but become more worldly. A young woman new to a shop might have been embarrassed to ask a male foreman for the ladies' room, as some working girls' auto-biographies report, but such maidenly reticence could hardly survive very long. Even gentle, naïve farm girls soon found out how to handle the inevitable, improper advances of foremen. They also learned the discipline of the clock, the managing of their own money, the excitement of life outside the home, the exhilaration of financial independence along with the drudgery of machine labor. Having learned something of the ways of the world, women could not be treated then, nor later in marriage, as the hopeless dependents Victorian ideals prescribed.

12   In time work transformed the outer woman, too. First to go were the hobbling, trailing skirts, which in a factory were a hazard and a nuisance. Even before the Civil War, Amelia Bloomer and other feminists had pointed out that women, if they were to work in the world as human beings, needed looser and lighter garments than those then in fashion. Until working women were numbered in the millions, no change took place. After 1890 women's skirts gradually crept up from the floor, and the neat and simple shirtwaist became the uniform of the working girl. A costume very like the original bloomer was widely worn by women factory workers during the First World War. Later the overall and the coverall continued the adaptation of women's clothes to the machine.

13   The most dramatic alteration in the image of woman came after the

First World War, when there was a new upsurge in women's employment. The twenties witnessed the emergence of the white-collar class,
and women were a large part of it. Over twice as many women entered
the labor force that decade as in the previous one; the number of
typists alone in 1930 was three-quarters of a million, a tenfold increase
since 1900. And woman's appearance reflected the requirements of
work. Except for some of the extreme flapper fashions, which were
transient, the contemporary woman still dresses much as the woman
of the 1920's did. In the 1920's women threw out the corset and the
numerous petticoats in favor of light undergarments, a single slip,
silk or rayon stockings, short skirts and bobbed hair. So rapid and
widespread was the change that an investigation in the 1920's revealed
that even most working-class girls no longer wore corsets, and the new
interest in bobbed hair resulted between 1920 and 1930 in an increase
of 400 per cent in the number of women hair dressers.

14   The physical freedom of dress that women acquired during the
1920's was but the superficial mark of a new social equality. The social
forces behind this new equality are several. Some of these forces, like
the growing number of college-trained women and the increasing
number of women in the working force, go back far into the past;
others, like the impact of the war and the arduous campaign for women's
suffrage, were more recent. But whatever the causes, the consequences
were obvious. Indeed, what is generally spoken of as the revolution in
morals of the 1920's is more accurately a revolution in the position of
women. Within a few short years a spectrum of taboos was shed. For
the first time women began to smoke and drink in public; cigarette
manufacturers discovered and exploited in advertising a virtually
untouched market. As recently as 1918 it was considered daring for a
New York hotel to permit women to sit at a bar. In the twenties,
despite prohibition, both sexes drank in public.

15   Perhaps most significant, as well as symbolic, of the new stage in the
position of women was their new sexual freedom. The twenties have
long been associated with the discovery of Freud and a fresh, publicly
acknowledged interest in sex. But insofar as these attitudes were new
they represented changes in women, particularly those of the middle
and upper classes. Premarital and extramarital sexuality by men had
never been severely criticized, and discussion of sexual matters was
commonplace wherever men gathered. Now, though, middle-class
women also enjoyed that freedom. For the first time, it has been said,
middle-class men carried on their extramarital affairs with women of
their own social class instead of with cooks, maids and prostitutes.

16   An easier sexuality outside of marriage was only the most sensational
side of the revolution in morals; more important, if only because more
broadly based, was a new, informal, equal relationship between the
sexes, culminating in a new conception of marriage. The day was long

since past when Jennie June Croly could be barred, as she was in 1868, from a dinner in honor of Charles Dickens at a men's club even though her husband was a member and she was a professional writer. (Indeed, so thoroughly has such separation of the sexes been abandoned that the new Princeton Club in New York City has closed all but one of its public rooms to any man who is not accompanied by a women!) And at least in the gatherings of the educated middle class, talk between the sexes was often free, frank and wide-ranging. The same mutual acceptance of the sexes was visible in the prevalent talk about the "new marriage," in which the woman was a partner and a companion, not simply a mother, a social convenience and a housekeeper.

17   The reality of the new conception of marriage was reflected in the sharp increase in the divorce rate. Because marriage, legally as well as socially, in the nineteenth century was more confining for women than for men, the early feminist had often advocated more liberal divorce laws. And even though divorce in the nineteenth century was more common in the United States than in any European country, the divorce rate in the 1920's shot up 50 per cent over what it had been only ten years before. One sign that women in the 1920's were seeking freedom from marriage if they could not secure equality in marriage was that two thirds of the divorces in that decade were instituted by women.

18   By the close of the twenties the ordinary woman in America was closer to a man in the social behavior expected of her, in the economic opportunities open to her and in the intellectual freedom enjoyed by her than at any time in history. To be sure there still was a double standard, but now its existence was neither taken for granted nor confidently asserted by men.

19   In truth, the years since the twenties have witnessed few alterations in the position of women that were not first evident in that crucial decade. The changes have penetrated more deeply and spread more widely through the social structure, but their central tendency was then already spelled out. Even the upsurge in women's employment, which was so striking in the twenties, continued in subsequent years. Each decade thereafter has counted a larger number of working women than the previous one. During the depression decade of the 1930's, even, half a million more women entered the labor force than in the prosperous twenties. By 1960 some 38 per cent of all women of working age—almost two out of five women—were employed outside the home.

20   The movement of women out of the home into remunerative work, however, has been neither steady nor unopposed. Undoubtedly one of the underlying conditions is an expanding economy's need for labor. But something more than that is needed to break society's traditional habits of mind about the proper work for women. Certainly here the feminist demands for equality for women played a part. But a social

factor of equal importance was war. By their very disruption of the steady pulse of everyday living, wars break the cake of custom, shake up society and compel people to look afresh at old habits and attitudes. It is not accidental, for instance, that women's suffrage in England, Russia and Germany, as well as the United States, was achieved immediately after the First World War and in France and Italy after the Second.

21   At the very least, by making large and new demands upon the established work force, war draws hitherto unused labor into the economic process. During the Civil War, for example, young women assumed new roles in the economy as workers in metal and munitions factories, as clerks in the expanded bureaucracy in Washington and as nurses in war hospitals. Moreover, when the war was over women had permanently replaced men as the dominant sex in the teaching profession. Furthermore, since many women found a new usefulness in the Sanitary Fairs and other volunteer work, the end of hostilities left many women unwilling to slip back into the seclusion of the Victorian home. It is not simply coincidental that the women's club movement began very soon after the war.

22   When the First World War came to the United States, feminist leaders, perhaps recalling the gains of the Civil War, anticipated new and broad advances for their sex. And the demand for labor, especially after the United States entered the war, did open many jobs to women, just as it was doing in contemporary Great Britain and Germany. All over the United States during the war customary and legal restrictions on the employment of women fell away. Women could be seen doing everything from laying railroad ties to working in airplane factories. The war also brought to a successful climax the struggle for the suffrage. Pointedly women had argued that a war for democracy abroad should at least remedy the deficiencies of democracy at home.

23   If politically the war was a boon to women, economically it failed to live up to feminist anticipations. The First World War, unlike the Civil War, did not result in a large permanent increase in the number of working women. Indeed, by 1920 there were only 800,000 more women working than in 1910. But as a result of wartime demands, women did get permanent places in new job categories, like elevator operators and theater ushers. (But women street car conductors disappeared soon after the armistice.) Certain traditional professions for women, like music teaching, lost members between 1910 and 1920, while professions that required more training and provided steadier income, like library and social work and college teaching, doubled or tripled their numbers in the same period.

24   The Second World War, with its even more massive demands for labor and skills, brought almost four million new women workers into the nation's factories and offices. Once again jobs usually not filled by

women were opened to them. For example, the number of women bank officers rose 40 per cent during the four years of the war and the number of women employees in finance has continued to rise ever since. Furthermore, unlike the situation after the First World War, the female work force after 1945 not only stayed up but then went higher.

25   Measured in the number of women working, the changes in the economic position of women add up to a feminist success. Twenty-four million working women cannot be ignored. But weighed in the scales of quality instead of quantity, the change in women's economic status is not so striking. It is true that women now work in virtually every job listed by the Bureau of the Census. Moreover, the popular press repeatedly tells of the inroads women are making into what used to be thought of as men's jobs. Three years ago, for example, a woman won a prize as the mutual fund salesman of the year. Women are widely represented in advertising and in real estate, and even women taxicab drivers are no longer rare. Yet the fact remains that the occupations in which the vast majority of women actually engage are remarkably similar to those historically held by women. In 1950 almost three quarters of all employed women fell into twenty occupational categories, of which the largest was stenographers, typists and secretaries—a category that first became prominent as a woman's occupation over a half century ago. Other occupations which have traditionally been women's, like domestic service, teaching, clerical work, nursing and telephone service, are also conspicuous among the twenty categories. Further than that, the great majority of women are employed in occupations in which they predominate. This sexual division of labor is clearly evident in the professions, even though women are only a small proportion of total professional workers. Two thirds of all professional women are either nurses or teachers; and even in teaching there is a division between the sexes. Most women teach in the primary grades; most men teach in high school. Women are notoriously underrepresented in the top professions like law, medicine, engineering and scientific research. No more than 7 per cent of all professional women in 1950 were in the four of these categories together. Only 6 per cent of medical doctors and 4 per cent of lawyers and judges were women. In contrast, almost three quarters of medical doctors are women in the Soviet Union; in England the figure is 16 per cent. In both France and Sweden women make up a high proportion of pharmacists and dentists; neither of those professions attracts many women in the United States.

26   One consequence as well as manifestation of the sexual division of labor in the United States has been the differences in pay for men and women. That difference has been a historical complaint of feminist leaders. In 1900 one study found women's wages to be, on the average, only 53 per cent of men's. The reason was, of course, that women were concentrated in the poorer paying jobs and industries of the economy.

The disparity in pay between the sexes has been somewhat reduced today, but not very much. In 1955 among full-time women workers of all types the median wage was about two thirds of that for men. In short, women are still supplying the low-paid labor in the economy just as they were in the last century. (In substance, women workers and Negroes of both sexes perform a similar function in the economy.) The willingness of women to supply cheap labor may well account for their getting the large number of jobs they do; men often will not work for the wages that women will accept.

27   Today, there does not seem to be very much disparity between men's and women's wages for the same work, though the sexual division of labor is so nearly complete that it is difficult to find comparable jobs of the two sexes to make a definitive study.

28   There has been no improvement in women's position in higher education; indeed, it can be argued that women have failed to maintain the place reached much earlier. As we have seen, the United States led the world in opening higher education to women. This country also led in broadening the social base of education for women. No other country educated such a large proportion of women in its universities and colleges as did the United States. At the close of the nineteenth century, one third of American college students were women; by 1937 women made up almost 40 per cent of the students in American institutions of higher learning. In Germany, just before Hitler took power, no more than one out of ten university students was a woman; in Swedish universities in 1937 only 17 per cent of the students were women; in British universities the ratio was 22 per cent.

29   But since the Second World War the gap between American and European proportions of women in higher education has narrowed considerably. In 1952-1953 women constituted only 35 per cent of the American college population, while France counted women as 36 per cent of its university students and Sweden 26 per cent. The *number* of women in American colleges, of course, is considerably greater than it was in the 1920's and 1930's, but in proportion to men, women have lost ground in America while gaining it in Europe.

30   A further sign of the regression in the educational position of women in the United States is that in the early 1950's women earned about 10 per cent of the doctoral degrees in this country as compared with almost 15 per cent in the 1920's.

31   How is one to explain this uneven, almost contradictory record of women in America? How does it happen that a country with a kind of built-in feminism from the frontier falls behind more traditional countries in its training of college women; that a country with one of the highest proportions of working women in the world ends up with such a small proportion of its women in medicine, in law and in the sciences? Perhaps the correct answer is that the question should not be asked—at least not by Americans. For like so much else in American

society, such contradictions are a manifestation of the national avoidance of any ideological principle, whether it be in feminist reform or in anything else. To be sure there has been no lack of feminist argument or rationale for women's work outside the home, for women's education and for other activities by women. But American women, like American society in general, have been more concerned with individual practice than with a consistent feminist ideology. If women have entered the labor force or taken jobs during a war they have done so for reasons related to the immediate individual or social circumstances and not for reasons of feminist ideology. The women who have been concerned about showing that women's capabilities can match men's have been the exception. As the limited, and low-paying, kind of jobs women occupy demonstrate, there is not now and never has been any strong feminist push behind the massive and continuing movement of women into jobs. Most American women have been interested in jobs, not careers. To say, as many feminists have, that men have opposed and resisted the opening of opportunities to women is to utter only a half truth. The whole truth is that American society in general, which includes women, shuns like a disease any feminist ideology.

32   Another way of showing that the historical changes in the status of women in America bear little relation to a feminist ideology is to examine one of those rare instances when women did effect a social improvement through an appeal to ideology, for instance, the struggle for the suffrage. By the early twentieth century the feminist demand for the vote overrode every other feminist goal. Once women achieved the vote, it was argued, the evils of society would be routed, for women, because of their peculiar attributes, would bring a fresh, needed and wholesome element into political life. In form, and in the minds of many women leaders, the arguments for the suffrage came close to being a full-blown ideology of feminism.

33   In point of fact, of course, the Nineteenth Amendment ushered in no millenium. But that fact is of less importance than the reason why it did not. When American women obtained the vote they simply did not use it ideologically; they voted not as women but as individuals. Evidence of this was the failure of many women to vote at all. At the end of the first decade of national suffrage women still did not exercise the franchise to the extent that men did. Nor did many women run for or hold political offices. The first woman to serve in Congress was elected in 1916; in 1920, the first year of national women's suffrage, four women were elected to Congress, but until 1940 no more than nine women served at one time in the House of Representatives and the Senate together. That we are here observing an American and not simply a sexual phenomenon is shown by a comparison with European countries. In nonfeminist Germany, where the ballot came to women at about the same time as in the United States, the first Reichstag after

suffrage counted forty-one women as members. In 1951 seventeen women sat in the British House of Commons as compared with ten in the United States House of Representatives. Twice the number of women have served as cabinet ministers in Britain between 1928 and 1951 as have served in the United States down to the present.

34   Another instance in which social change was effected by feminist ideology was prohibition. The achievement of national prohibition ran second only to the suffrage movement as a prime goal of the organized women's movement; the Eighteenth Amendment was as much a product of feminist ideology as the Nineteenth. Yet like the suffrage movement, prohibition, despite its feminist backing, failed to receive the support of women. It was *after* prohibition was enacted, after all, that women drank in public.

35   In the cases of both suffrage and prohibition, women acted as individuals, not as members of a sex. And so they have continued to act. It is not without relevance that the women's political organization that is most respected—the League of Women Voters—is not only nonpartisan but studiously avoids questions pertaining only to women. To do otherwise would be feminist and therefore ideological.

36   One further conclusion might be drawn from this examination of the nonideological character of American women. That the changes that have come to the position of women have been devoid of ideological intent may well explain why there has been so little opposition to them. The most successful of American reforms have always been those of an impromptu and practical nature. The great revolution of the New Deal is a classic example. The American people, like F.D.R. himself, simply tried one thing after another, looking for something—anything —that would get the nation out of the depression. If lasting reforms took place too, so much the better. On the other hand, reforms that have been justified by an elaborate rationale or ideology, like abolition, have aroused strong and long-drawn-out opposition. By the same token, when women became ideological in support of suffrage and prohibition, they faced their greatest opposition and scored their most disappointing triumphs.

37   The achievement of the suffrage in 1920 is a convenient date for marking the end of the first phase in the changing position of women, for by then women were accorded virtually the same rights as men even if they did not always exercise them. The second phase began at about the same time. It was the participation of married women in the work force. During the nineteenth century few married women worked; when they did it was because they were childless or because their husbands were inadequate providers. Even among the poor, married women normally did not work. A survey of the slum districts in five large cities in 1893 revealed that no more than 5 per cent of the wives were employed. Only Negro wives in the South and immigrant wives

in big northern cities provided any significant exceptions to this generalization.

38   Before the First World War, the movement of wives into the working force was barely noticeable. During the 1920's there was an acceleration, but as late as 1940 less than 17 per cent of all married women were working. Among working women in 1940, 48 per cent were single and only 31 per cent were married. The Second World War dramatically reversed these proportions—another instance of the influence of war on the position of women. By 1950 the proportion of married women living with their husbands had risen to 48 per cent of all working women while that of single women had fallen to 32 per cent. In 1960 the Census reported that almost 32 per cent of all married women were employed outside the home and that they comprised 54 per cent of all working women. No industrial country of Europe, with the exception of the Soviet Union, counted such a high proportion. Today, married women are the greatest source of new labor in the American economy. Between 1949 and 1959, for example, over four million married women entered the labor force, some 60 per cent of *all* additions, male and female.

39   Such a massive movement of married women out of the home was a development few of the early feminists could have anticipated. That it has taken place is at once a sign and a yardstick of the enormous change in women's position in society and in the family. In the nineteenth century work outside the home was unthinkable for the married women. Not only were there children to care for, but there were objections from husbands and society to consider. That is why the convinced feminist of the nineteenth century often spurned marriage. Indeed, it is often forgotten that the feminist movement was a form of revolt against marriage. For it was through marriage, with the legal and social dominance of the husband, that women were most obviously denied opportunities for self-expression. Even after the legal superiority of the husband had been largely eliminated from the law, middle-class social conventions could still scarcely accommodate the working wife. To the woman interested in realizing her human capabilities, marriage in the nineteenth century was not an opportunity but a dead end. And it was indeed a minor scandal of the time that many of the "new women" did in fact reject marriage. The tendency was most pronounced, as was to be expected, among highly educated women, many of whom felt strongly their obligation to serve society through careers. Around 1900 more than one fourth of women who graduated from college never married; more than half of the women medical doctors in 1890 were single.

40   Like other changes in the position of women, the movement of married women into the work force—the reconciliation of marriage and work—must be related to the social changes of the last three

decades. One of these social changes was the increase in contraceptive knowledge, for until married women could limit their families they could not become steady and reliable industrial workers. Information about contraceptive techniques which had been known for a generation or more to educated middle-class women did not seep down to the working class until the years of the Great Depression. In 1931, for instance, there were only 81 clinics disseminating birth control information in the United States; in 1943 there were 549, of which 166 were under public auspices. As the number of public clinics suggest, by the end of the 1930's birth control was both socially and religiously acceptable, at least among Protestants. And a method was also available then to Roman Catholics, since it was in the same decade that the rhythm method, the only one acceptable to the Roman Catholic Church, was first brought to popular attention with the approval of ecclesiastical authorities.

41   Another social force underlying the movement of wives and mothers in the work force was the growing affluence of an industrial society, especially after 1940. Higher health standards, enlarged incomes of husbands and a better standard of living in general permitted a marked alteration in the temporal cycle of women's lives. Women now lived longer, stayed in school later and married earlier. In 1890 half the girls left school at 14 or before—that is, when they finished grammar school; in 1957 the median age was 18—after graduation from high school. The girl of 1890, typically, did not marry until she was 22; the age of her counterpart in 1957 was 20, leaving no more than two years for work between the end of school and marriage. Among other things this fact explains the fall in the proportion of single women in the work force in the United States as compared with other industrial societies. Few other countries have such an early median age of marriage for girls.

42   Early marriages for women produce another effect. With knowledge of contraceptive techniques providing a measure of control over child-bearing, women are now having their children early and rapidly. When this tendency is combined with a younger age of marriage, the result is an early end to child-bearing. In 1890 the median age of a mother when her last child was born was 32; in 1957 it was 26. A modern mother thus has her children off to school by the time she is in her middle thirties, leaving her as much as thirty-five years free for work outside the home. And the fact is that almost half of working women today are over forty years of age. Put another way, 34 per cent of married women between the ages of thirty-five and forty-four years are gainfully employed.

43   Unquestionably, as the practical character of the woman's movement would lead us to expect, an important force behind the influx of married women into the work force is economic need. But simple poverty is not the only force. Several studies, for example, have

documented the conclusion that many women who work are married
to men who earn salaries in the upper income brackets, suggesting
that poverty is not the controlling factor in the wife's decision to work.
A similar conclusion is to be drawn from the positive correlation between education and work for married women. The more education a
wife has (and therefore the better salary her husband is likely to earn)
the more likely she is to be working herself. Many of these women work
undoubtedly in order to raise an adequate standard of living to a
comfortable one. Many others work probably because they want to
realize their potentialities in the world. But that women are so poorly
represented in the professions and other careers suggests that most
married women who work are realizing their full capabilities neither for
themselves nor for society.

44   Over sixty years ago, in *Women and Economics*, the feminist Charlotte
Perkins Gilman cogently traced the connection between work and the
fulfillment of women as human beings. In subsequent writings she
grappled with the problem of how this aim might be realized for
married women. As a mother herself, raising a child under the trying
circumstances of divorce, Gilman knew first hand that work outside
the home and child-rearing constituted *two* full-time jobs. No man, she
knew, was expected or required to shoulder such a double burden.
Gilman's remedies of professional domestic service and kitchenless
apartments never received much of a hearing, and considering the
utopian if not bizarre character of her solutions, that is not surprising.
Yet the problem she raised remained without any solution other than
the eminently individualistic and inadequate one of permitting a
woman to assume the double burden if she was so minded. Meanwhile,
as the economy has grown, the problem has entered the lives of an ever
increasing number of women. Unlike most of her feminist contemporaries, who were mainly concerned with the suffrage and the final
elimination of legal and customary barriers to women's opportunities,
Gilman recognized that the logic of feminism led unavoidably to the
working mother as the typical woman. For if women were to be
free to express themselves, then they should be able to marry as well
as to work. Women should not have to make a choice any more than
men. To make that possible, though, would require that some way
be found to mitigate the double burden which biology and society
had combined to place only on women.

45   As women moved into the second stage of their development—
the reconciliation of work and marriage—the problem which Gilman
saw so early was increasingly recognized as the central issue. Virginia
Collier, for example, in a book *Marriage and Careers*, published in
1926, wrote that since so many married women were working, "The
question therefore is no longer should women combine marriage with

careers, but how do they manage it and how does it work." Interestingly enough, her study shows that what today Betty Friedan, in *The Feminine Mystique*, has called the "problem that has no name," was already apparent in the 1920's. One working wife explained her reasons for taking a job in these words, "I am burning up with energy and it is rather hard on the family to use it up in angry frustration." Another said, "I had done everything for Polly for six years. Suddenly she was in school all day and I had nothing to do. My engine was running just as hard as ever, but my car was standing still." A year after Collier's book appeared, President William A. Nielson of Smith College observed "that the outstanding problem confronting women is how to reconcile a normal life of marriage and motherhood with intellectual activity such as her college education has fitted her for." That the issue was taken seriously is attested by an action of the Board of Trustees of Barnard College in 1932. The board voted to grant six months' maternity leave with pay to members of the staff and faculty. In announcing the decision, Dean Virginia Gildersleeve clearly voiced its import. "Neither the men nor the women of our staff," she said, "should be forced into celibacy, and cut off from that great source of experience, of joy, sorrow and wisdom which marriage and parenthood offer."

46   With one out of three married women working today, the problem of reconciling marriage and work for women is of a social dimension considerably larger than in the days of Charlotte Gilman or even in the 1930's. But the fundamental issue is still the same: how to make it possible, as Dean Gildersleeve said, to pursue a career or hold a job while enjoying the "experience . . . joy, sorrow and wisdom" of marriage and parenthood. The practical solutions to this central problem of the second stage in the changing position of women seem mainly collective or governmental, not individual. Child-care centers, efficient and readily available house-keeping services, and emergency child-care service such as the Swedes have instituted are obviously a minimal requirement if women are to have the double burdens of homemaking and employment lightened. The individual working woman cannot be expected to compensate for the temporary disabilities consequent upon her role as mother any more than the individual farmer or industrial worker can be expected single-handedly to overcome the imbalance between himself and the market. Today both farmers and workers have government and their own organizations to assist them in righting the balance.

47   But as the history of farmers and industrial labor makes evident, to enact legislation or to change mores requires persuasion of those who do not appreciate the necessity for change. Those who would do so must organize the like-minded and mobilize power, which is to say

they need a rationale, an ideology. And here is the rub; in pragmatic America, as we have seen, any ideology must leap high hurdles. And one in support of working wives is additionally handicapped because women themselves, despite the profound changes in their status in the last century, do not acknowledge such an ideology. Most American women simply do not want work outside the home to be justified as a normal activity for married women. Despite the counter-argument of overwhelming numbers of working wives, they like to think of it as special and exceptional. And so long as they do not advance such an ideology, American society surely will not do so, though other societies, like Israel's and the Soviet Union's, which are more ideological than ours, obviously have.

48   Perhaps the kind of gradual, piecemeal advance toward a feminist ideology that Mrs. Rossi proposes in other pages of this issue may contain the seeds of change. But a reading of the past reminds us forcefully that in America the soil is thin and the climate uncongenial for the growth of any seedlings of ideology.

Discussion of Theme

1. Why during the last two centuries have American women been more highly valued than their counterparts in Europe? How have they benefited from this situation?
2. What effect did the Industrial Revolution have on women's place in society?
3. Women's clubs have in the past been responsible for many social improvements. Name some. What purpose do these clubs often serve today?
4. What changes in attitudes about sex and marriage occurred in the 1920s? What brought these changes about? What are the effects today?
5. What is the greatest problem facing the majority of working women today? Is there any solution?

Discussion of Rhetoric

1. What is Degler's purpose in this article: to inform, to entertain, or to persuade? Give reasons for your answer.
2. How objective is the author? Does he ever permit his own personality or views to intrude into the discussion?
3. What purpose is served by the anecdotes in his article? Do they entertain? Convince? Are they relevant to the topic, or are they distracting?
4. Is there an introduction, body, and conclusion to this essay? If so, where are the divisions?

Writing Assignments

1. Account for the fact that in many jobs women do not receive as much compensation as men doing the same work.
2. In a theme, define one of the following terms: "The All-American Woman"; "The All-American Man."
3. Describe the American woman as she is presented on daytime television programs.

Library Exploration

For provocative views of women's place in society, read Betty Friedan's *The Feminine Mystique* or Simone de Beauvoir's *The Second Sex*.

Vocabulary

disparities (2): dissimilarities; inequalities
impetus (4): driving force
axiomatic (5): taken for granted
exodus (7): mass departure
sinew (8): muscle fiber
imbued (8): saturated
venerable (8): impressive by reason of age
reticence (11): reserve; restraint
remunerative (20): profitable; gainful
manifestation (26): demonstration; appearance; display
millennium (33): a period of perfection or freedom from all the ills
                 of human existence
ecclesiastical (40): pertaining to the church ·

63

ART, SCIENCE, AND THE NEW VALUES

Harry S. Broudy

Is the new morality here to stay? *questions, particularly as they affect*
Are the old values gone forever? *the college student.*
The following article considers these

1   I shall discuss sexual behavior as one example of the transvaluation of values made necessary by science-technology, because of all the acts in our physiological repertoire, none is so intense in its demands and rewards, and yet, for the individual if not the race, so postponable. It thus comes under the dominion of choice and morality. Further, because it is involved with life-giving and life-sustaining, church, state, and family are inordinately concerned with the most private of intimacies. And in modern times, at least, it has become inextricably woven with romance, glamour, status, and sanity.

2   But once science made it reliably possible to sever the bond between sex and life-giving, the moral meanings of sexual behavior had to be redefined, for it released the sexual act from a great part of its burden of social consequences. The moral dimension of sex now has to be sought more in personal relations and individual character rather than in social consequences. Sex morality is now personal rather than tribal.

3   The easy evasion of pregnancy has made it possible to reduce the the domain of moral responsibility in the personal domain also. The James Bond or Playboy philosophy of sex is not so implausible, if the human context of sex is reduced to the hedonic and aesthetic properties of *love-making*. (Note that one *makes* it.) Can the human context be reduced so radically? The evidence of civilized society seems to be against it. We cannot refrain from humanizing even the most obviously physiological functions: eating becomes dining just as lust, before we know it, turns into love and romance. Birth and death have been ritualized no end; other physiological functions such as digestion and elimination have defied human sublimation, so we devote our efforts to keeping them out of sight and conversation. When these and other vegetative functions get out of kilter to the point where life or death depends solely on them, we are in the nadir of humanness. Surgeons

and nurses, in doing what they must under these circumstances, make short shrift of personal dignity. Because civilization consists pretty largely of transforming physiological necessities into human possibilities, science, in making it possible to demoralize sex, does not make more plausible that we shall use the new freedom to do so. On the contrary, the new sexual freedom can be used not to demoralize sex but to moralize it far more profoundly than was heretofore possible, once the human relationships that sex engenders become objects of choice rather than forced upon us by biological accidents or the fear of them. Sex relationships become a challenge to integration with all other values, and, above all, a challenge to be consonant with the type of personality one has chosen to become.

4   But how does one bring about this reflected choice unless the experience is there to be reflected upon? And how does one control the consequences of such experiences so that they remain developmental rather than destructive? What social institutions have we developed for this form of character development? Lacking appropriate institutions—for the ones we have are predicated on equating sex with reproduction—our adolescents have coped with the situation in a clumsy way. Sometimes they establish Bohemian regions within cities or on the unofficial spaces of the campus. Sometimes they leave home for the anonymity and freedom of the city. But by and large it is technology in the form of the automobile and contraceptive devices that furnish the means of escape from parental surveillance, albeit not from guilt feelings.

5   These solutions are satisfactory to nobody, and I suggest that art has yet to come up with a life style that satisfactorily embodies the new value possibilities in sexual relations. The James Bond and Playboy images are bids in that direction, but they exemplify the demoralization of sex rather than its new moralization. No new life style for the contemporaneous woman has yet emerged. The roles of wife, prostitute, and casual companion we are familiar with, but a variety of free-spirited heroines served up by current fiction and film must still be classified as the probings of art to find such a new form.

Discussion of Theme

1. What are the new values referred to in the title of this article?
2. According to the author, how has the pill affected sexual morality?
3. What are some of the values college students have adopted in their search for a meaningful life? How adequate have these values been?
4. Is the current sexual revolution merely a passing phase or will it have a lasting effect on certain areas of morality?

Discussion of Rhetoric

1. Note the use of parentheses in paragraph 3. What does this suggest about the author's attitude toward the subject and assumed relationship to the audience?
2. In paragraph 4, the author writes that the young can ". . . escape from parental surveillance, albeit not from guilt feelings." Is this a dubious assumption as it stands? Is it a loaded statement?
3. In what sense is paragraph 1 an introduction? Is paragraph 5 an effective conclusion?
4. Is the author impartial and impersonal in his discussion of a search for new values, or is he advocating a particular set of ethics for his reader? How can you tell?

Writing Assignments

1. If you disagree with the author, present a rebuttal in a theme.
2. What is your mother's role as a woman? How will your daughter's role differ from hers?
3. In general, are the moral standards of your generation higher or lower than those of your parents' generation?

Library Exploration

1. Read one of Ian Fleming's James Bond novels, paying particular attention to the morality and values of its hero. Is Bond the forerunner of the new man of the future?
2. For some controversial views on sexual morality, read some of the writings of Albert Ellis.

Vocabulary

inordinately (1): excessively
hedonic (3): relating to pleasure
nadir (3): lowest point
engenders (3): produces
albeit (4): however; although

64

THE NEW ARISTOCRATS

Paul Goodman

*The author of this article, unlike
many of his generation, sees hope
and promise in the youth of today.*

1   Predictions about the future of America during the next generation
are likely to be in one of two sharply contrasting moods. On the one
hand, the orthodox liberals foresee a Great Society in which all will
live in suburban comfort or the equivalent; given a Head Start and
Job Training, Negroes will go to college like everyone else, will be
splendidly employed and live in integrated neighborhoods; billboards
will be 200 yards off new highways, and the arts will flourish in many
Lincoln Centers. On the other hand, gloomy social critics, and orthodox
conservatives, see that we are headed straight for 1984, when everyone's
life will be regimented from the cradle to the grave by the dictator in
Washington; administrative double talk and Newspeak will be the
only language; Negroes will be kept at bay by the police (according to
the social critics) or will be the pampered shock troops of demagogs
(according to the conservatives); we will all be serial numbers; civil
liberties and independent enterprise will be no more.

2   Yet these predictions have much in common. They assume the
continuation of the same trends and attitudes that are now in full
sway. There will be increasing centralization in decision making,
increasing mass education as we now know it, a stepped-up rate of
technical growth and growing Gross National Product, and more use of
a technological style—of "planning" or "social engineering," depending
on one's bias—with heavy use of computers. These same premises are
seen by some as enriching and great, and by others as menacing and
empty.

3   Oddly, however, both kinds of prediction describe the play and
leave out Hamlet; namely, the next generation itself, the young people
who are going to be the heirs to all this greatness or the slaves of this
social engineering. I have not seen a single forecast that takes into
account that present high school and college students will be of some
importance in shaping society 20 years from now. Commencement

speakers are eager to pass on the torch and they seem to be sure that there are ready hands to receive it. Yet the evidence is that students are not at all happy with the present trends and attitudes, whether the prediction is gloomy *or* rosy. For instance, in 1956, surveys showed that college students admired and wanted to work in big corporations, but last year (at Harvard) more seniors opted for the Peace Corps than for careers in business. Allow me a small personal example: My book *Growing Up Absurd* sells 1000 copies a week, of which the majority, my publisher guesses, are bought by high school students. This gives one pause; I wouldn't have thought they could read the words. Maybe they can't, but they get the message, that the conditions of our society are too inhuman to grow up in. For collegians that message is dated; they take it for granted.

4   I do not intend to predict what the future might look like if we take young people into account. I don't know (although I give plenty of advice, which they disregard). What I want to show, however, is that point by point, with remarkable precision, articulate students—and an indeterminate number of others—*live, feel and think in direct opposition to the premises on which both the rosy and the gloomy predictions are based.* It is so in their community life, their ethics and their politics. If only because of sheer numbers, the temper of young people must make a difference for the future. And it is whistling in the dark to think that their opposition is a "generational revolt" that will be absorbed as they grow older and wiser, for it is endemic in our system of things. If the planners continue to treat this temper as if it did not exist, the result will be still deeper alienation and worse ultimate disruption. My experience in Washington, as a Fellow of the Institute of Policy Studies, is that social and educational planners have about as much information of what happens on college campuses as the State Department has about Vietnam.

5   *Community.* About 50 percent of all Americans are now under 26. Of the college-age group, nearly 40 percent go to college—there are 6,000,000 in 2000 institutions. Of the present collegians, it is estimated that five percent are in some activity of the radical youth movement, usually "left" but sometimes "right." This does not seem a big proportion, but it has increased at least tenfold in the last decade, and it and the number of its alumni will certainly increase even more rapidly in the next years. We are thus speaking of several million people.

6   More important, they are the leaders. Radical collegians are not only middle class but they are also disproportionately the best academically and from the most prestigious schools. Unlike Negro youth, who are now causing such turmoil, collegians are a major economic force, looming large among the indispensable inheritors of the dominant power in society. And although—or perhaps because—they do not share a common ideology but rather a common sentiment and style, in

showdown situations like the troubles in Berkeley, they have shown a remarkable solidarity and a common detestation for the liberal center, crossing even the apparent chasm between extreme right and extreme left.

7   A chief reason for their solidarity and their increase in numbers is mass higher education itself. For most, going to college has little academic value—indeed, one of their shared sentiments is resistance to being academically processed for the goals of the "system." In my opinion, about 15 percent, instead of 40 percent, ought to be in colleges; the rest, including most of the bright, would be better educated in other environments. Nevertheless, *the major colleges and universities are, in fact, many hundreds of physical and social communities of young people, with populations of a few thousand to 25,000, sharing a subculture, propagandizing one another and learning to distrust anybody over 30. Such collections of youth are a phenomenon unique in history.*

8   Consider some details from San Francisco State College, where I was hired as a teacher by the Associated Students last spring. With 15,000 students, the Associated Students collect $300,000 annually in dues, more than half of which is free and clear and which they use for untraditional purposes. These purposes include organizing a tenants' league, helping delinquents in a reformatory, running a tutorial program for Negro and Mexican children (with 300 collegian tutors), sponsoring a weekly television program on KQED, running an "experimental college" with offbeat courses, and hiring their own professors. They apply on their own for institutional grants from the Ford Foundation and the Poverty Program. In the fall of 1966, the experimental college registered 1600 students!

9   Or consider the college press, with its fairly captive audience of a couple of million, many of them daily. In a few cases, e.g., Harvard and Columbia, publication has gone off campus and is not under the tutelage of "faculty advisors." Increasingly, college papers subscribe to news services and print (and edit) national and international news; and they also use syndicated material, like Art Buchwald, Jules Feiffer, Russell Baker. Occasionally, the college paper is the chief daily of its town (e.g., the Cornell *Sun*). More important, there is a national student press service that could be a powerfully effective liaison for mobilizing opinion on common issues. Last winter I wrote a fortnightly column on student matters for a tiny college in Vermont, which the enterprising editor at once syndicated to 50 other college papers. On this model there could spring up a system of direct support, and control, of students' "own" authors, just as, of course, they now indirectly support them through magazines whose main circulation is collegiate.

10   Nor are these young people properly called "youth." The exigencies of the American system have kept them in tutelage, doing lessons, till 23 and 24 years of age, years past when young industrial workers

used to walk union picket lines or when farmers carried angry pitch-
forks, or young men are now drafted into the Army. Thus, another
cause of their shared resentment is the foolish attempt to arrest their
maturation and regulate their social, sexual and political activity.

11   More than other middle-class generations, these young live a good
deal by "interpersonal relations" and they are unusually careless,
in their friendships, about status or getting ahead. I do not mean that
they are especially affectionate or compassionate—they are averagely
so—but they have been soaked in modern psychology, group therapy,
sensitivity training; and as a style they go in for direct confrontation
and sometimes brutal frankness. Add to this the lack of embarrassment
due to animally uninhibited childhood, for their parents, by and large,
were permissive about thumbsucking, toilet training, masturbation,
informal dress, etc. They are the post-Freudian generation in this
country—their parents were analyzed from 1920 to 1940. The effect
of all this psychology—for example, long sessions of mutual analysis
or jabber about LSD trips—can be tiresome, at least to me; but it is
fatal to suburban squeamishness, race and moral prejudice, and to
keeping up appearances. Still another cause of resentment at the colleges is the impersonality and distance of the teachers and the big
classes that make dialog impossible. Students are avid for dialog.
Sometimes this looks like clamoring for "attention," as our statesmen
say about the demonstrators, but it is really insisting on being taken
seriously as troubled human beings.

12   Middle-class privacy also tends to vanish. An innovation of the
Beats was the community use of one another's pads, and this spirit
of sharing has persisted in off-campus university communities, which
are very different from paternalistic dormitories or fraternity row.
In big cities there are rapidly growing bohemian student neighborhoods,
usually—if only for the cheaper rent—located in racially mixed sections. Such neighborhoods, with their own coffeehouses and head-
quarters for student political clubs, cannot be controlled by campus
administration. In the famous insurrection of Berkeley, Telegraph
Avenue could easily rally 3000 students, ex-students, wives and pals.
(The response of the University of California administration has been,
characteristically, to try to root up the student neighborhood with
Federally financed urban renewal.)

13   Inevitably, sexual activity and taking drugs loom overlarge in the
public picture: for, whereas unkempt hair, odd company and radical
politics may be disapproved, sex and drugs rouse middle-class anxiety,
a more animal reaction. The statistics seem to show, however, that
quantitatively there are not many more sexual goings on than since the
Twenties. The difference is that the climate has finally become more
honest and unhypocritical. Sexuality is affirmed as a part of life rather
than as the Saturday religion of fraternity gang bangs covered by

being drunk. Since there is more community altogether, sex tends to revert to the normalcy of back rural areas, with the beautiful difference of middle-class prudence and contraceptives. (Probably, since there is less moralism, there are more homosexual acts, though not, of course, any increase of homosexuality as a trait of character.) In the more earnest meaning of sex, love and marriage, however, the radical young still seem averagely messed up, no better than their parents. There is no remarkable surge of joy or poetry—the chief progress of the sexual revolution, so far, has been the freer treatment of small children that I mentioned above. The conditions of American society do not encourage manly responsibility and moral courage in men, and we simply do not know how to use the tenderness and motherliness of women. The present disposition of the radical young is to treat males and females alike; in my observation, this means that the women become camp followers, the opposite of the suburban situation in which they are tyrannical dolls. I don't know the answer.

14   Certainly the slogan "Make love, not war"—carried mainly by the girls—is political wisdom, if only because it costs less in taxes.

15   The community meaning of the widespread use of hallucinogenic drugs is ambiguous. (Few students use addictives; again, they are prudent.) I have heard students hotly defend the drugs as a means of spiritual and political freedom, or hotly condemn them as a quietist opiate of the people, or indifferently dismiss them as a matter of taste. I am myself not a hippie and I am unwilling to judge. It seems clear that the more they take pot, the less they get drunk, but I don't know if this is an advantage or a disadvantage. (I don't get drunk, either.) Certainly there is a difference between the quiet socializing of marijuana and the alcoholic socializing of the fraternities, suburbs and Washington. Also, being illegal and hard to procure, the drugs create conspiracy and a chasm between those who do and those who don't. As usual, the drug laws, like other moral laws, fail to eradicate the vice they intend to eradicate, but they produce disastrous secondary effects.

16   The LSD cult, especially, must be understood as part of a wave of religiosity in young persons that has included Zen, Christian and Jewish existentialism, a kind of psychoanalytic yoga, and the magic of the Book of Changes. On the campus, a young Protestant chaplain— or even a Catholic—is often the center of radical activity, which may include a forum for psychedelic theory as well as peace and Negro rights. Certainly the calculating rationalism of modern times is losing its self-evidence; and it is not the end of the world to flip. Personally, I don't like it when people flip, it is eerie; I like people to be in touch, and I think the heads are mistaken when they think they are communicating. Also, in our overtechnological society, I am intensely suspicious of Dr. Tim Leary's formula to "turn on, tune in and drop out" by chemical means. Yet by and large, the public repression in this

field is grossly disproportionate to the occasional damage that has been proved; and frankly, the burden of proof is the other way: If we do not want young people to live in harmless dreams, we have to provide something better than the settled arithmetical delusions of Mr. McNamara, not to speak of Herman Kahn, author of *On Thermonuclear War*.

17   The shagginess and chosen poverty of student communities have nuances that might be immensely important for the future. We must remember that these are the young of the affluent society, used to a high standard of living and confident that, if and when they want, they can fit in and make good money. Having suffered little pressure of insecurity, they have little psychological need to climb; just as, coming from respectable homes, they feel no disgrace about sitting a few nights in jail. By confidence they are aristocrats—en masse. This, too, is unique in history. At the same time, the affluent standard of living that they have experienced at home is pretty synthetic and much of it useless and phony; whereas their chosen poverty is not degraded but decent, natural and in many ways more comfortable than their parents' standard, especially if they can always corral obvious goodies such as hi-fi equipment and motorcycles. Typically, they tour Europe on nothing, sleeping under bridges; but if they get really hungry, they can drop in at American Express to pick up their mail. Most of the major satisfactions of life—sex, paperback books, guitars, roaming, conversation, games and activist politics—in fact, cost little.

18   Thus, this is the first generation in America selective of its standard of living. If this attitude became general, it would be disastrous for the expanding Gross National Product. And there is obvious policy and defiance in their poverty and shagginess. They have been influenced by the voluntary poverty of the beat movement, which signified withdrawal from the trap of the affluent economy. Finally, by acquaintance they experience the harsher tone of the involuntary poverty of the Negroes and Spanish Americans whose neighborhoods they visit and with whom they are friends.

19   In a recent speech, Robert Hutchins pointed out that business can no longer recruit the bright young. He explained this by the fact that the universities are rich and can offer competitive rewards. But I do not think this is the essence, for we have seen that at Harvard, business cannot compete even with the Peace Corps. The essence is that the old drive to make a *lot* of money has lost its magnetism. Yet this does not seem to mean settling for security, for the young are increasingly risky. The magnet is a way of life that has meaning. This is a luxury of an aristocratic community.

20   *Ethics.* The chief (conscious) drive of the radical young is their morality. As Michael Harrington, author of *The Other America*, has put it, "They drive you crazy with their morality," since for it

they disregard prudence and politics, and they mercilessly condemn day-to-day casuistry as if it were all utterly phony. When politically minded student leaders, like the Students for a Democratic Society, try to engage in "tactics" and "the art of the possible," they may temporarily gain in numbers, but they swiftly lose influence and begin to disintegrate. Yet indignation or a point of honor will rally the young in droves.

21   Partly, the drive to morality is the natural ingenuousness of youth, freed of the role playing and status seeking of our society. As aristocrats, not driven by material or ulterior motives, they will budge for ideals or not at all. Partly their absolutism is a disgusted reaction to cynicism and the prevalent adult conviction that "Nothing can be done. You can't fight city hall. Modern life is too complex." But mostly, I think, it is the self-righteousness of an intelligent and innocent new generation in a world where my own generation has been patently stupid and incompetent. They have been brought up on a literature of devastating criticism that has gone unanswered because there is no answer.

22   The right comparison to them is the youth of the Reformation, of *Sturm und Drang*, and of Russia of the Seventies and Eighties, who were brought up on their own dissenting theologians, *philosophes* and intelligentsia. Let us remember that those students did, indeed, ultimately lead revolutions.

23   The philosophical words are "authenticity" and "commitment," from the existentialist vocabulary. And it cannot be denied that our dominant society is unusually inauthentic. Newspeak and double talk are the lingua franca of administrators, politicians, advertisers and the mass media. These official people are not even lying; rather, there is an unbridgeable chasm between the statements made "on the record" for systemic reasons or the image of the corporation, and what is intended and actually performed. I have seen mature graduate students crack up in giggles of anxiety listening to the Secretary of State expound our foreign policy; when I questioned them afterward, some said that he was like a mechanical man, others that he was demented. And most campus blowups have been finally caused by administrators' animal inability to speak plain. The students have faithfully observed due process and manfully stated their case, but the administrators simply cannot talk like human beings. At this point it suddenly becomes clear that they are confronting not a few radical dissenters but a solid mass of the young, maybe a majority.

24   Two things seem to solidify dissent: administrative double talk and the singling out of "ringleaders" for exemplary punishment. These make young people feel that they are not being taken seriously, and they are not.

25   In principle, "authenticity" is proved by "commitment." You must not merely talk but organize, collect money, burn your draft

card, go South and be shot at, go to jail. And the young eagerly commit themselves. However, a lasting commitment is hard to achieve. There are a certain number of causes that are pretty authentic and warrant engaging in: Give Negroes the vote, desegregate a hotel or a bus, commute Chessman's sentence to the gas chamber, abolish grading and get the CIA out of the university, abolish HUAC, get out of Vietnam, legalize marijuana and homosexuality, unionize the grape-pickers. But it is rarely the case that any particular authentic cause can really occupy the thought and energy of more than a few for more than a while. Students cool off and hop from issue to issue, then some become angry at the backsliders; others foolishly try to prove that civil liberties, for instance, are not so "important" as Negro civil rights, for instance, or that university reform is not so "important" as stopping the bombing of Hanoi. Others, disillusioned, sink into despair of human nature. And committed causes distressingly vanish from view at the June vacation, when the community disperses.

26   Shrewder psychologists among the young advocate getting involved only in what you "enjoy" and gravitate to—e.g., don't tutor unless you like kids—but this is a weak motive compared with indignation or justice.

27   The bother is that, except with a few political or religious person-alities, the students' commitments do not spring from their own vocations and life ambitions; and they are not related in a coherent program for the reconstruction of society. This is not the fault of the students. Most of the present young have unusually little sense of vocation; perhaps 16 continuous years of doing lessons by compulsion has not been a good way to find one's identity. And there *is* no acceptable program of reconstruction—nobody has spelled it out—only vague criteria. Pathetically, much "definite commitment" is a self-deceptive way of filling the void of sense of vocation and utopian politics. Negroes, who are perforce really committed to their emancipation, notice this and say that their white allies are spiritually exploiting them.

28   It is a difficult period of history for the young to find vocation and identity. Most of the abiding human vocations and professions, arts and sciences, seem to them, and are (to a degree) corrupt or corrupted: law, business, the physical sciences, social work—these constitute the hated System. And higher education, both curriculum and professors, which ought to be helping them find themselves, also seems bought out by the System. Students know that something is wrong in their schooling and they agitate for university reform; but since they do not know what world they want to make, they do not know what to demand to be taught.

29   *Politics.* It is not the task of age 18 to 25 to devise a coherent program of social reconstruction; for instance, to rethink our uses of technology, our methods of management, our city planning and international

relations. They rightly accuse us of not providing them a program to work for. A small minority—I think increasing—turns to Marxism, as in the Thirties; but the Marxist theorists have also not thought of anything new and relevant to overripe societies. Most radical students, in my observation, listen to Marxist ideological speeches with polite lack of interest—"they are empty, man, empty"—and they are appalled by Marxist political bullying. On the other hand, they are disgusted with official anticommunism. By an inevitable backlash, since they think all American official speech is double talk, they disbelieve that Communist states are worse than our own.

30   What the American young do not know, being themselves pushed around, itemized and processed, is that they have a right to a say in what affects them. They believe in democracy, which they have to call "participatory democracy," to distinguish it from double-talk democracy. Poignantly, in their ignorance of American history, they do not recognize that they are Congregationalists, town-meeting democrats, Jeffersonians, populists. But they know they want the opportunity to be responsible, to initiate and decide, instead of being mere personnel. Returning from their term overseas, the first thousand of the Peace Corps unanimously agreed that exercising responsibility and initiative had been the most worthwhile part of their experience, and they complained that back home they did not have the opportunity.

31   The primary area for seeking democracy would be, one would imagine, the universities, for that is where the students are and are coerced. And the radical students, who, we have seen, are among the best academically, have campaigned for *Lernfreiheit*—freedom from grading, excessive examination, compulsory attendance at lectures and prescribed subjects—and also for the ancient privilege of say in designing the curriculum and evaluating the teachers. But unfortunately, as we have also seen, the majority of students do not care about higher education as such and are willing to put up with it as it is. They are in college for a variety of extrinsic reasons, from earning the degree as a union card to evading the draft. There is no mass base for university reform.

32   So instead of working in their own bailiwick, activist students have mainly sought participatory democracy for poor people, organizing rent strikes, opposing bureaucratic welfare procedures, and so forth. But there is an inherent dilemma in this. Negroes claim, perhaps correctly, that middle-class whites cannot understand their problems; if Negroes are going to run their own show, they have to dispense with white helpers. The present policy of the Student Nonviolent Coordinating Committee is that Negroes must solve their own peculiar problems, which are the only ones they care about and know anything about, and let their young white friends attend to changing the majority society. There is something in this. Certainly one would have expected

Northern students to get their heads broken in the cafeteria at Tulane or the University of Mississippi, where they could talk with their peers face to face, as well as on the streets of country towns. And white Southern liberals have desperately needed more support than they have gotten.

33   But pushed too far, the rift with the middle-class students consigns poor people to a second-class humanity. The young Negroes cannot do without the universities, for there, finally, is where the showdown, the reconstruction of society, will be—although that showdown is not yet. Consider: Some pressing problems are universal; the poor must care about them, e.g., the atom bomb. Many pressing problems are grossly misconceived if looked at at short range from a poor man's point of view; only a broad human point of view can save Negroes from agitating for exactly the wrong things, as they have agitated for educational parks, when what is needed in schooling is a small human scale. Also, there is something spurious in Negro separatism, for a poor minority in a highly technological society will not engineer the housing and manufacture the cars that they intend to use. Finally, in fact, the Negroes are, perhaps unfortunately, much more American than Negro. Especially in the north, they are suckers for the whole American package, though it makes even less sense for them than for anybody else. The Negro subculture that is talked up has about the same value as the adolescent subculture; it has vitality and it does not add up to humanity.

34   As in other periods of moral change, only the young aristocrats and the intellectuals can *afford* to be disillusioned and profoundly radical. And in a high technology, only the students will be able to construct a program.

35   In their own action organizations, the young are almost fanatically opposed to top-down direction. In several remarkable cases, e.g., Tom Hayden, Bob Moses, Mario Savio, gifted and charismatic leaders have stepped down because their influence had become too strong. By disposition, without benefit of history, they are reinventing anarchist federation and a kind of Rosa Luxemburgian belief in spontaneous insurrection from below. In imitating Gandhian nonviolence, they do not like to submit to rigid discipline, but each one wants to make his own moral decision about getting his head broken. If the Army really gets around to drafting them, it will have its hands full.

36   All this, in my opinion, probably makes them immune to take-over by centralists like the Marxists. When Trotskyites, for instance, infiltrate an organization and try to control it, the rest go home and activity ceases. When left to their own improvisation, however, the students seem surprisingly able to mount quite massive efforts, using elaborate techniques of communication and expert sociology. By such means they will never get power. But, indeed, they do not want power, they want meaning.

37   *Parallel Institutions.* The operative idea in participatory democracy
is decentralizing, to multiply the number who are responsible, initiate
and decide. In principle, there are two opposite ways of decentralizing:
either by dividing overcentralized organizations where it can be shown
that decentral organization is more efficient in economic, social and
human costs, or at least not too inefficient; or by creating new small
enterprises to fill needs that big organizations neglect or only pretend
to fulfill.

38   Obviously, the first of these, to cut the present structures down to
human size, is not in the power of the young. But it happens that it does
require a vast amount of empirical research and academic analysis to
find if, where and how decentralizing is feasible; and in current
American academic style, there is no such research and analysis. So
on 150 campuses, I have urged students to work on such problems.
They seem fascinated, but I do not know if they are coming across.
(To say it wryly, there is a fine organization called Students for a
Democratic Society, but it is not enough evident that they are scholars
for a democratic society.)

39   The other way of decentralizing, by creating parallel enterprises,
better suits the student zeal for direct action, and they have applied it
with energy and inventiveness. They have set up a dozen little "free
universities" that I know about—probably there are many others—in
or next to established institutions, to teach in a more personal way and
to deal with contemporary subjects that are not yet standard curriculum,
e.g., Castro's Cuba, Psychedelic Experience, Sensitivity Training,
Theater of Participation. Some of these courses are action sociology,
like organizing labor or community development. In poor neighborhoods, students have established a couple of radio stations, to broadcast
local news and propaganda and to give poor people a chance to talk
into a microphone. They have set up parallel community projects to
combat the welfare bureaucracy and channelize needs and grievances.
In the South, they have helped form "freedom" political machines,
since the established machines are lily white. They have offered to
organize international service projects as an alternative to serving in
the Army. (I have not heard of any feasible attempts at productive
cooperatives or planned urban communities of their own, and students
do not seem at all interested in rural reconstruction, though they should
be.)

40   Regarded coldly, such parallel projects are pitifully insignificant and
doomed to pass away like so many little magazines. And, in fact, at
present, the most intense discussions among student radicals, causing
deep rifts, are on this theme. Some, following older thinkers like
Michael Harrington and Bayard Rustin (director of a civil rights and
poverty research institute) want to engage in "coalition politics," to
become effective by combining with the labor unions and leftish

liberals in the Democratic Party, to get control of some of the Federal money and to campaign for A. Philip Randolph's (president of the Brotherhood of Sleeping Car Porters) 185-billion-dollar budget to eliminate poverty. This involves, of course, soft-pedaling protests for peace, community action and university reform. Recent history, however, has certainly not favored this point of view. Federal money is drying up and radical coalition people who go to work for the Government get fired; nor is it evident that, if it were spent for liberal social engineering, Randolph's budget would make a better world—even if the money were voted.

41   Others, for example one wing of SDS, say that the use of participatory democracy and parallel institutions is not for themselves but to consolidate people into a political party; it is not to provide models for the reconstruction of society but, as a kind of initiation rite, to get into the big game of numbers and power. This seems to me to give up on the authenticity, meaning and beautiful spontaneous motivation that have, so far, been the real power of the radical young and the source of what influence they have had. And it presupposes that the young know where they want to go as a party, rather than in what direction they *are* going as a movement. But they don't know; they (and we) will have to find out by conflict.

42   In my opinion, it is better to regard the parallel institutions as a remarkable revival of a classical American movement, populism, that seemed to have been dead. It is now reviving on the streets and among citizens who storm city hall because they feel they have been pushed around; in such a movement, the young are natural leaders. The principle of populism, as in 1880, is to get out from under the thumb of the barons and do it yourself. And perhaps the important step is the first one, to prove that self-help is possible at all. There may be hope of bringing to life many of our routinized institutions if we surround them with humanly meaningful enterprises. The most telling criticism of an overgrown institution is a simpler one that works better.

43   This was John Dewey's vision of the young 60 years ago: He thought of an industrial society continually and democratically renewed by its next generation, freely educated and learning by doing. Progressive education, free-spirited but practical, was a typical populist conception. And it is useful to regard the student movement as progressive education at the college and graduate-school level; for at this level, learning by doing begins to be indistinguishable from vocation, profession and politics. It is the opposite of the mandarin establishment that now rules the country, and of the social engineering that is now called education. Maybe this time around, the populist movement will succeed and change what we mean by vocation, profession and politics.

44   So, describing radical students—and I do not know how many others

—we have noticed their solidarity based on community rather than ideology, their style of direct and frank confrontation, their democratic inclusiveness and aristocratic carelessness of status, caste or getting ahead, their selectivity of the affluent standard of living, their effort to be authentic and committed to their causes rather than merely belonging, their determination to have a say and their refusal to be processed as standard items, their extreme distrust of top-down direction, their disposition to anarchist organization and direct action, their disillusion with the system of institutions, and their belief that they can carry on major social functions in improvised parallel enterprises.

45 Some of these traits, in my opinion, are natural to all unspoiled young people. All of them are certainly in contradiction to the dominant organization of American society. By and large, this is as yet the disposition of a minority, but it is the only articulate disposition that has emerged; and it has continually emerged for the past ten years. It is a response not merely to "issues," such as civil rights or Vietnam, but to deeply rooted defects in our present system, and it will have an influence in the future. It will make for a more decent society than the Great Society and it may well save us from 1984.

Discussion of Theme

1. What (or who) is responsible for the particular style of the young people Goodman calls the new aristocrats?
2. Is the author's view of today's youth a realistic one?
3. Are, as the author states, "the conditions of our society . . . too inhuman to grow up in"? What are the new aristocrats doing to change these conditions?
4. What is participatory democracy? What method of achieving it does the author recommend?

Discussion of Rhetoric

1. Describe the author's style. Note especially diction, sentence structure, and tone.
2. What is the central thesis of this article? Is it stated or implied?
3. Is there a conclusion to this selection? Where does it begin?
4. This selection is divided internally into four parts. Does the author prepare you for such a division?

Writing Assignments

1. Goodman suggests that the nature of college education be changed. Discuss his suggestions, and present your reaction to them. If you disagree with him, write a rebuttal.
2. How serious is the drug problem on campus? Is it exaggerated?

Are there other, more serious problems that we should be considering? Give your views in a theme.

3. Should colleges and universities accept money from the government for war-related research?

Library Exploration

1. Read *Growing Up Absurd* by Paul Goodman for an extended treatment of some of the ideas in this article.
2. For another view of the purposes of education, read something by John Dewey, an American educator and the founder of progressive education.

Vocabulary

orthodox (1): conventional

demagogs (1): leaders who make use of popular prejudices and false promises to gain power

endemic (4): native to

tutelage (9): guardianship; guiding influence

exigencies (10): requirements; demands

casuistry (20): the reasoning about or resolution of questions of right or wrong by applying general principles of ethics

Index